SEVENTH EDITION

VETERINARY SURGERY

by

E. R. FRANK, B.S.A., D.V.M., M.S.
Professor Emeritus of Veterinary Surgery
Kansas State University

CBS Publishers & Distributors Pvt. Ltd.
New Delhi • Bengaluru • Chennai • Kochi • Kolkata • Mumbai
Hyderabad • Uttarakhand • Nagpur • Patna • Pune • Jharkhand

ISBN: 81-239-1443-1

First Indian Reprint: 1981
Reprint: 2002

Authorised reprint from English language edition published by
Burgess Publishing Company, Minneapolis, Minnesota, USA

Published by **Satish Kumar Jain** and produced by **Varun Jain** for
CBS Publishers & Distributors Pvt. Ltd.,
4819/XI Prahlad Street, 24 Ansari Road, Daryaganj, New Delhi - 110002
delhi@cbspd.com, cbspubs@airtelmail.in • www.cbspd.com
Ph.: 23289259, 23266861, 23266867 • Fax: 011-23243014

Corporate Office: 204 FIE, Industrial Area, Patparganj, Delhi - 110 092
Ph: 49344934 • Fax: 011-49344935
E-mail: publishing@cbspd.com • publicity@cbspd.com

Branches:

- ***Bengaluru:*** 2975, 17th Cross, K.R. Road, Bansankari 2nd Stage, Bengaluru - 70 • Ph: +91-80-26771678/79 • Fax: +91-80-26771680 E-mail: cbsbng@gmail.com, bangalore@cbspd.com
- ***Chennai:*** No. 7, Subbaraya Street, Shenoy Nagar, Chennai - 600030 Ph: +91-44-26681266, 26680620 • Fax: +91-44-42032115 E-mail: chennai@cbspd.com
- ***Kochi:*** Ashana House, 39/1904, A.M. Thomas Road, Valanjambalam, Ernakulum, Kochi • Ph: +91-484-4059061-65 Fax: +91-484-4059065 • E-mail: cochin@cbspd.com
- ***Kolkata:*** 6-B, Ground Floor, Rameshwar Shaw Road, Kolkata - 700014 Ph: +91-33-22891126/7/8 • E-mail: kolkata@cbspd.com
- ***Mumbai:*** 83-C, Dr. E. Moses Road, Worli, Mumbai - 400018 Ph: +91-9833017933, 022-24902340/41 • E-mail: mumbai@cbspd.com

Representatives:

- Hyderabad: 0-9885175004
- Patna: 0-9334159340
- Jharkhand: 0-9811541605
- Nagpur: 0-9021734563
- Pune: 0-9623451994
- Uttarakhand: 0-9716462459

Printed at:
India Binding House, Noida, UP (India)

DEDICATION

to my wife, Jean

PREFACE

In preparing this the Seventh Edition new material has been added together with some fifty new illustrations. The illustrations are particularly valuable in the clarification of the written text. There is revision of some of the material in the previous edition and elimination of techniques that failed to give the desired results.

The purpose of this book is to present a survey of the field of large animal surgery. It was a rather difficult task to select those subjects that seem to be the most important at the present time. To present the material that seemed most essential, conciseness was a prime requisite so that many things had to be omitted in this text.

If teachers of surgery are to accomplish their responsibility, they must acquaint their students with the fundamental principles of surgery. They must instruct students in methods which will enable them to recognize surgical disorders and teach them what surgery can accomplish in the treatment of various conditions.

While the use of the sulfonamides and antibiotics have received a great deal of credit for the results obtained in some cases, they have not had the influence that has been assumed by some surgeons. These agents must not be allowed to displace sound surgical principles.

The surgeon must be interested in investigational work, as from this, is established our sound surgical procedures. Due to the importance of surgical pathology in the teaching of surgery, numerous illustrations together with case histories of neoplastic and other lesions are included in the text. We must be interested in the diagnosis upon which depends the selection of those measures which will meet the conditions that require treatment.

The author is indebted to many of his colleagues in the various Departments of the College of Veterinary Medicine for advice and help in the preparation of this edition. The College Photographer, Mr. F. J. Hanna has always given excellent cooperation and exhibited a great deal of interest in the taking of the pictures.

It is a pleasant duty to acknowledge my indebtedness to the Burgess Publishing Company for their cooperation and meticulous attention they have given to the many details in the production of this and the other editions.

E. R. F.

TABLE OF CONTENTS

Chapter I
ANESTHESIA

Anesthesia for operations on animals is essential for a number of reasons. It is just as essential to control pain in animals during an operation as it is in humans. From a surgical standpoint the operation can be performed more efficiently if the animal is under complete control and the operator is sure the patient will not make a sudden move. The veterinary surgeon is confronted with the problem of using anesthetics upon several different species of animals in which the reaction to a given anesthetic may differ widely. There is also a difference in size and temperment as well as anatomy and physiology. The anesthetic that is efficient for one species might be harmful to a member of another species. The safety of the anesthetic for the patient must always be the first consideration of the operator. It does not make any difference how well the operation was performed if the patient dies from the anesthetic.

When giving an anesthetic to a human the anesthetist can expect some cooperation from his patient. This is not true in our animal patients as they will usually resist from fear any restraint necessary to the administration of the anesthetic. In some cases it may be advisable to give a sedative to control the struggling, as an adjunct to the local anesthetic or before the administration of a general anesthetic.

Generally speaking the anesthetic agents are of two distinct types, local anesthetics which exert their action upon the sensory nerves. The general anesthetics are those which have their action on the central nervous system bringing about a loss of consciousness and insensibility to pain of the entire body.

There are a number of points to consider in choosing the anesthetic or combination of anesthetics to be used in any given case. The disposition of the animal may determine the choice as to whether a local or general anesthetic may be used. Also the extent and location of the operation may be the determining factor. If the operation is in an area where a number of vital structures are situated it may be advisable to use a general anesthetic to prevent any movement on the part of the animal during the operation. In those horses that are used to being handled, nerves may be blocked to certain areas or the tissue to be invaded may be infiltrated and the horse operated in a standing position.

Anesthesia, Local and General

Anesthesia is divided into three types according to the anatomical division of the nervous system involved.

Local Anesthesia is that type of anesthesia in which only the peripheral nervous system is brought under the influence of the anesthetic.

General Anesthesia is that type of anesthesia in which the nervous system consisting of the brain and spinal cord and the peripheral nervous system, consisting of afferent nerves, efferent nerves and tactile end organs are brought under the influence of the anesthetic.

Spinal anesthesia, blocking nerves within the spine in the subarachnoid space.

Important Facts in Relation to Local Anesthetics

All local anesthetics are protoplasmic poisons and produce anesthesia by coming into combination with the tissue cells. Cocain and its substitutes possess a marked affinity for nerve tissue and toxic symptoms arise from the action of these substances upon the higher nerve centers. It is obvious that the safety and efficiency of any local anesthetic depends upon maintaining it in the area where its action is desired. Also it is important to keep it from reaching and exerting any action upon the higher nerve centers. It is well to remember that other things being equal the rate of absorption and the toxic action of local anesthetics varies with the concentration. The total amount of the drug required to produce a toxic effect is many times greater with a weak solution than with a strong solution. It is also true the potency of local anesthetic solutions varies almost directly with their concentration. Thus the toxic effects of a local anesthetic are only remotely related to the total amount of the drug used but is dependent more upon the above mentioned factors. If the local anesthetic solution is injected slowly its toxic action is diminished.

Local anesthetic solutions have a special predilection for the sensory nerves. They affect the motor nerves but to a lesser extent. Thus an extremity may be completely anesthetized and yet retain the power of voluntary action.

The Desirable Properties of Local Anesthetics

A local anesthetic, if it is efficient, must have certain requisites. When it is injected into the tissues it should not cause pain at the time of injection or after its action has ceased. It should not be absorbed rapidly from the tissues and must be compatible with adrenalin. The solutions should not deteriorate when sterilized by boiling. It should be efficient in paralyzing nerve endings in rather dilute solutions. The relative toxicity is one of the most important features and it has been shown that procaine is the least toxic.

Cocain

There are two official preparations of the drug, the alkaloid and the hydrochlorid. Cocain was the first one of our local anesthetics and with the exception of butyn has the greatest potency and also is the most toxic of any local anesthetic known. It is absorbed very rapidly from the mucous membrane and denuded surfaces but not from the unbroken skin. Cocain has a strong affinity for nerve tissue and is a strong protoplasmic poison, first stimulating and then paralyzing the nerves. It is a marked stimulant to the central nervous system and in the human is probably the most dangerous of the habit forming drugs.

The crystalline form of cocain hydrochlorid is stable for a long period but in solution is not entirely stable. The solution may be sterilized by boiling without greatly lowering its efficiency. This drug is very efficient upon mucous membranes but should not be used except in small doses in the tissues, due to its toxicity.

A number of compounds have been developed synthetically that are less toxic than cocain. Some of the compounds discovered are: Beta-eucain, Tropacocain, Stovain, Alypin, Apothesin, Allocain-S, Hiavanin, Quinin and Urea Hydrochlorid, Tutocain and Procain. Of the local anesthetics procain is probably the most popular for general use.

NOVOCAIN HYDROCHLORIDE (PROCAIN). Novocain, a white crystalline powder, is chemically closely related related to stovain and alypin. Its solutions possess slight antiseptic properties, may be repeatedly sterilized by boiling without marked effect upon the anesthetic properties and may be kept for long periods of time without undergoing any change.

Locally it exerts a prompt and pronounced anesthetic action which is intensified by the addition of adrenalin, more so than with any of the other local anesthetics. There is no after pain or tendency toward the production of tissue necrosis as with cocain.

Novocain is but mildly toxic. It is perhaps because of its low toxicity more than to any of its many other favorable qualities, that this drug has become the most widely used of all the local anesthetics. The toxicity is further reduced by the addition of adrenaline, two to five drops of 1 to 1000 solution of adrenalin to each 30 cubic centimeters of novocain solution which retards its absorption.

BUTYN. As a local anesthetic for topical application on mucous membranes it is an excellent substitute for cocain. For ophthalmic work a two percent solution is used and the best results are obtained when several installations are made about three minutes apart. A committee of the section on Ophthalmology of the American Medical Association reports the successful use of butyn in practically all operations on the eye and in some the nose and throat. It also concludes that it is more powerful than cocain, it acts more rapidly and the action is more prolonged. It is also less toxic than cocain, does not dry the tissues or produce the ischemic action of cocain.

Methods of Producing Local Anesthesia

Cold has been known for a number of years as a method of producing local anesthesia. It was not used extensively and such drugs as ether, ethyl bromide, ethyl chlorid, methyl chlorid and liquid carbonic gas are the ones that have been used most frequently for this purpose. While this method has been used for some rather extensive operations its real value lies in the performance of superficial minor operations.

Pressure may be used to produce numbness and if continued long enough, anesthesia of the area is obtained. This method was used for many years but gradually fell into disrepute as more efficient methods were developed.

TOPICAL ANESTHESIA. Local anesthetics may be applied in their natural form, powders, crystals, ointments or solutions to the mucous membranes or denuded surfaces. In such cases the method is referred to as topical anesthesia. All of the regular local anesthetics may and should be used in greater strength as topical applications than when injected subcutaneously.

The indications for the use of topical anesthesia in animals is rather limited. It is very beneficial for examination of the eye, some minor operations, and removal of foreign bodies from the cornea. The interior of the larynx and the laryngeal saccule may be anesthetized by the application of an anesthetic on the mucous membrane. If the horse resists the irrigation of the nasolacrimal canal it may be first irrigated with a topical anesthetic. For topical anesthesia a two percent solution of Butyn is as efficient as any of the local anesthetics.

Infiltration Anesthesia consists in bringing the local anesthetic into actual or close contact with the sensory nerve supply by injecting the anesthetic solution into the tissues. The operative area should be prepared in the usual manner. To start the infiltration a fine needle is used to make a small weal in the dermis. A larger and longer needle is then used to infiltrate the skin and underlying tissue along the proposed line or lines of incision. When using infiltration anesthesia the tissue should be infiltrated with a sufficient quantity of the anesthetic solution, so there is complete anesthesia of the tissues.

Regional anesthesia consists in interrupting the nerve or nerves at any point along their course proximal to their peripheral nerve ending. This form of anesthesia may be obtained by injecting the anesthetic solution directly in contact with the nerve, termed perineural anesthesia or injecting the anesthetic solution into the nerve, intraneural anesthesia. If this form of local anesthesia is to be effective the anesthetic solution must be strong enough to interrupt sensation at the point where it comes into contact with the nerve. When the anesthetic agent is absorbed by the nerve there is produced a temporary paralysis of its function resulting in anesthesia of those parts supplied by the nerve. To accomplish this it is usually advisable to use a four or five percent solution of the local anesthetic. The amount of the anesthetic solution to use will depend upon the size of the nerve to be anesthetized and will vary from three to five cubic centimeters for small nerves to ten to twenty cubic centimeters for the large nerves. Also if the nerve can not be very accurately located it may be advisable to use a large quantity of the solution so it will come in contact with the nerve. If asepsis is observed in making the injection of the anesthetic solution this procedure should not result in any permanent injury to the nerve. Complete anesthesia should occur in ten minutes and persists for about one hour.

Probably in the horse we find the greatest and most frequent indication for the use of regional anesthesia. It is especially indicated for the location of the seat of some cases of obscure lameness in the horse. Also by blocking the nerves to certain areas operations may be performed with the animal in the standing position. In some incurable conditions causing lameness, it should be determined by blocking the nerves if a neurectomy of the nerve supplying the area will be successful in relieving pain. If the lameness is not relieved by blocking the nerve supplying the area no benefit will be derived from a neurectomy of that nerve.

A fine sharp needle 24 gauge is used to block the nerves. Anesthesia of the area supplied by the blocked nerve may be determined by pricking the skin with a sharp needle. It is one of the methods that may be used to determine if the nerve or nerves have been blocked.

Distribution of Sensory Nerves of Front Limb of Equine

MEDIAN NERVE. This nerve receives its fibers chiefly from the eighth cervical and first thoracic roots of the brachial plexus. It is the largest branch and descends to the lower part of the limb accompanying the chief arterial blood supply. At a variable distance above the carpus the median nerve divides into two branches the medial and lateral volar nerves.

The lateral branch of the median nerve is joined by the ulnar nerve to form the lateral volar nerve. About the middle of the metacarpus the medial volar nerve detaches a large branch which descends obliquely downward and outward over the flexor tendons to join the lateral nerve near or just below the middle of the metacarpus. The two volar nerves each divide near the fetlock into two branches a dorsal digital branch and posterior digital branch. The dorsal digital branch distributes its branches in the skin and corium of the hoof on the anterior surface of the digit. The posterior digital branch supplies innervation to the skin and corium of the hoof and other structures of the posterior portions of the foot.

DIGITAL NERVES. Blocking of the digital nerves is usually performed to confirm or disprove a diagnosis of navicular disease. Just below the fetlock joint the nerves lie in rather close contact to either edge of the deep flexor tendon. To block these nerves two to four cubic centimeters of a four percent solution is injected over each nerve. The area anesthetized will be confined to the posterior part of the foot.

VOLAR NERVES. The area to inject the volar nerves is located about two inches above the fetlock joint. This is above where the nerves start to divide and below where the anastomotic branch passes from the medial to the lateral volar nerve.

The area anesthetized by blocking the volar nerves is the foot, pastern region and fetlock joint except for a narrow area on the anterior surface. If the horse moves sound after blocking the volar nerves it is definite evidence that the seat of the lameness is in the desensitized area. By blocking only one of the volar nerves it may be determined if the painful lesion is confined to one side. This is important if a neurectomy is to be performed as the operator can definitely determine upon what nerves it is necessary to perform the neurectomy operation. In some painful conditions affecting the feet, as acute laminitis, it is possible to obtain temporary relief from the severe pain by blocking the volar nerves. This relief from severe pain may be the turning point in the recovery of the animal.

ULNAR NERVE. The site for blocking the ulnar nerve is located about four inches above the accessory carpal bone of the posterior aspect of the forearm. By careful palpation, a groove may be felt between the flexor carpi ulnaris and ulnaris lateralis muscles. The needle is inserted through the skin and antebrachial fascia to the nerve which is found just beneath the fascia. If the anesthetic solution is injected so it comes in contact with the nerve four to six cubic centimeters of the four percent solution is sufficient.

MUSCULO - CUTANEOUS NERVE. If complete anesthesia of the fore limb below the carpus is to be obtained it is necessary to block the musculo cutaneous nerve, median and ulnar nerve. The musculo-cutaneous nerve may be anesthetized on the surface of the radius halfway between the elbow and carpus and just in front of the cephalic vein.

MEDIAN NERVE. This rather large nerve is located most easily about two inches below the elbow joint. It is usually found behind the posterior border of the radius and anterior to the muscular portion of the flexor carpi radialis muscle. The needle is inserted through the skin, posterior superficial pectoral muscle and the antebrachial fascia to the nerve, the needle may have to be inserted as much as one and one-half inches. The median nerve is large and not too definitely situated so it is advisable to inject ten to twenty cubic centimeters of the four percent solution of the local anesthetic.

BLOCKING NERVES TO THE HIND LIMB. The indications for blocking the nerves of the posterior limb are not as numerous as those of the anterior limb. The results from blocking the plantar nerves are more variable than the corresponding volar nerves of the anterior limb. The location and technique of blocking the plantar and digital nerves of the posterior limb corresponds very closely to the technique of blocking the corresponding nerves of the anterior limb.

TIBIAL NERVE. The tibial nerve of the posterior limb corresponds very closely in size and distribution to the median nerve of the anterior limb. This nerve may be most easily located about four inches above the summit of the tuber calcis. The nerve can usually be palpated between the thumb and fingers. This is accomplished by placing the fingers on one side and the thumb on the other side of the achilles tendon. Then with the fingers and thumb palpate deeply into the tissue immediately posterior to the deep digital flexor muscle. The nerve about as large as a lead pencil may be palpated through the skin and fascia and use ten cubic centimeters of a four percent solution of the local anesthetic to inject around the nerve.

DEEP PERONEAL NERVE. This nerve is located on the lateral side of the tibia lying along the edge of the tibialis anterior muscle. Its location is most easily determined by palpating for the septum that separates the long and lateral digital extensor muscles. The depth the needle will have to be inserted will depend upon the muscular development of the patient. On the average the needle will need to be inserted from one to one and one half inches. The needle is started distal to the most prominent development of the muscles and along the anterior surface of the septum dividing the two muscles. Due to its location it is not as easy to block this nerve as those nerves which are more superficial. This nerve is about the same size as the ulnar nerve of the anterior limb so four to six cubic centimeters of the anesthetic solution is used.

Paravertebral Lumbar Anesthesia

Paravertebral, block is made close to the spinal column at the emergence of the nerve trunks from the intervertebral foraminae. By using this method of anesthesia the region of the flank of the bovine may be anesthetized for Caesarean section and rumenotomy. When the paravertebral lumbar nerves are blocked all of the tissue in the abdominal wall including the peritoneum is anesthetized.

ANATOMY. In the bovine the paralumbar fossa is the region where most of the operations are performed in the abdominal wall. The nerve supply to this area is derived from the ventral branches of the last thoracic and first two lumbar nerves. Occasionally the last thoracic and first two lumbar intervertebral foramina are double in the cow. The interverbral foramina of the last thoracic vertebrae is posterior to the head of the last rib. In the lumbar vertebrae the intervertebral foramina are located between the bases of the transverse processes and usually on the same level.

After the spinal nerves pass through the intervertebral foramina they divide into dorsal and ventral branches. The nerve supply of the skin, fascia, muscles and peritoneum is derived from the ventral branches of the three nerves.

To block the nerves it is necessary to inject the anesthetic solution at the point where the nerves emerge from the intervertebral foramina. This is most easily accomplished by using a one inch, sixteen gauge needle to pass through the skin. Then a twenty or twenty-two gauge needle four inches long is passed through the larger needle and muscle to the point of injection. It is usually necessary to insert the needle about two and one-half inches in an animal in average condition. A two percent solution of a local anesthetic is the strength of solution usually used.

The points to insert the needle are most easily determined by locating the spinous processes of the first two lumbar vertebrae and the head of the last rib. To locate the head of the rib follow the last rib upward with the fingers until the head is felt about two inches lateral to the median line. This is the place on the skin to insert the needle to block the last thoracic spinal nerve. The areas on the skin to insert the needle to block the first two lumbar nerves are found by drawing imaginary lines transversely from the posterior borders of the first and second lumbar spinous processes. The needle is inserted on these lines at a point two inches lateral to the median line. Before inserting the needle a small area on the skin should be shaved, cleansed thoroughly, and an efficient skin antiseptic applied. With the sixteen gauge needle inserted through the skin the smaller longer needle is passed through it. The direction of the longer needle should be downward and parallel to the median plane for about two inches. As the needle is inserted more deeply into the tissues a small amount of the anesthetic solution is injected ahead of the needle. In the average case the needle will have to be inserted about two and one-half inches before reaching the nerve. If the point of the needle strikes the rib or the transverse process it should be directed backward to the posterior edge of the bone. When the operator feels the needle is in proper position, five cubic centimeters of the anesthetic solution should be deposited over the nerve. The remainder of the anesthetic solution is deposited in the tissue around the nerve as the point of the needle is pushed back and forth. In most cases it will be advisable to inject five cubic centimeters over the third lumbar nerve to anesthetize a cutaneous branch of this nerve. The tissues in the operative area should be tested in five to ten minutes to see if anesthesia is complete. In most cases a slight lateral curvature of the back may be noticed on the side that was anesthetized because the motor nerves are also affected.

Spinal Anesthesia

Spinal anesthesia is the instroduction into the spinal canal of a local anesthetic solution, which by coming into contact with the spinal nerves and nerve roots temporarily paralyzes them and produces anesthesia of those parts supplied by the sensory portions of the nerves. Spinal anesthesia is produced by injecting the anesthetic solution into the subarachnoid space where it mixes with the cerebrospinal fluid. By means of spinal anesthesia it is possible to render the entire body insensible to pain.

In epidural or extradural anesthesia the needle does not penetrate the meninges so the anesthetic solution comes in contact with the nerves after they pass through the dura mater. Epidural anesthesia is most useful in the bovine and equine to control straining for the manipulations necessary to correct a mal-position of the fetus. It is also ideal to control straining while a prolapsed rectum, vagina or uterus is returned to its proper position. According to Benesch epidural anesthesia does not inhibit the normal involution of the uterus.

Epidural Anesthesia in the Bovine

The method of anesthesia was first intro duced into this country by Benesch of Vienna in 1926. This form of anesthesia soon became very popular with the veterinarians of this country.

Bovine

Epidural anesthesia is used more in the bovine than any of the other species. This is because there are more indications for its use in this species and also because its members are more numerous. In the bovine the needle may be inserted into the vertebral canal between the last sacral and first coccygeal vertebrae or between the first and second coccygeal vertebrae. These two points may be determined by grasping the tail and elevating it dorsally and moving it from side to side. By palpation movement will be detected at either of these two points and also a distinct depression will be felt between the vertebrae. Of the two points probably the one between the last sacral and first coccygeal is the preferred one. The area should be prepared as for an aseptic operation. The patient will not object to the introduction of the needle if an insensitive weal is first made in the skin with a fine needle. Then a two inch 16 gauge needle may be started through the skin at approximately a 45° angle. The depth the needle will need to be inserted will vary with the breed, whether dairy or beef, and the age of the animal. In the average case the depth will vary from one and one-eighth inches to one and one-half inches. The needle should be inserted until the point is felt to strike the bottom of the vertebral canal and then retracted a short distance. The ease with which the anesthetic solution is injected through the needle is another important guide that the needle is in the vertebral canal. A glass syringe may be used to inject the anesthetic solution. With a glass syringe there is practically no friction between the plunger and barrel so it is readily determined if any pressure is required to inject the anesthetic solution into the vertebral canal. If pressure is required the needle is probably not in its proper position or possibly the needle has passed through the canal and the point may be in the intervertebral cartilage. Of the local anesthetics procaine hydrochloride is probably the most widely used because of its low toxicity and dependable anesthetic action.

The strength of the anesthetic solution will vary with the preference of the operator. To control the straining in replacing prolapsed organs, rectum, vagina and uterus, a one percent solution will control straining. This amount will also anesthetize the tissues for some minor operations in the perineal region. For more painful and extensive operations as caesarean section in the small heifer a dosage of 40 cubic centimeters of a two percent solution should be used. In larger heifers it is usually advisable to use 50 cubic centimeters of a two and one-half percent solution of the local anesthetic. For the more extensive operations as amputation of the udder it is necessary to use 40 to 50 cubic centimeters of a three percent solution.

Equine

The equine is usually more susceptible to the introduction of the needle so it is advantageous to first anesthetize the skin. In the equine the first coccygeal vertebrae is usually fused to the last sacral vertebrae so the needle will have to be introduced into the vertebral canal between the first and second coccygeal vertebrae. The distance the needle will need to be inserted is slightly less than in the bovine. In a 1000 pound horse in average condition the needle will have to be inserted about one and one-eighth inches. The dosage is approximately the same as indicated for the various procedures in the bovine. Due to the more nervous temperament of the equine it may be necessary to quiet the patient with nembutal or chloral hydrate.

Porcine

Epidural anesthesia is not as frequently indicated in swine as in some of the other species. Also the procedure is slightly more difficult in this species because of the thick layer of fat over the vertebrae. The thickness of this layer of fat will vary with the condition of the animal. In the porcine the place to insert the needle into the vertebral canal is between the last lumbar and the first sacral vertebrae or the lumbo-sacral space. The point to insert the needle on the median line is located by drawing an imaginary line across the anterior borders of the wings of the ilii. Then approximately two and one-half inches posterior to this line a needle is inserted through the skin on the median line. A three inch, eighteen gauge needle is directed in a downward and forward direction at about a 45° angle. The needle will have to be inserted from two to two and one-half inches in a 80 pound pig. As the needle is inserted through the tissues the point may strike the posterior edge of the spine of the last lumbar vertebrae which may be used as a guide to the lumbo-sacral space. The point of the needle may be felt to strike the edge of the opening before passing through the lumbo-sacral space. A few minutes after the injection of the anesthetic solution the tail will be relaxed. For operations we use a two percent solution of procaine hydrochloride and one cubic centimeter of the solution is used for each ten pounds of body weight. For operations posterior to the abdominal cavity a slightly smaller amount may be used. For a pig weighing eighty pounds six cubic centimeters is usually the correct dosage. This form of anesthesia has been used in swine for caesarean section, hernias and scirrhous cord operations. The anesthetic solution is usually injected with the patient standing on its feet and then is placed on the operating table. It is important not to place the patient with with the head lower than the posterior parts for the anesthetic solution may flow too far forward and affect some of the vital centers.

General Anesthesia

To produce general anesthesia it is necessary that the anesthetizing substance enter into the general circulation. It is only by this method that the higher centers can be brought under control. General anesthesia may be brought about indirectly by oral or rectal administration. It may be given directly by intraperitoneal or intravenous anesthesia.

Complete Anesthesia

Complete anesthesia is divided into three stages:

a. Stage of Induction
b. Stage of Maintenance
c. Stage of Recovery

Stage of induction is further divided into three periods:

a. Period of excitement, cerebral and muscular.
b. Period of rigidity.
c. Period of relaxation.

Stage of maintenance not subdivided.

Stage of Recovery is further divided into two periods:

a. Return of the reflexes.

b. Return of consciousness.

The state of induction extends from the beginning of the administration of the anesthetic to the point where general muscular relaxation has been brought about. This stage leading the patient as it does from consciousness to deep anesthesia is the most difficult and important of the three stages. The undervaluation of this is responsible for the failures which one sees in otherwise uncomplicated anesthesias.

The stage of maintenance extends from the completion of relaxation to the point where the anesthetic level which has been carried is permitted to drop with the view of allowing the patient to recover. The stage of maintenance should begin just before the time of the first incision and should cease shortly before the conclusion of the operative procedure.

The stage of recovery is the inverse of the stage of induction. The stage of recovery begins when the constant level which has been carried during the stage of maintenance is permitted to drop permanently. The stage of recovery ends with the return of consciousness.

Induction anesthetizes the patient

Maintenance keeps him anesthetized

Recovery returns him to consciousness

The stage of maintenance begins when general relaxation obtains and when a constant depth of anesthesia has been reached. It ends when the level which has been held is permanently permitted to drop. Maintenance keeps the patient so completely anesthetized throughout the operation that he will not inconveniently react to deeper stimuli. The amount of anesthetic required to keep the patient in the stage of maintenance will vary with the sensitiveness of the tissues. The skin and peritoneum are more sensitive and will react more energetically than the muscle and bone tissues. In the stage of maintenance the color, respirations, pulse and the eye signs are the most important.

The evidences of the stage of Recovery are shown by (a) the gradual and complete return of the reflexes, (b) the return of consciousness. One of the first signs to appear, upon allowing the patient to recover is slowing down of the respirations. The pupil which has been moderately dilated during the stage of maintenance will contract. There will be rolling of the eyeballs, also active lid and corneal reflexes.

The corneal reflex. This reflex is without doubt the most valuable eye sign which we have. When the cornea is touched and the degree of activity with which the eyelid then closes, constitutes one of the most unvarying signs of the depth of the anesthesia.

During the period of excitement and rigidity the corneal reflex is snappy: as relaxation comes on the sharpness of the reflex gradually decreases. When maintenance has been entered into, the reflex has either become quite sluggish or is absent. The reappearance of the corneal reflex and its variable activity during the stage of maintenance will give one a most satisfactory idea as to the exact depth of the anesthesia.

General Anesthesia for the Equine

The use of a general anesthetic in the equine is indicated when the operation is so extensive or in an area where the pain cannot be controlled by the use of a local anesthetic. Also some individuals are of such a temperment that it is necessary to give a general anesthetic before the operation can be performed. In some large animals the production of general anesthesia may be facilitated by the use of a basal anesthetic.

Before the administration of any general anesthetic the patient should receive a thorough physical examination. The use of a general anesthetic is contra-indicated if the patient is affected with any condition that markedly lowers its vitality and especially any affection of the circulatory or respiratory systems.

Chloroform

Of the inhalant anesthetics, chloroform is the most important one used in large animals. Excellent surgical anesthesia can be obtained in the horse by using chloroform. The horse tolerates chloroform anesthesia better than any other domestic animal and recovery is rapid and complete. Occasionally a horse is found to be quite resistant to the action of chloroform. When this is pronounced it is safer to resort to some other form of anesthesia.

The method of administering the chloroform will vary with the preference of the anesthetist. It may be administered by putting a definite quantity of chloroform into an inhaler or muzzle. If a muzzle or inhaler is not available a heavy towel can be fastened over the nose. The average initial dosage of chloroform for a one or two year old horse is one ounce and for an adult horse is one and one-half to two ounces. To prolong the period of anesthesia additional quantities of chloroform may be given from time to time. The stimulant stage can be shortened or abolished by giving chloral hydrate as a basal anesthetic. Chloral hydrate may be given intravenously or introduced into the stomach and the amount used will depend upon the size and vigor of the patient and the results desired.

Another method of administration that can be used is the use of drops. With this technique the patient is confined in lateral recumbency and the lower nostril is closed tightly with cotton. The inside of the upper nostril is coated with vaseline. A towel is applied over the upper nostril and the administration of chloroform is started with a few drops on the towel with each inspiration. As the symptoms indicate a tolerance for the chloroform the amount is increased until the stage of anesthesia is reached. Only enough chloroform should now be given to hold the patient in the stage of anesthesia.

Chloral Hydrate

Chloral hydrate belongs to the group of hypnotics. In moderate doses it depresses the cerebrum producing a deep sleep while in larger doses it may serve as a general anesthetic. The use of chloral hydrate for general anesthesia in large animals has been increasing in recent years. This increasing popularity is due to its ease of administration and wide range of safety.

Chloral hydrate may be administered, into the stomach, intravenously or intraperitoneally. For intravenous use a seven per cent solution is usually used although stronger solutions may be administered.

In giving the chloral hydrate the patient will pass through the same stages as in chloroform anesthesia, but the symptoms will not be so pronounced. There is some variation in the amount of chloral hydrate required in individuals of the same weight. To prevent the development of any unfavorable sequela from the effects of chloral hydrate only enough should be given to obtain the desired results. The amount of chloral hydrate used may vary from one-half ounce in a Shetland pony to more than three ounces in a draft horse. The stage of surgical anesthesia may be determined by the complete relaxation of the muscles and insensibility to pain in the operative area. The period of recovery from chloral hydrate is rather variable and may vary from one to several hours.

Chloral Hydrate and Magnesium Sulphate

In an attempt to reduce the irritant action and toxic action of chloral hydrate the use of magnesium sulphate has been recommended. A combination of equal parts of chloral hydrate and magnesium sulphate has been found to be superior to chloral hydrate alone. The dosage of the preparation when administered intravenously is approximately twenty grams of the mixture for each 220 pounds of body weight. The magnesium sulphate seems to hasten the action of the chloral hydrate and decreases its toxicity.

Another preparation recommended by Danks contains 12 percent of chloral hydrate and six percent of magnesium sulphate. To determine the irritant action of this preparation as compared with chloral hydrate it was injected into muscular tissue. It was found that when 125 cubic centimeters of a solution of chloral hydrate was injected into the tissues abscessation and sloughing of the tissues occurred. When 250 cubic centimeters of the combination of chloral hydrate and magnesium sulphate was injected into muscular tissue swelling occurred but this subsided in eight days. There was no evidence of abscess formation or sloughing of tissue. He recommended the rate of injection should not exceed one ounce per minute intravenously.

Chloral hydrate is an excellent hypnotic for its action to facilitate the handling of nervous or vicious individuals. In some unusual cases of viciousness best results may be obtained if the chloral hydrate is dissolved in the drinking water. It will probably be necessary to keep water away from the individual until they will drink water that contains chloral hydrate. In more quiet individuals the stomach tube may be passed and the solution of chloral hydrate introduced into the stomach or it may be given intravenously.

One other preparation that contains chloral hydrate, magnesium sulphate and pentobarbital sodium has been recommended by Millenbruck and Wallinga. They feel that the addition of pentobarbital sodium to chloral hydrate and magnesium sulphate results in a marked increase in the safety factor. They anesthetized more than fifty horses without observing any unfavorable results. The ingredients in the solution which they preferred consisted of chloral hydrate one ounce, magnesium sulphate one-half ounce and pentobarbital sodium 100 grains dissolved in 1000 cubic centimeters of distilled water.

According to their observations, in using this preparation there is an absence of the excitement stage. Also there seems to be a wide range of safety in its use. They also observed there was less struggling during the period of recovery. This preparation is given intravenously rather slowly until the horse begins to stagger. The flow of solution is increased until the horse is ready to fall and continued until proper narcosis is obtained. They observed the two most important signs to indicate surgical anesthesia are the corneal reflex and the slowing of nystagmus.

Groves reports that by adding ethyl alcohol to the mixture of chloral hydrate, magnesium sulphate, and sodium pentobarbital a more stable product is produced. He recommends a base mixture of chloral hydrate to gm. magnesium sulfate 30 gm and distilled water enough to make 350 cc. To complete the mixture ethyl alcohol 100 cc and sodium pentobarbital 50 cc is added. This mixture is very effective in producing anesthesia and is also economical. It is recommended to use 1 cc for each 3 lbs. of body weight for general anesthesia and 1 cc for each 10 lbs. of body weight for sedation.

Nembutal

The barbituric acid derivatives are effective sedatives and hypnotics. Nembutal is one of the barbituric acid derivatives used as a general anesthetic in large animals it is not generally used because of the expense and long period of recovery from its effects. In foals Fowler says it may be used as a general anesthetic in doses of five to twenty-five cubic centimeters and up to seventy-five cubic centimeters for older colts. In young calves and small cattle nembutal may be given intravenously with good results. The dosage will vary from fifty to one hundred and twenty-five cubic centimeters.

In mature horses excellent results have been obtained in using nembutal as a sedative. For a horse weighing a thousand pounds fifteen cubic centimeters injected intravenously will in a few minutes facilitate the handling of a nervous individual. For a larger and more nervous horse the amount used may be increased. The sedative dose for a horse suffering from pain in the digestive tract is usually fifteen to twenty-five cubic centimeters administered intravenously. It was observed by Danks that when pentobarbital sodium was used in horses and complete anesthesia was desired that one grain for each 15 pounds live weight was required, for incomplete anesthesia one grain for 20 pounds live weight and for hypnosis one grain for 25 pounds.

Bovine

Chloroform is recommended for use in the bovine but when used alone it is decidedly dangerous in action. The toxic action appears to affect the circulatory system with particular severity and death is generally due to simultaneous failure of the circulatory and respiratory systems. For the purpose of safeguarding the heart it is well to inject one-fourth to one-half grain of atropine sulphate fifteen to thirty minutes before the administration of chloroform. By this procedure the margin of safety is increased and excellent anesthesia can be developed and maintained for operative procedures.

Probably the safest general anesthetic for use in the bovine is chloral hydrate, or the chloral hydrate solution and magnesium sulphate. The chloral hydrate may be administered in the stomach or given intravenously. If the chloral hydrate is to be administered intravenously a twelve percent solution may be used with a six percent solution of magnesium sulphate. The safety of the chloral hydrate may be increased by withholding food from the patient for twenty-four hours before the operation. Chloral hydrate should not be used for complete general anesthesia for caesarean section if the fetus is alive. As a general rule the fetus is killed by the chloral hydrate. In those animals that are fat the safest procedure would be to just give enough of the chloral hydrate to control the struggling and complete anesthesia of the operative area with a local anesthetic. The approximate intravenous dose of chloral hydrate is based on 10 gram of chloral hydrate for each 220 pounds of live weight. For some individuals the dosage will be less while other patients will be more resistant to the action of chloral hydrate and require more than the suggested dose.

The use of chloral hydrate is indicated to facilitate the handling of those individuals that become excited and vicious when an attempt is made to restrain them. The chloral hydrate may be put in their drinking water after water has been withheld until they will drink water containing chloral hydrate. Usually in fifteen to twenty minutes the vicious animal may be restrained without difficulty.

Porcine

General anesthesia is required to some extent in the porcine, and ether, chloroform and chloral hydrate may be used. With ether and chloroform a fair margin of safety exists but care must be taken in administering these drugs or respiratory and circulatory failure will occur with slight overdosage.

Chloral hydrate may be introduced into the fasted stomach or emptied rectum using ten to twelve grams of the crystals well diluted with water to a fifty pound animal.

The chloral hydrate and magnesium sulphate solution may be injected into the ear vein until the proper degree of anesthesia is obtained. It has also been observed that good surgical anesthesia is produced when the chloral hydrate and magnesium sulphate is administered intraperitoneally. This method is much simpler than by the intravenous route. The dose of chloral hydrate to produce surgical anesthesia may be based on two grains for each pound of body weight.

It was observed by Danks that pentobarbital sodium may be given to swine with good results. When the pentobarbital sodium is injected into the ear vein there is an interval of from two to four minutes between time of injection and development of anesthesia. If the anesthetic solution is injected intraperitoneally the time interval is from 10 to 14 minutes. The duration of surgical anesthesia is the same for the chloral hydrate and magnesium sulphate as it is for the pentobarbital sodium from one and one-half to four hours.

Ovine

The demand for general anesthesia in the ovine is very limited but occasionally a case is presented where its use is advisable. The ovine exhibits a marked susceptibility to the action of chloroform and ether. Chloroform anesthesia is usually followed by delayed toxemia characterized by extensive degeneration of the liver, kidneys and cardiac muscle. Chloral hydrate is usually satisfactory when given intravenously in doses of five to ten grams. Nembutal may be used to quiet the patient and a local anesthetic to infiltrate the tissues in the operative area.

Tranquilizers

The tranquilizing agents are referred to as "ataraxics" which means, freedom from confusion. These new drugs act on the lower nervous centers, the thalmus, hypothalamus and reticular formation. The drugs that exert their action on the autonomic nervous system through the hypothalamus and reticular formation are reserpine and other Rauwolfia alkaloids and phenothiazine derivatives. Those drugs acting on the central nervous system exert a specific effect on the thalamus as, mephenesin and other propanoidiol derivatives. Rauwolfia and reserpine act on the cardiovascular and central nervous system. The conventional doses of these drugs lower the arterial blood pressure and slow the heart rate producing a sedative effect.

Mephenesin is a synthetic ether derived from glycerol. It is a relaxant producing skeletal muscular relaxation without loss of consciousness. This compounds action is rather brief so its value is rather restricted.

Maprobamate (Equanil) is a new longer acting propanediol derivative. The muscle relaxing action is similar to that of mephenesin but is more potent and of longer duration. It is safe, effective, generally uniform in action and practically free of any side reactions.

Chlorpromazine is a synthetic phenothiazine derivative and has a depressant effect on the central nervous system of domesticated animals. It may be used to tranquilize the highstrung, vicious or those animals that are difficult to handle. Also it may be used as an adjunct to a general anesthetic as the animal then requires a smaller amount of the general anesthetic. Also the combined use of phenothiazine tranquilizers and a general anesthetic may increase the margin of safety. But the combination should be used with caution until one has become experienced in using them. When a tranquilizer is given intravenously it should be given slowly and with caution.

Some of the phenothiazine derivatives as mepazine, perphenazine, sparine, compazine and vesprin have been developed in an attempt to remove some of the objectionable side effects of chlorpromazine. By using one of the phenothiazine tranquilizers before giving a general anesthetic it is felt that animals recover with less struggling than is usual with only a general anesthetic.

Promazine hydrochloride produces a consistent response in the equine in obtaining the desired degree of tranquilization. The equine responds to the administration of promazine hydrochloride by muscular relaxation. The intravenous dosage is based on 0.5 mg. per pound of body weight or approximately 500 mg to the average equine administered intravenously. The maximum effect is obtained in fifteen minutes. It has also been observed that it requires 40 percent less of the general anesthetic to produce surgical anesthesia. The recovery from general anesthesia is obtained with less struggling, no excitement and in a shorter period of time. The promazine hydrochloride may be used to control nervous or patients difficult to handle for many minor procedures.

In the bull the use of promazine hydrochloride in a dosage of 500 mg intravenously will produce a relaxation of the retractor penis muscle. It may also be used to control vicious and unruly animals. The dosage in many cases will be determined by the results that are desired and will not be the same for each individual.

When using tranquilizers in swine the recommended dosage should be observed very carefully and in hot humid weather should be reduced by 25 to 30 percent. The proportion of body weight to fat should be considered in calculating the dosage for aged boars or fat hogs. For example a 700 pound boar or sow may be tranquilized with the dosage recommended for a 400 - 500 pound animal. After treatment the animals should be kept in a cool, dark place away from noise and left alone for twelve to eighteen hours. If there is hyperexcitability and the value of the animal justifies the expense Cogentin (Merck) may be used. Hysteria in sows is sometimes observed at farrowing time and if not controlled they may eat, destroy or injure their pigs. This hysteria in sows has been controlled by giving 100 mg intramuscularly and in a few minutes the sows would permit the pigs to nurse.

REFERENCES

Abstract- Chloral- magnesium Anesthesia, J.A.V.M.A., XCV, 749, August, 1939, pp. 151.

Bemis, H. E., Guard, W. F., and Covault, C. H., 1924, Anesthesia, General and Local, J.A.V.M.A., lXlV, January, 1924, N. S. 17, (4), pp. 413.

Danks, A. G., Anesthesia in Horses and Swine, Cornell Veterinarian, Vol.XXXlll, October, 1943, No. 4.

Farquharson, J., Paravertebral Lumbar Anesthesia in the Bovine Species, J.A.V.M.A., Vol. XCVll, (1940), pp. 54-57.

Foley, E. J., McDonald, G. F., D.V.M., Robertson, W. G., PhD., and Segrist, J. C., D.V.M., Use of Perphenazine in Feed Lot Cattle, Veterinary Medicine, October, 1958.

Fowler, George R., General Anesthesia in Large Animals, J.A.V.M.A., XCVl, 755, February, 1940, pp. 210.

Gans, Joseph H., The Pharmacology of Preanesthetic Agents, The Cornell Veterinarian, July, 1958, pp. 300-304.

Groves, Lawrence W., Large Animal Anesthesia, J.A.V.M.A., Vol. CXlV, July, 1951, pp. 50.

Raker, C. W., V.M.D., and English, Blair, Promazine Its Pharmacological and Clinical Effects on Horses, J.A.V.M.A., 134, January, 1959, pp. 19-22.

Raker, C. W., V.M.D., and Sayers, A. C., V.M.D., Promazine as a Preanesthetic Agent in Horses, J.A.V.M.A., 134, January, 1959, pp. 23-24.

Scheidy, Samuel F., and McNally, Kendall S., Smith, Kline and French Laboratories, The Cornell Veterinarian, July, 1958, pp. 331-346.

Chapter II
SURGICAL TECHNIQUE, SUTURES AND SUTURING AND RESTRAINT

Asepsis is the protection of wounds that have been made either for an operation or from injury, against infection from bacteria. In performing an operation that requires incising of the skin, the sterilization of the skin is relative and not absolute for the field is never completely aseptic. However by proper preoperative cleansing of the patients skin and the operators hands, also the sterilization of instruments, ligatures and operating equipment proper healing of the operative wounds is obtained. The operative area must also be protected from infection until healing has occurred. If the surgeon is to be successful he must be familiar with the principles and practice of sterilization, the preparation of the patient and operator and the instruments, suture materials and dressings. His knowledge must also include the best information, and practice in the technique of making, handling and closure of wounds.

Preoperative Preparation of the Hands

The skin has a bacterial flora that is composed of both transient and resident bacteria. If the hands are comparatively clean there should be few transient bacteria present but when present are rather easy to remove. The resident bacteria are located in the crevices of the skin, glands and hair follicles and are more difficult to remove or destroy.

In the preparation of the hands the finger nails should be cut short and the dirt cleaned from beneath and around the nails. The hands should be scrubbed in a routine manner using preferrably a cocoanut oil soap. All soaps are germicidal due to their cleansing action but this soap has a definite bactericidal effect due to its chemical nature. The scrubbing should be continued until all portions of the hands have been gone over at least thirty times with a brush. A stiff lather is maintained at all times. If this procedure is continued for at least seven minutes all gross dirt, transient bacteria, fats, and about half of the resident bacteria will be removed. All of the lather should be removed by a good rinse in running water.

A good germicide should then be used for its effect on the remaining resident bacteria. One method that may be used is to immerse the hands into a 70 percent by weight concentration of ethyl alcohol. This exact concentration is very important for it has been proven that a 70 percent by weight solution is 30 times as powerful as a 60 percent by weight solution or 40 times as effective as an 80 percent by weight preparation. This concentration may be prepared by the following formula.

Ethyl alcohol (95% at 25 C)____815 cc
Cold distilled water q.s. ad__1000 cc

To maintain the efficiency of the alcohol the hands should be wiped dry so the alcohol will not be diluted by any water. This efficiency may be increased by friction with gauze for one minute with the alcohol and it will be equal to 6.5 minutes of scrubbing with soap and water.

A preparation with a higher bactericidal efficiency than the ethyl alcohol is composed of,

Ethyl alcohol (95%)	675 cc
N prophyl alcohol (C.P.)	250 cc
Distilled water	250 cc

Mixing of the ingredients should be made at a temperature of 25 C. If the hands are rubbed with this preparation for one minute it is equal to eleven minutes of scrubbing.

A method of hand disinfection recommended by Kelly consisted in using hot saturated solutions of potassium permanganate. The stain of the potassium permanganate was removed with oxalic acid. This procedure usually required from two and one-half to five minutes depending upon the temperature of the solutions. This procedure is considered to be equal to scrubbing for twenty to thirty minutes.

The chlorine compounds are used as disinfectants for the skin and when properly used are very effective. One popular and efficient preparation is the lime paste.

Chlorinated lime (30%)______200 gm
Sodium bicarbonate ______200 gm
Sodium carbonate (C.P.)______ 80 bm

This preparation should be stored as a dry powder for the chlorine content is lost rapidly when the mixture comes in contact with water. In using this preparation the powder is mixed in the hands with enough water to make a thin paste. If the hands are rubbed with this paste for four minutes it is equal to twenty minutes of scrubbing.

After using one of the above methods of disinfecting the hands the margin of safety may be increased by the use of a 1-1000 solution of bichloride of mercury in alcohol for one minute. The mercuric salt forms a film on the skin.

The use of the most effective method of disinfection of the skin will not make the hands sterile. As all of the bacteria on the hands cannot be removed it is also necessary to use sterile rubber gloves if the operation is to be aseptic.

Preparation of the Field of Operation

In all operations on our animals it is usually necessary to shave the operative area. After shaving, the skin should be thoroughly washed with soap and water to remove all dirt, most of the fats and practically all of the transient bacteria. The soap is rinsed off and the skin dried.

Probably the most efficient method of preparing the skin before the operation is to use a piece of gauze and scrub it with 70 percent by weight of alcohol or the mixture of the two alcohols may be used. The alcohols should be allowed to dry slowly for their efficiency as skin disinfectants will depend upon the time they are in contact with the skin.

Another method of skin disinfection consists in applying U.S.P. tincture of iodine to the skin and allowed to dry slowly. The iodine is then washed off by the use of alcohol which makes a very effective method of skin disinfection.

The prevention of contamination of the operative area from the skin of the patient is very difficult. Most of the resident bacteria of the deeper portions of the skin are located in the sebaceous glands and hair follicles. The greatest danger of contamination from these bacteria will be in those areas where these structures are the most numerous. To prevent contamination of the deeper tissues in the operative area it is important to discard the scalpel that is used to make the skin incision. Also the surface and cut edges of the skin should be kept covered during the operation. After the operation is completed and just before the closure of the skin the drapes used during the operation should be removed. The perspiration is removed, the skin is cleansed as for the operation and sterile drapes put on. After this procedure there is little chance of contaminating the area from the needles passing through the skin.

Rubber Gloves

For many of the operations performed it is desirable to wear sterile rubber gloves. The use of sterile rubber gloves are essential for the operator and his assistants if the operation is to be aseptic.

If rubber gloves are to be properly sterilized the preparation of the gloves before they are put in the sterilizer is of the utmost importance. To permit the interchange of air and steam in the fingers and palm of the glove it is necessary to place a gauze sponge in the cuff. A convenient method of making a powder puff of the sponge is to place about one gram of talcum powder in its meshes. When the gloves are placed in the sterilizer they should be put on edge with the thumbs up. This will insure a clearance of the air. The rubber gloves should be sterilized for 30 minutes at 250 F.

After the hands have been prepared in the manner described the rubber gloves may be put on either dry or wet. In using the gloves dry they are prepared in the usual manner, placed in a sterile container and sterilized with steam. When they are to be used the hands are powdered and the dry gloves put on. For the wet glove technique the gloves are removed from their sterile container before the operation. They are then placed in a sterile basin containing a germicidal solution. When the operator is ready the gloves are filled with the germicidal solution. The hands are then forced into the distended gloves after which the hands are raised to allow any excess solution to run out. With this technique any small openings in the glove will be detected when the germicidal solution is put in. Also it has been demonstrated the germicidal solution in contact with the hand will keep it sterile during the operation. It has also been observed the hands seem to be in better condition after the operation.

Sterilization of Instruments

Before instruments are ready to be sterilized they must be free of all spots of pus, blood, feces, or grease. To cleanse the instruments they may be placed to soak in a solution of soap, rinsed and polished. Surgical instruments are usually of three kinds, those which will withstand sterilization by moist heat and those with sharp cutting edges that corrode when exposed to moist heat. Also there are some instruments not resistent to heat that require chemical sterilization.

The use of boiling water is a frequent means of sterilizing instruments. This method has its limitations as the maximum temperature attainable is 212 F. at sea level which does not kill some spores. The efficiency of this method of sterilization can be increased by making sure there are no air pockets and all instruments are covered with water. Also the germicidal action may be increased and the corrosive action of the water decreased by adding 2 percent sodium carbonate or 0.1 percent sodium hydroxide to the water to alkalinize it. The advantage of alkalinizing the water is the boiling of the instruments can be reduced from thirty to fifteen minutes.

Another method of heat sterilization which is the most effective is that of saturated steam under pressure. However when instruments are sterilized by this method corrosion may occur because of the condensation of steam on them. In sterilizing instruments by steam under pressure the steam may be used at 250 F. for fifteen minutes.

Dry heat may also be used for sterilization of instruments and is very efficient when properly used. However the temperature must be carefully controlled or it will draw the temper of any cutting edge and the instrument is ruined.

Sterilization of Instruments by Chemicals

The use of chemicals for the sterilization of instruments is not often effective for several reasons. If the chemicals are used in the concentrations recommended they are bacteriostatic rather than germicidal. Also most chemicals are selective in their action destroying some organisms and only inhibiting the action of other organisms. The action of some chemicals depends upon an exact concentration and any deviation from this destroys their efficiency. Any blood, pus, grease or tissue on the instruments will decrease their reliability. The use of chemicals to sterilize instruments should be limited to those instruments that will be injured by heat.

A number of chemicals have been tested for their efficiency in the sterilization of instruments and formaldehyde was one of the few that was found suitable. Formaldehyde may be used in either an aqueous or alcoholic solution. For these solutions to be reliable the instruments must be free of all pus, blood, feces or anything that will prevent the germicide coming in contact with the metal. To destroy spores it is necessary that the instrument remain in the solution for eighteen hours. The drug may be irritating to the tissues of some individuals so the formaldehyde should be all allowed to evaporate or be rinsed from the instruments. Any of the following formula may be used and they can be easily and economically prepared.

a. Sodium tetraborate __________ 50 gm
   Formalin (10%) q.s. ad _____ 1000 cc

b. Formalin (38%) __________ 130 gm
   Potassium nitrite __________ 0.15 gm
   Sodium hydroxide __________ 0.012 gm
   Ethyl alcohol C.P. (95%)
   q.s. ad _____ 1000 cc

c. Formalin (38%) __________ 135 cc
   Sodium hydroxide __________ 10 gm
   Distilled water q.s. ad _____ 1000 cc

One of the best commercial chemical germicides is the Bard-Parker solution which is non-corrosive and instruments may be kept in it continuously for long periods of time.

For the disinfection of bulky rubber goods they may be immersed in an alkaline solution of formaldehyde for two hours.

Formalin (38%) __________ 135 cc

Sodium hydroxide______________10 gm
Distilled water q.s. ad.______1000 cc

Also another method is to thoroughly cleanse the rubber goods to be sterilized and soak them in a solution of chlorinated lime that contains 1:1000 free chlorine.

Sterilization of Surgical Dressings

It has been conclusively demonstrated that saturated steam under pressure is the most reliable method of sterilizing textiles. The equipment does not need to be very elaborate as some of the most complicated is the least efficient. If pressure cookers are operated efficiently they will produce the desired results. When saturated steam comes in contact with textiles it enters into it very readily. Saturated steam at 250°F. is very bactericidal as it will destroy spores in thirteen minutes.

To obtain maximum results from the use of saturated steam the packages must be placed so there is free access of the steam to them. If the packages are crowded together it will be difficult for the steam to come in contact with the contents. All utensils may be wrapped and sterilized with saturated steam at 250°F. for thirty minutes.

CONCLUSION: The development of a good routine method of aseptic technique in surgery is not difficult to develop. The improved results following surgical operations will more than justify any slight expense that is needed to obtain the necessary equipment.

Sutures and Suturing

Suture, when used as a verb, means to stitch or sew. In surgery it means the stitching together of the edges or lips of a wound to effect union. The ideal suture is one which will remain intact long enough to secure rest to the divided structures and which will cause a minimum amount of reaction in the tissues. As a general rule the quickest healing is obtained when the least amount of suture material is used. Surgery may be said to have progressed with improvement in the choice and preparation of sutures.

Ligature, when used as a noun, means the thread or cord with which an artery or vein is tied to prevent or control hemorrhage. It is also applied to a cord, thread, or wire used to remove tumors.

A variety of suture materials are available for suturing. Some are not absorbed as silk, linen, silkworn gut, horsehair, and the various metallic sutures. Unabsorbable suture material must not be used in the tissues if there is a possibility of infection as it may be the source of a chronic discharge for months. Absorbable sutures are those which, during the healing process of wounds, are absorbed by the tissues in which they are embedded. The most commonly used are catgut and kangaroo tendon.

Catgut

Catgut is made from the submucous layer of the small intestines of the sheep. Catgut may be used either plain or chromic and the object of chromicising catgut is to delay its absorption. The chemicals used to chromicise catgut are chromic acid, iodine, tannin, formalin, and others. The rate of disintegration of catgut varies a great deal depending upon the tissues in which the catgut is embedded. A double strand of small catgut engenders less reaction than a single strand of large suture material because it is easier for the tissue wandering cells to attack the former. Also smaller sizes of chromic catgut last as long as or longer than larger sizes for they are more thoroughly impregnated with the chromicising material. Plain catgut causes great reaction, is quickly absorbed, and is not as reliable as chromic catgut. It is customary to designate chromic catgut as "ten-day," "twenty-day," or "forty-day." These terms are used to indicate the relative resistance that the sutures offer to absorption when embedded in normal muscular tissue of aseptic wounds.

Kangaroo Tendon

The best kangaroo tendons come from the tail of the small kangaroo. These tendons have great tensile strength and are supposed to be absorbed more slowly than catgut. They are rather expensive and are used more by specialists for certain operations.

Silk

Silk is probably the best known and one of the oldest materials used as a suture or ligature. There are two varieties, "braided silk" and "twisted silk." Because of its pliability, ease of handling, and because it is easily tied into a tight knot that shows little tendency to slip, silk is still extensively used in surgery. However, due to its capillarity silk is unsuited for closing the skin as it may act as a wick and carry infection into the deeper tissues. When silk sutures are placed in aseptic wounds they become encapsulated and remain permanently in the tissues. If the silk is embedded in infected tissue the bacteria are harbored in its interstices and there is a persistent discharge until the silk comes away by itself or is surgically removed.

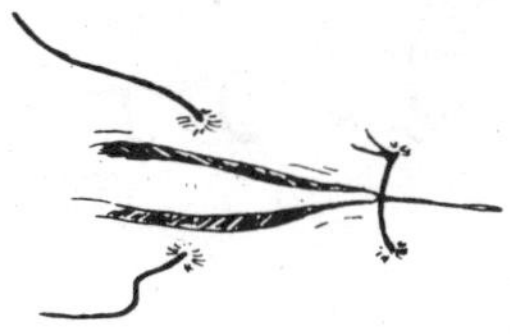

FIG. 1. Interrupted suture.

Silkworm Gut

Silkworm gut is, essentially, unspun silk that is made from the thick fluid secreted by the silk worm. It is readily sterilized by boiling, is non-irritating to the tissues and is not absorbed. It is almost an ideal suture for skin and tension suture as it has no capillarity so does not carry infection into the deeper tissues. Its stiffness is overcome by soaking in warm sterile water before use, which also facilitates tying it and prevents splitting.

FIG. 2. Continuous suture

Linen

This is linen thread and is ordinarily used in its greyish white form. A form known as "Pagenstecher's Linen" is a linen thread impregnated with celluloid. This is to overcome capillarity and thus prevent infection from being carried into the wound by the strand. The coating increases the tensile strength and overcomes any tendency to irritate the tissue.

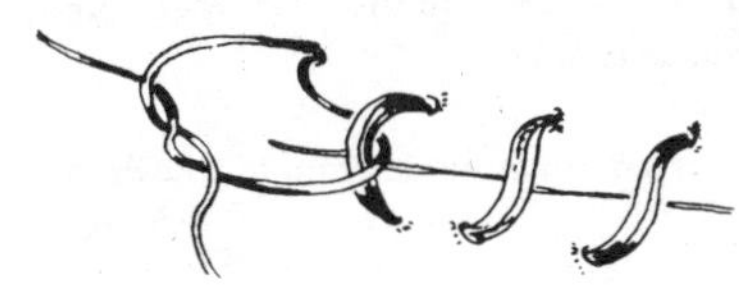

FIG. 3. One method of ending a suture with double thread.

Metallic Sutures

Wire sutures are made of silver, aluminum, bronze, copper and steel wire. The use of steel wire may be objectionable due to its stiffness which may make it difficult to use. However in infected wounds it will maintain the integrity of the wound and may not be extruded from the wound. Tantalum and steel will remain embedded in the tissues forever and at the same time cause the least reaction.

A suture is designated "continuous" when it is inserted so as to consist of a series of stitches; the suture running continuously from one stitch to the other, and only the first and last stitches of the series are tied.

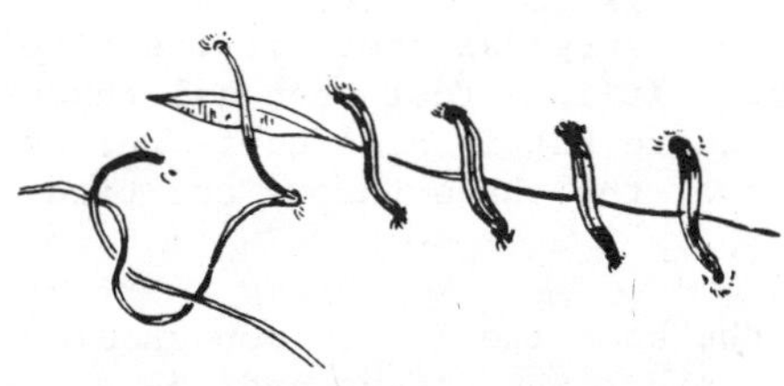

FIG. 4. Another method of ending a suture with double thread.

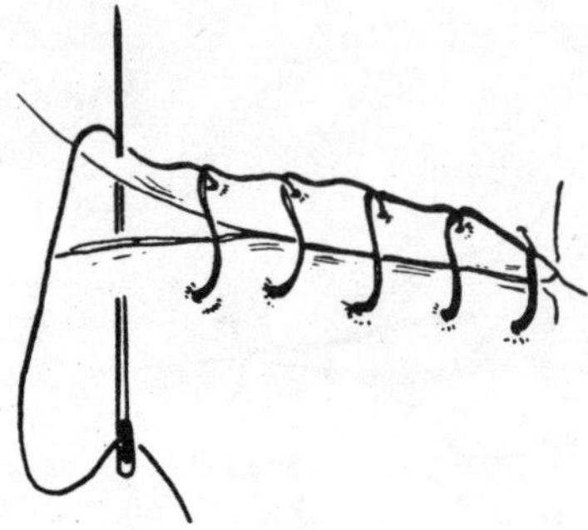

FIG. 5. Lock stitch.
The lock stitch is used to prevent the pouch effect that may occur when a continuous suture is drawn too tight.

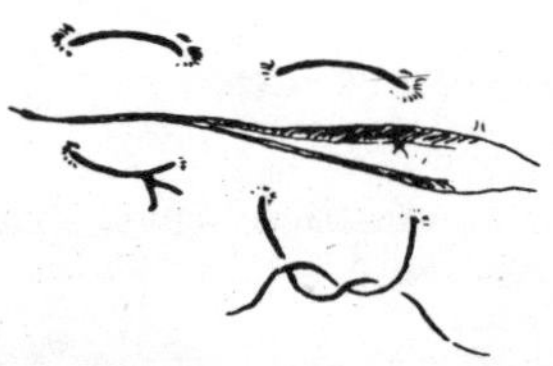

FIG. 6. Mattress suture.
This suture is used in the skin when there will be too much tension for interrupted or continuous sutures.

(These drawings were made from Markowitz)

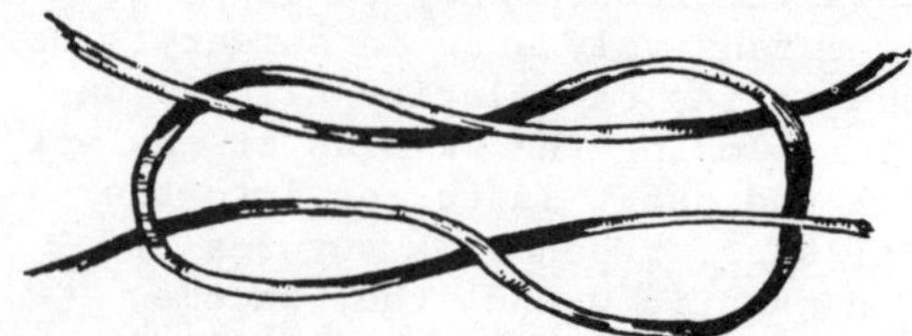

FIG. 7. Granny Knot

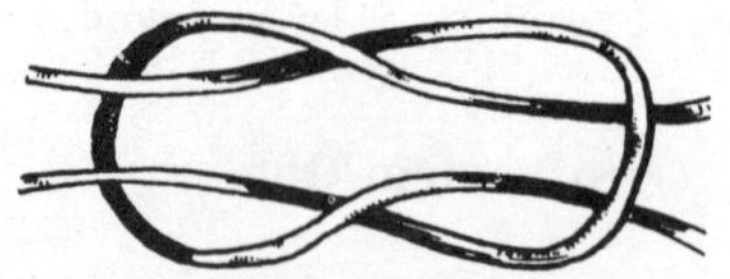

FIG. 8. Reef Knot

FIG. 9. Triple Throw Knot

Knots

The important principles of tying the simple knots should be understood by the surgeon. The reef knot or square knot is supposed to be the ideal knot but probably in the largest percentage of cases the "granny" knot is sufficient. Probably the safest of all surgical knots is the triple throw knot. It is safest when all throws are tied square but is also quite reliable if any two of the three throws are tied square.

In tying the knot the first loop should lie flat against the tissue and the second loop must be brought down flat and snugly upon the first so the completed knot will be tied securely.

Sutures

Sutures may be classified according to the manner in which they are inserted in the tissues.

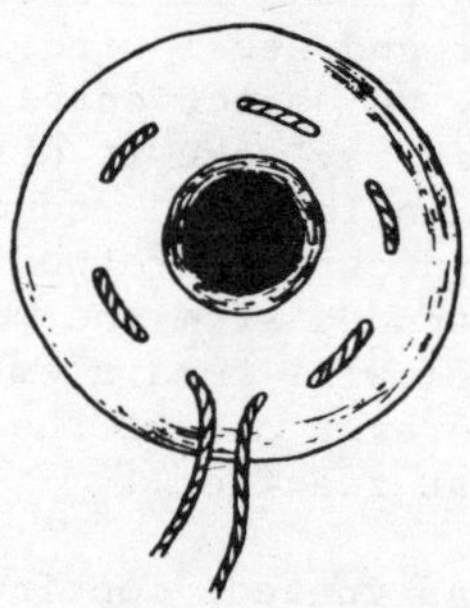

FIG. 10. Purse String Suture.
This suture is most useful around the anus to prevent a recurrence of a prolapse.

Interrupted sutures are inserted in the tissues in such a manner that each stitch is self contained and tied independently of the other. These stitches are termed interrupted sutures. Nothing is gained by tying sutures too tight as they merely cut through the tissues.

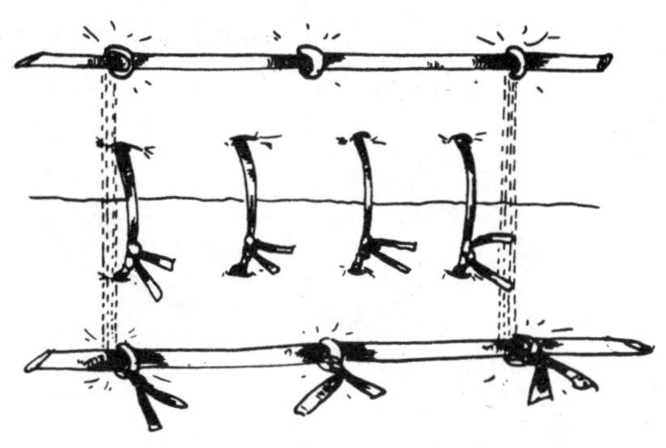

FIG. 13. Quill Suture.
Is made by passing several double interrupted sutures through the lips of the wound half an inch or more apart and tying the ends over a quill, piece of cotton, roll of gauze, or catheter and placed on either side in a line parallel to the wound.

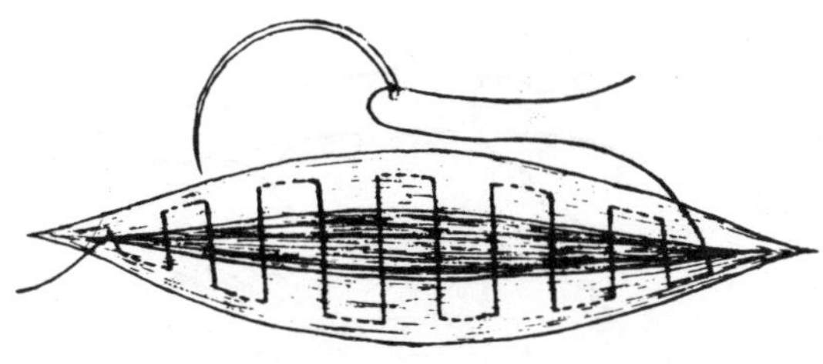

FIG. 11. Subcuticular Suture.
Used in holding edges of skin incision together and does not leave any scar. When suture is removed it may be cut at one end and the entire suture is removed.

Tension sutures are non-absorbable sutures inserted at some distance from the traumatized area and passed through the skin and muscle. They are used to relieve some of the tension on the uniting sutures. Most of the strain is taken from traumatized tissue and is placed on healthy tissue.

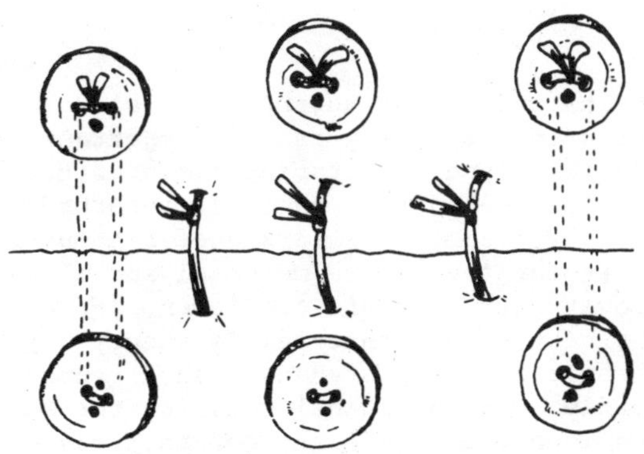

FIG. 12. Button Suture.
This interrupted suture which is usually inserted deeply through the tissues is used as a relaxation suture. The suture material is passed twice through each button.

Mayo's Running Loop Suture

This is a form of continuous suture that is used in suturing the skin down to the underlying tissue. It is indicated when the skin and subcutaneous tissue have been loosened from the muscle tissue. For healing to take place by first intention it is necessary to have the skin in firm contact with the underlying tissues. The mayo running loop suture is an efficient suture for holding the skin in close opposition with the underlying tissue. Before inserting this suture the edges of the skin incision should be held in opposition with interrupted sutures. A full curved needle threaded with a double strand of suture material is inserted an inch or so beyond the outer limits of the pocket carried through the skin and underlying tissue and caused to emerge about one inch from the point where it was inserted. The needle carries only one strand of the suture material through the tissue. The other strand is carried forward and a knot tied at the point of emergence of the needle. The needle is reinserted through the same opening from which it emerged and after passing through the tissue for an inch it is again brought to the surface and tied to the second strand. This process is kept up or continued until the suture has been carried completely across from one edge of the pocket to the other. Several such sutures spaced about one inch apart are inserted across the operative area.

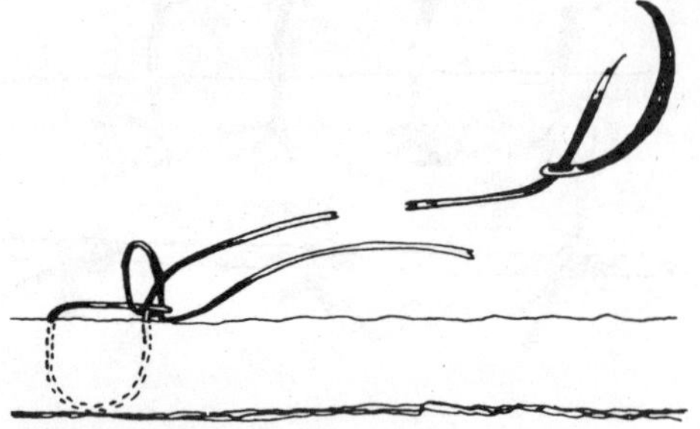

FIG. 14. Shows the method of inserting the Mayo Running Loop Suture.

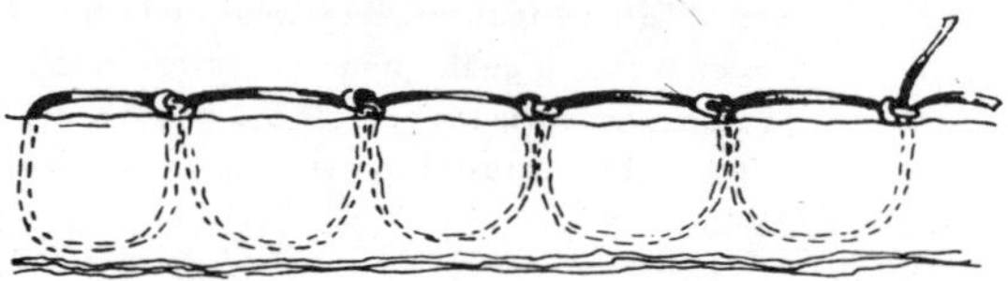

FIG. 15. Is a cross section of a series of Mayo Running Loop Sutures.

Surgery of the Alimentary Canal

The principles observed in suturing the stomach and intestines are also used in suturing the uterus. In 1826 Lembert observed that intestinal wounds heal by the adhesion of the inverted peritoneal surfaces and he designed the Lembert suture. The Lembert suture is the basis of all intestinal suturing. To be successful an intestinal suture must penetrate the tough submucosa of the intestinal wall. The intestinal wall is composed of mucosa, submocosa, muscularis, and serosa. The submucous coat which is found between the muscle and the mucous layers is the strongest tissue in the intestinal wall. This is the fibrous substance of which violin strings and surgical catgut are made. The serous coat is the quickest one to heal but it will do so only when its cells approximate each other, that is, serosa to serosa. The principle to observe in intestinal surgery is to turn the bowel wall in so serosa and serosa are in contact. After one half hour a deposit of fibrim occurs due to clotting of blood plasma, later a collagenous exudate forms that prevents leakage. This important fact makes possible intestinal surgery. Even the most delicate suturing would not prevent leakage were it not for the astounding ability of the serous coat to seal itself so rapidly and completely. The serous coat heals by granulation from the subserous connective tissue. This begins in twenty-four hours and is complete in about a week.

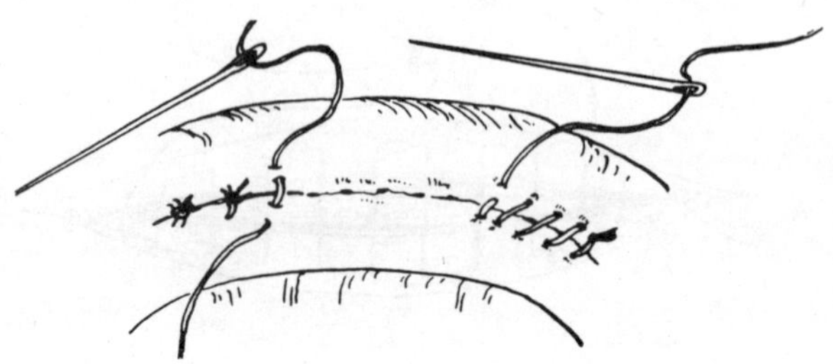

FIG. 16. Interrupted Lembert Stitch and continuous Lembert suture.
(Redrawn from Gould)

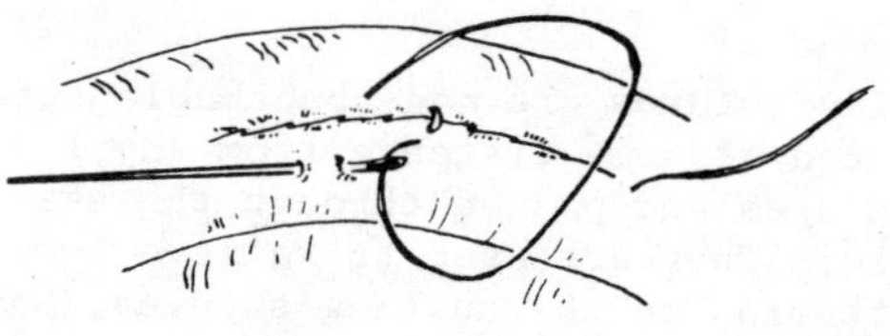

FIG. 17. Cushing right angle suture, reinforcing a Connell suture line already laid.
(Redrawn from Gould)

The nature of the suture material used in intestinal suturing is very important. For this type of suturing plain catgut should not be used, as it is absorbed too quickly. Some operators prefer to use linen for the suture material and it is slowly extruded into the lumen. Probably the best suture material is twenty-day chromic catgut fastened to an atraumatic needle. In intestinal suturing the sutures should not be too tight for they may cut through the tissues and a leak will develop.

In using the Connell suture the sutures should be inserted close to the margin of the opening and only a small amount of tissue is included in each stitch.

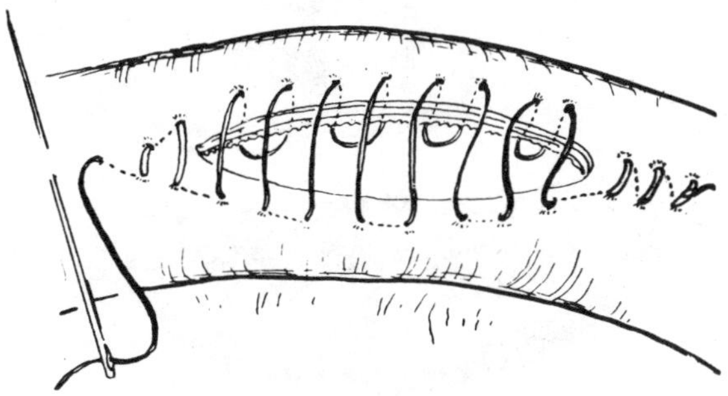

FIG. 18. Connell suture for closing a longitudinal cut in the intestine. It should begin and end at some distance from the opening.

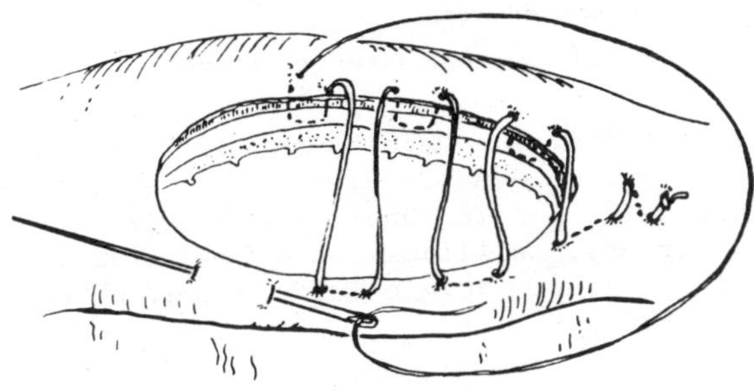

FIG. 19. Cushing right angle suture. The stitches do not penetrate to the lumen. (Redrawn from E. A. Printy's "Surgical Technique - The Laboratory of Surgical Technique." Chicago, 1925.)

Intestinal Anastomosis

In large animals an intestinal anastomosis is indicated in intususception, injury to a portion, or there may be gangrene of the intestine in a strangulated hernia.

There are three methods of performing an intestinal anastomosis, the end-to-end, the lateral, and end-to-side. The objection to the lateral anastomosis is that it is a mechanical and not a physical procedure. However, in a few months the lateral anastomosis becomes straight again. The end-to-end anastomosis is considered the physiological operation as the contents are carried forward by a normal physiological process. When the intestine is of small diameter there is a possibility of a cicatricial contraction at the site of the anastomosis. However, this is not a common complication.

In resection of the bowel it is important to determine the extent to which the intestine is affected and how much should be removed. All affected tissue must be removed to be sure that all the sutures will be placed in good healthy tissue. The vessels supplying the portion of the bowel to be removed should be ligated.

It is important to trim the mesenteric fat from the ends of the bowel to be inverted. The Carmalt forceps with longitudinal striations are now applied and are placed straight across or at an angle. In cutting the bowel obliquely the acute angle is at the mesenteric border. If the operator fails to do this the antimesenteric segment may slough from lack of circulation.

End-to-End Anastomosis

In large animals the intestine is large enough so there is little danger of a stricture as the result of cicatricial contraction after healing occurs.

Kerr and Parker devised an aseptic method of anastomosing intestine that is applicable in an end-to-end, end-to-side, or between bowel of unequal diameters. By this method of operating the handling of the intestines is reduced to a minimum. Also the small peritoneal defect is obliterated when the end of the intestine is sutured. The serous surfaces are approximated at a uniform distance from the edge of the incision. With the inversion of the ends of the intestine, the folded wall provides an ideal area for the insertion of the sutures, also the ends of the intestine can be held in an ideal position for suturing.

The ends of the intestine are inverted after a basting stitch is applied over a Carmalt clamp. As the clamp is removed the stitches are drawn tight and the edges of the incision are automatically inverted and held in a straight line. The ends of the intestine are thus closed without any chance for leakage of the intestinal contents. Also the suture ends were not tied but left long. The inverted segments of the intestine are now placed side by side and sutured together with a Cushing stitch around their entire circumference. After this is accomplished the inverting basting stitches are removed thus re-establishing the continuity of the lumen of the intestine.

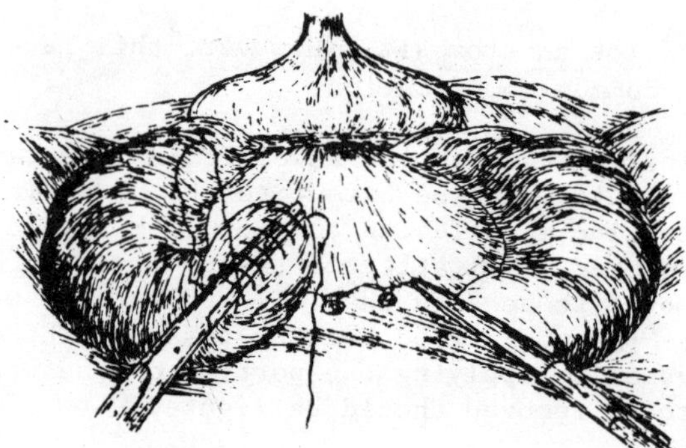

FIG. 20. The end of the intestine is closed with the basting stitch over the Carmalt clamp.

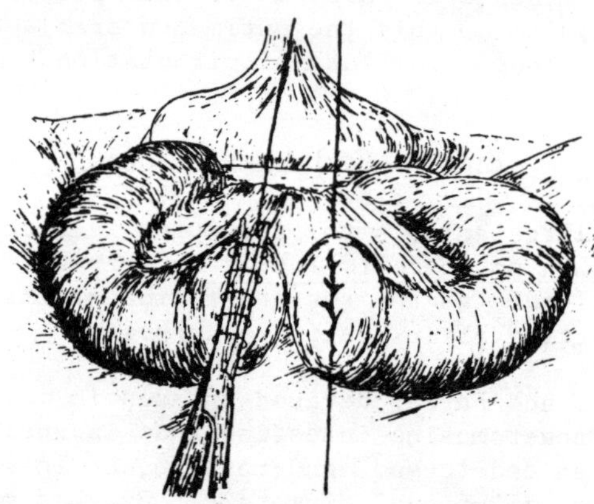

FIG. 21. The clamp has been withdrawn, the end of the intestine has been inverted by tightening of the basting stitch.

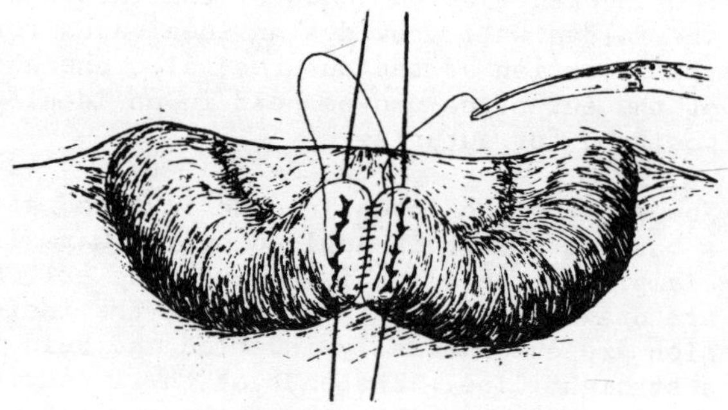

FIG. 22. The ends of the intestine are placed together and the suture is started.

REFERENCES

Gould, A. H. Technic of Operations Upon Intestines and Stomach. Saunders, Philadelphia, (1906).

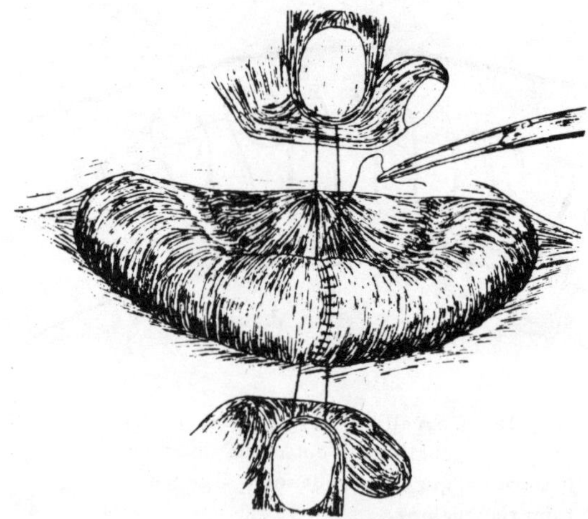

FIG. 23. Anastomosis of the intestine is complete, the basting stitches are now removed.

(These illustrations were taken from technique by Kerr.)

Kerr, H. H. The Development of Intestinal Surgery, J.A.V.M.A. (1923), 81, 641-646.
Markowitz, J. Textbook of Experimental Surgery. William Wood & Co: (1937).
Printy, E. A. Surgical Technique, Chicago, (1925).

Restraint

The success of an operation is determined in many cases by the method of restraint that is used to control the patient. Restraint is the act or method by which an animal is hindered from motion or action. In treating or operating on animals it is practically always necessary to use methods of restraint, but they should be applied in as humane a manner as possible. There is no general method of restraint that can can be used by all operators and will be equally successful. For what is a successful method for one operator may be a failure when used by another. Also the method of restraint used will depend upon individual peculiarities of the patient. If the method of restraint used is not efficient the operator is in constant danger of bodily injury. Also the patient may be able to produce self-inflicted injuries that might prove fatal and cause financial loss to the owner.

Horse

Many of the operations on the horse may be performed with the patient in the standing position. Horses differ a great deal in temperment, some are very nervous and excitable and will resist many forms of restraint. Many of these horses if handled quietly may be operated on by the proper use of a local anesthetic. Other horses may have to be quieted with a hypnotic or general anesthetic. In applying any form of restraint it is best to start with the simplest and least drastic and use only the severe forms of restraint when necessary.

Twitch

This form of restraint is undoubtedly the one most frequently used on the horse in the standing position. The object of the twitch is to divert the animals attention by compressing the nerves of the upper lip. It is almost universally applied to the upper lip although it may be applied on the lower lip or ear. In applying the twitch it should exert only enough pressure on the tissues to detract the animals attention from the operator. With some horses it will be found the twitch makes them more unmanageable and then its use should be discontinued. The twitch may consist of several forms but the most common type is the stick with a loop made of either rope or a chain.

Another method of restraint that may be used and is sometimes very effective is applied in the following manner. The end of an abstetrical chain is fastened on one side of the halter and then the free end is passed under the upper lip over the gums of the incisor teeth and through the

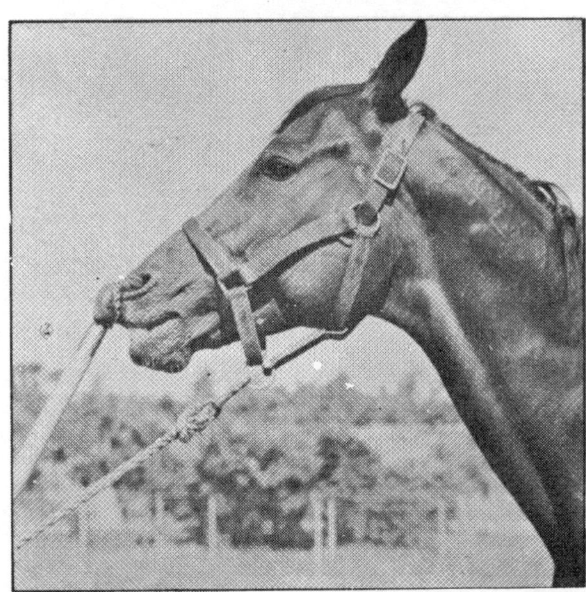

FIG. 24. Twitch in position on upper lip

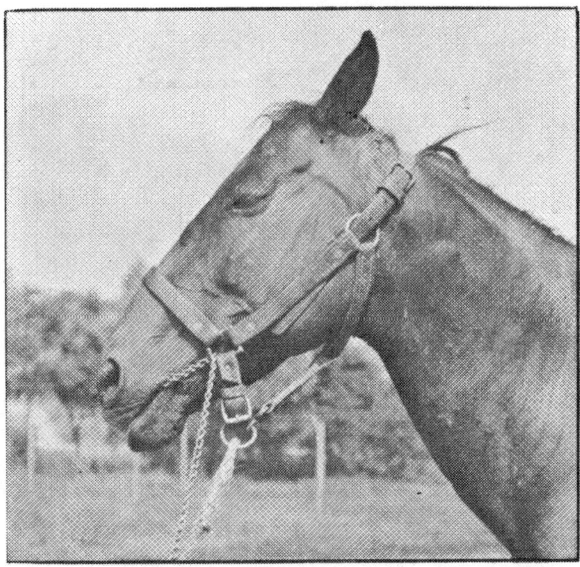

FIG. 25. Chain in position above upper incisor teeth.

ring in the halter on the opposite side. By pulling on the end of the chain pressure is produced on the sensitive tissue.

War Bridles

For some vicious horses and mules that are not restrained with the twitch the war bridle may be very effective. It may be almost indispensable for handling certain animals. As with other methods of restraint good judgment and extreme care must be used with the war bridle. Depending upon the type employed will determine how its action is obtained. The war bridle may be made from sash cord or other rope about that size.

Magner's War Bridle

A loop large enough to slip over the lower jaw is made in one end of the rope. The loop is placed around the lower jaw and the other end passed on the off side of the head over the poll then downward through the loop and traction is applied to the end of the rope. Pressure is produced on the spinal cord at the atlo-axoid space.

A more severe and effective war bridle is a modification of the Magner War Bridle. Its effectiveness is obtained by producing pressure on the spinal cord and the sensitive tissue above the upper incisor teeth

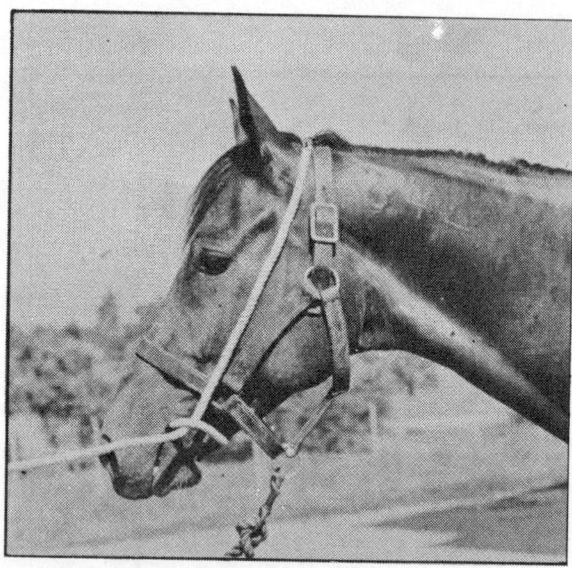

FIG. 26. Magner's War Bridle.

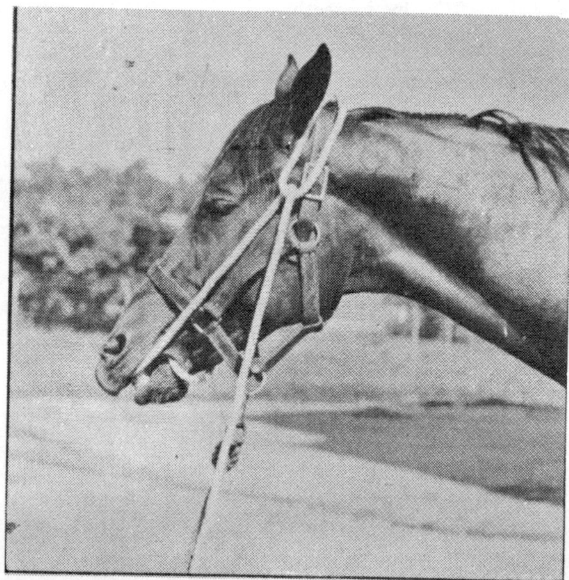

FIG. 27. Magner's Modified War Bridle.

A non-slip noose is placed around the lower jaw. The free end is then passed upward on the off side and over the poll. A bend is made in the cord in the rear of and slightly below the left ear. With the bend of the rope held here the free end of the cord is passed downward on the off side and under the upper lip over the gums of the incisor teeth, then upward to be passed through the bend in the cord. The free end of the cord is then passed downward through the loop around the lower jaw. The rope should fit snugly to the head at all points so any traction of the free end will exert the proper pressure.

Restraint of One Foreleg

With the horse in the standing position it may be desirable to restrain one or more legs. The lifting up of one front leg in conjunction with the use of the twitch or other procedure may assist materially in the restraint. When it is desirable to confine only one foreleg it may be held up by an assistant. Also it may be held in position by a knee strap. In some cases it may be desirable to use a rope to hold the foot up. The end of the rope is fastened around the pastern and the other end passed over the withers. With the rope held by an assistant the foot may be released very quickly if necessary.

Restraint of a Hind Leg

Usually the object of restraining one hind leg is to prevent the patient from kicking. In some cases it serves to divert the animals attention while an examination is being made. Also it may be used for restraint during a minor operation. However when animals object too vigorously to its use then it will have to be discontinued. In some cases the twitch is a valuable adjunct to the side line in the control of the patient.

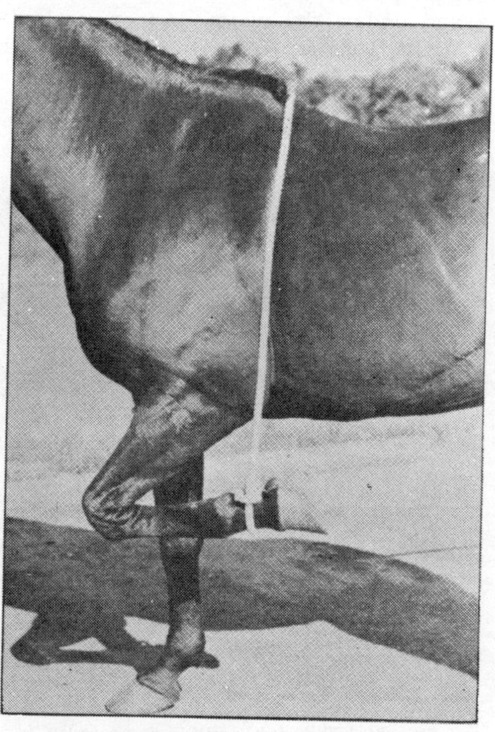

FIG. 28. Restraint of one foreleg.

The side line may be made by using twelve to fifteen feet of rope. A loop that will not slip and is large enough to fit loosely around the neck is made with the end of the rope. The rope is then passed backward between the hind legs and around the pastern of the leg to be restrained. In some cases it is best to use a hobble around the pastern to prevent any rope burns. The rope is then carried forward and passed through the loop around the neck. By pulling on the free end of the rope the foot may be pulled up to and held at any position. However it is usually held so the toe is just touching the ground.

Another method of using a side line is to fasten one end of the rope to a hobble that is around the pastern. The other end of the rope is passed forward between the front legs. If it is desired to secure the left hind pastern the free end is continued up on the right side of the neck, return to left side just back of withers downward and around that part of rope extending between the hobble strap and fore legs, this forms a half hitch over the shoulders that is adjustable.

The casting harness that is ordinarily used may provide a side line to one or both hind legs.

Sigler's Method of Restraint

To prevent a horse from either striking or kicking a single rope may be used. A long rope is doubled in the middle and the loop placed over the withers. The ends are taken down over the sides of the thoracic cavity and from behind forward between the front legs. Then around each front leg and back under the ropes on each side of the thoracic cavity. The ends of the ropes are passed back between the hind legs and around the hind legs, upward and inside of the horizontal ropes. The ropes are continued upward and the ends tied over the loin. To get the best results the ropes are pulled tight and snug to the body before being tied.

Restraint of the Horse in the Recumbent Position

For some operations and certain patients

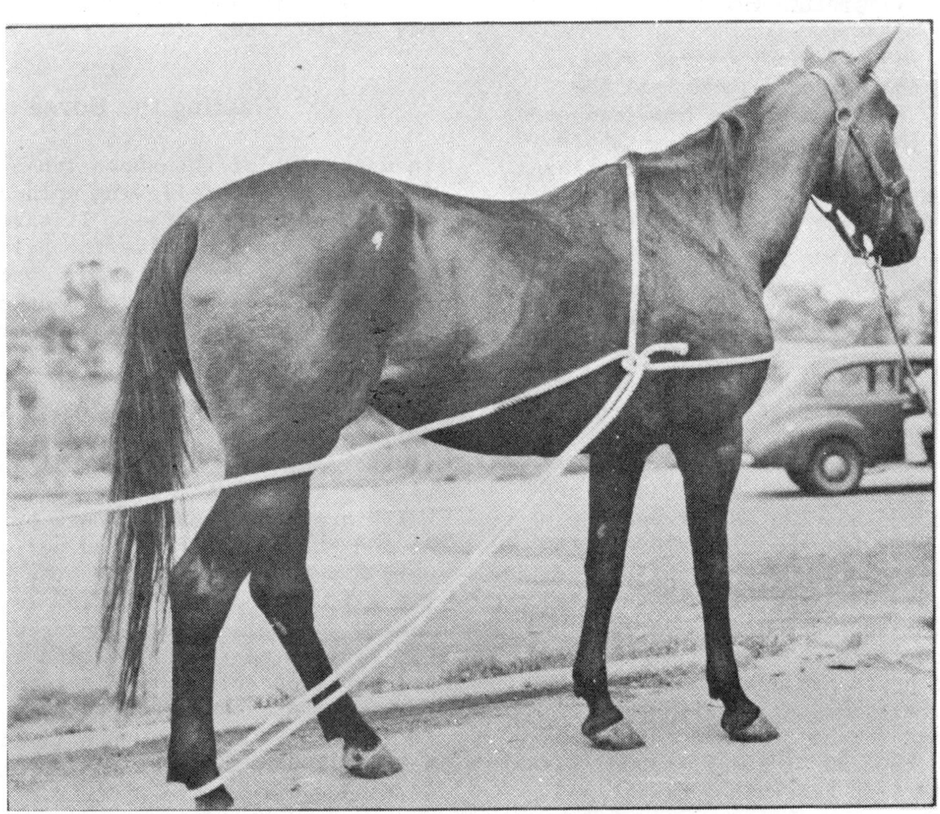

FIG. 29. One method of applying side line.

it is necessary to have then in the recumbent position. When available the operating table is usually selected and is the best means of restraint for those operations where it can be used. However in many cases an operating table is not available and a casting harness will have to be used. The place where the horse is to be cast should be selected with a great deal of care. If possible it should be smooth, free of stones or any hard objects and covered with grass. The choice of casting harness will depend upon the operator. There are many different types of casting harness some simple and others very complicated. The type that is chosen will depend somewhat upon the disposition and vigor of the patient. A great deal of the struggling of vigorous or vicious animals may be controlled by first giving a drug to quiet them. This may consist of fifteen to thirty cubic centimeters of Nembutal administered intravenously or one to two ounces of chloral hydrate may be given intravenously or into the stomach. By reducing the struggling of the patient the chance of any unfortunate accident is reduced and the work of confining the patient is simplified.

Operating Hood

The hood is made of heavy canvas with openings at the top to accommodate the ears. It is placed over the head and secured under the chin and throat. The hood acts as a protective covering preventing bruises when horses are cast and as a blindfold, acts as a form of restraint.

All Rope Casting Harness

The all rope casting harness may be made from eighty feet of half inch rope or two ropes forty feet long. It is not necessary to use hobbles with this harness. The rope is doubled in the center so the ends are even. Pass the doubled end around the breast and upon the opposite side to the rear of the withers where a bowline knot is tied. The advantage of this knot is, it will not slip, does not draw tight and lies flat on the back. Stand on the near side of the horse and one end of the rope is carried backward, passed between the hind legs and around the hind leg. The free end is then carried forward and passed under the loop encircling breast and withers. This rope is held until the opposite rope is adjusted in the same manner.

Knowles Casting Harness

The casting harness designed by W. F. Knowles is made in the large and small sizes. It is simple in construction light and easy to carry. As designed it consists of a flat webbing collar two main ropes and two hobbles made of webbing. The harness is shown in position in the following picture.

Another simple type of casting harness is that shown in Fig. 33. This harness consists of two six inch rings on each side. From these rings one strap passes over the back to act as a back band. There is also a broad breast strap passing around in front of the shoulders. It has a buckle so the size may be adjusted to the size of the horse. Another strap that is the belly band may also be adjusted to the size of the horse. A casting harness that can be readily adjusted to the size of the animal is very important. This is especially valuable in casting young mules as they may slip out of a harness that does not fit tight to the body. Fig. 33. The harness is in position and hobbles may or may not be used.

Casting the Horse

In using any of the above types of casting harness the following method may be used to cast the horse. If three men are available one man holds the halter rope and twitch if this is used. One man pulls forward on one rope and the other man pulls to the rear with the other one. When only two men are available one of the ropes may be tied forward to a post or tree. When ready to cast the man on the halter rope pushes the horse backward. At the same time the men pull on the ropes keeping them parallel with the body. The horse gradually settles back on his haunches and the man at the head pulls him over onto his side. The men on the ropes continue to pull until the hind legs are flexed. A half hitch is placed around the pastern of the upper hind leg. The leg may then be completely flexed by the rope passed around the pastern and hock in two Figure 8 loops then fixed with a clove hitch around the pastern. A loop is placed around the pastern of the fore foot and two half hitches are placed

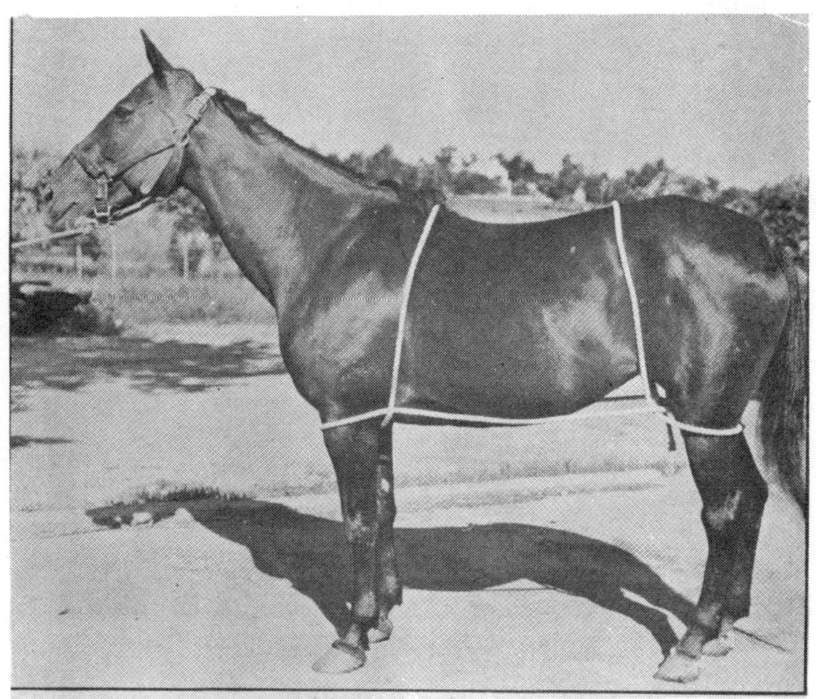

FIG. 30. Use of rope to prevent horse striking or kicking.

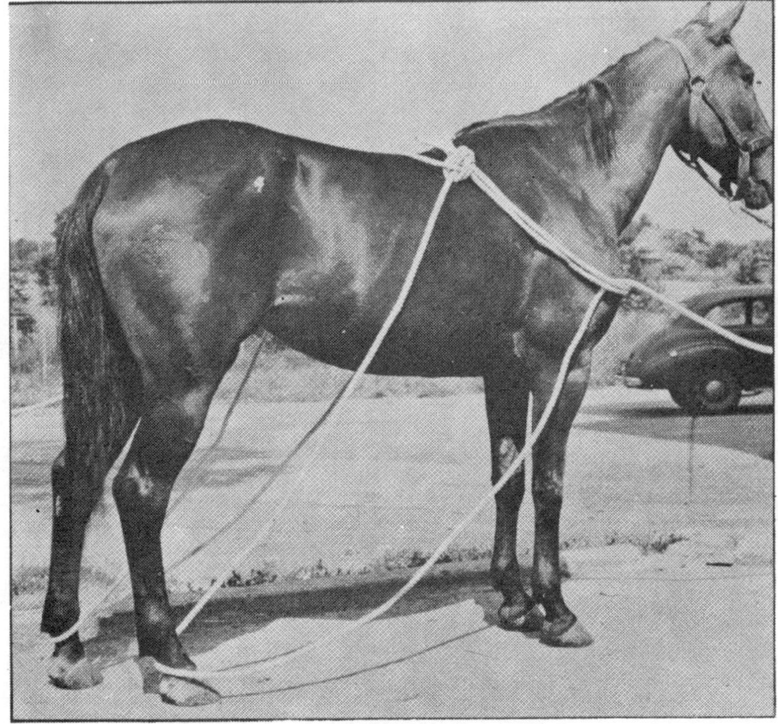

FIG. 31. All Rope Casting Harness.

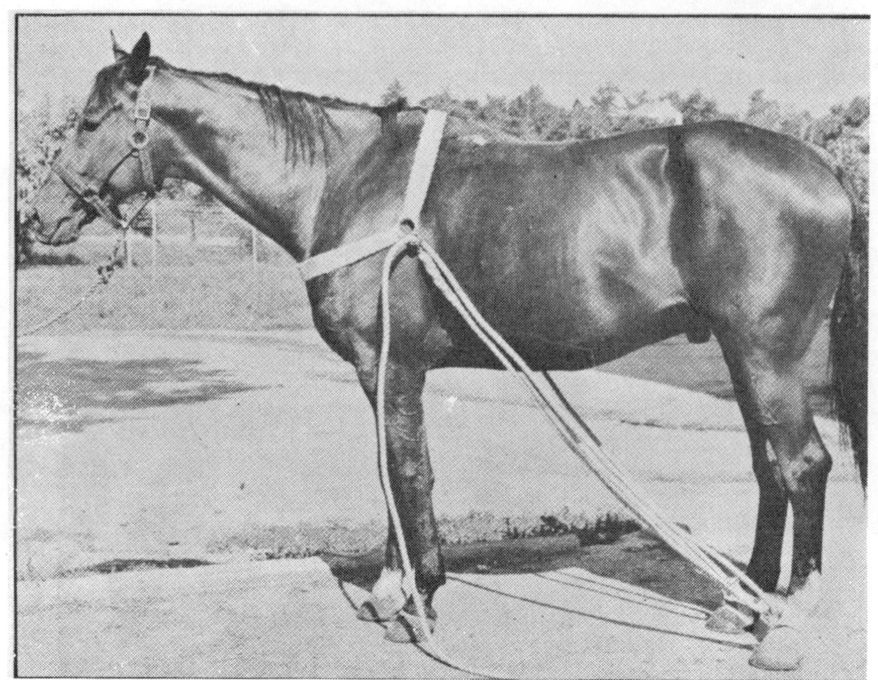

FIG. 32. Knowles Casting Harness.

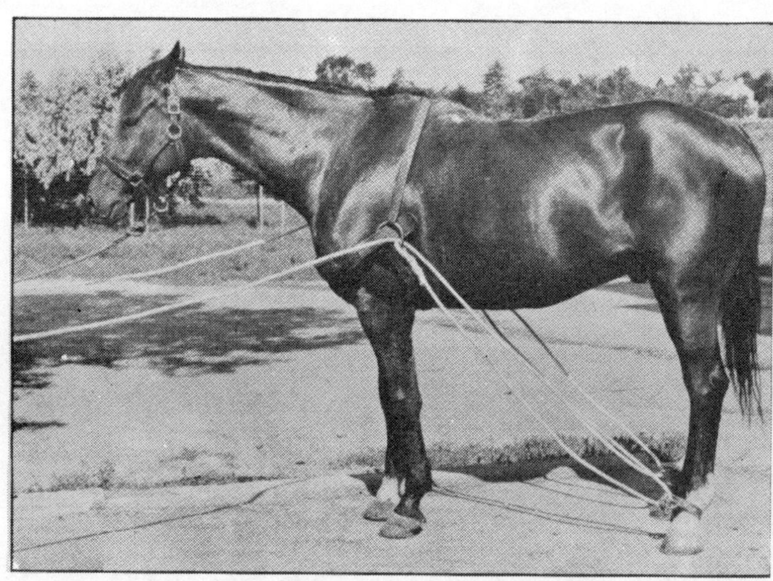

FIG. 33. Another type of Casting Harness.

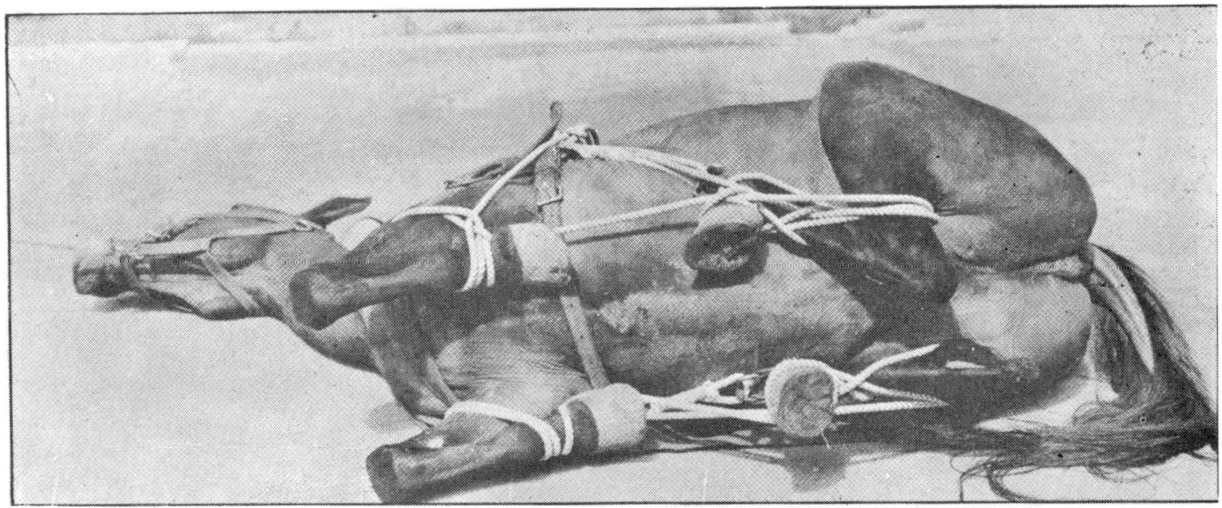

FIG. 34. Horse is cast and all four legs are completely flexed and tied.

around the pastern and fore arm completely flexing it. The free end of the rope is then fastened to the harness. The horse is then rolled over and the same procedure is used in tying the legs on the other side. When a horse is confined in this manner with his legs completely flexed and tied securely there is little chance of him injuring either himself or the operator.

The W Casting Harness

This is a type of casting harness that is a little more complicated than any of those previously described but is very efficient in the casting of a horse. In the first illustration is shown the arrangement of the harness on the right side of the horse. The harness consists of a broad heavy strap around the body. There are three rings on the strap for the ropes going to the front feet. The end of the rope is fastened to the ring on the left side. From here the rope passes through the hobble on the left front feet, then up through the ring in the median line, then down and through the hobble on the right foot. The end of the rope is passed through the third ring and up over the back to the left side. In the second illustration is shown the arrangement of the harness on the left side with this rope going to the left hind foot. The rope has a knot close to the end which acts as a lock when the foot is pulled up.

Before casting, the horse should be tied low down on a post with a good strong halter rope. When ready to cast the operator stands on the left side of the horse. The left hind leg is pulled up and the rope holds the foot in that position. Then before he has time to struggle the rope to the front feet is pulled up and the patient goes down on the left side. A loop is made in this rope and passed through a ring on the strap and the loop is placed around the pastern and the leg is tied in the usual manner. The halter rope can be untied passed through this ring and the head pulled up close to the body and tied there. With the other rope the left hind leg is tied in the usual manner.

To Raise Horse with Rope

This method may be used to raise a horse when slings are not available. In some cases it is more easily applied than the slings. The rope may be one-half inch or more in diameter and at least forty feet long. For a large horse it will need be longer than forty feet.

The rope is doubled in the center and

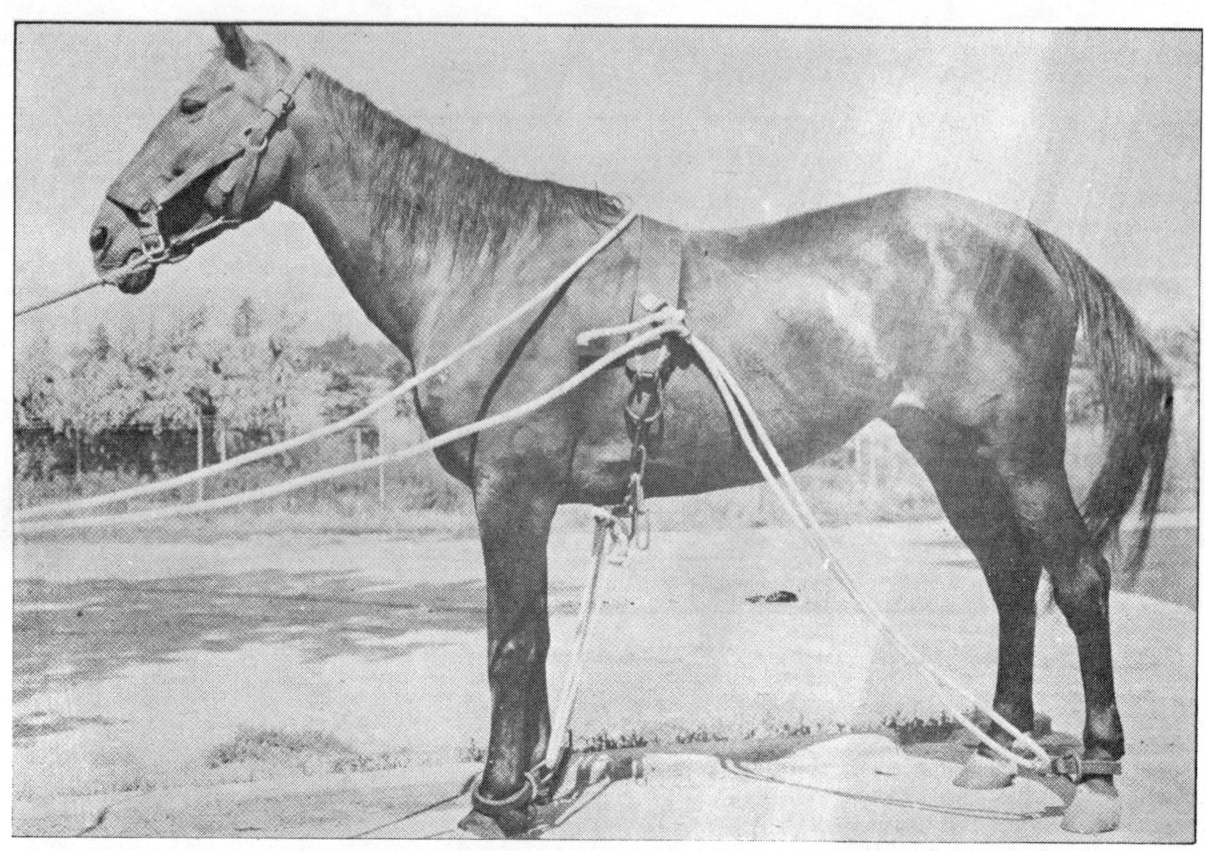

FIG. 35. View of W casting harness from the left side.

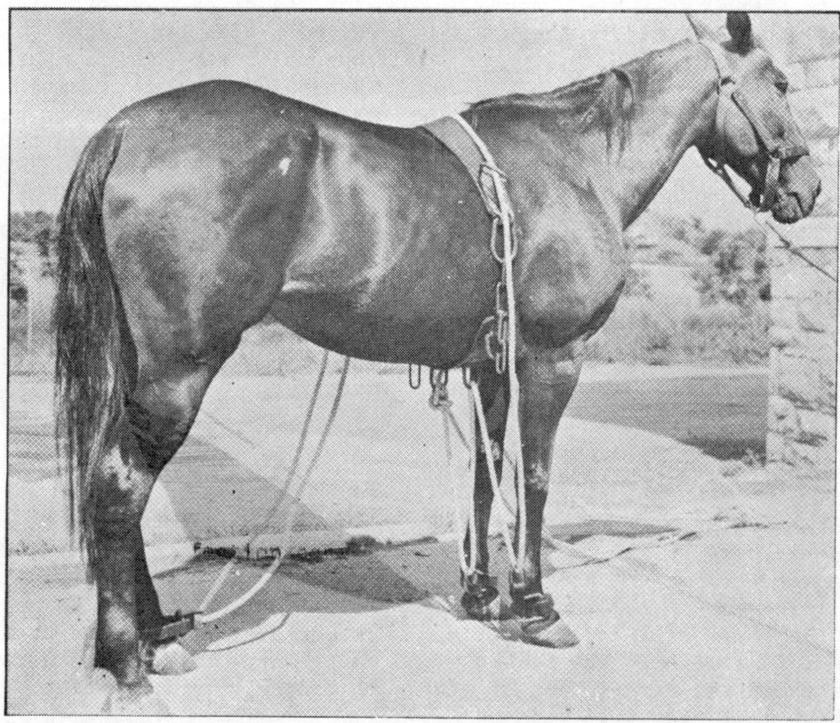

FIG. 36. View of W casting harness from the right side.

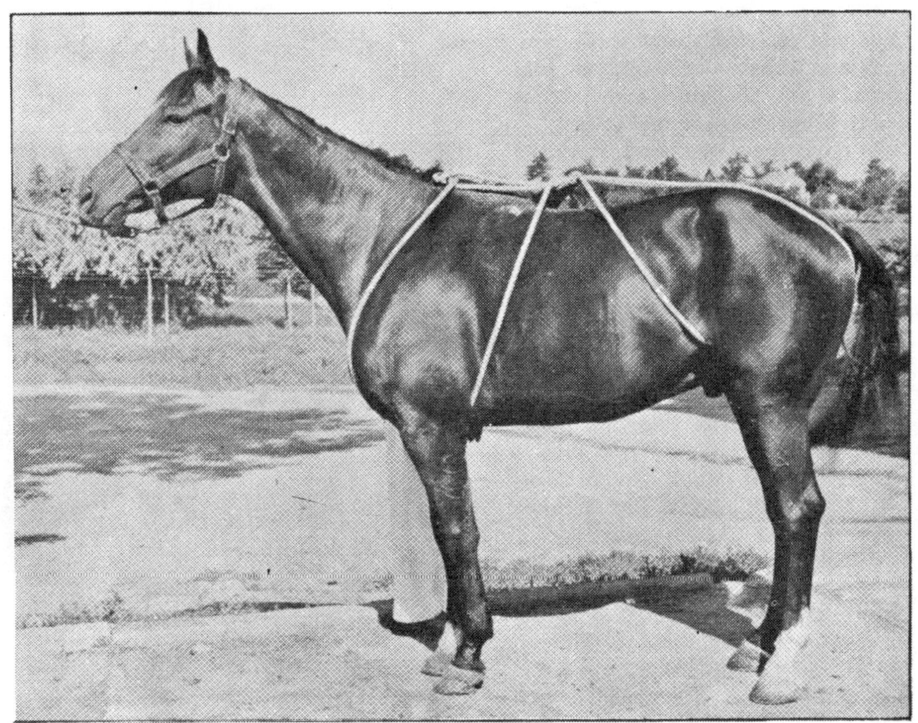

FIG. 37. Rope sling that may be used to raise horse.

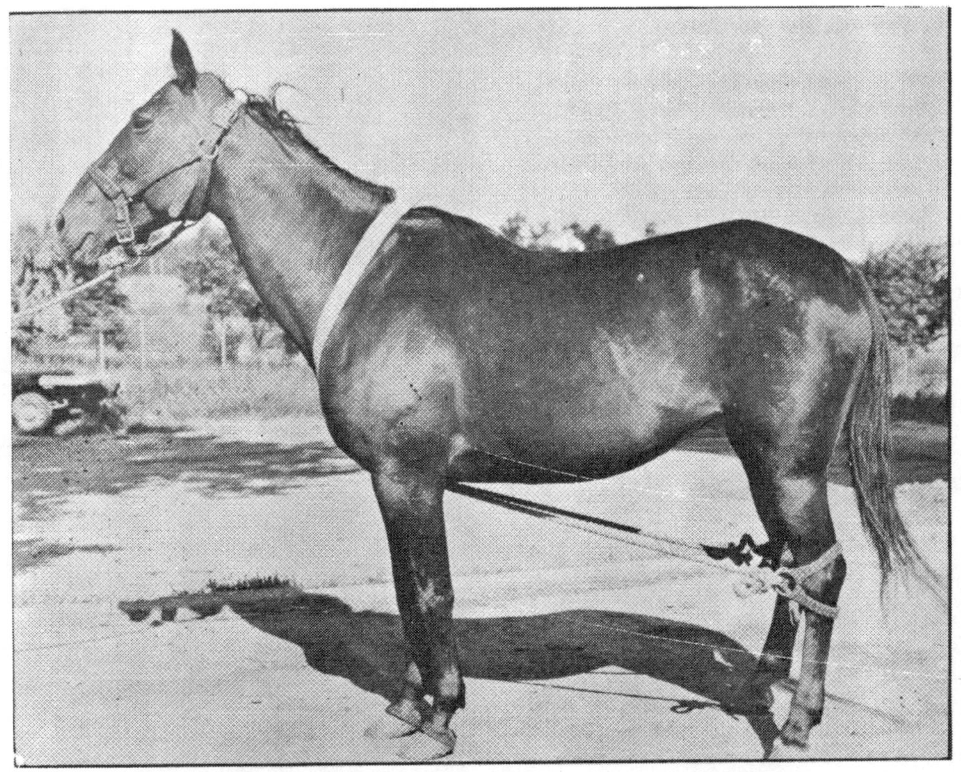

FIG. 38. Breeding hobbles, very efficient for restraint of hind legs.

passed over the neck so the loop rests on the neck where the collar would fit at the top. The free ends of the rope are passed between the front legs and across them once just before they pass between the front legs. The lower rope is brought up over the side of the thorax and passes over the back just posterior to the withers. The upper rope is brought up on the other side of the thorax and crosses the lower rope on the back. Continue the rope over the sides of the body and back between the hind legs, crossing the ropes at this point. The ropes are then brought up over the buttocks with one rope on each side of the tail and are carried forward along the spine and under ropes where they cross on back. After the ropes are drawn tight so they fit snugly to the body the ends are tied to the rope where it passes over the neck. In raising the horse, the hook of the block is inserted at the point where the ropes cross on the back. The chief advantage of this type of sling is the horse cannot fall out. Also this type of sling does not produce any pressure on the thoracic cavity thus interfering with the functioning of the heart and lungs.

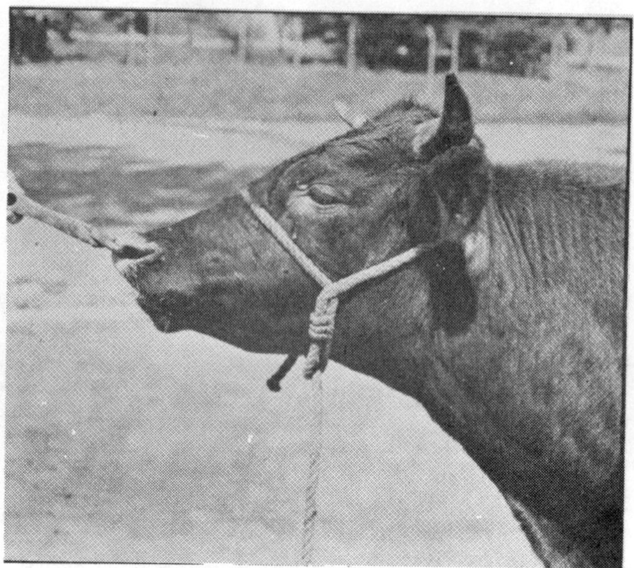

FIG. 39. Nose clamp applied to nose.

Restraint of the Bovine

The method used in restraining the bovine will depend upon size, strength and disposition of the patient. In some cases partial restraint in the standing position is sufficient while in other cases it will be necessary to employ complete restraint in the recumbent position. The bovine is very susceptible to pain and actively resist when any pain is produced so the restraint used must be efficient. Also the restraint used must be adequate to control the patient for you cannot reason with them like you can with a horse.

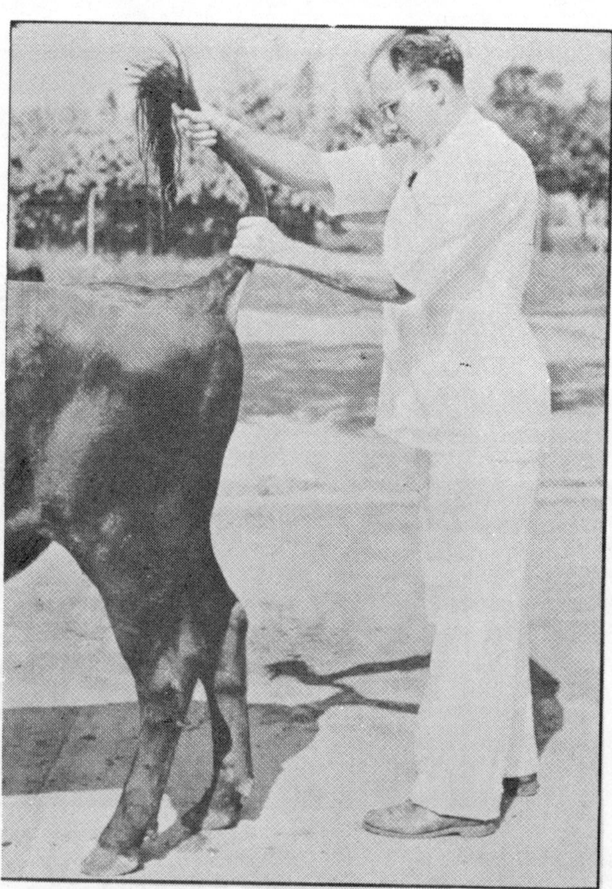

FIG. 40. Tail is extended up over the back and held firmly in this position.

Restraint of the Head

One efficient and simple method of controlling the head is to grasp the nasal septum. By a tight grasp of the nose producing pressure on the septum many animals can be controlled for minor operations. Another method of holding the nose is with the nose clamp or bull lead. A rope should be tied to the bull lead so it may be fastened to a post or other firm support. For in some cases the attendant is not strong enough to hold the bull lead with his hands.

STOCKS. - When available properly constructed stocks are the most efficient means of restraining the very nervous or vicious vigorous individuals in the standing position.

Restraining the Hind Legs

Some individuals will kick when the examination is made of the udder or any other part where the examiner can be reached by the hind feet. A number of methods that can be applied simply and easily are too well known to merit a description.

One rather efficient method to prevent a cow from kicking is to push the tail straight up over the back. This is accomplished by the assistant grasping the tail with one hand close to the body and the other hand six or eight inches higher up on the tail. The tail is then held in this position as firmly as possible. If this procedure is combined with the use of the bull lead it is very efficient in the control of animals for minor operations.

Restraint of the Bovine in Lateral Recumbency

As a general rule the bovine can be cast easier than the equine. The method most generally used is to use a single rope and make two half hitches around the body. For most animals it is advisable to put a halter on and fasten securely to some stationary object. The end of the rope is fastened to the horns or around the neck with a knot that will not slip. The first half hitch is made around the chest just back of the front legs and the second half hitch around the body in the flank region. After the half hitches are completed and drawn snug to the body the free end is carried backward. By exerting steady but firm traction on the end of the rope the body is gradually compressed! In a short time the patient lies down on its side and can be held there by tension on the rope. If an operation is to be performed the legs must be restrained. One method that is very efficient for animals that are not too large is the following. One assistant sits on the ground back of the hind legs and takes a firm hold on the upper hind leg pulling it backward. He places his feet against the other hind leg just above the point of the hock and pushes it forward. The operator can keep the patient from kicking the leg too high by standing on it, if possible during the operation. Another assistant grasps the upper front leg and flexes it firmly upon itself and at the same time kneeling and placing one knee on the patients neck.

When the patient is too large and strong or assistants are not available another method of restraint may be used. After the patient is in lateral recumbency the two front feet are tied together with a single rope, the legs are stretched forward and the rope tied securely. A single rope is used to fasten the two hind feet together and this rope is carried back stretching the hind legs backward and tieing it securely. With the animal stretched out in this manner it makes an efficient method of confining them in lateral recumbency.

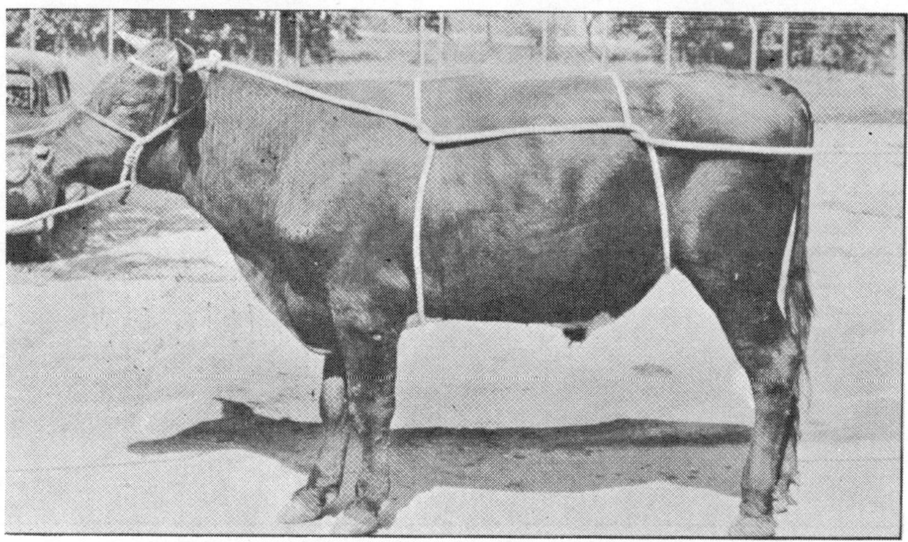

FIG. 41. The two half hitches in position.

FIG. 42. One method of restraint in the recumbent position.

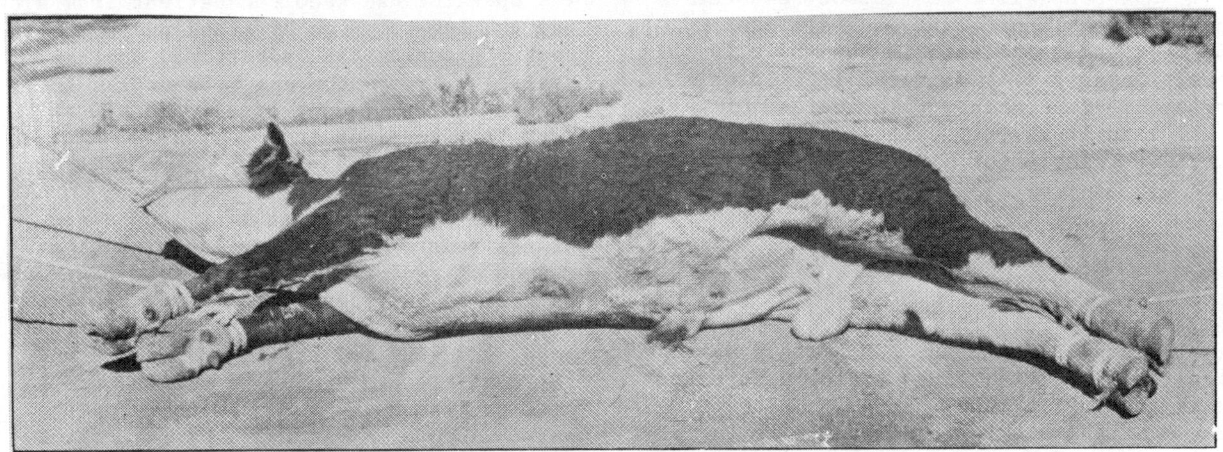

FIG. 43. The two front feet are tied together and ~~the~~ two hind feet, then the front and hind legs are stretched in opposite directions.

FIG. 44. Casting harness in position on the bull.

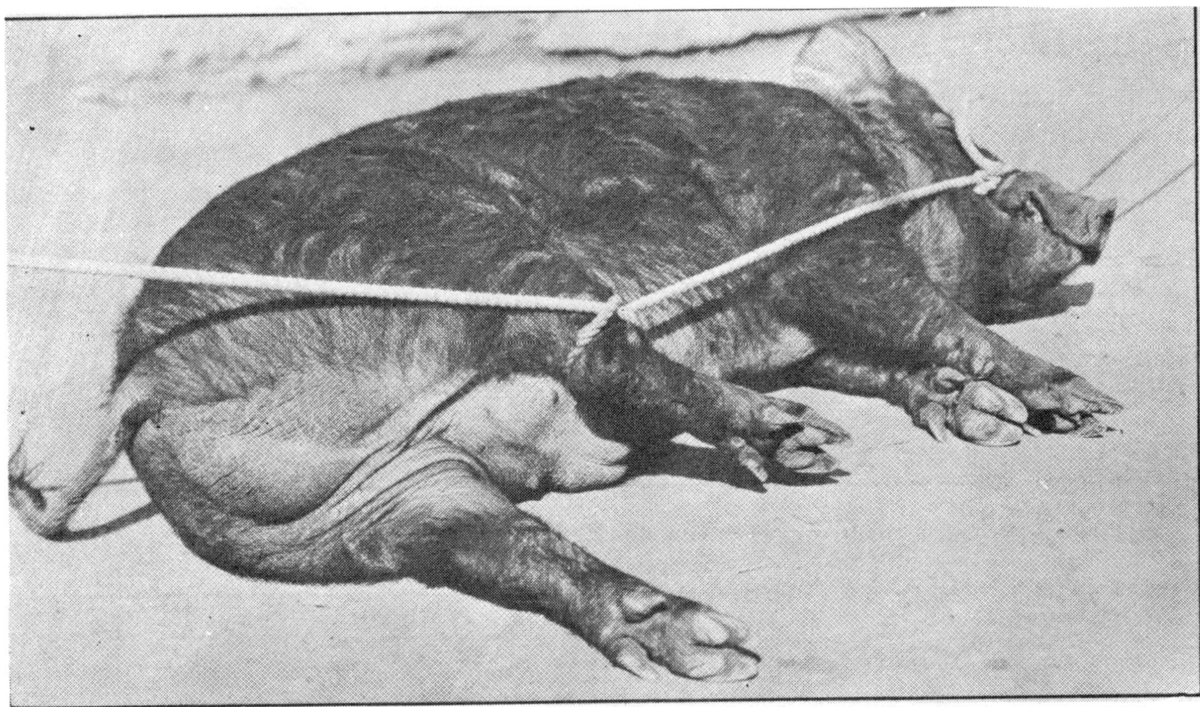

FIG. 45. The snout and hind leg are pulled as close together as possible.

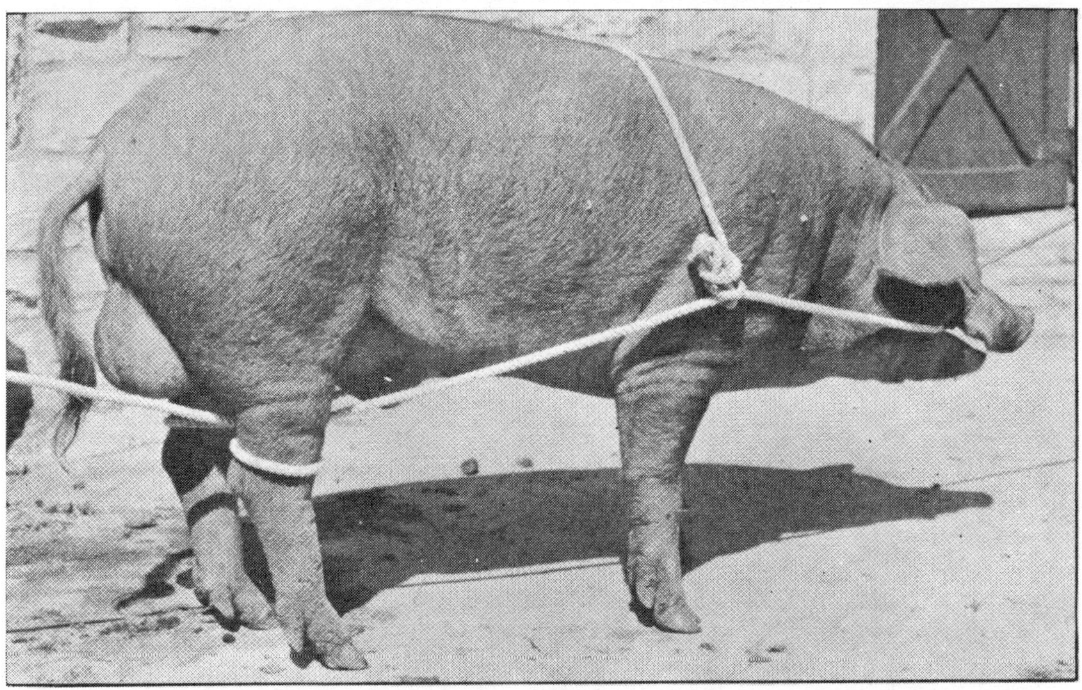

FIG. 46. The rope is passed through the mouth and fastened around both hind legs.

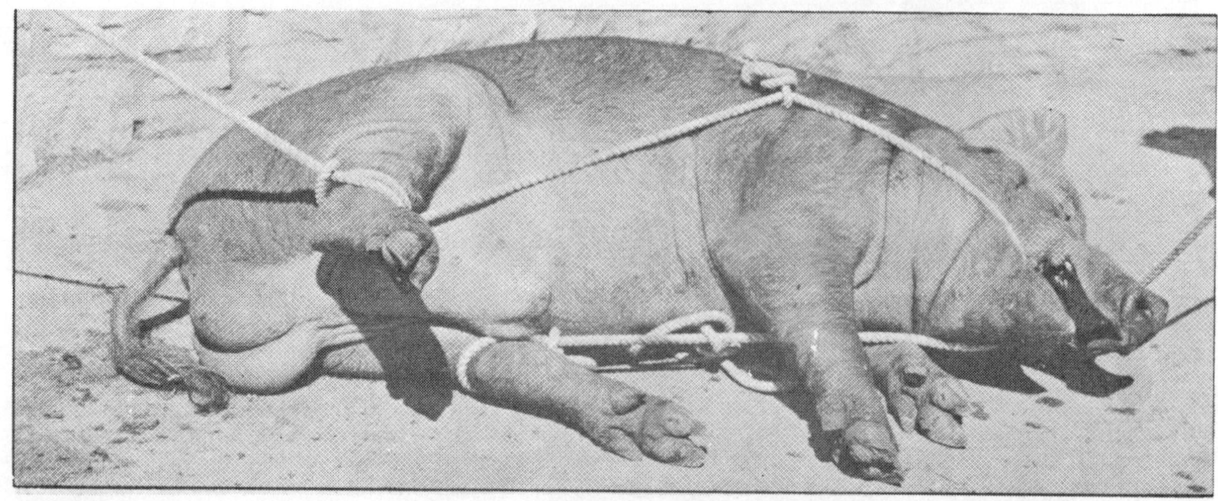

FIG. 47. The hind legs are pulled as far forward as possible.

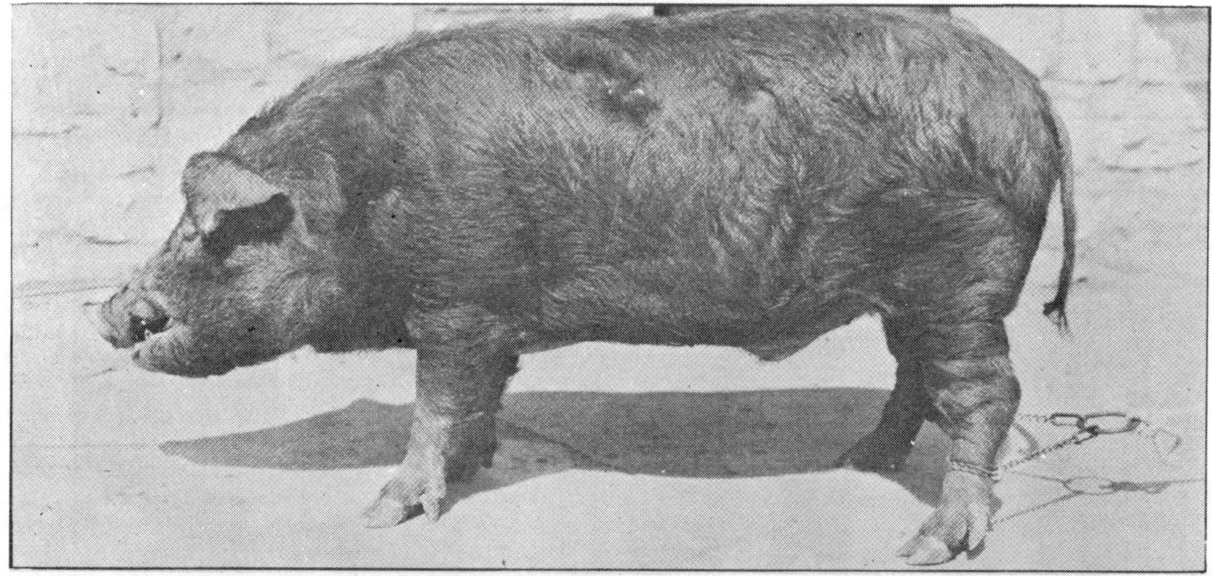

FIG. 48. The hobbles in position on the boar before casting.

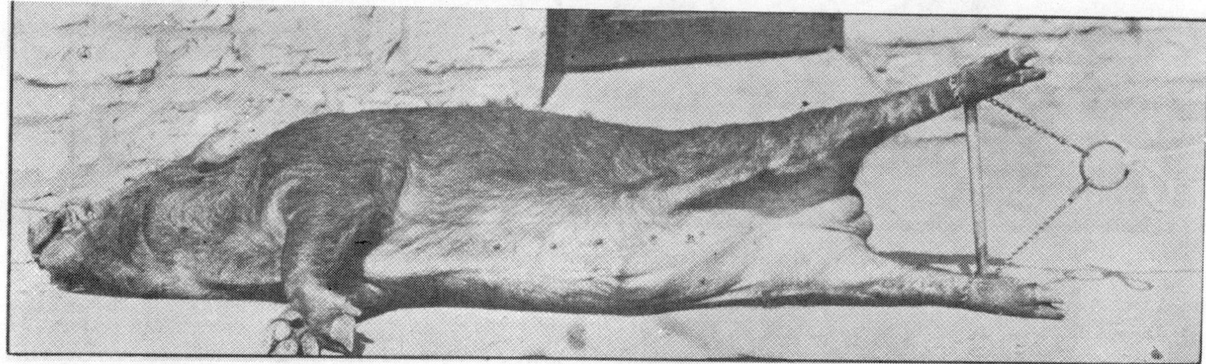

FIG. 49. The boar is stretched out and held securely in this position.

With some large bulls it may not be advisable to use the half hitches around the body for if they are used the penis may be injured. In some cases of torsion of the uterus in the cow the operator may want to roll the cow over and over. For cases like the above one of the methods of casting the horse may be used with good results. After the patient is down the bovine is tied the same as is shown for the horse.

Restraint of the Pig

Most small pigs are restrained by holding them by either the front or hind legs. If one of the hernia operations is to be performed they may be restrained on a flat surface or in a V shaped trough. The most difficult problem in restraint is presented when it is necessary to operate on a large boar. A number of methods have been devised for restraining the large boar in lateral recumbency. Some of the methods are rather difficult to apply and the restraint is not too efficient.

To apply any method of restraint it is first necessary to catch and confine the animal by the head. This may be accomplished by slipping a running loop made from a good strong one-half inch rope over the snout and back of the tusks and tightened. For one method of restraint the free end of the rope is carried back and passed around one hind leg above the hock. By pulling on the rope the snout and hind leg are brought as close together as possible. A clove hitch around the leg above the hock is used to fasten the rope so it will not slip. The disadvantage of this method of restraint is the lower hind leg is free. This permits the patient to struggle and also kick dirt and debris on the operator.

With the second method of restraint the rope around the snout is fastened to a post. The end of a one-half inch rope is fastened around one hind leg above the hock. The free end is carried forward and passed between the teeth and pulled back so the rope fits in the commissures of the mouth. Then the free end is brought back on the side of the body to the opposite hind leg and passed around it just above the hock. A short rope is placed over the back and fastened to the ropes passing along the sides. The object of this rope is to hold the other ropes up high enough so the patient cannot work the rope out of his mouth when he is in lateral recumbency. By pulling on the free end of the rope and working the rope through the mouth the hind legs are gradually pulled forward. When the hind legs are pulled well forward the rope is secured with a clove hitch above the hock joint. The objections to this method is the patient can still struggle and it also requires much effort on the part of the operator to cast a larger boar.

A method that is easy on both the patient and the operator was devised by Alcorn of Iowa. It also restrains the boar so there is a minimum of struggling. The rope that is around the snout is fastened approximately one foot above the ground to a post. For the hind legs a hobble is made using a piece of pipe one and one-fourths inches in diameter, and sixteen inches long. A strong ring two inches in diameter is welded on each end of the pipe. A piece of obstetrical chain or rope may be fastened to each ring. These chains or ropes are used to make hobbles to fasten around each hind leg just above the fetlock joint. To fasten the rope or chain around the leg a loop of chain or rope is passed through the ring. A foot is then slipped through this loop and it is pulled tight. The ends of the two hobbles are brought together and fastened to a long single rope or to a block and tackle. These are fastened about six feet off the ground to a solid post. As the rope is tightened the boar is stretched out, falls on his side and gradually rolls upon his back. The boar is held securely with little chance to do any struggling. By using this method of restraint one man can restrain a large boar with a minimum of effort.

REFERENCES

Arlein, Myron S. and Walter, Carl W., Aseptic Technique in Veterinary Surgery, J.A.V.M.A., CLL, (1943), pp. 41-47.

Brewer, J. H., The Antibacterial Effects of Organic Mercurial Compounds, J.A.M.A., CXll, (May, 1939), pp. 2009-2018.

Nye, R. N., The Relative in Vitro Activity of Certain Antiseptics in Aqueous Solutions, J.A.M.A., CVlll, (Jan. 1937), pp. 280-287.

Price, P. B., New Studies in Surgical Bacteriology and Surgical Technic, J.A.M.A., (Nov. 1938), pp. 1993-1996.

Sigler, T. A., Experiences of a General Practitioner, Veterinary Medicine, (July, 1941), pp. 348-364.

Spaulding, E. H., Studies on the Chemical Sterilization of Surgical Instruments, Surg., Gynec., & Obstet., LX1X, (Dec. 1939), pp. 738-744.

Walker, J. E., The Germicidal Properties of Soap, Joun. Infect. Dis., XXXV11, (1925), pp. 127-130.

Walter, C. W., The Relation of Proper Preparation of Solutions for Intravenous Therapy to Febrile Reactions, Ann. Surg., CV11, (Oct. 1940), pp. 603-617.

Walter, C. W., The Sterilization of Dressings and Dry Goods, Internat. Abstr. Surg., LXX1, (Nov. 1940), pp. 414-419.

Walter, C. W., Sterilization, Surg. Clinics of N. America, XX11, (April, 1942), pp. 333-356.

Walter, C. W., The Use of a Mixture of Cocoanut Oil Derivatives of a Bactericide in the Operating Room, Surg., Gynec. & Obster., LXV11, (Nov. 1938), pp. 683-688.

White, George R., Restraint of Domestic Animals, (1912).

Chapter III

WOUNDS AND INFECTIONS

A wound is a break in the continuity of tissue in any part of the body and is usually produced by an external instrument. In the repair of wounds the living cells promote this by their activity and growth and the role of the different cells varies only to meet the demands of the wound. When healing of the wound is complete the growth of new tissue from the cells stop. Every wound may be regarded as a new growth and our every effort should be directed to promote its growth. We know that if the proper treatment has been used that when healing is complete the process will be terminated. If the principles of wound healing are followed it is easy to determine if the wound is healing according to the natural process of repair. Also it is easy to determine when or if the treatment should be changed so that the wound will heal in the best possible manner.

Wounds may be classified as: incised wounds when it is due to a sharp cutting instrument. The edges of the wound are smooth and there has been a minimum amount of damage to the tissues.

Abrasions are wounds in which the superficial layers of tissue have been destroyed by friction exposing the sensitive tissue. These wounds are very sensitive, bleed very little, but heal slowly.

A contusion is a traumatic rupture of continuity of tissue without a complete separation of tissue. It is accompanied by an effusion of blood or lymph and swelling. All surface contusions must be considered potentially as more serious injuries to the underlying soft parts until the latter are excluded. A mistaken diagnosis of contusion may be made when in reality there is a fracture.

Swelling is a constant symptom of contusion and is caused by the interference with the circulation brought about by the effusion of blood or lymph.

Contusions are accompanied by hemorrhage of varying amounts. Hemorrhage should be distinguished from congestion in that the former, means the extravasation of blood from its normal vessels and the latter means simply the accumulation of a greater amount of blood than normal in the vessels.

By extravasation of blood is meant a large quantity of blood has spread between tissue planes. By hematoma is meant a circumscribed collection of blood in any tissue. The course of a contusion in the large majority of cases is resolution and absorption. Contusion wound is produced by traumatism and the wound may be open or closed depending on whether the skin is broken. When this type of wound is produced, there is rupture of the capillaries, small arteries, veins and lymphatics. The swelling that occurs as a result of the traumatism is due to the escape of blood and lymph into the tissues.

Lacerations are wounds in which the edges are torn and irregular due to the tearing of the tissues. In most cases the wounds are due to barb wire and there is extensive damage to the tissues.

Avulsions are wounds in which there is actual loss of tissues due to the tearing action of the object which in many cases is barb wire. There is in many cases very little pain with this very extensive type of injury.

Penetrating wounds are those wounds in which a small external opening is produced but the foreign object may penetrate deep into the tissues. These wounds are very dangerous as they may injure tendon sheaths, joint capsules or other important tissues. Also virulent organisms as anaerobe infections may be introduced into the tissues where conditions are ideal for their development.

Kinds of Repair

Granulation tissue is essential to the healing of every wound. There is no difference except in degree when a wound heals by first, second or third intention.

Besides the essential part granulation tissue plays in healing of a wound it is in the absence of epithelial and endothelial protection the body's best defense against the invasion of bacteria. Therefore, protection of the granulation tissue and its surface cell medium from traumatization and insults of any nature becomes of paramount importance in the consideration of wound healing.

When a wound heals by first intention it is the closest approach to perfection that can be obtained in wound healing. The wound heals without any infection present, also the tissues are approximated so accurately there is no apparent defect. Only enough granulation tissue is formed to join the opposed surfaces.

Healing of a wound by second or third intention occurs where there is a severe infection present or there is extensive loss of tissue and a large amount of granulation tissue is required to close the defect. The resulting scar may be rather large and interfere with movement of the part. Even though satisfactory healing is obtained in healing by secondary intention it requires a longer period of time and more care by the surgeon.

Bacterial Inflammation

Bacterial inflammation is usually an indication of infection. With every surgical procedure there is a possibility that infection will be introduced into the wound. The prevention of postoperative infection in wounds and the use of anesthetics has extended the possibilities of operative procedures. Also infection is of interest to the surgeon for surgery is indicated in those diseases that will respond to surgical therapy.

ASEPSIS AND ANTISEPSIS. The prevention of infection during an operation under present surgical technic is the accepted procedure. It is just as important to wear gloves to prevent contamination of the hands whenever there is a possibility of touching infection as it is to wear gloves during an operation. This procedure is to prevent the hands from becoming contaminated and the skin harboring infection.

The object of modern aseptic surgery is to prevent infection of the wound both during and after the operation. If sterility of the area is maintained, healing by first intention is obtained.

SURGICAL BACTERIOLOGY. In surgical bacteriology the knowledge of bacteriology should be used in the diagnosis and treatment of surgical infections. Some of the surgical infections occur in wounds and other infections may develop spontaneously or after apparently slight injuries. When abscesses develop they require incision for drainage and treatment.

The pyogenic bacteria (pus forming) are the most important in the acute surgical infections. Those organisms that produce pus are the staphylococcus, streptococcus, colon bacillus, and pyocyaneous bacillus.

Staphylococcus exist in at least three forms, the aureus, albus, and citrus; these terms are based on the color the colonies produce on culture.

The staphylococcus is found as a normal inhabitant of the skin so it is difficult to determine whether the organism isolated on culture is pathogenic or one of accidental contamination. When the staphylococcus is pathogenic there is usually rapid suppuration, with a tendency to localize and form a thick creamy pus. When the abscess breaks and drains to the outside, healing usually occurs without difficulty. It is also known that septicemia and pyemia may occur with staphylococcus infection, as it has been recovered from the blood stream in such cases.

STREPTOCOCCUS. It may be found as a normal inhabitant of various parts of the body. When the streptococcus becomes virulent, it tends to spread involving extensive areas of tissue and producing necrosis of tissue rather than abscesses. If pus is formed, it is usually watery at first then may become thick.

B. Coli is normally found in the posterior part of the intestinal tract and may escape into the abdominal cavity producing peritonitis. When pus is produced by B. Coli it has an offensive fecal odor and is thin and watery.

B. pyocyaneus in itself is of very little pathogenic importance but may occur in a mixed infection. When present, the infection may be recognized by its musty odor and by the greenish or bluish color to the purulent discharge.

Acute Surgical Infections

The surface of the body may be invaded by infection without the apparent presence of a wound. In many cases the infection usually staphylococcus or streptococcus gains entrance to the tissue through an imperceptible wound or slight trauma. When the infection gains entrance to the tissue it is called invasion. The infection may be capable of producing systemic effects which may not be noticeable. However, the systemic effects are very important as they indicate an invasion of the entire body by the organism or its products. When the organism invades the blood stream it is called a septicemia and the mortality may be high in these cases. The local effects of surgical infections may be classified into cellulitis and suppuration.

CELLULITIS AND SUPPURATION. Cellulitis occurs when infection enters the tissues and the local evidence is an area of inflammation known as cellulitis. It is important to recognize the difference between cellulitis and suppuration as the treatment is different for each condition. If an incision is made into an area of cellulitis, it may result in the spreading of the infection. In most cases of cellulitis, the inflammatory reaction in the affected tissue is so sudden and severe that it is difficult to differentiate from a traumatism. There is a marked swelling of the affected tissues, it is sensitive and redness is observed where the skin is white. Due to the increased flow of blood and exudation to the part, heat will be felt radiating from the tissue. The swelling may extend beyond the cellulitis and is called lymphedema. If the swelling of the tissues becomes so tight that the arterial blood supply is closed, this tissue may become necrotic. Palpation of the affected tissue will usually induce symptoms of pain on pressure.

SUPPURATION. In many cases the cellulitis will disappear without suppuration but quite frequently there is suppuration. When suppuration or abscess formation occurs a softened area can be felt, in which there is formation of pus, which is composed of dead bacteria, leucocytes, necrotic tissue and exudate.

When suppuration occurs, there is cellulitis and also pus formation which is manifested by fluctuation. When fluid is present a wave like sensation, called fluctuation, is felt as pressure is applied by the fingers to opposite sides of the swelling. Occasionally inflammatory tissue, lipomas, and cysts, will give a sensation of fluctuation. Before making an incision to drain any swelling, it is advisable to insert a needle to see if pus is present. A large bore needle should always be used as thick pus might fail to enter a small needle and an improper diagnosis would be made.

EXTENSION OF INFECTION. The acute surgical infections may extend to other parts of the body by way of the lymphatic or venous systems, also by direct extension. Infection may enter the lymphatic vessels and they will provide a pathway of extension to other parts of the body. This is shown by the fact that there is involvement of the regional lymph node with development of an acute lymphadenitis.

PHLEBITIS. Infection may enter the venous system and be carried to other parts of the body. If a chill occurs, it is usually due to the entrance of bacteria into the blood stream. When infection is carried to other parts of the body, it is usually by way of the blood stream. If inflammation of the vein occurs, it may be shown by swelling and tenderness along its course. This is called phlebitis. The blood in an inflamed vein may become thrombosed producing thrombophlebitis. If a portion of the thrombus should break off, it might be carried by way of the blood stream to the heart, brain or lungs.

DIRECT EXTENSION. Probably in most cases the infection spreads in all directions by invading adjacent tissue until arrested by the defenses set up by the tissues. When direct extension occurs by way of the fascia or tendon sheaths, it produces a very serious condidion.

SEPTICEMIA. When there is an extension of an infection from a local process over the body the systemic manifestations are those of septicemia. The term septicemia implies that bacteria have entered the blood stream but it may not be possible to obtain a positive culture from the blood. Even though a blood culture is not obtained, the clinical symptoms of septicemia are so characteristic that a diagnosis of septicemia is justified. The characteristic symptoms of septicemia may occur in the following order. (1) Fever is practically always present in a systemic infection and may be of the intermittent type. Fever seems to be an indication that the body is building defenses against the infection. If the infection is one that is developing very rapidly the animal may die before it has a chance to develop any resistance. Fever seems to be a part of the accelerated metabolism, which is set up by the body to fight the infection. If the temperature becomes abnormally high it may prove harmful rather than beneficial in combatting the infection. (2) Chills may be observed in those cases in which the infection has gained entrance into the blood stream. The chill may cause spasmodic contractions of the muscles and the patient to shake rather vigorously. Due to the peripheral vaso-constriction the extremities are cold while the temperature of the deeper tissues may be rather high. (3) Leukocytosis occurs in the presence of infections and the activity of the bone marrow is evidenced by the appearance of the younger forms in greater numbers. The leucocyte count may be rather high with 20,000 or more per cubic millimeter. If the infection develops very rapidly and overcomes the resistance of the patient, leukocytosis may be absent. In some of the cases, leukocytosis may be one of the first indications of infection before there is an increase in temperature or any other signs. (4) The general attitude of the patient may be one of depression and listlessness. But in some cases the patient may be more alert and restless. (5) Metastatic foci may occur in septicemia with abscesses and infection occurring in various parts of the body. Some of the metastatic foci may be inaccessible, while abscesses may be incised and drained or other treatment that is indicated may be used.

The acute surgical infections may terminate in a number of ways due to immunity and resistance of the tissues. In the case of cellulitis, the swelling in the tissues may gradually subside without leaving any trace of the intense inflammatory reaction that occurred in the tissues. The invasion of the tissue by bacteria is frequently terminated by suppuration. In some cases local necrosis of tissue occurs when the invading organism is unusually virulent.

When death occurs from a general invasion of the body with infection, it may be due to lack of resistance. The fatal termination of the infection may occur in a few hours or days. In some cases death may be preceded by the development of pyemia and infective foci that are inaccessible to treatment.

Repair of Tissue

The science of surgery is dependent upon the ability of tissue to repair injuries whether it is accidental or intentional. If best results are to be obtained in the treatment of wounds the surgeon must know which tissues will be regenerated in the wound. During the process of wound healing only three tissues are regenerated, epithelium, blood vessels and fibrous tissue. The objective of wound treatment is to provide conditions that will result in the regeneration of those tissues and continuity and function of the injured tissues. If new tissue is to be formed it is essential that it have a rich blood supply. However after the new tissue is formed only those vessels that are not necessary to maintain the new tissue are obliterated. Regeneration of tissue occurs as soon as the exudative phase is complete.

The skin and mucous membrane are regenerated by almost the same process from around the edges of the wound and from any epithelium present in the wound. However, the regenerated skin does not contain sebaceous glands or hair follicles. Regenerated fibrous tissue will restore the injured continuity of injured muscle, fat, liver, spleen, kidney, lung and the serosal surfaces are reunited and replaced by it.

The process producing the fibrous tissue of the scar and called fibroplasia starts with the multiplication of mononuclear cells and fibroblasts. Fibroplasia establishes continuity and provides strength for the sutured wound while it is responsible for the granulation tissue in the open wound. The period of multiplication of fibroblasts lasts only a day or two then from the fourth day on the process consists in the formation of fibrils of reticulin.

In approximately two weeks the reticulin fibrils are enlarged to form fibers that become differentiated according to their function in the area. The differentiation of the fibers in the wound restores it to its original strength. As a general rule it requires longer for differentiation to occur in the fibrous tissue then it does in the epithelium. In healing of the skin the continuity may be established in a few weeks but it may require several months before the original strength is restored. For those tissues that were originally strong such as tendons, ligaments and fascias it requires a long time for differentiation to occur to the original strength restored. But the original strength of muscle tissue and intestine is restored by the reticulin as its strength is equal to the strength of the connective tissue in these tissues. In an intentional wound the original strength is restored more quickly if the tissues are divided in the direction of their fibers.

When organs are injured the only function of the fibrous tissue in the scar is to establish continuity while function is performed by hypertrophy of the parenchymatous tissue.

Fibroplasia

When any of the deeper tissue in a wound is injured or destroyed it is replaced by fibrous tissue during the healing process. If there is any infection or necrotic tissue in the wound it stimulates the formation of more fibrous tissue and the size of the scar is increased. When the injury occurs to the tissue some fibrous tissue is generated but there is some absorption during the period of differentiation. The regenerated tissue continues to exist only so long as it is necessary to assist in maintaining function. If there is an excessive amount of fibroplasia as a result of the injury or due to infection in the tissue, then the reabsorption that occurs may not remove the excessive fibrous tissue that interferes with function. If infection is controlled in a wound it will help to prevent the formation of an excessive quantity of fibrous tissue.

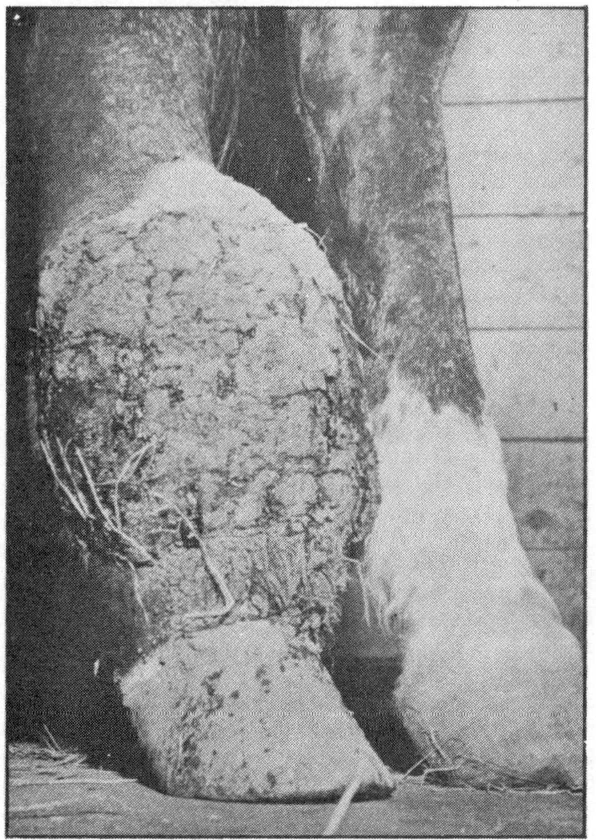

FIG. 50. Extensive formation of inflammatory tissue after severe injury to anterior surface of metatarsus.

Exudative Phase

With the formation of the wound the exudative phase of wound healing occurs. It is during this phase that hemorrhage is controlled, fibrin is formed and bacterial invasion is overcome, dead tissue is liquefied and there is sloughing of foreign bodies. Also during this phase there are chemical changes taking place in the area of new cells. The proper care of wounds is directed toward shortening the exudative phase so that tissues will regenerate in as short a time as possible.

Hemorrhage is controlled by the retraction of the blood vessels and maintained by the deposition of fibrin in the cut ends of the vessels. With the deposition of fibrin the tissues are sealed together. Thus a water tight and air tight seal is formed and prevents leakage from hollow viscera and is responsible for making possible successful operations on these structures. Fibrin is also responsible for enclosing loose matter and bacteria and holding it in one location in the wound.

The resistance to bacterial invasion of the wound is accomplished by the vascular and cellular reaction. After dilatation of the vessels there is an exudate poured into the tissues producing an edema. Phagocytosis and anti-bacterial substances slow the development of and destroy bacteria. The enzymes liberated by the leucocytes liquefy dead tissue and thus reduce the food available for bacteria. As toxic products are formed they are carried away by the blood stream. With the liquefaction of the tissue proteins the acidity of the tissue proteins approaches neutrality and new capillaries begin to develop from the blood vessels in the surrounding healthy tissue. When the chemical environment becomes favorable and there is adequate nutrition from the new capillaries it stimulates fibroplasia.

In a wound that is sutured and healing occurs by first intention the exudative phase lasts about four days. During this period the wound has only the strength supplied by the sutures and fibrin. Also during this period the tissues are weaker due to the edema and liquefaction which lowers the capacity of the tissues to hold sutures.

Antiseptics and Wound Healing

It is very questionable if antiseptics should be used in the treatment of fresh wounds. The popular antiseptic dusting powders should not be used on fresh wounds as they combine with the exudate to form into a hard inert crust.

The only value antiseptics have in treating wounds is to destroy bacteria on the surface of the skin. Antiseptics have very little if any value in destroying bacteria in the muscle tissue of a wound or in the hair follicles. The skin must be clean if the antiseptic is to exert any bactericidal activity.

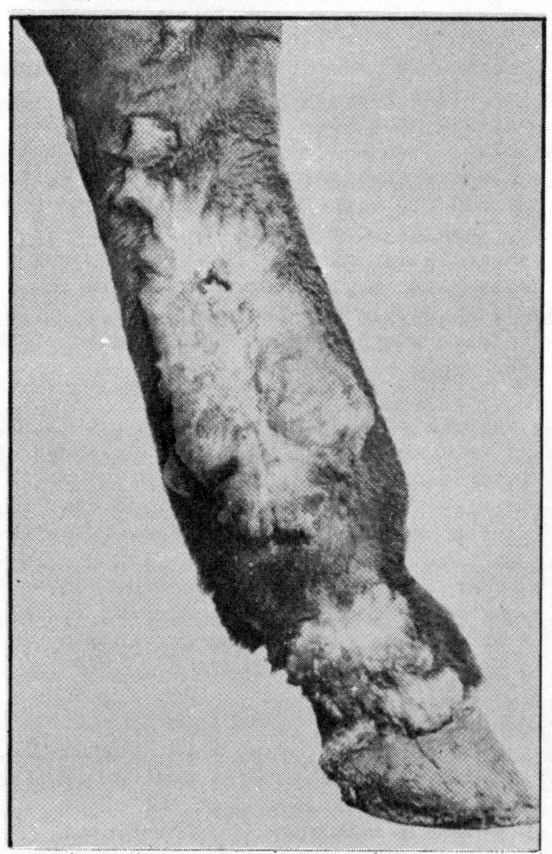

FIG. 51. Too strong antiseptics produce fibrous tissue and the wound will not heal.

The antiseptic should be mixed with a grease solvent so the dirt and grease will be removed. However soap and water is very efficient in removing the dirt, grease and bacteria on the surface of the skin. There are antibacterial powerful detergent preparations that are very efficient in cleansing the skin of grease and dirt. All of the antiseptics that contain alcohol or acetone are very detrimental to wound healing as they destroy cells. Although it is well known that antiseptics will not destroy bacteria in the presence of blood but they are still recommended by some manuals and textbooks.

If the bacteria are on the surface of the wound they may be removed with running water. Antiseptics will not destroy the bacteria that are ground into the soft tissue of the wound. The various solutions of antiseptics as iodine, mercury, acriflavines and others when used in wounds destroy cells in the wound and delay healing.

Relationship Between Epithelization and Fibroplasia and the Control of Epithelization

Epithelization is a surface phenomena requiring a suitable granulating base.

If epithelization is to occur over a wound there must be a suitable granulating surface. When the granulating surface is below the skin edges or are above them the new epithelium will not grow over it until this irregularity is corrected. When the granulation tissue is too high it may be reduced surgically or by the use of caustics. If the granulation tissue is too low it may be due to bacteria present on the surface and the puddling of pus or to sloughing tissue. It may be possible to stimulate the proper development of the granulation tissue by the use of mild irritants.

It is only by providing the proper conditions for epithelization that it occurs readily as there are no drugs that stimulate the rate of epithelization. However a proper rate of epithelization can be maintained by keeping the granulation tissue at the proper height and by reducing the bacteria on the surface. Epithelization may cover a large area if there is sufficient elasticity of the surrounding skin. In some areas of the body and where the area is too large to epithelize spontaneously it may be necessary to do skin grafts.

Contraction

Contraction of the tissue begins with the appearance of the granulation tissue. It is a very important and powerful force in the closing of wounds and results from the inward movement of the surrounding healthy tissue. This contraction starts at a maximum rate with the appearance of the granulation tissue but slows up as the wound is closed. This contractile force can close a large wound if it is located in an area where the tissues are freely movable. However, very little contraction occurs if the tissues in the wound are fixed to the underlying structures or are stretched across bony areas. When wounds occur in such an area the regeneration of tissue must close the wound with the formation of as large a scar as the original wound. The tuber coxae and lower parts of the limbs are areas where contraction cannot exist.

In wounds such as shown in Fig. 52, there is a gradual contraction of the wound and the edges of the skin heal together with little scar formation.

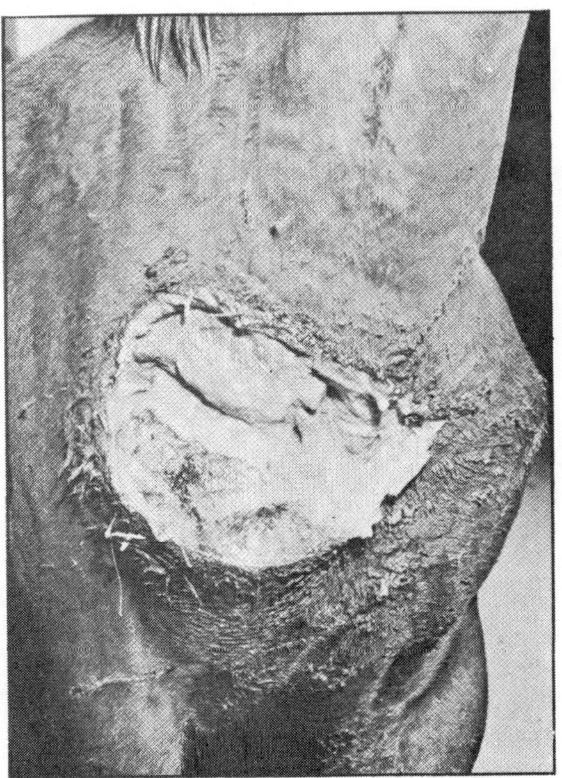

FIG. 52. Extensive laceration at point of shoulder in yearling, wound heals well.

On wounds below the hock and knee the tissues are fixed to the underlying structures so it is very important to keep the edges of the tissues in close apposition. As soon as a wound occurs an antiseptic pack should be placed over the wound and bandaged in position with bandages applied with pressure. The pressure bandage prevents the formation of an excessive amount of tissue between the edges of the wound. For those wounds from the knee to the elbow or hock to stifle bandages are not necessary except in special cases. When wounds occur above the elbow and stifle joints they may be treated as open wounds as the tissues are freely movable and contraction will close a large wound. The difference in the movability of the tissues in different portions of the body is the determining factor in choosing how a certain wound will be treated.

There is no treatment known that will hasten the contraction of the tissues. At various times hormones, plant substances and vitamins are publicised as stimulants to the whole process of wound healing. Also there is no product known that will stimulate the regeneration of tissue.

Suturing Wounds

In large animals many of the wounds are lacerated and very extensive and should not be sutured. A wound should not be sutured unless it possesses certain properties. It should be practically free of crushed tissue, the edges should have an adequate blood supply and the wound should be practically free of foreign bodies. The last and most important point is the wound should contain the minimal number of bacteria. Only those wounds that are incised under proper antiseptic precautions, possess these properties.

When traumatic wounds are to be sutured the crushed tissue is debrided to reduce its amount and the wound irrigated to remove the bacteria. Primary suturing of traumatic wounds should not be performed ten hours after the injury as the bacteria are multiplying in the tissues.

As tension reduces the blood supply to the edges of the wound the tissues should not be sutured under tension. If tension is used on the sutures it may cause sloughing of more skin. Experience has shown the incidence of infection in wounds closed under tension is far higher than in wounds closed without tension.

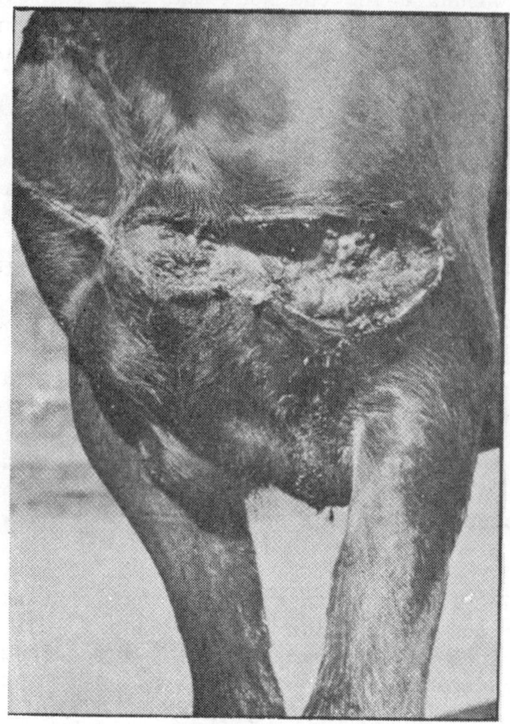

FIG. 53.

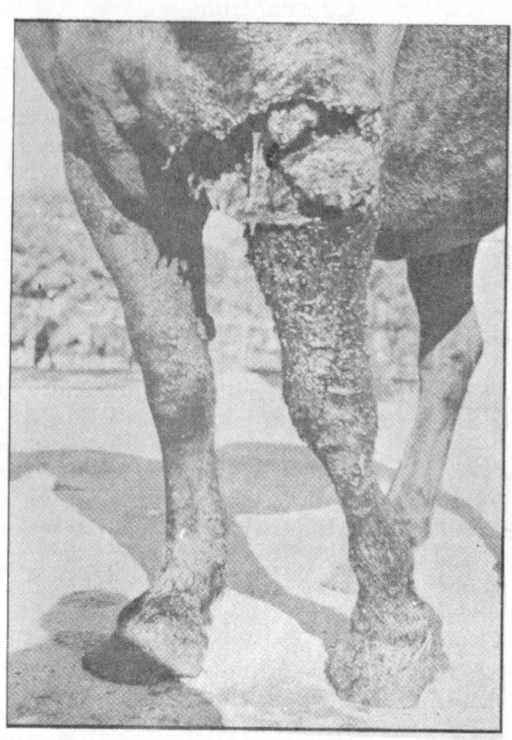

FIG. 54. Wound lacerated, extensive injury to muscle tissue.

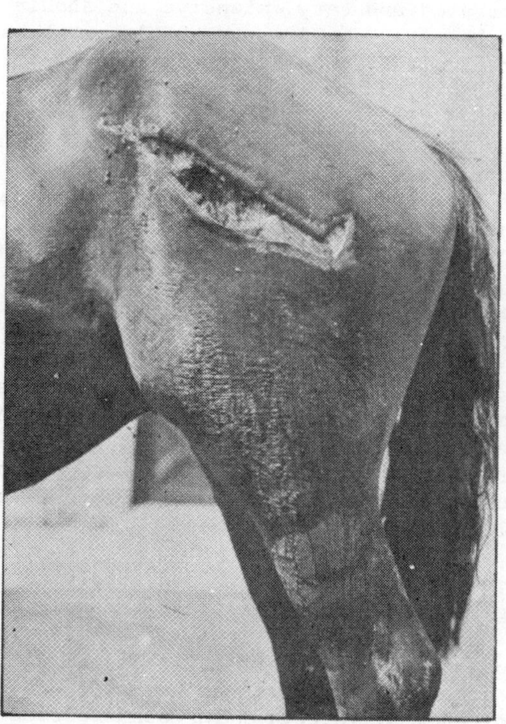

FIG. 55.

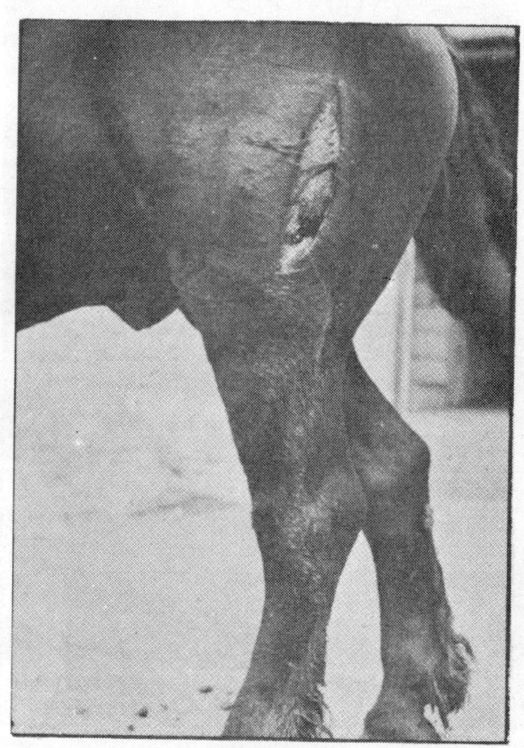

FIG. 56.

In Figures 53, 54, 55 and 56 are shown excellent examples of the types of wounds that heal better if they are not sutured. It is very important to treat as open wounds those in which the deeper tissues have been injured and are infected. Those wounds in the region of joints usually heal with less interference of movement if the wound is treated without suturing. A wound that has invaded a bursa or tendon sheath should never be sutured. When bursas or tendon sheaths become contaminated they are very difficult to treat. Where ever possible the edges of the tissues should be approximated to prevent contamination of tissue at the maximum points of advancement. Sutures should never be used to bridge across the defect as they are left exposed to infection. When sutures become infected they act as a wick to carry infection back into the edges of the wound. The wound invariably becomes infected, the sutures have to be removed and the wound is more extensive than it was originally. For those wounds that are extensive and have angles, the size of the wound may be reduced by suturing the angles and leaving the center open. When the edges of the sutured angles can be approximated the prerequisites for successful healing have been made.

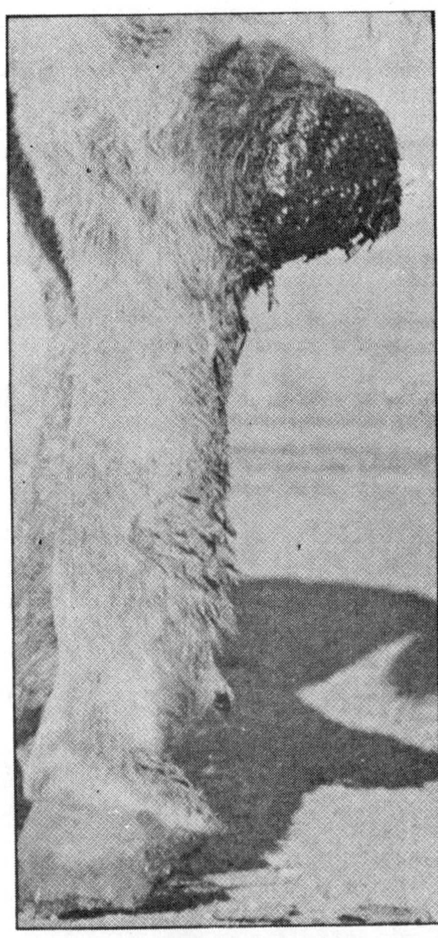

FIG. 57. A mass of exuberant granulation tissue that developed from a wound two inches long.

Exuberant Granulation of Tissue

There is a tendency for wounds below the knee and hock to develop exuberant granulation tissue. This type of tissue is unhealthy tissue and wounds will not heal until it is removed. If the wound is located where there is movement, as produced by a tendon, there is an even greater tendency toward the stimulation of excessive granulation tissue. When wounds occur below the knee and hock they should receive special care until a healthy layer of granulation tissue has been formed. This is accomplished by keeping the tissue clean and healthy and the use of a pressure pack. By keeping the wound under pressure it will prevent the development of any excessive amount of granulation tissue.

Exuberant granulation tissue may be removed in a number of ways depending upon the amount that has developed. If there is only a small amount present it may be removed by applying powder copper sulphate. This is bandaged in position and left on for forty eight hours. When the bandage is removed a thin layer of granulation tissue is removed. In some cases it may be necessary to use the copper sulphate several times. The exuberant granulation tissue may be removed surgically and a pressure pack applied until the tissue is healthy. If there is a large amount of granulation tissue present an escharotic may be used by mixing hydrochloric acid and sulphur until a paste is formed or sulphuric acid may be used with the sulphur. A liberal application of vaseline should be applied to the normal skin around the area before the escharotic paste is applied to the granulation tissue. In a few days a thick layer of necrotic tissue may be removed and if necessary the escharotic paste may be used until all of the exuberant granulation tissue has been removed.

In the case shown in Fig. 57 it was very difficult to get complete healing of the wound by the usual methods of treatment. After the granulation tissue was reduced to the size of a dollar a liberal application of formalin was made on the tissue. This was repeated several times before there was complete healing.

In some wounds the destruction of tissue has been so extensive that it is necessary to assist the tissues in the healing process. The extensive destruction of tissue in Fig. 58 occurred when the mare ran through a barbed wire fence. It was necessary to use pressure bandages to bring the edges of the skin together. By this procedure excellent healing was obtained in this very extensive wound as shown in Fig. 59. Due to the destruction of the normal muscle tissue and its replacement by fibrous connective tissue there was some interference with the normal extension of the limb. When a wound in which there has been extensive destruction of tissue does not receive assistance in the healing process the edges of the skin may not heal together.

Healing Under a Scab

The formation of a scab occurs most frequently on small wounds. The scab is formed from the wound exudate and healing takes place under the scab. A careful examination should be made of the scab to see if it is firmly attached. If the scab is loose it should be removed as there is infection under it. When there is infection present healing of the wound is retarded.

Wounds in certain locations and other wounds when they have reached a certain stage of healing seem to heal best if they are covered with a firm scab. The value of forming a scab on a wound is illustrated by the following case. A stallion was presented for the treatment of a purulent discharge from the sheath. Examination of the sheath revealed the discharge was due to suppurating areas on the prepuce. There were seven of these area each about one inch in diameter. Treatment consisted in applying a two per cent solution of formalin to the areas daily until a firm scab was formed. Healing of these wounds then occurred without further treatment. Some

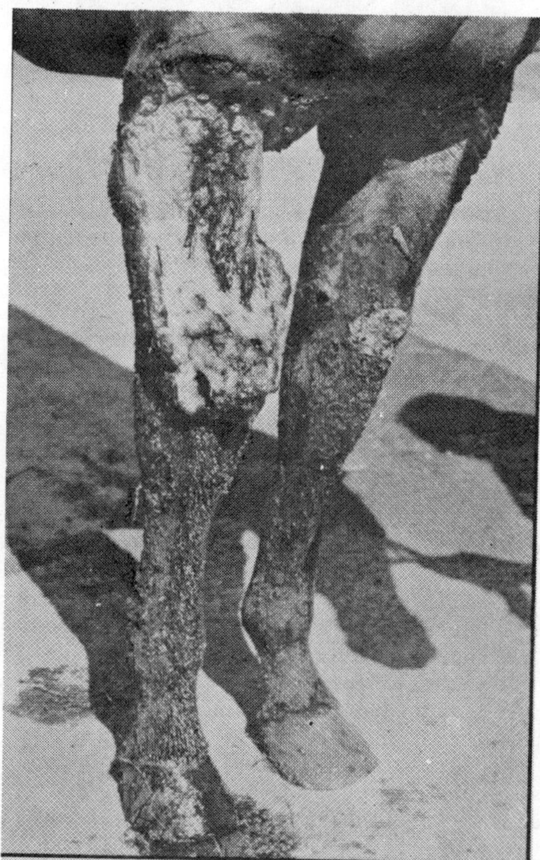

FIG. 58. Avulsion wound, in which there has been an actual tearing away of tissue.

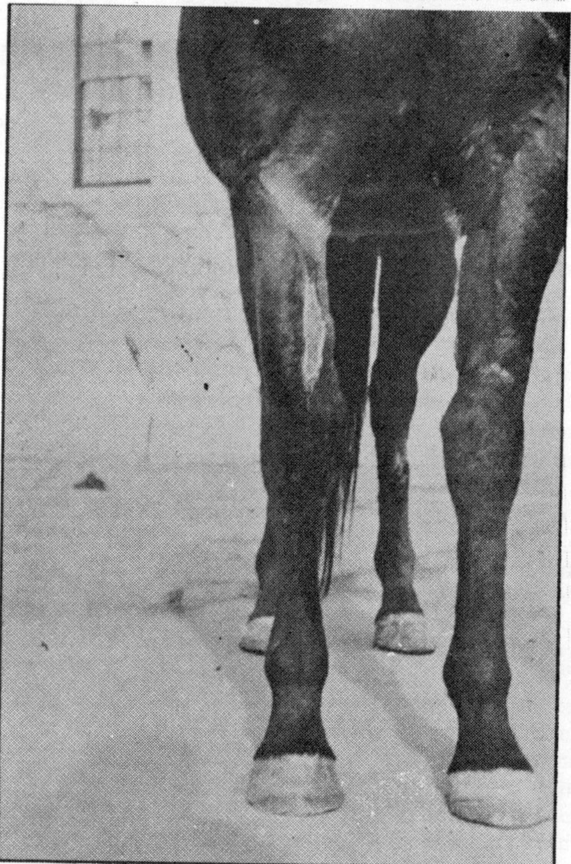

FIG. 59. Extensive wounds will heal if they receive proper care.

wounds of the limbs heal more rapidly when they are painted once daily with equal parts of a forty per cent solution of formalin and tincture of iodine until a firm scab is formed.

Wounds of the Axillary Region

Wounds in the axillary region may be puncture wounds or lacerated wounds. This area is located between the elbow and the sternum. Quite frequently a wound in this area permits air to enter the tissues. It may spread rather rapidly under the skin to other portions of the body and the air may be felt in the subcutaneous tissue of the shoulder, neck, head, trunk, and even extend to the hindquarters. The air in the tissue does not require any particular treatment as it is absorbed in a few days.

Wounds in the axillary region are treated the same as wounds in other parts of the body. However, healing is rather slow due to the frequent movement of the tissue.

Wounds on the Flexion Surface of Joints

Lacerations of the anterior surface of the hock joint are of frequent occurrence. These are in many cases very deep and extensive and the usual cause is barbed wire.

When wounds occur where there is normally a great deal of movement of the parts they must be watched closely. If there is any formation of exuberant granulation tissue it should be removed. This may be removed by the use of powdered copper sulphate, burnt alum, phenol, or other escharotics.

Even though it delays healing of the wound, the animal should receive a normal amount of daily exercise. If the granulation tissue develops without movement it is likely to break open when the patient is exercised, also exercise seems to toughen the developing tissue. The antiseptic used daily should be one that has a tendency to prevent the development of exuberant granulation tissue. In this area there is a tendency toward the development of keloids if the wound is allowed to heal with infection present in the tissues. This tendency is usually absent if infection is not present. A keloid is in the nature of a fibroma which occurs from a stimulus of injury to the tissues and it has a tendency to recur after removal. Keloids have very little practical importance unless they become extremely large.

Periosteum and Bone Wounds

When injuries of the periosteum occur they should be treated carefully to prevent infection of the bone. Infection causes destruction of bone and may burrow through the cortex and strip the periosteum as well as the endosteum. This will give rise to a necrotic piece of bone called a sequestrum. When this occurs treatment consists in waiting until there is complete separation of the sequestrum when it is removed. The area will then fill in with granulation tissue which is changed to osteoid tissue and bone.

When the periosteum is exposed or injured the area should receive protection from further injury or irritation. If wounds of this type are improperly treated it may result in the development of an osteoma. The periosteum is very susceptible to infection and exposure of a fresh surface may permit the infection to invade the deeper tissue. The above procedure was followed in Fig. 61 and in a few weeks exfoliation of the periosteum and endosteum occurred. This sequestrum was removed and beneath was a smooth even covering of healthy granulation tissue which gradually changed to osteoid tissue and bone.

In some cases a severe injury to the periosteum may develop into an osteoperiostitis with the formation of an exostosis. This occurs when the wound is improperly treated and the infection is not destroyed.

Wounds Below the Fetlock

Injuries due to barbed wire, the sharp edge of a disc, corn sled knife, and other sharp objects, are of frequent occurrence just below the fetlock joint. When injuries occur in this region of the limb the great digital sheath is frequently opened. Also the deep digital flexor tendon is often severed. When this occurs the outstanding sign is the extreme dorsal flexion of the phalanges.

The most serious complication that may occur as the result of the injury is the entrance of the infection into the very extensive great digital sheath. This sheath extends from the distal fourth of

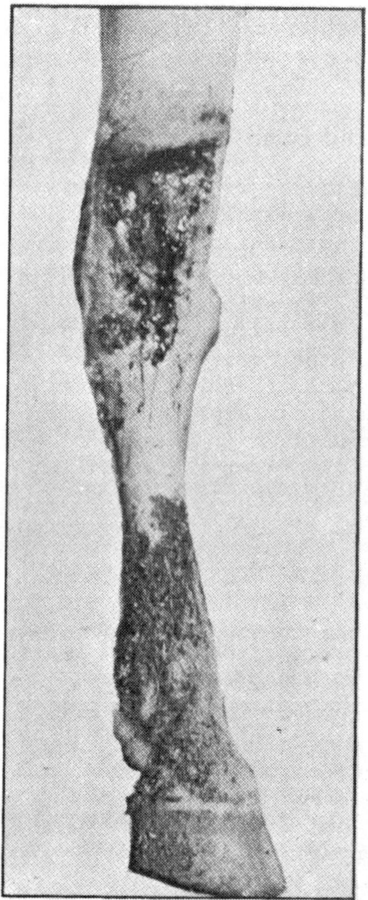

FIG. 60. A wound on the flexion surface of the hock joint.

FIG. 61. A wound in which the periosteum is exposed.

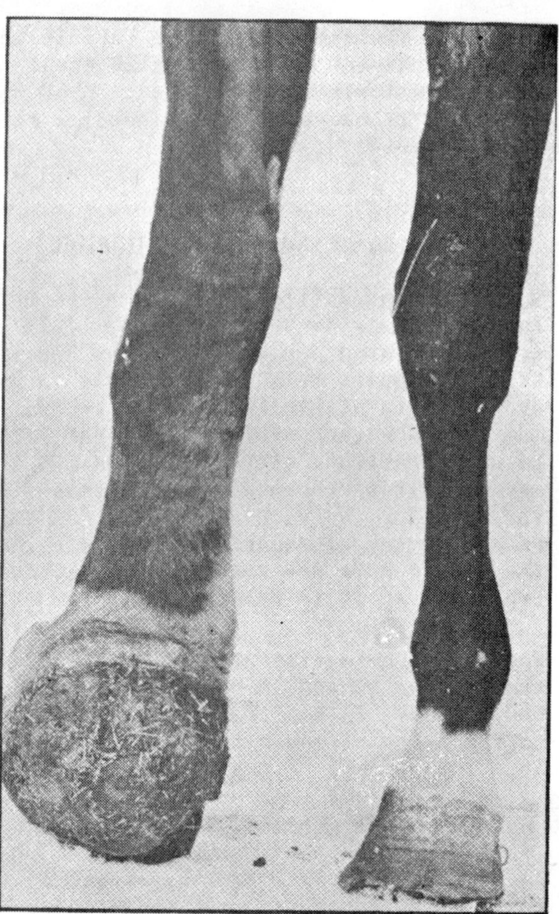

FIG. 62. An exostosis that developed from a severe injury of the periosteum.

the metacarpus to the distal end of the second phalanx. When the tendon sheath and that portion of the sheath above the fetlock joint becomes infected, there is distention of the sheath above the fetlock joint and it is sensitive on palpation. Also the animal hesitates to put any weight on the limb. The absence of swelling of the sheath below the fetlock joint is due to the three annular ligaments which bind it tightly to the digital ligament. When the infection gains entrance to the proximal portion of the sheath drainage is impossible due to the close binding of the sheath by the ligaments and the inflammatory swelling of the tissues.

When there is definite evidence that infection has gained entrance to the proximal portion of the sheath early surgical drainage of the sheath is indicated. If the pressure of the excess fluid in the sheath is maintained in the sheath it will disturb the delicate blood supply of the tendon tissue. When this disturbance in blood supply is maintained for too long a period of time it may result in an early breakdown of the tendon tissue. After drainage of the infection from the sheath it is indicated to use penicillin in the sheath. This method seems to shorten the prolonged period of suppuration which usually followed just surgical drainage. The use of some of the sulfonamides internally may also be indicated in some cases to help overcome infection.

Injuries to the Foot

Severe injury to the foot of the horse is of common occurrence due usually to barbed wire. Quite frequently the wire will be caught medial to the lateral cartilage and the horse in attempting to free the foot will pull it along the wire producing severe lacerations of the tissues. The laceration may extend through the coronary band in front and the digital cushion posteriorly. Hemorrhage may be rather profuse as injury of the extensive coronary plexus in this area usually occurs.

TREATMENT. If the coronary band has been lacerated this portion should be removed as it will produce an inferior quality of horny wall. When not more than one inch is removed a normal coronary band is usually regenerated, but it is necessary to maintain a pressure pack over the area if regeneration is to take place.

The infection and tissue debris in the depths of the wound should be removed by flushing out with a mild antiseptic solution. An antiseptic pack should be bandaged tightly over the area to keep the edges of the wound close together. The object of this pack is to keep an antiseptic in contact with the area and also to keep the edges of the wound close together. When this is done there is little opportunity for the development of an excessive quantity of granulation tissue.

In wounds on the lower part of the limb there sometimes develops the problem of stimulating the formation of epithelial tissue. The formation of epithelial tissue may proceed normally for a time then becomes stationary. This retarding of epithelization may be referred to as regeneration fatigue. Epithelization seems to vary a great deal in different individuals, as in some individuals wounds in any part of the body will heal slowly while in other individuals the same type of wound will heal rapidly. When wounds begin to heal slowly the epithelium may be stimulated by the use of an irritant. One irritant may be effective for only a short period of time then another will have to be used. Infection in the area tends to inhibit regeneration principally through injury to the newly forming cells. So a wound that is free of infection will heal more rapidly than one where there is infection present.

Puncture Wounds

This type of wound is usually caused by a sharp pointed body. These wounds are characterized by a small external opening that extends a variable depth into the tissue. Most puncture wounds are serious as they may introduce infection deep into the tissue. Another complicating factor may be the introduction of a foreign body into the tissue. When a foreign body is present the wound does not heal until this is removed.

PROGNOSIS. Prognosis is always guarded as frequently a virulent infection is introduced into the tissues.

TREATMENT. It is advisable to administer a prophylactic dose of tetanus anti·toxin in wounds of this type. Depending upon the location of the wound, hot antiseptic compresses may be applied or the part may be immersed in hot antiseptic solutions. This treatment should be used for one hour periods two or three times a day. If the swelling and inflammation does not subside pus has probably collected in the wound. A careful examination will usually disclose there is a soft area where the wound should be opened for drainage. The depths of the wound should be examined for the presence of a foreign body.

Open Joint

As a general rule penetrating wounds that involve a joint cavity are the most serious wounds occurring in animals. The seriousness of the injury will depend upon the joint affected as some of the joints are more extensive and complicated than others.

There are two different types of wounds produced; first, the extensive wounds which open the articulation with provision for good drainage. In the second type of wound there is a small opening into the joint cavity with no provision for drainage.

ETIOLOGY. Penetrating wounds may be caused by a cutting instrument, sharp pointed objects, or severe bruises of the tissue or a septic wound in the region of a joint may result in infection of the joint cavity.

SYMPTOMS. The severity of the signs will depend upon the virulence and degree of infection. Also the reaction in some individuals is more severe than it is in others. There are usually marked general systemic disturbances which may seem out of proportion to the small wound. The most pronounced signs do not occur until about the second or third day after the injury and then there is a marked increase in the respirations and the temperature may be from 104° to 106°. The pulse rate is markedly increased with a tendency to become wiry. As the signs increase in severity the appetite becomes variable and sweating is usually observed. If the condition is very painful there is almost constant movement of the affected limb and when the pain is severe and continuous the animal tends to become exhausted.

DIAGNOSIS. Diagnosis is based not only upon the location of the wound and the severity of the signs, but also upon the discharge of synovia. When the joint is moved the synovia may be expelled in a stream. Due to the inflammation there is an increased secretion of synovia and it may coagulate around the edges of the wound. A probe should never be used to see if the wound involves the joint cavity as it may be the means of introducing infection into the cavity.

PROGNOSIS. Prognosis is always guarded as it is impossible to foretell what the results of the treatment will be in open joints. Even if the infection is overcome, ankylosis of the joint may occur which is an unfavorable result if free movement of the joint is essential. This is not so serious in a joint where there is little movement.

Suppuration may ensue upon the initial stage and the presence of pus in a joint is always serious. Unless speedily cured, suppuration results in disintegration of a joint and even of nearby bone and transformation of the synovial membrane into granulation tissue. This is followed by healing by scar formation and a solid immobilization of the joint - ankylosis.

Whenever a suppurating joint has been opened it should be kept open and subjected to active motion. Such treatment helps drainage and subdues infection. It restores to usefulness, in some instances, joints which under less heroic methods would become permanently stiff.

TREATMENT. The skin area around the wound should be shaved, cleansed, and thoroughly disinfected. A variety of methods have been recommended for the treatment of open joints. In most cases good results are obtained if they are presented for treatment before the articular cartilages are infected, eroded and eventually destroyed.

During the acute stage of the infection hot applications should be applied to the area, and best results are usually obtained when the applications are applied for one hour periods three times daily.

The most difficult problem to decide is whether to enlarge a small opening of the joint capsule. Even though infectious material has been introduced into the joint cavity it may not be necessary to enlarge the opening for recovery to occur.

Frost recommends the following treatment in open joints. A solution containing one part Lugol's solution and three parts glycerine is injected into the joint cavity. This injection should be repeated two or three times a day. Enough of the solution should be used to thoroughly fill the joint cavity. The longer the solution is retained in contact with the infected membrane the better the results. This solution does not irritate the tissue but is an excellent antiseptic and the period of congestion and inflammation is shortened.

When there is definite indication of an open joint penicillin may be injected into the joint cavity. By using penicillin early it may prevent the development of infection. The use of penicillin is also indicated after infection has developed in the joint in an attempt to prevent injury to the tissues of the joint. Also some of the sulfonamides may be indicated internally to help in combating the infection.

FIG. 63. A portion of the muscle is protruding through the wound.

Wounds of the Tibial Region

Injuries in the region of the tibia are of rather common occurrence. The medial side of the tibia is covered only by the thin skin and fascia. A bruise or injury on the medial side of the tibia may produce a painful periostitis which is treated by antiphlogistic measures.

The muscles in this region are covered by a strong fascia which when injured may cause a very troublesome type of wound. If the wound involves the skin, fascia, and muscle, it may permit some of the muscle tissue to protrude through the wound. The almost constant movement of the muscle irritates the edges of the wound stimulating the formation of exuberant granulation tissue. Also the presence of muscle tissue in the opening prevents the closing of the wound.

TREATMENT. All exuberant granulation tissue may be removed surgically. Also it is necessary to remove the muscle tissue that extends outside of the fascia. To obtain healing of the wound it is necessary to keep an antiseptic pack over the wound under pressure. The pack may be maintained in position by using a splint. If tacks are driven into the splint they will keep the bandages from slipping forwards. Pressure should be maintained on the wound until the wound is almost closed.

Cutaneous Habronemiasis, Summer Sores

The so called summer sores develop as the result of the presence of Habronema larvae in the skin or wound when ordinary wounds are exposed to flies. Some animals may develop summer sores every summer while other individuals never have them.

In some cases the condition is first observed as a subcutaneous nodule of a size varying from a hazel nut to a hen's egg. There is usually some inflammatory reaction in the tissue and they seem to cause the animals a great deal of distress. They rub these areas and finally the tissue breaks open and ulcerates. These area are then characterized by the rapid development of exuberant granulation tissue. Nodules may continue to form close to these areas, they break open and ulcerate joining the original area and a large raw surface is created.

Summer sores occur most frequently on the lateral side of the fetlock joints, on the sides of the neck, the medial canthi of the eyes, knees and hocks and the collar bed. They may also develop on areas where there is friction from the harness or those sites that are kept moist with sweat.

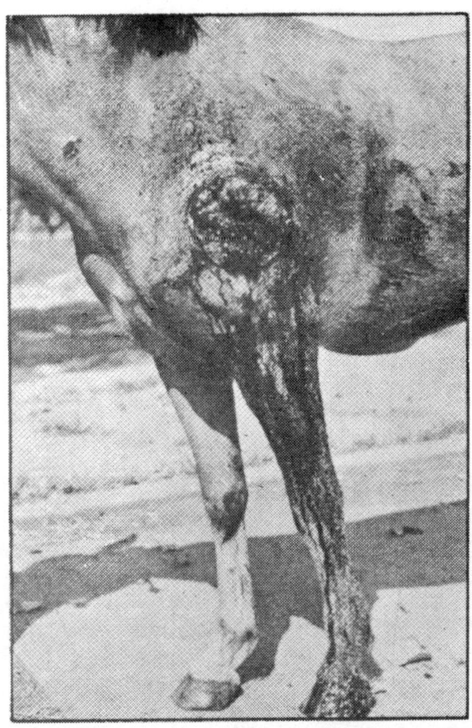

FIG. 64. A summer sore showing the exuberant granulation tissue.

SIGNS. One of the chief characteristics of a summer sore is that it does not heal with the usual forms of treatment. Also there is the rapid proliferation of exuberant granulation tissue. On examination this tissue will have many caseous or caseo-calcerous nodules all through it. In some cases the itching is intense and the affected individual may produce considerable damage to the area from rubbing. The exudate from the sore may at first be thin and copious and later becomes thick.

DIAGNOSIS. Summer sores present a very characteristic appearance with their reddish brown granulation tissue. The diagnosis may be confirmed by finding the larvae in the affected tissue.

TREATMENT. Where possible it is desirable to place the affected individuals in a dark stall where they can be protected from flies. The usual methods of treating wounds seem to exert little benefit on summer sores. Underwood recommends the use of glycerine to which has been added a good fly repellant. We have had the best results by keeping a pack on the wound, where this is possible, then keeping the pack moistened with the camphor phenol antiseptic. The largest percentage of the summer sores will heal with this method of treatment and a few will be resistant.

Wounds Due to Wire

Occasionally in the bovine we find wounds produced by wire that is around the distal part of the limb. These wires are found most frequently around the claws and one or both may be affected, also the wire may be around the leg above the fetlock joint. These wounds are usually produced by baling wire that becomes wrapped around the part. If the wire is not removed at this time the pressure of the wire produces an inflammatory reaction of the tissue. With the production of inflammatory tissue the wire becomes tighter and more pressure on the skin is produced. In a short time pressure necrosis occurs in the skin and the wire cuts through the skin. A narrow wound is produced in the skin as shown in Fig. 65, which indicates the location of the wire in the tissue. As long as the wire remains embedded in the tissue there is more inflammatory tissue produced and the wire cuts in deeper. The lameness becomes very pronounced with the animal placing very little or no weight on the limb. In some cases as in Fig. 65 the wire may be in

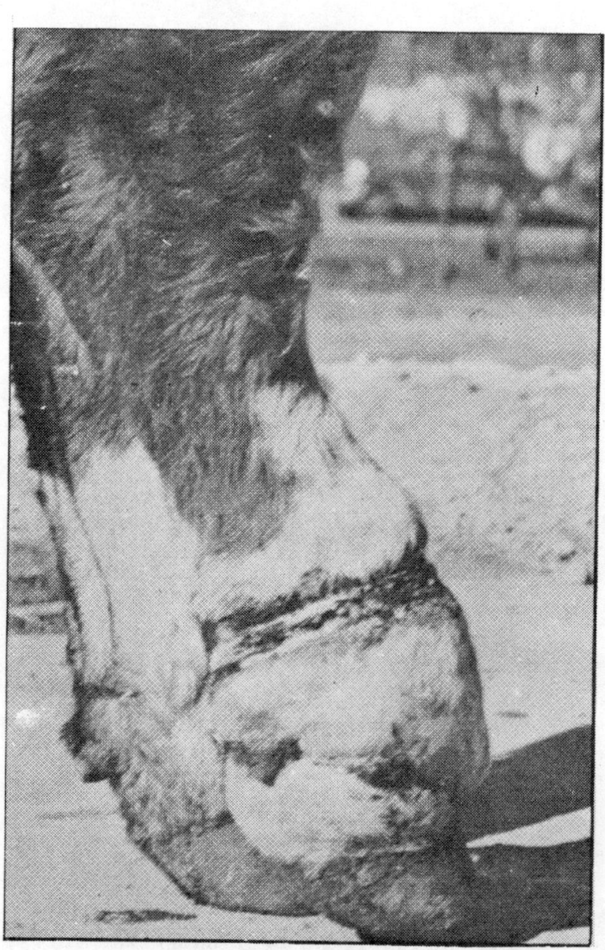

FIG. 65. Type of wound produced by wire when it has cut through the skin.

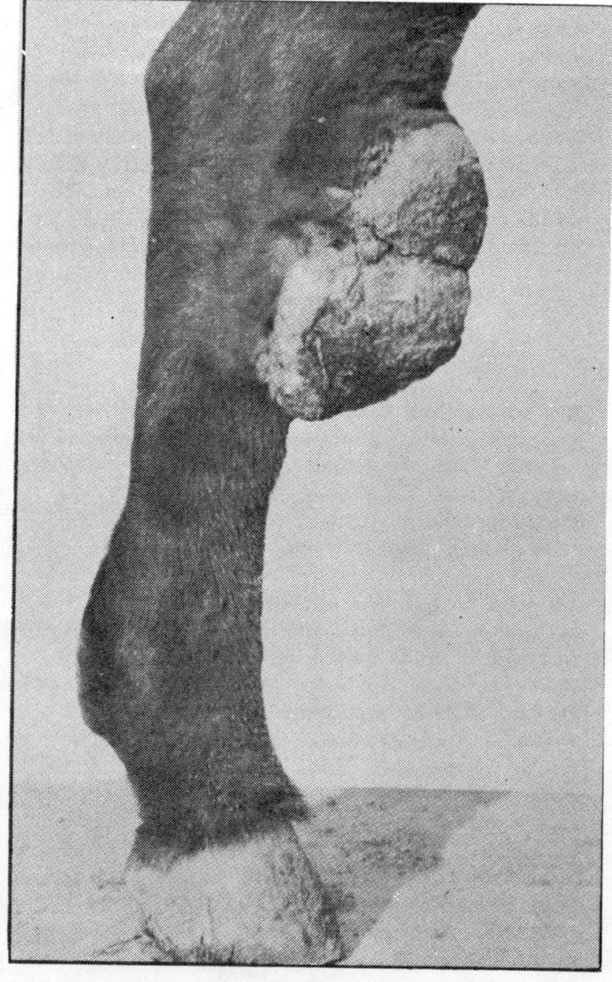

FIG. 66. A Jack Sore.

the tissue one and one-half inches. The wire may be grasped by inserting a pair of forceps into the depths of the narrow wound. By lifting the wire up it can be cut in two and pulled out of the tissues. The wounds produced by the wire may be treated with mild antiseptics. After the wire or wires are removed from the tissue there is a gradual decrease of the inflammatory tissue. If the damage to the structures affected has not been too extensive there is a gradual but slow return to normal of the damaged tissues.

Jack Sores

The above term is used for those sores that appear on the legs of Jacks below the knees and hocks. These sores seem to be the result of feeding the Jack too much grain and a lack of the proper amount of exercise. If the amount of grain fed is reduced and the Jack receives more exercise it will prevent the development of the sores. The grain fed should be reduced and the Jack forced to take more exercise as soon as edema and swelling of the legs occur below the hock and knee. If the above precautions are not observed an open wound will develop on the legs. These wounds occur most frequently on the anterior surface of the hock joint and the lateral side of the fetlock joint on the front limb. If these are not treated there is gradually developed a mass of fibrous tissue due to the chronic inflammation in the area. A typical so called, "Jack Sore" is shown in Fig. 66 on the anterior surface of the hock joint. It is very difficult to obtain healing of these sores after they have developed to the size shown in the picture. However, the mass of fibrous tissue may be removed surgically down to the normal tissue. The wound may then be treated as any other large wound below the knee and hock with the usual antiseptics and pressure packs.

Foreign Bodies

When a foreign body produces a wound the possibility of infection increases with the extent of tissue damage and the presence of bacteria. The possibility of infection also increases with the interference with the blood supply. When there is complete destruction of the blood supply for a period of time or even partial interference, it results in infection. An efficient blood supply is the best

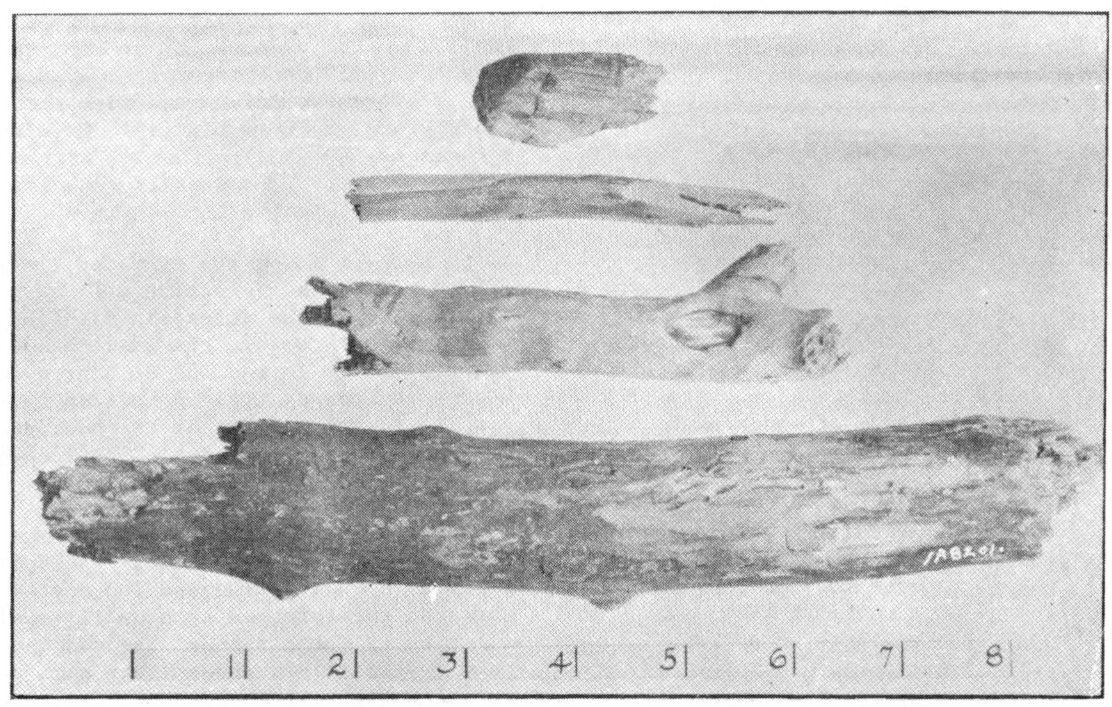

FIG. 67. A few examples of foreign bodies that have been removed from wounds with a chronic purulent discharge; the small piece of wood was removed from a wound medial to the scapula.

assurance against the development of infection in a wound.

The possibility of a foreign body initiating infection in a wound will depend on its physical properties. When a foreign body helps to initiate an infection, thereafter it becomes the nidus of this infection which persists until the foreign body disappears from the wound. If foreign bodies do not aid the onset of infection they gradually become encapsulated in fibrous tissue. If a foreign body does aid in the development of infection, it usually has a rough surface; is porous and composed of organic material; is partially soluble and this soluble portion is irritating to the tissues.

If the foreign body has an insoluble smooth surface, non-porous and chemically inert, it is rarely responsible for the development of infection in a wound.

Quite frequently pieces of wood or cornstalks will enter the tissues and a portion will break off and remain as a nidus of infection. The original opening in the skin will almost completely close except for a small opening through which there is an almost continuous discharge of pus. In some cases there may be a discharge that is serous in character with a gradual decrease in amount until the foreign body becomes encapsulated. All wounds that have an almost continuous purulent discharge should be examined for the presence of a foreign body.

One case was interesting due to the location of the foreign body. There was an opening just anterior to the edge of the scapula and about six inches below its dorsal edge. This opening had been discharging purulent material for five months when the horse was presented for examination. The owner expressed the opinion the horse had been shot as there was a crease on the side of the neck from the atlas to the opening at the edge of the scapula. This crease was about one-fourth inch wide and devoid of hair its entire length. A probe introduced through the opening and medial to the scapula revealed a hard object four inches from the edge of the scapula. When removed the hard object was a piece of wood one inch wide, two inches long and one-fourth of an inch thick. After the opening was enlarged and the foreign body removed the discharge ceased and the opening closed in a short time.

A horse was presented with the history of having had a severe and extensive wound with barbed wire in the region of the lateral cartilage. The wound healed very well except for one opening which discharged purulent material. When the horse was presented for examination the opening had been discharging purulent material for approximately seven months. The wound had been treated very extensively for quittor as the location of the opening and the chronic discharge was suggestive of quittor. The various treatments failed to have any effect on the purulent discharge.

When a metal probe was inserted through the opening a grating sound suggestive of metal could be heard. An incision was made in the skin large enough to permit the introduction of a finger. A hard object could be felt with the finger and this was removed with forceps. The foreign object was the barb from a barbed wire and apparently slipped off the wire when it made the wound. The discharge ceased with the removal of the foreign object and the opening closed with very little after-treatment.

Abscess

The abscess is characterized by a localization of infection and presence of pus in a cavity. In animals a number of organisms may be pyogenic in action; the staphylococci, streptococci, Corynebacterium pyogenes, Corynebacterium pseudotuberculous, Escherichia coli, Pseudomonas aeruginosa, Actinomyces bovis, Actinobacillus lignieresi, and other organisms may also be a factor.

As an abscess forms the tiny capillaries are closed so the infection will be kept localized. If the infection is highly virulent the clots in the small blood vessels may be forced out or destroyed. When this occurs septic emboli may be carried to other parts of the body producing abscesses, pyemia or septicopyemia.

When infection occurs in tissue the bacteria are in the center of the inflammatory area destroying tissue. The body defenses become active and leucocytes surround the infected area until local immunity is established. The dead and many living polymorphonuclears remain in the necrotic cavity and these together with cellular debris, lymph and serum, produce suppuration or the formation of pus. The wall of the cavity is composed of granulation tissue that contains polymorphonuclear leucocytes, lymphocytes, fibroblasts and endothelial cells. These cells aided by humoral antibodies bring about local immunity.

When infection with pathogenic bacteria occurs in tissue there are five classical signs indicative of the inflammatory reaction of the tissues.

1. Redness is evident on inspection but can be determined only when the swelling lies adjacent to the surface.
2. Heat is almost constantly present in inflammation and is due to the increased flow of blood through the affected part. The determination of the sensation of heat is extremely valuable in diagnosing inflammation even though no redness is present.
3. Swelling always occurs except in those locations where the anatomy of the parts prevents expansion. In inflammation the swelling is due to cellular outflow, vasodilatation and extravasation of fluids. When potential spaces exist in the inflamed area these may become distended with transuded fluid as, a bursa, synovial sheath of a tendon, joint and peritoneal or pleural cavities. The swelling is confined to the area of the inflamed tissue. Its greatest single cause is capillary permeability and clinically this is manifested by edema of the tissue. This edema is an important clinical feature of local inflammation. In some cases it may be the sole sign which gives an indication as to the inflammatory nature of the swelling.
4. Pain always exists to some degree in the inflammatory area when it is located in regions supplied by nerve endings.
5. Loss of function of the part is usually due primarily to pain but in the later stages may be due to destruction of tissue.

The presence of pain, heat, flunctuation and edema are of the greatest clinical significance but since any one or more of them may be absent the importance of those present requires investigation.

Some of the special signs noticed in inflammatory swellings is the shape which

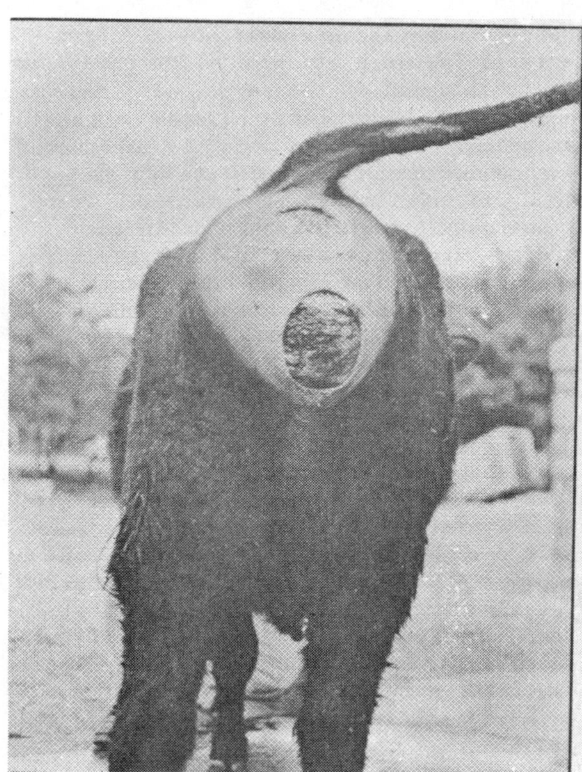

FIG. 68. Abscess between the pelvis and rectum and vagina forced the tissues posteriorly.

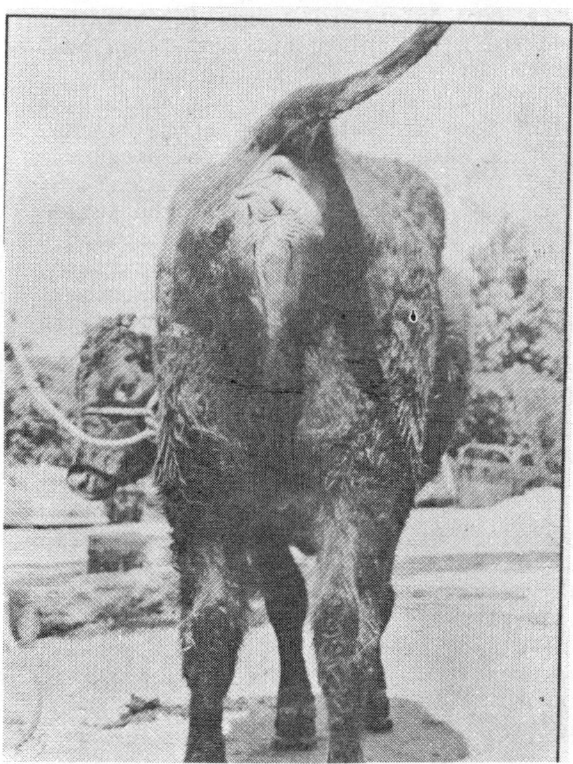

FIG. 69. After the pus was evacuated the tissues returned to their normal position.

tends to assume a spherical form owing to the regular spread of the reactionary process. In the early stages the mass is firm and tense but when necrosis, liquefaction and pus formation occur an area of softening appears. Abscesses of sufficient size may exhibit to the practised touch fluctuation, a wave like impulse transmitted through a soft-walled sac of fluid in response to pressure. Probably the outstanding characteristic of an inflammatory swelling is the absence of a definite edge as the mass seems to blend into the surrounding tissue.

An abscess may occur in most any location on the animal body. In some cases they occur in unusual areas and a careful examination is necessary to determine the presence of an abscess.

Ferguson records two abscesses that occurred in unusual situations and produced unusual signs. The outstanding signs observed in one case in a mare was her inability to eat or drink. She had not been eating normally for some time and for a week had refused to swallow either food or water. With the aid of a light the oral cavity was thoroughly examined. A slightly swollen and highly inflamed area was observed on the right posterior region of the hard palate. The swelling was incised and a liberal quantity of fetid pus drained out. In a week by appropriate treatment the mare regained her ability to swallow food and water in a normal manner. The other case was a gelding the owner reported as not passing a normal quantity of manure and was slightly lame in the left hind leg. A rectal examination revealed a large swelling on the left dorsal surface of the rectum approximately twelve inches anterior to the anus. This large swelling was diagnosed as being an abscess and an incision into the abscess through the rectal wall permitted the pus to drain into the rectum. As the swelling subsided manure was passed normally and the lameness disappeared.

DIAGNOSIS. Diagnosis is based upon finding some of the outstanding signs as previously described. Also when the pus is deeply situated or in an unusual location it is a good procedure to insert a hollow instrument into the swelling. If pus is obtained it is definite indication of an abscess.

TREATMENT. The skin over the swelling should be shaved or clipped closely and an efficient skin antiseptic applied. If the pus is rather deeply situated the tissue along the proposed line of incision should be infiltrated with a solution of a local anesthetic. To obtain rapid and complete healing of the abscess the incision should be made so it provides for complete drainage of the cavity. After the pus is removed the cavity is packed with gauze that has been saturated with tincture of iodine. This is used to destroy any infection that may be present in the lining membrane of the cavity. The gauze is removed in forty-eight hours and the cavity is flushed out with a mild antiseptic solution. After care consists in keeping the opening free for drainage and removing any exudate that collects in the cavity.

Shock

The word shock is used in practically all of those cases where there is acute peripheral circulatory failure regardless of the cause. Until we understand the fundamental mechanism of shock it will be impossible to even attempt to define the syndrome. It has been shown that a reduction in the volume of circulating blood is the most important factor in the initiation of shock.

There is general agreement on the characteristic features of shock which occurs in practically all of the cases. In traumatic shock there is an acute collapse of the peripheral circulation which is manifested by a reduction in the velocity of the blood flowing through the tissues. There is not only a marked reduction in the cardiac output but also in the circulating blood volume. The oxygen concentration of young venous blood is markedly reduced and also there is a decrease in the carbon dioxide combining capacity of the blood. In all cases there is a low or falling blood pressure.

It has been determined that all of the above changes are present and responsible for a diminished secretion of urine, muscular weakness and decreased oxygen consumption. With the sympathetic nervous system dominance, there is a vaso-constriction, pale, cyanotic mucous membranes with cool skin, sweating and rapid shallow pulse. All of the above changes are present in shock regardless of the reason for its development.

It is important to remember that a number of factors may be responsible for the development of shock but the primary cause is usually loss of whole blood or plasma. It may also be due to toxemia from bacteria or chemical poisons. The site of final action of any agent is on the peripheral circulatory system.

A great many theories have been advanced in an effort to explain shock and there is universal agreement that traumatic shock results from more than one etiologic agent. There are three theories that are most widely accepted in an effort to explain the cause of shock. The first theory is that the most important factor is the reduction in volume of circulating blood. This reduction in volume may be due to loss of blood or plasma at the point of injury whether due to traumatic or thermal injury. In the late stages of traumatic injury there may be permeability in non-traumatized regions of the body. If shock is allowed to progress the cardiac output of blood continues to decrease even though there is no further decrease in the amount of circulating blood. While reduction in the volume of blood is considered to be the chief cause in producing shock there is also good evidence that trauma of tissues increases the severity of the symptoms and in some cases may be the chief factor. There may also be products liberated from the severely damaged and devitalized tissue such as occur in burn and crushing injuries. If bacterial infection develops in wounded or burned tissue, it is an important factor in the development of shock.

It is a well-known fact clinically that a severe infection can cause all the features of traumatic shock due to the bacterial toxins.

The neurogenic theory as a cause of shock is that vasodilation occurs as a result of diminished constrictor tone. This type of shock is due to direct injury to the nervous system or may be reflex in action. However when blood declines due to this cause it is less serious than when associated with a decrease in the volume of blood.

After the critical point has been passed in a decrease in the cardiac output, lower blood pressure and a reduction in blood volume a tissue anoxia may develop that results in metabolic changes and severe damages to important organs as heart, brain and adrenala. If this damage is prolonged it may result in the state termed irreversible shock.

TREATMENT OF SHOCK. For some time it was believed that failure to respond to shock treatment was due to the escape of the infused fluid and the patients blood through damaged capillaries. This theory cannot apply to shock due to toxemia as the fluid loss has been insignificant and fluid therapy would be useless. It is well known that excessive loss of plasma may occur in burns or into extensively damaged tissue or when compression maintained for some time is released suddenly. Also it is generally agreed that recovery occurs when the deficiency in blood volume is restored but that recovery will not occur even when large amounts are restored but too late. When the shock occurs as a result of local trauma there is a continuous loss of fluid into the injured area especially when it is due to a burn. As soon as shock is recognized transfusions should be given before hemodilution occurs. Also the quantity of isotonic salt solution or glucose solution which is given intravenously should not exceed the amount of plasma or whole blood that is used.

When blood or plasma fails to cure shock resulting from blood volume deficiency no other fluid or drug will alter the course of events except in shock resulting from dehydration.

The most challenging problem in the treatment is where irreversibility to blood volume irreplacement is due to excessive blood loss. When this occurs there is a degree of damage to important organs which does not respond to treatment by any known therapeutic method.

Blood Transfusion of Large Animals

Probably the indirect method of blood transfusion is the most practical in the average case in large animals. It is a therapeutic measure that has considerable value in many cases.

In the indirect method of blood transfusion blood is taken from an apparently healthy animal and injected into the recipient. Coagulation of this blood may be prevented by the use of sodium citrate or defibrination. If sodium citrate is used in a concentration of 0.3 per cent of volume of blood this will completely inhibit the coagulation reaction. By this procedure the calcium of the blood becomes changed by the citrate to a soluble compound calcium-sodium citrate.

To citrate the blood one gram of sodium citrate may be added to one ounce of sterile distilled water. This is sufficient for nine ounces of blood. The container must be kept in motion as the blood flows in to insure a thorough mixing of the blood and citrate solution.

Defibrinated blood may be used instead of the citrated blood. The fibrin is removed from the blood by agitating it during the course of fibrin formation. The partly filled container should be shaken beyond the average clotting period of the blood obtained. The blood of the horse should be agitated for fifteen minutes and ox blood for ten minutes. The fibrin which is formed should now be removed by straining thru very fine sterile cheese cloth so that all fibrin is removed.

If direct transfusion is to be used it is very important the donor is not affected with any disease. The technique of direct transfusion is very simple and easy to do. All the equipment necessary is two large needles or trocars and cannulas, sterile rubber tubing long enough to reach from the donor to the recipient. The rubber tubing should contain a short section of glass tubing so the progress of the blood may be observed. The needle or trocar is inserted into the jugular of the donor at its upper extremity and the other needle is inserted into the jugular of the recipient near the entrance to the thorax.

Saline Transfusion

When blood is not available saline solutions which are isotonic may be used. Their use may result in saving the life of an animal which is in a state of shock or has lost an excessive amount of blood. The effect from the use of the saline solutions is very short due to their rapid elimination. If gelatine or gum acacia is added to the extent of six or seven per cent the rapid elimination is retarded.

The physiological saline solution may be used which contains .85 per cent sodium chloride or one of the following may be used.

Ringer's Solution
- Sodium chloride - - - - - -0.85
- Potassium chloride- - - - -0.83
- Calcium chloride- - - - - -0.025
- Sodium bicarbonate- - - - -0.02
- Aquae - - - - - - - - - - -100.00

Locke's Solution
- Sodium chloride - - - - - -0.90
- Potassium chloride- - - - -0.042
- Calcium chloride- - - - - -0.024
- Sodium bicarbonate- - - - -0.02
- Dextrose- - - - - - - - - -0.10
- Aquae - - - - - - - - - - -100.00

The amount of the solution to give in a transfusion will depend upon the indications for giving it. If severe hemorrhage has occurred the transfusion should be continued until the pulse has returned to normal. The transfusion should be given slowly to permit the circulatory system time to adapt itself to the increased volume of fluid. In a case of poor quality of blood it might be advisable to remove some of the patients blood and replace it with normal blood.

Coagulation of the Blood

Occassionally in horses it is desirable to stimulate the clotting time of the blood. Excessive or profuse hemorrhage may occur where it is impossible to use methods that are ordinarily used to control hemorrhage. The clotting time of horse blood is unusually long and a dangerous and often fatal hemorrhage may occur if something is not used to hasten the clotting of the blood. The average clotting time of normal horse blood is eleven and one-half minutes.

Recently, Roberts conducted a rather extensive series of investigations on the value of some of the drugs used to stimulate coagulation. Any drug or preparation that is used to stimulate coagulation should not produce any toxic effects. This point is especially important in those cases where the vitality of the patient is already weakened from loss of blood.

Some of the drugs that were the most efficient and least toxic to the patient are as follows.

SODIUM CITRATE, one to two ounces may be used made up in a twenty per cent solution. This solution was given intravenously and lowered the clotting time of the blood 59.2 per cent. Sodium iodide, one ounce was dissolved in a pint of water and administered intravenously. This drug did not produce any toxic symptoms and lowered the clotting time 67.4 per cent.

FORMALIN, the most desirable results were obtained when eight to sixteen cubic centimeters were used in 100 cubic centimeters of water. The average decline in coagulation time was 67.3 per cent.

GELATINE, is usually recommended for intravenous injection to combat shock. As gelatin is not a complete protein there is little danger of it producing shock. After the preparations are made up they should be sterilized for twenty minutes at 15 lb. pressure. Probably for the average case 500 cc of a 5 per cent solution is sufficient. It was found the coagulation time was reduced 76 per cent. This preparation is probably the least toxic to the patient as no unusual symptoms were produced following its administration.

Gangrene

Strictly speaking gangrene and necrosis mean the same thing, death of tissue. The two terms necrosis and gangrene are frequently used interchangeably but necrosis refers more to death of small localized areas of tissue while gangrene is applied to the death of large masses of tissue. Gangrene is fundamentally due to either lack of arterial blood supply, insufficient pathway for venous return, a combination of the two or actual destruction of the cells by a toxic substance. The main pathologic types of gangrene are the moist or wet gangrene and dry gangrene.

DRY GANGRENE. This type of gangrene occurs when there is adequate venous return and arterial occlusion. The amount of tissue involved is usually more extensive when sudden occlusion takes place. The part affected changes color, pale to greenish blue and then black and becomes mummified. There is generally a well identified line of demarcation between living and dead tissue. The part usually falls away after time, leaving a conical stump. In Fig. 70 is shown a typical case of dry gangrene in a cow due to ergot poisoning. Ergot poisoning is a frequent cause of dry gangrene of the extremities in animals.

Ergot develops as a fungus upon grains such as rye, wheat, and barley also upon many types of grass, red top, timothy, wild rye, brome, quack grass, needle grass and possibly on other kinds of grasses. The gangrene follows chronic poisoning and is probably due to prolonged powerful constriction of the arterioles.

MOIST OR WET GANGRENE. The essential difference between moist and dry gangrene is that in the former, infection and venous stasis are present. The area is cold, swollen and may be covered with large blebs. There is a change in color from dark red to green, purple and black and has no definite edge of demarcation. The types of gangrene, which are usually moist are gas gangrene, infectious gangrene, traumatic gangrene with laceration of veins as well as arteries. In the bovine the udder is frequently affected with moist gangrene especially if the tissue is endematous and filled with fluid when the gangreneous process begins. Amputation of the affected portion of the udder may be performed or extensive incisions into the gangrenous tissue will provide drainage for the very toxic products formed in this tissue. If the patient survives that period in which there is absorption of toxic products the gangrenous tissue gradually separates from the healthy tissue.

BACTERIAL GANGRENE. This is gangrene produced by the anaerobic organisms and is called gas gangrene. It occurs frequently among domestic animals and castration wounds are the ones most often affected. The infection frequently develops in the tissue around sitfasts on top of the neck of horses. The infection may gravitate down the side of the neck and shoulder in the subcutaneous tissue producing extensive swelling. The infection destroys the blood supply to the skin and as gangrene of the skin occurs it gradually sloughs away. If the animal survives the infection even though the skin loss has been extensive the area will gradually heal and skin will cover the area.

Sinus

A sinus is a tract leading from a suppurating cavity to the surface and usually the source of a chronic discharge purulent in nature. This condition may be due to the presence of a foreign body in the tissues or necrosis of bone or soft tissue. In some cases an abscess will rupture but drainage is not fully established with the result there is a chronic discharge. Some of the chronic infections as actinobacillosis may form sinuses if drainage is incomplete or infection is not destroyed. If epithelial cells line a tract they produce a continuous secretion.

A fractured portion of the wing of the ilium may result in an external opening

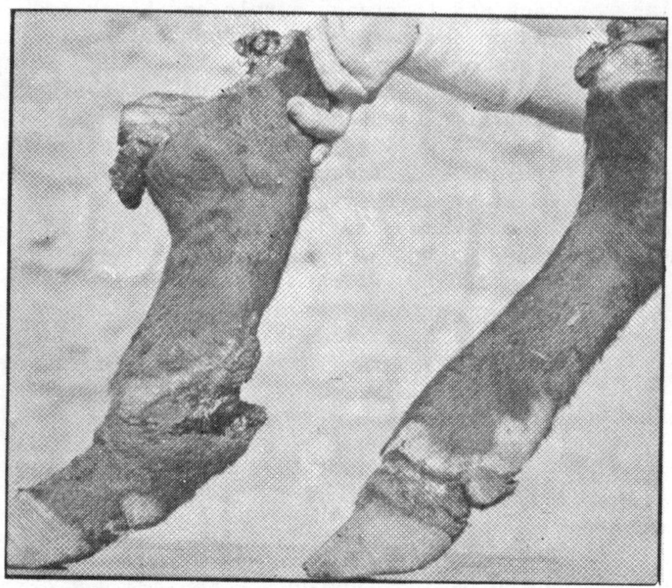

FIG. 70. A clear line of demarcation shows where the circulation is closed in one limb, in the other limb separation of the tissue has occurred.

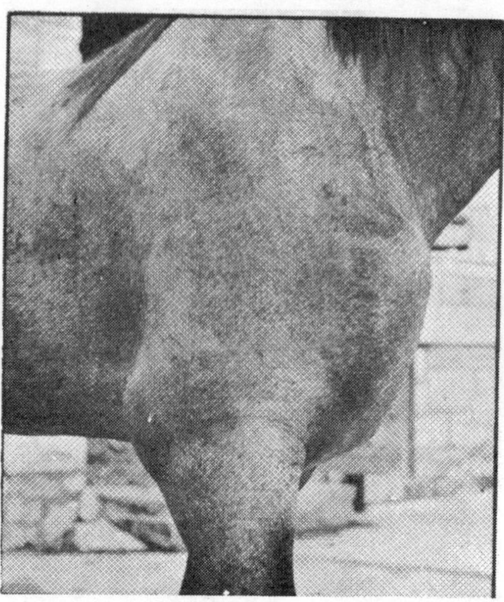

FIG. 72. Extensive swelling and edema that sometimes occurs in this type of infection.

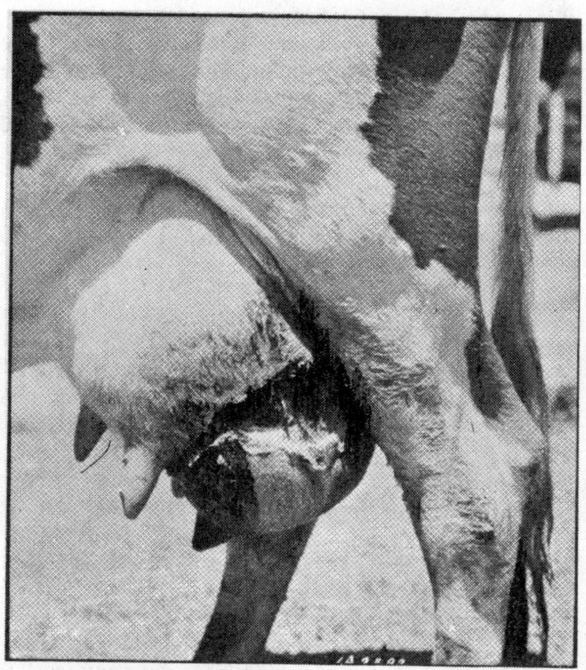

FIG. 71. Gangrenous mastitis, note separation of gangrenous and healthy tissue.

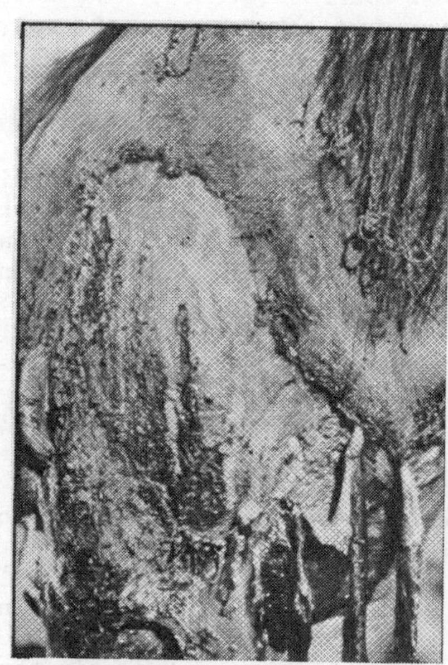

FIG. 73. The affected skin usually sloughs off as shown in this case.

discharging to the outside on the lateral surface of the thigh between the patella and tuber coxae.

An opening discharging along the lower border of the mandible is indicative of an infected alveolus and diseased tooth and complicated in some cases with necrosis of bone.

Treatment of a sinus consists in first determining the cause of the discharge. If due to the presence of a foreign body, wood, bone, or tooth they must be removed and complete drainage established. When due to a mass of chronic infected tissue, if possible, this tissue should be removed as it results in quicker healing.

When a tract is lined with epithelial cells they may be removed by dissection or destroyed with an escharotic.

Fistula

A fistula is an abnormal passage leading from an internal organ to the exterior or between endothelial or epithelial lined cavities. These abnormal communications may be produced intentionally, may occur through injury or are a congenital condition and in some cases infection in an organ may result in the development of a communication to the exterior.

In domestic animals a fistula is frequently found, the origin of which is difficult to determine. A chronic discharge occurring through an opening on the internal surface of the thigh posterior to the stifle joint may be a rectal fistula. These are due to a perforation of the rectum. From the rectum the tract passes through the periproctal tissue and pelvic cavity and may pursue a tortuous course between the adductor muscles of the limb to perforate the skin. Because of the inaccessability of the origin of a rectal fistula, treatment is impossible but healing may occur spontaneously.

An opening with a chronic discharge and located in the lumbar region of a horse may originate from a suppurating process in the pelvis of the kidney. From the kidney the infection usually pursues a course between or around the transverse processes of the lumbar vertebrae through the masculature and skin to discharge to the exterior. Extirpation of the affected kidney would be the only effective method of treatment.

Ulcer

An ulcer may be defined as an open circumscribed lesion located on a free surface and which fails to undergo the natural process of healing. A wound does not become an ulcer until the repair which should normally produce healing is interrupted. The ulcers that occur externally may be classified as specific infective ulcers, neoplastic ulcers, trophic and regional ulcers.

The base of the ulcer may or may not be depressed. The edge may be undermined, punched out, heaped up, or rolled. Flat edges covered with growing epithelium are evidence that destruction has ceased and that healing is going on. The discharges may be abundant or scanty, and if purulent indicate a pyogenic infection; if serosanguineous, usually due to a streptococcic infection.

Some varieties of cancer break down as they grow and form ulcers.

DIAGNOSIS. The important point in diagnosing an ulcer is to determine the cause of the ulcer. It is rather easy to determine the presence of an ulcer.

TREATMENT. The treatment that is used to obtain healing of the ulcer will depend upon its cause. If it is produced when too strong antiseptics are used on a wound, the fibrous tissue must be removed surgically before healing of the area will occur. The use of another antiseptic may be all that is necessary to obtain healing of some ulcers due to infection. Ultraviolet light may be all that is necessary in some cases. When the ulcer is due to neoplastic tissue this must be surgically removed.

Miscellaneous Infections

There are a number of miscellaneous infections that are primarily of medical rather than of surgical significance. However most of them require surgical treatment at some time so the surgeon should know when surgery is indicated to obtain the best results.

Gas Gangrene

The most important anaerobic organisms producing gas gangrene Cl. perfringens (welchii), Cl. novyii (edematiens), Cl. septicum (vibrion septique) and Cl. histolyticum these are named in the order in which they are usually found infecting wounds developing gas gangrene. Gas gangrene is frequently found in wounds that are rather extensive and considerable contamination has occurred. Also those wounds in which there is some gangrenous tissue seems to provide ideal conditions for the development of these organisms. When a puncture wound is produced some of the gas gangrene organisms may be introduced into the tissues and symptoms may develop ten or twelve hours after the injury.

SIGNS. The first sign that may be noticed is a hot, painful edematous swelling around the wound which tends to spread rapidly with well defined and raised borders. The temperature is usually high, and there is also dyspnea and anorexia with symptoms of toxemia. In some cases the infection is highly toxic and the animal may be dead in twenty-four to seventy-two hours after the first signs are noticed. If the edges of the wound are opened a reddish fluid containing tissue debris and gas escapes. When the infection is introduced into the heavy musculature the swelling becomes very extensive and the skin is drawn tight. Crepitation due to gas in the tissues may be observed within ten to fifteen hours. If there is an open wound a clear or slightly turbid brownish exudate drains from the wound and a very offensive odor characteristic of putrefying tissue is present. Also gas bubbles may be seen in the discharge. When a true gas gangrene infection is present it invades principally muscle tissue. The muscle fails to bleed when cut transversely apparently because of vascular thrombosis or compression due to edema.

TREATMENT. The treatment that is used will depend upon the location of the affected tissue.

When malignant edema occurs following castration the edema of the tissue is found extending forward from the scrotum along the sheath and ventral surface of the abdominal cavity. The scrotal wounds should be opened and the affected portions of the cords removed.

If the wounds are located where a pack can be maintained on the area an ice pack can be used with very good results. The ice pack should be kept in continuous contact with the area until the swellings subside. The packs should contain a liberal quantity of crushed ice.

One treatment that is recommended is to use a 1:5000 solution of acriflavine. A syringe and long needle is used to inject ten cubic centimeters at points three inches apart around the periphery of the swelling and also into the swelling. The average amount used will vary from two hundred and fifty to five hundred cubic centimeters of the solution.

Another method of treatment is to inject oxygen from an oxygen tank into and around the affected tissue. This is repeated each day until improvement is noted. When this method is used the tissue should not be incised as it will permit the escape of the oxygen.

In many cases incisions can and should be made into the affected tissue and then the tissue is thoroughly irrigated with hydrogen peroxide, one per cent solution of chlorine, or one or two per cent solution of potassium permanganate.

Diffuse Suppurative Inflammation

The above named condition usually is caused by streptococci, and it is commonly referred to as phlegmon or diffuse cellulitis. It is a severe and frequently fatal infection. In this type of infection there is a tendency for it to spread along the fascia involving, veins and lymphatics, and with rather widespread destruction of tissue. The destruction of tissue may be very extensive with little tendency toward pus formation: any exudate is usually serosanguineous in character. This infection has a tendency to invade tendon sheaths, muscle septa, bursae and joints.

SIGNS. In the severe cases there is evidence of absorption of toxins with a marked rise in temperature, 105° to 106°, pronounced depression, and loss of appetite. If the infection is introduced through an external wound the tissues in this region become hot, swollen, and painful. When the wound is on a limb the swelling usually extends upward, with involvement of the lymphatic vessles, producing a lymphangitis. The most severe and fatal cases of suppurative inflammation encountered have been those involving the tissues of the head.

PROGNOSIS. Prognosis is unfavorable due to the rapid progress of the infection and the failure of the tissues to set up an adequate defense reaction.

TREATMENT. In this condition there is a tendency for the infection to spread through connective tissue to break in and out of tissue spaces, and invade the blood stream. All of this tends to make the treatment difficult. In some cases the best results are obtained if the tissues are not invaded surgically. However, if any soft spots develop they should be opened so that bacteria and their toxic products can be drained from the tissues. Then hot applications to the area may result in marked improvement. The speed of recovery will depend upon the amount of dead tissue which is cast off or absorbed, and upon the persistence of the infection in scattered areas.

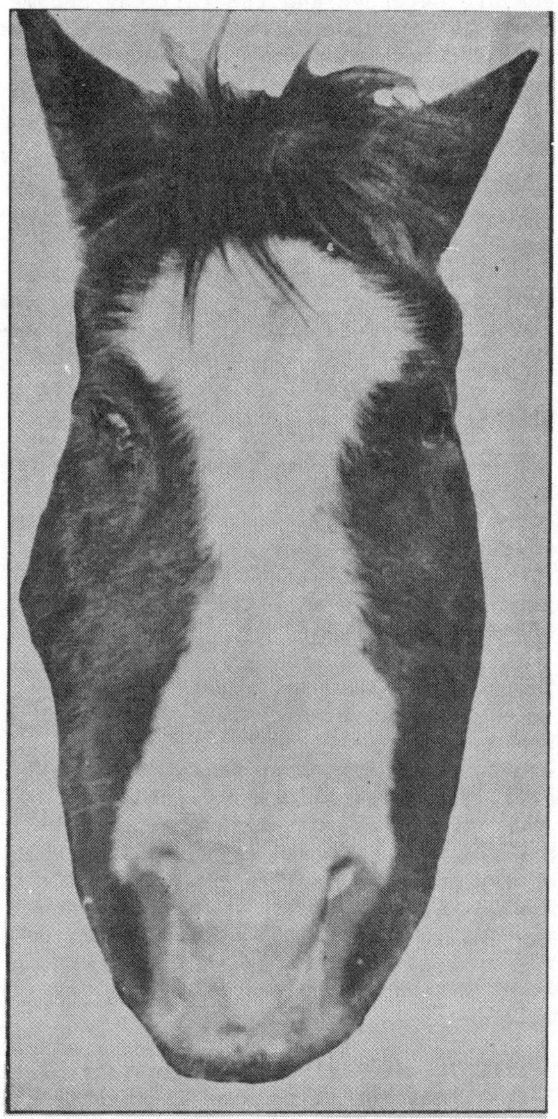

FIG. 74. The infection originated at the roots of the fourth and fifth upper cheek teeth with death occurring in seventy-two hours.

The treatment that has given us the best results for the diffuse suppurative inflammation that develops in the mandibular space of the bovine, has been through the use of sulfamerazine. If the temperature is 106° the dosage of sulfamerazine the first day will be one grain for each pound of body weight. This amount may be given at one dose due to its slow elimination. The next two days the daily dosage will be three-fourths of a grain for each pound of body weight, and for the next three days the daily dosage will be one-half grain for each pound of body weight. We have found that five to six days of treatment is sufficient to control this infection. Palpation of the most ventral point of the swelling will usually disclose a space between the skin and underlying tissue, and when the skin of this area is incised, a thin, watery, dark colored fluid will be obtained that has a very fetid odor. The amount of this fluid will vary with the size and extent of the swelling.

Tetanus

Tetanus is important from a surgical standpoint in that it usually occurs as a result of wound infection. The etiological

FIG. 75. The infection developed in the mandibular space with death of the animal in five days.

factor in tetanus is the tetanus bacillus, an anaerobic spore forming organism. The organism is widely distributed and is found most frequently in the soil which has been fertilized with manure, is found in the intestinal tract of horses and also other domestic animals. Since the tetanus bacillus is an anaerobic spore forming organism it may remain in the contaminated soil indefinitely. The spores are very resistant to unfavorable influences and will survive boiling in water for one hour.

Infection occurs most frequently in puncture and deep wounds in which there is necrotic tissue and pyogenic organisms present. It also occurs in wounds where there is gangrenous tissue as in sitfasts on the dorsal surface of the neck. When pyogenic organisms are present in the wound they consume the oxygen in the tissues and create anaerobic conditions which are necessary for the growth of the tetanus organism. The tetanus bacillus tends to remain localized in the wound and does not enter the blood stream or other tissues in the body. In the United States tetanus is more prevalent in the south and particularly in those states bordering on the Gulf of Mexico. The mechanism by which the toxin produces its fatal effect is still in confusion. The tetanus toxin is fixed by the tissues and only when more than a lethal dose is given can any of it be recovered from the circulating blood and lymph. It has also been observed that the toxin does not travel up the spinal cord to the brain.

Of our domestic animals the equine is the most susceptible to tetanus and puncture wounds of the feet are the most dangerous to the animal. However, in those sections in the United States especially in the southern states where tetanus is the most prevalent, prophylactic treatment against tetanus is a routine part of the treatment of wounds. Tetanus has been observed to occur in the bovine following retained placenta, dehorning, castration and wounds. In pigs tetanus occurs most frequently following castration. Lambs may develop the infection after castration or docking. Tetanus occurs frequently in lambs when ligatures have been used for castration and docking. The tissues where the ligature closes the circulation provides an ideal medium for the development of the infection. In some cases tetanus may occur without any history or evidence of a wound but the infection may have been introduced through a very small opening.

SIGNS. Quite frequently the period of incubation of tetanus is from seven to ten days after an operation although in some cases it may be several weeks or months before the signs are observed. The symptoms will vary a great deal depending on whether the disease develops slowly or rapidly. In the equine typical signs are seen when a sudden loud noise is produced. The signs may consist of mild tonic spasms of the skeletal muscles and the appearance of the third eyelid a variable distance over the eyeball. The spasms may be limited to the muscles of the neck and head so the animal has difficulty in eating. As the spasms increase in severity and become more generalized the head and neck are extended and the tail may become stiff and extended backward, with all legs stiff and spread apart. If the patient can be persuaded to walk they move with difficulty due to the stiffness of the legs.

In the bovine the symptoms may not be detected unless the animal is observed very closely for signs of tetanus. At first the animal may be more alert than normal with the ears more erect. The tail in one case curled upward in a very striking manner. The head and neck may be extended with the third eyelid extending up over the cornea.

The symptoms in sheep, goats and swine are similar to those observed in the other domesticated animals. However, the signs frequently become generalized with the affected animal standing stiff legged or lying on its side with all four legs extended and stiff.

The prognosis is usually determined by the rapidity with which the signs develop. When the signs are generalized and severe, death may occur in two or three days. If the signs are mild and develop rather slowly and never become generalized the prognosis is generally favorable. However some cases may die rather suddenly when they seem to be recovering from the disease. In cattle, sheep and swine the prognosis is unfavorable as the percentage of recoveries in these species is very small.

TREATMENT. The value of tetanus anti-toxin in the treatment of tetanus is questionable as very little difference in the mortality rate has been noted in the treated and untreated cases. Udall states that in the equine there is nothing to indicate that

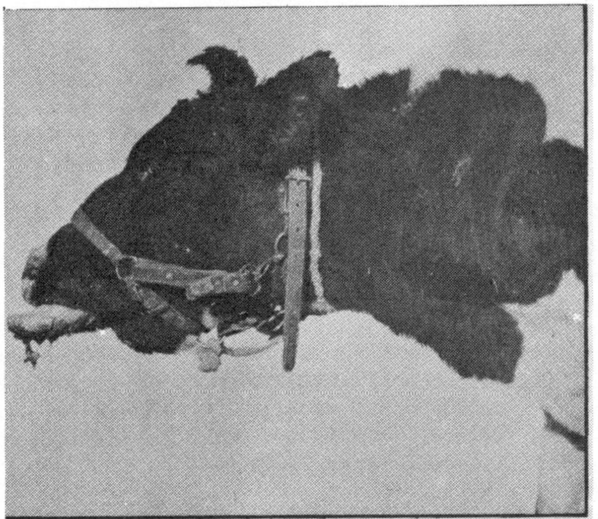

FIG. 76. A pronounced case of wooden tongue.

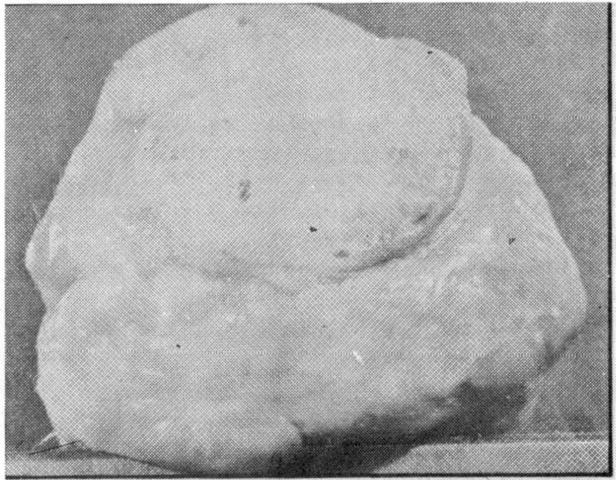

FIG. 78. Granulation tissue that developed in dorsal wall of pharynx due to Actinobacillosis ligniersi infection, produced a marked dyspnea.

FIG. 77. Actinobacillosis of the subcutaneous tissue.

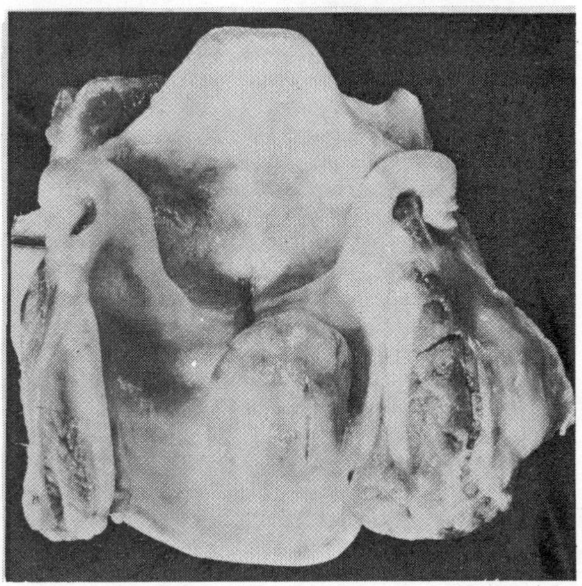

FIG. 79. Tissue that developed in the larynx, producing dyspnea, due to Actinobacillosis ligniersi infection.

large doses of antitoxin lowers the mortality rate in tetanus. As the infection remains locally in the wound it is an important part of the treatment to treat the wound. This should consist in opening the wound and removing all of the infected tissue. If possible the affected animal should be kept where there is very little noise and the stall can be kept dark. The use of procaine hydrochloride intravenously has resulted in a big increase in recoveries according to the experience of Burns of Georgia. He recommends giving intravenously 100 to 150 cc of a two and one-half per cent solution of procaine hydrochloride intravenously daily for two days then every other day for two or three doses. One of the tranquilizers may be used to control the tetanic spasms.

Actinobacillosis

Actinobacillosis is of frequent occurrence in the bovine. It is caused by Actinobacillus Lignieresi. The term actinomycosis is used frequently to designate infection in both the soft and bony tissue. As a general rule actinobacillosis is found involving the soft tissue, and actinomycosis affecting the bony tissue. Actinobacillosis is found most frequently in the soft tissues of the head, but may become rather generalized involving soft tissues in almost any part of the body. The actinobacillosis abscess usually develops rather slowly so that a very thick firm capsule is formed. When an inexperienced examiner palpates one of these abscesses, he may conclude that it does not contain pus because it is so firm. When the abscess is opened, the pus is non-odorous, very thick and tenacious, may be white or with a slightly yellowish tinge and contain a variable quantity of mucus.

One of the most frequent locations for actinobacillosis abscesses are at the posterior borders of the mandibles in the subcutaneous tissues. There may be one or a number of abscesses, one or two rather large, and a number of smaller ones. Occasionally a series of small abscesses will be found on the side of the mandible. The tongue is frequently affected and due to its loss of pliability is named "Wooden Tongue". The owner may notice that there is excessive salivation, and the affected individual requires a much longer time to eat its feed. Also there may be a marked loss in weight, and a cow in production may not give as much milk. If the anterior portion of the tongue is affected, it may protrude from the mouth all or part of the time. Palpation of the tongue may reveal hard nodular areas scattered throughout the tissue. In other cases the tongue will be thickened, stiff, and very firm. If the deeper tissue of the tongue is affected, a swelling of the tissues in the mandibular space will also be observed If the subcutaneous tissue of the muzzle is affected, there is a marked increase in its size.

The affected animal may show dyspnea which is suggestive that the infection may be in the post-pharyngeal region.

With the mouth held open with a speculum a manual examination of the interior of the pharynx may be made. If there is a large abscess in the post-pharyngeal region, the roof of the pharynx will be pushed downward. This will be recognized by the convex curvature of the roof of the pharynx just above the posterior end of the soft palate. If the abscess has been ruptured for some time, exuberant granulation tissue will have developed around the edge of the opening in the pharynx. Either one of these conditions will produce dyspnea. Occasionally it is found that the infection has invaded the tissue of the soft palate producing a marked increase in its size and dyspnea. If the examination of the pharynx fails to reveal any reason for the dyspnea, a finger may be introduced for diagnostic purposes into the animal's larynx; occasionally a large nodule will be found that is a result of infection with Actinobacillus Lignieresi. During the examination of the pharynx a neoplasm that is producing the dyspnea may be palpated.

If one or both posterior limbs are enlarged or thickened, it may be due to infection of the skin and subcutaneous tissue. The examination of the limb will reveal that the subcutaneous tissue is thickened, edematous and fibrotic with many small nodules, containing the characteristic pus.

TREATMENT. Actinobacillosis responds readily to the internal administration of iodine. It may be administered either intravenously or into the stomach. The method of administration is not as important as that the patient shall receive sufficient iodine to overcome the infection. A mild infection may respond to one ounce while an extensive involvement of tissue may require one or more pounds of iodine.

The subcutaneous abscesses are opened with a liberal incision and all of the pus removed. The lining membrane of the cavity is destroyed by either curretting or by the use of escharotics. One method that is effective is to pack the cavity for forty-eight hours with gauze that has been thoroughly moistened with tincture of iodine.

In a case of "wooden tongue" the internal administration of iodine is usually very effective treatment. Its administration should be continued until the tongue has returned to normal. If treatment is discontinued too soon, the patient will fail to show much or any improvement, and the owners will get the impression that these cases do not respond to treatment.

Penicillin has been used in the treatment of "wooden tongue" with good results, as described in the following case. A bull was presented for examination with the history that he was not eating and there was excessive salivation. Examination of the tongue revealed the anterior eight inches was thicker and wider than normal. The affected portion of the tongue was so stiff the tongue could not be used for the prehension of food.

Treatment consisted in infiltrating the affected portion of the tongue with six million units of penicillin. The next day the patient was eating in a normal manner. The examination of the tongue revealed most of the swelling had disappeared and the tongue was pliable. In two days the tongue was again infiltrated with six units of penicillin. The patient was sent home and was alright for one year when the tongue was affected to about the same extent as the first time. The tissue did not respond as readily to treatment as it did the first time. Probably the tongue would not have been affected the second time if the patient had previously received iodine for one month in addition to the penicillin.

The abscesses dorsal to the pharynx should be opened if possible. A hook bladed knife is carried into the mouth with the hand, and an incision is made at the most prominent point in the dorsal wall of the pharynx. The pus is very thick but with pressure exerted with the fingers, it may be forced into the palm of the hand. By removing all of the pus in this way, it prevents any from being aspirated into the lungs. The patient should receive some iodine so that any residual infection in the tissues may be destroyed. If it is impossible to open the abscess, the infection usually responds to the internal administration of iodine. When the abscess has ruptured previous to the examination, the examination will reveal exuberant granulation tissue around the edge of the opening. Due to the location of the granulation tissue, it may be very difficult to remove it surgically. The operator will have to use considerable ingenuity in some cases to remove all of the tissue. When all of the tissue is removed the dyspnea disappears.

When there is extensive involvement of the subcutaneous tissue and skin, the administration of iodine should be continued until the tissues are normal.

Actinomycosis

Actinomycosis is due to Actinomyces bovis, an infection that most frequently invades the bones of the head in the bovine. The mandible is the bone most frequently affected, less frequently the bones forming the maxillary sinus. This infection is subacute or chronic, and is slowly progressive producing marked inflammatory reaction in the tissue. The changes in the one characterized by a certain amount of destruc-

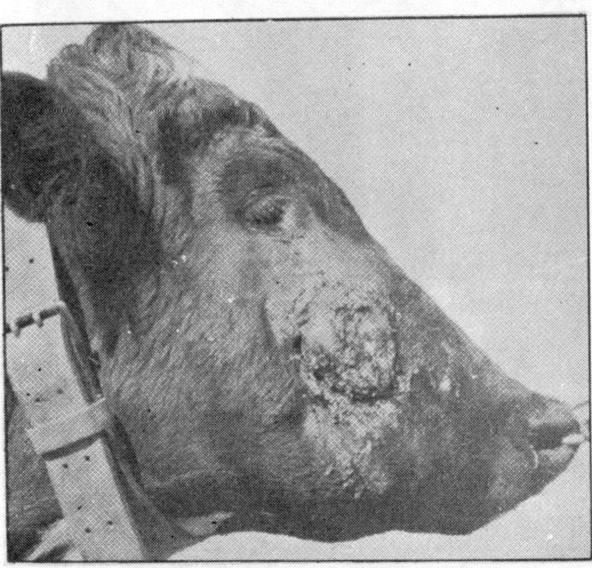

FIG. 80. Actinomyces bovis infection in the maxillary sinus and exuberant granulation tissue.

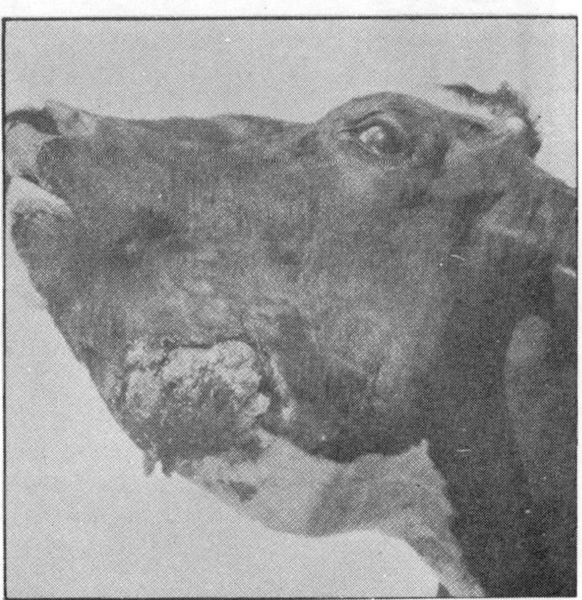

FIG. 81. Extensive involvement of the mandible with Actinomyces bovis infection and exuberant granulation tissue.

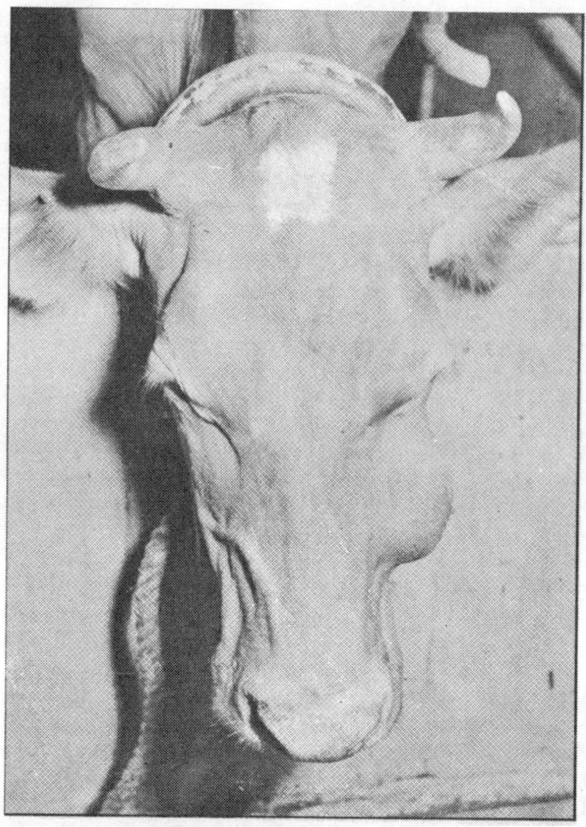

FIG. 82. Actinomycosis of the maxillary sinus.

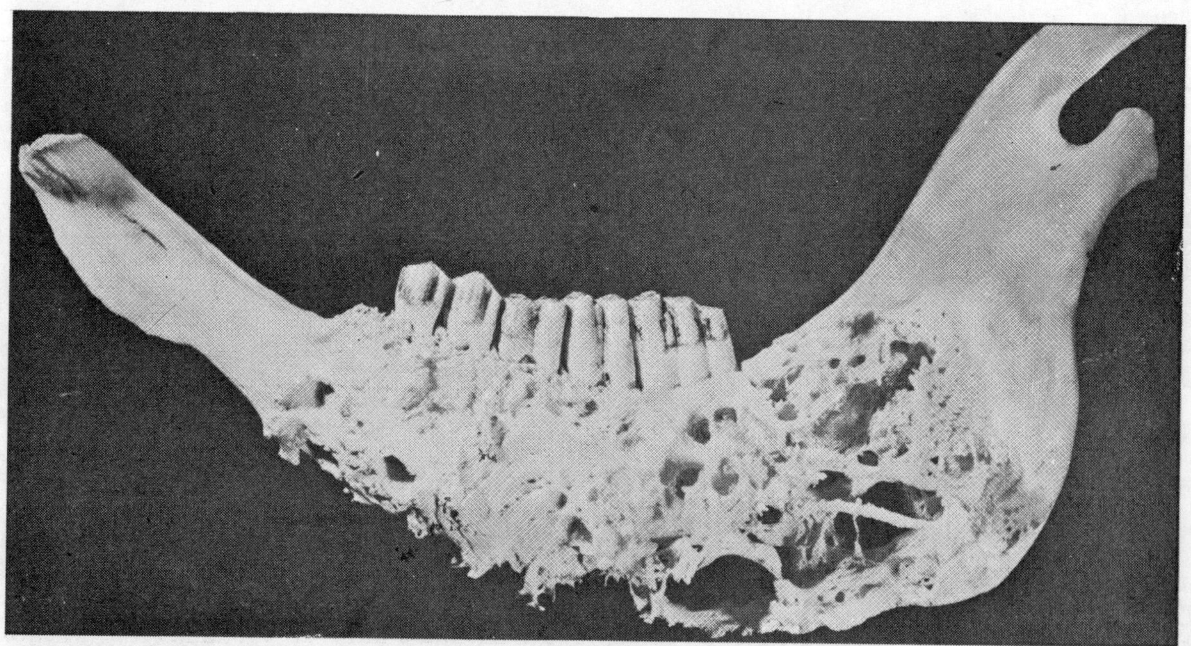

FIG. 83. Actinomyces bovis infection of the mandible with extensive osteoporosis of the bone.

tion of the medulla and cortex with an extensive periosteal reaction, and the formation of the sequestra. With the destruction of the bony tissue of the mandible the teeth become loose and sensitive so that the affected animal does not eat well, with a gradual loss in condition. As the infection progresses the extensive periostitis stimulates an inflammatory reaction in the subcutaneous tissue and skin producing a marked enlargement of the region. When the infection penetrates the mucous membrane or skin, there is a tendency to the formation of exuberant granulation tissue. The granulomatous tissue is very vascular and bleeds profusely when injured.

The infection may gain entrance to the maxillary sinus and also involve the tissues of the hard palate and maxilla. The sinus may become filled with exuberant granulation tissue. The external changes in the tissues may not give a true indication of the very extensive involvement of the various bone structure.

Symptoms in the early stage of involvement of the mandible may consist in an occasional loss of a bolus of food from the mouth. There may be excessive salivation, or the animal will lap up water with the tongue. These symptoms are an indication that the teeth are sensitive. Palpation of the mandible will reveal a thickening of the tissue and in some cases separation of the gum away from the teeth. As the infection progresses there is a gradual thickening or enlargement of the mandible. If the maxillary sinus is involved, there is a gradual bulging of the maxilla over the sinus. Examination of the swelling will usually reveal that the bone is softer than normal, or it may be absent.

Actinomyces bovis occasionally invades the genital tract of either the male or female, lesions occurring in the prepuce, glans, penis, and uterus.

TREATMENT. In the early stage penicillin has given very good results. The penicillin can be given intramuscularly using from one million to three million units daily depending upon the value of the animal and the extent of involvement of tissue. Also streptomycin may be used in either the early stage or the chronic one in which there is extensive involvement of tissue. The dosage of streptomycin will depend upon the extent of the infection and the changes that have occured in the tissue. From five to ten grams are injected at one time so as to thoroughly infiltrate the tissue. This dosage may be repeated once or twice a week as seems to be indicated.

REFERENCES

Amadon, Roger S., The Physiological Background of Transfusion Therapy, J.A.V.M.A., Vol. XClV, N. S., Vol. 47, No. 1.

Blood and Saline Transfusion in Horse and Cattle Practice, University of Pennsylvania Bulletin, Vol. XXXVl, (June 15, 1936), No. 3.

Ferguson, T. H., and S. E., Obscure Abscesses in Equine, North American Veterinarian, Vol. XV, (October, 1934), pp. 21-23.

Forssell, G., Some Views on the Treatment of Wounds, The American Veterinarian, Vol. XXlll, pp. 30-37.

Glenney, W. E., Malignant Edema in Large Animals, North American Veterinarian, Vol. XX, (1939), pp. 19-21.

Gordon, G., Malignant Edema, North American Veterinarian, (December, 1939), pp. 23.

Harvey, S. C., The Velocity of the Growth of Fibroblasts in the Healing Wound, Arch. Surg., (1929), 18:1227.

Hutyra, Marek, Manninger, Habronema, Special Pathology and Therapeutics of the Diseases of Domestic Animals, 4th Ed., Vol. 111, pp. 727-730.

Lyon, B. M., Blood Transfusion in Horses, North American Veterinarian, 20, (1939), 4, pp. 41-42.

Roberts, Stephen J., Intravenous Injections, American Journal of Veterinary Research, lv, (1943), No. 12, pp. 226-239.

Chapter IV

NEOPLASMS AND CYSTS

The terms neoplasm and tumor are frequently used synonymously. The nature of tumor growth is different from that of normal tissues and from inflammatory hyperplasia; it is something new and foreign to the organism in which it occurs. When the growth is malignant the term "cancer" is commonly used. The term neoplasm means a new growth and neoplasia means the formation of new tissue. Some neoplasms apparently originate following an injury to tissue or they may result from chronic irritation so that they may represent in their very earliest stages a reparative process. When a swelling occurs in a location where it should not be, or a wound fails to heal according to the natural laws of repair, a careful examination should be made for the presence of neoplastic tissue.

The external appearance of tumors present extremely wide variations exceeding those of normal structures. However, the gross variations are many times very distinctive so that the presence of neoplastic tissue may be recognized by inspection and palpation of the tissue. In some cases the color of the neoplastic tissue is very distinctive as the normal color undergoes some change. The blood content and hemorrhage may determine the color of most neoplasms. Melanoma is a brown or black neoplasm derived from pigment producing cells. The pigment of melanoma is the product of a special metabolic function of the cell.

The consistence usually yields significant indications of the nature of many neoplasms, as osteomas and chondromas have almost a stony hardness, but some fibromas may simulate chondromas. Some neoplasms may be softened by edema, hemorrhage, necrosis, mucous degeneration or cyst formation and some become very hard from fibrosis or calcification. Ulceration is frequently seen in neoplasms of the skin and mucous membrane. When ulceration occurs it may transform a comparatively harmless neoplasm into a fatal process through local or general infection, suppuration, absorption of toxic products and hemorrhage.

A neoplasm has an independent manner of growth which is manifested by a proliferation of tissue that has no purpose and apparently no natural termination or limit of growth. If a neoplasm occurs in a gland the activity of the latter may be perverted or it may be stimulated to excessive activity. Neoplastic tissue serves no useful function and is parasitic in nature as it derives all of its blood supply from its host. The growth of some neoplasms may be expansive starting from an isolated group of cells and pushing contiguous tissue before it. Usually neoplasms of this type are well encapsulated and appear to be isolated from the surrounding tissue. In other neoplasms the growth is infiltrative as single cells or groups of cells push their way through destroying adjacent tissue. In some neoplasms growth is extensive beginning in a small focus and gradually incorporating the surrounding normal cells into the neoplastic tissue.

The benign tumor resembles the tissue from which it originated, is encapsulated and freely movable in the tissue. As a general rule growth is slow and there is usually little danger to the host. If death should occur it would be caused by interference with the vital function of some organ because of the location and size of the growth rather than from destruction of tissue. The benign tumor can usually be completely removed with no tendency toward recurrence. However, if they do recur their growth may be very rapid.

The malignant neoplasm is characterized by a rapid growth and because of its infiltrative manner of development is fixed in the tissue. The cells of the malignant neoplasm, usually atypical to some degree, may be of the embryonic type and have a tendency to invade the surrounding tissue. Because of this infiltration of cells into the surrounding tissue the macroscopic boundary may not be the microscopic and all of the neoplastic cells will not be removed. If this occurs the remaining cells act as a focus of growth and the malignant neoplasm recurs. After an attempt at surgical removal there seems to be more of a tendency toward metastasis, and a fatal termination. The removal in these cases should be early and complete.

When the word metastasis is used it means there has been a dissemination of neoplastic cells into other portions of the body. This metastasis may occur in two ways, by the lymphatic system or by the blood stream. Metastasis by the lymphatic system is usually observed in carcinoma and it may take place in two ways, by embolism or permeation. If it occurs by embolism cells or groups of cells break off and are carried by the lymph vessels to anatomically related lymph glands. In metastasis by permeation the cells grow along the wall of the lymph channel and infiltrate the superficial lymphatics of the surrounding tissue. The permeation is carried along the deep fascia upon which the lymphatics lie finally involving the lymph glands. In blood stream metastasis a group of cells break off after penetrating a thin walled vein and are carried to the lungs.

DIAGNOSIS. The clinical manifestations are of first importance in the diagnosis of a tumor. A swelling or enlargement, a sore which does not heal, an abnormal or bloody discharge, are important signs in the diagnosis. It is very desirable that the gross diagnosis of tumors be developed as highly as possible. The method of gross diagnosis has the advantage in that the diagnosis can be made with the eye and by palpation. It will not only reveal the character but usually the extent of the process. One of the most important aids in the diagnosis is a biopsy, obtaining some of the tissue from the live host for examination under the microscope.

TREATMENT. The best method of treatment for neoplasms is early complete surgical removal. Some of the neoplasms are very vascular and proper precautions should be made to treat shock. The symptoms of shock may develop during the progress of the operation or afterward if the mass of tissue to be removed is very large or if excessive hemorrhage occurs.

Classification and Nomenclature

The histogenetic method of classification seems to be the most accurate method. Therefore the main classes of tumors are named from their histological structures while the specific forms are named where possible by their histogenesis. The behavior of a tumor is mainly determined by the properties of the tissues of origin and when the origin is known the course can often be predicted and the cause determined.

Group I Type Connective Tissue

1. Fibroma, composed of connective tissue.
2. Chondroma, composed of cartilage.
3. Osteoma, composed of bone.
4. Myxoma, composed of mucous tissue.
5. Lipoma, composed of fat tissue.
6. Melanoma is a tumor derived from pigment producing cells.
7. Sarcoma, a cellular tumor composed of anaplastic tissue of any of the above types.

Group II Type Epithelium, Pavement or Glandular

1. Papilloma, a tumor of pavement epithelium.
2. Adenoma, a benign tumor of glandular epithelium with supporting tissue in normal arrangement.
3. Carcinoma, a tumor of glandular epithelium with supporting tissue in normal arrangement.

The variable structure of many simple tumors requires complex terms for the accurate designation of structure; a sarcomatosis quality is designated as fibro, chondro or osteosarcoma.

Fibroma

Fibroma is a term applied to tumors composed chiefly of connective tissue. Fibromas are circumscribed tumors, which may arise wherever fibrous connective tissue is found; when composed chiefly of connective tissue they are called pure fibromas. The neoplastic connective tissue is also observed in various benign and some malignant neoplasms as fibrolipoma, neurofibroma or adenofibroma. The gross appearance of true fibroma is usually characteristic as they are circumscribed, encapsulated, may be lobulated and on section exhibit a grayish translucent appearance. There is no sharp dividing line between chronic inflammatory tissue and a fibroma although characteristic examples of each are widely different.

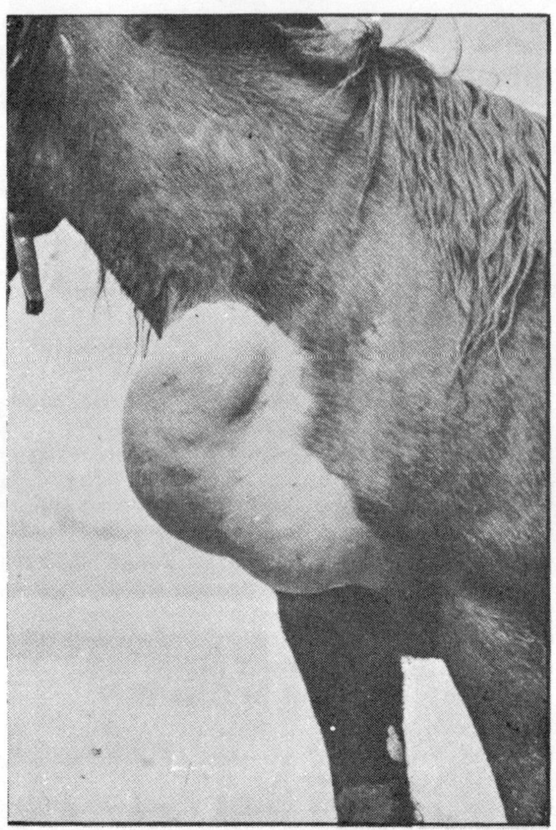

FIG. 84. Fibroma is a circumscribed encapsulated neoplasm that is easily removed surgically.

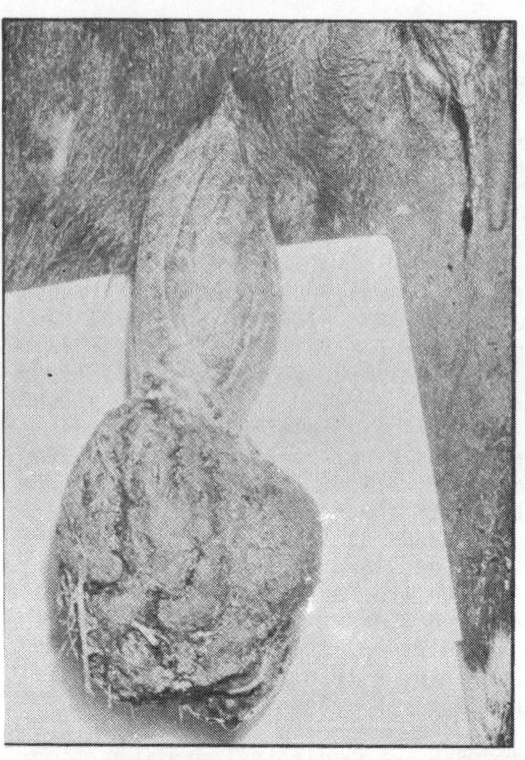

FIG. 85. Fibroma that would become as large as a basketball, was attached to area lateral to vulva.

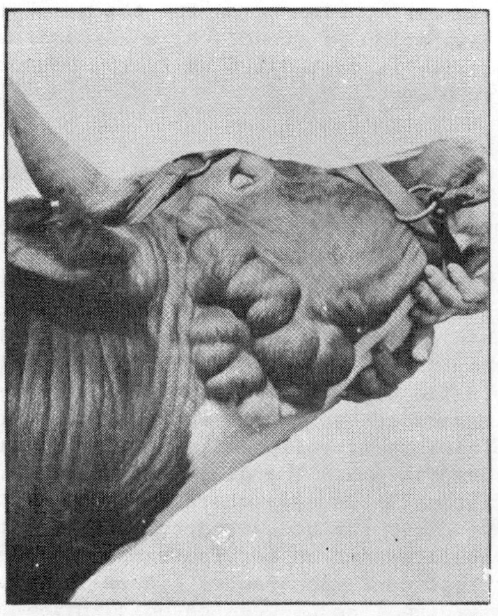

FIG. 86. Fibrolipoma, first noticed when the bull was three months of age and reached size shown in picture at sixteen months of age.

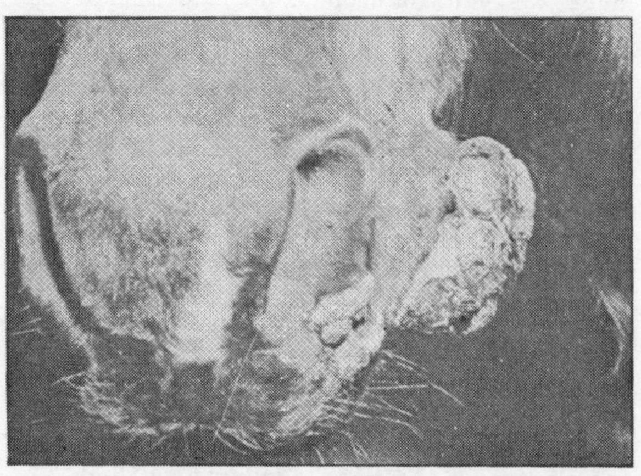

FIG. 87. Neurilemmoma involving tissue at commissure of the mouth.

In some cases a chronic productive inflammation may change into a fibroma. The most frequent location is the head, neck, shoulder and leg or any area where there is constant irritation. The well encapsulated fibroma is readily separated from the surrounding tissue and with no tendency toward a recurrence.

Neurilemmoma

Neurilemmoma is also known as Schwann-Cell tumor; either of these terms may be used to describe a neoplasm which is thought to develop from the neurilemmal cells. The neurilemmoma in structure looks very much like the fibroma microscopically. As a general rule the neurilemmomas are located along the course of a nerve or some nerve tissue. Neurilemmomas have a tendency to recur after removal.

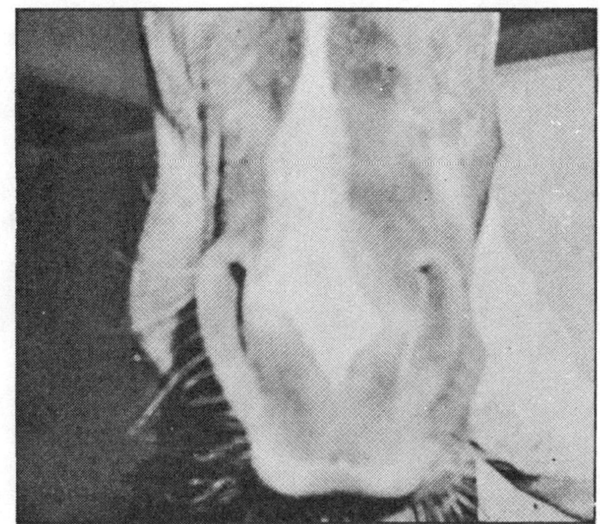

FIG. 88. Ameloblastoma in the mouth producing a bulging outward of the cheek.

ADAMANTINOMAS

Ameloblastoma

The adamantinomas are among the rare tumors and have been known to occur in several species. These tumors are also called ameloblastoma and enameloblastoma. They originate from the enamel organ the embryological predecessor of a tooth. The ameloblastoma shown in Fig. 89 occurred in a one year old colt and seemed to originate from the enamel organ of the tush in the interdental space. After the neoplasm was removed it was found that it originated in a smooth cavity about one inch long and one inch deep. The cavity was curretted to be sure all of the neoplastic tissue was removed. There was no recurrence of the neoplasm.

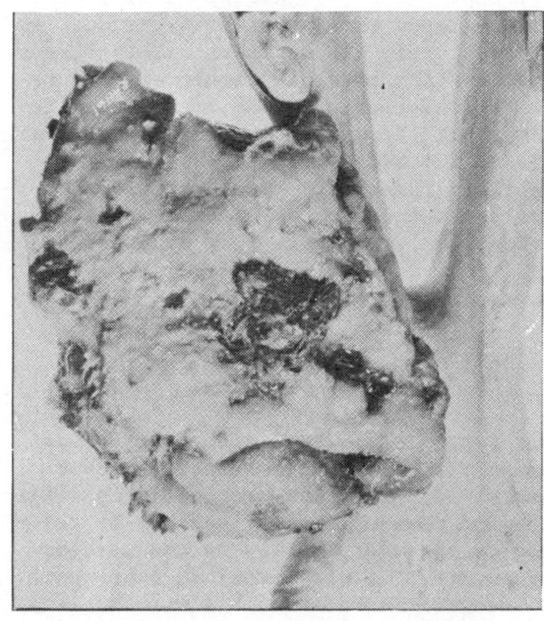

FIG. 89. Shows the approximate location of the ameloblastoma in the interdental space.

Lipoma

Lipomas occur rather frequently and may be found most any place within the body. The simple solitary lipoma the most frequent form of fatty tissue tumor usually occurs in the subcutaneous tissue. In Fig. 90 is shown a lipoma in the subcutaneous tissue that the owner first noticed as a swelling about two inches in diameter. In six years there was a marked increase in size of the swelling to one that was fifteen inches long and twelve inches wide. There is known cause for the formation of lipomas.

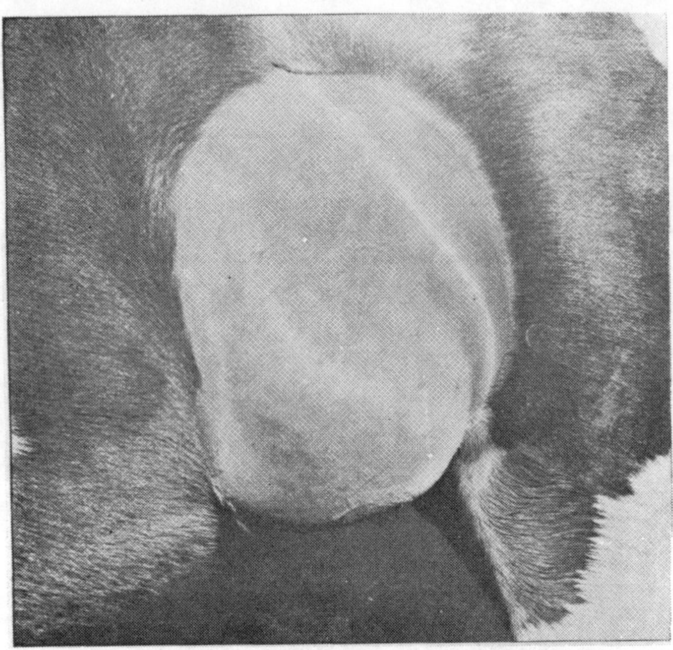

FIG. 90. Location of the lipoma in the subcutaneous tissue of the flank region, it was fifteen inches long, twelve inches wide, six inches thick in center, weight 19 pounds.

Lipomas exhibit all of the characteristics of adult fat but they do not arise from adult fat. The consistency of the lipoma will depend upon the amount of fibrous tissue scattered through the fat tissue. As a general rule lipomas have a thin fibrous capsule which makes it rather easy to remove by enucleation. One interesting feature about lipomas is the fat is not available to the body during starvation. In treating lipomas they must be removed surgically as they are not sensitive to irradiation. It was rather easy to enucleate the lipoma from its position in the subcutaneous tissue.

Osteoma

This type of neoplasm is one of the most commonly seen benign connective tissue tumors. It is formed from osteogenic tissues and thus originated usually in relation to bone, especially on the head or extremities. A circumscribed overgrowth of bone occurs under such a wide variety of conditions and the distinctions between inflammatory and neoplastic hyperplasia of tissue are so often obscure that it has not been possible to exactly define the limits of an osteoma. Those chronic processes which result in bone formation from trauma, inflammation and disturbances of nutrition are common.

Osteoma is the term applied to tumors composed of bone. Exostoses are circumscribed masses which project above the bony surface. Traumatic exostoses constitute a well defined class; they may occur at the seat of fractures when an excessive callus forms, after trauma of the periosteum or bone and along the elveolar borders. The bones of the head are the seat of a variety of bony overgrowths which may be difficult to classify.

In the horse the dental alveoli, sinuses of the head and mandible are common sites of osteomas. When osteomas occur on the premaxilla and mandible as in Figs. 92 and 93 they usually have a narrow base of attachment and are easily removed with a bone saw. If a pressure pack can then be applied to the area and maintained in position it usually heals over with healthy tissue. In some cases there may be a tendency for it to recur but not as large as before removal. If the operation is repeated several times it may result in a complete disappearance of the osteoma.

Rhabdomyoblastoma

Myoma, a tumor of muscle tissue occurs in two types, leiomyomas, containing smooth muscle tissue and rhabdomyoma composed of striated muscle tissue. Tumors of striated muscle tissue occur under a wide variety of conditions which are difficult to enterpret. Rhabdomyosarcomas of the voluntary muscles arise from the adult tissues and form an important group of malignant neoplasms of the trunk and limbs. In form rhabdomyomas appear as single or multiple, modular or voluminous, flat or rounded, circumscribed or diffuse and even polypoid growths. The course of rhabdomyoma is usually progressive and in the sarcomatous and teratoid forms it is rapid. Rhabdomyomas, benign or malignant, occur in nearly every organ of the body which contains muscle tissue. Those of the skeletal muscles and the tongue are of chief importance.

Treatment consisted in surgical removal of all of the affected portion of the tongue. It was necessary to remove all of the tongue anterior to the frenum linguae. A dorsal and ventral incision were made and

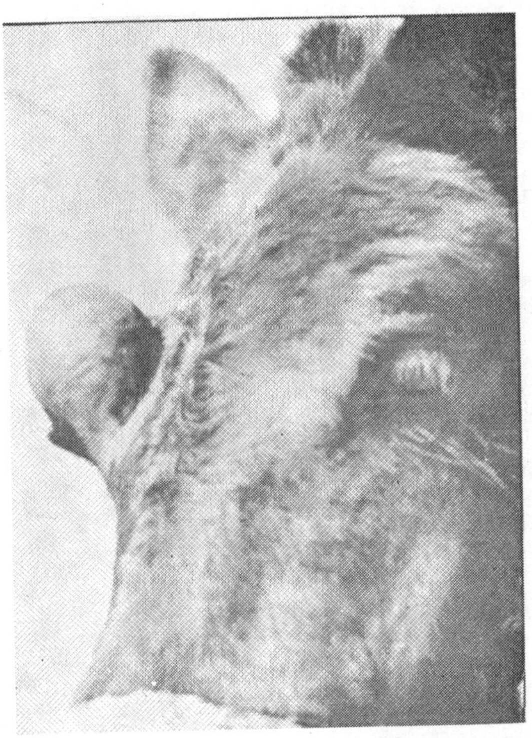

FIG. 91. Osteoma on the supra-orbital process.

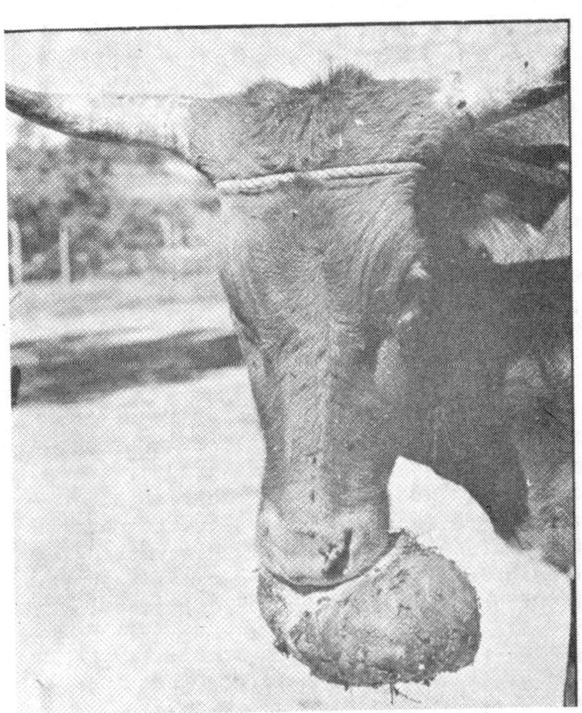

FIG. 93. Osteoma of the mandible.

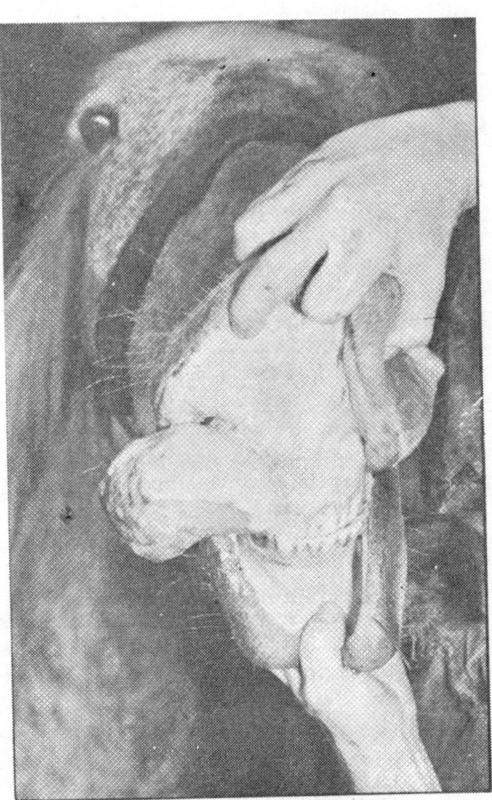

FIG. 92. Osteoma of the premaxilla.

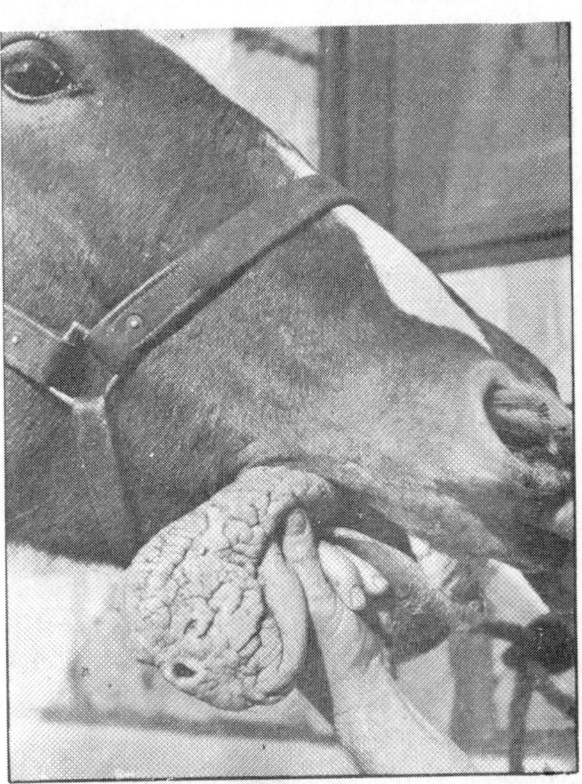

FIG. 94. Rhabdomyoma involving all of the free portion of the tongue.

directed posterior so as to meet in the center of the tongue thus providing a dorsal and ventral flap. The two edges are then approximated using interrupted sutures of silk. For a few days the horse had some difficulty in eating and drinking, but this was only a temporary condition. The owner reported two years later the loss of the free portion of the dongue did not affect the horse's ability to eat or drink or his general condition.

Sarcoma

Sarcoma is a malignant type of tumor composed of cells of the connective tissue type. The majority of the sarcomas are bulky, soft and vascular. This soft consistency reflects the cellular character of rapidly growing tumors. However, some sarcomas fail to reveal the usual features as a fibrosarcoma is firm, resistant and non vascular; osteogenic sarcoma may be as hard as ivory. As a rule the gross appearance depends largely upon the tissue of origin as fibrosarcoma, chondrosarcoma, osteosarcoma, liposarcoma and lymphosarcoma. Sarcomas are usually single but multiple tumors arise in nerve trunks and the skin.

The growth of sarcomas is usually rapid and locally destructive. The abundant blood supply favors extremely active cell growth so the tumors may reach a large size. Due to the infiltrative type of growth on the periphery the tumor fuses with the surrounding tissue so it may be difficult to extirpate completely, therefore it frequently recurs after removal. Metastasis is observed in the advanced stages of most sarcomas, and it is characteristic of the disease for the embolic cells to travel by way of the blood vessels.

In Fig. 95 the owner said a small swelling was first noticed when the colt was six months of age and at this time the swelling was opened. The wound was treated with various antiseptics but this treatment seemed to stimulate it to increase rapidly in size. All of the neoplastic tissue was surgically removed and the area treated as an open wound.

A mule twenty-two years of age was presented for examination with the following history. For two weeks the owner had noticed a swelling along the ventral surface of the body. The mule had a good appetite but he was losing weight rapidly. Also when he was forced to exercise, he would tire quickly and respirations were labored.

Examination of the mule revealed edema along the ventral surface of the region of the thoracic and abdominal cavities. There was also a large firm swelling of the tissues at the anterior extremity of the sternum and at the entrance to the thoracic cavity. Forced mild exercise would cause pronounced dyspnea and labored abdominal respirations. A tentative diagnosis of a neoplasm in the thoracic cavity was made because of the similarity in symptoms of other cases we have had with neoplasms in the thoracic cavity. A post mortem examination revealed the thoracic cavity was almost filled with a clear watery fluid. A large mass of the neoplastic tissue was around the vessels and trachea at the entrance to the thoracic cavity. The neoplastic tissue was also involving the anterior superficial pectoral muscles. Microscopic examination of the tissue revealed it was a sarcoma.

Wounds that fail to heal or openings that do not close should be examined carefully for any evidence of neoplastic tissue. When neoplastic tissue is present it will be found that the tissue present is thicker and more firm than normal tissue. In Fig. 96 the opening through the cheek would not heal because of the sarcomatous tissue that involved the edges of the opening.

Fibrosarcoma is the most common type of sarcoma found in domesticated animals, particularly in horses and mules. They may arise wherever fibrous connective tissue is found. Thus they occur in the subcutaneous and submucous tissue, the fascia, intermuscular septums, periosteum, and in parenchymatous tissue. In some cases the tumor grows so rapidly that death occurs from metastasis to some of the internal organs. It exhibits malignant powers principally by infiltrating into the surrounding tissue, and recurrence after removal is common. Usually the more rapid growth and presence of secondary nodules helps to differentiate it from the well encapsulated fibroma.

Fibrosarcomas are the most frequent type of tumors found in mules. They may occur on the ears, mouth, neck, shoulders, forelimbs, and sheath. If they are on areas where the tumors are easily injured they may be covered with blood. The term, blood wart, is frequently used to designate these fibrosarcomas. It has been observed that when fibrosarcomas are removed, particularly in mules, they invariably return. Usually they grow rapidly, and they may appear on various parts of the body.

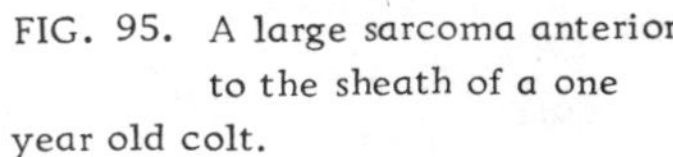

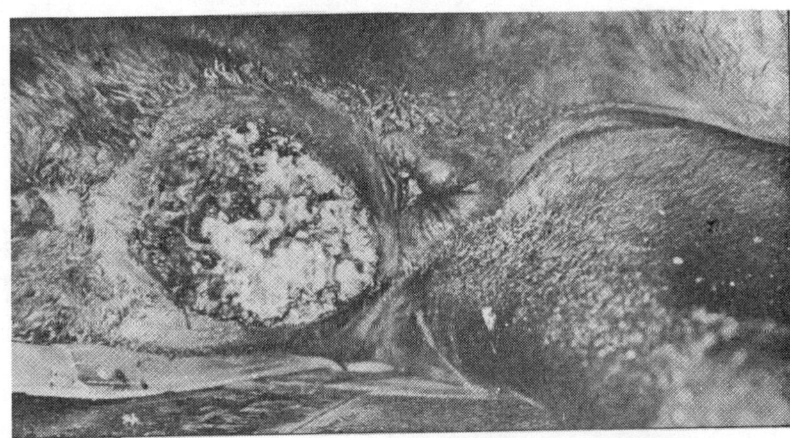

FIG. 95. A large sarcoma anterior to the sheath of a one year old colt.

FIG. 96. An opening in the cheek that would not heal due to a sarcoma involving the tissue.

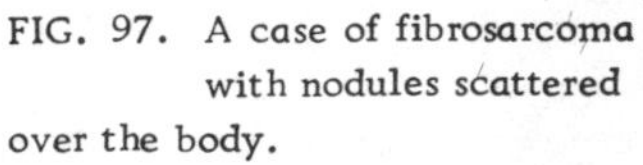

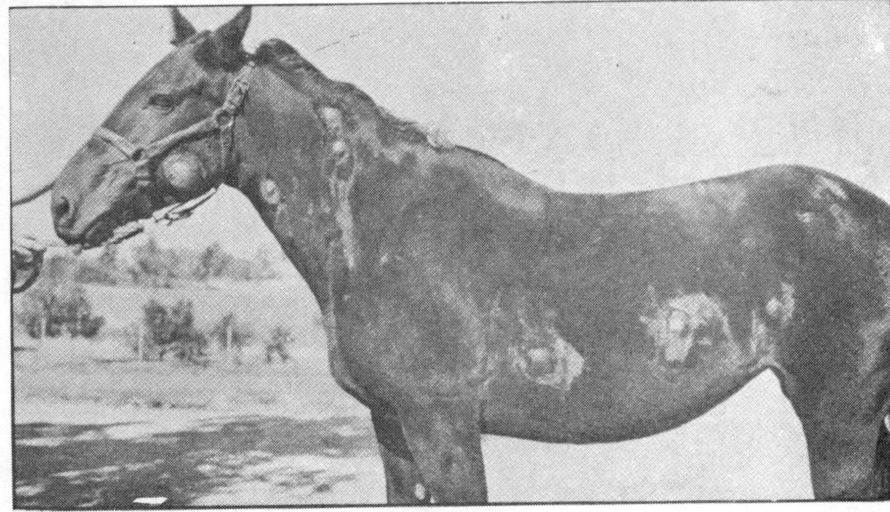

FIG. 97. A case of fibrosarcoma with nodules scattered over the body.

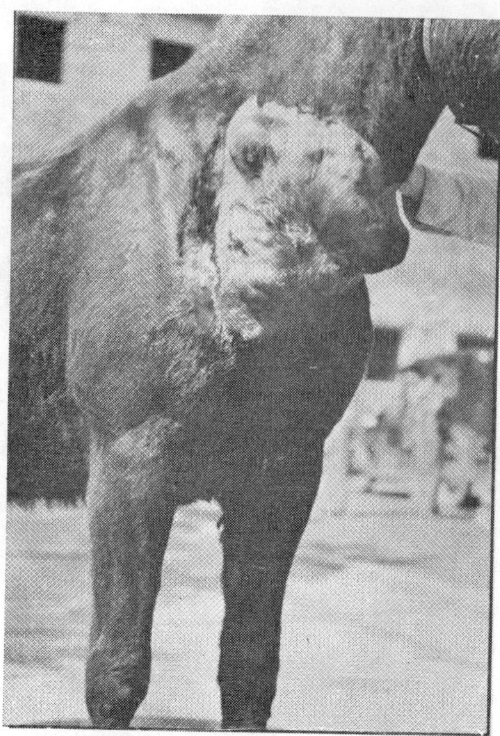

FIG. 98. A good example of the nodular type of growth of fibrosarcomas.

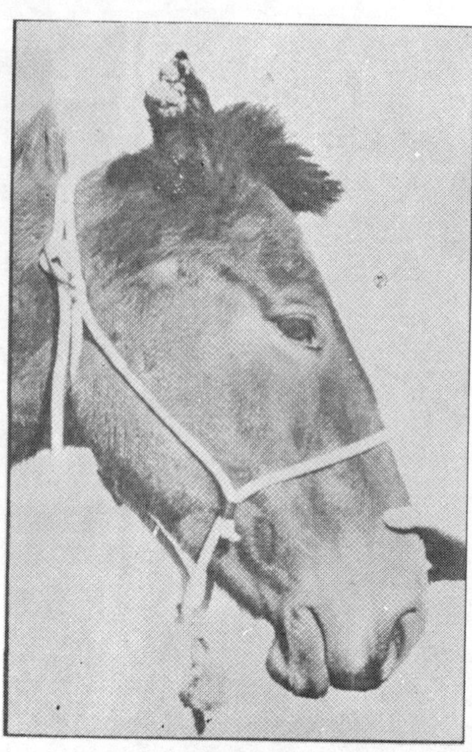

FIG. 99. Fibrosarcoma of the ear, when surgically removed they invariably recur.

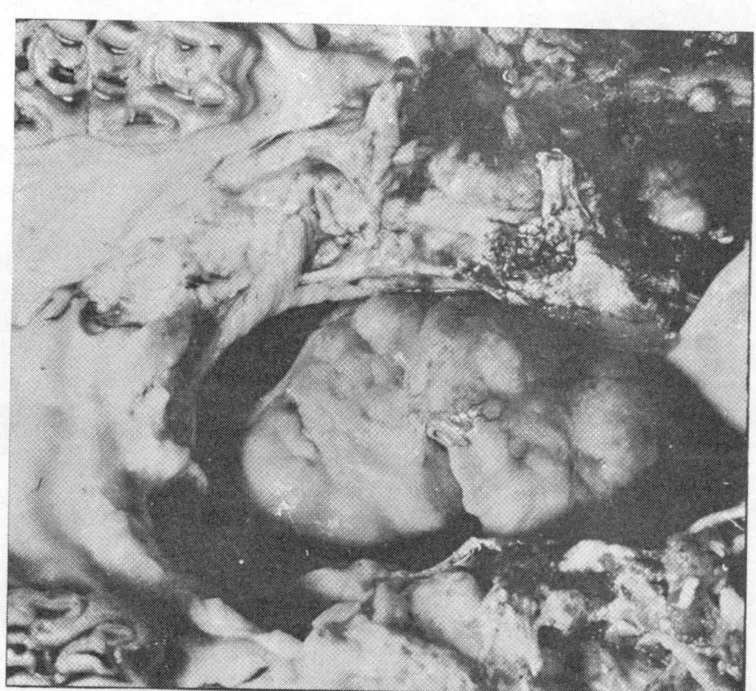

FIG. 100. A portion of a fibrosarcoma partially closing the posterior nares in a ten year old mule.

FIG. 101. A fibrosarcoma developing in the mandibular space in a two year old mule.

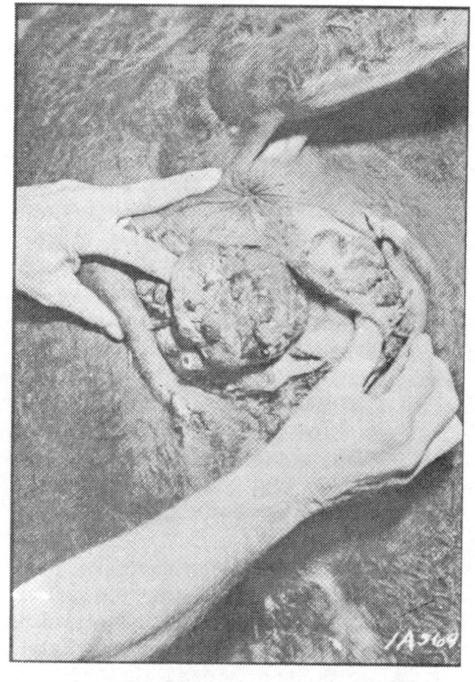

FIG. 102. Fibrosarcoma in the vagina.

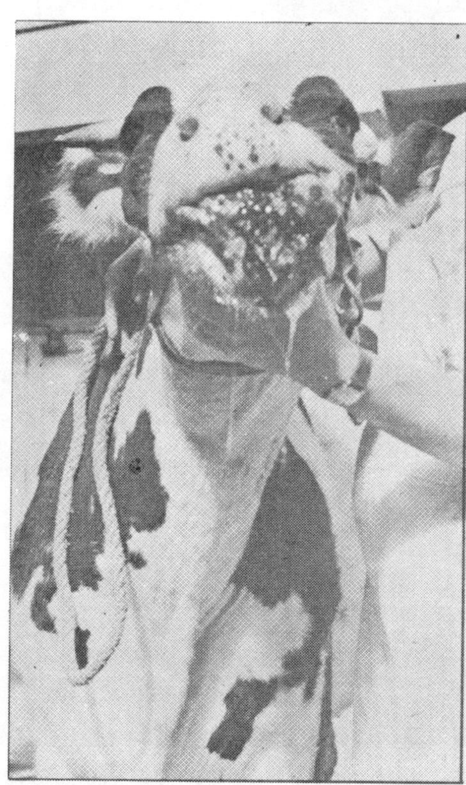

FIG. 103. Fibrosarcoma involving body of mandible.

FIG. 104. Fibrosarcoma in the maxillary sinus of a mule.

The case in Fig. 98 shows the nodular type of growth of many fibrosarcomas. Approximately two years before this picture was taken two separate tumors were removed from this area. The area remained smooth for almost two years when the tumors became more numerous and larger than before. All of the neoplastic tissue was again removed and the area healed. However in less than a year tumors had appeared again in the original area and also on the sheath and posterior limbs.

A mule was presented for examination with a history of having some difficulty in respiration for about a year. Also there was a bilateral muco-purulent nasal discharge and a gradual loss of condition for a year. This fibrosarcoma had originated in the posterior compartment of the maxillary sinus on the right side and it had developed a very extensive growth.

A fifteen year old draft horse was presented with the following history. For approximately six months the owner observed the horse had several hemorrhages from the left nostril. On two occasions the owner thought the horse was going to bleed to death. The examination revealed that the left side of the nasal cavity was completely closed as there was no air passing through it. Digital examination through several trephine openings revealed that the tumor had originated in the posterior compartment of the maxillary sinus on the left side. The tumor had become so extensive that it had destroyed the medial wall of the maxillary sinus and completely filled the posterior portion of the nasal cavity.

A Duroc sow one year of age was presented at the clinic with the history of losing flesh rapidly and having difficulty in eating. Examination of the mouth revealed a neoplasm attached to the posterior end of the hard palate and almost closing the fauces.

The patient was confined on the operating table in ventral recumbency. With the mouth held open with a hog speculum the base of the neoplasm was infiltrated with a one per cent solution of procaine hydrochloride. A piece of obstetrical wire was doubled and the looped end passed through a hollow pipe. A pair of long forceps were used to carry the wire loop to the back of the mouth and place it around the base of the neoplasm. The base of the neoplasm was quickly cut through with a sawing movement of the wire. The slight hemorrhage

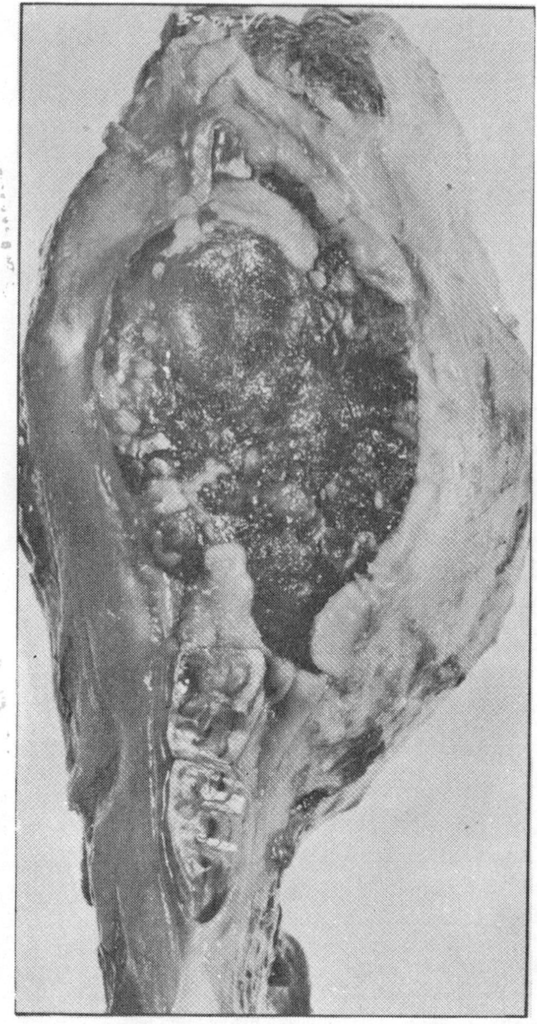

FIG. 105. Fibrosarcoma that occurred between the two plates of bone of the mandible.

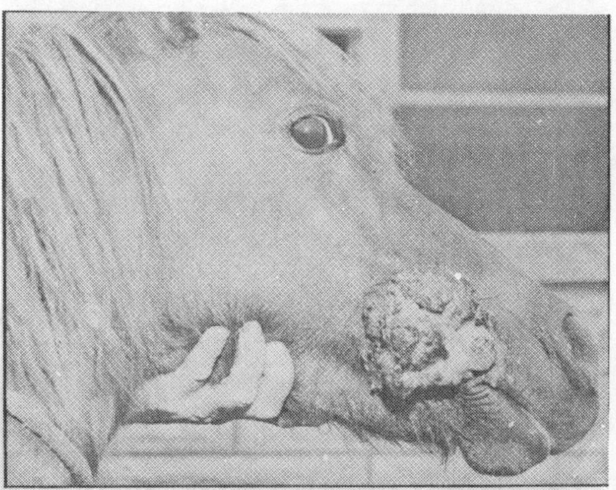

FIG. 106. Fibrosarcoma, surgically removed several times but would recur in a short time.

that occurred was controlled by applying the actual cautery to the bleeding surface. In a few days the sow recovered from the operation and was eating in a normal manner. Microscopic examination of the tissue revealed an osteogenic sarcoma.

An aged thoroughbred mare was presented for examination with the history of having had a slight continuous blood stained discharge from the left nostril for a year. A careful examination of the teeth and head failed to reveal any cause for the discharge. To permit of a more thorough examination of the nasal cavity a resection of the nasal septum was performed. With a portion of the nasal septum removed and a light inserted into the nasal cavity it was possible to examine the cavity very thoroughly. There seemed to be some extra tissue present on the floor of the nasal cavity. A small piece of this tissue was removed with a currette for a biopsy. The laboratory reported the tissue as a chondrosarcoma. A post mortem examination revealed that the posterior compartment of the maxillary sinus was completely filled with the neoplastic tissue, also there was extensive involvement of the ethmoid and posterior part of the nasal cavity.

The neoplasm in Fig. 107 occurred in a six year old Hereford cow. For a month the owner had noticed the cow was slightly unsteady on her legs. This unsteadiness was noticeable in the posterior limbs. He also noticed when a sudden noise was made, as clapping the hands, the cow would tremble all over and fall to the ground. After the above signs were observed for a month the cow became paralyzed in the posterior limbs. She was able to get up on her front feet but could not arise on her posterior limbs. During all this time her appetite was normal and there was no loss in condition. Due to the apparently incurable condition the cow was euthanized. A post-mortem examination revealed a neoplasm in the vertebral canal pressing on the spinal cord at the second thoracic vertebra.

In Fig. 108 the sarcoma involved the alveoli of the fourth and fifth cheek teeth of the mandible. The sarcoma is a malignant type of tumor composed of cells of the connective tissue type. Usually the sacromatous tissue is bulky, soft and vascular. This soft consistency reflects the cellular character of rapidly growing neoplasms. Metastasis is observed in the advanced stages of many sarcomas. After the large mass of neoplastic tissue was removed more of the soft vascular could be palpated in the alveoli. The bone of the mandible was thinner than normal, pliable and was fractured. The necropsy revealed metastasis had occurred to the kidneys.

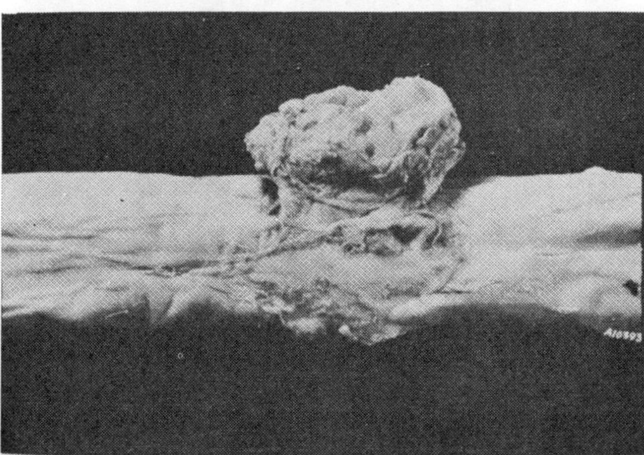

FIG. 107. Neurosarcoma that was pressing on the spinal cord.

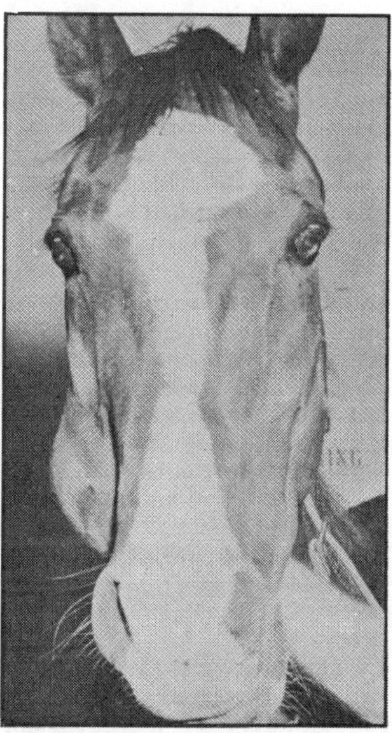

FIG. 108. Bulging of the cheek on the right side due to a sarcoma.

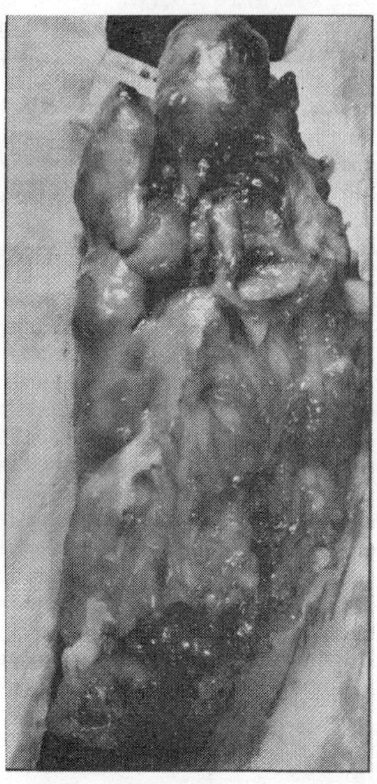

FIG. 109. The approximate location of the sarcoma on the side of the mandible.

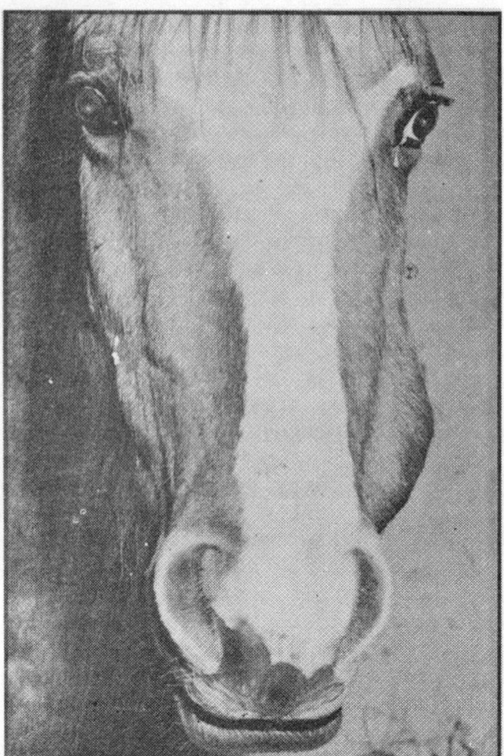

FIG. 110. The bulging outward of the cheek from the second to fifth cheek tooth due to a neurofibrosarcoma.

Neurofibrosarcoma

Neurofibrosarcomas have a tendency to recur after removal. The neurofibrosarcoma shown in Fig. 110 was attached to the tissue on the lateral side of the maxilla. Neoplastic tissue that contains nerve tissue is very persistent about recurring after removal.

Undifferentiated Neoplasms

Horses are presented occasionally with an excessive growth of new tissue on the lateral side of the fetlock joint of either the front or posterior limb. This tissue seems to develop following an injury of the area. Due to the location of this rather vascular tissue it is frequently injured and becomes covered with blood so the term, "bloody wart", is erroneously used to describe the condition. The diagnosis on microscopic examination of the tissue in the cases treated has varied from fibroma, fibrosarcoma to exuberant granulation tissue. In operating on these cases the incisions should extend out into the normal tissue. Also deep enough to be sure all of the abnornal tissue is removed.

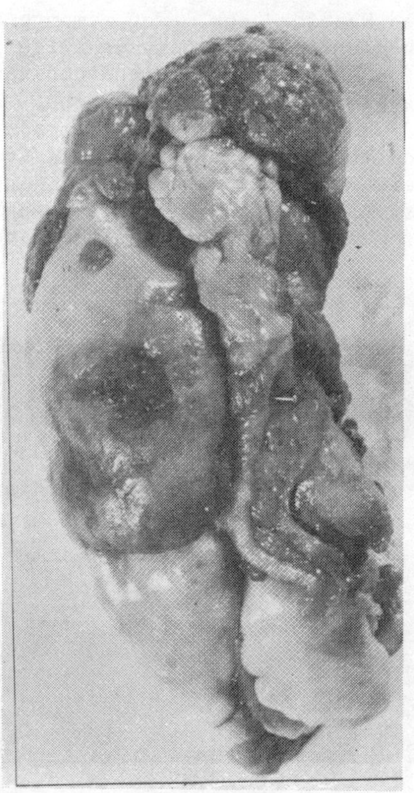

FIG. 111. Neurofibrosarcoma that was removed from case shown in Fig. 110.

Although care is used to remove all of the pathological tissue in most cases there is a reoccurrence of the condition. This tendency to recur after removal is typical of fibrosarcomas. Probably the most important point to remember in these cases is that they are not "bloody warts" but neoplastic tissue with a tendency to recur after removal.

Osteogenic sarcomas are frequently found arising from the aveoli of the teeth. A two year old horse was presented for an examination of the teeth. Examination of the mouth revealed a mass of tissue approximately eight inches long, three inches wide, and one inch thick lying on the table surface of the lower cheek teeth on the right side. The neoplasm apparently originated from the alveoli of the teeth as the second, third, and fourth cheek teeth on that side were loose, and the alveoli contained soft spongy tissue. Microscopic examination of this tissue revealed it as an osteogenic sarcoma.

Neoplasms of the Pharynx

Pharyngeal tumors occur rather frequently in the bovine but only rarely in other species of animals. The most commonly encountered neoplasms in the bovine have been fibromas and fibrosarcomas; other enlargements have been due to Actionobacillus lignieresi.

SIGNS. The outstanding sign is a variable degree of dyspnea depending upon the size and location of the enlargement. A very pronounced dyspnea may develop very suddenly. If the enlargement becomes large enough it may not cause difficulty in breathing but also in swallowing. Large bulls have been observed to show the following signs: periodic attacks of difficult breathing, protruding eyes, whirling around in a circle, shaking the head violently and finally falling to the ground, and recovering their equilibrium in a few minutes.

DIAGNOSIS. A diagnosis is made upon finding the enlargement in the pharynx. With a speculum holding the mouth open a thorough manual examination of the pharynx of the bovine may be made through the mouth. In the equine the manual examination of the pharynx is more difficult because of the long soft palate.

PROGNOSIS. Prognosis is favorable unless the neoplasm is malignant.

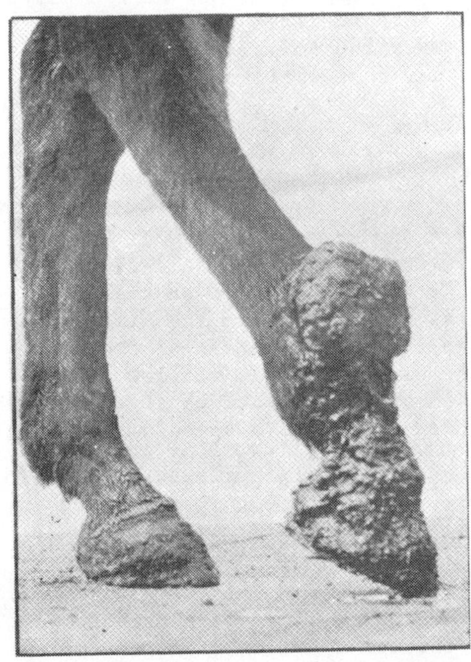

FIG. 112. Neoplastic tissue that has a tendency to recur after surgical removal.

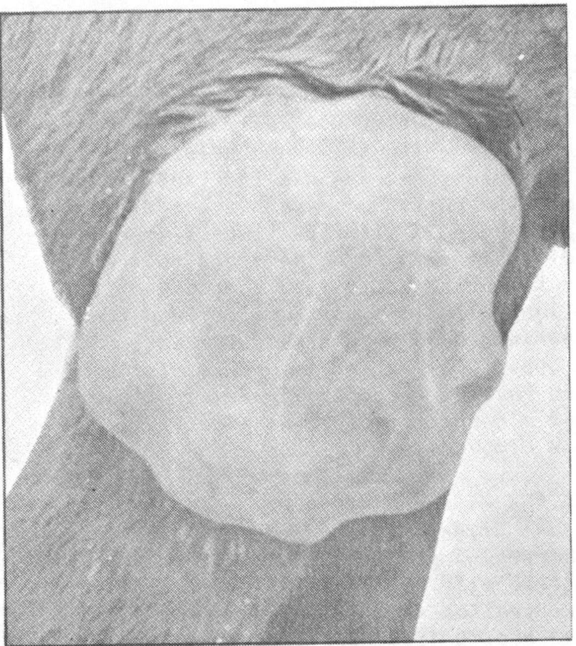

FIG. 113. Myxosarcoma weight ten pounds on the lateral side of right posterior limb of equine.

TREATMENT. Most of the neoplasms in the pharynx may be removed by means of a wire carried in through the mouth. A piece of obstetrical wire is doubled and the looped end passed through a hollow pipe. With the mouth held open with a mouth speculum the looped end is carried back to the pharynx and placed around the base of the neoplasm. With a sawing movement of the wire the neoplasm is incised as close to its attachment to the pharynx as possible.

In one case in a two year old bull it was necessary to pass the wire through the nostril. This was due to the location of the neoplasm which was attached to the dorsal surface of the pharynx and partially covered by the soft palate. The looped wire was passed through a small size stomach tube and this in turn was passed through the nostril. With the hand in the mouth it was possible to place the wire around the base of the neoplasm to remove it. This neoplasm was demonstrated to be a fibrosarcoma.

The following case was described by Hudson in the February 1939 issue of the Veterinary Journal. The subject was a large Shire gelding. For some time the owner had noticed a peculiar rumbling noise when the horse was feeding and at times he would appear to choke. It was also noticed that occasionally fluids were returned through the nostrils. The horse was also losing condition.

To thoroughly relax the animal and prevent any struggling, two ounces of chloral hydrate in solution was administered intravenously. With the mouth held open with a speculum the hand was inserted through into the pharynx. A rather large polypus could be felt with the fingers. This polypus seemed to be attached to the side of the pharynx close to the epiglottis. A long wire loop was carried into the pharynx and placed around the base of the polypus. By sawing movements of the wire the base of the polypus was cut through and a neoplasm about the size of an egg was removed.

In the Michigan State College clinic unusual signs were shown by a mare with a pharyngeal polypus. The mare entered the clinic with a history of difficulty in respiration after drinking. The signs had been noticed for approximately six weeks. When the mare was offered water and drank a small amount she immediately extended her neck, opened her mouth as though she was attempting to inspire air. However, she was unable to inspire any air, and she collapsed in a few minutes. Apparently normal respiration was resumed in a short time and she was able to get up. The cause of the respiratory trouble was diagnosed as a pharyngeal polypus. This diagnosis was confirmed on autopsy when a polypus as large as a hen egg was found just ventral to the epiglottis.

In the Iowa State College clinic a horse was presented with the history of making a noise on inspiration and it seemed to be increasing in severity. The horse would cough and choke and apparently get something out so it would obtain some relief. One outstanding sign was the coughing of solid material through the nasal passage after mastication and the attempt to swallow. With the mouth held open with a speculum a pedunculated growth about the size of a baseball was felt attached to the floor of the pharynx. The point of attachment was posterior to the base of the tongue, anterior to the epiglottis and to the right of the median line. The location of the polypus permitted it to move over onto the opening of the glottis and esophagus when the horse swallowed. A piece of obstetrical wire was doubled and the looped end passed through a pipe. The looped end was carried through the mouth to the pharynx and placed around the attachment of the polypus. With a sawing movement of the wire the attachment of the polypus was cut through close to the pharyngeal wall. When the polypus was incised it contained numerous small abscesses.

Pharyngeal Cyst

Cysts are swellings with a wall and the contents may be fluid or semi-fluid and may occur in any location on the body. A horse was presented with the history of from one-third to one-half of the water and food the horse tried to swallow was returned through the nasal cavity. With the mouth held open with a speculum examination of the pharynx with the hand revealed a soft swelling on the ventral surface of the pharyngeal cavity. The swelling was located half way between the base of the tongue and the larynx.

A piece of obstetrical wire doubled was passed through a hollow piece of tubing that was long enough to reach the pharynx. The looped end of the wire was carried into the pharynx with the hand and placed around the cyst. By sawing movements with the wire, tissue holding the cyst, was cut through and the cyst removed. The patient was then able to swallow food and water in a normal manner.

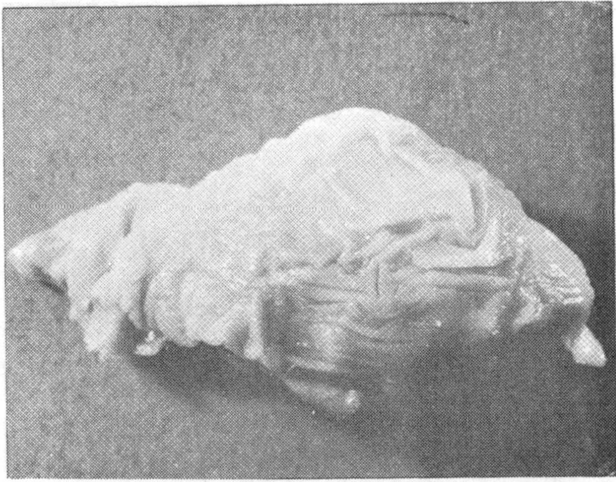

FIG. 114. Cyst removed from ventral surface of Pharyngeal cavity.

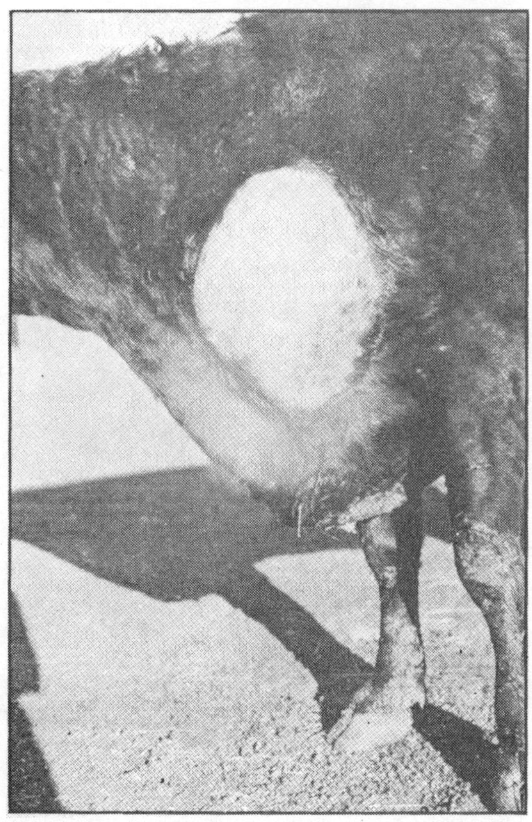

FIG. 115. A large lymphoma involving the prescapular lymph gland.

Lymphoma and Lymphosarcoma

A few important physiological properties influence the origin of tumors of lymphoid tissue. In the first place lymphoid tissue responds to irritation with inflammatory hyperplasia more actively than any other tissue. Second, the lymphoid tissues are relatively mobile rather than fixed, hence tumors and tumor-like processes in lymphoid tissue are frequent, and as a rule tend to become widely diffused.

Simple Lymphoma

Local or regional, circumscribed chronic enlargements of lymph nodes which are self-limiting and do not lead to systemic invasion are rather common pathological conditions. Lymphomas develop rather slowly and if the affected tissue is not removed they may become enormous. The lymphoma shown in Fig. 115 was approximately fifteen inches long and six inches in diameter at its base. The only successful method of treating lymphomas is extirpation of the affected tissue.

Lymphocytoma

A true malignant neoplasm arising in lymphatic tissue from proliferation of atypical lymphoid cells. Lympocytoma is distinguished from other forms of lymphoma by its local destructive capacity and by true metastasis to distant organs. The tumors arise in a chain of lymph nodes or in a localized lymphatic structure and rapidly produce bulky growths which obliterate the outlines of the separate nodes and infiltrate surrounding tissues. The development of lymphoid tissue may be local but wide spread extensions are frequently observed. In its entire scope the luekemic process illustrates many phases of hyperplasia of lymphoid tissue. Due to the widespread involvement of tissue the signs in different cases will vary a great deal. The most recognized sign of lymphocytoma is an increase in size of one or more of the external lymph glands. In some cases the external lymph glands may become enormous in size. When lymphoid tissue develops in the orbital cavity posterior to the eyeball there is a gradual protrusion of the eyeball. Only one eye may be affected but frequently in a short time the other eye may present the same appearance. Extensive edema of the brisket, neck and mandibular space together with marked distension of

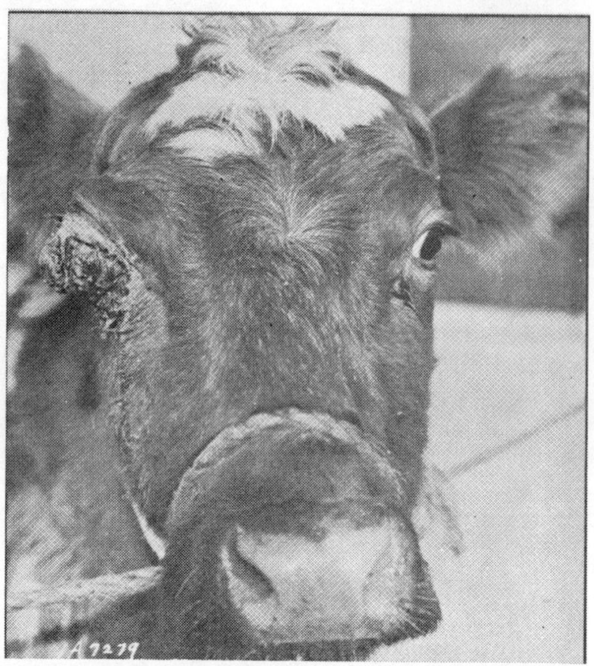

FIG. 116. Protrusion of right eye due to lymphoid tissue in orbital cavity.

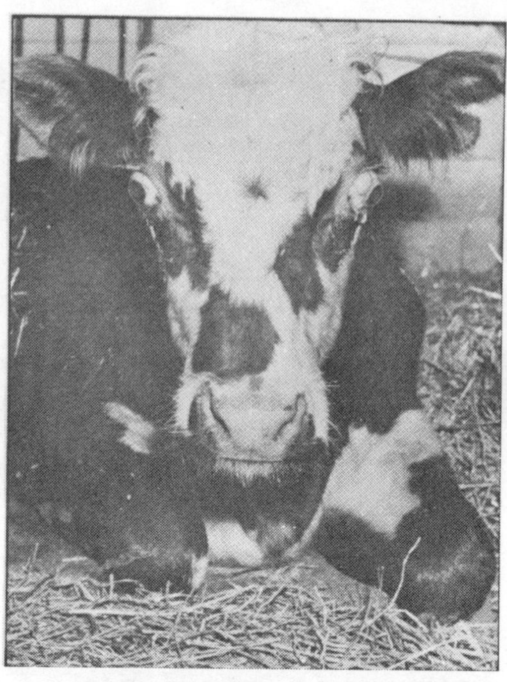

FIG. 117. A steer with protrusion of both eyeballs due to lymphoid tissue in the orbital cavities.

the jugular veins may occur due to large masses of lymphoid tissue in the anterior portion of the thoracic cavity. The tissue may be located so that it interferes with the return of the blood to the heart. The lungs may be involved with lymphoid tissue scattered throughout the lung tissue.

Probably the digestive tract is affected more frequently than any other tissue and the abomasum is the portion that is usually affected. In some cases the abomasum becomes enormous with its walls several inches thick. The patient may have a good appetite but there is a gradual loss in condition. All of the mesenteric lymph glands may be enlarged. Occasionally the reticulum, omasum and rumen may be affected. The urinary system may be involved with either the kidneys or bladder affected or both organs may be involved at the same time. The uterus may be so extensively involved that in some cases it is enormous in size.

Paralysis of the posterior limbs is frequently observed in animals affected with lymphocytoma. The paralysis may be caused by lymphoid tissue in the vertebral canal pressing on the spinal cord. Also masses

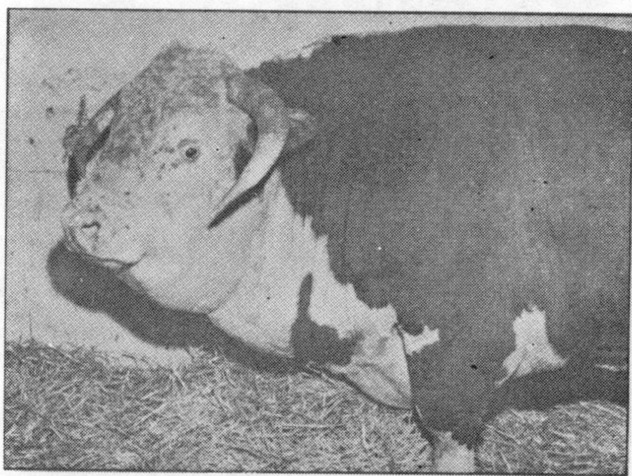

FIG. 118. A case of lymphocytoma in which there were masses of lymphoid tissue in the thoracic cavity that interfered with the return of the blood to the heart and caused the extensive edema of the brisket and neck.

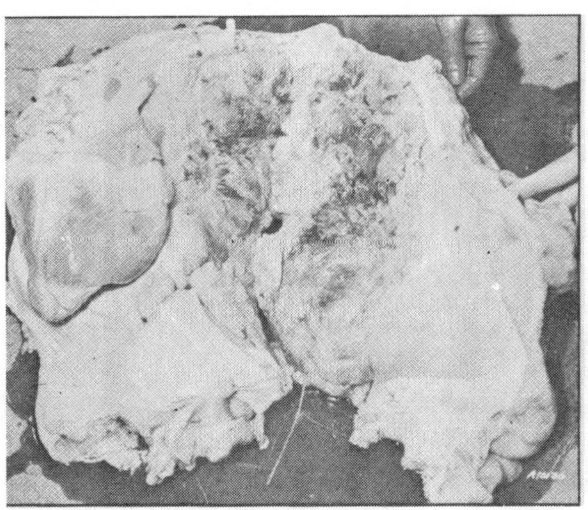

FIG. 119. Large mass of lymphoid tissue, weight 60 pounds, in the thoracic cavity in a case of lymphocytoma.

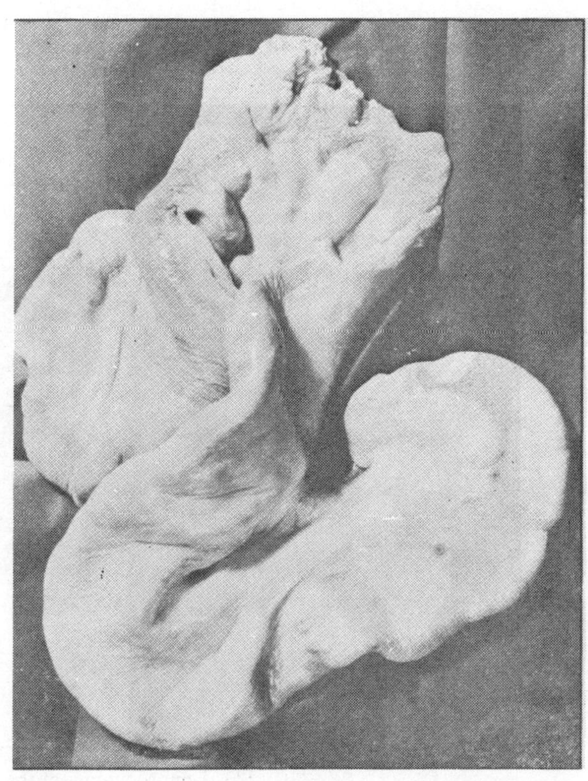

FIG. 120. Lymphocytoma of the uterus.

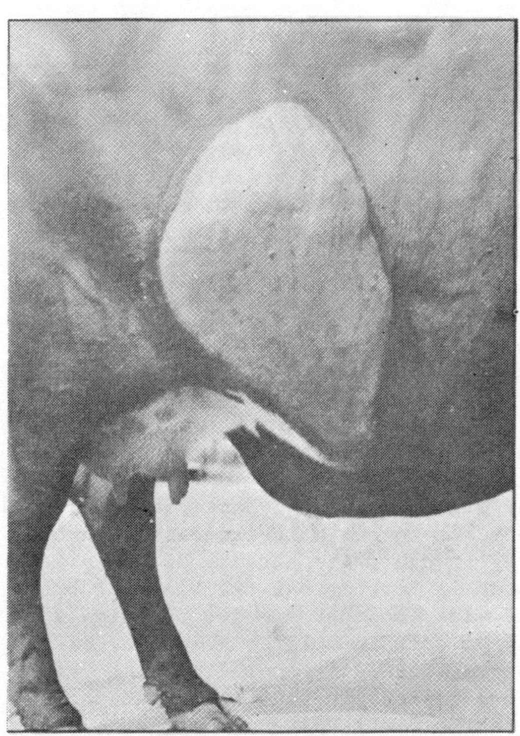

FIG. 121. Extensive involvement of the prefemoral lymph gland in a case of lymphocytoma.

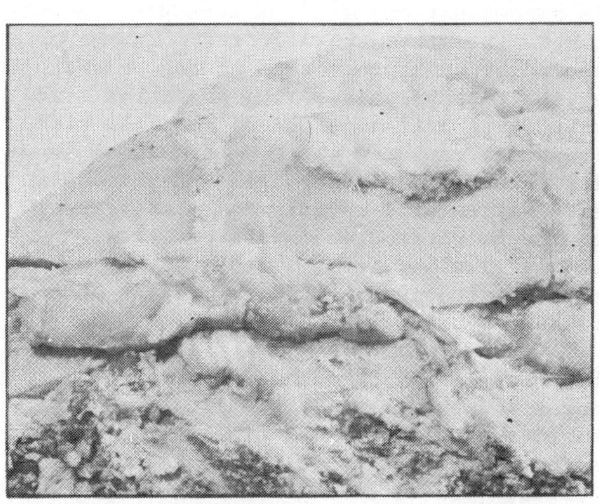

FIG. 122. Lymphoid tissue in the vertebral canal that produced pressure on the spinal cord and posterior paralysis.

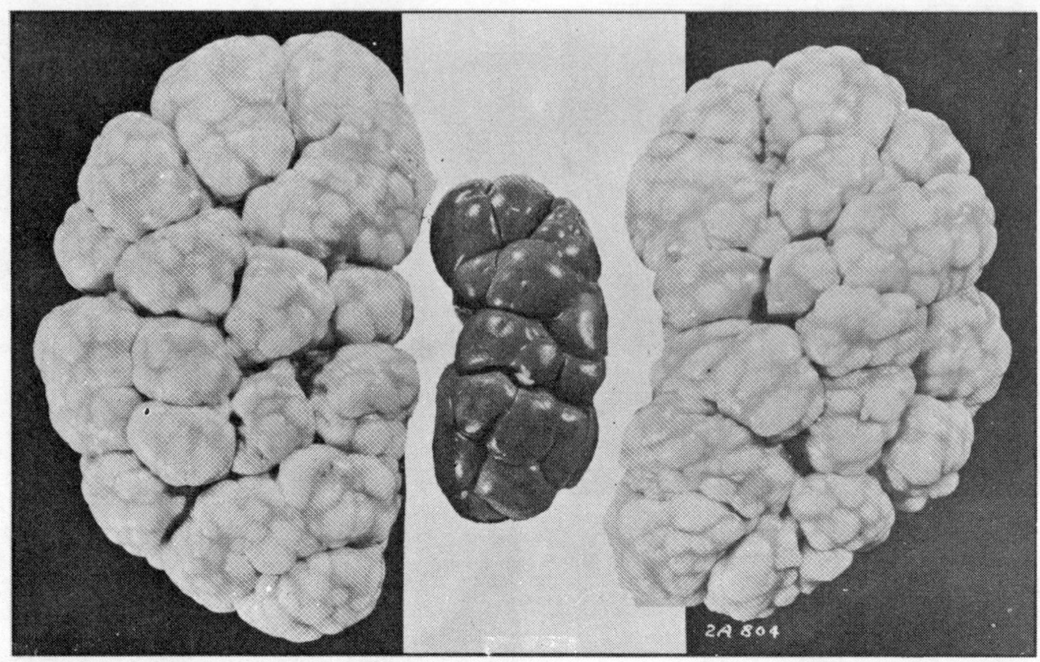

FIG. 123. Lymphocytoma of the kidneys of a two year old heifer, kidney in center is a normal kidney.

of lymphoid tissue in the pelvic cavity may produce pressure on nerves to muscles of the posterior limbs. Paralysis has also been observed when lymphoid tissue was in the muscle tissue and involving the nerves of the muscles. In many of the cases there is a combination of signs depending upon the tissues that are affected. In one case there may be a protrusion of one or both eyes with paralysis of the posterior limbs developing over a period of several weeks. The owner may have noticed the animal showing rather indefinite signs and a rectal examination will reveal masses of tissue in the pelvic and abdominal cavities. A rectal examination of another animal may reveal extensive involvement of the uterus, bladder or kidneys.

Lymphocytoma is occasionally observed in mules and in these individuals there is a history of gradual loss of condition. The affected animals usually have a good appetite, seem to feel good but they are thin and do not improve in condition. A rectal examination usually reveals the presence of neoplastic tissue in the abdominal cavity, and it is usually a lymphocytoma. In one case in a mule there was extensive involvement of the spleen that could be felt on rectal examination. One mule was presented with a history of excessive straining when defecating. A rectal examination revealed a large mass of tissue on the right side of the abdominal cavity. The post mortem examination revealed that this neoplastic tissue was producing a partial stricture of the intestines.

Melanoblastomas

The melanotic tumors or melanoblastomas occur more frequently in the horse than in any other species of domesticated animals. They also occur more frequently in old grey or old white horses, but they may be found in horses that are black or brown, and also in other species of animals that may be dark in color. Melanomas are observed frequently on the skin of red pigs, and occasionally they have been found on Ayrshire cattle.

Melanoblastomas are neoplasms composed principally of pigment producing cells called melanoblasts. The pigment produced is called melanin. It has been suggested by Feldman that the benign neoplasm of this type be designated a melanoma, and that the malignant neoplasm be called a malignant melanoma. A melanoblastoma is very malignant. It is one of the most rapidly fatal neoplasms known.

This type of neoplasm is found most frequently in the region of the anus, vulva, perineum, ventral surface of the tail, scrotum and sheath, but they may be found in other parts of the body. Melanomas usually increase in size rather slowly and remain localized. Malignant melanomas grow rather rapidly with a tendency to metastasize to other parts of the body.

The pressure of the neoplasm on the rectum produced a partial obstruction and defecation was accomplished only with difficulty. Surgical removal of the neoplasm was performed with the patient in the standing position. Anesthesia of the operative area was obtained by injecting fifteen cubic centimeters of a one per cent solution of procaine hydrochloride into the epidural space. However, it was necessary to inject additional quantities of the anesthetic solution epidurally during the operative procedure. The total quantity used was eighty cubic centimeters. A vertical incision six inches long was

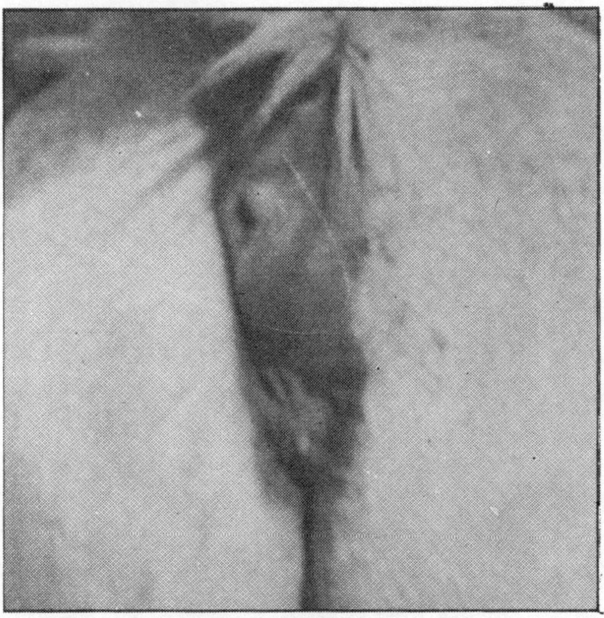

FIG. 124. The rectum is pushed over by a melanoma between it and the pelvis.

made in the skin lateral to the anus. The melanoma was removed in pieces and the total amount of tissue removed weighed sixteen hundred grams. To control the profuse hemorrhage that occurred, it was necessary to tamponade the cavity tightly with gauze.

This gauze was removed in forty-eight hours and the area treated as an open wound. The removal of the melanoma permitted the rectum to return to its normal position and defecation to occur without difficulty.

Melano-sarcomas occur frequently around the anus and ventral surface of the tail as shown in Fig. 125. Surgical interference in cases of this type are contra-indicated as complete removal of the neoplastic tissue is impossible and the surgical procedure may stimulate more rapid growth of the neoplastic tissue or metastasis to other portions of the body.

A cecal trocar was introduced into the abdominal cavity of Fig. 126 and a clear watery fluid was obtained. A rectal examination revealed a large lobulated mass of tissue anterior to and below the brim of the pelvis. The tentative diagnosis of malignant melanoma was justified because of the gray color and age of the patient.

The post-mortem examination revealed an extensive involvement of the various tissues with melanomas as shown in Fig. 127. Only about one-half the number present in the abdominal cavity are shown in the picture. It was conservatively estimated that fifty gallons of fluid was present in the abdominal cavity.

In Fig. 128 there is extensive swelling of the tissues medial to the point of the shoulder joint. About three months previously an abscess had been opened in this area and apparently good healing had occurred. In two months the area began to enlarge and in another month reached the proportion shown in the picture. When a trocar was introduced into the depths of the tissue black fluid was obtained. An incision was then made and some of the deeper tissue removed. It was demonstrated to be a melanoma.

A twelve year old grey mule with an unusual history was presented for examination. The owner first noticed the mule would not walk in a straight line, and the hair on the left side of the head, the ear, forehead, and upper eyelid was moist and warm to the touch. The hair on the other half of the

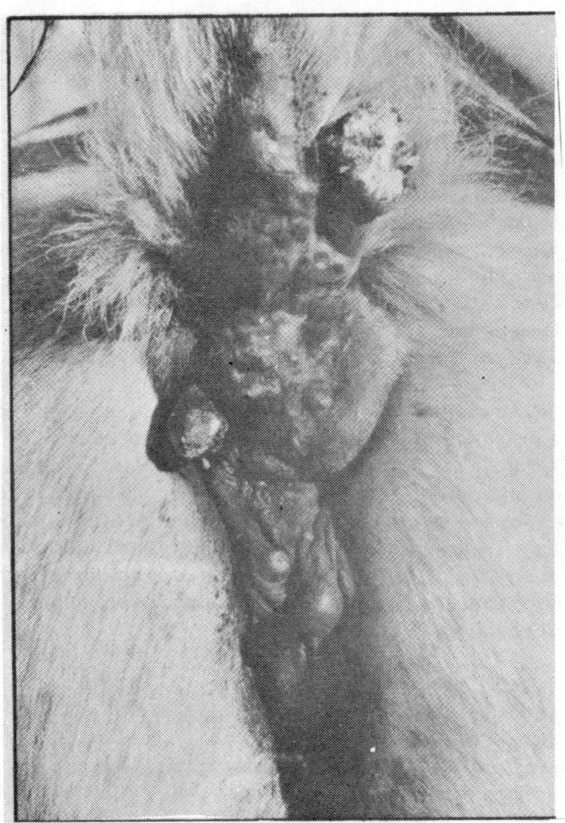

FIG. 125. A typical case of multiple melanomas involving the ventral surface of the tail, anus and vulva.

FIG. 126. A posterior view of a twelve year old mule with a bilateral distension of the abdominal cavity.

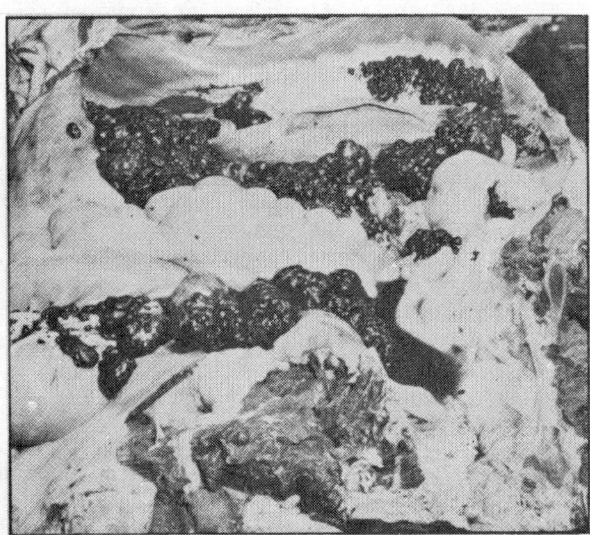

FIG. 127. The interior of the abdominal cavity showing the extensive involvement of the tissues.

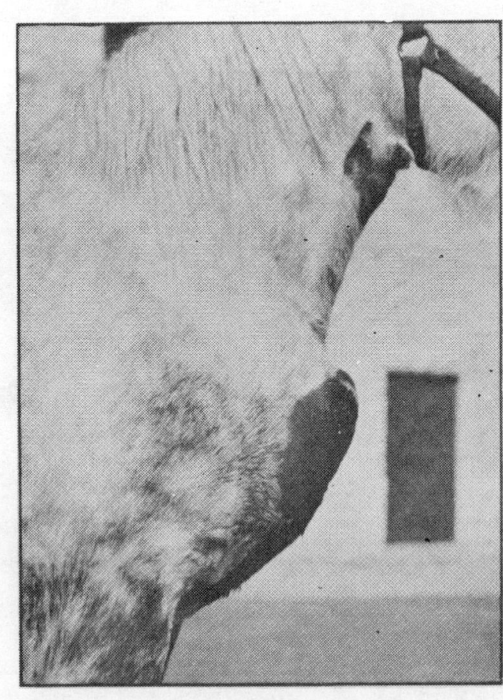

FIG. 128. A melanoma medial to the shoulder joint.

head was dry and cool. In about a month it was noticed that he was having some difficulty in breathing and, if forced to extra effort in pulling, it was very pronounced.

The mule was euthanized and a careful postmortem examination was performed. A melano-sarcoma the size of a hazel nut was found between the cerebral hemispheres and

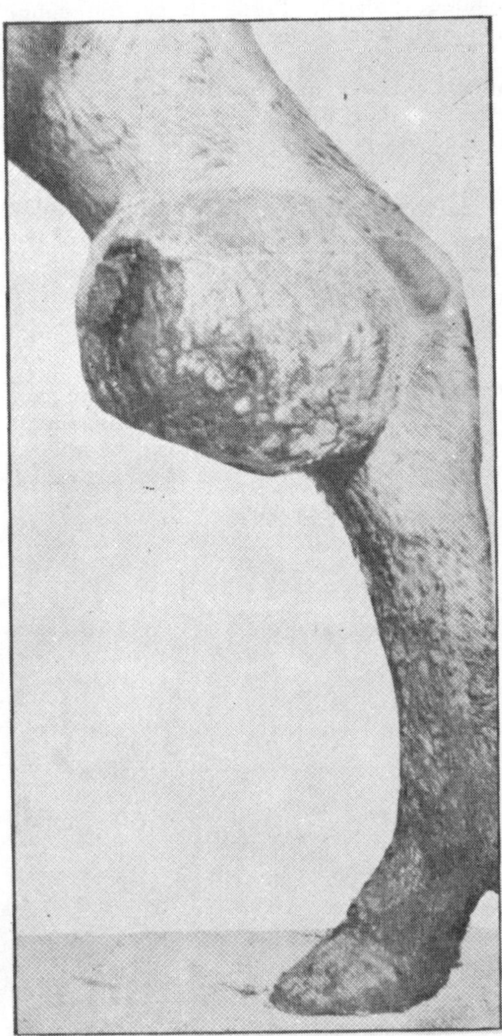

FIG. 129. Melanoma on posterior limb of a cow.

in contact with the dorsal surface of the corpora quadrigemina. In this position it could have exerted pressure on the thalamus, the heat regulator, and this may have produced the signs noticed around the head. There was a large mass of the melano-sarcoma at the entrance to the thoracic cavity. This was pressing on the trachea thus producing the difficulty in breathing.

Warts

A wart may be a true papilloma or if multiple they may be due to a filtrable virus. The larger warts are covered with an excessive number of epidermal cells. The base peduncle of the larger warts is composed of fibrous tissue derived from the dermis.

FIG. 130. When young animals are so extensively affected with the large warts they are very difficult to treat.

TREATMENT. Excellent results have been reported from the use of wart vaccine when the warts are small. The dosage recommended of the vaccine is twenty-five cubic centimeters administered subcutaneously, divided among two or three sites. It is recommended that this dosage be repeated once or twice at weekly intervals if the complete disappearance of all of the warts is to be obtained. For the larger warts it may be necessary to remove then surgically.

Nephroblastoma

Embryoma

The nephroblastomas also known as Wilm's tumor arise during fetal life close to the kidney. There is good evidence that they develop from renal blastema from which the kidney is formed. In the case shown in Fig. 131 the dark hair shows the extent of the tumor which was covered with skin. It extended from the last rib to the tuber coxae and to the midline. Also it extended into the abdominal cavity and was in contact with the kidney. The colt was one month old when presented for examination and died four days later after a little exertion. The tumor which was outlined by the dark hair on the skin was noticed at time of birth and developed very rapidly during the fourth week of life.

FIG. 131. Dark hair in flank region indicates location of Nephroblastoma in abdominal cavity.

Hemangioma

This neoplasm is usually benign and consists of endothelium lined bloodspaces filled with normal circulating blood. The hemangioma shown in Fig. 132 originated in

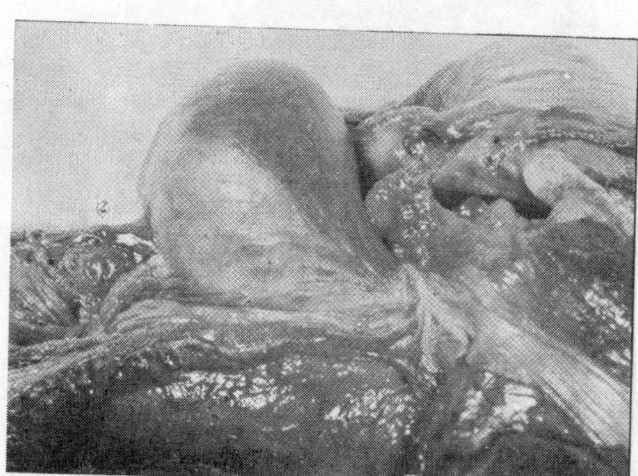

FIG. 132. Lateral view of pear shaped hemangioma with its movability could close entrance into larynx or oesophagus.

FIG. 133. Dorsal view of hemangioma with its pear shape and position dorsal to larynx, it was freely movable.

the wall of the pharynx lateral to the epiglottis. It was pear shaped, freely movable and the horse was unable to swallow either food or water. At times there would be definite interference with inspiration. A trachea tube was inserted but was removed in three days as the breathing seemed to be normal. The horse died rather suddenly two days later from suffocation.

Papilloma

Papilloma. The term papilla indicates a small projection and a papilloma is a tumor composed of a large number of these projections. In many cases the complicated architecture of these tumors may resemble a dahlia. The papillary projections which are characteristic of papillomas often produce a branching effect even in the very small almost minute tumors. Papillomas quite frequently develop near the cornea-scleral junction. Some may be very small and fragile while others may grow to a large size. In operating on the small neoplasma on the cornea the prognosis is more favorable as to the probability of its recurrence when it is a papilloma rather than a carcinoma.

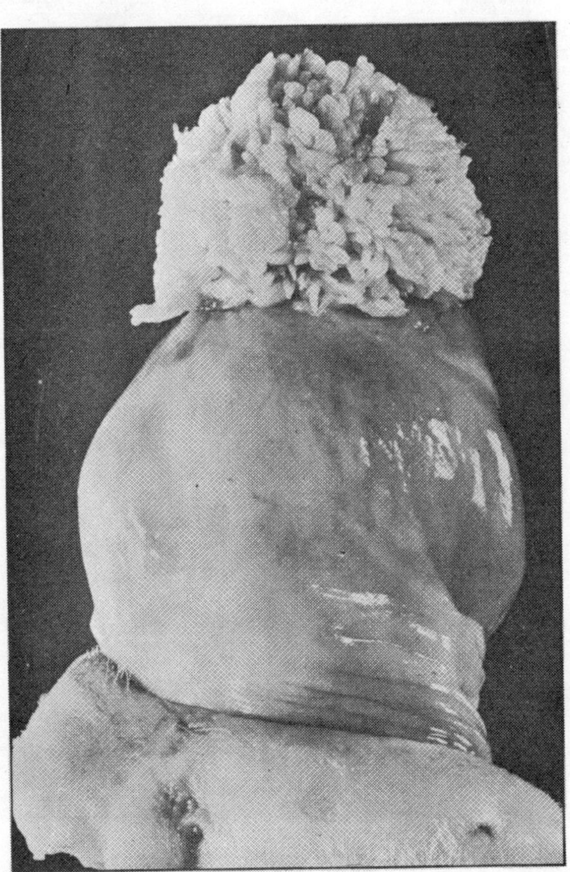

FIG. 134. Papilloma on the cornea.

Epithelioma. This, sometimes termed squamous - celled carcinoma is the commonest malignant neoplasm affecting the orbit. Usually it appears first on the membrane nictitans or in the conjunctiva at the cornea-scleral conjunction. When the early lesion appears, it presents a nodular surface and is highly vascular. It increases rapidly in size and may invade all of the tissues in the orbit.

Hemorrhagic Cyst or Hematoma

A seven year old horse was presented for examination with the history of difficulty in breathing. This difficulty in breathing had become very pronounced over a period of six months. Examination revealed there was no air passing through the right side of the nasal cavity. In ten days it was necessary to use a trachea tube as there was a rapid increase in the patients difficulty to breathe. A necropsy revealed a hemorrhagic cyst or hematoma in the maxillary sinus on the right side. The tissue extended into the nasal cavity and produced enough pressure on the nasal septum to force it over against the medial wall of the maxillary sinus on the left side. One portion of the cyst or hematoma extended posteriorly and closed the posterior nares.

Carcinoma

Carcinoma is a tumor process characterized by atypical and destructive proliferation of epithelium. The destruction of tissues by carcinoma is a common event. Carcinomas occur so frequently in and on various portions of the animal's body that they undoubtedly are the most important neoplasms of domesticated animals. Wherever carcinomas are found they have a tendency to invade the surrounding tissue.

Metastasis - apart from the continuous permeation of lymphatics and tissue spaces - is a highly significant property of carcinoma. It gives rise to emboli which pass through the blood or lymph vessels and originate distant secondary tumors. Induration of the affected tissue is probably the most constant and significant feature

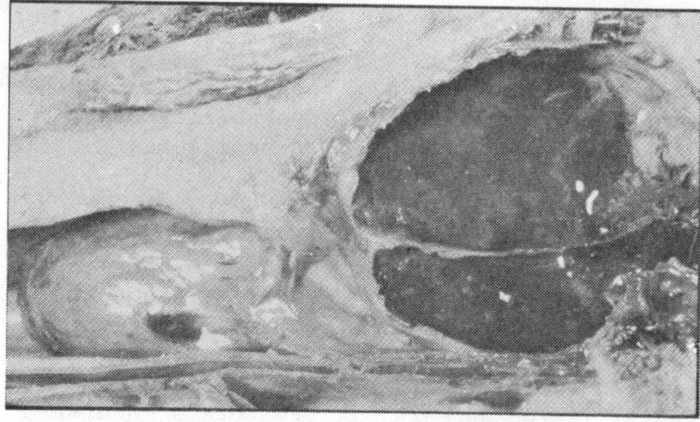

FIG. 135. Hemorrhagic cyst or hematoma in the maxillary sinus with a portion in the nasal cavity.

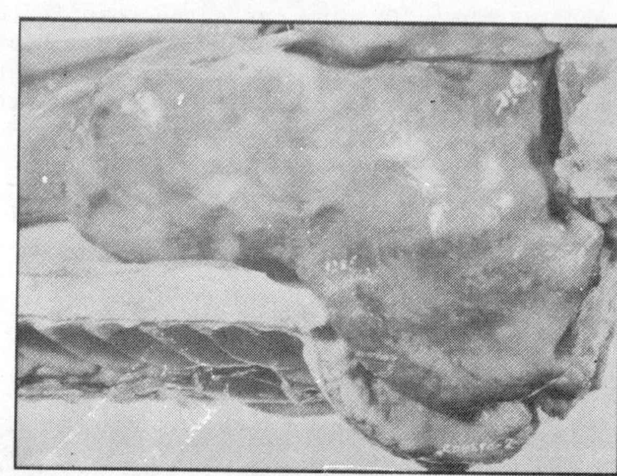

FIG. 136. Portion of cyst or hematoma that was in nasal cavity and extended into and completely filled posterior nares.

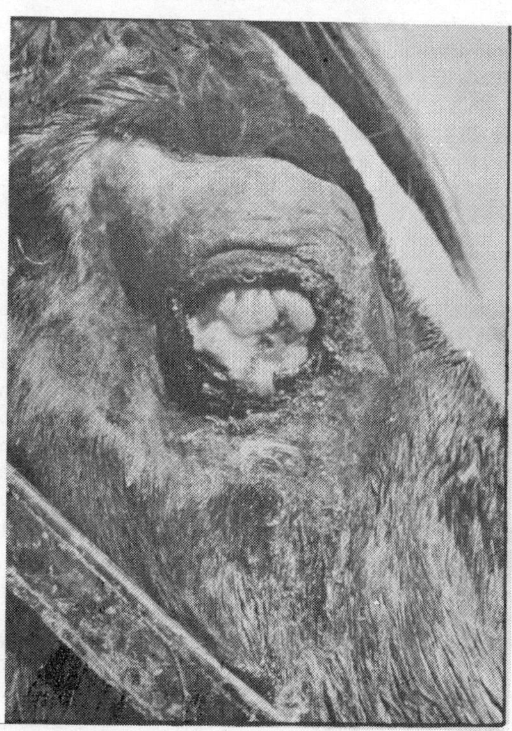

FIG. 137. Carcinoma that developed in the orbital cavity of a horse after injury to the eye.

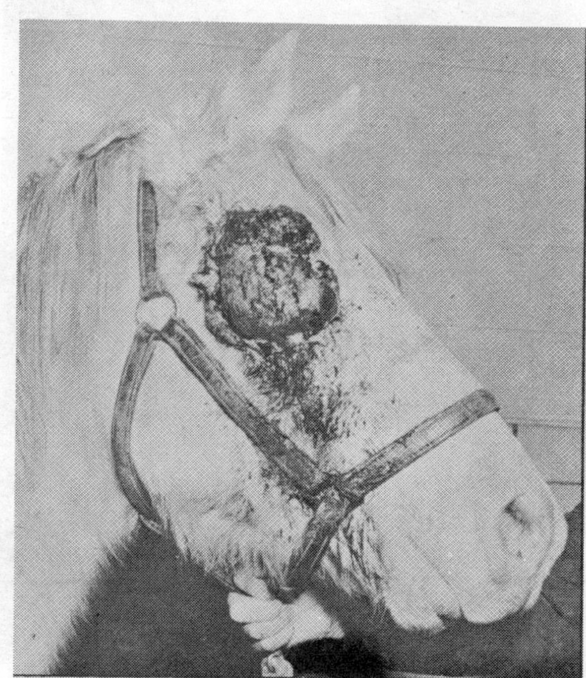

FIG. 138. Carcinoma involving the orbital cavity of a mare.

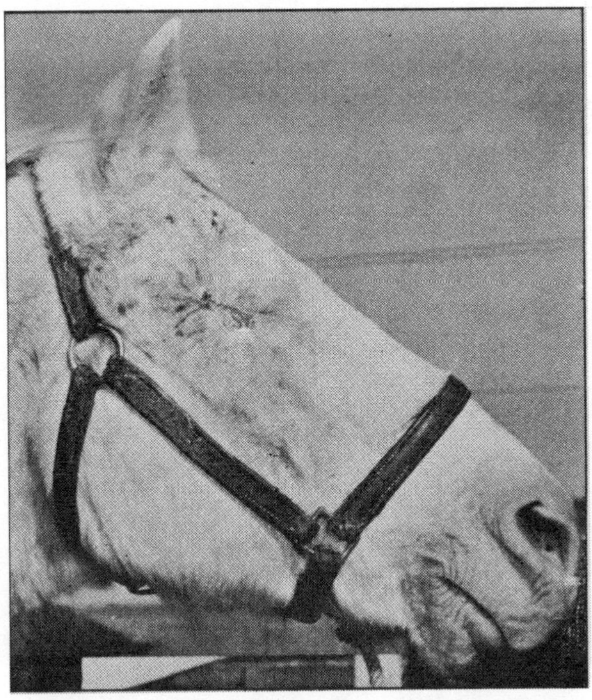

FIG. 139. Two months after the operation the skin had healed over the orbital cavity.

of large and even of miniature carcinomas. It is often of great diagnostic significance. The induration of carcinoma is a peculiar physical quality owing to its extreme density and its presence in suspicious lesions must be strong evidence of carcinoma. It must be distinguished from the less resistant and more diffuse induration of chronic productive inflammation.

Equine

In the horse the eye is a frequent location for carcinoma. When carcinoma affects the eye or orbital cavity of the horse there is usually a history of some injury to the tissue.

The mouth, sinuses and alveoli of the cheek teeth are frequently the site of origin of carcinomas. A ten year old saddle horse was presented at the clinic with the following history. When the horse was exercised after being on pasture he showed unusual signs. Before traveling one hundred yards he began to wheeze and cough, foam came from the mouth and nose and he continued to do this for about one-half hour. Then all of the described signs disappeared and he seemed normal as long as he was not exercised. However after resting one-half hour and then exercised he exhibited the same signs. Also when eating it was noticed that he seemed to choke on the first few mouthfuls of feed. He continued to show these signs for about six months before he was presented for examination.

Examination of the nasal cavity revealed a thickening of the mucous membrane covering the turbinates. This thickening was more pronounced on the left side of the nasal cavity. When the horse was exercised he showed the same signs as described by the owner. Whenever the horse was eating or drinking it was noticed that some food and water returned through the nasal cavity.

A resection of the nasal septum was performed to permit a more thorough examination of the nasal cavity and to provide for a freer passage of air through the nasal cavity. Examination of the nasal cavity after resection of the nasal septum revealed gangrene of the mucous membrane covering the turbinates in the posterior part of the nasal cavity. The nasal cavity was irrigated daily with mild antiseptic solutions and the gangrenous mucous membrane was removed as it loosened from the turbinates. From day to day it was noticed that more food and water was returned through the nostrils and it seemed to require more effort for the horse to swallow. Palpation of the post-pharyngeal region did not reveal any enlargement. After the horse had been in the hospital thirty days he seemed to be unable to swallow either food or water. The horse died very suddenly thirty-four days after he was admitted to the hospital.

A post-mortem examination revealed that the posterior compartment of the maxillary sinus on the left side was full of neoplastic tissue that apparently originated in the alveolus of the fifth cheek tooth. The post-pharyngeal region was filled with another mass of the same kind of tissue. This tissue was responsible for the difficulty and finally inability to swallow. There was a large mass of the same type of tissue in the abdominal cavity around and involving the tissue of the right kidney. A microscopic examination of the neoplastic tissue revealed it was a carcinoma.

The signs in a seventeen year old horse affected with carcinoma were observed over a period of six months. For approximately four months a slight mucus discharge was present each day from the right nostril. At various times a few pus cells were seen in the mucus but in a few days the discharge would be clear mucus. The fifth month after the first sign was observed the right eye became affected. The fluid in the posterior chamber became cloudy and there was also a marked increase in the fluid in the anterior and posterior chambers of the eye. During the next month there was a gradual protrusion of the right eye from the orbital cavity, then the left eye began to show the same signs. At this time a dyspnea developed and this condition became progressively more pronounced until it was necessary to use a trachea tube. The animal was destroyed and a post-mortem examination revealed that a carcinoma was responsible for the signs shown. Neoplastic tissue was present in the sinuses, orbital cavities, ethmoid cells, cranial cavity and other parts of the head.

An aged mare was presented for examination with an enlarged mammary gland. According to the owner the mammary gland had been gradually increasing in size for about a year. There were several external openings in the mammary tissue with a purulent discharge. There was also some edema in the subcutaneous tissue anterior to the mammary gland. Microscopic examination of the affected tissue revealed it to be a carcinoma. Treatment consists in extirpation of the mammary gland using the same technique as described for removal of the mammary gland of the cow.

Bovine

Carcinoma is the most common type of neoplasm occurring externally in the bovine. Carcinoma of the bovine horn is of rather rare occurrence. A number of cases have been reported as occurring at the base of the right horn in work animals in India.

A grade Shorthorn cow, nine years of age, was presented for the examination of an unusual horn growth. According to the owner the horn had been injured at two different times and the last time it was loosened at its attachment to the head. Following this injury there was a rapid proliferation of the horn-like tissue. This growth was only attached to the skin

FIG. 140. Mammary gland of a mare affected with carcinoma.

FIG. 141. Carcinoma of the bovine horn.

as it was slightly moveable. The growth was removed by an incision through the skin around the base of the horn, removing about one-half inch of skin. In approximately six months the cow was returned to the clinic with a growth similar in size and shape to the first one. This was removed in the same manner but taking a wider strip of skin around the base. The area then healed completely over and has shown no evidence of recurring. A diagnosis of a squamous cell carcinoma of the bovine horn was made after a microscopic examination of the tissue.

In the bovine carcinomas occur most frequently in the region of the orbital cavity on the eyeball, the membrane nictitans and the lower eyelid. If the neoplasm is allowed to develop it may invade the sinuses and the surrounding bony structures.

The Hereford breed seems to be most susceptible to carcinoma in and around the orbital cavity. In some sections of the country carcinomas occur almost as frequently in the Holstein as the Hereford breed. The neoplasm is practically always unilateral as it is rare to find both eyes affected with carcinoma. If the neoplasm becomes very extensive metastasis may occur to other portions of the body. In some cases it will be found that the neoplasm has invaded the sinuses producing an inoperable condition.

TREATMENT. If the owner is a close observer and finds the neoplasm when it is small, complete removal may be all the treatment necessary. If it occurs on the cornea the neoplasm should be removed close to the cornea with a sharp instrument. The wound is then cauterized with silver nitrate. When the neoplasm occurs on the third eyelid it may be necessary to remove only a portion of the third eyelid. If the neoplasm is attached on the edge of the eyelid only this portion is removed. However, if the cartilage is affected all of the third eyelid is removed.

Extirpation of the Eye

This operation is indicated in the largest percentage of cases when a carcinoma involves the eyeball and its appendages. The operation may be performed with the animal in the standing position or cast in lateral recumbency.

OPERATION. The eyelids are shaved, cleansed thoroughly and painted with a good skin

FIG. 142. Carcinoma on the cornea.

antiseptic. The operation may be performed by using a local anesthetic in the tissues. The eyelids are anesthetized by injecting a one per cent solution of a local anesthetic about one-half inch from their edge. Anesthesia of the area is completed by injecting twenty cubic centimeters of a two per cent solution of a local anesthetic into the muscles medial to the eyeball.

Nerve Block of the Eye and Associated Structures

In the March, 1951, issue of the Journal of the American Veterinary Medical Association, Peterson describes a technique for blocking the sensory nerve supply to the eye and associated structures. He recommends the use of an 18 gauge needle 4.5 inch needle and bent so that it is slightly curved. The needle is inserted so the anesthetic solution is deposited just anterior to the foramen orbitorotundum where practically all of the nerves are emerging that innervate the tissues of the eye. A short 16 gauge needle is inserted through the skin in a depression posterior to the point where the supraorbital process meets the zygomatic arch. The tissue in this area is anesthetized by infiltration with a solution of a local anesthetic. The 18 gauge needle is now inserted through the opening that was made in the skin and with the concave portion of the needle directed posteriorly. Also the hub of the needle is slightly higher than the point. The needle is then inserted until it strikes the coronoid process of the mandible. By working the needle the point slips by the anterior border of the coronoid process and is then inserted medially until it strikes the bony plate forming the floor of the pterygopalatine fossa. The depth the needle will need to be inserted will vary with the size of the head but the distance is usually from three to four and one-half inches. It is then recommended to inject fifteen cubic centimeters of a two per cent solution of a local anesthetic. By this procedure all of the nerves passing through the foramen orbitorotundum are anesthetized.

To prevent twitching of the eyelids, it is necessary to block the auriculpalpebral branch of the facial nerve. This nerve may be anesthetized by inserting the needle posteriorly in the subcutaneous tissue lateral to the zygomatic arch. The needle is inserted a distance of two to three inches depositing the anesthetic solution as the needle is pushed through the tissue.

The edges of the eyelids are sutured together with a continuous suture of tape or silk, leaving the ends several inches long. The purpose of this suture is to facilitate the application of traction on the tissues during the dissection. Starting the incision through the eyelids at one of the canthi it is made about one-fourth of an inch from the edge through the skin and subcutaneous tissue to the conjunctive. The incisions through the two eyelids are united at an equal distance beyond each canthi. In some cases the lower eyelid is extremely involved with neoplastic tissue and it may be necessary to remove practically all of the lower eyelid. The hemorrhage that occurs should be controlled by the application of forceps to the bleeding blood vessels. By careful dissection the eyelids are separated from the conjunctiva back to its attachment to the eyeball. With a pair of curved sharp scissors each of the eye muscles is severed close to their attachment to the eyeball, also the optic nerve is cut close to the eyeball. During the dissection and removal of the

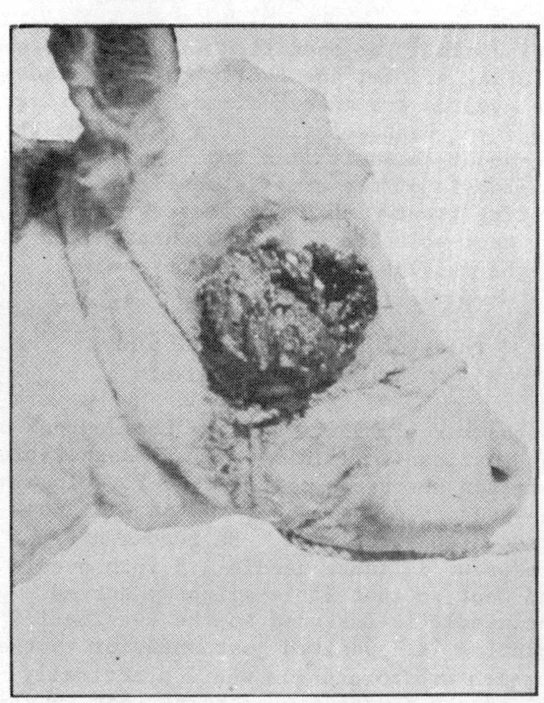

FIG. 143. When carcinomas in the orbital cavity become as extensive as this one they are inoperable.

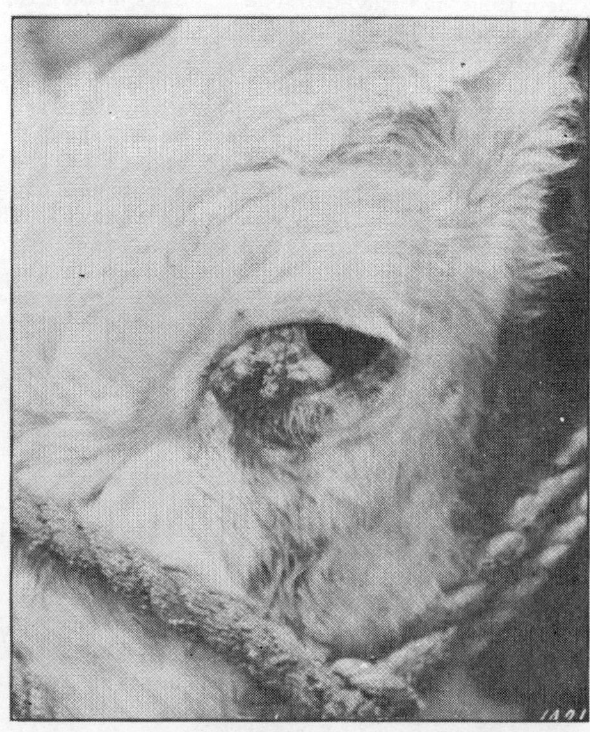

FIG. 144. A carcinoma on the third eyelid.

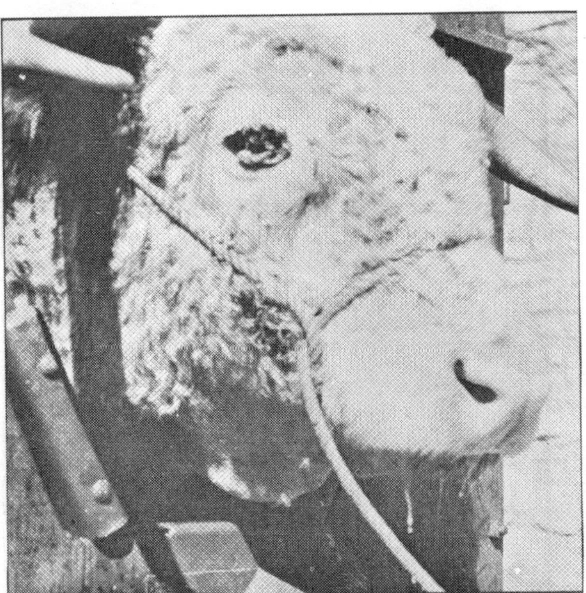

FIG. 145. Carcinoma of the third eyelid.

FIG. 146. Extensive involvement at base of ear and post-pharyngeal region with a carcinoma.

eyeball and its appendages careful palpation is made during the procedure to be certain all of the neoplastic tissue is removed. All of the muscle and fat that is healthy should be left in the oribital cavity. The hemorrhage that occurs in the depths of the cavity may be controlled during the operation by using a pressure pack of gauze or cotton. In suturing the edges of the eyelids together the best results are usually obtained if rather wide suture material, such as umbilical tape, is used. The edges of the eyelids are brought into close apposition by interrupted sutures placed one-fourth of an inch apart. In tying the sutures care should be taken not to tie them too tightly or suture necrosis may develop and delay healing of the wound. At the medial canthus an opening one inch long is left for drainage and treatment of the cavity. The temporary pack is now taken out and all blood carefully removed. If the blood is left in the wound it may become infected and delay healing. To prevent infection from developing in the orbital cavity one of the antiseptic ointments may be used. The ointment that is used should be nonirritating so there is no interference with healing of the tissues. A rather liberal quantity of this paste is placed in the cavity. To maintain the paste in contact with the tissues gauze is packed rather tightly into the cavity. The pressure maintained by the gauze is also important in preventing further hemorrhage. This gauze should be removed after forty-eight hours.

After care consists in keeping the opening at the medial canthus free of exudate so that there is free drainage at all times. Also the cavity should be examined frequently for the presence of any loose tissue. In eight to ten days the edges of the eyelids should be healed together and the sutures may be removed. However, in some cases the eyelids may not have healed together when the sutures are removed but healing will occur even after the sutures are removed. If care was taken to remove all neoplastic tissue the possibility of its recurring is remote. The technique used in this operation is also used in other species when it is necessary to remove the eye and its appendages.

In Fig. 146 carcinoma involved most of the post-pharyngeal region. Cases of this type are inoperable and euthanasia of the patient is advisable. Carcinomas are occasionally seen in the region of the anus and vulva of the bovine. In our experience the Ayrshires are most often affected but we have also observed it in the Holstein breed. In cases of this

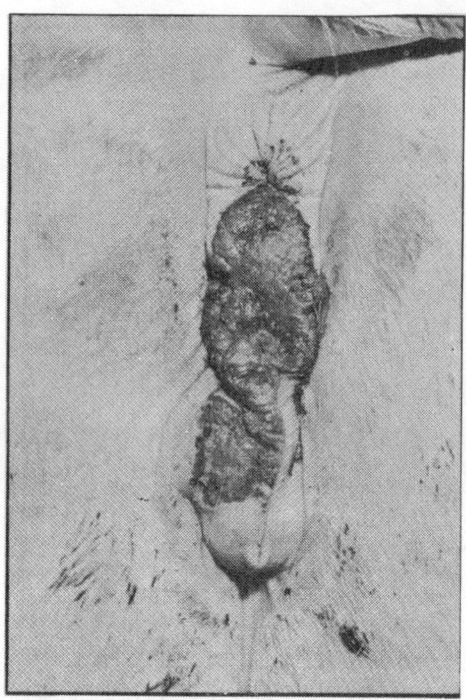

FIG. 147. Carcinoma of anus and vulva.

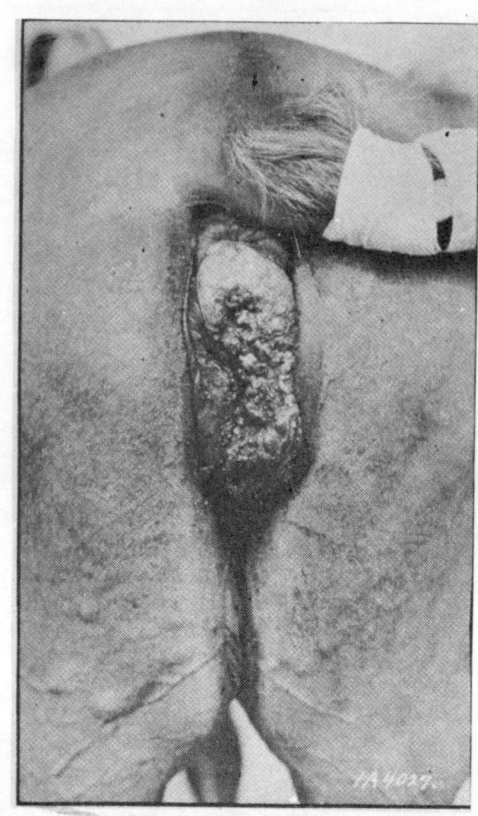

FIG. 148. Carcinoma involving the anus and vulva of a mare.

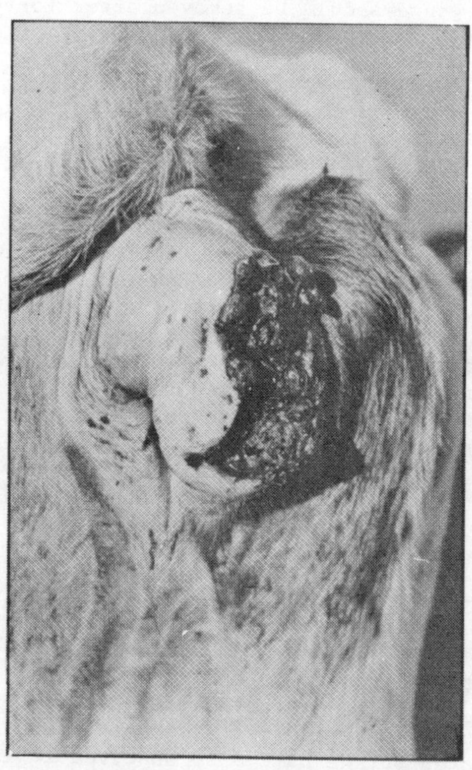

FIG. 149. Carcinoma involving the anus and vulva of Ayrshire cow.

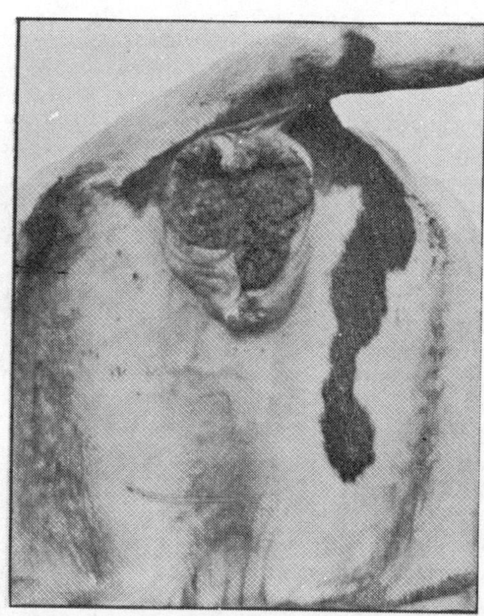

FIG. 150. A carcinoma that involves the anus and vulva of a Holstein.

type the carcinoma can be surgically removed. However, we do have carcinomas occurring in the region of the vulva that have become so extensive when they are presented for treatment that they are inoperable. A rectal examination may reveal there is metastasis into the pelvic and abdominal cavities.

Cyst

A cyst is a swelling with a wall and the contents may be fluid or semi-fluid. They may result from new growths or from distension of pre-existing ducts or spaces. Retention cysts occur when there is obstruction of the duct of a gland. Exudation cysts are formed when there is an accumulation of fluid in a pre-existing cavity, hydrocele. Congenital cysts may be due to the failure of an embryonic cavity to close. The cysts of new formation may be dermoid cysts that contain sebaceous material and hair. They occur in the ovary, testes, and skin. Some cysts occur due to foreign bodies which have become encapsulated as parasitic cysts. There may be cystic degeneration of a new growth.

Treatment of cysts may consist of excision of the wall, as in retention cysts. When the cyst involves an organ, as in dermoid cysts of the testes, the latter should be removed. In general the treatment of a cyst consists in the evacuation of its contents, and removal of the cyst.

REFERENCES

Bank, W. C., D.V.M., The Use of Radioactive Cobalt in Treating Ocular Carcinoma in Cattle, 37, (1956), 114-118, The North American Veterinarian.

Hall, Rodney E., Pharyngeal Polypus in Horse, Iowa State College Veterinarian, Vol. XX, (1958), 33.

Lundvall, R. L., D.V.M., M.S., and Campbell, Richard L., D.V.M., Chlorpromazine Hydrochloride for the Examination of the Penis in Bulls, J.A.V.M.A., 131, (July 15, 1957), pp. 86-87.

McEntee, Kenneth, Fibropapillomas of the External Genitalia of Cattle, Cornell Veterinarian, XL, (1950), 305-312.

Peterson, D. R., Nerve Block of the Eye and Associated Structures, J.A.V.M.A., Vol. CXVIII, (March, 1951), No. 888, pp. 145.

Chapter V
FRACTURES AND DISLOCATIONS

Injuries to the body of large animals that affect the bony skeleton present many difficult problems in treatment. A fracture in large animals is usually due to external violence or extreme muscular action. If the bone is fractured from twisting, the line of fracture is usually oblique. Movement and weight bearing depend upon the integrity of the bony skeleton, and when a fracture occurs, some of these functions are seriously impaired. The responsibility of the surgeon is greater in these cases, as poor end results may be accompanied by a permanent disability. In some cases the movements of the animal are not controlled after the fracture, and the ends of the bone may cause irreparable damage to the soft tissue. Also a fracture that is simple when it occurs, may become compound due to the struggling of the animal.

Definitions

A fracture is the breaking of a bone or cartilage.

An epiphyseal separation is a fracture in which the line of fracture lies wholly or partly in the epiphyseal line.

A sub-luxation is a complete dislocation in which the normal relationship of the articular surfaces is disturbed, but in which they are partly in contact.

A sprain is a temporary subluxation in which the articular surfaces have returned to their normal positions, and in which there has resulted more or less damage to the ligaments, tendons, and muscles around the joint.

A sprain fracture is a sprain in which a small portion of one of the bones, usually a ligamentous insertion, has been pulled off.

Etiology of Fractures

The causes of fractures may be divided into predisposing or indirect and exciting or direct causes.

The predisposing causes may be divided into external and physical or physiologic. Under physical or natural predisposing causes we include the liability of certain bones to fracture because of their exposed positions, shape, osseous structures or functions as levers.

Direct or Exciting Causes

These may be divided into external violence and muscular action. Most fractures are the result of external violence, which may be either direct or indirect. A fracture by direct violence is one in which the bone is broken immediately beneath the point of impact. These fractures are always accompanied by injury to the overlying soft tissues, and are often compound. In fractures from indirect violence the tissues are injured by the displacement of the fragments. These fractures are not often compound, and when they are compound, the compounding is from within, that is by the ends of the fragments being forced through the skin.

Classification of Fractures

Depending upon whether or not the fracture communicates with the outside air, fractures are classified as simple and compound. Simple fractures are those in which there is no wound. The term simple, as used in fractures, has no reference to the treatment; for a simple fracture may be very difficult or impossible to treat. Compound fractures are those in which there is an open wound extending through the skin and down to the bone injury. A primary compound fracture is one in which the wound occurs at the time of fracture either from external violence or from within by forcing of the end of a fragment through the skin. A secondary compound fracture is one in which a simple fracture has been rendered compound either by a surgical operation or by the sloughing of tissues over the site of the fractures.

DEPENDENT UPON THE DEGREE OF THE FRACTURE: Fractures may be classified as complete and incomplete, dependent upon whether or not the continuity of the bone has been completely interrupted. A subperiosteal fracture is one in which there is no obvious displacement of the fragments, and in which the periosteum is assumed to be intact. It may be incomplete or complete as regards the bone.

A greenstick fracture is an incomplete fracture of the shaft of a long bone in which the cortex is broken on the convexity of the curve in the broken bone while the bone on the concave surface is bent, and the bone is usually split longitudinally in either direction from the site of the fracture.

Dependent upon the direction and character of the line of fracture, fractures are classified as longitudinal, transverse, oblique, and spiral. Comminuted fractures are those in which there is not only a break in the continuity of the bone, but the bone is broken into three or more fragments. An impacted fracture is one in which one fragment has been driven into the other fragment and remains embedded there.

DEPENDENT UPON THE PORTION OF BONE INVOLVED: In descriptions of fractures the site of the fractures is usually stated as fracture of the shaft or lower end of the humerus or fracture through the neck. If the fracture line lies entirely within a joint cavity, it is called an intraarticular fracture, while if it involves both intraarticular and extraarticular portions of the bone, it is called a true articular fracture.

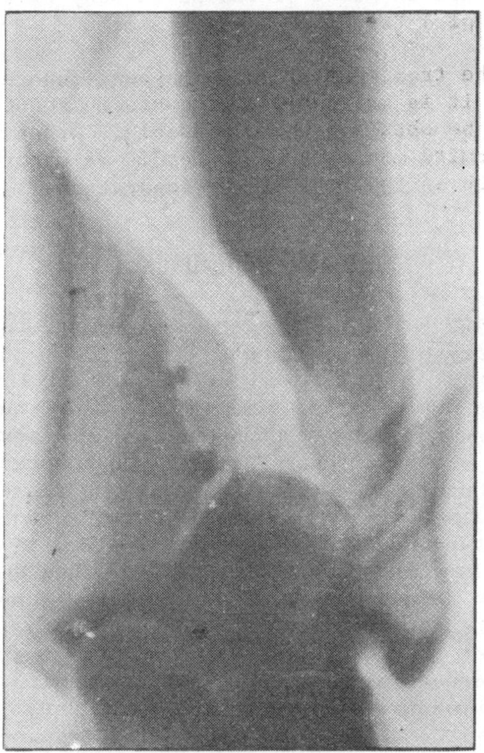

FIG. 151. A true articular fracture, at distal end of tibia, good functional recovery.

Epiphyseal Separations

Epiphyseal separations are fractures in which the fracture line lies wholly or partly within the epiphyseal line, and the epiphysis may be wholly or partly separated from the shaft. Not infrequently in an epiphyseal separation a portion of the cortex of the shaft is split off with the epiphysis. The differential diagnosis between an epiphyseal separation and a fracture can, in many instances, be made only by an X-ray, but in a fracture near a joint in a young animal in which the line of acute point tenderness lies at about the level of the epiphyseal line of the involved bone, an epiphyseal separation should be suspected. The symptoms are identical with those of a fracture except that if the fragments be moved upon one another, a soft cartilaginous crepitus is

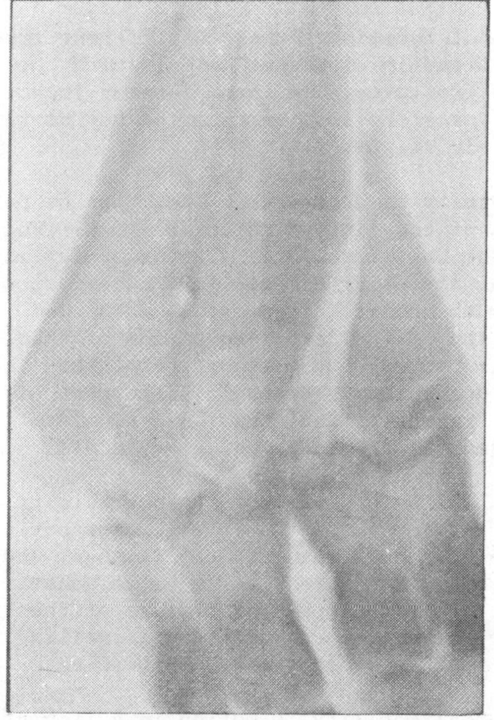

FIG. 152. Epiphyseal separation in a two year old heifer with a portion of the shaft split off.

obtained in place of the harsh bony crepitus of a true fracture.

In the treatment of an epiphyseal separation it is advisable that anatomic reduction be obtained where possible. Otherwise deformity may occur as a result of abnormal growth at the site of the separation.

Signs of Fractures

HISTORY - The history should include a history of the accident.

PAIN - Pain at the time of the injury and afterward, both spontaneous and upon movement of the fractured limb, is a constant accompaniment of fracture; but the degree of pain varies considerable in different fractures and in different animals with similar fractures. The examiner should learn as accurately as possible the character and location of the pain. The amount of tenderness varies greatly in different animals, and also varies with the amount of injury to the soft parts and with the time elapsing after the injury. If fractures are not seen until some hours after the injury, and if there is considerable swelling and damage to the soft tissue, there may be tenderness over a wide area.

Loss of function varies in different fractures and in different animals with the same fractures. In incomplete or impacted fractures the loss of function may be relatively slight.

Deformity is a change in the shape or position of the limb which is due to alteration in the bony structure. The deformity may be a shortening of the limb, a deviation from the normal alignment, an abnormal torsion of the limb, separation of the fragments or abnormal posture of the limb. The deformity is due to displacement of the fragments, and cannot occur unless the fragments are displaced.

SWELLING - The swelling in the vicinity of a fracture is the result of extravasation of blood and serum into the tissues, and in severe fractures it may be so great that it is the dominant feature of the injury. There may be additional swelling due to the shortening of the muscles.

Abnormal mobility is motion in a limb at a point or in a direction in which it does not normally occur, and ranks next to deformity in the diagnosis of fractures. Whenever it can be demonstrated, it is a pathognomonic sign of a fracture which is located at a point approximately the center of the abnormal motion. In the examination for abnormal mobility in a limb the movements should be carried no further than is necessary to make the diagnosis. In most cases this can be done without causing damage to the soft tissues or increasing the pain.

CREPITUS - In fractures crepitus is the grating sound or sensation produced by the friction of one segment moving on the other. The crepitus of a fracture is a harsh grating sensation, and may be distinguished from the soft cartilaginous crepitus which occurs in epiphyseal separations. When a true bone crepitus is heard, it is diagnostic of fracture. To produce crepitus the ends of the fragments must be in contact and then moved upon one another. However, with the X-ray, the fracture can be definitely determined so crepitus is not always necessary to make a diagnosis. When the ends of the fragments are in contact, crepitus may be felt or heard during the examination to demonstrate false motion.

The X-ray has extended our knowledge of fractures and helped to improve our methods of treatment. It is an excellent means of aiding in diagnosis and in clearing up some points about the injury which cannot be determined by a physical examination. This is especially true of fractures without displacement or small fractures in the region of joints that are impossible or difficult to diagnose without an X-ray.

Repair of Fractures

With the breaking of a bone there is a variable amount of soft tissue damage and rupture of blood vessels in the surrounding area. This consists not only of the bone itself and periosteum, but also the muscles and connective tissue around the bone. When the fracture occurs as the result of direct violence, there is damage to the soft tissue and to traumatism from the ends of the fragments. The rupture of blood vessels of the bone and surrounding tissue results in an extravasation of blood into the area. This blood eventually clots, and the fibrin clot contracts and the ends of the bone are surrounded by a blood clot. As with any other blood clot in the tissue it tends to become organized by the ingrowth of young blood vessels and fibroblasts. Usually a blood clot may be either absorbed or is replaced by scar tissue that varies a great deal in extent. The scar tissue is the result of the maturation of the granulation tissue.

When a blood clot occurs in the subcutaneous tissue, it usually disappears; but with blood clot in the case of a fracture, there is a normal tendency for the granulation tissue to form a callus and this to be replaced by bone. The difference seems to be determined by the presence of bone in the hematoma. This may consist of bone or the mineral in the bone matrix, the osteogenic cells or osteoblasts, which normally cover the surface and line the spaces in the bone.

When a bone is broken, the ends do not heal in the strict sense of the word there is no tendency for actual growth to take place from the end of bone fragment; but under favorable conditions the continuity of the bone becomes reestablished by the soldering together of the ends of the fragments by new tissue which is formed around and between them. This is also true of cartilage when it is cut. The ends do not heal together, but repair takes place by ingrowth of other tissue which binds the surfaces together.

In the case of a fracture then we have, first, the hematoma, in which the blood clots and becomes organized. The difference between this and the ordinary blood clot is that from the sixth to the tenth day after the injury, the fibrin clot begins to undergo a change into a tissue which is called a callus. The characteristics of callus which distinguish it from other forms of granulation tissue are that it contains areas of cartilage and areas of calcification and ossification. The amount of cartilage varies considerably, and seems to be due to an attempt on the part of nature to immobilize the fragments by the formation of a temporary semirigid tissue. Usually the more perfectly the fracture is reduced and immobilized the less the amount of cartilage that is produced. The invasion of the clot by connective tissue takes place from all sides, that is from the surrounding tissues and from the periosteum and from the medullary canal. If the fragments are separated, the cartilage is formed in the space between the fragments and at various points in the organized hematoma. These cells swell, assume a mature or senile appearance and the semifluid or gelatinous intercellular material tends to solidify and become cartilaginous in character. This is not true cartilage, but is better called chrondroid tissue. These islets may coalesce so that the fracture is surrounded by a large mass of this tissue. This temporary healing of the fracture by a mass of chrondoid tissue or cartilaginous callus serves to immobilize the fragments to a considerable degree. In addition to the cartilage in the callus there is also a variable amount of calcification and ossification. The bone that is formed differs from normal bone in that it is irregular in its structure and is a type of spongy bone. Thus we have the two bone ends surrounded by and imprisoned in a mass of callus which consists of connective tissue, cartilage, and spongy bone. So far the ends of the fragments have acted as dead pieces of bone which they really are.

With the formation of the callus there is a beginning formation of true bone. This usually begins beneath the periosteum around the fragments and also at some distance from the site of the fracture. This true bone is in the beginning cancellous in character and consists of fine trabeculae. It begins at the sixth to the tenth day, and gradually grows down toward the ends of the fragments to invade and replace the callus. With the invasion of the callus by the ultimate bone which is to heal the fracture, there is a tendency to resorption of excess callus around the site of fracture. Eventually the true bone growing from beneath the periosteum of each fragment meets and fuses across the defect. This bone which is first spongy in character becomes transformed into dense cortical bone. Also there is an attempt by nature to restore the normal form of the original bone.

FACTORS RESPONSIBLE FOR NON-UNION:

1. Time element in the treatment of fractures is very important as every hour that elapses after the injury adds to the swelling. If there is overriding, the time element adds to the shortening and to the muscle spasm which must be overcome if reduction is to be obtained. The swelling incident to the extravasation of blood renders reduction more difficult while if the patient is treated immediately, the reduction could be accomplished with ease.

2. Position of the bone fragments may determine if union will result. If the gap between the ends is longer than the tissues are able to form a callus or the distance is greater than can be transversed by bone from the fragments, non-union will result.

3. If the parts are not immobilized as nearly absolute as possible, any movement will tend to break apart the callus. While it is true the callus is of such a nature that it heals rapidly after injury and possibly the formation of a larger callus. However, the lack of immobilization may result in involution of the callus and the formation of fibrous tissue and a fibrous union.

4. If muscle tissue or fascia is interposed between the fragments, the new bone growing from either fragment may be unable to penetrate this tissue and non-union may occur.

5. Compound fractures heal more slowly than do simple fractures because the blood escapes and a hematoma is not formed. Also in these fractures there is unuslly extensive damage to the soft parts, the blood supply to a rather large area may be destroyed which results in necrosis of this tissue. In these cases repair is inadequate or fibrosis may only occur, or the granulating tissue may be unable to bridge the gap. So in these cases non-union may be due to the extensive damage to the soft tissue or to incomplete reduction and immobilization.

Infection by pyogenic organisms may in some cases stimulate the formation of bone. However, infection more often in acute fractures tends to cause non-union because of rapid autolysis of the fibrin clot, and thus removes the framework that is to form the callus. This is the result of action from the leucocytes which have accumulated in the area as the result of the infection.

Infection of a compound fracture has been accepted as an adequate explanation of the non-union so commonly observed. In exceptional cases virrulent infection may destroy so much bone and the gap may be filled with such dense cicatricial tissue that non-union is almost inevitable. In most cases non-union is due not to the infection, but to the inadequate immobilization permitted because of the infection. Immobilization may have been inefficient from the beginning because attempts were made to dress or irrigate the wound at regular intervals, or there may have been failure to continue immobilization for a sufficiently long period. An infected fracture is exactly like a simple fracture except that each stage of repair is prolonged.

Fractures of the Bones of the Head

Fracture of the bones of the head usually occurs as the result of a severe blow. A horse may throw itself over backwards striking the head on the ground or other hard surface. The fracture that occurs may involve the cranial bones so there is a permanent central nervous system injury. Some injuries may cause a depression of a portion of the frontal, malar, maxilla or nasal bones. In many cases it is possible to elevate the fractured portion of the bone to its normal position. In some cases a fracture may occur rather easily. A horse was being ridden at a slow trot, stumbled and struck the nose on the ground. Examination revealed a fracture of the nasal process of the premaxilla as shown in Fig. 153. This was a green stick type of fracture and when the parts were returned to their normal position, the different pieces meshed together so tight, the parts were held without any splint.

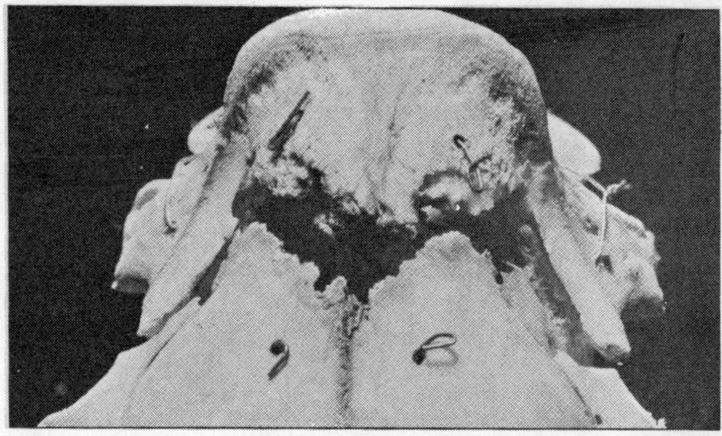

FIG. 153. Fracture of the skull that occurred when six months old colt fell over backwards striking head on hard ground.

Fracture of the Body of Premaxillae

Unusual case of fracture of the premaxillae was presented with all of the incisor teeth reflected upward except one incisor tooth. The treatment of this case was simplified because the one incisor tooth was still in place. This fracture apparently occurred when the halter rope was caught under the incisor teeth and the patient exerted vigorous efforts to get the rope out of its mouth. Enough of the body of the premaxillae was included in the fracture to hold the incisor teeth together. The portion of the bone holding the incisor teeth was returned to its normal position. The bones were held in close and firm apposition by a No. 18 stainless steel wire fastened around the corner incisor tooth, that was not included in the fracture, and a lateral incisor tooth. A good callus was formed and the patient made an uneventful recovery.

Fracture Through the Symphysis Mandibulae

Fracture through the symphysis mandibulae of the bovine does not occur very often. It would seem that fracture through the symphysis would occur frequently as the two halves are not completely fused even in mature animals. The fracture shown in Fig. 158 occurred when the patient became excited and was difficult to control. The fracture was immobilized by fastening a No. 25 stainless steel wire around the intermediate incisor teeth.

Bilateral Fracture of Mandibles in Interdental Space

Fracture of one or both mandibles occurs most frequently in colts and calves. The fracture usually occurs from kicks or running into posts or some solid object.

FIG. 154. Fracture of the nasal process of the premaxilla with displacement of body of premaxilla.

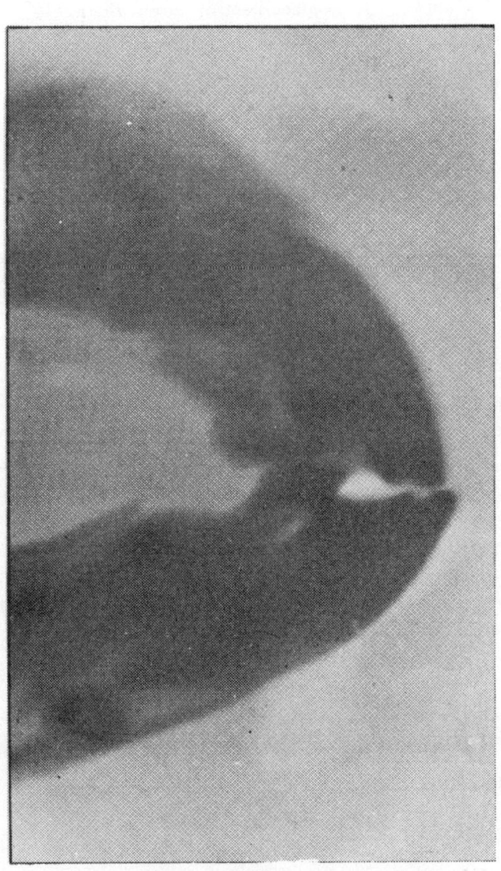

FIG. 155. After body of the premaxilla was elevated to its normal position.

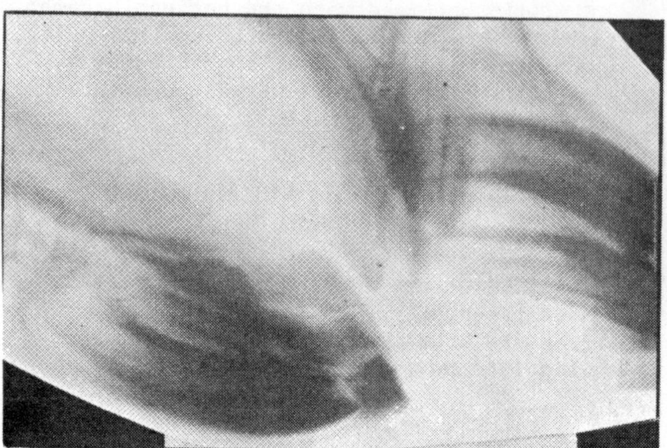

FIG. 156. Fracture of body of premaxillae with displacement of incisor teeth.

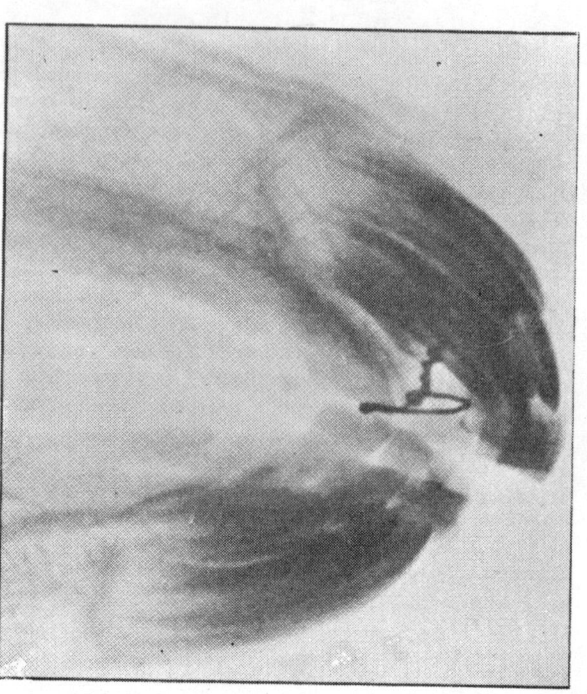

FIG. 157. After the fracture was reduced and the incisor teeth are in normal position.

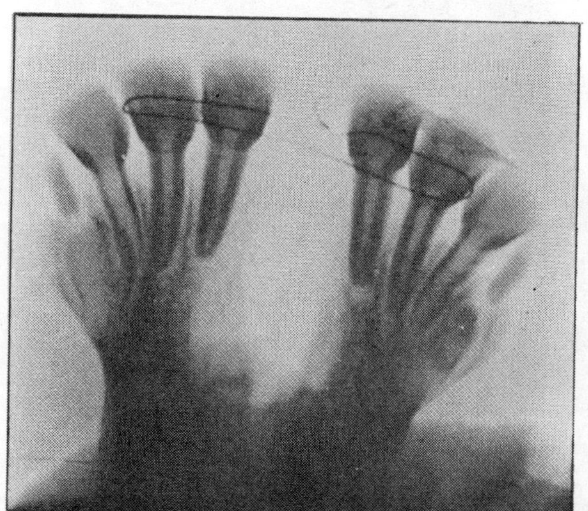

FIG. 158. Fracture through Symphysis Mandibularis in four year old cow.

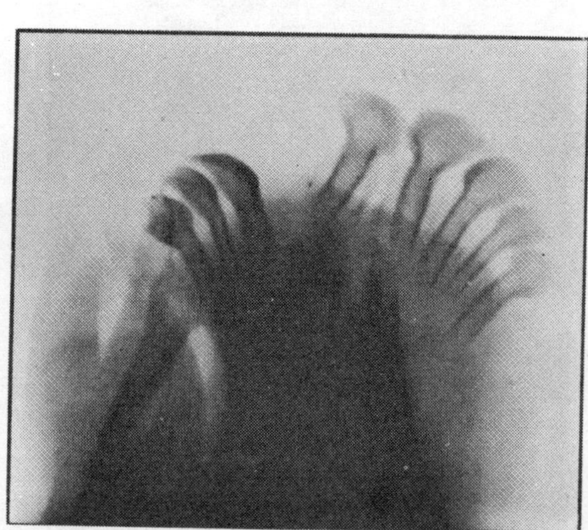

FIG. 159. Fracture of body of mandible with displacement of five incisor teeth.

TREATMENT. To control the patient a sufficient amount of a general anesthetic may be used. The fracture may be immobilized by using a No. 25 stainless steel wire, passing it between the first and second cheek teeth and around the corner incisor tooth. To facilitate passing the wire between the cheek teeth a stab wound is made through the cheek opposite to the separation between the two teeth. Then a one-eighth inch drill bit is introduced through the wound and a hole is drilled through between the teeth. A curved needle carrying the wire is passed through the opening and around the corner incisor tooth. The ends of the bones are put in close apposition and the body of the mandible placed in its normal position, the wire is pulled tight and the ends tied. A callus should be developed in two to four weeks and the wire or wires may be removed.

Fracture of Body of Mandible

Frequently colts and calves in running and playing or are frightened run into a solid object and fracture a portion of the body of the mandible. In Fig. 159 is shown a fracture of the body of the mandible with displacement of five of the incisor teeth, that occurred in calf three months of age. A piece of No. 25 stainless steel wire was passed around the intermediate incisor teeth and tightened until the displaced teeth were in their normal position and wire was tied. In approximately one month there was a good strong callus.

Fractures of the Scapula

Fractures of the scapula occur only occasionally in large animals. When a fracture does occur it is usually through the neck and not the body of the bone. If the fracture occurs through the body there is little displacement and usually lack of crepitation. It may be rather difficult to make a definite diagnosis of fracture. When the fracture occurs through the neck crepitation will be heard and also increased mobility of the parts.

The only way to treat fractures of the scapula is by complete rest as it is impossible to use a splint to immobilize the part.

Fractures of the Humerus

Fractures of the humerus usually occur in large animals from extreme muscular action or a traumatism. The fracture may occur through any part of the bone. If the fracture is oblique the sharp ends produced may cause extensive damage to the soft tissue. This injury of the soft tissue will cause excessive swelling in this area. Lameness is very pronounced with the limb held in a typical position as in Fig. 161. The joints of the limb are extended with the front of the hoof resting on the ground. Crepitus may or may not be present depending upon the position of the ends of the bones. A fracture of the humerus is a serious condition in large animals as it is impossible to immobilize the bones with splint or bandage. However if the fracture is transverse with little or no displacement of the bones, good healing may occur if the animal is kept quiet. In young animals, both colts and calves, we have had good recoveries. Also in the cow good functional healing has occurred but our cases in the mature horse have been unsuccessful.

Fractures of the Ulna

In the horse fractures of the ulna usually occur as the result of falls or kicks. The fracture may involve the joint but usually the olecranon process is the part affected. When this occurs there is marked lameness, swelling and intense pain is shown on palpation of the region. The upper portion of the fragment is pulled forward by the muscles as shown in Fig. 162. Due to the displacement of the bones by the pull of the muscles it is impossible to hold them in a position until union is complete.

As a general rule the prognosis is unfavorable in horses with fracture of the olecranon process. However, the case shown in Fig. 163 made a good functional recovery. For a short time after the fracture occurred he was confined in slings but did not seem to do well. He was then turned loose in a small lot and in a month was using the limb in a normal manner at the walk. The use of slings seems to be contra-indicated in fractures of the olecranon process.

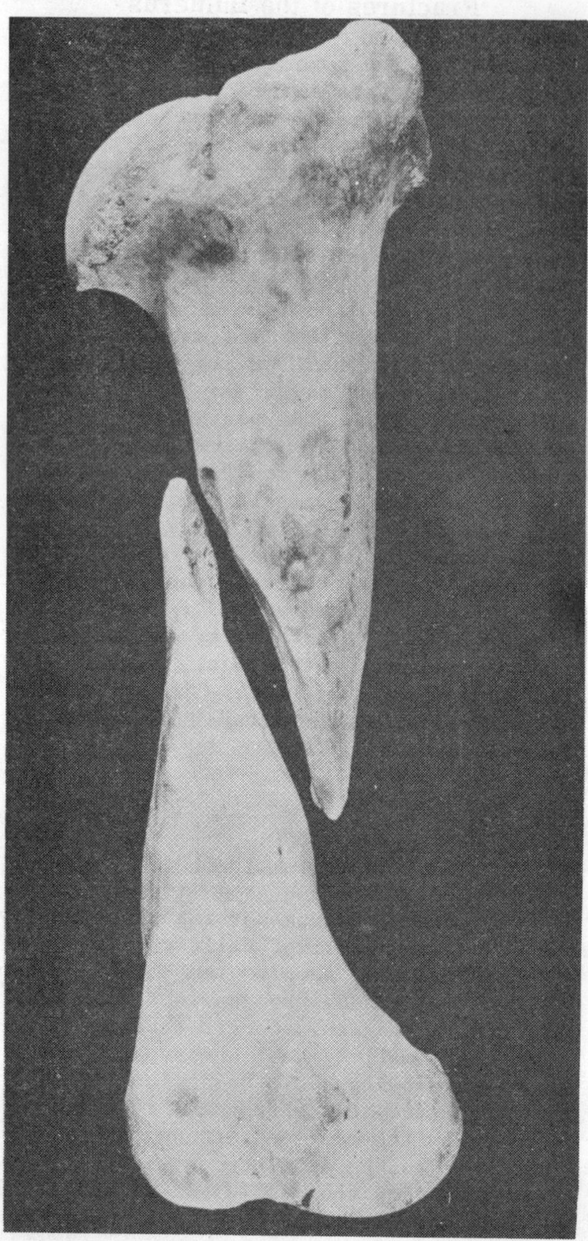

FIG. 160. Oblique fracture of the humerus, there was extensive swelling of the soft tissue.

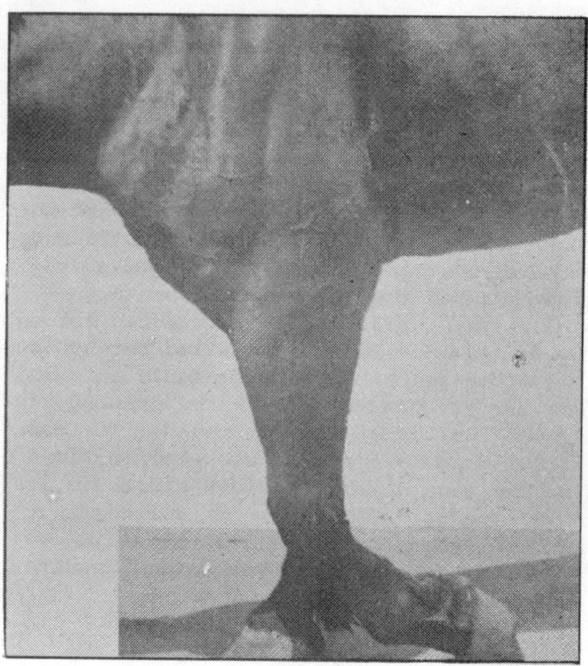

FIG. 161. Typical attitude of the limb in fracture of the humerus.

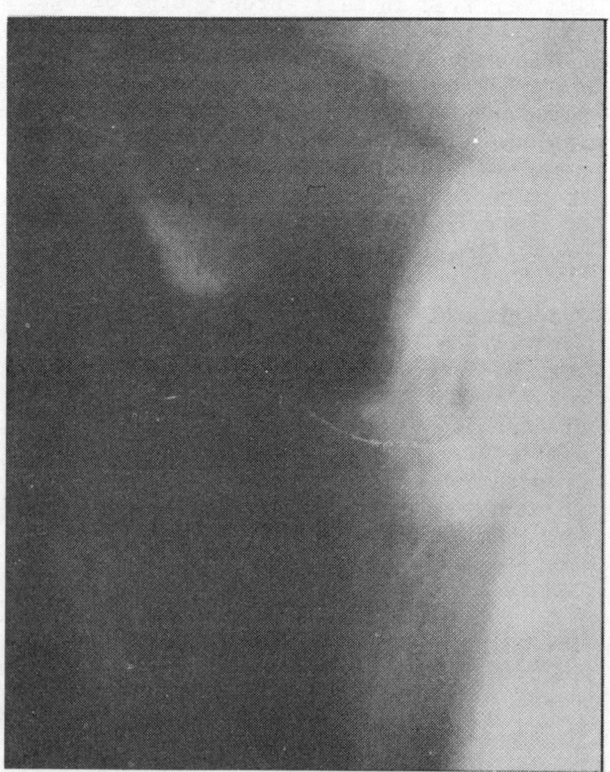

FIG. 162. Fracture of the olecranon process with displacement of the parts.

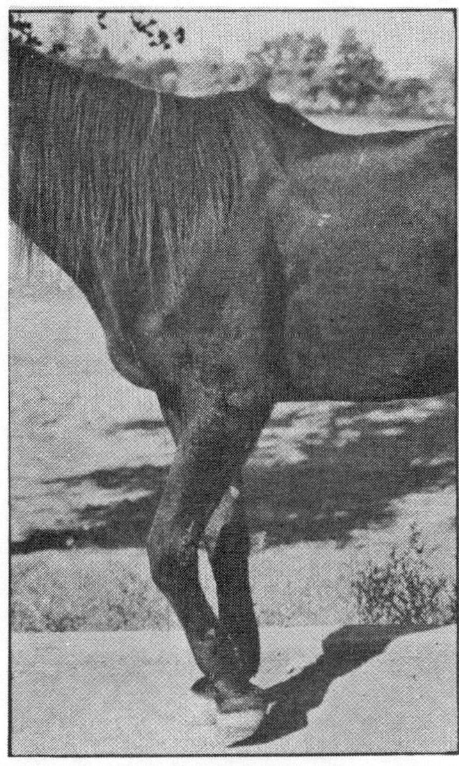

FIG. 163. The attitude of the limb when the olecranon process is fractured.

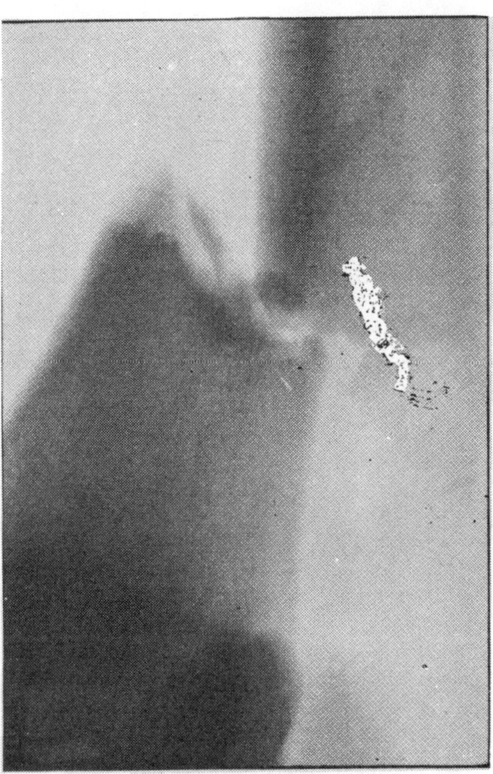

FIG. 164. A complete fracture of the large metacarpal bone.

Fractures of the Radius

Fracture of the radius does not occur as frequently as some of the other long bones of the limbs particularly the tibia. In the colt fracture of the radius and ulna may occur as the result of a kick or other traumatism. In these cases there is usually a marked displacement of the ends of the bone. According to some writers, complete fractures of the radius are generally regarded as incurable. However Miars records good recovery in a twenty year old horse and a six months old colt. If the parts can be held in apposition until a strong callus forms, a good recovery is usually obtained.

Fractures of the Carpal Bones

Fracture of the carpal bones is of frequent occurrence in the equine. Any one of the carpal bones may be affected but the third, radial and intermediate and the distal end of the radius are most frequently fractured. The carpal fractures occur more frequently in horses used for racing where there is extreme flexing and extension of the joint. Also the concussion of these bones from the added weight of the rider may be a contributing factor.

When fracture of a carpal bone occurs there is lameness and inflammatory swelling of the tissues over the fracture. This swelling of the tissues is suggestive of the presence of a fracture but a radiograph is necessary to definitely identify a fracture and determine its extent. It may be necessary to take radiographs from several different angles to obtain all of the necessary information as to the location of the fracture. Palpation of the swollen tissue may reveal a sensitive area that indicates the exact location of the fracture. Lameness may be present all of the time or may be intermittent depending upon the size and location of the fracture. It would be unusual for a carpal fracture to heal without removal or fixation. When a slab fracture is present there may be a question as to whether it should be removed or fixed in position with a bone screw. Before using a bone screw careful consideration should be given to the possibility it may stimulate an excessive amount of calcification. Quite frequently there is a definite displacement of the fragment and surgical removal is necessary.

FIG. 165. Slab fracture of third carpal bone.

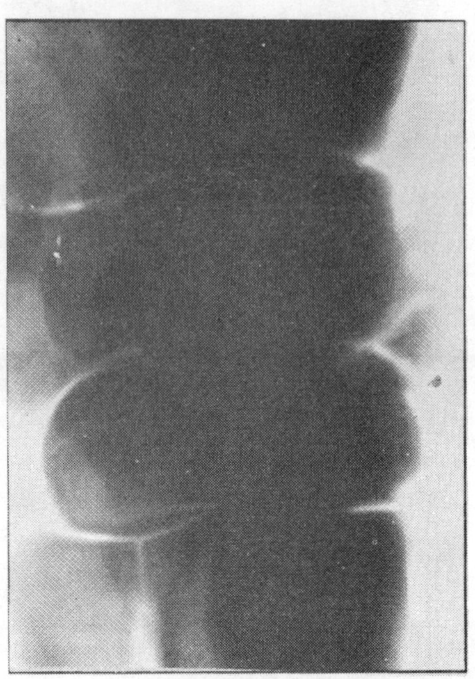

FIG. 166. Chip fracture of intermediate carpal bone.

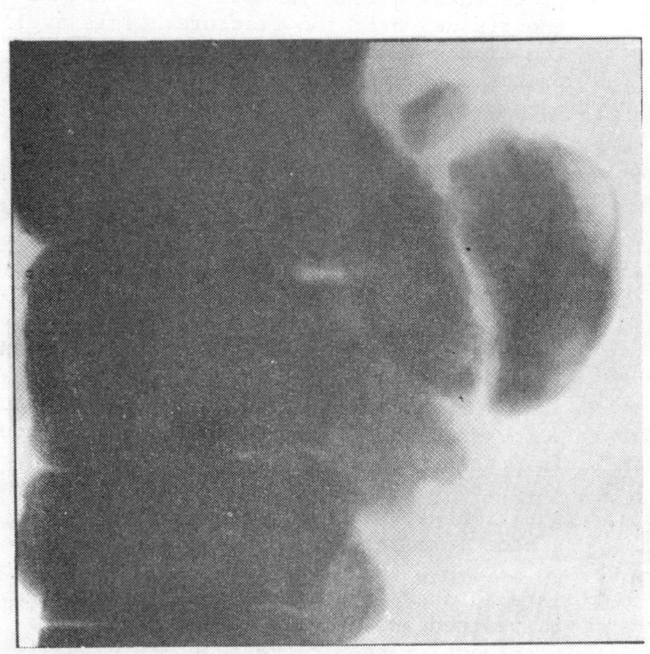

FIG. 167. Fracture of accessory carpal bone.

FIG. 168. Fracture of the second metacarpal bone.

TREATMENT. The operative area may be prepared by clipping and shaving before the patient is confined in lateral recumbency. All preparations should be made to perform an aseptic operation. Anesthesia of the tissues in the operative area may be obtained by infiltration of the tissues dorsal to the area. The patient may be controlled during the operation by using enough of a general anesthetic, the one that is used will depend upon the preference of the operator. Hemorrhage may be controlled by the use of a tourniquet and the use of ligatures when necessary. The skin incision over the affected area should be liberal enough to provide good access to the fracture. Continue the incision through the subcutaneous tissue, the fibrous portion of the joint capsule and the synovial membrane. The edges of the tissues should be reflected to provide a good view of the carpal bones. All of the bone fragments should be removed and a periosteal elevator will help in finding those in which separation of the fracture line has not occurred. Any rough fracture surfaces should be made smooth with a currette. The joint capsule should be closed with catgut sutures inserted in the fibrous part of the joint capsule. The subcutaneous tissue is closed with catgut and the skin with either silk or nylon. A dry sterile pack is bandaged over the wound. To prevent flexion of the carpus a metal splint is placed on the posterior surface of the limb and bandaged in position. The pack over the wound may be changed every three days until the wound is healed, also the splint. Until the wound has healed the patient should be closely confined as any unnecessary movement during this period may stimulate irritation of the tissues. For the first two months after the wound has healed exercise should be limited to walking. For the next four months exercise may be gradually increased but training should not be started until six months after the operation.

Fracture of Accessory Carpal Bone

Fracture of accessory carpal bone does occur and the lameness is continuous. If the examination reveals an inflammatory reaction around the accessory carpal bone a radiograph will reveal the fracture. Usually the fragment is not displaced so treatment consists in keeping the patient confined in a box stall.

Fracture of Metacarpals or Metatarsals

Fracture of the small metacarpal or metatarsal bones is of frequent occurrence in horses used at fast gaits. The cause of these fractures is not definitely known but trauma may be the causative factor in most of the cases. Occasionally a horse will kick into a solid object producing a compound fracture of one of the small metatarsal bones. Most of the fractures occur at the distal end of the bones but it may involve any portion. If the fracture occurs in the portion of the bone in close contact with the third metacarpal or metatarsal good healing may occur. When the distal free end is fractured the formation of a good callus would be unusual. The presence of inflammatory tissue over the fracture, some sensitiveness of the area and lameness suggests the presence of a fracture. A radiograph will reveal the fracture.

TREATMENT. The operation may be performed with the patient standing or in lateral recumbency depending upon the case. Anesthesia of the operative area may be obtained by blocking the volar or plantar nerves and infiltration of the tissues dorsal to the operative area. If it is desired to confine the patient in lateral recumbency a general anesthetic may be used.

Operative area should be prepared for an aseptic operation. Depending upon the amount of inflammatory or fibrous tissue surrounding the fracture will determine the location of the incision in the skin. It may be necessary to cut some of the fibrous tissue so the fragment may be removed. If the end of the bone is rough it should be made smooth. The skin incision is closed with closely placed sutures. A snug fitting bandage is placed over the wound to control the hemorrhage. The bandage is changed in two days and the wound is kept bandaged until it is healed. It is best to limit exercise for sixty days.

Fracture of the Proximal Sesamoids in the Equine

Fracture of one or both proximal sesamoids is of frequent occurrence in horses used for racing. As a general rule in the Thoroughbred the fractures usually occur in the fore limbs while in the Standardbred the incidence of fracture is greater in the

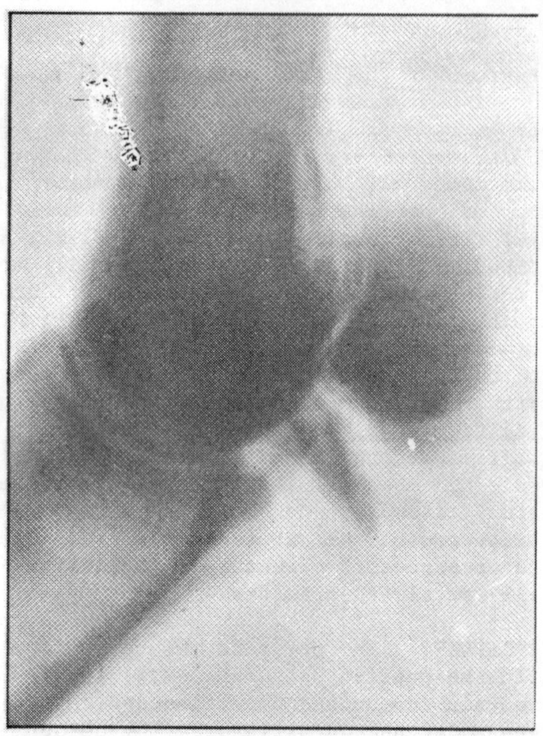

FIG. 169. Fracture of the lateral proximal sesamoid.

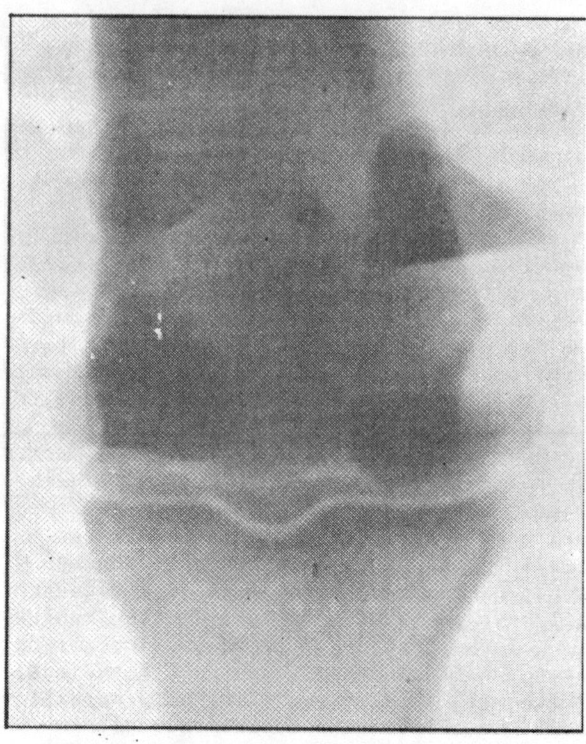

FIG. 170. Fractures of the two proximal sesamoid bones.

hind limb. The exact cause of the fractures has never been determined. However any unusual strain occurring on the tissues in the sesamoid area may be responsible for the fracture. Some of the contributing factors have been, stepping on an uneven surface, leaving the toes too long producing more strain on the posterior surface of the fetlock joint, trauma to the sesamoid area. Also muscle fatigue may be an important factor, as more strain is placed upon the ligaments and other supporting structures of the sesamoid area.

DIAGNOSIS. The signs of the fracture will depend upon: the location of the fracture, the size of the fragment, displacement of the fracture portion and probably the causative factor. A variable amount of swelling will be found over the fractured sesamoid. Also the pain in the region of the fracture will vary depending upon whether it is a recent or chronic fracture and the size of the fracture. To make a definite diagnosis it is necessary to make radiographs from a sufficient number of angles so the location and size of the fragment may be determined.

TREATMENT. Conservative methods may be used but the results are only satisfactory in a small percentage of the cases. If the fractured portion is small and the parts are in apposition complete recovery may occur with rest. The structure of the sesamoid bone is such that a good bone callus may not develop, the union is apt to be fibrous in nature. The patient may seem to be alright but when the tissues are subjected to the strain of training and racing the lameness will recur. In most cases time will be saved, if not more than one-third of the proximal portion of the sesamoid bone is fractured, by an operation.

OPERATION. The ideal time to operate is within thirty days from the time of the fracture. However operations have been successful when performed several months after the fracture. It is essential for the operation to be performed aseptically and all the necessary preparations should be made to achieve this objective. The tissues in the operative area may be anesthetized by blocking either the volar or plantar nerves. Anesthesia to control the patient will depend upon the preference of the operator. The patient is confined in lateral recumbency with the operative area in the most accessible position for the operator. The skin incision approximately three inches long through the skin and subcutaneous tissue is made halfway between the posterior border of the third metacarpal or metatarsal bone and the suspensory ligament. To expose the sesamoid bone the incision is continued through the joint capsule from the base to the top of the sesamoid bone. In some cases it may be desirable to flex the fetlock joint so the sesamoid bone may be examined more thoroughly, by inspection and palpation. The bone fragment or fragments should be removed as carefully as possible. Any attachments of soft tissue should be cut with scissors or scalpel with a small blade. In some cases a bone chisel may be useful to divide any fibrous attachment of the fragment. If the remaining fracture surface is rough a currette may be used until it is smooth. For some fractures on the ventral surface of the sesamoid bone a longitudinal incision on the posterior surface of the fetlock joint will provide the best approach to the fracture.

All incised tissues should be sutured separately with catgut except the skin which may be sutured with nylon. A dry bandage is applied over the wound, this bandage may be changed in three days. The patient is confined in a box stall for one week and then careful exercise. After four to six months of controlled exercise the patient may be put into training.

Fracture of the Phalanges

When fracture of one of the phalanges occurs it is usually due to a false step, a twist or may be traumatic. Fractures of these bones occur more frequently in horses used at fast gaits. If a severe lameness appears suddenly while the horse is in motion and examination reveals pain and swelling of the pastern, a tentative diagnosis of a fracture is justified. However, if there is absence of crepitation and increased mobility, an X-ray may be necessary to confirm the diagnosis.

In simple fracture of the first phalanx, good healing should be obtained by immobilization. When the fracture is comminuted and intra-articular healing may occur but it may produce a chronic lameness.

Fractures of the second phalanx are very unfavorable as it is usually a comminuted fracture. The callus that develops is usually very extensive and results in a permanent lameness.

In most fractures of the third phalanx good recovery may be expected as the fracture is held in position by the horny hoof. Fractures of the third phalanx occur most frequently in race horses or those horses used at fast gaits. When the fracture occurs there is marked lameness and the animal may refuse to bear any weight on the limb. According to the owner the horse was running down a steep hill, slipped and fell. When he got up the foot was held off the ground and he refused to put it down to the ground.

SIGNS. In fracture of the third phalanx the horse becomes lame and the lameness is characteristic of a foot lameness. Until healing occurs the lameness remains about the same, it does not get any worse nor does it show any improvement. One outstanding sign is that when pressure is applied on the sides of the foot with the hoof testers the horse shows definite evidence of pain.

TREATMENT. Rest is the only treatment necessary as the wall provides the best possible splint for the third phalanx. In the fracture shown in the picture Fig. 173 the lameness disappeared in two months.

In Fig. 175 the line of fracture is on the median line and extends up to the articulation.

When the horse was presented for examination for a persistent type of lameness he had been lame for approximately three months. When the hoof testers were applied to the lateral and medial sides of the foot there was evidence of pain. A radiograph of the foot revealed a definite fracture of the third phalanx. It was about one year before the horse recovered from the lameness.

Fractures of the Pelvis

In large animals fractures of the pelvis usually occur as the result of falls on hard surfaces. They have also been observed to occur in cows that were being ridden or were riding cows in oestrum. One of the most frequent fractures that occur are those involving the tuber coxae or external angle of the ilium. This fracture occurs when the animal strikes the tuber coxae against the side of the doorway, from traumatism or falling on a hard surface. After the acute signs of inflammation subside, lameness disappears

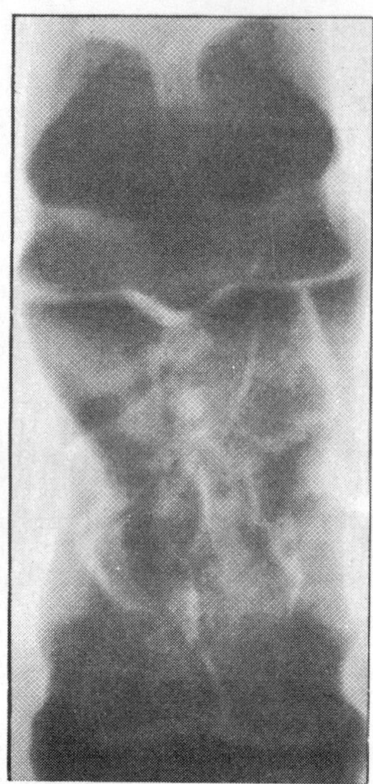

FIG. 171. Comminuted fracture of first phalanx.

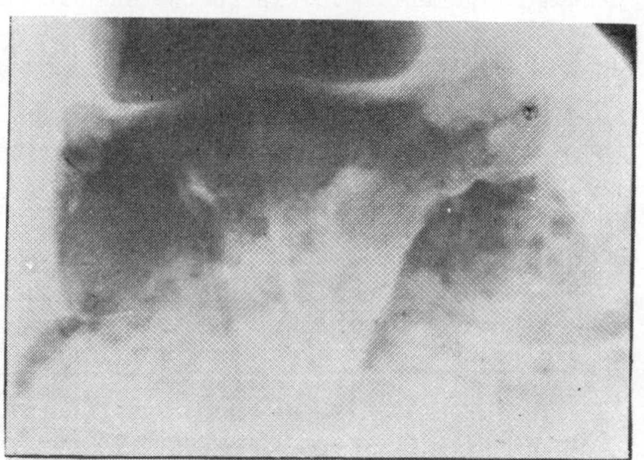

FIG. 173. Line of fracture is shown on medial side of third phalanx.

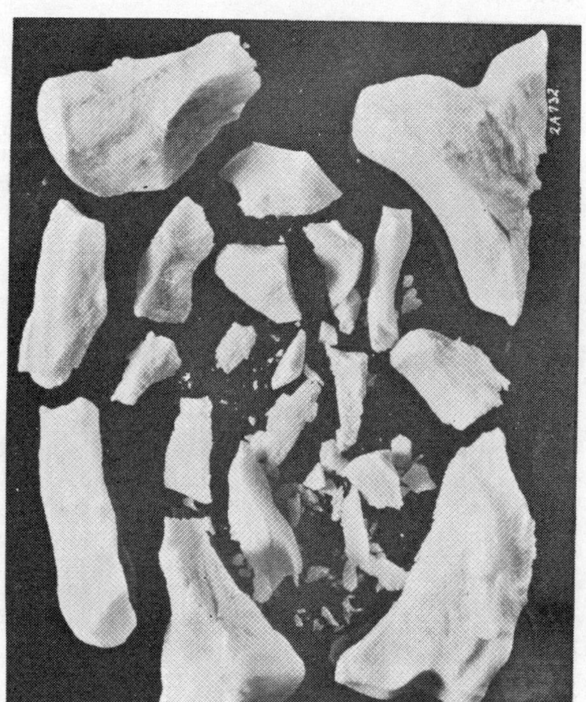

FIG. 172. Comminuted fracture of the second phalanx that occurred during a polo game.

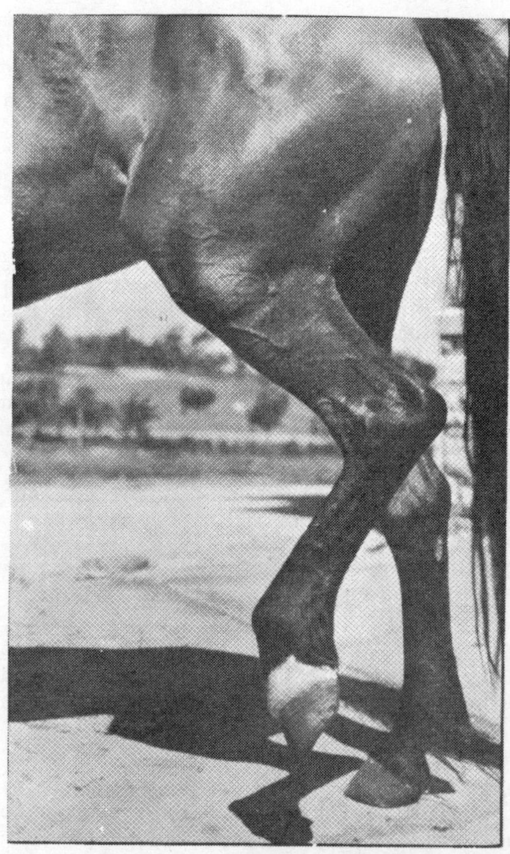

FIG. 174. Attitude of the limb twenty-four hours after fracture of the third phalanx.

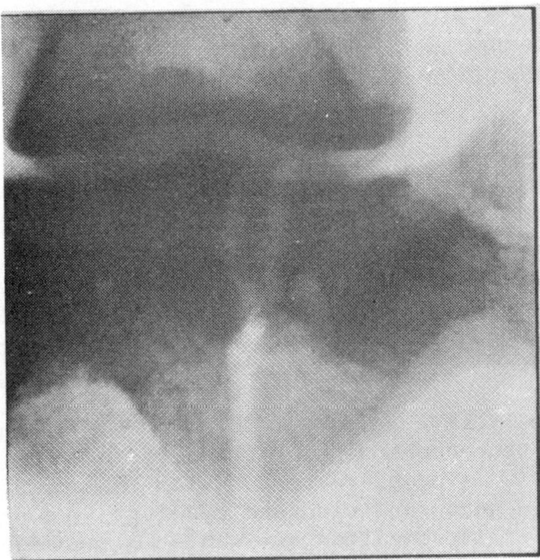

FIG. 175. Line of fracture through median line of third phalanx.

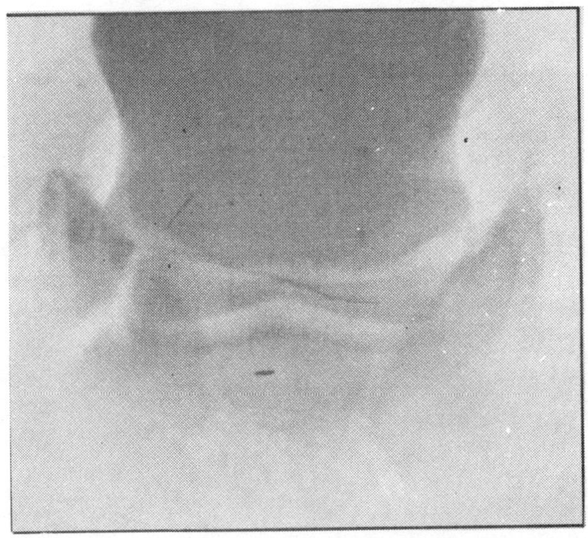

FIG. 176. Fracture of the lateral angle of the third phalanx, it was necessary to perform a posterior digital neurectomy for the lameness, after healing occurred.

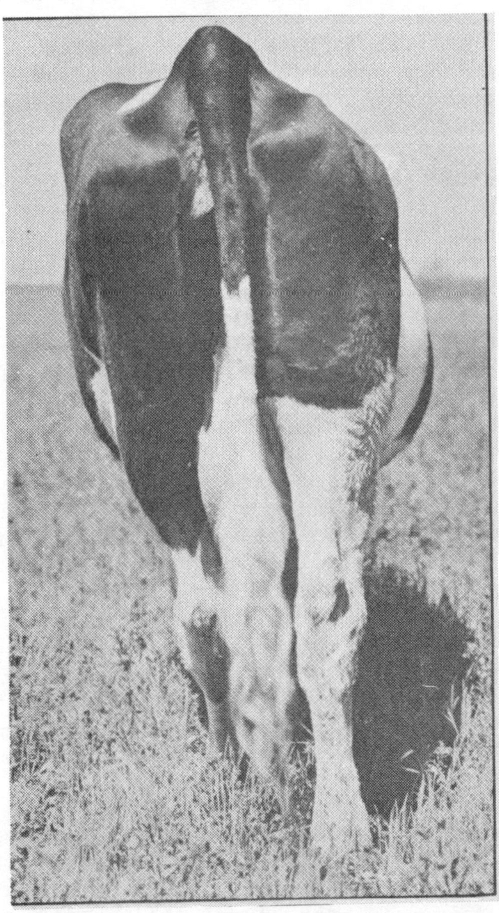

FIG. 177. Fracture of the right tuber coxae, with displacement of the fractured portion.

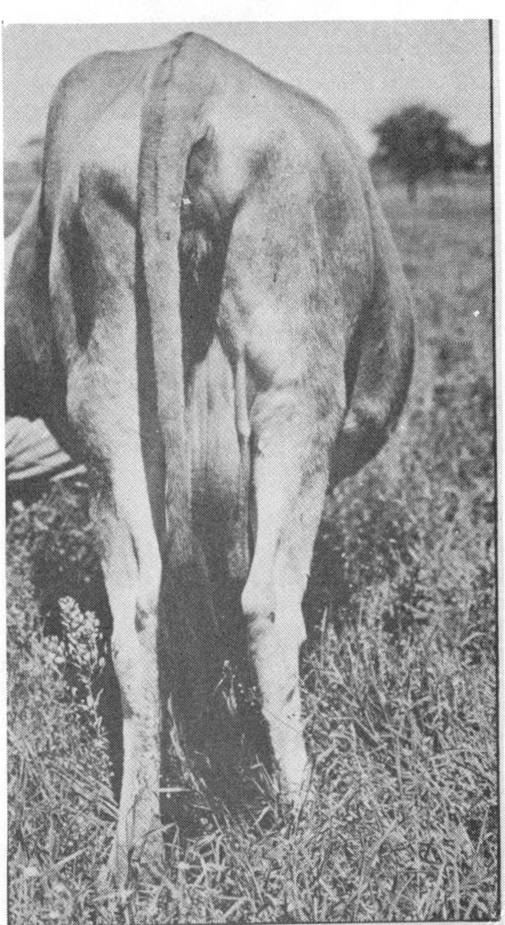

FIG. 178. Fracture through the shaft of the ilium, with displacement of the ends of the bones.

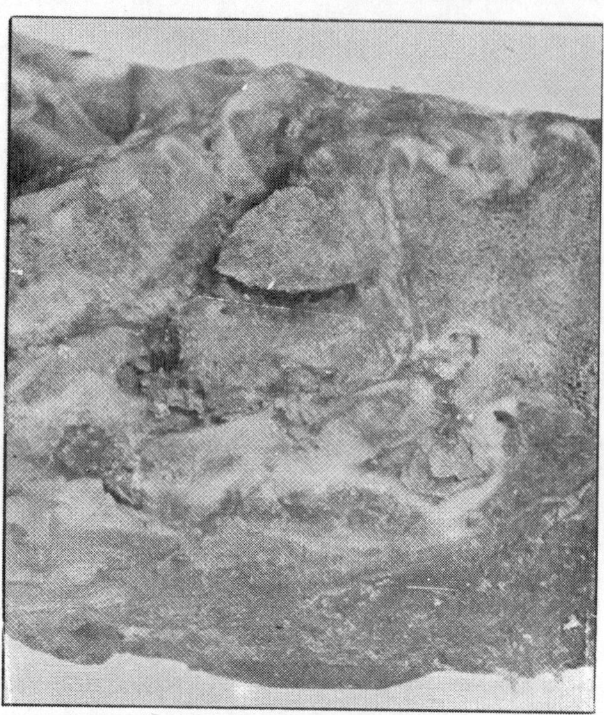

FIG. 179. Fracture of 6th lumbar vertebrae in a yearling colt that produced posterior paralysis.

and only the deformity remains. In some cases rather extensive fractures of the pelvis occur without any opportunity for a fall or traumatism to occur. Fractures have been observed to occur through the shaft of the ilium with displacement of the ends of the bones which resulted in a marked deformity of the pelvis. Fractures both multiple and comminuted may involve one or all of the bones of the pelvis.

The signs of a fracture of the pelvis, depending on its location, will vary a great deal. In some cases the affected animals show an inability to support weight on that side. In many cases of fracture of the pelvis the animals refuse to get up or to support any weight by the hind limbs.

Diagnosis of a fracture of the pelvis is usually determined by inserting one hand in the rectum and noting any movement as the weight is shifted from one leg to the other. If there is displacement of any of the bones this is readily determined. Any sounds of crepitation may be detected with movement of a limb or shifting of the weight from one limb to the other. In some cases a swelling will be felt along the line of fracture. Fractures of the external angle are readily observed as the fragment is pulled forwards and downward by the muscles.

PROGNOSIS. In most cases of fracture of the pelvis the prognosis should be guarded. Fractures involving the external angle of the ilium usually do not give any trouble except for the deformity. Some fractures of the pelvis will heal but the patient is always affected with a permanent lameness.

TREATMENT. The only form of treatment that can be recommended for fractures of the pelvis is complete rest. When the animal is in good condition and recovery is doubtful it is sometimes advisable to recommend slaughter so the meat may be used for food.

Fracture of the Femur

In large animals fracture of the femur may be due to a fall or to extreme muscular action when the animal is confined, particularly by a casting harness. Fractures may occur in any portion of the femur or only the trochanters may be affected. In a few rare cases comminuted fractures have occurred with the bone broken into many pieces.

Fracture through the epiphyseal cartilage between the head and neck of the femur usually occurs before the animal is three years of age. After three years of age ossification of the cartilage has occurred and it is rare for a fracture to occur at this point. When a fracture does occur through the epiphyseal cartilage the neck is displaced upward and the leg appears to be shorter than normal.

SIGNS. The diagnosis of fracture through the shaft of the femur should offer no difficulty. There is marked swelling of the soft tissue, increased mobility and crepitation if the ends of the bone are in apposition. When fracture of the great trochanter occurs there is swelling and marked lameness when the limb is carried and a shortening of the forward stride. If the lameness becomes chronic there is atrophy of the gluteal muscles and a marked depression over the trochanter.

PROGNOSIS. In large animals the prognosis is very unfavorable in fracture of the femur. Fractures of the shaft in swine and calves in many cases will heal if the ends are in apposition and the animal is kept quiet.

TREATMENT. In large animals consists in keeping the animals quiet and the horse may be placed in slings.

Fracture of the Tibia

The tibia is the bone that is most frequently fractured in the horse. The fracture may be due to traumatism, slipping or twisting of the leg while in motion. When fracture of the tibia occurs in the young animal it frequently occurs through the epiphyseal cartilage. In many cases the fracture is oblique and if movement is not controlled the sharp ends cause severe damage to the soft tissue and a compound fracture may be produced. Those fractures of the tibia in the mature horse due to kicks may produce a subfacial fracture of the bone. It may be a week or several weeks later before there is definite evidence of a fracture.

When fissuring of the bone occurs there will be a linear distribution of pain along the fissure line. When pain seems to be present in a line along the shaft of the bone it is considered to be diagnostic of a fissure of the bone. In complete fractures of the tibia there is increased mobility and crepitation when the ends of the bone are in contact.

PROGNOSIS. The prognosis in fractures of the tibia in large animals should be guarded. This guarded prognosis is indicated for in many cases the soft tissue has been extensively damaged. Also some individuals are difficult to handle and it is almost impossible to immobilize the bone so healing can occur.

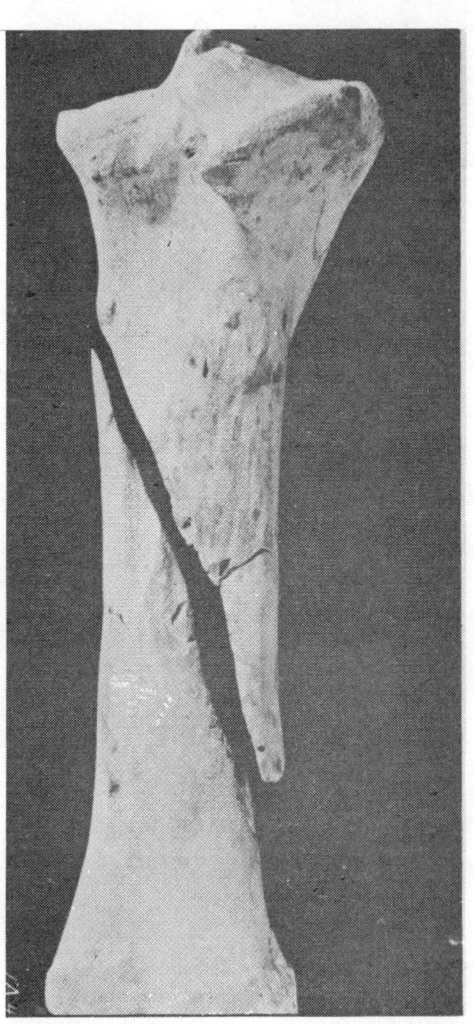

FIG. 180. Oblique fracture of the tibia, very sharp ends.

FIG. 181. A comminuted fracture of metatarsus, horse struck by automobile.

SYMPTOMS. These will vary with the degree of fracture and in most cases it will be impossible for the animal to place or support weight on the limb. When a transverse fracture occurs and the foot is lifted, the lower portion of the limb dangles. When fracture of the tibia occurs in large animals there is usually displacement of the ends of the bone. This produces marked evidence of mobility at that point.

Fracture of the Hock

Fracture of any of the tarsal bones is of rather rare occurrence. When fracture of any of these bones occurs it is usually the tibial tarsal or fibular tarsal. The tuber calcis may be fractured from external violence as kicks or blows with the Achilles tendon torn away from the tuberosity.

SIGNS. The signs will resemble those of rupture of the Achilles tendon. The animal is unable to bear any weight on the limb as all of the joints are excessively flexed.

The prognosis is unfavorable in these cases although some recoveries have been reported.

Fractures of the bones below the hock are similar to those occurring below the knee. However in fractures of the metatarsus, the splint must extend up onto the tibia for at least half its length. The purpose of this procedure is to prevent the lower portion of the limb from turning laterally or medially.

PROGNOSIS. In large animals the prognosis will depend upon a number of factors. The most important is the type of fracture and the extent to which the soft tissue has been damaged. A comminuted compound fracture with extensive injury to the soft tissue is very unfavorable. A fracture through the epiphyseal cartilage in young animals is favorable as healing usually takes place rapidly.

The disposition of a certain animal may influence the prognosis. Some individuals will resist all methods of restraint to keep them quiet so healing can occur. Some fractures will heal in horses due to their ability to be confined in slings almost indefinitely. The same type of fracture in the bovine might be unfavorable due to the movement that occurs when they are getting up and down.

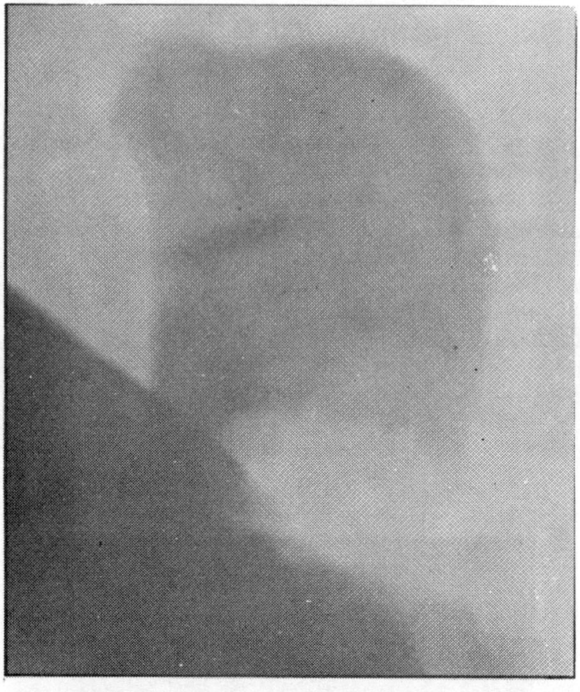

FIG. 182. Fracture of the fibular tarsal bone.

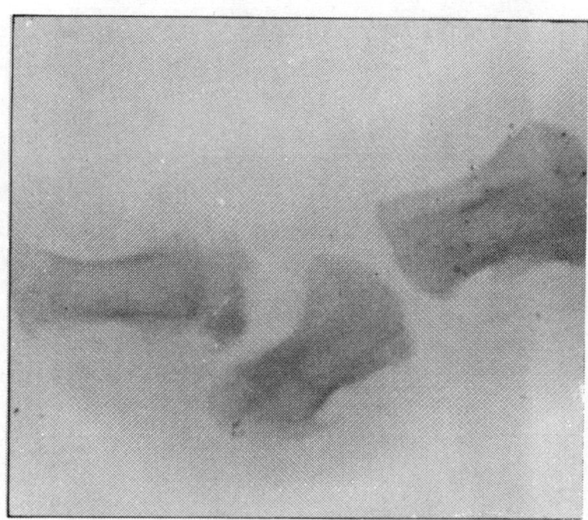

FIG. 183. Fracture of the fourth coccygeal vertebrae, producing a crooked tail.

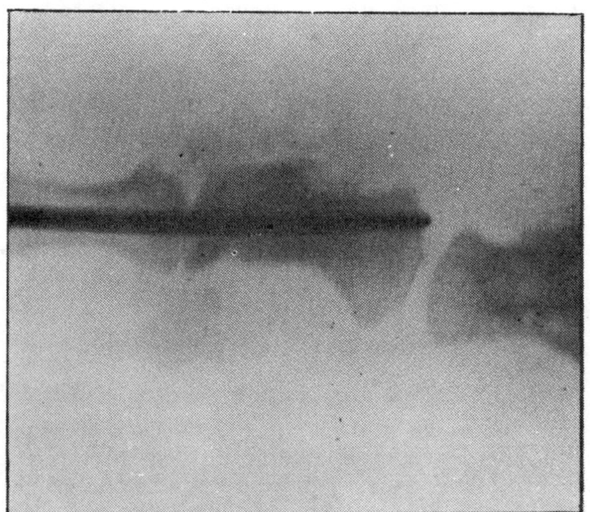

FIG. 184. A pin has been introduced through the vertebrae to hold the ends in apposition, pin left in permanently.

Treatment of Fractures

When a bone is broken the object of the treatment is to obtain union of the fragments in a good functional position, restoration of movement in the joints and power in the muscles of the limb as soon as possible. Union is usually most rapidly and surely obtained if the broken ends are placed in contact and immobilized until they are firmly united by a callus. In simple fractures without displacement, it is only necessary to immobilize the fracture until union occurs. When displacement of the broken ends has occurred, an attempt should be made to at least get the bones into a good functional position. A good functional position means that if union occurs the function of the limb will not be impaired even if the fragments are not in their normal position.

A variety of materials and methods have been used for immobilizing the fracture until a strong callus is formed. Of the various materials probably plaster of paris has been used more than any other. In large animals it is difficult to keep the patient absolutely quiet until the plaster of paris has had time to set. In many fractures it is necessary to change the splint or examine the fracture frequently which is difficult to do with plaster of paris.

One convenient form of splint material is that used by Alcorn of Iowa. This splint is made of galvanized iron gauge, twenty to twenty six. The edges of the splint may be turned back one-fourth of an inch several times to strengthen the splint. This material can be shaped to any size or shape of limb and should be bent like this ∩ so it will remain in position on the limb.

In applying the splint Alcorn states the cast should not extend below the foot. When the splint extends below the foot and the patient steps on it there is movement of the splint. This more or less continual movement of the splint interferes with the formation of the callus. The splint should be fastened to the toe by screws or bandages. If there is a shoe on, or if one can be put on, small pieces of iron bent at right angles can be inserted between the shoe and wall to support the splint. In bandaging the splint to the limb the fetlock joint and pastern are drawn forward and only the toe can be placed on the ground. This prevents the patient from putting weight on the heel and prevents stretching of some of the tendons. If the patient is allowed to put full weight on the heel many times when the splint is removed the fetlock sinks below its normal position. The limb should be covered with a thick layer of cotton to prevent pressure necrosis of the soft tissue from the splint. This necrosis of skin and soft tissue is most apt to occur in young colts where there are bony prominences, particularly the knee and hock joints.

In fractures involving either the tibia or metatarsus, the splint should extend from the foot to the proximal end of the tibia. This should be made so it conforms to the normal shape of the limb. By having the splint this length and shape it will prevent the lower portion of the limb from twisting either laterally or medially. As a general rule best results will be obtained in the horse if they are confined also in slings. This will keep them quieter and they are not getting up and down. The bovine will be getting up and down frequently so in fractures of the tibia a Thomas splint should also be used. This will provide additional support to the metal splint.

When a fracture is compound it may be desirable to leave an opening in the bandage for treatment of the wound. Some fractures in large animals require a great deal of ingenuity to reduce and immobilize the bones so a good strong callus will be formed.

Dislocations

In comparison with the large number of fractures, dislocations are rather rare injuries. Usually about 90% of the dislocations occur in the upper portion of the extremity.

ETIOLOGY - The predisposing causes are instability of the joint and exposure of the joint to injury.

In a traumatic dislocation the articular surface of one of the bones entering into a joint is violently pushed or pulled away from its fellow and forced through the joint capsule and into the surrounding tissue where it comes to rest, and is fixed by muscle spasm.

When the dislocation occurs, it is obvious that not only must the capsule of the joint be ruptured to permit the passage of the articular surface of the dislocated bone.

Also the ligaments of the joint must be ruptured to a variable degree, and many of the muscles which control the joint are either stretched or torn. The degree of displacement and the extent of damage to the soft tissue vary directly with the severity of the dislocating force and with the size of the joint. In cases of very severe violence the end of the bone may be forced through the skin, and a compound dislocation is produced.

Repair of Dislocations

If the dislocation is reduced without excessive trauma, and if the joint is immobilized, the extravasated blood will be absorbed; and the tear in the capsule will heal by the formation of granulation tissue and a scar as does any other tissue. The ligaments and tendons also tend to heal by scar tissue. Tears in the muscles will heal, and muscles which are torn off from their insertions also tend to heal by scar tissue.

SYMPTOMS. Deformity - The pathognomonic signs of a dislocation are the identification of the articular end of the displaced bone in an abnormal position and the demonstration of its absence from its normal position. This is usually determined by inspection and palpation. In addition to the deformity due to the displacement of the articular end of the bone, there is also a deformity of the limb as a whole which is characteristic of the given dislocation. This fixation of the limb in an abnormal attitude is one of the most important points in the differential diagnosis between a dislocation and fracture. Whereas, in a fracture, the limb can be moved freely, and even false motion may be obtained; in a dislocation it may be found the limb is fixed in some abnormal posture. There may be shortening or apparent lengthening of the limb. It is also characteristic of most dislocations that once the dislocation is reduced, there is little tendency for it to recur; whereas in a fracture the opposite is true.

Dislocation of the Shoulder Joint

Dislocation of the scapulo-humeral joint may occur in any of the domestic animals, but occurs most commonly in ruminants, horses and dogs. It usually occurs during excessive flexion of the shoulder and elbow joint so the head of the humerus is thrust forward and upward.

In the Veterinary Bulletin, December, 1927, Colonel Behney describes the occurrence and successful treatment of a case. He states that a valuable jumping horse tripped while attempting a difficult jump and fell with all his weight on the right shoulder. The horse rose without assistance, but would not bear any weight on the affected limb. Upon flexion and extension the pain was severe, but abduction and adduction were comparatively easy. Palpation disclosed an abnormal prominence below and anterior to the articular end of the scapula and showed intense pain on palpation.

TREATMENT. Attempts were made to reduce the luxation in the standing position by extending the leg forward but was unsuccessful. The animal was cast in the usual manner. A rope was passed over the withers, the ends crossed in front of the pectoral region carried between the front legs, crossed over the withers and tied to the rope crossing the neck. Another rope was fastened to the cross over the withers and tied to a post. A hobble was fastened to the pastern and to this a chain block and fall was attached to affect extension. The operator stood over the joint to replace the head of the humerus and supervise the direction of extension. As the bones were brought into position a loud clicking sound was heard and the enlargement disappeared. The horse got up without any difficulty and walked perfectly sound. Recovery was apparently complete as he was able to jump as good as ever afterward.

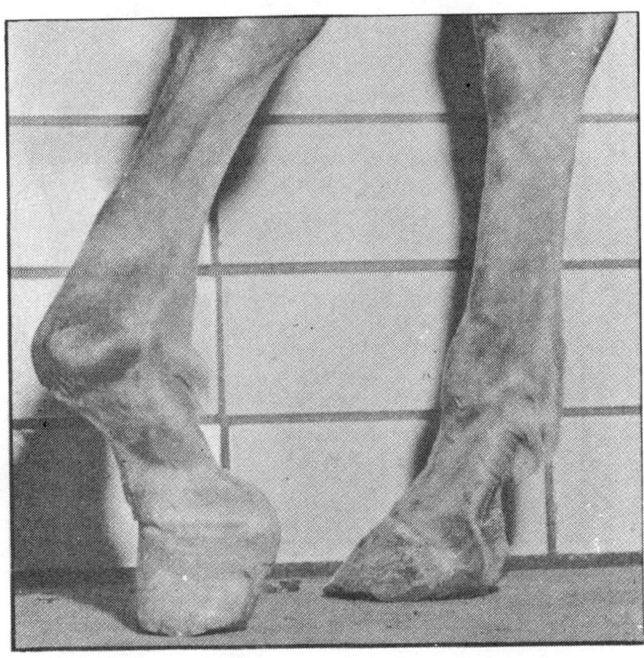

FIG. 185. Dislocation of metacarpo-phalangeal articulation in colt.

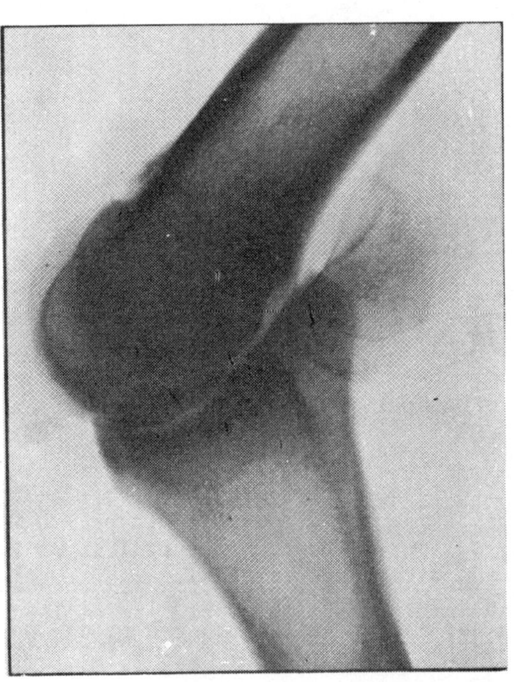

FIG. 186. Radiograph of the dislocation of the metacarpo-phalangeal articulation.

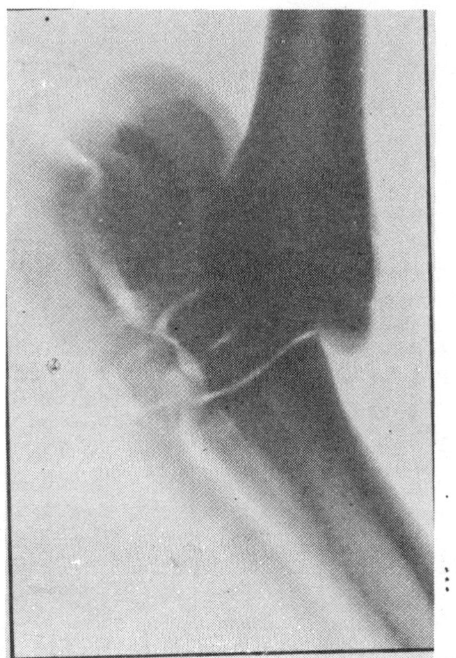

FIG. 187. Dislocation of the tibio-tarsal articulation.

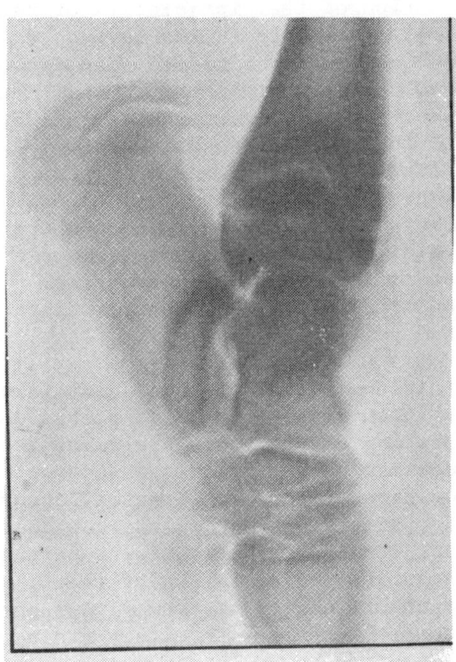

FIG. 188. After the dislocation of the tibio-tarsal articulation was reduced.

Dislocation of Metacarpo-phalangeal Articulation

Dislocation of the metacarpo-phalangeal articulation or fetlock joint is sometimes observed in colts about one year of age. The typical appearance of the joint when the dislocation occurs is shown in Fig. 185 and the radiograph is shown in Fig. 186. To reduce the dislocation a metal splint is placed on the posterior surface of the limb and bandages are used to reduce and hold the joint in its normal position. Usually in two to three weeks the splint may be removed.

Dislocation of the Tibio-tarsal Articulation

Dislocation of the tibio-tarsal articulation occurred in a two year old pony. The dislocation is shown in the radiograph Fig. 187 and after the dislocation was reduced in the radiograph Fig. 188. The dislocation was rather easily reduced by the use of traction. As traction was being exerted a clicking sound was heard and a radiograph revealed the articular surfaces were in normal position. A splint was placed on the limb for two weeks.

Dislocation of the Hip Joint

Dislocation of the hip joint is of rather frequent occurrence in the bovine, the cow is the one usually affected, and is considered rather rare in the equine. The frequency of its occurrence in the bovine is due to the difference in anatomy of the hip joint. In the bovine the acetabulum is comparatively shallow, its superior border is deeply notched, and the articular head of the femur has a smaller radius of curvature. The ligament is entirely intra-articular and sometimes absent while the accessory ligament is always absent.

When dislocation of the hip joint takes place in the cow, it usually occurs during parturition or when they are in oestrum. The cow may calve without assistance, but dislocation of the hip joint may occur during parturition. When the cow does not get up, it may be confused with parturient paresis. When dislocation of the hip joint occurs during oestrum, it usually happens when the cow is either riding or is being ridden by other cows.

SYMPTOMS. When the dislocation occurs, the head of the femur may be pulled upward and forward until it comes to rest upon the shaft of the ilium. When this occurs, the symptoms are limited abduction, easy adduction, shortening of the limb, prominence of the great trochanter with displacement upward and forward. If the head of the femur lodges in obturator foramen, its round surface may be felt in the foramen on rectal examination. The limb in these cases will appear to be longer than normal. Many cows affected with dislocation of the hip joint refuse to get up and will make no effort to stand when put in slings. One cow remained down for six weeks before she would get up. When they do get on their feet, the ability to support weight may be only partially interfered with. When they walk, the affected limb is moved with the stifle and hock joints extended. The long axis of the limb points in an outward and forward direction with foot of the affected limb in front of the opposite hind foot. When heifers less than three years of age show the characteristic symptoms, it may not be a dislocation but a fracture. In young animals fracture through the epiphyseal cartilage between the hand and neck of the femur is of frequent occurrence.

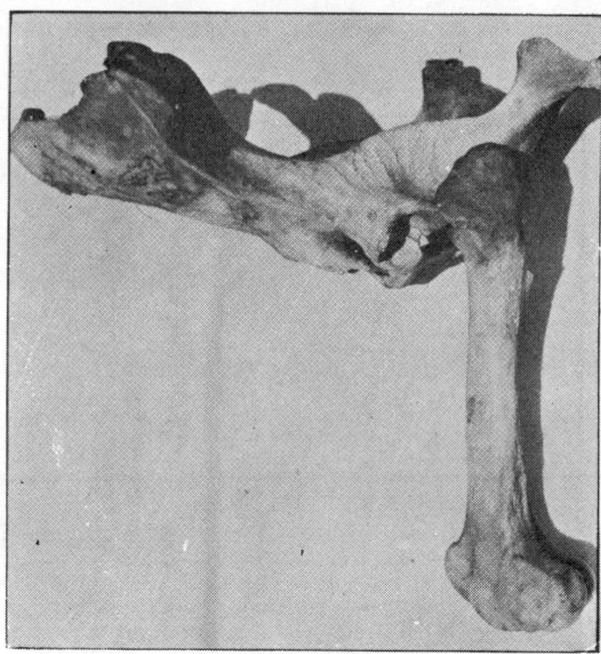

FIG. 189. When dislocation of the head of the femur occurs in the Bovine, the head may lodge in obturator foramen.

PROGNOSIS. A guarded or unfavorable prognosis should be given for even though the dislocation is reduced, it may be impossible to prevent it from reoccurring.

TREATMENT. The following method of treatment has been recommended by H. Holroyd. The patient should be cast in lateral recumbency with the affected limb uppermost. A piece of wood four feet long and 3x2 is placed between the leg and udder. This is held firmly in position by fastening a rope at each end and is then made secure to a solid object. A rope is fastened to the limb above fetlock joint, and steady traction is applied keeping the foot as close to the ground as possible. To reduce the dislocation traction may be exerted at right angles to the body, or it may be directed forward or backward until reduction is obtained. When the operator is sure the dislocation is reduced, all traction should stop.

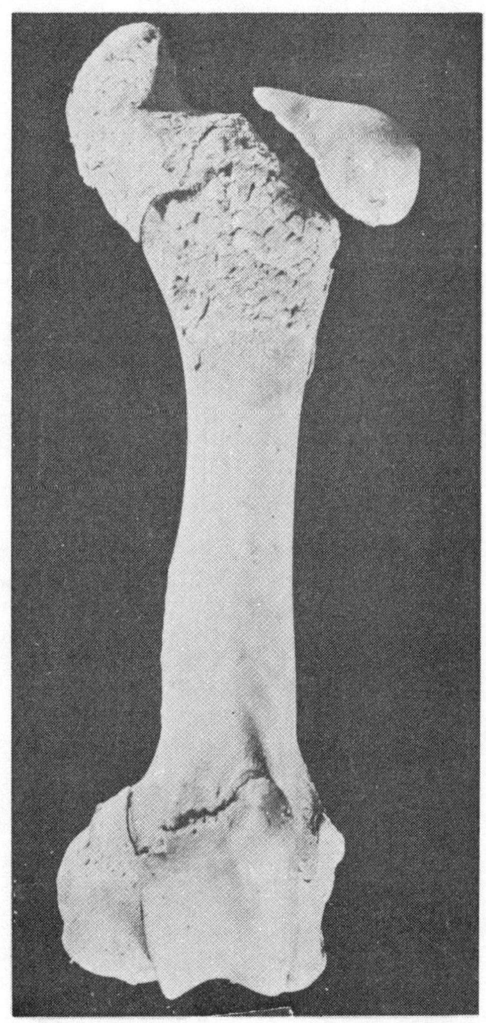

FIG. 190. Fracture through the epiphyseal cartilage that occurred in two year old heifer.

The after treatment recommended is to keep the patient quiet in a single stall for four or five days. For the next ten days the patient may be allowed more freedom with complete recovery in three weeks. The author reports a high percentage of recoveries in uncomplicated cases.

Reichel describes two methods of immobilizing fractures in large animals. For those fractures below the carpel and tarsal joints the unpadded plaster of paris cast is applied directly to the skin with the animal in dorsal recumbency. When the fracture is dorsal to the carpus and tarsus the transfixation of the bone is accomplished with Steinmann pins. By using this method the animal has more freedom of movement of the limb. However the insertion of the pins through the bone makes this more dangerous because of possible injury and infection in the bone. After the pins are in position they are bridged by two lateral splints to immobilize the fracture between the pins. The circular fixation is accomplished with an unpadded plaster of paris cast around the limb.

REFERENCES

Adams, O. R., Preliminary Report on Repair of Coxofemoral Luxation Subluxation in Cattle J.A.V.M.A., Vol. 130, (1957), 515.

Bruce, Ralph A., Bilateral Coxofemoral Luxation in a Bull, Vet. Med. 37 (1942), 488.

Churchill, E. A., Surgical Removal of Fracture Fragments of the Proximal Sesamoid Bone, J.A.V.M.A., 128 (June 15, 1956), 581-582.

Frost, J. N., and Sunderville, Earl, Luxation of the Coxofemoral Articulation, Cornell Veterinarian, (1932), 41-43.

Greenough, P. R., Dislocation of the Hip in the Cow, The Veterinary Record, Vol. 72, No. 10, pp. 180-181.

Peters, J. E., Fractures of the 3rd. Phalanx and Sesamoids in the Race Horse, J.A.V.M.A., 114 (1949), pp. 405-408.

Reichel, Ernest C., Treatment of Fractures of the long Bones in Large Animals, J.A.V.M.A., 129, (1956), pp. 8-15.

Sevelius, Fritz, Vet. Surg., and Tufvesson, Gunnar, Vet. Med. Dr., Treatment for Fractures of the Sesamoid Bones in Horses, Vol. 142, (May 1, 1963), pp. 981-988.

Wheat, J. D., and Rhode, E. A., The Surgical Treatment of Fractures of the Proximal Sesamoid Bones in the Horse, 132, J.A.V.M.A., (1958), pp. 378-382.

Chapter VI

AFFECTIONS OF THE HEAD AND NECK

Conchal Cyst or Dentigerous Cyst

A small opening in the skin on the posterior edge of the ear of the equine discharging a thick viscid liquid that accumulates on the hairs indicates the presence of a conchal or dentigerous cyst. The amount of this liquid that is discharged will be determined by the extent of the cyst and in some cases it is rather profuse. A small probe may be passed through the opening to the bottom of the cyst to determine its extent. The tract and the termination of the cyst which may be sac like is composed of a thick wall and a secreting membrane lining the entire structure.

TREATMENT: The conchal cyst is located in the subcutaneous tissue and should be completely removed. If any of the secreting tissue is not removed it may be the source of a persistent discharge. Most of the cases can be operated with the patient in the standing position. The tissues are infiltrated with a local anesthetic. The incision through the skin is made over the cyst from the opening over the entire length of the tract. All of the tissue composing the cyst should be removed. The edges of the skin may be united with closely placed interrupted sutures.

Dentigerous Cyst

The dentigerous cyst is characterized by the presence of a small molar like tooth. This tooth may be palpated in the subcutaneous tissue in the lower portion of the tract.

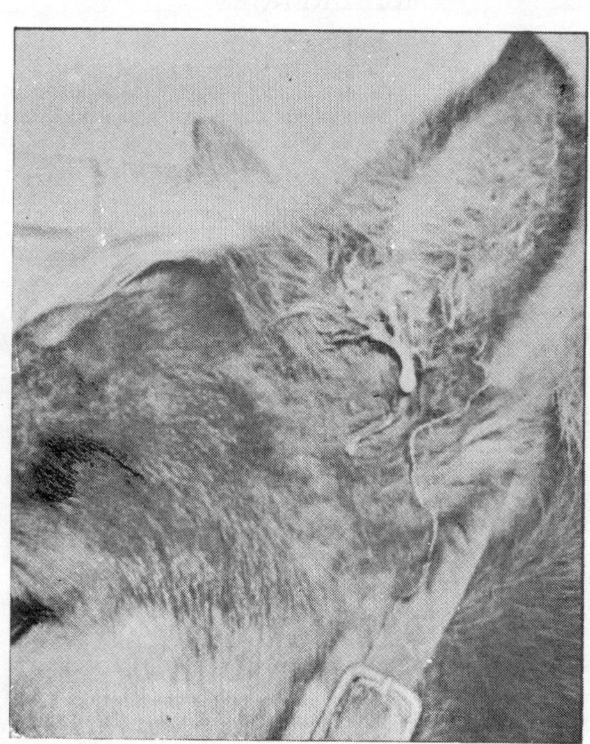

FIG. 191. Conchal fistula, note droplet of characteristic discharge on hair.

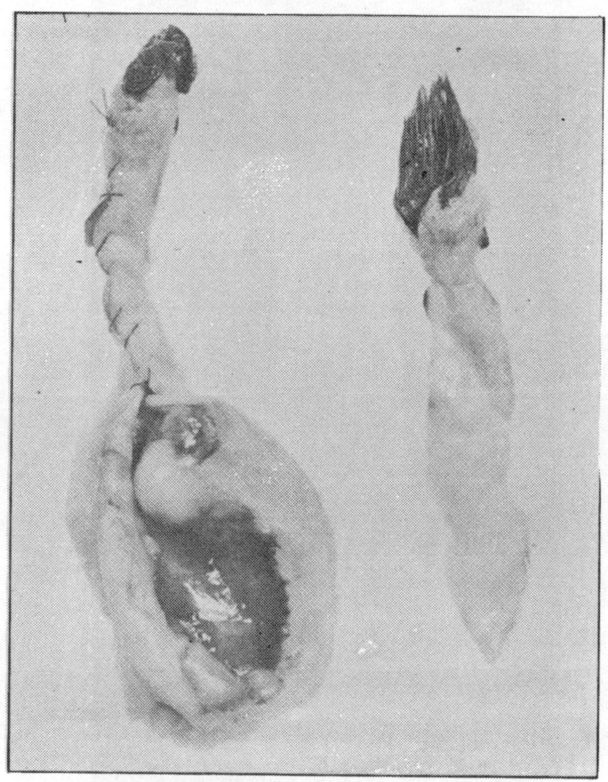

FIG. 192. A case of bilateral conchal fistulas, profuse discharge from the one on the left.

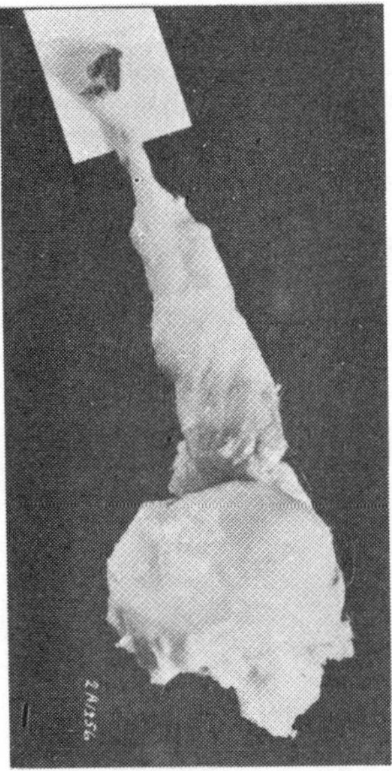

FIG. 193. Dentigerous cyst, the large swelling indicates location of molar-like shaped tooth.

OPERATION. The operation is performed in a manner similar to that for a conchal cyst. The tissues may be anesthetized by infiltration with a local anesthetic. In the dissection of the dentigerous cyst it will be found the tooth is firmly attached to the underlying tissue. This attachment may be fibrous in character or fragile bony like tissue. Either one of these attachments may be cut or broken rather easily. The edges of the skin may be united with rather closely placed interrupted sutures.

Otitis Media

Otitis media is an inflammation of the middle ear that affects suis most frequently but it also occurs in other species of animals.

ETIOLOGY. Apparently due to infections of the respiratory tract gaining entrance to

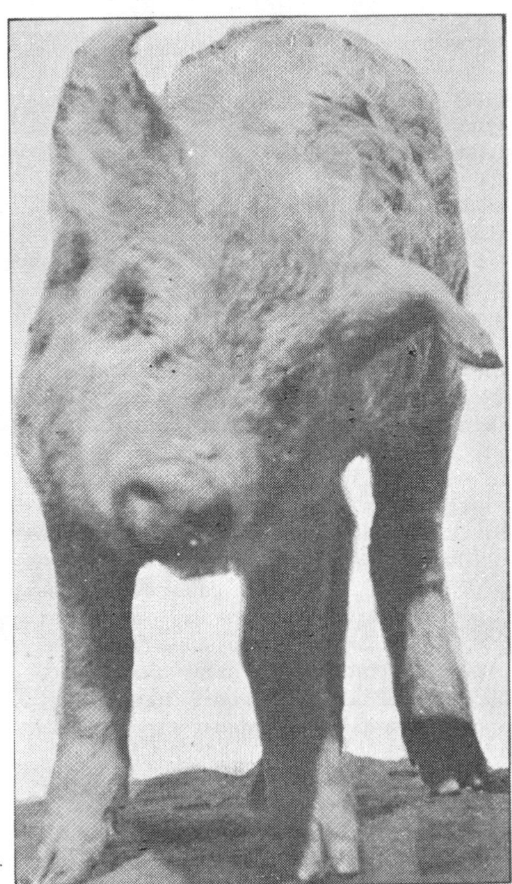

FIG. 194. The characteristic tilting of the head with the affected ear down in a unilateral case of otitis media.

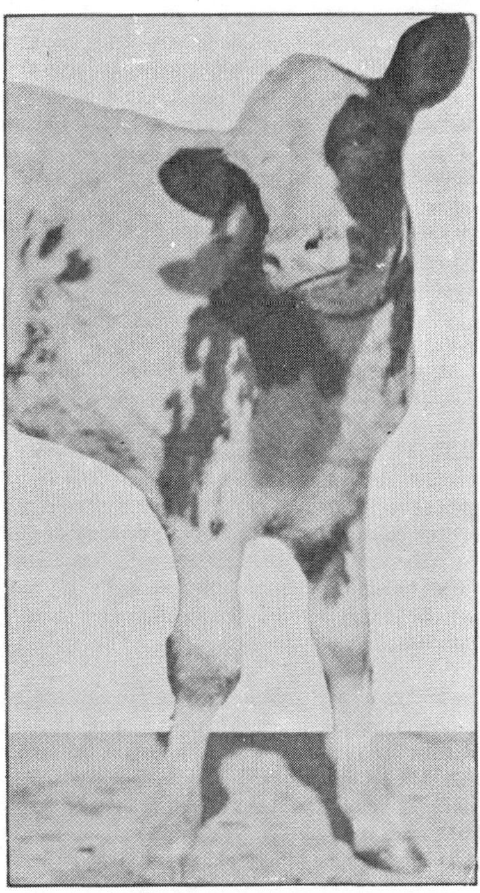

FIG. 195. Otitis media in a calf, note tilting of the head.

the middle ear by way of the eustachian tube. Frequently occurs following a respiratory infection as influenza. Bacteriological examination of some of the cases has revealed streptococci and staphlococci as the organisms most frequently present.

SYMPTOMS. The symptoms vary a great deal in different outbreaks. In some herds only one or two will be affected, in other herds six or eight, while in some herds twenty-five per cent of the pigs have been affected. Some pigs that are affected may have a temperature of 106° with a complete loss of appetite. If the condition is unilateral the head is tilted to one side with the affected ear down. If both ears are affected the head is extended with the nose to the ground. One veterinarian reported that of eighty-five head of six weeks old pigs that were in good condition, twenty-five per cent were affected and all died.

The first symptoms noticed were that they held their heads twisted over until the ears were about straight up and down and moved in a circle toward the ear that was down. They continue this circling until they are down and unable to get up. The temperatures of all ailing pigs were normal and their appetite was good as long as they could reach the feed. All affected pigs usually died within forty-eight hours after first symptoms were noticed. The largest and most thrifty pigs were the ones affected.

The chronic condition shows about the same symptoms except they are milder and have a longer course.

TREATMENT. If the treatment is to be effective it should be used while the inflammation is located in the eustachian tube and middle ear. The treatment should alleviate the inflammation of the middle ear and eustachian tube so there is free communication between the pharynx and middle ear.

A stiff slender probe may be used to puncture the tympanic membrane. Before the membrane is punctured it should be anesthetized with a mixture of equal parts of cocaine crystals, menthol crystals and phenol crystals. The tympanum offers only slight resistance when it is punctured.

Before injecting the antiseptic solution the nose should be lowered so there will be good drainage through to the outside. The antiseptic recommended most highly to use is liquid Bipp. This preparation consists of Iodoform, two ounces; Bismuth subnitrate, one ounce; and enough liquid paraffin to make it the right consistency to inject readily, through a dose syringe. When drainage is established through the eustachian tube no further treatment is indicated. Some of the chronic cases may be benefited with this type of treatment enough so they can be fattened for food purposes. Sulfonamides or antibiotics might prove to be of considerable value in these cases.

Affections of the Eye and Eyelids

Entropion

In this condition there is inversion of the palpebral border of one or both eyelids and one or both eyes may be affected. The lower lid is the one most frequently affected. The eye lashes on the edge of the lid are very irritating to the cornea and conjunctive. This irritation produces lachyrmation and conjunctivitis and if not relieved keratitis and ulceration of the cornea may occur. Entropion is usually congenital and is seen most frequently in lambs and occasionally in colts.

TREATMENT. The object of any form of treatment is to hold the edges of the lid in a normal position until they will remain there permanently. One simple form of treatment used in lambs is to pick up a fold of skin sufficient to draw the edge of the eyelid to a normal position and place one or two sutures through the fold of skin. Another method is to use metal wound clips to hold the fold of skin. These clips will drop off in a few days but sufficient irritation has been produced in the tissue to hold the edge of the lids in the normal position. Also a very fine needle may be inserted between the skin and conjunctiva and enough sterile liquid paraffin injected to cause enough swelling of the lid to draw the lid to a normal position. The swelling gradually disappears and a permanent cure is usually obtained.

The operative treatment consists in removing an elliptical piece of skin from the affected lid. Shave the hair from the operative area and paint with a skin antiseptic. Anesthesia for the operation may be obtained by infiltrating the tissue with a one per cent solution of a local anesthetic.

The amount of skin that is necessary to remove may be determined by picking up a fold of skin sufficient to draw the edge of the lid to a normal position. Remove the fold of skin with scissors or scalpel. The upper incision should be about one-fourth of an inch from the edge of the lid and should extend the entire length of the affected portion of the lid. In making the skin incision the operator must be sure the conjunctiva is not incised. After the elliptical portion of skin is removed the edges of the incision are approximated with closely placed interrupted sutures of catgut. The operative area is then covered with flexible collodion.

Ectropion

In this condition there is eversion of the eyelid usually the lower one. It may be congenital or occur when too much skin is removed in operating for entropion.

SYMPTOMS. The exposed conjunctiva becomes reddened and there is increased lachryma-tion.

TREATMENT. The operative area may be in the lid or the skin lateral to the lateral canthus of the eye. Either area may be prepared as described for the preceding operation and also anesthetized in the same manner.

One operation is to remove a triangular shaped area of skin and conjunctiva from the lower lid. The base of the triangle is toward the edge of the lid and about one-fourth of an inch from it. After the skin and mucous membrane are removed the edges of the triangle are sutured together. The suturing is started at the apex and closely placed sutures of catgut are used. The sutures may be covered with flexible collodion.

The second operation which may be performed consists in removing a triangular area of skin lateral to the lateral canthus of the eye, with one corner of the triangle involving the lateral canthus. The base of the triangle is upward. A narrow strip of tissue is removed from the edge of the lower lid so that the length will correspond to the length of the base of the triangle. Its length will be governed by the extent of the ectropion. The freshened edge of the lid is now sutured to the base of the triangle and the sides of the triangle are sutured together. The area may be covered with flexible collodion.

Pterygium

This condition results from a vascular thickening of the conjunctiva of the eyeball with extension onto the cornea. Its usual site is at the medial canthus and may affect one or both eyes. A true pterygium is rather loosely attached except at its apex and on the cornea it is folded upon itself.

TREATMENT. The best results are obtained by surgical removal of the tissue. The tissue may be anesthetized by the application of an efficient topical anesthetic. Grasp the tissue on the cornea with forceps and dissect it from the cornea to the corneal margin. A triangular shaped excision of the pterygium is then made with the apex toward the medial canthus. The edges of the conjunctiva are undermined and the edges sutured together.

Dermoid

This is frequently a congenital growth of more or less normal skin growing from the conjunctiva at the corneosclearl margin. In structure it is more or less like skin and from its surface protrudes numerous hairs. These hairs may be a source of irritation to the eye. Dermoids are seen only occasionally in the bovine.

TREATMENT. The eye should be anesthetized by using an efficient topical anesthetic as butyn or cocaine. The tissue is grasped with forceps and removed from the cornea and sclerd by careful dissection. If the cyst extends too deeply into the cornea it

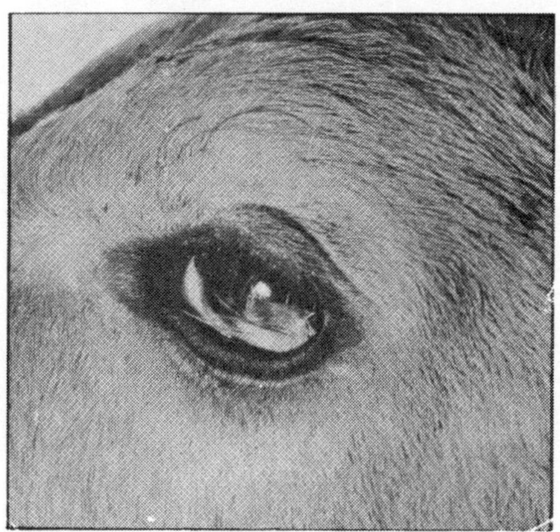

FIG. 196. A typical case of dermoid.

should not be completely removed as it may result in serious complications. Mild eye antiseptics may be used after the operation and good healing of the tissue should occur.

Removal of the Membrane Nictitans

The surgical removal of the membrane nictitans is indicated when it is hypertrophied and when it is affected with a neoplasm. The hypertrophy of the tissue may cause a protrusion of the membrane nictitans and produce an objectionable blemish. The most frequent neoplasm found affecting the membrane nictitans has been carcinoma.

TREATMENT. The membrane nictitans can be surgically removed with the horse in the standing position if the tissues to be removed are completely anesthetized.

Anesthesia of the mucous membrane may be obtained by injecting a one per cent solution of a local anesthetic into the subconjunctival tissue. The nictitans membrane is grasped between the thumb and finger so the outline of the semi-lunar cartilage may be followed so all of the cartilage is removed with the mucous membrane. With the thumb and finger following the edge of the cartilage a pair of blunt pointed curved scissors are used to cut the mucous membrane. Usually the hemorrhage that occurs requires no treatment but it may be desirable to apply pressure to the area for a few minutes if the hemorrhage is pronounced. No after-treatment is necessary in these cases.

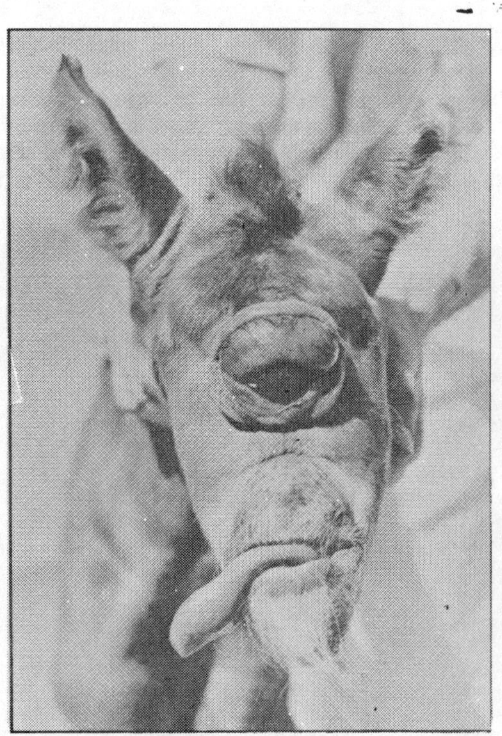

FIG. 197. Cyclops Equi.

Cyclops Equi

Cyclops equi is defined as the presence of one eye only, situated on the median line of the head. This condition is regarded as an anomaly, which is a malformation that involves an organ or a portion of the body.

When deviations from the normal result in malformations they occur in the course of embryonal development. Embryologists state that most of them have their origin within the first few weeks after fertilization. Some cases of Cyclops equi are born dead or die within a few hours after birth. However there is a case on record in which a horse reached maturity.

Ulceration with Perforation of the Cornea

One of the most common conditions affecting the eyes of the bovine is infectious keratitis. As a general rule the eyes of the young animal, particularly calves, are more severely affected than in the more mature animals. The most prominent symptoms are lacrimination and photophobia with opacity of the cornea. The opacity of the cornea is usually in its exact center and may be about the size of a pin head. Examination of the eye may reveal some hypertension and may be an indication of impending ulceration of the cornea. When ulceration occurs and hypertension is present it is usually responsible for failure of the ulcer to heal, and also for it to extend deeper into the tissue with eventual rupture of the cornea. In many cases granulation tissue develops in the wound in the cornea. Where the wound is small the grandulation tissue may be about one-eighth of an inch in diameter and three-fourths of an inch long. If the wound is more extensive a rather large amount of granulation tissue may be formed.

In the treatment of the granulation tissue it may be surgically removed if it is of

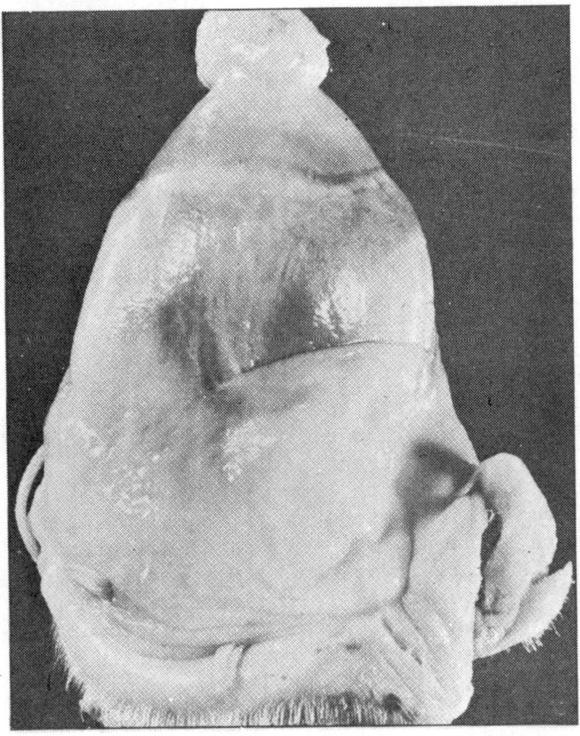

FIG. 198. Exuberant granulation tissue frequently develops in a wound produced by rupture of the cornea.

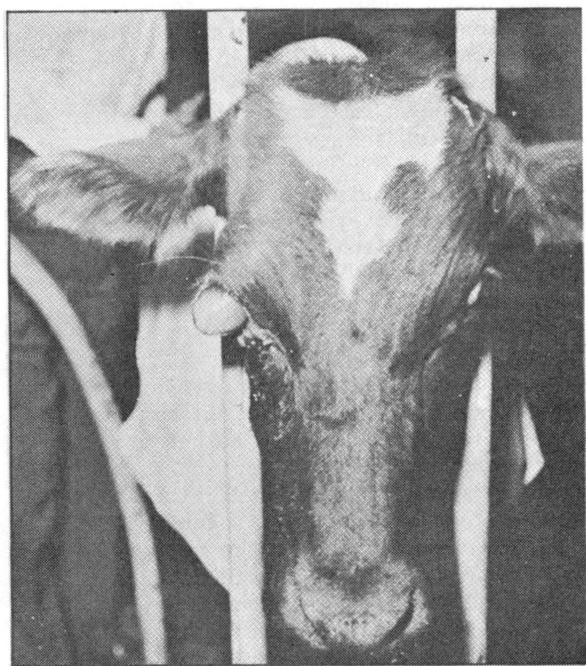

FIG. 199. Hydrophthalmus.

rather small diameter. When the granulation tissue is rather extensive the inflammation of other tissues has damaged the eye so the sight is destroyed. Extirpation of the eye is indicated when the sight has been destroyed and the changes that have occurred are rather extensive.

Hydrophthalmus

This condition is seen only occasionally in the bovine but more frequently in the equine, dog and cat. Hydrophthalmus may be congenital or acquired. In acquired hydrophthalmus there is an interference with the drainage system of the eye and a gradual increase in the fluid contents of the eye. The eyeball may bulge in all directions with stretching of the eyelids and an exophthalmus. With the exposure of the cornea there is drying of the tissue and interference with its nourishment and it presents an opaque appearance. In many cases the cornea is insensitive, the lens becomes detached and may be found adhered to the cornea in the anterior chamber.

Treatment is of no value in these cases and extirpation of the eye is indicated, to improve the appearance of the animal.

Injuries of the Cornea

Injuries to the cornea usually occur when foreign bodies as awns from grass, pieces of chaff and portions of stems of grasses adhere or become imbedded in the cornea. If the foreign body penetrates deep into the cornea and carries infection it may cause extensive damage to the tissue. When present for a number of days a surrounding area of infiltration appears with the formation of a small ulcer. Foreign bodies are frequently responsible for the development of ulcers on the cornea. When foreign bodies are in contact with the cornea the eye becomes very sensitive and this condition is manifested by lacrimination and photophobia.

To examine the eye the cornea and conjunctiva are anesthetized with a two per cent solution of butyn sulphate. When the tissues are anesthetized the lids are separated with the fingers. If the foreign body is just in contact with the cornea, it may be removed with a little absorbent cotton wound on a forcep or applicator.

The cotton should not be used with any pressure but rather with a brushing motion to remove the foreign body. If the foreign body has become imbedded in the corneal tissue a small forcep or curette may be efficient in its removal.

After care consists of using an anesthetic and antiseptic eye ointment on the cornea night and morning.

Opacities of the Cornea

The lack of transparency or opacity of the cornea is the result of inflammation due to ulceration or injury to the cornea. If the opacity is a grey spot it is called a macula and when dense and white it is a leucoma. The opacities interfere with vision when located in the pupillary area. When the opacity is located where it does not interfere with vision it may be regarded as a blemish that reduces the sale value or appearance of the eye.

TREATMENT. The treatment for corneal opacities will be most successful in those cases where they are superficial and recent. In some cases an ointment of yellow oxide of mercury (3%) or a (3%) ointment of ammoniated mercury or a (2%) quinine bisulphate ointment may be used twice a day on the opacity. If the ointments do not produce the desired results dionine in a (2 to 10%) solution may be used to produce a marked reaction in the tissue. If the above measures should not prove successful it would be necessary to perform an operation which, in our large animals, is impractical.

Dacrocystitis

Dacrocystitis occurs when the conjunctiva is irritated from dust or other foreign material, or where there is closure of the lacrimal canal. There is usually a conjunctivitis with a profuse discharge from the eye either watery or purulent in character.

TREATMENT. It is indicated to determine if the naso-lacrimal canal is open by irrigating it with a mild antiseptic solution. The canal is irrigated by inserting the end of a naso-lacrimal tube into the opening on the floor of the nasal cavity at the junction of the skin and mucous membrane. Digital pressure should be applied over the tube to prevent the escape of the fluid. If the patient is sensitive to the pressure in the canal ten cubic centimeters of a two per cent solution of butyn sulphate may be injected into the canal. After the canal is open there is a rapid improvement in the appearance of the eye and a freedom from any discharge over the face. If there is any irritation of the cornea an antiseptic eye ointment should be used night and morning.

A very effective method of treating an inflammation of the cornea or other tissues of the eye is the use of corticosteroids. After the cornea and conjunctiva have been anesthetized with a two per cent solution of butyn sulphate the corticosteroid may be injected beneath the conjunctiva. If only a portion of the cornea is affected, as that covered by the lower eyelid, one-half to one cubic centimeter is deposited beneath the conjunctiva at three different points. If all of the cornea is affected the corticosteroid is injected beneath the conjunctiva of both the upper and lower eyelids. The treatments may be repeated at seven to ten day intervals depending upon the progress of the case.

Affections of the Nasal Cavity

Epistaxis

Epistaxis or bleeding from the nose may be due to injury to the nasal mucous membrane, tumors or ulcers. The distinguishing character is pure blood from the nostril, if it is frothy it is usually from the lungs, and if it contains food the blood probably originates in the stomach.

TREATMENT. Will depend upon the source and severity of the hemorrhage. Sometimes one or more two ounce doses of hydrogen peroxide injected forcibly up into the nostril will cause the hemorrhage to stop. If this is not sufficient, a large piece of gauze to which a piece of suture material long enough to protrude beyond the nostril is forced up the nostril with the stomach tube. This gauze is then removed in twenty-four or forty-eight hours by pulling on the suture material.

Another recent recommendation is to give intravenously one ounce of sodium citrate dissolved in three ounces of sterile distilled water. Arrest of hemorrhage should occur in fifteen to thirty minutes. If this should result in hypocalcemia, calcium gluconate or chloride should be given as an antidote.

Atheroma

Atheroma is a sebaceous cyst that occurs in the false nostril of the equine. These cysts vary in size from a pigeon egg to a large chicken egg. The contents may be like water in the small cyst and the large cyst may be filled with a thick, greasy dark grey material. The presence of the cyst is readily diagnosed.

TREATMENT. The skin over the cyst is prepared for the operation and the tissues may be anesthetized by infiltration with a local anesthetic. The incision through the skin exposes the wall of the cyst. The cyst wall should be separated from the surrounding tissue so that all of the wall can be removed. It may be desirable to establish drainage into the nasal cavity. The edges of the skin incision may be united with closely placed interrupted sutures.

Congenital Atresia of the Naso-lacrimal Duct

Congenital atresia of the naso-lacrimal duct is seen in the equine and one or both sides may be affected. Colts are usually presented for treatment when they are six to twelve months of age. At this age the affected individuals have developed a marked purulent discharge from the medial commissure of one or both eyes. Examination usually reveals there is no opening of the naso-lacrimal duct on the floor of the nasal cavity at the junction of the skin and mucous membrane.

TREATMENT. The patient should be confined in lateral recumbency. The puncta or ocular openings of the duct are two in number, one in the upper and one in the lower eyelid, just within the free margin of the eyelid and one-fourth inch from the medial commissure. The doubled end of a No. 25 stainless steel wire is passed into the puncta of the lower eyelid and directed medially for a distance of about one-fourth of an inch then down the canal. Normally the opening of the naso-lacrimal duct is on the floor of the nasal cavity at the junction of the skin and mucous membrane. When the opening has failed to develop normally the position of the end of the canal may vary a great deal in position. In some cases the end of the wire is palpated on the medial side of the ventral turbinate. The wire is most easily palpated by moving it forward and backward and it will be felt beneath the mucous membrane. The mucous membrane can be incised with the No. 12 Bard-Parker curved blade. With the finger guiding the blade an incision three-fourths of an inch long is made through the mucous membrane. A pair of curved forceps is inserted through the incision to grasp the wire. The wire is pulled through until about two inches is left in the tissues. Cut the wire so about one inch extends anterior to the incision, an interrupted catgut suture is placed around this portion of the wire. The wire through the incision will help to develop a permanent opening. When the catgut is absorbed the wire will fall out.

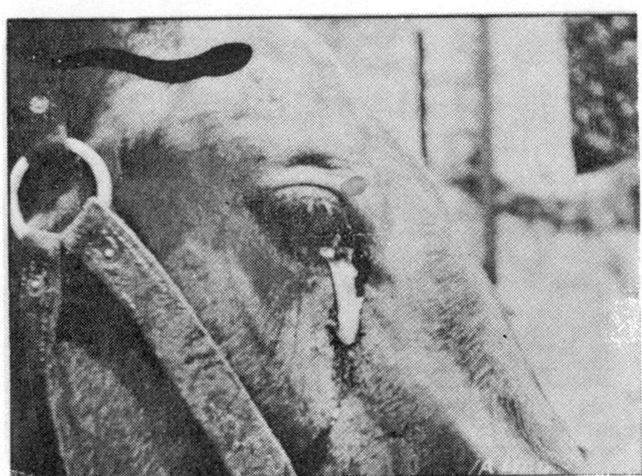

FIG. 200. Congenital atresia of naso-lacrimal duct; the left side was also affected.

Injuries of the Lips and Cheek

Injuries to the lips and cheek occur quite frequently due to the bit, nails, sharp hooks, or other trauma. Despite the constant mobility, contamination of the wound by feed and organisms, they usually heal rapidly. This is due to the good blood supply of these tissues.

Perforating wounds of the cheek will heal if they are not sutured but kept clean and all loose or necrotic tissue removed. If it is necessary to suture wounds such as those occurring at the commissures, the mucous membrane and skin should be sutured separately. It is also desirable to put in tension sutures to take the strain from the uniting sutures and to act as a brace to the area.

If healing is to take place the parts must be kept as immobile as possible. This is best accomplished by cross tying the horse and feeding with a stomach tube for approximately seven days.

The following semi-liquid diet will provide the necessary requirements to maintain an average sized horse.

Wheat flour - 600 gms
Wheat bran - 200 gms
Water - 9 liters

This is boiled for twenty minutes and allowed to cool, then add the following:

Molasses - 500 cc
Evaporated milk - 500 cc
Sodium chloride - 8 gms
Ethyl alcohol - 60 cc

This may be administered once or twice a day.

Paralysis of the Facial Nerve (Branch of the Seventh Cranial)

Facial paralysis occurs occasionally in both equine and bovine but we have not observed it in any of the other species. The paralysis may be unilateral or bilateral and either central or peripheral in origin. This nerve arises behind the pons and enters the internal auditory meatus traverses the facial canal of the petrous temporal bone and emerges at the stylomastoid foramen. After its emergence the nerve lies on the guttural pouch under cover of the parotid gland. As it passes forward it crosses the ramus of the mandible about one and one-half inches ventral to the tempero-mandibular articulation. Below this point it divides into superior and inferior buccal branches. The symptoms of facial paralysis are due to the lack of function of these muscular branches. The facial nerve also supplies innervation to the muscles of the cheeks, ears and eyelids.

ETIOLOGY. When the paralysis affects the peripheral nerves it is usually due to traumatisms or pressure upon the nerve where it crosses the border of the mandible or wounds which may divide some of the branches of the facial nerve. If there is complete unilateral paralysis it may be due to neoplasms within the facial canal, diseases of the petrous temporal bone or middle ear or neoplasms or abscesses in the subparotid region. When there is bilateral central paralysis it may be due to neoplasms, abscesses, hematomas or degenerative processes at the base of the brain.

SYMPTOMS. When the nerve paralysis is unilateral in the equine and anterior to the

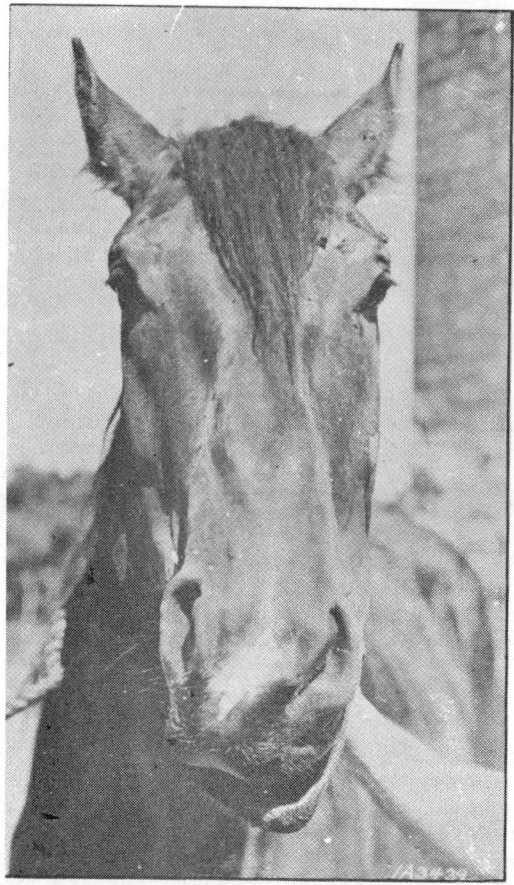

FIG. 201. Unilateral paralysis of facial nerve with upper lip pulled to sound side and lower lip drooping.

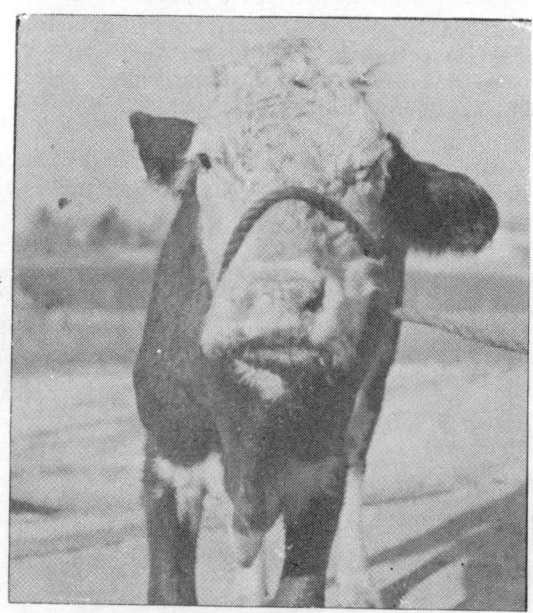

FIG. 202. Injury of the facial nerve has occurred posterior to the eye and ear branches, the ear is drooping and there is ptosis of the upper eyelid.

eye and ear branches, the tip of the nose and upper lip assume an oblique position toward the sound side. Examination of the cheek will disclose food between it and the cheek teeth on the affected side. In the bovine the oblique position of the lips is not noticed due to the stiffness of the muzzle. When the fingers are inserted between the cheek and teeth there is less resistance on the paralyzed side and food is found between the cheek and cheek teeth. The affected individual will usually lose large amounts of feed from the affected side when ruminanting.

In central paralysis there is a lack of function of all the structure supplied with motor fibers, such as drooping of the ear, ptosis of the upper eyelid and paralysis of the muscles of the cheek, lips and nostrils. Due to the relaxation of the cheek a variable quantity of food is found between the cheeks and cheek teeth.

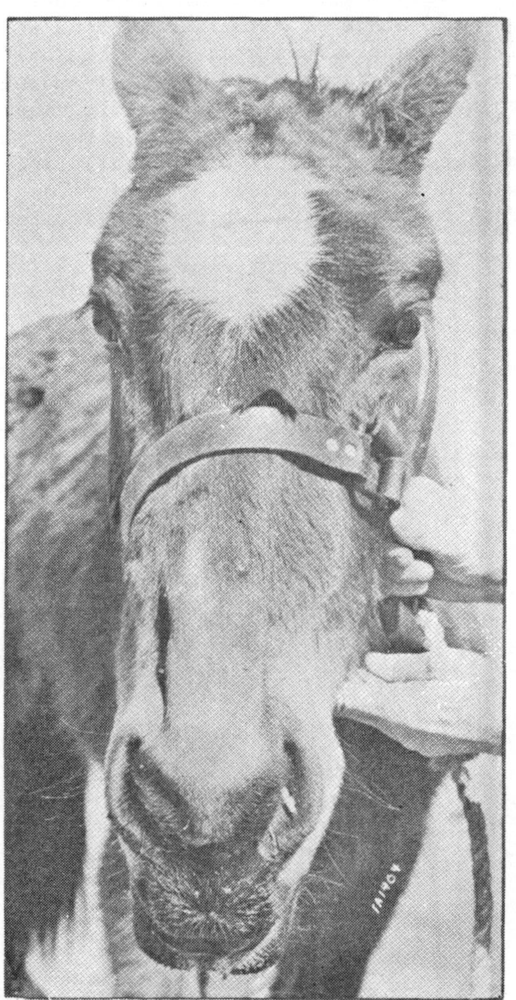

FIG. 203. Bilateral paralysis of the facial nerve, note the relaxation of the lips and drawing in of the nostrils on inspiration.

When the paralysis is bilateral and central in origin both the upper and lower lips may hang relaxed. There is marked respiratory difficulty due to the collapse of the nostrils on inspiration and choking may result when a fast gait or heavy work is attempted. When the animal attempts to drink, the mouth is put deep into the water and considerable difficulty is noted as water is swallowed. When the horse is affected there is difficulty in prehension and the horse will have to pick up feed with his teeth.

PROGNOSIS. The prognosis depends upon the cause and some cases recover in a few days without treatment. If the paralysis is central the prognosis is less favorable due to the difficulty of treatment. The prognosis should always be guarded as it is impossible to determine the extent of the injury to the nerve or nerves.

TREATMENT. The food should be removed frequently from between the cheeks and teeth to prevent decomposition and possible sloughing of the mucous membrane. In case of bilateral paralysis in the horse the collapse of the paralyzed nostrils may be relieved by the use of sutures. This is accomplished by picking up a fold of skin on the dorsal surface of the nasal cavity, sufficient to bring the nostrils up to the normal position. One or two mattress sutures are placed through the two layers of skin and this will prevent the nostrils from collapsing. The sutures may be left in position until the affected muscles have regained their function.

Plastic Surgery for the Lips in Facial Paralysis in the Equine

In some cases of facial paralysis in the equine the condition may be objectionable to the owner or he may want to show the horse and would like to have the deviation of the lips corrected. Fortunately the drooping of the ear occurs in a very small percentage of the cases. Attempts to correct the drooping of the ear have not been successful.

The deviation of the upper lip may be corrected by removing three elliptical areas of skin. The first elliptical area is removed ventral to the posterior edge of the nostril. In the average sized horse the incisions will be approximately one and one-half inches long and three-fourths of an inch apart at the widest point, terminating at the edge of the lip. The incisions extend only through the thickness of the skin and the elliptical area of skin is removed. After the skin is removed the edges of the skin are approximated with closely placed interrupted sutures using No. 1 chromic catgut. The posterior incision for the next elliptical area to be removed is one inch anterior to the posterior incision of the previous area. The second elliptical area is the same size as the first one and after the skin is removed the edges are united with the interrupted sutures. The location of the third area to be removed is determined by picking up a fold of skin sufficient to bring the lip to its normal position. Usually a smaller area of skin will need to be removed than in the first two areas.

The lower lip presents a different problem from that of the upper lip as it is drooping. The three elliptical areas of skin removed from the lower lip are ventral to those removed from the upper lip. The elliptical areas of skin removed are the same width as the areas removed from the upper lip but only one-half as long. The incisions are approximately three-fourths of an inch long and terminate when the edges of the incisions are the widest apart and at the edge of the lower lip. For approximately ten days the grain and hay should be placed on a flat surface. The water container should be removed as soon as he finishes drinking. For the best results it is essential the patient is confined so that he cannot rub the operative areas.

Nasal Polypi

Nasal polypi occur frequently in the nasal cavity of the equine but are only seen occasionally in the bovine. Nasal polypi originate from the submucous connective tissue of the nasal cavity and are composed of inflammatory tissue. When they originate in one of the alveoli they may contain some bony tissue. The nasal polypi have a polypoid type of growth and occur unilaterally.

Some of the polypi are very extensive and have produced sufficient pressure to cause complete atrophy of the turbinates. Nasal polypi vary a great deal in shape consistency and place of attachment. Some polypi will be round with a wall about one-half inch thick and containing a small amount of a thin yellowish fluid. These are usually lightly attached to the nasal septum. In some cases the polypus will have a large enlargement at the nostril, then a long narrow band of tissue which extends along

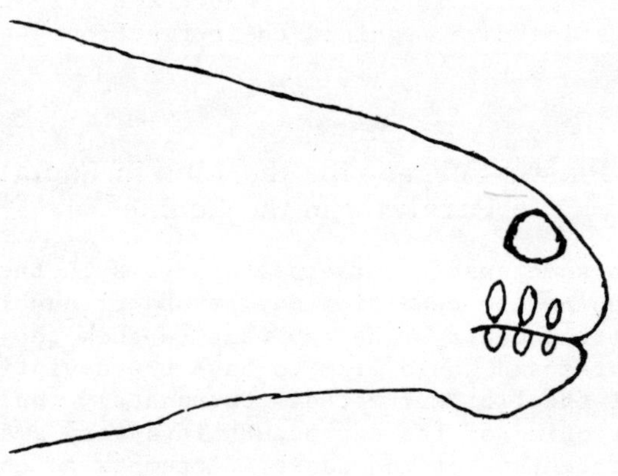

The approximate location of the operative areas to correct deviation of lips.

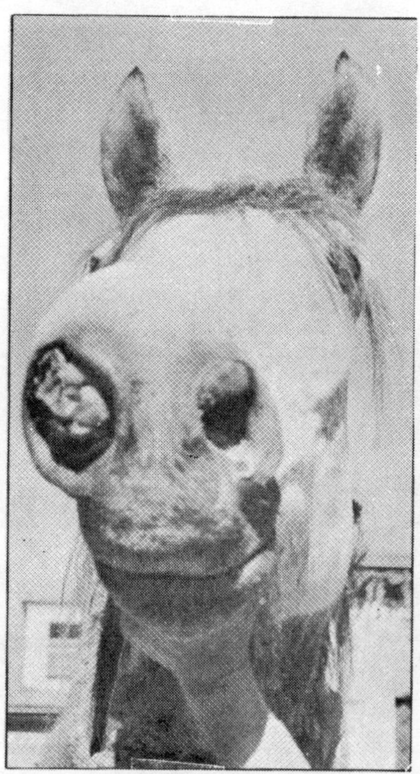

FIG. 204. Nasal polypus that is occluding right side of nasal cavity.

the floor of the nasal cavity to be attached in the posterior part of the nasal cavity. In other cases the polypus will be a large mass of tissue that completely fills the nasal cavity and seems to originate in the alveolus of the third cheek tooth. During the operation for the removal of nasal polypi the hemmorhage may be rather profuse but stops as soon as the operation is complete.

OPERATION. In removing a nasal polypus it is usually necessary to trephine into the nasal cavity. Anesthesia of the nasal cavity may be obtained by blocking the maxillary nerve on the side to be operated. The trephine opening should be made far enough lateral from the median line so the nasal septum will not be injured. By introducing a finger through the trephine opening the cutting edge of any instrument used can be directed so that normal structures will not be injured. In some cases it is necessary to divide the polypus into several pieces before it can be removed. There is little tendency for the polypus to recur if all of the tissue is removed.

Necrosis of the Turbinates

This above condition practically always occurs in the horse. It may result from excessive pressure on the turbinates, from pus in the turbinate portion of the frontal sinus, or from pus in the maxillary sinus.

OPERATION. Consists in first blocking the maxillary nerve, also a sedative dose of chloral hydrate if the patient is nervous. It is also best to perform a tracheotomy. Make a trephine opening where the nasal bones start to diverge and far enough from the median line to avoid injury to the nasal septum. Cut the cartilaginous anterior end of the turbinate loose from its attachment anteriorly and with a nasal septum chisel cut the attachment of the turbinate from the lateral wall of the nasal cavity. Divide the turbinate transversely at the height of the trephine opening and pull it through the nostril. Profuse hemorrhage occurs so it is necessary to tamponade the cavity tightly with gauze. It is impossible to completely remove the ventral turbinate due to its anatomical location.

The Sinuses

When it is necessary to invade the sinuses of either the equine or bovine it is essential that the operator have a thorough understanding of the complicated anatomy of these structures.

ANATOMY. In the equine the two sinuses of greatest surgical importance are the frontal and maxillary. According to Sisson the frontal sinus in the horse consists of two portions; namely, the frontal part and the turbinate parts, so designated because the former is bounded by the frontal bone while the latter is located in the dorsal turbinate bone. The frontal part, with the head held in a horizontal position, extends as far forward as a line drawn from the medial canthus of one eye to that of the opposite side. It is separated from the sinus of the opposite side by a complete bony septum.

The turbinate part of the frontal sinus is located in the posterior part of the dorsal turbinate. The anterior limit may best be determined by passing the thumb and index finger backward along the nasal bones and at the point where the fingers start to deviate from each other will be found the anterior limit of the turbinate part of the frontal sinus. An important surgical point to bear in mind is that this turbinate part is separated from the nasal cavity by the thin tissue of the dorsal turbinate. The frontal and maxillary sinus in the horse communicates through a large fronto-maxillary opening which is situated ventral to the osseous lacrimal canal. The frontal sinus in the horse has no direct communication with the nasal cavity.

The maxillary sinus occupies a large portion of the region immediately anterior to the orbital cavity and even under this space. Its anterior limit corresponds quite generally to a line drawn from the anterior extremity of the facial crest to the infra-orbital foramen. Medially the maxillary sinus is in contact with the ventral turbinate. The maxillary sinus of the horse is divided into anterior and posterior compartments, the former constituting the inferior maxillary sinus and the latter the superior maxillary sinus. This septum is said to be absent in the mule. The complete bony septum in the equine is between the anterior and posterior parts, and is about two inches from the anterior end of the facial crest, and from here it is directed inward, backward, and upward.

The posterior compartment of the maxillary sinus has passing through it the bony infraorbital canal which serves for the passage of the large sensory infraorbital nerve. This compartment communicates with the nasal cavity through a very narrow slit located at the posterior part of the middle meatus. The anterior compartment of the maxillary sinus is partially divided by the bony partition which arises from its floor and which serves to carry along its upper border the infraorbital canal into a lateral or maxillary part and into a medial or turbinate part. The turbinate part communicates with the nasal cavity by means of a narrow slit in the middle meatus. The roots of the last four cheek teeth project into the maxillary sinus, that is, the third partially in the anterior compartment, the fourth entirely so, and the fifth is usually on the dividing line between the anterior and posterior compartments. The sixth is in the posterior compartment.

Surgery of the sinuses is more frequently indicated in the equine than any of the other species. This is due to the frequency of alveolar periostitis permitting infection to gain entrance to the maxillary sinus.

CYSTS - Congenital cysts may occur in both the maxillary and frontal sinus of the equine and are occasionally seen in the bovine. They may consist of from one to any number of teeth that are incompletely developed and usually imbedded in embryonic tissue. The sinus is usually filled with a yellowish fluid. Usually these cysts do not manifest their presence until the animal is three or four years of age. The pressure of the fluid in the sinus produces a non-inflammatory rounded bulging of the bones over the sinus. As the pressure increases in the maxillary sinus there may be interference with the functioning of the bony naso-lacrimal canal. Also enough pressure in the maxillary sinus to push the medial wall over against the nasal septum occluding that side of the nasal cavity may occur.

Prognosis will be determined by the extent of the involvement of the sinus and whether all of the tissue can be removed without extensive damage to normal structures.

Treatment would consist in trephining of the sinuses to permit complete removal of the process and any teeth that are present.

When there is bulging of the bones over a sinus it may be due to a neoplasm, a cyst or pus. In Figs. 206 and 207 both horses were two years of age and each horse had a different condition. The only way to determine the cause of the bulging of the bones is to invade the sinus.

Empyema of the Sinuses of the Equine

Infection frequently gains entrance to the frontal sinus of the horse and it is difficult to obtain adequate drainage from this sinus unless certain guides are borne in mind. The frontal sinus has a frontal portion and a turbinate portion, the latter directly continuous of the former, and in turn separated from the nasal cavity only by the thin wall of the dorsal turbinate - It is evident that the logical route for the outflow of cavity material is through the nose, accomplished by making an artificial opening through the medial wall of

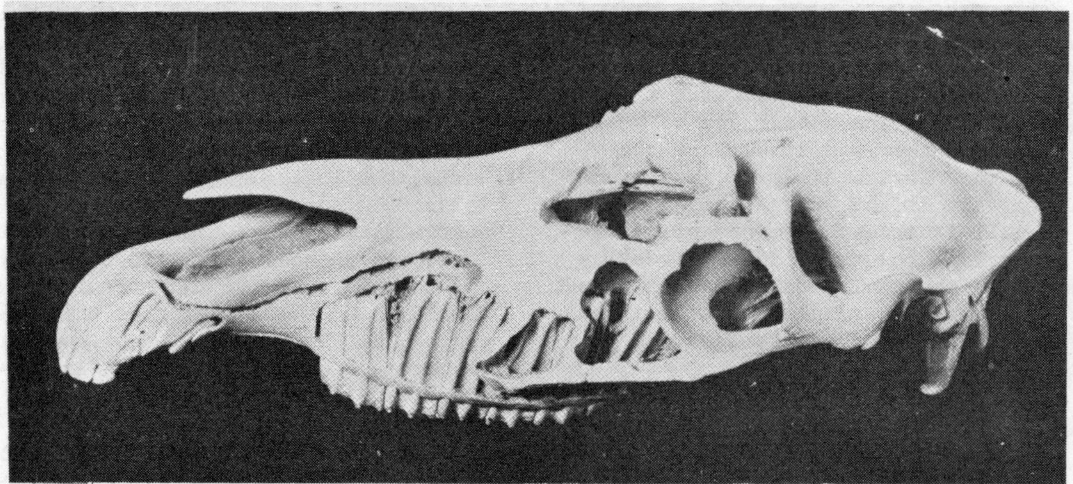

FIG. 205. Skull of horse with sinuses opened to show anatomy and extent of both the frontal and maxillary sinus.

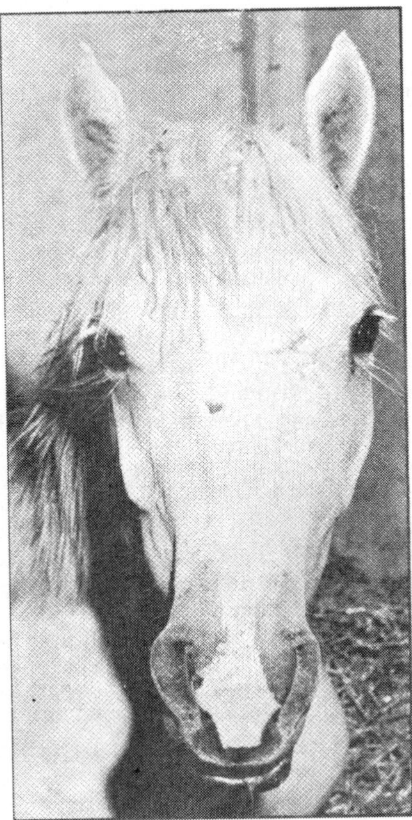

FIG. 206. Cyst in the maxillary sinus on the left side that has produced a bulging of the bones.

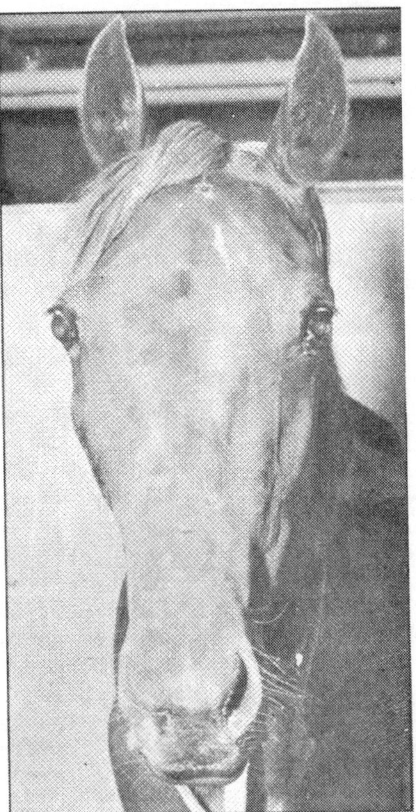

FIG. 207. Fibrosarcoma in maxillary sinus on right side produced bulging of bones and protrusion of right eye.

the dorsal turbinate at a point corresponding to the anterior limit of the turbinate portion of the frontal sinus.

It has already been indicated that to locate the anterior limit of the turbinate portion of the frontal sinus, the operator should pass the thumb and index finger backward along the nasal bones, and where they begin to diverge there is located the anterior limit of the cavity.

First make a trephine opening two inches posterior to the anterior limit of the turbinate portion of the frontal sinus as indicated by the thumb and index finger. This trephine opening should be about one inch from the middle line, pass the index finger of the left hand through this trephine opening, in a forward direction into the cavity of the turbinate portion of the frontal bone and press it against its medial wall so that the end of a female catheter, passed with the right hand into the nasal cavity, may be distinctly felt. The point of the female catheter is then forced from the nasal cavity into the turbinate portion of the frontal sinus by breaking down the relatively thin partition separating the two. In order to keep the opening thus made from closing, a piece of twisted gauze should be passed through it - and it should be long enough so that one end will emerge from the nostril and the other from the trephine opening. Tie the two ends over the outside of the face.

Though the foregoing step will permit of free drainage from the frontal sinus, it does not drain the communicating posterior compartment of the maxillary sinus. This compartment should therefore be drained just posterior to the septum dividing it from the anterior compartment, but as the position of this septum is variable, we cannot always determine the exact place to trephine in relation to it. The best plan, therefore, is to make a trephine opening into the posterior compartment of the maxillary sinus at some point anterior to the rim of the orbital cavity and about midway between the facial crest and the position of the osseous lacrimal canal. The finger may be introduced into this trephine opening and by palpation we may determine the exact location of the anterior limit of the posterior compartment of the maxillary sinus, so that a second trephine opening may be made for effective drainage. This compartment of the maxillary sinus also has a very shallow depression medial to the infraorbital canal, but it seldom or never requires a separate drainage opening. In many instances, if the fifth or sixth cheek teeth have been removed, the passageway thus created will provide an excellent drainage opening.

To obtain drainage from the anterior compartment of the maxillary sinus demands steps independent from those taken for the frontal sinus and the posterior compartment of the maxillary sinus. In fact, the anterior compartment of the maxillary sinus is seldom involved in an infection of the other sinuses. It is usually an independent empyema. To drain it, the operator must remember that it is partially divided into a lateral or maxillary portion, and a turbinate portion by the bony septum that carries along its superior border the infraorbital canal. Each of these cavities requires separate drainage. The lateral or maxillary portion is effectively drained by making a trephine opening in the angle formed by the anterior extremity of the facial crest and an imaginary line drawn from it to the infraorbital foramen. In old horses - because the roots of the teeth are not very long - we may then break through the bony septum which carries the infraorbital canal and thus establish good drainage from the turbinate portion. In young horses the roots of the teeth prevent this, and therefore by means of a grooved instrument passed through the trephine opening first made, over the infraorbital canal, thus entering the turbinate portion of the anterior compartment of the maxillary sinus and forcing the tip of the instrument through the medial wall of the ventral turbinate into the nasal cavity. The opening thus made should also be kept open by means of a twisted gauze passed through it and the ends tied on the outside of the animal's face.

Bovine

Infection of the frontal sinus in the bovine occurs most frequently following the dehorning operation, especially in animals mature enough so there is an opening from the frontal sinus into the horn process.

Sinuses of tne Bovine

The frontal sinus of the bovine is very different from that of the horse. It corresponds to the anterior surface of the cranium and also extends into the horn core.

ANATOMY. The anterior limit of the frontal sinus corresponds to an imaginary line passed through the middle of the orbits. Medially it is separated from the sinus of the opposite side by a complete septum. Posterior this sinus extends to the region of the pole. Laterally it extends to a point anterior to the external ear. The outstanding difference between the sinus of the horse and the ox is that in the latter it is separated by many bony septa which makes complete drainage almost impossible. As in the horse the frontal sinus of the ox has a turbinate portion. It is separated from it by a complete septum, so that this does not have the same surgical significance as in the horse. It is well to bear in mind, however, the frontal sinus of the ox communicates normally with the nasal cavity, through the ethomid cells. As these openings are very small and when the mucous membrane lining them is swollen, they are virtually closed. Another anatomical point to bear in mind is that one of the numerous compartments of the frontal sinus is virtually back of the orbital cavity. It is known as the post-orbital diverticulum, and is separated from the temporal fossa by only a very thin plate of bone, so that when this breaks down infection readily involves the region in back of the eye.

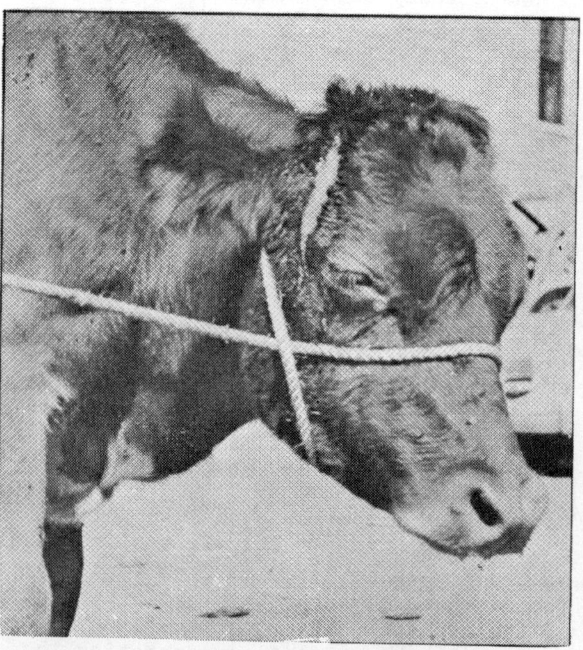

FIG. 208. Empyema of the frontal sinus.

SIGNS. The signs of pus in the frontal sinus of the bovine may be rather obscure until bulging of the frontal bone occurs or a thickening of the frontal bone in the region of the post-orbital diverticulum is observed. In some cases the pus will produce enough pressure to push the cranial plate of bone down upon the brain producing symptoms of a brain disturbance. The affected animal may be observed pushing against a wall or manger with the head. Also it may have fits or convulsions at rather frequent intervals. Sometimes the head is held extended and in the case of a cow in production there may be a decided drop in milk flow. If the thin plate of bone between the frontal sinus and the temporal fossa breaks down, pus accumulates in the region posterior to the orbit. This usually produces enough pressure to cause an exophthalmus or protrusion of the eyeball.

Trephining Frontal Sinus of Bovine for Empyema

To obtain drainage from the frontal sinus, it is necessary to make openings outwardly so the various compartments and diverticuli will drain. Such openings should be made where the frontal sinus has its deepest parts. When infection develops in the frontal sinus the pus is most frequently retained in the post-orbital diverticulum. This produces a marked thickening of the tissues on the affected side. A definite diagnosis can usually be made by palpation and observing the difference in thickness of the frontal sinus on the affected and normal sides.

To obtain complete drainage from the post-orbital diverticulum a trephine opening should be made medial to the bony ridge which marks the lateral limit of the frontal sinus. It is also made approximately one and one-half inches from the posterior edge of the orbital cavity when the head is held in the horizontal position. The other part of the frontal sinus may be drained by a trephine opening made posterior to a line passing through the center of the orbits and approximately one and one-half inches from the median line. The need for making a trephine opening at this point is indicated when there is a bulging of the tissues in this area. The other point to trephine is determined by passing the thumb and finger upward on each side of the nasal bones. At the point where the fingers start to diverge is the place to make the trephine opening. This will drain the turbinate portion of the frontal sinus. Occasionally this cavity becomes filled with pus and then causes a variable degree of dyspnea. In some cases the swelling of the tissues may become so extensive as to close that side of the nasal cavity.

If an abscess occurs in the temporal fossa as a result of the infection breaking through the thin plate of bone that limits the post-orbital diverticulum, the best that can be done is to make an incision at the most prominent part of the swelling and establishing fair but imperfect drainage through this incision. Usually this opening only gives relief until the animal can be marketed.

The indications for trephining the maxillary sinus of the bovine are not very numerous, but they do occur. In some cases infection has gained entrance producing pus, or the sinus may contain a clear, watery fluid. This is especially true in young animals. Enough pressure may be produced to push the turbinate over against the nasal septum completely occluding that side of the nasal cavity. In this case a distinct dyspnea is noticed and it will also be noticed that no air is passing through the affected side. If the infection is actinomycotic there is usually a pronounced bulging of the bones, and this type of case is usually hopeless to treat.

TREATMENT. To drain the maxillary sinus of the bovine more than a year old a trephine opening may be made just above and back of the facial tubercle. In animals under a year of age it is necessary to make the trephine opening about one inch higher due to the projection of the roots of the cheek teeth.

Resection of the Nasal Septum

The nasal septum is subject to injury from a traumatism on the nostrils or when fracture of nasal bones occur. Both conditions may produce fracture of the nasal septum and a thickening result, sufficient to produce dyspnea. Apparently one of the after effects of influenza is a thickening of the mucous membrane covering the turbinates which results in a pronounced respiratory noise or it may result in an inspiratory dyspnea.

Resection of the nasal septum is performed for the above conditions and also for diag-

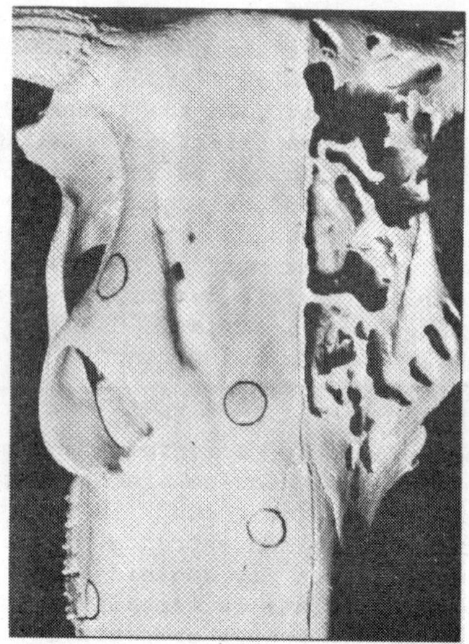

Fig. 209. The skull of the bovine with three circles indicating preferred points for trephining frontal sinus.

nostic purposes when it is impossible to determine by any other method what is affecting the nasal cavity.

OPERATION. A tracheotomy operation is performed to permit breathing as it is necessary to tamponade the nasal cavity to control hemorrhage.

Anesthesia of the operative area may be obtained by blocking both maxillary nerves. If the patient is of a nervous disposition, it is advisable to give a sedative dose of chloral hydrate, nembutal or combination of drugs to control struggling.

A trephine opening is made on the median line of the face at the point where the nasal bones start to diverge from each other. This is determined by placing the thumb and finger on either side of the nasal bones and passing them backward over the dorso-lateral surface. The trephine operation should be stopped as soon as the trephine has cut through the bone. This is to prevent injuring the mucous membrane and producing hemorrhage at this stage of the operation. A pair of compression forceps with jaws four inches long are inserted through the trephine opening and astride the nasal septum. The points of the forceps should reach the full width

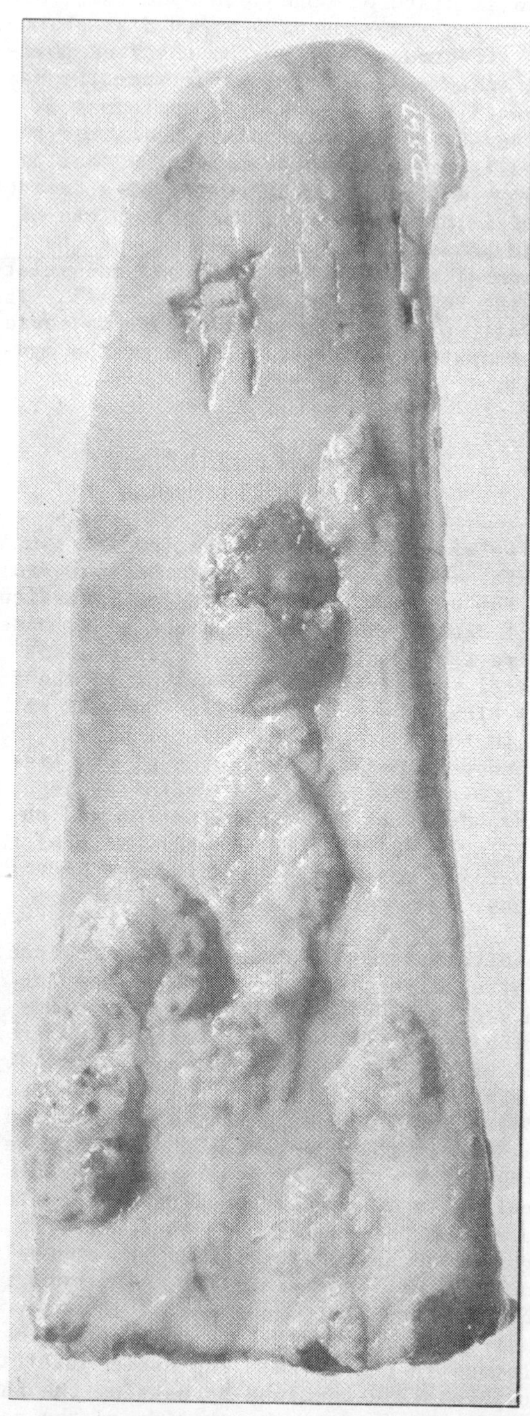

FIG. 210. Extensive granulomatous that were present on both sides of the nasal septum due to Mucormycosis infection.

of the nasal septum and are then closed tightly.

The nasal septum is then divided anteriorly by a curved incision, leaving at least two inches of the septum to support the nostril. Secure the cut end with a pair of forceps, then place a nasal septum chisel astride the septum and push it along the superior border of the nasal septum until the chisel comes in contact with the forceps. Withdraw the chisel and insert in the same manner along the floor of the nostril, cutting the septum free from the vomer bone. With a narrow chisel placed anterior to and in contact with the forceps, divide the septum transversely and remove the septum through the nostril. Tamponade the nasal cavity tightly with gauze which has been impregnated with some antiseptic as two parts boric acid and one part chlorinated lime. The gauze controls very nicely the severe hemorrhage that usually occurs. It is advisable to suture the nostrils shut to retain the tampon in position. The tampon may be removed in forty-eight hours and also the trachea tube.

After treatment consists in irrigating the nasal cavity with a mild antiseptic solution through the trephine opening.

Cleft Palate

The soft palate in the equine is well developed with a length of approximately six inches. It separates the cavity of the mouth from that of the pharynx except during swallowing. The soft palate serves as a flap or valve that permits food or water to enter the esophagus and prevents food from entering the nasal passages. When a cleft or split occurs in the soft palate, food or water gains entrance to the nasal passages and comes out the nose. The presence of food or water in the nasal cavity produces a chronic irritation of the tissues. This inflammation and also failure of some of the food to reach the stomach is responsible for the animal not doing well physically.

The repair of the soft palate should be made when the colt is only a few weeks old. At this age the parts are more accessible and the colt may nurse without interfering with the healing of the wound. In performing the operation special instruments will have to be made so one can operate in a narrow space and at great depth. To provide fresh surfaces on the edges of the soft palate it will be necessary to remove a thin layer of tissue. The tissue can be

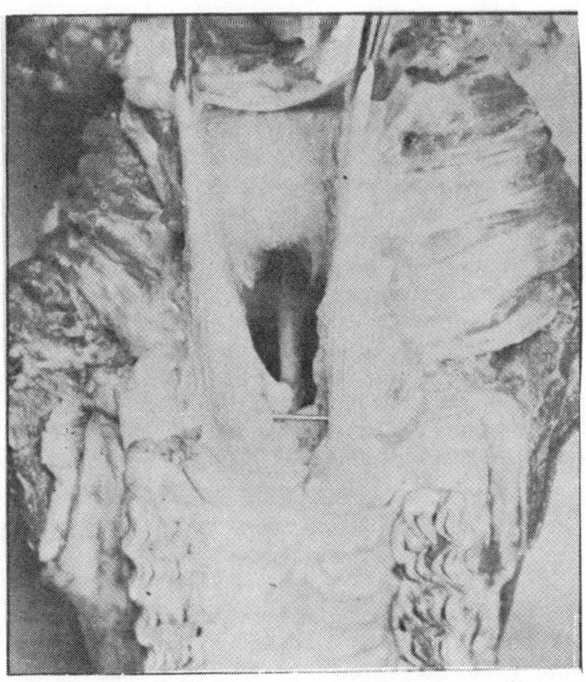

FIG. 211. Cleft soft palate.

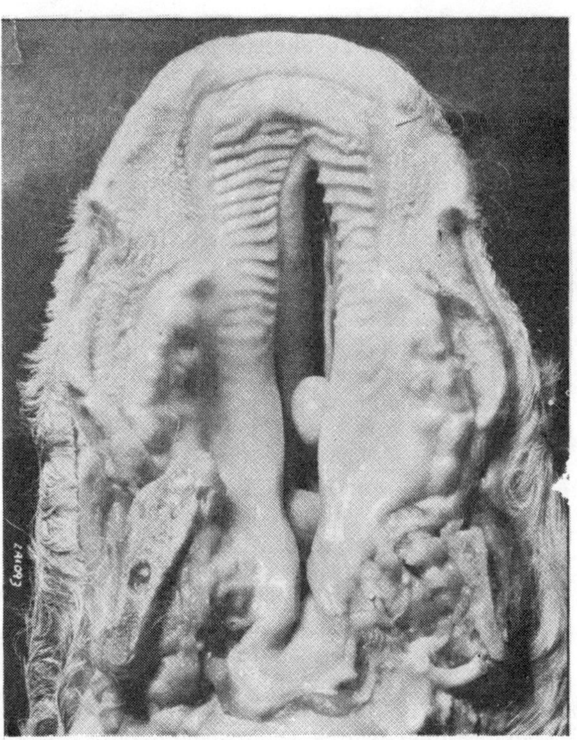

FIG. 212. Cleft in hard and soft palate that was present when calf was born.

removed by using a curved blade fastened to a long handle. A needle holder will need to be devised for holding a full curved needle so the sutures can be inserted where they are indicated. For suture material No. 1 chromic catgut is preferred so it will not be necessary to remove the sutures. The tediousness of knot tying can be eliminated by passing the suture material through split shot which can be crushed at the point where the knot would be tied. Several main sutures are inserted to prevent tension and some approximation of the edges. Also additional uniting sutures are inserted to bring the edges in close apposition. If the colt is confined on its back the blood and mucus will drain away from the operative area. When the patient nurses in a normal manner after the operation there is little need for any after care.

Palatitis

(Lampas, Lampers)

Palatitis is an inflammation and thickening of the hard palate immediately posterior to the superior incisors.

ETIOLOGY. This condition is observed most frequently in young horses during the development of the teeth. The palate may appear thickened because the teeth are still too short to extend below the soft tissue.

TREATMENT. The owner observes the projection of the tissue below the table surface of the incisor teeth and is convinced the condition should be treated. The usual forms of treatment have been to scarify or cauterize the first few bars of the palate to cause them to shrink below the level of the table surface of the teeth. However, such treatment is unnecessary and the owner should be advised to feed the horse soft feed for a short time.

Gnathitis

This is an inflammation of the mandible in the inter-dental space.

ETIOLOGY. The most frequent cause of injury to the tissues in the interdental space is severe use of curb bits. However, any bit may cause bruising of the tissues if extreme pressure is produced until the soft tissues are injured. In some cases injury to the periosteum and bone may occur.

SIGNS. The condition occurs most frequently in race, show and saddle horses. Horses that are affected are driven with difficulty and usually hold the head to one side. They may show sensitiveness when the bit is adjusted or may refuse to take the bit.

TREATMENT. A bit should not be used until the tissue is healed as its use delays healing. If pus has formed under the mucous membrane complete drainage must be established. When there is necrosis of bone the sequestra should not be removed until it is loose from the underlying tissue. Only mild antiseptics should be used in treating this condition.

Ranula

A ranula is a cystic tumor belonging to the class of retention cysts. It occurs under the tongue near the frenum. They increase in size slowly and have no tendenty to rupture.

SYMPTOMS. May cause disturbed prehension and mastication with increased salivation.

TREATMENT. Best method is complete removal of the entire cyst wall. The cyst may be freely opened and the cavity swabbed with tincture of iodine.

Tongue

Occasionally in cattle an individual is found that is persistent about sucking the milk from herself or another cow. A simple and effective method of stopping this is to insert two hog rings in the tongue. One ring is put in the ventral surface where the frenum joins the tongue, and another ring is put in two inches anterior to the first ring. The rings should not enclose too much tissue, or the excessive swelling that occurs will cause the rings to cut through the tissue. It is necessary that the rings remain in the tongue permanently if this persistent habit is controlled.

Dentition

In the domestic animals there are two sets of teeth, the milk teeth or temporary teeth, and these are replaced by the permanent teeth.

Horse

There are three pairs of incisor teeth in the upper and lower jaws, named the centrals, laterals, and corners. The incisor teeth of the lower jaw provide a fairly accurate guide as to the age of the animal.

In Sisson's Anatomy is given the following eruption table for the teeth.

A. Deciduous

Teeth	Eruption
First incisor	(Di 1) Birth or first week
Second incisor	(Di 2) 4-6 weeks
Third incisor	(Di 3) 6-9 months
Canine	(Dc)
First premolar	(Dp 2) Birth or
Second premolar	(Dp 3) first two
Third premolar	(Dp 4) weeks

B. Permanent

Teeth	Eruption
First incisor	(I 1) 2½ years
Second incisor	(I 2) 3½ years
Third incisor	(I 3) 4½ years
Canine	(C) 4-5 years
First premolar or wolf tooth	(P 1) 5-6 months
Second premolar	(P 2) 2½ years
Third premolar	(P 3) 3 years
Fourth premolar	(P 4) 4 years
First molar	(M 1) 10-12 months
Second molar	(M 2) 2 years
Third molar	(M 3) 3½-4 years

All the permanent incisor teeth should be present at five years of age. For the next three years the regular disappearance of the cups from the lower incisor teeth is a fairly accurate guide as to the age of the horse.

At six years of age the cups have disappeared from the centrals, at seven years old the cups have disappeared from the laterals. Also at this age a definite projection forming the so-called seven year notch is apparent at the posterior edge of the upper corner incisor. This is because the lower corner incisor tooth does not completely oppose the upper corner tooth. At eight years of age the horse has a smooth mouth and the seven year notch has disappeared.

Due to the wear of the incisors there is a gradual change in the shape of the table surface. In the young horse they are wider from side to side, then the centrals at nine years become triangular in outline. This occurs in the laterals at ten, and in the corners at eleven years. The so-called Galvayne's groove appears close to the gum of the corner incisor tooth and gradually extends downward so it is about half way down at fifteen years and has reached the table surface of the tooth at twenty years of age.

Bovine

The age of cattle can be approximated closely by the appearance, development, and subsequent wear of their permanent incisor teeth. However, the eruption of the permanent teeth may be subject to considerable variation. In the calf all of the eight temporary incisor teeth are present within the first month of age.

From 1½ to 2 years of age the central pair of temporary incisors are replaced by the permanent incisors.

The intermediate pair of permanent incisors erupt on the average from 2 to 2½ years of age, although some writers give from 2½ to 3 years of age.

The lateral pair of permanent incisors erupt on the average from 2½ to 3 years of age, again other writers give from 3½ to 4 years.

The corner pair of permanent incisors erupt from 3½ to 4 years of age, again other writers give from 4½ to 5 years.

Examination of the teeth of the bovine is not performed as frequently as it should be. When an individual is off feed or losing in condition examination of the teeth should be a regular part of the examination. It has been observed that cows off feed and losing in condition and some were even showing nervous symptoms because of defective teeth.

A case was presented with a history that the cow had been losing in condition for about three months. She had a good appetite but in drinking, lapped up water like a dog. It would require several hours for her to drink a gallon of water. Examination of the teeth revealed an elongated cheek tooth. When this was removed she drank water in a normal manner and there was a marked improvement in her general condition.

Foreign Bodies in the Mouth

Due to the habit of cattle licking or chewing on objects they frequently take these into their mouth. After they take an object into their mouth it may be impossible for them to get it out of their mouth. These objects may become wedged between the teeth or between the cheek and teeth. Some of the objects that have been removed from the mouths of cattle are tin cans that have been flattened, a portion of a corn cob, wedged between the upper cheek teeth transversely across the hard palate. A rather large piece of bone is probably the foreign object found most frequently in the mouth of the bovine.

SYMPTOMS. The most pronounced symptoms are the almost constant chewing movements they make attempting to get the object out of the mouth, excessive salivation, inability to eat, uneasiness and usually a very anxious expression. The above symptoms should suggest, to the examiner to make a very careful examination of the mouth. When the mouth is held open with a speculum the foreign object can be removed with the hand. In some cases it will facilitate the removal of the object if a pair of forceps are available as frequently the foreign object is wedged tightly in the mouth.

After the object is removed the soft tissues of the mouth should be examined to see if any treatment is required. Any swelling of the tissues will subside after the object is removed.

Ovine

The age of sheep may be judged fairly accurately with the eruption of the permanent incisor teeth. As in cattle there is considerable variation. The average period of eruption of the permanent incisor teeth is the same as given for the bovine.

In Circular No. 149, of Montana State College, some variations were noted on range sheep. They observed that sheep with all their permanent incisor teeth are usually three year olds and a typical three year old mouth is probably a two year old.

Affections of the Teeth

Examination

The ability to make a thorough examination of the teeth of the horse is acquired with experience and close observation. The requirements to acquire this ability consist of:

1. Complete knowledge of the eruption of the temporary and permanent teeth.
2. Know the normal number of permanent teeth.
3. The abnormal conditions that may be present should be known.
4. The history of the case is important.

To enable the examiner to make a complete examination it is necessary to use a speculum. A well developed sense of touch is important in the manual examination. A good light that can be placed over each tooth is especially valuable for the examination of the table surface of the teeth.

Supernumerary Teeth

Supernumerary incisors and molars are of frequent occurrence while canines are rarely found. The supernumerary teeth develop when more than one stalk grows from the permanent tooth germs.

SIGNS. The incisor arcades are most often affected and in some cases there may be a double row of incisors. However, in most cases there are only one or two extra incisors. Increase in the number of cheek teeth is of frequent occurrence. They may occur either medial or lateral to the normal cheek teeth but in most cases they are found posterior either above or below.

Due to lack of wear by any opposing teeth supernumerary teeth become elongated and should be cut off or removed as they may cause severe and extensive injury to the opposing soft tissue. If the supernumerary tooth is not causing any trouble it should be left alone. In the examination of the teeth the examiner should determine if there are any supernumerary teeth present.

Abnormal Position of Teeth

Brachynathism (Parrot mouth)

A congenital deformity in the length of the jaws with the upper longer than the lower. As the teeth are not in contact for wear they become elongated and the lower incisors may injure the soft tissues above. Also the affected animal may have

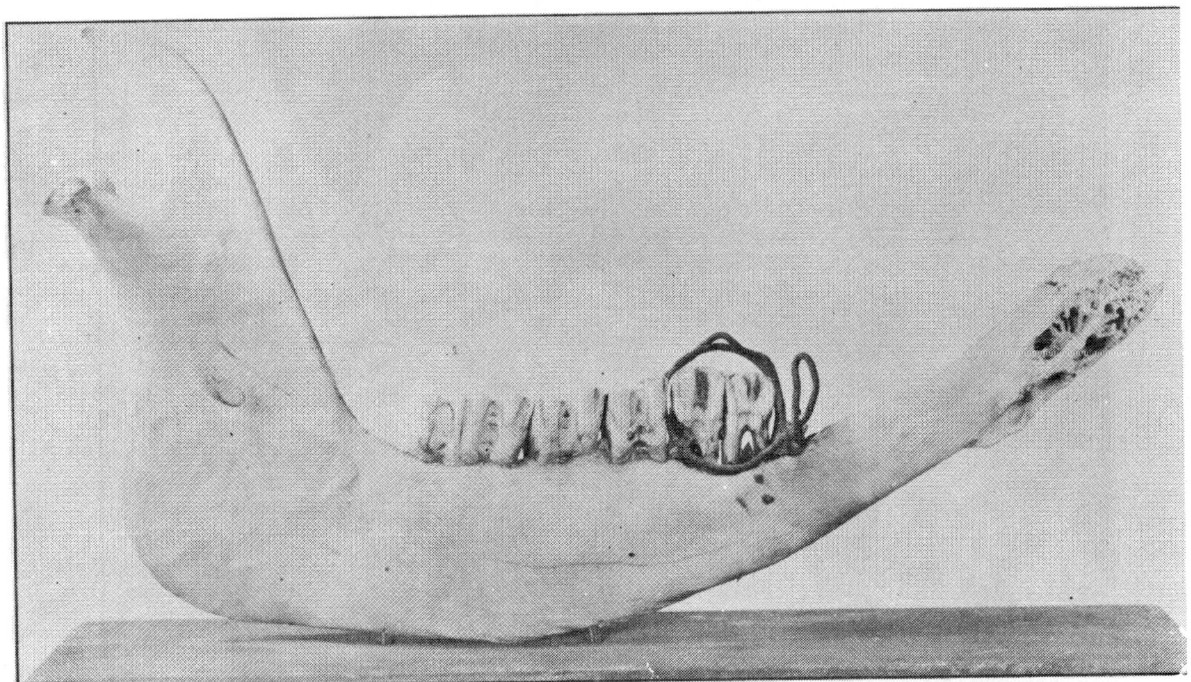

FIG. 213. One good example of why the teeth should be examined in the bovine.

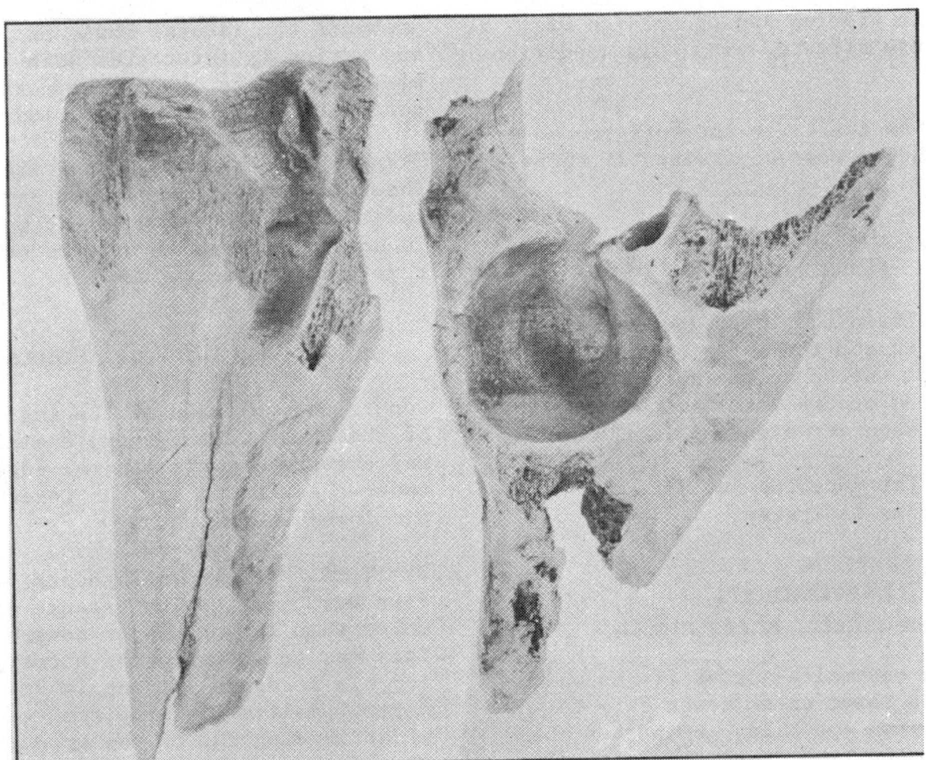

FIG. 214. Typical foreign bodies removed from the oral cavities of the bovine.

FIG. 215. Supernumerary molars are present posterior to the sixth cheek teeth in the lower arcades.

difficulty in grazing and prehension of food. A horse affected with this condition is unsound.

TREATMENT. As the lower incisors become elongated they should be frequently shortened.

Prognathism (Undershot)

In this condition the lower jaw is longer than the upper and the inferior incisors extend beyond the superior incisor teeth. This condition occurs most commonly in the dog, but is seen occasionally in the horse.

TREATMENT. The superior incisors should be shortened as indicated.

Parvinathism (Scissor mouth, shear mouth

Apparently a congenital deformity in which the upper and lower cheek teeth fail to meet properly on one side. Frost has observed this condition develop because of a sensitive cheek tooth in the opposite arcade. This results in the upper cheek teeth being beveled from the inside out and the lower cheek teeth are beveled in the opposite direction. This deformity prevents the lateral movement of the teeth and seriously interferes with mastication of food. It is one of the most serious deformities of the horse's mouth.

TREATMENT. The beveled portion of the cheek teeth must be removed and in most cases it is necessary to use molar cutters. In advanced cases it will be necessary to remove the cheek teeth close to the gums.

Sharp Enamel Points

Due to unequal wear of the table surface of the cheek teeth, sharp enamel points may occur along the lateral edge of the upper cheek teeth and the inner edge of the lower cheek teeth.

SYMPTOMS. Long enamel points may interfere with mastication because of pain produced when the cheeks or tongue are injured. This may be shown by the horse partly chewing his food and letting it drop from the mouth. Saliva may drip from the mouth while feeding due to the production of an excessive quantity of saliva. The horse chews rather cautiously on food sometimes holding his head to one side. Lacerations of the cheek or tongue may occur and in some cases large ulcer like area are produced in the mucous membrane.

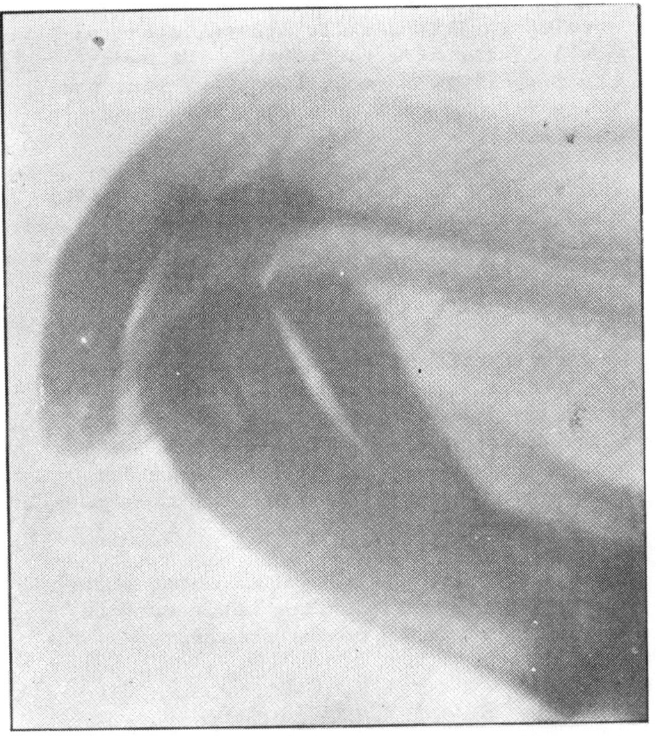

FIG. 216. Brachynathism of the incisor teeth the lower incisors can injure the soft tissues.

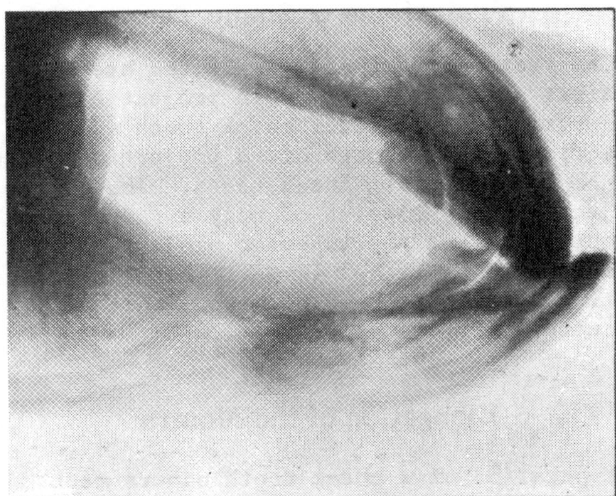

FIG. 217. Prognathism in a Shetland pony.

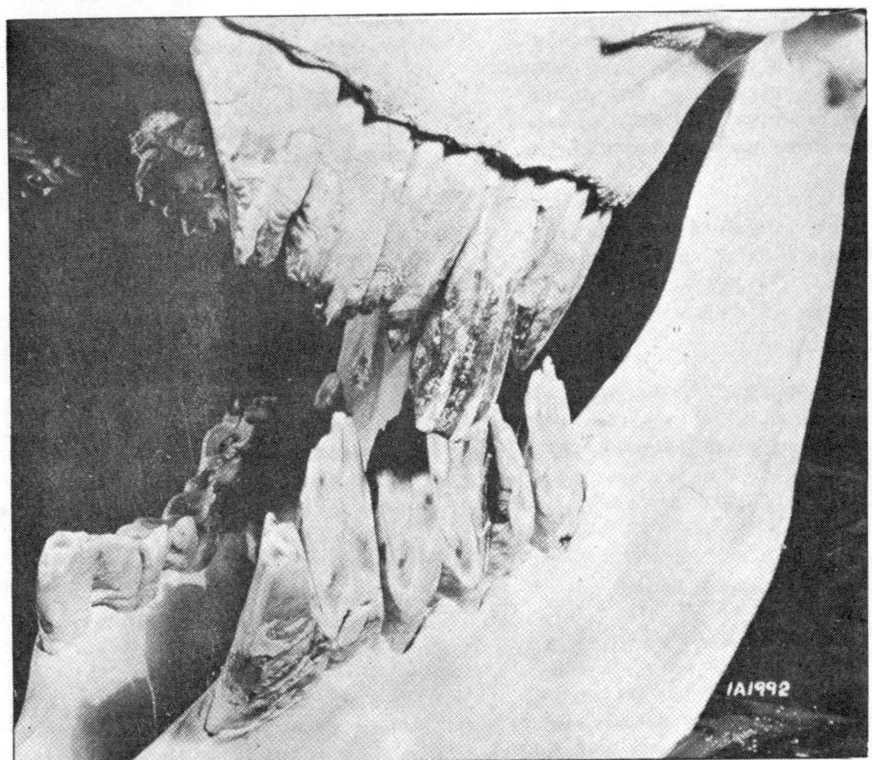

FIG. 218. A case of parvinathism affecting the cheek teeth on the left side.

TREATMENT. The extremely long sharp points are removed with a float and usually only a few strokes are necessary. The horse offers less resistance to the movements of the float if it is pushed the entire length of the arcade with each stroke. The operator can usually tell from the difference in the rasping sound of the float when the points have been removed.

Projections of Single Teeth

The teeth most commonly affected are the first superior cheek tooth projecting down in front of the lower cheek tooth and last inferior cheek tooth has a projection behind the last superior cheek tooth. These projections may consist of only a sharp point but sometimes the superior projection in front may be rather large. These projections should be removed with float, molar cutter or tooth chisel.

Elongation of the Molars

Elongation of a cheek tooth occurs most commonly where the opposite cheek tooth has been removed. It is also observed when the opposite cheek tooth is still in position but excessive wear of the cheek tooth has occurred. In these cases this cheek tooth seems to be of a softer texture. When the elongated cheek tooth develops from the inferior arcade, it may become long enough to injure the hard palate. A few cases have been observed where an opening was made through the hard palate into the nasal cavity.

SIGNS. Difficulty in mastication, passage of poorly masticated food, and gradual loss of condition. Palpation will readily reveal the presence of the elongated cheek tooth.

TREATMENT. The elongated cheek tooth is cut to the level of the other cheek teeth in the arcade. It is usually necessary to use a compound molar cutter to remove the elongations of the superior arcade.

Undulating Molar Tables

A wave like condition occurs along the molar arcade due to uneven wear of the teeth. This condition may be unilateral or bilateral and usually the lower row of cheek teeth is concave and the upper row convex. This abnormal shape of the table surface is most serious when an infundibulum is opened and alveolar periostitis develops. This usually necessitates removal of the affected tooth. The owner observes it is more difficult to keep the horse in good condition when this condition is present.

TREATMENT. It is advisable to shorten the elongated cheek teeth and remove any diseased teeth.

Step-Formed Tables

In this condition the cheek teeth become unequal in height. This is usually produced when several cheek teeth are absent alternately and the opposite cheek teeth become elongated. It is impossible for normal mastication to occur with this condition present.

TREATMENT. Cut the elongated cheek teeth so they are level with the table surface of the other teeth in the arcade.

Smooth Table Surface

In aged horses it is commonly observed the table surface of some of the cheek teeth is worn smooth. In some cases the table surface is smooth and concave. The owner observes the horse has difficulty in eating hay and the horse is not in good condition.

TREATMENT. It is impossible to correct the smooth condition of the teeth. The usual recommendation is to prepare the feed so it will require less mastication.

Irregularities in Structure of Teeth

Probably the most common defect in the development of the cheek teeth is the failure of complete cementation of the infundibuli. When the infundibuli are not closed with cement decomposing food material in the infundibuli breaks down the cement into the pulp cavity. When this occurs infection develops in the pulp cavity and the alveolus. This is considered to be the most common cause of alveolar periostitis.

One other defect that may occur in the tooth structure may be improper union of the dentinal folds. When this occurs the tooth may split so that only a thin piece breaks away from the tooth. In some cases the split extends from the table surface to the gum line and then breaks transversely.

When the part that is split falls away it causes no further trouble. In other cases the split may extend the entire length of the tooth and food will pack in between the two portions forcing them apart. The lateral portion may produce pressure on the aveolar periosteum with the development of a painful periostitis. If the sharp end of the lateral portion is forced out far enough it may produce painful laceration of the cheek. Also the splitting of the tooth may permit infection to gain access to the pulp cavity and the alveolus.

Chronic Ossifying Alveolar Periostitis

In chronic ossifying alveolar periostitis there is sometimes evidence of infection in the alveolus that is responsible for the periostitis and in other cases the periostitis seems to develop without infection. In the largest percentage of the cases it is seen in horses from two to three years of age. However it does occur in horses one year of age and it has been observed in horses four and five years old. The upper third cheek tooth is the one most frequently affected, in some cases the second and it is unusual for the first cheek tooth to be affected. A productive periostitis and ostitis develops that results in a variable amount of new bone tissue over the affected alveolus. The bone tissue can become so extensive the nasal cavity will be permanently closed on the affected side. Also the bony enlargement can become so prominent that it is a serious blemish.

In practically all cases the nutrition to the tooth is interfered with or destroyed and a normal tooth does not develop. Some teeth that are removed may only be a shell, in others the roots are short and knob like,

FIG. 219. Unusually extensive enlargement over the upper third cheek tooth of a five year old horse.

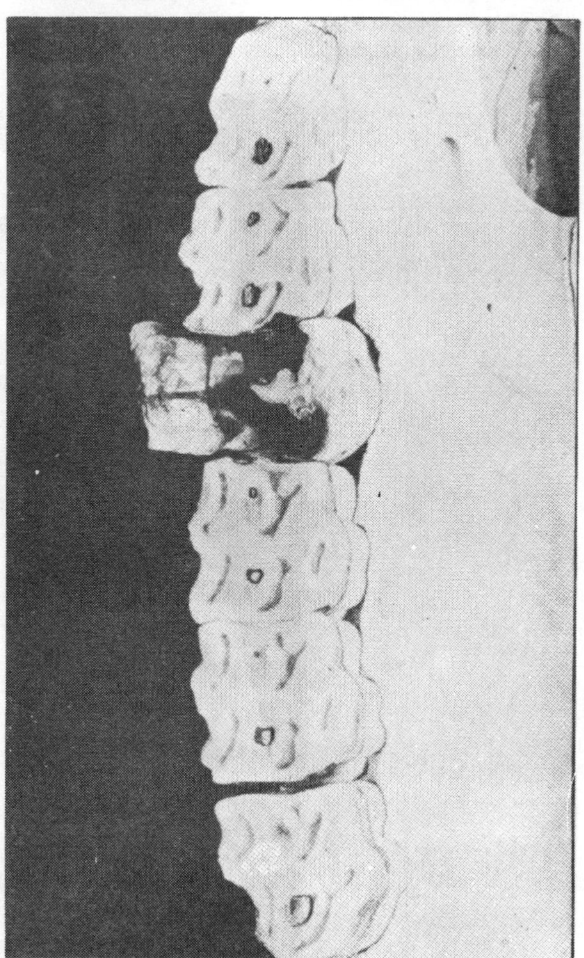

FIG. 220. Splitting of the cheek teeth is of frequent occurrence and produces a very painful condition.

while in other cases the permanent tooth has failed to develop.

TREATMENT. When the enlargement over the alveolus is barely noticeable a mild blister may be tried. However when the enlargement becomes pronounced and before it has a chance to become extensive the tooth should be removed. A trephine opening is made over the center of the enlargement and on the base line. The base line for making trephine openings for the upper teeth is on a line drawn from the medial canthus of the eye to a point just above the infraorbital foramen. A complete discussion of repulsion of the teeth will be given under the treatment of alveolar periostitis.

Affections of the Alveolar Periosteum

Alveolar periostitis is an inflammation of the periosteum lining the alveolus and is the most common condition affecting the teeth of the horse.

ETIOLOGY. In the largest percentage of cases food material and infection gain entrance to the alveolus through an imperfectly closed infundibulum. In some cases the infection may reach the alveolus between the gum and tooth. Food of poor quality may be a contributing factor during the first few years of the horse's life. Many cases of alveolar periostitis occur in young horses that are in poor condition.

SIGNS. When either the fourth, fifth, or sixth upper cheek teeth are affected the first sign that may be noticed is a unilateral purulent nasal discharge. The odor is very fetid and characteristic of necrosis of bone. The horse may hold its head to one side when eating grain or when drinking cold water it may show evidence of pain. Occasionally a suppurative opening will develop to the outside from infection in the maxillary sinus. The owner may notice the horse is not doing well and tires quickly. When splitting of the tooth occurs food packs in between the two por-

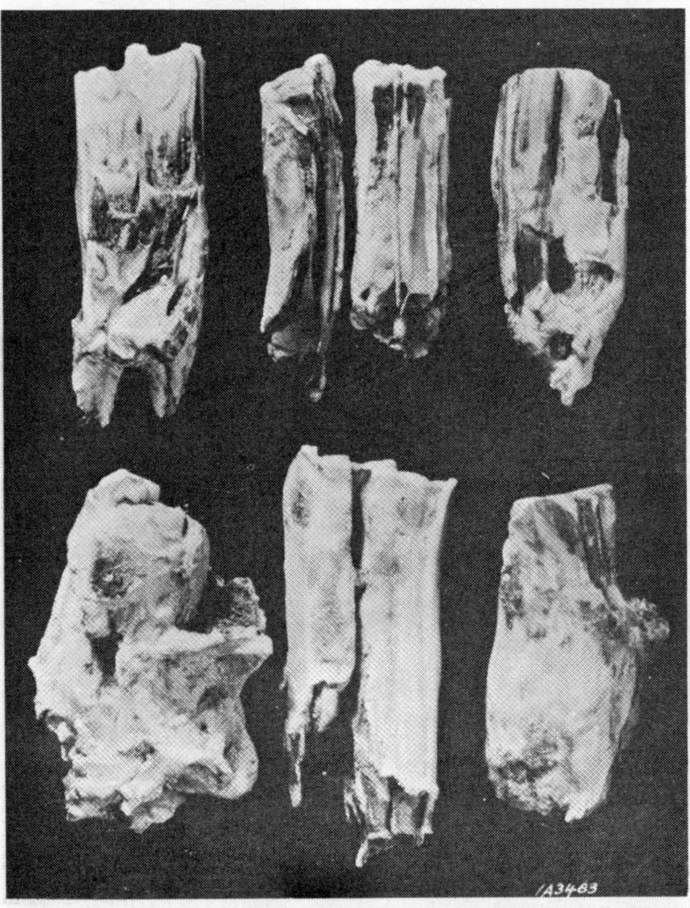

FIG. 221. Examples of some of the changes that occur in the cheek teeth due to the inflammation and infection in the alveolus.

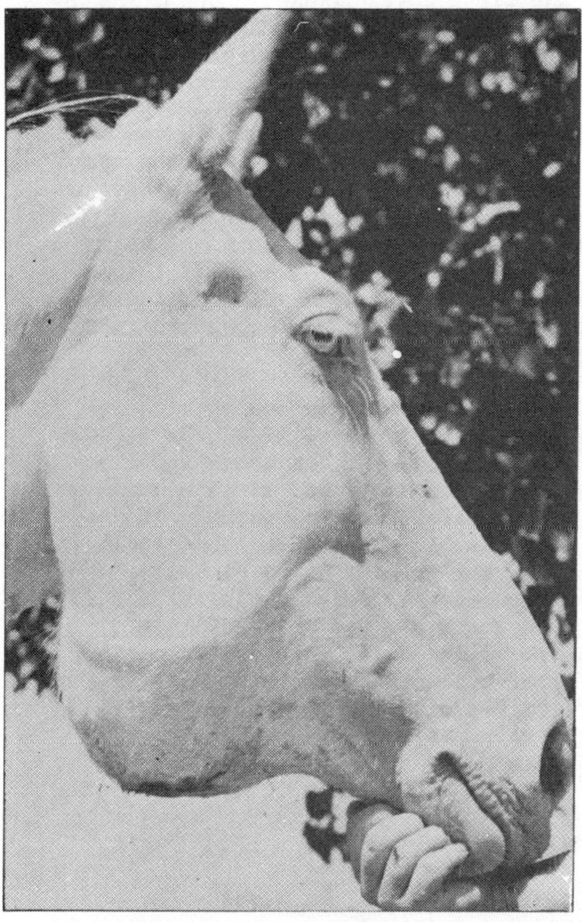

FIG. 222. Unusual case of thickening of the mandible due to inflammation and infection in the alveolus.

tions forcing the sharp edge of the lateral portion of the tooth into the cheek. This may result in severe and painful lacerations of the cheek. When this condition is present the horse eats with difficulty and the food is poorly masticated.

The usual symptoms of alveolar periostitis of the lower cheek teeth is a thickening of the mandible. The rapidity of the development of ostitis and tumefaction of the mandible is dependent upon the virulence of the infection that may gain entrance to the alveolus. Another symptom commonly observed is the so-called dental fistula. The dental fistula has an opening on the ventral border of the mandible or it may be on the lateral or medial side.

DIAGNOSIS. The affected tooth in some cases may be easily recognized. The nutrition to the tooth is destroyed with death and splitting of the tooth occurring. The gum may be swollen, reddened or definitely retracted from the affected tooth. The open infundibulum may be easily recognized or the opening may be so small that only a very fine needle can be passed into it. Some pressure may be required to force the needle into the infundibulum if it is packed tightly with food. In the lower jaw the same symptoms are observed with the tumefaction of the mandible. This tumefaction may extend along the ventral border of several teeth but it has been observed the ostitis and tumefaction also extends upward over the affected tooth.

TREATMENT. Removal of the affected tooth is the only effective method of treatment. If the crown is long enough to grasp with the forceps a large percentage of the affected cheek teeth can be extracted. William's molar extractor is an excellent instrument for extraction of cheek teeth. The jaws are short, thick, and shaped properly for grasping and maintaining their hold on the tooth. Extreme care must be used in the use of this extractor as the long handles provide the operator with a powerful leverage. In adjusting the extractors on the tooth the operator must be sure the extractors are on the right tooth. The operator will find an artificial light will help in determining when the extractor is properly placed. When the extractor is grasping the tooth firmly, the handles are slowly rotated in a small arc. At this time care must be used or the tooth will be crushed or fractured. As the tooth loosens blood appears around the crown of the tooth and then a sucking sound is heard as the tooth moves in the alveolus. When it is sufficiently loose a fulcrum is placed under the extractors close to the tooth and it is elevated, out of the alveolus.

The aftercare following extraction will depend upon the amount of infection present. In the case of an upper cheek tooth if the nasal discharge is profuse it is well to trephine into the sinus to provide complete drainage and thorough antiseptic treatment. If a lower cheek tooth is extracted it is advisable to trephine the mandible if there is extensive tumefaction. For in many cases there is some necrotic bone and infected tissue to be removed and complete drainage can then be established.

Repulsion of Teeth

When the tooth cannot be extracted, it is usually necessary to repell the tooth. To properly repell the tooth the horse must be confined on the table or the ground. A general anesthetic should not be used as blood and other fluids may gravitate into the lungs. It may be necessary to quiet a nervous horse with chloral hydrate and then block either the infraorbital or the mandibular alveolar nerve.

Nerve Blocking for Upper Cheek Teeth

The infraorbital nerve supplies the upper cheek teeth, canine, and incisor teeth, and maxillary sinus. To inject the anesthetic over the nerve the needle is inserted at a point about one inch below the lateral canthus of the eye. This point is below the facial crest and the needle is inserted where it will not injure the transverse facial vessels. A Bemis nerve blocking needle is used which is four and one-half inches long, sixteen gauge, and for the average sized horse it will have to be inserted about three inches. The needle is directed in a medial anterior direction and continue pushing the needle until it strikes the perpendicular portion of the palatine bone close to the maxillary foramen. The point of the needle should be moved around until it strikes the nerve, which will be shown by the horse jerking his head. If the needle strikes the internal maxillary artery or vein, which are below the nerve, the point of the needle should be directed higher. When the point of the needle is over the nerve, 10 cubic centimeters of a two per cent solution of a local anesthetic should be injected. Anesthesia should occur in five to ten minutes and its completeness can be tested by pricking the skin of the lip on the side of injection with a sharp needle.

Location of trephine opening, superior teeth. A base line is established from the medial canthus of the eye to a point just above the infraorbital foramen and continued beyond the root of the first cheek tooth. This line indicates the location of the osseous lacrimal canal, and to prevent injury to this canal all trephine openings should be placed below this line. In older animals it may be necessary to trephine well below this line as the teeth are shorter and the bones of the face may sink in sharply.

For the first cheek tooth a line is drawn through the center of the tooth and the trephine opening made just below the base line. There is a backward curvature of the second, third, fourth, and fifth cheek teeth and a line is drawn upward from a point on the posterior border of the tooth. This pronounced backward curvature of the second, third, fourth, and fifth cheek teeth is present up to about eight years but after this age they gradually become straighter. After eight years of age the trephine opening is placed more over the center of these teeth.

In young horses the trephine opening is made just below the base line. It is seldom the sixth cheek tooth needs to be repelled, but when it does, it is necessary to use a specially curved punch. The trephine opening for the sixth cheek tooth is made into the frontal sinus on a line drawn between the medial canthi of the eyes and about one and one-half inches from the median line. The curved punch is passed through the trephine opening and the fronto-maxillary opening and lateral to the infraorbital canal to the root of the tooth.

Nerve Blocking Lower Cheek Teeth

To block the mandibular alveolar nerve which supplies the lower cheek teeth, canine, and incisor teeth, requires injection of the nerve on the medial side of the mandible. To locate the mandibular foramen, an imaginary line is drawn from the lateral canthus of the eye across the mandible. Another imaginary line is extended backward along and beyond the inferior lateral border of the upper cheek teeth. In Figure 223 is shown the position of these lines on the mandible. Where the two lines cross on the mandible corresponds very closely to the position of the mandible foramen on the medial side. The needle is started at the lower border of the mandible and the point of the needle is kept close to the medial side of the mandible until the point is reached where the two lines crossed. Usually about twenty cubic centimeters of the two per cent solution of a local anesthetic is injected at this point.

The base line for the inferior cheek is the ventral border of the mandible. The trephine openings can be made on the ventral border of the mandible. In young horses the teeth may extend almost to the ventral

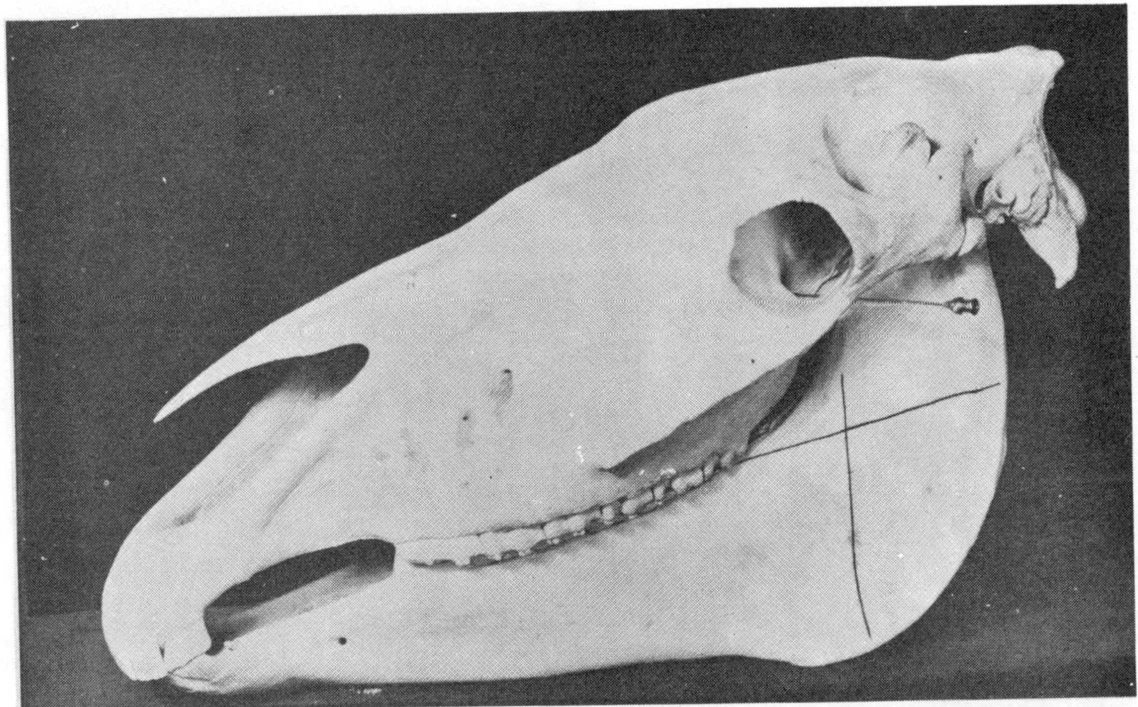

FIG. 223. Needle is shown in proper position to block the Infraorbital nerve.

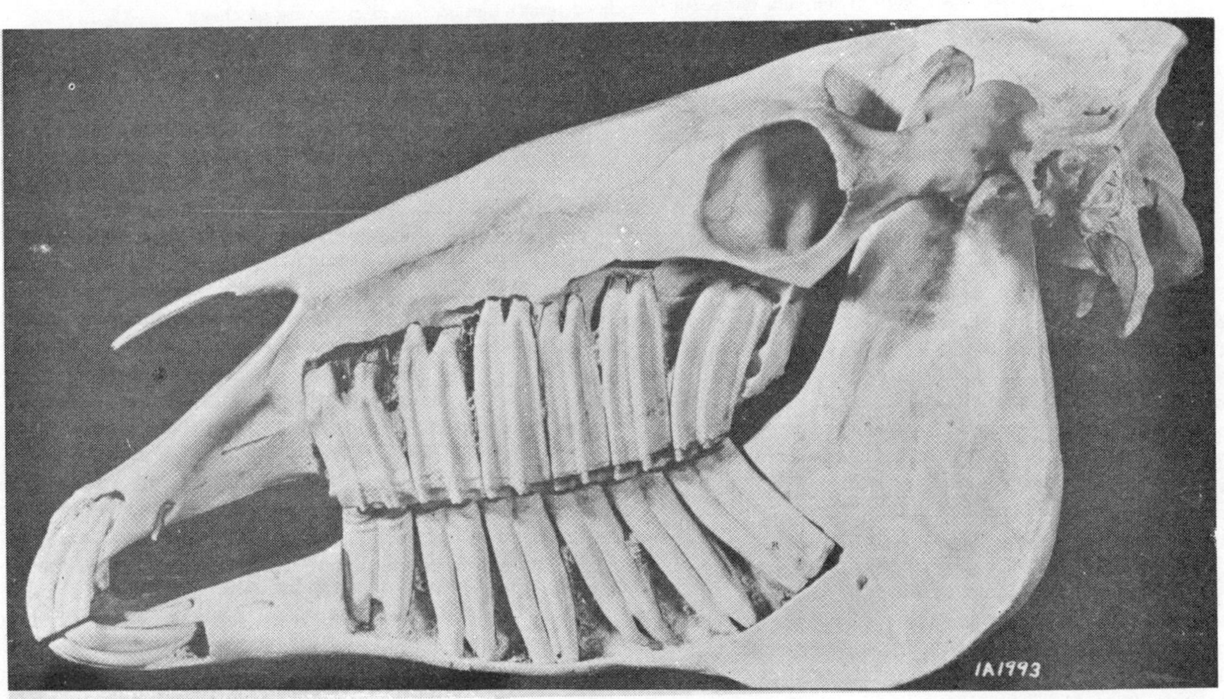

FIG. 224. Skull of five year old horse that shows length and backward curvature of cheek teeth at this age.

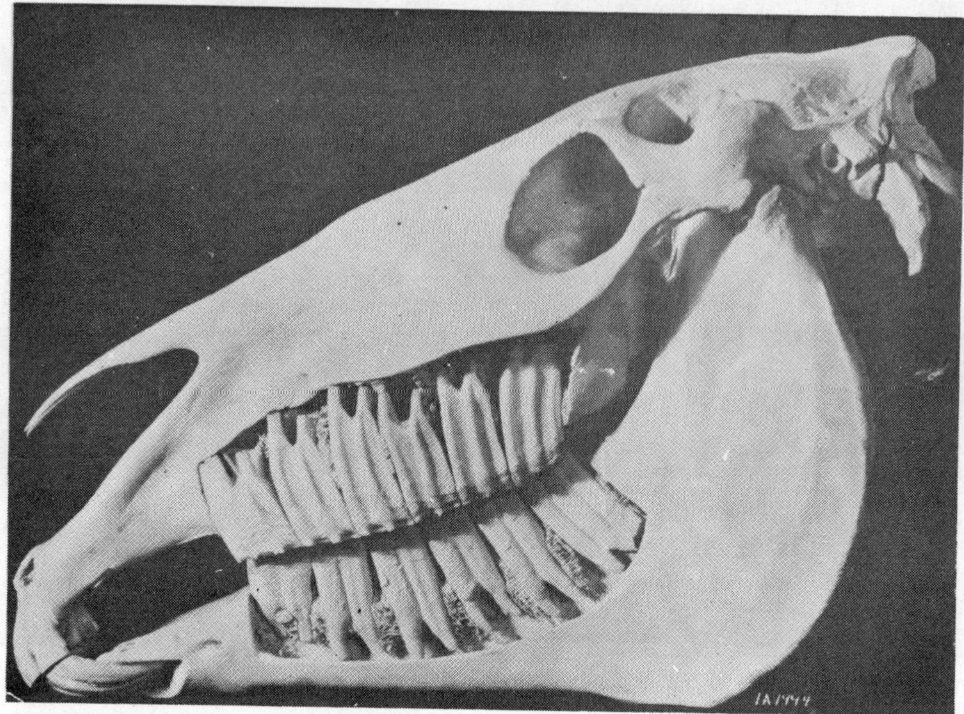

FIG. 225. Skull of ten year old horse that shows length and backward curvature of cheek teeth at this age.

border so it is necessary to make the trephine opening as close to it as possible.

Location of Trephine Opening, Lower Cheek Teeth

For the first cheek tooth the trephine opening is made below the table surface of the tooth. The trephine opening for the second, third, fourth, and fifth cheek teeth, is made below the posterior border of the tooth. The above rule is used on horses less than nine years of age. With increase in age the trephine opening is made more directly below the center of the tooth. The teeth are not so long as the five year old, and the backward curvature is not so pronounced. The placing of the trephine opening for the fourth and fifth teeth may be complicated by the external maxillary artery and vein, and the parotid duct. To make the trephine opening in the proper place it may be necessary to push these structures forward or backward. The trephine opening for the sixth tooth is on a line drawn through the center of the tooth to the point at the greatest curvature of the mandible. The skin and muscle are divided on this line at the point where the two plates of bone separate at the root of the tooth. This incision should terminate about one or one and one-half inches from the border of the mandible to prevent injury to the masseteric artery. Some of the branches of the seventh nerve may be in this area and care should be observed not to injure any nerve tissue.

After the trephine opening is made a punch is inserted through the trephine opening and placed over the root of the tooth to be removed. If the operator will place one hand in the horse's mouth and over the affected tooth he can determine if the punch is placed properly. It is also important to determine if the punch is directed in the same direction as the axis of the tooth. In the case of a lower tooth where the mandible is excessively tumefied proper placing of the punch is facilitated by moving the root of the tooth. This is accomplished by placing the extractors on the crown and rotating the tooth.

When the operator is satisfied the punch is properly placed it usually only requires a few sharp blows with a mallet to repell the tooth. After the tooth is removed a careful examination is made of the alveolus for any necrotic bone, pieces of the root of the tooth, or any infective tissue that should be removed.

A roll of gauze, approximately one inch long or long enough to fit tightly between the teeth on either side of the alveolus, is obtained. The roll should be large enough to fill the opening into the alveolus to prevent food material from passing into the alveolus. Narrow strips of muslin are fastened around the roll and passed through the alveolus to the outside. The roll of gauze is adjusted in the alveolus, and it should be below the table surface of the surrounding teeth. The strips of gauze are pulled tight and fastened around a roll of muslin over the trephine opening. Depending upon the amount of infection present the gauze is changed daily, or every other day, and the alveolus irrigated with an antiseptic solution. As the alveolus fills in with granulation tissue the strips of muslin passing through the alveolus are not used. The roll of gauze should be long enough so it can be wedged tightly between the two teeth on either side of the alveolus as it will be held in position. If the alveolus is filling in with healthy granulation tissue, the formation of the tissue should not be interfered with by too frequent treatments. The gauze should be maintained in the alveolus until it is completely closed with granulation tissue. If this procedure is neglected, food material and infection may gain entrance to the sinus or mandible and be the source of a chronic discharge. In the average case the alveolus should be completely closed with granulation tissue in ten days to two weeks. If the operator has been careful about the extraction or repulsion of teeth and the aftercare, uniformly good results should be obtained in these operations.

Odontomata (Tooth Tumor)

An odontomata is a tumor composed of tooth tissue.

SYMPTOMS. The presence of an odontomata may not be suspected until an attempt is made to remove the affected tooth. In other cases it may interfere with mastication.

TREATMENT. If the tooth is not causing any trouble it is best to leave it alone. In removing the tooth it may be necessary to split or break it in pieces before it can be removed. In some cases it may be desirable to remove the external alveolar plate to facilitate its removal.

Bishoping

The above term is used when an attempt has been made to make a horse's teeth look younger by a renewal of the cups in the incisor teeth. The operation usually consists in cutting deep cuts in the corners, smaller ones in the laterals, and only a slight depression in the centrals. The artificial cups are then stained a dark color. The attempt to make the teeth of old horses appear younger is easily detected because of the change in the shape of the table surface of the tooth. Also the cups are not lined with enamel.

Affections of the Horn

The horns consist of the cornual processes of the frontal bones which are osseous continuations of the bones of the skull. In the older animals the cornual processes become excavated to become continuous with and form a portion of the frontal sinus. The horn proper is secreted by the coronary corium and is attached closely to the cornual process.

Separation of the horn from the cornual process sometimes occurs as the result of a blow or striking the horn against a hard object. The accident is not very serious except for the profuse hemorrhage that occurs. However, the new horn that is formed is of poorer quality and less attractive in appearance.

TREATMENT. Clean the exposed horn core and cover with a dressing, as, pine tar.

Dehorning of the Bovine

Removal of the horns from cattle is commonly practiced for a number of reasons. They are less dangerous and are not able to gore other individuals. Dehorned cattle are easier to handle and do not interfere with other cattle around the feed trough. If the operation is properly performed there is a marked improvement in the appearance of a group of feeder steers.

The ideal time to dehorn or prevent horns from growing is when the calves are less

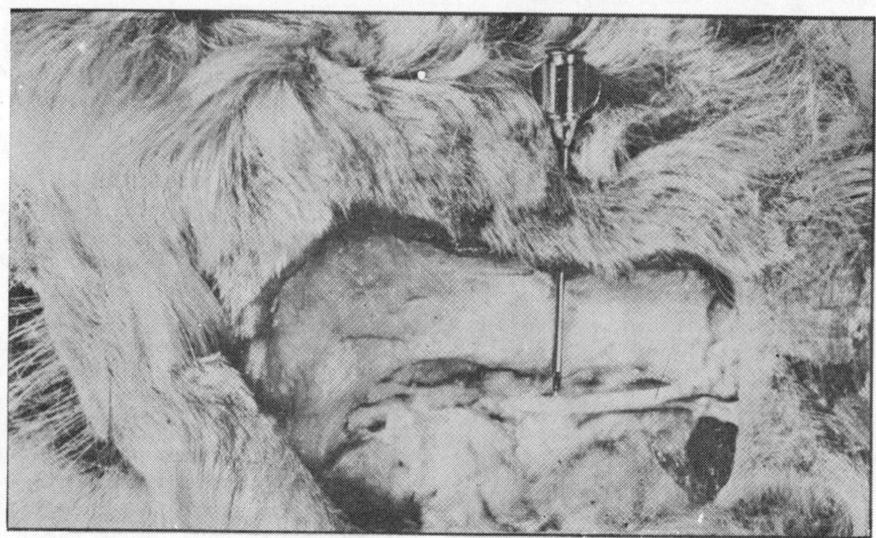

FIG. 226. Needle is in proper position to block the Nerve Cornualis just below the lower lateral border of the frontal bone.

than a week old or preferable to five days of age. At this age the horn buttons may be felt on each side of the poll. The hair may be clipped from around the base of these buttons so they are thoroughly exposed. Then a sharp knife is used to remove these buttons at the same time removing about one-eighth inch wide piece of skin with the base of the button. This should remove the horn forming portion of the skin. A stick of caustic soda or potash is used to cauterize the edges of the skin. After using the caustic the calves should not be out in a rain for twenty-four hours as some of the caustic may be washed onto the eye. The action of the caustic on the cornea might produce a partial or complete blindness.

As the calves increase in age the horns become larger and more firmly attached to the underlying tissues. The method that is used to dehorn older calves will depend upon the development of the horns. There are a wide variety of calf dehorners available that are efficient in removing the horns. Regardless of what type of instrument is used some of the skin, at least one-half inch, should be removed with the horn. The dehorning saw may also be used for removing the horns of the older calves.

ANESTHESIA. The dehorning operation may be performed painlessly under the influence of a local anesthetic. This may be accomplished by infiltrating the skin and periosteum along the proposed line of incision. Or the operative area may be anesthetized by blocking the Nerve Corualis. This nerve is located a little lateral and ventral to the lower lateral edge of the frontal bone. This ventral edge is easily palpated and is an important guide in blocking the nerve.

To determine the proper point to insert the needle, an imaginary line is drawn from the middle of the base of the horn to the middle of the anterior edge of the supra-orbital process. Approximately half-way between the base of the horn and the edge of the orbit the operator should palpate for the ventral lateral edge of the frontal bone. A needle is inserted through the skin at this point and in young animals the point should be inserted until it can be palpated below the ventral edge of the bone. As the animals mature the nerve is found deeper in the tissue so in the cow the needle will need to be inserted about three-fourths of an inch. For a large bull it may be necessary to insert the needle into the tissue from one to one and one-half inches. To block the nerves five cubic centimeters of a four per cent solution of a local anesthetic is deposited over each nerve. If the anesthetic solution is deposited over the nerve complete anesthesia of the operative area occurs in five to ten minutes.

OPERATION. The type of instrument that is used to remove the horns will depend upon the preference of the operator and either the clippers or dehorning saw may be used.

Which ever instrument is used at least one-half inch of skin is removed with the horn. If this rule is followed the horn forming cells are removed which prevents the development of any unsightly stubs or scurs afterward. Also the artery cornualis which passes lateral to the base of the horn and supplies the corium of the horn is exposed. The most efficient method of controlling the rather profuse hemorrhage that occurs is to grasp this artery with forceps. If a slow but steady traction is applied to the artery it stretches and then breaks under the skin. The pressure of the tissue on the end of the artery prevents further hemorrhage.

AFTER-TREATMENT. As a general rule no after treatment is necessary. However, if cattle are dehorned during warm weather there is danger of the wounds becoming infested with screw worms. To prevent this a good fly repellant should be used.

Necrosis of the Cornual Process

Necrosis of the cornual process has only been observed in a few cases in the bull. This condition is characterized by the rubbing of the base of the affected horn very vigorously. If the horn cannot be rubbed on a solid object a hind foot may be used. Due to the severe inflammation of the cornual process there is a gradual increase in size of the base of the horn. The intense pain affects the appetite which may be variable or there is a complete loss of appetite. There may be some loss in general condition.

Treatment consists in removal of the affected horn.

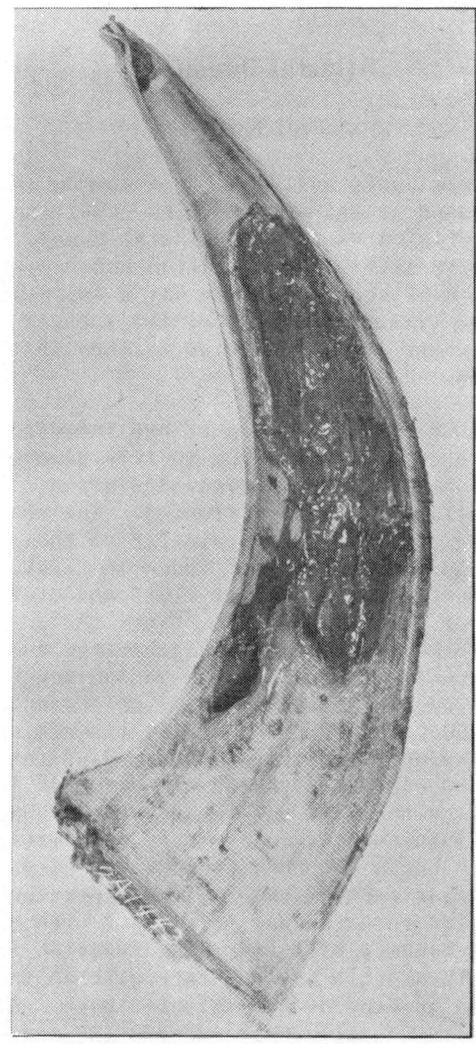

FIG. 227. Necrosis of the cornual process.

Dehorning the Caprine

There is a marked difference in the anatomy and shape of the head of the caprine as compared with the bovine head. The horns are closer together and the base of the horns are attached to the flat surface of the frontal bones.

Anesthesia for the operation may be obtained by blocking the nerve Cornualis halfway between the base of the horn and the edge of the orbit. These two structures are much closer together than they are on the bovine head which may confuse the operator. An imaginary line is drawn from the middle of the edge of the orbit to the middle of the base of the horn. The point to insert the needle on this line is halfway between the edge of the orbit and the base of the horn. The needle is inserted through the skin until the point is along the lower lateral edge of the frontal bone. The nerve is anesthetized by injecting three cubic centimeters of a three per cent solution of a local anesthetic. The horns may also be anesthetized by infiltrating the skin and underlying tissue around the base of the horn. At least one-half inch of skin should be removed around the base of the horn. A scalpel is used to cut through the skin, then a dehorning saw is used to remove the horn level with the surface of the frontal bone. The slight hemorrhage which occurs may be controlled by bandaging antiseptic packs over the wounds.

Atlantal Bursitis

Poll Evil

The term "poll evil" has from common usage been used as the name for the condition that originates in the atlantal bursa. There is little justification however, for the use of such a term as being descriptive of the tissues affected or the changes that occur in the affected tissues in this region.

ETIOLOGY. Recent research has indicated that the bursitis is due to infection of the bursa with Actinomyces Bovis and Brucella in the cases studied. The reaction of the bursa is similar to those of synovial membranes. There is first an increase in formation of fluid and distention of the fibrous sac. Later the bursal wall becomes edematous, degenerated and thickened. If the irritation causing the reaction continues, symptoms of pressure will occur as the surrounding tissues are compressed, motion of joints may be inhibited because of pain. In cases of long standing the wall may be many times the normal thickness. After the inflammation of the bursa has been present for some time that part of the funicular portion of the ligamentum nuchae in contact with the bursa becomes affected. The reaction in the ligament is inflammatory with an increase in size of the affected part. Also there is usually some degeneration and necrosis of the tissue of the ligament. As the bursal wall becomes thickened from the inflammation there is a tendency for the surrounding tissue to become adhered to it thus producing a parabursitis. With the gradual distention of the bursa it tends to penetrate the soft tissue and may come to the surface to rupture. One or more openings may discharge material from the bursa to the outside. The contents of the bursa before rupturing is a variable quantity of a yellowish fluid and many rice like bodies or larger masses composed of fibrin. After the bursa ruptures other organisms gain entrance to the bursa and the discharge is soon purulent in character.

SIGNS. The signs vary with the tissues affected and the extent to which they are involved. In some cases the owner has noticed a soft fluctuating swelling on one or both sides of the median line. This swelling may be painless or it may be very sensitive on palpation. Some horses will keep the head extended and are very reluctant to move the head or flex it on the neck.

In those cases which manifest the more typical signs there is usually a large amount of inflammatory tissue and there may be one or more openings on either side discharging a variable quantity of purulent material. In exceptional cases the inflammatory swelling may produce enough pressure on the ligament between the atlas and axis to affect the spinal cord producing nervous symptoms.

PROGNOSIS. In most cases of poll evil the prognosis is favorable. However, in those horses showing nervous symptoms it is unfavorable.

TREATMENT. In some early cases of bursitis favorable results have apparently been obtained by the use of iodine internally and also applied locally to the area.

However, in most cases the quickest and surest method of producing complete recovery is by the so-called radical poll evil operation. Only by this method can all the affected tissue be removed.

FIG. 228. A typical case of aseptic bursitis with head extended.

An area three inches wide extending from a point two inches in front of the occiput backward a distance of twelve to fifteen inches is shaved on the median line. The horse is placed on the operating table in lateral recumbency or cast on the ground. An efficient skin antiseptic should be applied to the shaved area. Complete anesthesia may be obtained by infiltrating the skin and subcutaneous tissue along the proposed line of incision. A one per cent solution of procaine hydrochloride or some other efficient local anesthetic may be used. If necessary or desirable one to two ounces of chloral hydrate may be administered into the stomach or intravenously to quiet the patient.

An incision is made in the median line through the skin and subcutaneous tissue down to the ligamentum nuchae. This incision extends from a point about two inches in front of the occiput backward usually a distance of twelve to fifteen inches. The skin is then dissected away from the ligamentum nuchae leaving the edges of the skin as thick as possible. At the posterior end of the incision where the ligament is normal in size it is entirely loosened from the surrounding structures so the fingers can be inserted around it. Hemorrhage is controlled by grasping all the bleeding vessels of any size with forceps. The ligament nuchae is now dissected free from all the surrounding tissue forward to where it attaches to the occiput. The ligamentum nuchae is now freed from its attachment to the occiput by cutting as close to the bone as possible. Because of its elastic structure the end of the ligamentum nuchae retracts four or five inches as soon as it is cut through. The free usually unaffected end of the ligamentum nuchae is now divided at the posterior end of the skin incision by an incision directed upward and backward. By careful palpation the depths of the area is carefully searched for any diseased tissue. Healthy tissue feels firm, smooth and is elastic while diseased tissue is hard, non-elastic and many times roughened. In some cases the bursa has become very extensive and it should all be removed. If all the diseased tissue is carefully removed, recovery from the operation is uneventful and complete.

The skin incision is closed with interrupted sutures placed one and one-half inches apart starting at the posterior commissure. Before the incision is closed the cavity is tamponaded tightly enough with gauze to control the hemorrhage. The gauze is first lightly sprinkled with an antiseptic powder composed of equal parts of chlorinated lime and boric acid. In forty-eight hours the gauze is carefully removed through the anterior opening of the incision. All the hay, grain and water is placed on the ground so the horse will have to keep his head down some of the time. By this means almost perfect drainage is provided from the operative area. The sutures are not removed until the sixth or seventh day. If any adhesions have developed between the edges of the skin these are broken or cut so the edges can spread apart. Usually at this time the edges of the skin will be firm so that if they were left thick enough they will not stand up straight and even. The interior of the cavity is wiped free of all exudate and scabs with dry cotton. An antiseptic oil such as the camphor-phenol preparation is then applied to the area. This procedure is repeated every day or every other day depending upon the progress of the case. The wound gradually fills in from the bottom with healthy granulation tissue. In three to four weeks the edges of the skin are drawing close together and the hair should be closely clipped along the edge. If this is not done infection and pus will be held in contact with the newly developing tissue and delay healing. In four to six weeks the operative area should be completely healed.

Affections of the Guttural Pouches

Infection and inflammation of the guttural pouches may result in the collection of pus in the pouches.

ETIOLOGY. Infection and inflammation of the pharynx may extend up the eustachian tube to the guttural pouches. Infection of the pouches may occur during the course of an infectious disease like influenza or strangles. Infection of the pouches usually becomes chronic because of lack of complete drainage.

SIGNS. It is observed that in some cases there is a nasal discharge when the head is lowered during feeding or drinking. If the pouches are greatly distended there may be some interference with swallowing and breathing. Pressure on the distended pouch may cause a nasal discharge. If the pus remains in the pouch for some time it becomes inspissated and may form into firm bodies called chondroids.

A tentative diagnosis of pus in the guttural pouch may be confirmed by passing a catheter into the pouch. A mare metal catheter as shown in Fig. 229 can usually be passed easily into the guttural pouch. In passing the catheter it is essential that it is started on the floor of the nasal cavity. Also the curved end of the catheter should be directed either up or down, preferably up, when it is inserted into the nasal cavity. The catheter is then passed along the floor of the nasal cavity until the operator feels the point pass over a ridge of bone which is the pterygoid process. Just as soon as the end of the catheter passes over this ridge of bone the catheter is rotated so the point is directed outward. The end of the catheter may be felt to strike the medial edge of the pharyngeal opening into the Eustachian tube and then enters the Eustachian tube. This opening is about fifteen inches from the nostril. After the catheter enters the Eustachian tube it is easily passed along the tube into the guttural pouch. If there is pus in the guttural pouch that is thin enough to enter the openings in the end of the catheter, pus will be obtained by this method. This of course is definite evidence of infection in the guttural pouch.

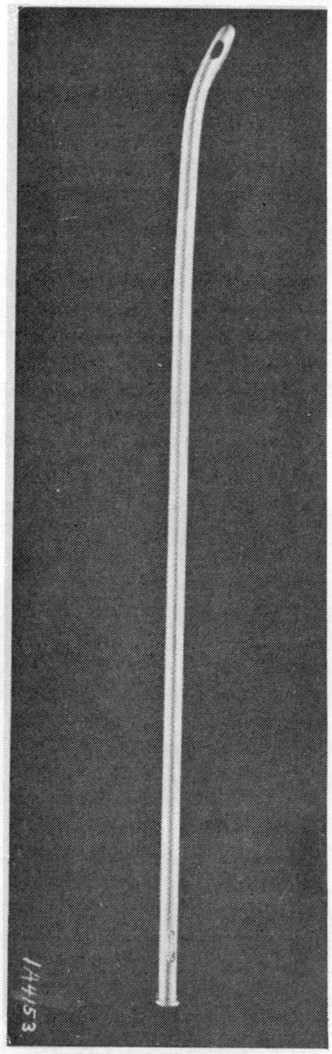

FIG. 229. A mare catheter that shows the ideal curve at the end.

PROGNOSIS. Prognosis is favorable when complete drainage and removal of contents is performed.

TREATMENT. Opening and draining the guttural pouches is the only successful method of treatment for the accumulated pus.

When the pouches become distended with pus they are best opened at the lowest point. To accomplish this an incision is made in the long direction of the neck lateral to the omo-hyoidens and sterno-hyoideus muscle. The incision extends through the skin and subcutaneous tissue. Blunt dissection is then used to break through the remaining tissue to the bottom of the distended pouch. An opening large enough to provide liberal drainage is made on its ventral surface. The usual irrigation with antiseptics and treatment of the wound is employed.

To remove chondroids or inspissated masses of pus, it will be necessary to enter the pouch from above.

OPERATION. The operative area is prepared by shaving and application of an efficient skin antiseptic. Anesthesia may be obtained by infiltrating the tissue with a local anesthetic.

The skin incision three or four inches in length is made about one inch anterior to and parallel with the anterior border of the atlas. The heavy fascia is carefully incised and dissect the posterior border of the parotid gland loose from the atlas. The gland is raised upward and forward and the auricular nerve is drawn backward.

One or two fingers or a blunt instrument is used to break through the areolar tissue into the region posterior to the occipito-mandibularis muscle. The carotid artery and its branches can be recognized as thin walled structures. A blunt pointed instrument may be used to open the pouch. The fingers are inserted into this opening to enlarge it until the whole hand can be introduced. The material in the pouch can be removed through this opening. If desirable another opening may be established through the bottom to provide complete drainage. After removal of the contents the wounds are treated as indicated.

Tympanites or Emphysema of the Guttural Pouches

Tympanites or emphysema of the guttural pouches is usually observed in young colts. Usually only one guttural pouch is affected but it may occur bilaterally. The air apparently enters the pouches during expiration or when the animal is swallowing. In some cases infection is present in the affected pouch and the distension may be due to the formation of gas. In one case in a one year old colt the two pouches were continuous with the distension most pronounced in the dorsal portion of the pouch on the left side.

The guttural pouches may vary a great deal in size due to congenital defects and in some cases become very extensive, one recorded case had a capacity of six quarts. When the guttural pouches become distended with air or gas they are recognized as a diffuse, painless, elastic, tympanic swelling in the parotid region. Only one pouch may be distended but it may produce enough pressure on the tissues to produce a bulging in the area of the other guttural pouch. However when a needle is inserted into the obviously distended pouch and the air removed the swelling subsides on both sides.

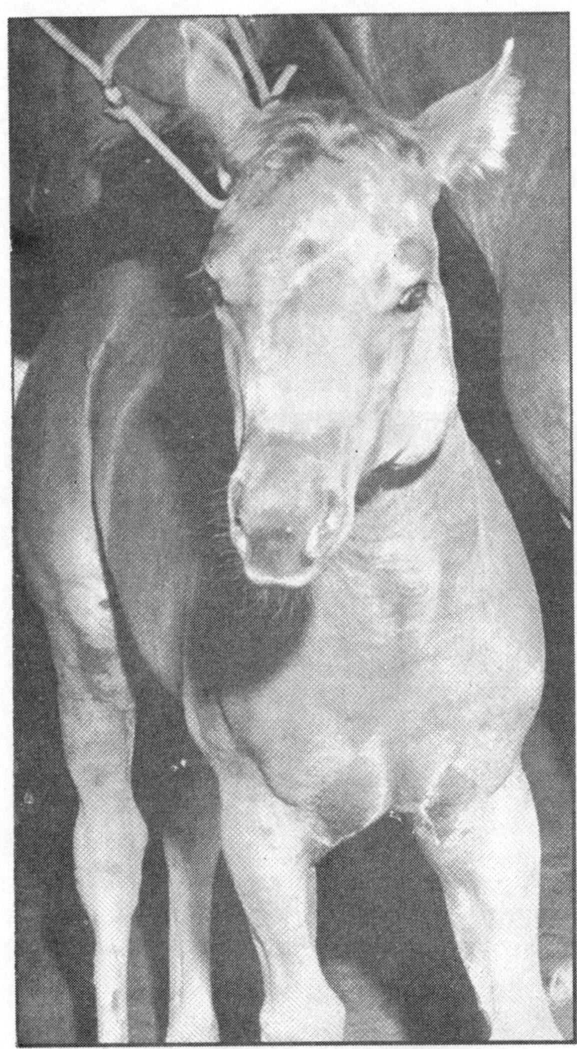

FIG. 230. Emphysema of guttural pouch on the left side.

TREATMENT. The treatment of a case of emphysema of a guttural pouch will depend upon the cause of the distension of the pouch. If the pouch extends posterior from its normal position and most of the distension is in this portion it probably indicates the pouch is more extensive than normal. The excess portion of the pouch should be removed. The incision through the skin should be made over the most ventral and prominent part of the pouch. Incise through the skin making the incision about three inches long and continue dividing the tissues until the pouch is exposed. The pouch can be separated from the surrounding tissue by blunt dissection. Continue the separation of the pouch until all of the excess portion is free from the surrounding tissue. The pouch is grasped with forceps and by some tension the excess portion of the guttural pouch is removed. The wound is treated as an open wound.

If the distension of the pouch is not too pronounced and it is in over the normal position of the pouch it is usually an indication of infection in the pouch. The pouch should be opened and antiseptics, such as tincture of iodine applied to the membrane lining the pouch. If the pouch is markedly distended anterior to its normal position it may indicate a congenital deformity that will not respond to treatment.

Parotid Gland

Parotitis is inflammation of the parotid gland. This condition may occur in all species of animals, but is not common to any one of the species. The inflammation may result from a foreign body in the duct producing closure or swelling from infection of the tissue may close the opening of the duct into the mouth.

SYMPTOMS. When affected with inflammation the gland is swollen, painful and the outline of the gland is easily palpated. If the condition is bilateral the head is held extended and if only one side is affected the head is held toward the sound side.

TREATMENT. If the swelling is due to obstruction of the duct and the obstruction can be removed the swelling may subside. Any inflammation of the gland should be treated with antiphlogistic measures, as hot packs. All abscesses should be opened with care to avoid injury to large blood vessels.

Salivary Calculi

Salivary calculi usually occur in Stenson's duct and vary a great deal in size. They occur most frequently in the bovine, but are also found in other species. When several are present they become faceted from attrition but an isolated calculus is usually oval in shape. They are usually smooth on the surface and a grey or yellowish-grey in color.

ETIOLOGY. The usual cause of salivary calculi is a foreign body as bacteria, spicule of grass, awn of oats, barley or wheat.

SYMPTOMS. The presence of a calculus is revealed by a hard painless swelling along the course of the duct. When several are present a grating sound is heard when they are palpated. In some cases a rather large calculus is present but is not causing any trouble.

TREATMENT. If the calculus is located close to the end of the duct it may be forced into the mouth. In some cases it may be necessary to enlarge the opening of the duct in the mouth or an incision may be made through the duct and over the calculus. When the calculus can be removed through the mouth there is no possibility of a fistula developing.

When this is impossible an incision will have to be made through the skin. The skin should be pushed upwards over the calculus and an incision made through the skin and duct to the calculus. After removing the calculus the duct should be sutured with fine suture material placing the sutures close together. The skin is sutured with a separate row of sutures. Healing by first intention may occur if food and water is withheld for three or four days and if the animal is kept away from where others are feeding. When healing by first intention does not occur a fistula usually forms which is very difficult to heal.

Salivary Fistula

Whenever the parotid duct or one of its radicles is injured it may permit enough

FIG. 231. Salivary calculi of Equine origin, the largest one weighs one pound and three ounces.

saliva to escape that a permanent fistula develops. Several different procedures are recommended for closing the fistula. Probably the most efficient method is to stop the flow of saliva by destroying the secreting tissue of the gland. One method is to ligate the duct between the gland and fistula. The duct must be isolated and ligated with a broad tape. If the ligature is pulled too tight it may cut through the duct before the function of the gland is destroyed.

Undoubtedly the most efficient method of destroying the function of the gland is to inject irritants into the gland. To do this most efficiently the irritant should be injected into the duct and it then penetrates to all parts of the gland. The duct is isolated most easily at the border of the mandible or where it crosses Viborg's triangle. After the duct is identified a needle is passed into its lumen with the point directed toward the gland. The walls of the duct should be pressed firmly around the needle to prevent any back flow of the solution. For large animals ten cubic centimeters of Lugol's solution should be injected slowly. After the injection the needle is removed and a tape is tied tightly around the duct to retain the solution. It is usually advisable to keep the animal off feed for two or three days. The inflammation which is started by the irritant soon destroys the secreting cells of the gland. The inflammation of the tissue produces swelling of the gland and sensitiveness to palpation, may cause a slight rise in temperature and a stiff carrriage of the head for a few days. If the one injection is not sufficient it may be repeated. When it is impossible to inject the solution through the duct it may be injected into the gland substance. The solution should be injected in numerous points over the gland with each point about one inch apart. Inject one or two cubic centimeters at each point using a total quantity of about fifteen cubic centimeters of the Lugol's solution. This method is not as efficient in destroying the secreting tissue as when it is injected into the duct.

Laryngeal Hemiplegia
Roaring

Laryngeal hemiplegia is apparently a complete or partial loss of function of the intrinsic muscles of the larynx, unilateral or bilateral, permitting the vocal cords to partially obstruct the lumen of the larynx producing an inspiratory dyspnea. The noise that occurs on inspiration may vary from a slight whistle to a pronounced roaring sound. It may require fast or hard work to produce the slightest sound while in other cases a pronounced roar is evident at rest. The character and volume of sound produced may be dependent upon the degree of nerve paralysis and whether it is unilateral or bilateral. It is also noticed that horses used at fast gaits or those that have to exert vigorously are unable to continue due to their inability to obtain all the air they need.

ETIOLOGY. One of the most commonly accepted theories is that the constant pulsation of the aorta against the left recurrent laryngeal nerve is responsible for its loss of function. The left recurrent laryngeal is the motor nerve to the intrinsic muscles of the larynx. Quite frequently following recovery from an infectious disease as influenza or strangles it is observed the horse is affected with laryngeal hemiplegia. Over extension of the head may cause injury to the recurrent nerve.

Examination of the patient should be as complete as circumstances will permit. In some cases it is almost impossible to get the patient to show any respiratory difficulty at the time of the examination. For these cases the observations of the owner or trainer may be accepted. The trachea should always be examined for any evidence of deformity as a flattened trachea will cause a pronounced respiratory difficulty. A neoplasm in the nasal cavity or pharynx may cause some unusual respiratory sounds. In some show horses extreme flexion and arching of the neck while they are being shown may cause some respiratory difficulty.

OPERATION. The operation for laryngeal hemiplegia has progressed from the removal of the vocal cords and arytenoid cartilages to the removal of the laryngeal saccule. In the operation it is essential that all of the laryngeal saccule is removed. Any portion of the laryngeal saccule that is not removed may be responsible for the development of pockets that prevent the operation from being successful.

The horse may be operated upon in the standing position, on the table in lateral recumbency or in dorsal recumbency. It has been found by most operators that the operation is most easily and quickly performed with the patient in the standing position. Most of the patients offer little or no resistence to the operation if care has been taken to anesthetize the tissues. A few patients may need to have their attention diverted with a twitch. For the very nervous individual that is difficult to control it may be desirable to use a tranquilizer.

The operative area from the thyroid cartilage to the trachea is prepared for an aseptic operation. Anesthesia of the skin and muscle tissue may be obtained by local infiltration with a local anesthetic along the proposed line of incision which is on the median line. Before making the skin incision it may be desirable to elevate the head. The skin incision which is made on the median line extends from the thyroid cartilage posterior for a distance of approximately three inches. The incision is continued through the muscle tissue, dividing the fibres where possible, until the larynx is exposed. After the crico-thyroidean ligament is identified by palpation it is incised from the thyroid cartilage to the cricoid cartilage on the median line. The mucous membrane of the larynx and laryngeal saccule is anesthetized by repeated applications of a topical anesthetic. A pledget of cotton grasped with forceps may be moistened with the anesthetic solution and then applied until anesthesia is obtained. A finger is introduced to the bottom of the saccule and the forcep introduced alongside of the finger to make sure the anesthetic solution is in contact with all of the saccule. After the anesthetic has been applied numerous times to the saccule the forceps are rotated until the saccule clings to the cotton. The saccule may be gradually everted and completely everted after several attempts have been made to produce eversion. To assure complete removal of all of the saccule the mucous membrane is incised on the dorsal edge of the vocal cord. The incision at one end of the vocal cord is continued to the side of the larynx.and terminates at the other end of the incision. By making the incision in this manner the mucous membrane is incised around the opening into the laryngeal saccule. This incision is made with the No. 12 curved Bard-Parker blade attached to the No. 3 metal handle. The index finger is used to guide the blade as it is drawn through the tissue. By incising the mucous membrane around the opening into the laryngeal saccule it prevents leaving any mucous membrane to form pockets that would prevent the operation from being successful. A burr may be introduced to the bottom of the saccule and twisted until the mucous membrane clings to the burr and then it is gradually everted. Any tissue that prevents the saccule from being removed is cut with scissors with narrow blades. Some operators will only remove the saccule from the affected side while other operators will remove both saccules.

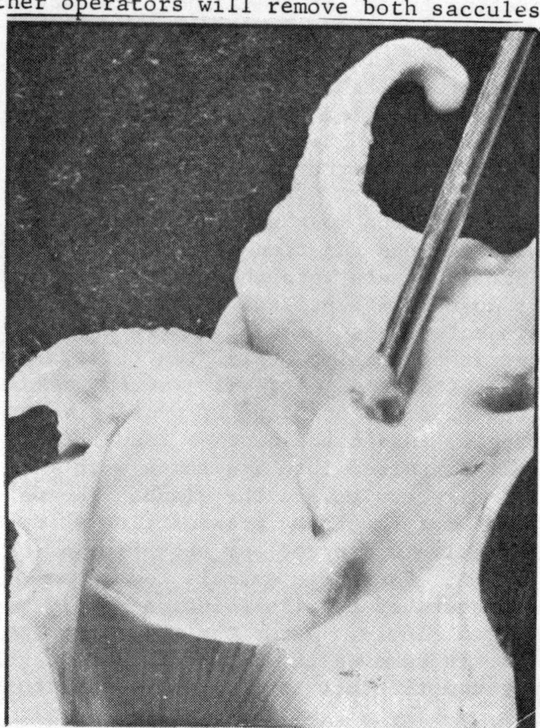

FIG. 232. The saccule is everted by the burr and is ready to be removed.

After care consists in keeping the patient quiet in a box stall for one month. The external wound is treated as an open wound with the removal of the exudates and the application of antiseptics. When horses of the heavier breeds are operated either a laryngeal or trachea tube should be put in position. The tube should be used until the patient can breathe easily with the tube closed. It is usually necessary to keep the tube in position for one week and should be cleansed daily. In some cases it may be desirable to put the feed and water on a platform so the patient can reach them easily.

After four weeks in the box stall the patient may be allowed some mild exercise. It should be at least six weeks after the operation before the patient is worked. Some cases show complete recovery in one or two months, in others the improvement is gradual over a period of six months or a year after the operation. Horses used at fast work do not show as high a percentage of recoveries as horses worked at slower gaits.

Ventriculo-Chordectomy in Goats - Debleating

This operation consists in removing a section of tissue from both vocal cords. When the operation is properly performed it stops the bleating of goats.

OPERATION. The operative ares is the same as for the roaring operating in the equine. An area in the median line extending from the body of the thyroid cartilage to the trachea is shaved and prepared for an aseptic operation. The skin and subcutaneous tissue along the proposed line of incision which is made on the median line is infiltrated with a one per cent solution of a local anesthetic. The incision will extend from the thyroid cartilage to the trachea.

The patient is confined in dorsal recumbency with the head held slightly extended. A mid-line incision is made through the skin and subcutaneous tissue from the thyroid cartilage to the trachea. The outline of the crico-thyroidean ligament is then determined by palpation. After the ligament is definitely identified it is incised on the mid-line from the thyroid cartilage to the cricoid cartilage. It is also necessary to continue the incision and divide the cricoid cartilage. A Covault ovariectomy hook is introduced flatwise through the incision into the larynx until the end is anterior to the vocal cord. The instrument is then turned until the point of the hook is in contact with the wall of the larynx. It is then drawn slowly backward until it comes in contact with the vocal cord. With a gradual pull on the vocal cord it stretches until the part grasped by the hook is pulled out to the incision. A pair of scissors are used to remove the piece of vocal cord grasped by the hook. For the operation to be completely successful the piece of vocal cord removed must extend completely through the cord. A section is removed from the other vocal cord with the same technique. The skin incision is treated as an open wound and heals in a few days.

Hyoid Bone

Injuries and fractures of the hyoid bone occur rather rarely in horses and cattle. The injuries or fractures are usually due to blows or may be caused by rough handling of the tongue.

SYMPTOMS. The most pronounced symptom is the difficulty or inability to swallow. Although there may be excessive salivation and swelling of the tissues.

PROGNOSIS. Healing of the affected tissues usually occurs in two to four weeks.

TREATMENT. The treatment consists in giving food through a stomach tube until the patient is able to swallow. The wound receives the treatment that is indicated in the particular case.

A two year old colt was presented for treatment with the following history. He had been running and playing in the corral when he had attempted to stop in front of a picket fence. However, he slipped in the mud and his head went over the top of the fence. The sharpened end of a one by four board was forced up into the mandibular space producing a very extensive injury of the soft tissue. Examination of the depths of the wound revealed a loose piece of bone which was removed and proved to be the body of the hyoid bone. Separation through the epiphyseal cartilages had occurred at the articulations with the thyroid cornua and the lingual process.

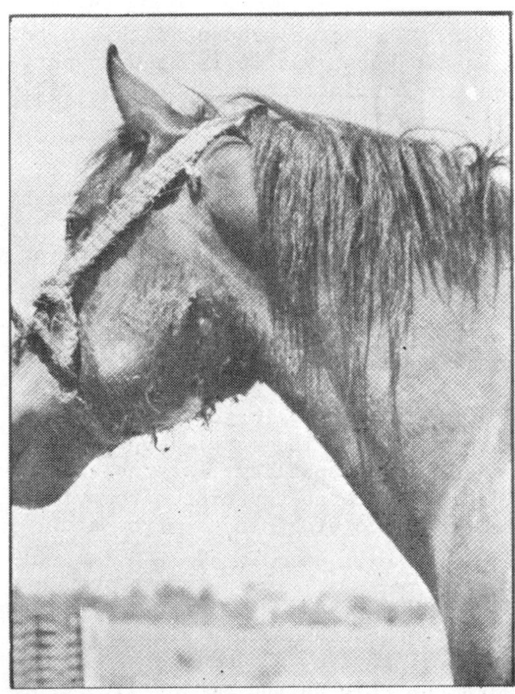

FIG. 233. The location of the wound in the mandibular space.

SIGNS. The outstanding sign was the horse's inability to swallow either food or water. Also there was the extensive wound in the soft tissue.

TREATMENT. The most important part of the treatment was the daily injection of water and food into the stomach through a stomach tube. The food material used is that described on page 137. This procedure was repeated daily for eight days when he recovered his ability to swallow food and water.

The wound had perfect drainage and healed very nicely with very little treatment. The horse did not lose any weight during the period of artificial feeding and made an uneventful recovery.

Cribbing in Horses

Wind Sucking or Aerophagia

Cribbing and wind sucking are practically the same. In cribbing the horse grasps the manger or some other object with the incisor teeth, arches the neck, makes peculiar movements with the head and attempts to swallow air. Wind sucking is the same habit, but the attempt is successful.

ETIOLOGY. The actual cause of this condition is not known but it is thought nervousness or confinement producing a stable habit are contributing factors.

TREATMENT. The most successful form of treatment is the operation recommended by Forssell of Stockholm. The operation may be performed under general anesthesia or local anesthesia and chloral hydrate. Shave the skin on the ventral surface of the neck from the larynx to the middle of the neck and from one jugular furrow to the other. After the skin is cleansed with alcohol it is painted with a good skin antiseptic. The muscles operated on are the sterno-cephalicus, sterno and omohyoideus and sterno-thyroideus removing at least six to eight inches from each muscle.

TECHNIQUE OF OPERATION. The horse is confined in dorsal recumbency with the head extended slightly. An incision is made through the skin on the median line from the thyroid cartilage and extending backwards for a distance of sixteen inches. The skin and fascia are dissected and reflected back on each side until each jugular vein is well exposed.

It is well to start with myectomy of the omo-hyoideus carefully separating it from the external maxillary vein. The muscle is lifted up at the external angle of the skin wound and divided transversely. Grasping the cut end of the muscle it is dissected and lifted up and resected where it is covered by the sternocephalicus. The sterno-hyoid is dissected free and divided transversely in the lower angle of the skin wound and the omo-hyoideus is removed on the other side. The sternocephalicus is freed from the surrounding structures still enclosed in its fibrous sheath. Divide the muscle at the lower angle of the skin wound and again just before the tendon disappears in the parotid region. The other side is operated on in the same manner. Both sterno-thyroids are now resected. Any large bleeding vessels are ligated. The edges of the skin are sutured together leaving an opening at the lower end of the incision for drainage. Treatment of the wound is that usually employed in the care of wounds. Usually the sutures can be removed in about two weeks.

RESULTS. Forssell states that 80 per cent of the cases operated on have become sound, 10 per cent have showed some improvement and 10 per cent have continued crib biting. A higher percentage of recoveries will be obtained if the patient is unable to grasp any object with his teeth for at least six months after the operation.

Torticollis

This is a twisting or distortion of the neck occurring usually in the horse.

ETIOLOGY. The usual history is that the horse fell with the head and neck under the body. It may occur while the horse is confined in the stall or running loose with long rope attached to the halter and he steps on the rope with the hind foot throwing himself with the head under the body. In attempting to jump over a gate or fence the horse may fall with the head and neck under the body. The distortion that results may be due to, spasm or paralysis of the neck muscles, subluxation of some of the vertebrae and in some cases all the causes are present.

SYMPTOMS. If the horse has been down for some time it may be difficult to get him to

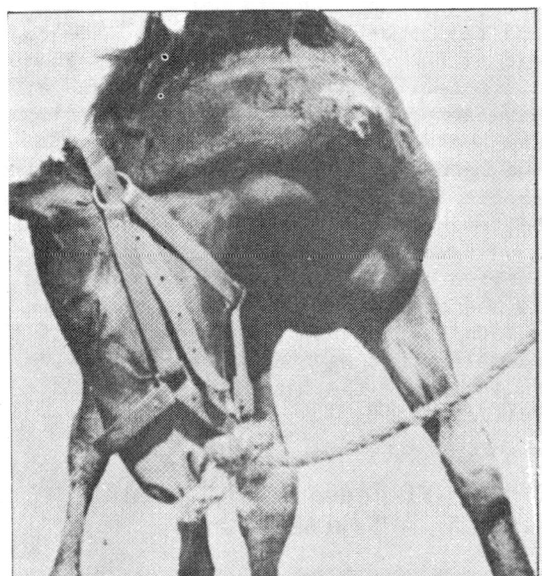

FIG. 234.

FIG. 236.

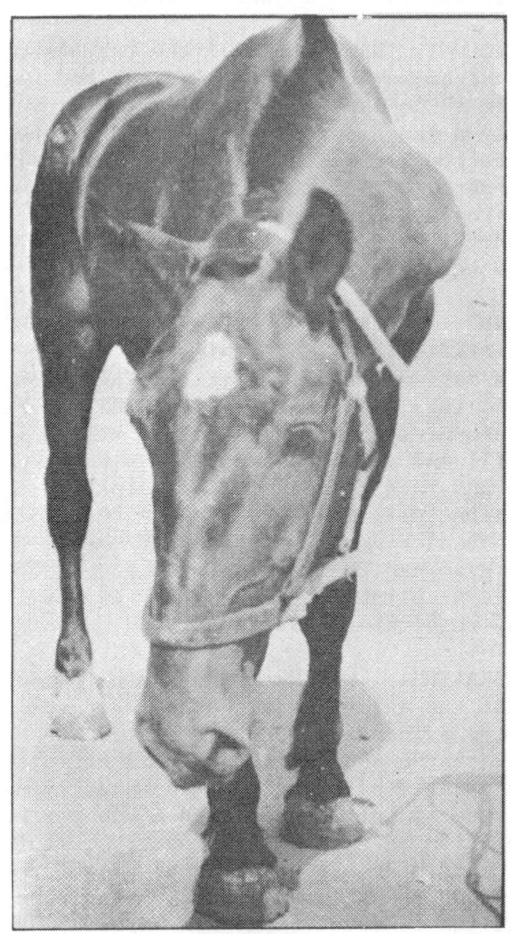

FIG. 235.

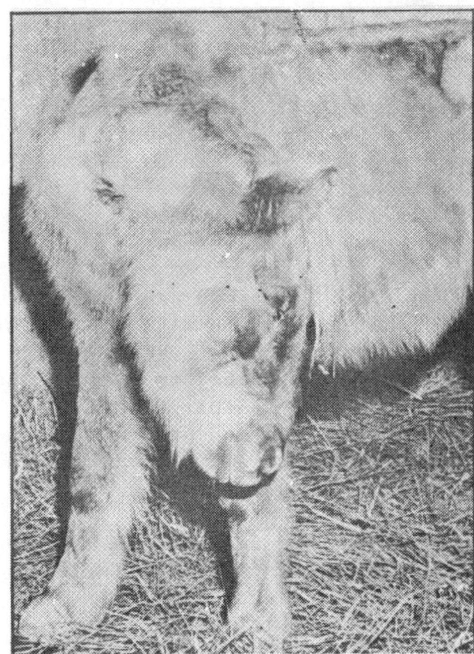

FIG. 237.

Figures 234, 235, 236 and 237 show four different attitudes of the head and neck in cases of torticollis.

stand. The head is carried to the right or left and it is usually deviated downward. The most prominent point of the convexity is about the middle of the neck.

PROGNOSIS. In most cases recovery occurs but some never make a complete recovery.

TREATMENT. When the condition first occurs the tissues are very painful and if attempts are made to straighten the neck the horse shows evidence of severe pain. Some individuals may fall over backwards or throw themselves. Until acute pain subsides massage of the affected muscles with gradual straightening of the neck seem to be beneficial. At this time a well padded halter may be put on with a rope long enough to pass through a pulley and a weight attached to pull the head to a normal position.

If it is apparently due to a subluxation it may be necessary to put well padded splints along either side of the neck as it is necessary to hold the parts in their proper position if healing is to occur.

Tracheotomy

This operation is indicated in cases of temporary stoppage of the respiratory tract, such as severe swelling and edema of the larynx, partial or complete ossification of the laryngeal cartilages and in some cases of flattening of the trachea.

The trachea is most superficial about the junction of the upper and middle third of the neck and this area can be determined by palpation. It is the preferred place to perform a tracheotomy unless the obstruction is below this area.

OPERATION. The operation can be performed in the standing position with the use of a local anesthetic in the tissues. The operative area should be prepared in the usual manner for an aseptic operation. Infiltrate the skin, subcutaneous tissue and underlying tissue with a one per cent solution of a local anesthetic.

An incision one and one-half inches long is made in the median line thru the tissues down to the sterno-thyro-hyoideus muscle. The two portions of the muscle are separated and the trachea exposed by cutting thru the loose areolar tissue covering it. A scalpel blade is inserted thru the inter-annular ligament between two tracheal rings. With the index finger of the other hand guiding the cutting edge of the scalpel a half moon shaped section of one tracheal ring is cut thru. The incision should be long enough to admit the trachea tube but should not extend thru more than one-half of the ring. The cut edge of the section of the ring is grasped with a pair of rat tooth forceps and a corresponding section of cartilage removed from the adjacent tracheal ring in the same manner. A sterilized self retaining trachea tube can now be inserted. Daily the tracheal tube should be removed, the wound carefully cleansed with an antiseptic solution and a sterilized tube inserted. The use of the tube should be discontinued as soon as possible to prevent some of the sequellae that may occur from excessive irritation of the mucous membrane and cartilage.

Flattened or Collapsed Tracheal Rings

The above condition occurs occasionally in the equine and equi-asini but is of rather rare occurrence in the bovine.

ETIOLOGY. Traumatism of the trachea may fracture several tracheal rings and permit them to collapse. The injury may involve only a few rings or the trachea may be affected for a distance of six to twelve inches. During the drouth when feed was scarce cases of complete collapse of the trachea were of frequent occurrence in the old equine and equi-asini.

SIGNS. The injury to the trachea results in difficulty in breathing and when due to traumatism there is local inflammation, swelling, and pain. The dyspnea may be pronounced when the animal is standing still and in some cases it may be necessary to put in a trachea tube. Palpation of the trachea will usually disclose the flattened tracheal rings. Occasionally horses will be examined for some ailment and found to have a collapsed trachea that is not causing any respiratory difficulty.

OPERATION. The operation may be performed with the animal in the standing position by using a local anesthetic. After the areas are shaved and painted with an efficient skin antiseptic the skin and underlying tissue is infiltrated with a one per cent solution of a local anesthetic. One incision is made along each side of the trachea through the skin and underlying tissue until the tracheal rings are exposed. A long straight needle threaded with silver wire is passed through the center of the sharp edge of a tracheal ring, the lumen and the opposite side of the ring. It is returned in the same manner through the next tracheal ring. Another method of inserting the sutures is to use a long hollow needle passing the wire through the lumen of the needle. The silver wire sutures are inserted through all of the affected tracheal rings. After all of the silver wire sutures are in position they are tightened until the tracheal rings assume a normal shape. Each silver suture is twisted and the ends left long enough to protrude out through the incision. The edges of the incisions are sutured with a continuous suture leaving an opening at the bottom for drainage. The silver wire sutures are removed in a week to ten days. The wounds are treated as indicated until healed.

If there is extensive flattening of the trachea as from the larynx to the thorax surgical treatment is not usually successful.

Region of the Neck

Affections of the Oesophagus

The entrance into the oesophagus of the bovine from the pharynx is quite large and easily dilated permitting the hand to be introduced rather easily. The oesophagus is from three to three and a half feet long in the medium sized animal and the average diameter is two inches. At its origin the oesophagus is almost dorsal to the cricoid cartilage in the median plane. From its position on the median plane the oesophagus reaches the left side of the trachea and continues in this position along the cervical region. After the oesophagus reaches the left side at approximately the fourth cervical vertebrae it is accompanied by the left carotid artery and the vagus, sympathetic and left recurrent laryngeal nerves. To reach the oesophagus it will be necessary to go through the skin, cervical fascia, cervical paniculus muscle, and then crossing the jugular furrow obliquely from above anteriorily and below posteriorily is the omohyoideus muscle. A large mediastinal lymph gland is immediately dorsal to the posterior part of the oesophagus and when it becomes enlarged it is frequently responsible for bloating of the affected individual. The oesophagus is very rarely injured externally but obstruction occurs frequently in large animals due to various objects. The species most frequently affected is the bovine, the equine is next and other species only occasionally have foreign bodies lodged in the oesophagus.

In the equine the most frequent cause of choke is fine dry feed composed of bran or chop, oats and sometimes hay. The tendency to choke occurs most frequently in aged horses that are greedy eaters but it has occurred in a wide variety of ages. The symptoms in the equine appear very suddenly and when choke occurs the horse will stop eating and make violent attempts to swallow. There is a peculiar anxious expression and in most cases there is excessive salivation. Arching of the neck with the nose drawn toward the chest may occur in some cases while in other individuals the head and neck are extended. If the choke occurs in the cervical region it can be palpated. When choke occurs in the bovine tympanites may be responsible for the death of the animal.

Treatment in the equine consists in first removing all food and water, and keeping the patient quiet for twenty-four hours. In some cases it may be desirable to give a sedative to relieve the spasmodic contractions of the oesophageal muscles. Within twenty-four hours there is in many cases relief from the choke without any further treatment. When the choke is composed of fine material a stomach tube is passed down to the mass. Then a pint of water is pumped down the tube and siphoned off bringing some of the food material out with it. By repeating this procedure many times most of the cases of choke due to fine material may be relieved. If the choke is due to some solid material and is in the cervical portion of the oesophagus it may be removed with the wire described under choke in cattle. For example a bolus composed of hay has been removed from the oesophagus of a young colt with a loop formed of baling wire.

In the bovine choke on foreign bodies is of frequent occurrence due to their habit of swallowing rather large objects. The bovine chokes most frequently on apples, pieces of turnip, potatoes, beets, portions of an ear of corn, pieces of hedge apples, silage, pieces of baling wire lodged transversely across at the entrance to the oesophagus. Added to these there are many other kinds of foreign bodies that have been removed.

The signs are similar to those described for the horse. In the bovine there may be bloating of the rumen which may be fatal if it is not relieved. If necessary a trocar can be inserted into the rumen to relieve the tympany. When the choke is in the cervical portion of the oesophagus it can usually be palpated.

Treatment in the bovine is different from that for the equine due to the nature of the foreign body. If the symptoms are suggestive of a choke at the entrance into the oesophagus a speculum should be used to keep the mouth open. An examination with the hand will reveal food material at the entrance into the oesophagus. After the food is removed a piece of baling wire will be felt fixed transversely across the lumen of the oesophagus. The wire is usually removed rather easily as the ends are not too firmly fixed in the tissues. For the solid objects a wire bent double will either remove them or loosen the object so that it will pass into the stomach. The size of the wire will be determined by the size of the animal. For the calf a piece of baling wire may be used and a number nine wire is indicated for the older animal. It is not always necessary but may facilitate the passing of the wire to have the mouth held open with a speculum. The looped end is passed into the oesophagus and beyond the object. The foreign body may be removed as the wire is pulled out or it may be dislodged so it passes into the stomach.

When the choke is due to ensilage the best results have been obtained by injecting water into the mass. A hypodermic needle is introduced into the ensilage and water is forced through the needle with some pressure. The point of the needle is moved frequently so the water reaches all parts of the material and the choke is relieved as the material passes into the stomach. A hard bolus of medicine became lodged in the oesophagus of a Shetland pony and all attempts to dislodge it failed. It was necessary to introduce a dental pick with a strong sharp point into the bolus to break it into small pieces before it passed into the stomach.

In those cases in which there is an anatomical defect in that the mucous membrane has failed to develop for a short distance the following history is typical. This anatomical defect usually occurs in the oesophagus just before its entrance into the thoracic cavity. The symptoms of choke are usually observed when the animal is about one year of age when it is beginning to eat large quantities of dry hay and grain. When they first start choking it may occur only once a month, then after a few times it occurs more frequently and there is a gradual increase in the amount of food material that forms the choke with each succeeding attack of choking. We do not know of any way of correcting the anatomical defect in the mucous membrane.

FIG. 238. Absence of mucous membrane in oesophagus, responsible for recurrent attacks of choking.

A case of choke in an eight year old cow occurred in which the foreign body was lodged at the thoracic portion of the oesophagus. A stomach tube was passed but no amount of pressure would dislodge the foreign body. A rumenotomy was performed and after removing some of the contents of the rumen a hard object could be palpated protruding a short distance into the rumen from the lower end of the oesophagus. A hook was carried in with the hand and fastened into the object. Considerable traction was required to remove it. The foreign body was a beet five and one-half inches long and the largest diameter was three inches.

Stricture of the Oesophagus

The entrance to the oesophagus of the bovine is large enough to admit the hand and is easily dilated. A five year old cow was presented for examination with the history of apparently having a good appetite but had been losing condition for approximately three months. On clinical examination the patient seemed to be apparently normal. She had a ravenous appetite and would pick up a mouthful of hay greedily. However, it was observed that after the hay was masticated thoroughly she would hold it in her mouth for a short time, then allow it to fall to the ground. After observing her do this repeatedly a thorough examination of the mouth was indicated. With the mouth held open with a speculum it was easy to examine the mouth, pharynx, and entrance into the oesophagus. Because of a definite stricture at the entrance into the oesophagus it was only possible to introduce two fingers. This stricture accounted for her inability to swallow a bolus of hay.

In a short time another cow was presented with almost the same history and loss of condition. However, a clinical examination revealed the stricture was not as pronounced as in the first case. Although she was able to swallow the bolus of hay there would be a marked period of time in the interval between the masticating of the food and when it passed down the oesophagus.

Rupture of the wall of the oesophagus is occasionally observed in the bovine. The passage of food material into the tissues is responsible for extensive swelling of the area. Also due to the bacteria that gain entrance to the tissues there is an extensive inflammatory swelling of the tissue. There is little that can be done except to remove the food material from the wound with the hope that the animal will pass for food. Usually the rupture of the wall of the oesophagus has produced so much damage to the tissues that it is impossible to repair the wound surgically.

Raker and Sayers cite a case of rupture of the oesophagus in a mare in which two openings were present and seemed to be due to traumatic injury. An attempt was made to suture the dorsal opening but it was not successful. The mare was treated by permitting the wounds to heal without suturing. To maintain the mare in a good state of nutrition all of the saliva was collected and mixed with the ration. An adequate ration was prepared and fed by gravity through a stomach tube passed through the wound. With this method of treatment the oesophageal and skin wounds were completely healed in 67 days.

Dilation of the oesophagus may develop because of a stricture of the oesophagus. The entire wall of the oesophagus may dilate due to the accumulation of food above the stricture.

A diverticulum occurs when there is a rupture of the muscles with a protrusion of the unbroken mucous membrane through the opening. It occurs most frequently in the thoracic portion of the oesophagus.

SYMPTOMS. The symptoms of the two conditions are practically the same. When solid food is swallowed both the dilatation and diverticulum fill with food until the oesophagus is closed. If additional food is swallowed, symptoms of choking develop and food mixed with saliva is regurgitated and appears in the mouth and nostrils. As a general rule liquid or simi-liquid material passes into the stomach without difficulty.

Oesophagotomy

The oesophagotomy operation should be performed only as a last resort when all other methods have failed to move the foreign body. This operation can only be performed in the cervical portion of the oesophagus and there is always the danger that an oesophageal fistula will develop after the operation. When an oesophageal fistula does develop it presents a condition that is very difficult to correct surgically.

Operation: By palpation it will be possible to determine the location of the foreign body in the oesophagus. The skin over the foreign body is prepared for an aseptic operation.

The patient should be confined in lateral recumbency on the right side. Determine by palpation the location of the foreign body in the oesophagus and prepare the skin over the area for an aseptic operation. Anesthesia for the operation may be obtained by local infiltration of the tissues or a general anesthetic may be used. The skin incision, four or five inches long, is made along the jugular furrow and above the jugular vein. Incise the cervical fascia and the panniculus muscle. If the operation is performed in the proximal part of the neck it will be necessary to divide the omohoideus muscle transversely but if the operation is performed in the distal portion of the neck it will be possible to dissect under the ventral border of the muscle by blunt dissection. During the progress of the dissection it is important to control the hemorrhage. It is very important during the dissection of the tissues in the lower part of the neck not to separate the tissues away from the trachea. If the separation occurs a space must be provided for secretions to gravitate downward along the side of the trachea. In the depths of the wound it will be possible to recognize the carotid artery by its pulsation and the trachea by the tracheal rings. The oesophagus will be found on the lateral side of the trachea and it will be recognized as a firm muscular tube with the mucous membrane feeling like a firm structure when the oesophagus is rolled between the finger and thumb. A pair of forceps inserted in under the oesophagus can be used to elevate it up into the incision. Every effort should be made to dislodge the foreign body or cut it into smaller pieces before performing an oesophagotomy. When all known methods have been used and failed to dislodge the foreign body, an incision may be made through the wall of the oesophagus on its dorsal side. The opening should be made only large enough to permit the removal of the foreign body. After removing the foreign body insert the sutures in the mucosa so that the subcutaneous surfaces will be brought into close opposition by closely placed sutures, using either silk or chromic catgut. The edges of the muscles are approximated with closely placed sutures and the skin wound may be closed with interrupted mattress sutures.

The patient should be kept away from other animals when they are being fed and watered. Also no food and water should pass through the oesophagus, for as long as possible, to keep from disturbing the wound. Every effort should be made to prevent the formation of an oesophageal fistula.

Bleeding of Swine

There are various methods that may be used to obtain blood from swine. The pure bred breeder may and usually does object to some of the methods that have been used, as cutting a piece from the end of the tail or from the dew claw. When one of the ear veins is nicked it may bleed so profusely that it is objectionable to the owner. A method of bleeding from the anterior vena cava has proven to be very satisfactory in the smallest pig to the mature animal. It is necessary to understand the anatomy of the area where the needle is to be inserted if blood will be obtained consistently and without injury to other vessels. The blood is obtained from blood vessels in an area which is anterior to the first rib, ventral to the trachea and dorsal to the cariniform cartilage of the sternum. In the arch formed by the first two ribs the anterior vena cava is formed with the uniting of the right and left deep and superficial jugular veins. Deeper than the jugular veins are the common carotid arteries which are found in contact with the ventral and lateral surfaces of the trachea.

Shock may occur if the blood is withdrawn too rapidly so it is important to use the proper gauge needle. For small pigs it is recommended to use a 20 gauge needle one and one-half inches long, for the larger animals an 18 gauge needle four inches long is adequate but some individuals may require a needle four and one-half inches long. A syringe is attached to the needle to exert suction to facilitate the filling of the syringe with blood from the bloodvessel.

The small pigs are easily bled when they are held in dorsal recumbency. For the large hogs a one-fourth inch rope is fastened around the upper jaw and posterior to the tushes. The hog is then pulled to within two feet of a strong post and the rope fastened about three feet from the ground. The skin where the point of the needle is to be inserted should be cleansed with a good skin antiseptic. With the glass syringe producing a little suction the needle is inserted through the skin on either side of the point of the cariniform cartilage toward the base of the ear. When the pig is confined in dorsal recumbency the needle is directed inward, downward and backward to the area between the first two ribs. When the animal is in the standing position the needle is directed inward, upward and backward until the needle enters the anterior vena cava between the first two ribs. If the needle is directed to the right of the median line there is less danger of injuring the phrenic nerve or some of the lymph vessels. If the operator is unable to introduce the needle into the anterior vena cava one of the ear veins may be nicked. There are three veins, one is close to the outer edge, one about the middle of the ear and the third vein about one inch from the dorsal edge of the ear.

REFERENCES

Bemis, H. E., Surgery of the Head of the Horse, J.A.V.M.A., Vol. LXX (November, 1926), pp. 210-228.

Carle, B. N., D.V.M., and Dewhirst, Wm. H., M.A., A Method of Bleeding Swine, Berkley, Calif., J.A.V.M.A. (1942), pp. 495.

Emmerson, M. A., Nerve Blocking in the Dehorning of Cattle, University Pennsylvania Bulletin (October, 1933).

Gibbons, W. J., Choke in Eleven Day Old Colt, Cornell Veterinarian, Vol. XXVI (1936), No. 3, pp. 281-282.

Gibbons, W. J., Dehorning Cattle, Cornell Veterinarian, Vol. XXII (April, 1932), No. 2, pp. 186.

Guard, W. F., Flattened or Deformed Trachea, J.A.V.M.A., Vol. XXIX, N. S., 32, 6, (1931, Dec.), pp. 814-817.

Guard, W. F., Otitis Media, Reprint from Veterinary Medicine, (April, 1923).

Hoerlein, Alvin B., D.V.M., Hubbard, Earl D., D.V.M., M.S., Getty, Robert, D.V.M., M.S., PhD., The Procurement and Handling of Swine Blood Samples on the Farm, J.A.V.M.A. (1951), pp. 357.

Merillat, L. A., Animal Dentistry (1919), Alexander Eger.

Raker, Charles, W., V.M.D., and Sayers, Allen, V.M.D., Esophageal Rupture in a Standardbred Mare, J.A.V.M.A., 133, (October, 1958), pp. 371-373.

Shigley, J. F., Choke in Eleven Day Old Colt, Cornell Veterinarian, Vol. VIII (1918), No. 4, pp. 302.

Udall, D. H., The Practice of Veterinary Medicine, 3rd Rev. Ed. (1939).

Chapter VII
AFFECTIONS OF THE SHOULDER AND FRONT LIMB

When an improperly fitted collar is used or the hair on top of the neck is cut too short the superficial protective layer of skin is rubbed off. The hair should be left at least one inch long or longer to provide a protective pad for the skin. The Malpighian layer of the skin is exposed when the superficial layer is removed and the area is very sensitive. As soon as this layer is exposed a serous discharge occurs which dries and forms a scab. Dirty collars, collars too tight at the top, high humidity and collar pressure may also be contributing factors.

SIGNS. The presence of this sensitive area may be manifested by the animal tossing its head while at work or the horse will resent any manipulation of this area, as when the collar is put on.

TREATMENT. An antiseptic astringent agent is indicated in the treatment of this condition as 20% of tannic acid in glycerine, also one ounce of pyoktanis blue, three pints of alcohol and water to make a gallon, if a more astringent action is desired six ounces of tannic acid may be added.

Phlegmon

Frequently a traumatism of the tissues on top of the neck to one side of the median line. The area is swollen and extremely sensitive - it involves the skin and subcutaneous tissue.

If this condition is not treated properly it may become rapidly worse and healing is delayed. Some form of antiphlogistic treatment should be used as hot water or antiphlogistine packs until the inflammation and sensitiveness have subsided.

Sit Fast

When extreme pressure of the collar occurs on the tissues on top of the neck the blood supply to the area is destroyed. Gradually an area of dry gangrene develops varying in diameter and depth - this is called a sitfast. This area is cone shaped in form with the base of the cone on the surface. With the development of this tissue separation of the dead and healthy tissue occurs. At the apex of the cone persistent adhesions develop between it and the ligamentum nuchae. This area seems to provide ideal conditions for the development of two serious infections - tetanus and malignant edema.

PROGNOSIS. Is favorable if secondary infection does not develop. Depending upon the depth of the sitfast recovery usually occurs in two to four weeks.

TREATMENT. A prophylactic dose of tetanus antitoxin should be administered and the horse tied so he cannot roll in the dirt and manure and the wound become infected in this manner. Also a fly repellant should be used to prevent flies from carrying infection to the area. The hair is closely clipped around the area and also the edges of the sitfast are removed. Then

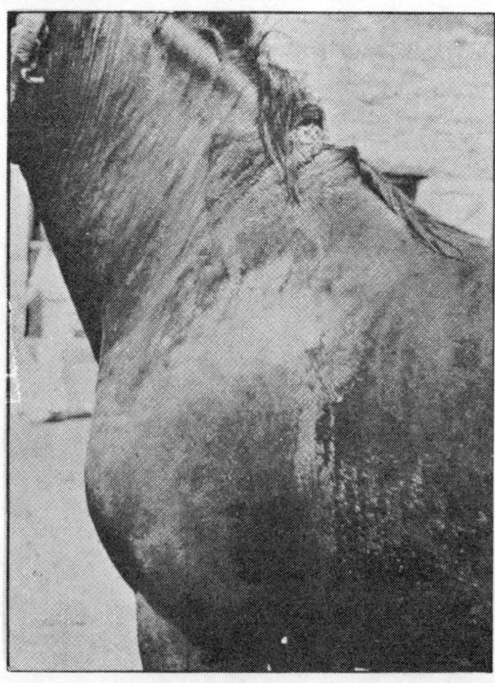

FIG. 239. The usual location of a sitfast on top of the neck.

some dry antiseptic powder as salicylic acid, boric acid, acetanilid, burnt alum or calomel, (the preferred salicylic acid) is packed tightly and deeply into the space between the healthy and gangrenous tissue. Every day the space is wiped clean with dry cotton and packed again with the dry antiseptic powder. This is repeated every day until the sitfast can be lifted out, usually with very little traction. After the sitfast is removed it is noticed the cavity is lined with healthy granulation tissue. Each day the cavity is cleaned out with dry cotton and dusted with a dry antiseptic powder. From now on the cavity fills in rapidly with healthy granulation tissue and complete healing soon occurs.

Hematoma of the Shoulder

The hematoma occurs quite frequently in the spring before the tissues in the collar bed have become toughened to hard work. Probably occurs more commonly in young horses but affects horses of any age when they are forced to do heavy work to which they are not accustomed.

SIGNS. A subcutaneous, fluctuating sac, that is non-inflammatory suddenly appears in the collar bed where the draft occurs. The greatest quantity of fluid is found at the lowest point of the sac. The contents of the sac is watery in consistency, blood tinged with usually some fibrin formation.

TREATMENT. If there is inflammation and thickening of the underlying muscle tissue do not open the hematoma for ten days or two weeks. As surgical interference at this time seems to delay healing.

The skin should be shaved over the lower lateral extent of the swelling. A local anesthetic should be injected along the proposed line of incision. A liberal incision is made into the swelling to one side of the collar bed and the contents evacuated. One or two fingers should be inserted into the cavity to remove any fibrin that is present. The cavity is then packed with gauze soaked in a preparation of 3 parts of glycerine and 1 part of Lugol's solution and removed in 24 hours. Then every day the owner should press the palm of his hand down over the area and force out any fluid that may be present. It will usually be advisable to rest the horse two weeks or longer depending upon the amount of traumatism to the underlying tissues.

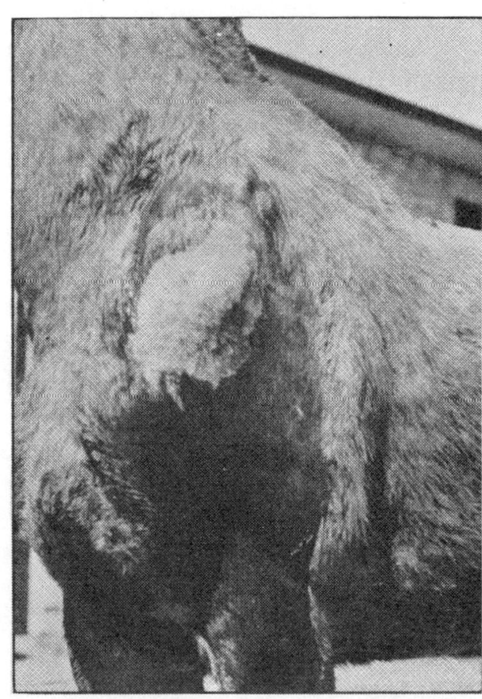

FIG. 240. The usual location of a hematoma in the collar bed.

Collar Gall, Callous, Bull's Eye Shoulder, Cicatricial Tissue

This condition occurs in the collar bed of the shoulder where the draft comes. Extreme pressure of the collar or movement of the collar over the skin may produce an abrasion of the skin resulting in the formation of a callous. It may start as a surface irritation with exudation of serum and if not treated properly an abraded, hairless area develops. Due to this irritation and inflammation of the tissue a variable amount of fibrous tissue is formed. In some cases abrasion of the skin does not occur but some irritation causes the formation of fibrous tissue in the subcutaneous tissue. When the horse is not worked for some time all the swelling in this area disappears and only by careful palpation can you detect this tissue. However, when the animal is worked the area becomes edematous, sensitive and greatly enlarged.

In other cases there is a large abraded area and underneath is a large mass of cicatricial or fibrous tissue.

TREATMENT. If it is desired to work the horse, much of the irritation to the area can be reduced by cutting a hole in the

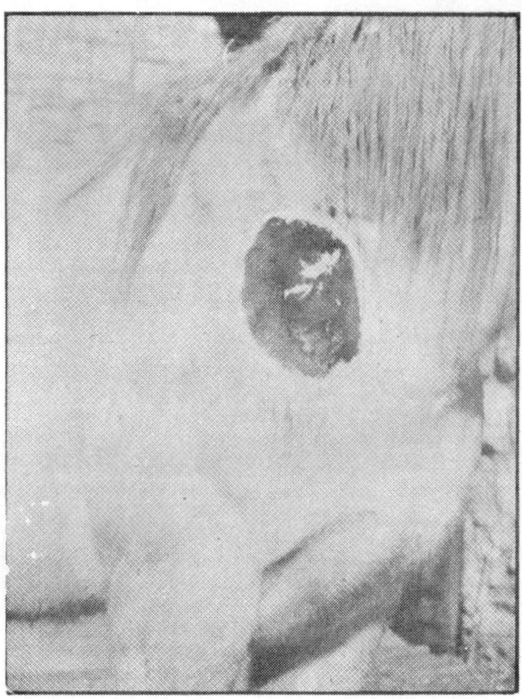

FIG. 241. A mass of cicatricial tissue in its usual location.

pad over the area. If permanent results are desired it can only be obtained by surgical removal of the abraded area of skin and all the underlying fibrous tissue. The operation is usually performed in the winter time when the horse can be rested for at least two months and all the inflammation in the tissue has disappeared.

The operation can be performed in the standing position and under the influence of a local anesthetic. Anesthetize the tissue by injecting the skin along the proposed line of incision around the area and also the underlying tissue with a one per cent solution of procaine. A circular incision is made thru the skin around the tissue to be removed. As the tissue to be removed is dissected away, careful palpation is made to determine if all the cicatricial tissue is being removed. The area is permitted to heal as an open wound and very smooth healing results in six to eight weeks. The wound may be treated by dusting it daily with an antiseptic.

Brachiocephalic Abscess

This is a deep seated abscess in the prescapular lymph gland which is situated beneath the brachiocephalic muscle. It may occur during or following an attack of strangles or influenza but in many cases there is no definite history to explain its occurrence.

SIGNS. The lymph gland is deeply situated usually four or five inches so that during the inflammation it develops a very thick wall. Usually when the patient is presented for examination a hard pointed enlargement is noted medial to the point of the shoulder. There is no fluctuation and practically no pain on palpation.

TREATMENT. An exploratory puncture should be made to determine the location of the abscess. In some cases this is difficult to do because of its deep situation and small size as a rule. Some of these abscesses only contain a teaspoonful or tablespoonful of pus. The pus should be removed by inserting a scalpel along side of the needle until the pocket is reached. The opening should be enlarged until all of the pus is evacuated. The cavity is then packed with gauze saturated with tincture of iodine. The gauze is removed in twenty-four hours and the wound flushed out daily with a mild antiseptic solution.

In some cases a large quantity of pus, as much as one or two gallons, accumulates medial to the shoulder joint. In these cases there is pronounced displacement of the shoulder joint laterally and on movement the leg is abducted as much as possible. These cases make remarkably quick recoveries even though it is impossible to establish complete drainage.

Supraspinous Bursitis

Fistula of the Withers

A similar condition exists at the withers that is true at the poll in regard to terminology. The term fistula of the withers does not accurately describe the tissues primarily involved in this condition or the changes that occur in the tissues as the result of the infection. The funicular part of the ligamentum nuchas which arises from the occipital protuberance inserts into the summits of the vertebral spines at the withers. A bursa which corresponds to the atlantal bursa at the poll, the supraspinous bursa is usually over the third and fourth thoracic spines but in some cases it may be over the second and may even extend over to the fifth thoracic spine.

Recent research on the two conditions called poll evil and fistula of the withers has revealed they are caused by the same organisms Actinomyces bovis and Brucella. With the development of infection in the bursa there is an increase in the formation of fluid and a distention of the bursa. The bursa is under considerable tension because of the overlying tissue and the pressure from within the bursa. When inflammation of the bursa occurs the wall becomes thickened and edematous with necrosis in the later stages. Due to the variable position of the bursa there is considerable variation in its size and location. The bursa may change its position so it has no further contact with the ligamentum nuchae. Usually the longer the inflammation is present in the bursa the more extensive the dilatations become, as pockets are forced between the tissue layers. These pockets and compartments are the rule in the advanced cases. Frequently they open into other sacs through small openings and the bilateral distentions may communicate under the ligamentum nuchae. If the distentions extend into loose tissue the bursa may become very extensive. However when it is in tissue that does not permit extensions it may rupture in a short time after the infection develops in the bursa. The contents of the bursa before rupture is a yellowish fluid which contains rice like bodies composed of fibrin. As soon as the bursa ruptures other organisms gain entrance to the bursa and the contents become purulent so there is a change in the character of the discharge. As a general rule the ligament is not affected but necrosis may occur in a few cases. The infection may also invade the spines of the vertebrae producing necrosis of the tops of the affected spines.

SIGNS. The signs of supraspinous bursitis vary according to the location and extent of the bursa. Also the virulence of the organisms and resistance of the tissues to infection may be important factors in the variations of the signs. Before any swelling is observed the horse may be stiff in the front legs or show pain when the withers are palpated. If the bursa is surrounded by tissues that prevents its expansion, the bursa may rupture before any swelling is observed. When this occurs there will be one or more tracts from the bursa and through the skin discharging purulent material to the outside. Occasionally a case is observed where the bursa after becoming distended has slipped from its position beneath the ligament to lodge in the subcutaneous tissue. When the infection develops slowly and the distentions can extend between tissue layers the characteristic swellings may appear at most any location in the region of the withers.

PROGNOSIS. The prognosis is favorable in the largest percentage of the cases.

TREATMENT. Before treatment is started on a case a careful examination should be made to determine if possible just what has occurred in the tissues. The simplest cases to treat are those in which the slightly distended bursa has moved from its position beneath the ligament and can be palpated in the subcutaneous tissue. If the appearance of the animal is highly important a horizontal incision is made through the skin. When the incision is made in this manner hair will hide the scar of the incision. After the incision is made through the skin the bursa is grasped with forceps and carefully dissected free from the surrounding tissue. The area is then treated as an open wound.

When the bursa is unable to distend due to unyielding tissue it may rupture before any swelling is observed. One or more openings may appear in the skin on each side of the withers discharging material to the outside from the bursa. This case and others have responded to treatment with

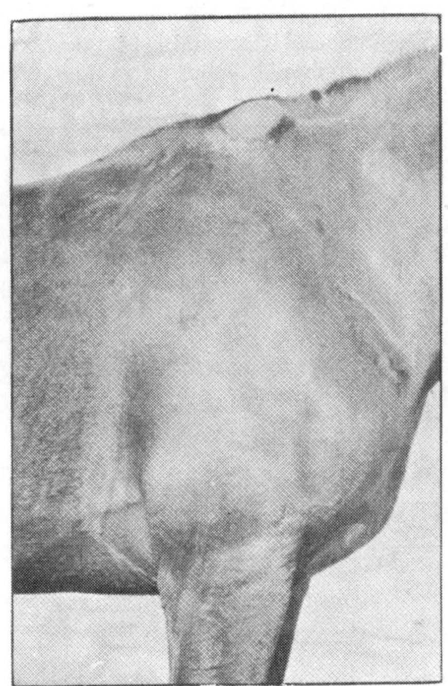

FIG. 242. The supraspinous bursa has moved from beneath the ligament to the subcutaneous tissue.

sodium iodide. The usual dosage is one ounce of sodium iodide dissolved in one pint of distilled water and administered intravenously. This treatment may be given two or three times a week until at least eight ounces have been administered. However some cases may require additional amounts to obtain complete recovery. The use of one of the sulfonomides or antibiotics is indicated for the secondary infection.

The longer the inflammation is present in the bursa the more extensive it may become if dilatation or extensions can be forced between the tissue layers. One or more swellings may occur in most any location in the region of the withers. Some of the dilatations may be deeply situated while others will be located beneath the skin. The various sacs may communicate through very small openings so it is necessary to establish drainage from each sac for complete recovery. These cases also receive iodine either intravenously in the form of sodium iodide or in the feed. As the infective agent in these cases are anaerobic, oxidizing antiseptics are used to irrigate the bursa and its dilatations.

Other types of cases that are sometimes observed are those in which necrosis of the ligament has occurred. All of the necrotic portion of the ligament should be removed. Necrosis of the tops of the spines may be manifested by a persistent chronic discharge. When this has occurred

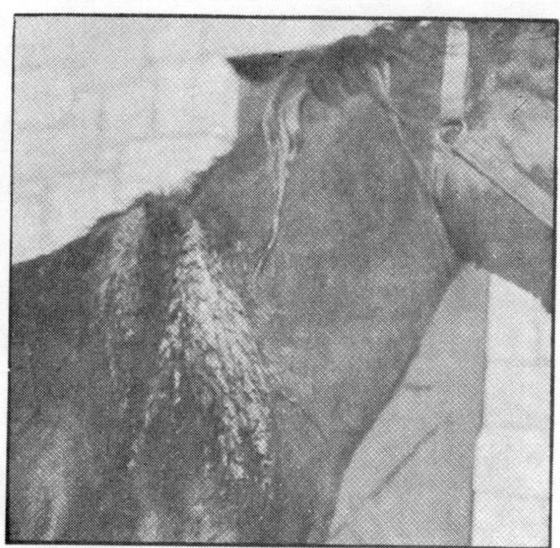

FIG. 243. Two openings discharging purulent material to the outside.

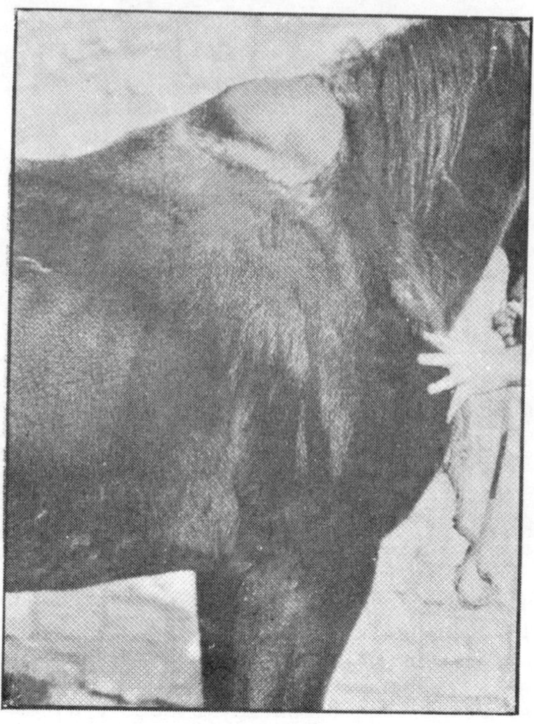

FIG. 244. A large swelling lateral to the median line.

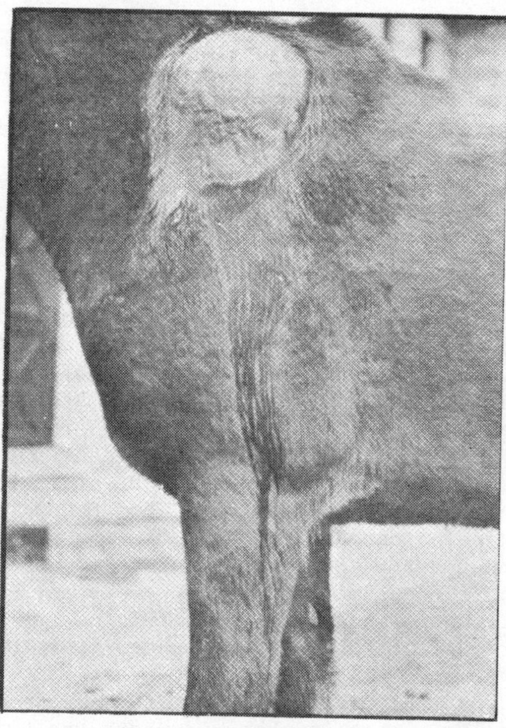

FIG. 245. A large swelling anterior to the scapula.

a digital examination of the tops of the spines will disclose some are very rough and pitted. It will be necessary to wait until their is separation of the necrotic and healthy bone when the necrotic portion may be removed.

Antibiotics are now used in the treatment of supraspinous bursitis with excellent results. The use of antibiotics has reduced the amount of surgery necessary in these cases. Also these cases now recover in a shorter period of time than with the various treatments used in the past. When the case is presented for treatment there may be one or more openings discharging purulent material to the outside or it may be necessary to establish drainage. In either case the patient receives the antibiotic of choice intramuscularly every other day until the desired results are obtained.

Spondylarthritis

Spondylarthritis is an inflammation of the joints between vertebrae. Any of the vertebral articulations may be affected but those most frequently involved are in the cervical or lumbar region. One case in which the articulation between the last cervical and first thoracic vertebrae was affected was observed in the equine. The owner first noticed the horse was standing and also walking with the anterior limbs held as close together as possible as shown in Fig. 246. The horse had a good appetite and would eat readily if the food was placed so he did not have to lower his head and neck. It was also noticed the horse always held his head and neck in the same fixed position with the neck held parallel with the ground. He was bright and alert and was normal except for the position of the anterior limbs and the head and neck. About four weeks after the horse was first observed to hold his anterior limbs together he would stand with the legs crossed as shown in Fig. 247. He would hold them crossed for a variable length of time. Horses have been observed to stand with the anterior limbs crossed with a neoplasm in the brain but they were also depressed. This horse was never depressed and seemed to be a normal alert horse at all times.

The necropsy revealed pronounced inflammatory changes in the articulation between the last cervical and first thoracic vertebrae. There was also an extensive periostitis of both vertebrae and a marked increase in their size. The horse walking with the legs held as close together as possible and crossing the legs was an attempt to relieve the pressure of the scapulae on the sensitive area.

Paralysis of the Suprascapular Nerve

Atrophy of the Shoulder, Sweeney, Shoulder Slip

The suprascapular nerve, a branch of the brachial plexus passes between the supraspinatus and subscapularis muscles and over the coracoid border of the scapula to innervate the supraspinatus and infraspinatus muscles.

ETIOLOGY. The condition seems to occur more frequently in young horses used in ploughing, especially those that are forced to walk in a furrow or on the ridge. Injury to the nerve may occur during extreme backward movement of the shoulder causing overstretching of the nerve or violent adduction of the shoulder against the thorax may bruise the nerve. Due to the location of the nerve on the anterior border of the scapula it is subject to a blow in this region or it may occur from collar pressure.

SIGNS. If the injury to the nerve is severe, abduction of the shoulder joint occurs when the greatest weight is placed on the limb. When the acute signs subside atrophy of the supraspinatus and infraspinatus muscles may occur producing a flat or depressed surface on each side of the spine of the scapula. In some cases in spite of the loss of function of the atrophied muscles there may be no change in action.

PROGNOSIS. If the injury to the nerve is severe and complete, atrophy of the muscles occurs in a week prognosis is unfavorable as it may indicate permanent injury to the nerve. If the atrophy is incomplete slow recovery may take place.

When only atrophy of the muscles is present it is necessary to differentiate from other diseased conditions that may be causing lameness as the atrophy may be due to lack of use.

TREATMENT. If injury to the nerve is due to traumatism of the tissues antiplogistic measures should be used to relieve the inflammation. In cases where slight injury to the nerve has occurred complete recovery

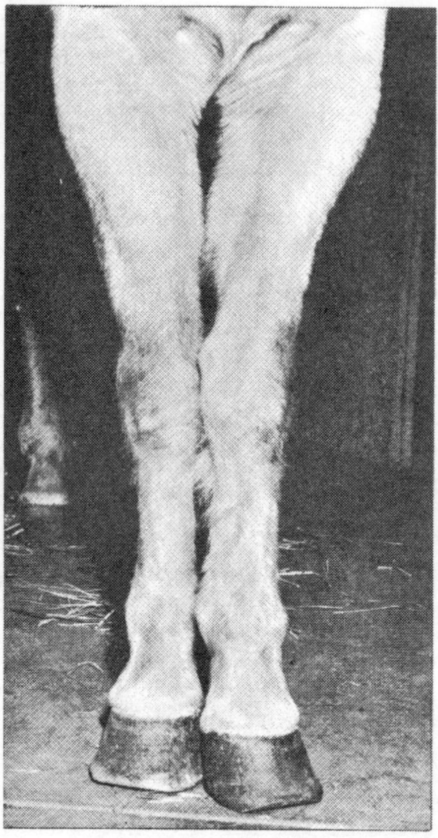

FIG. 246. Legs would be held as close together as possible when standing or walking.

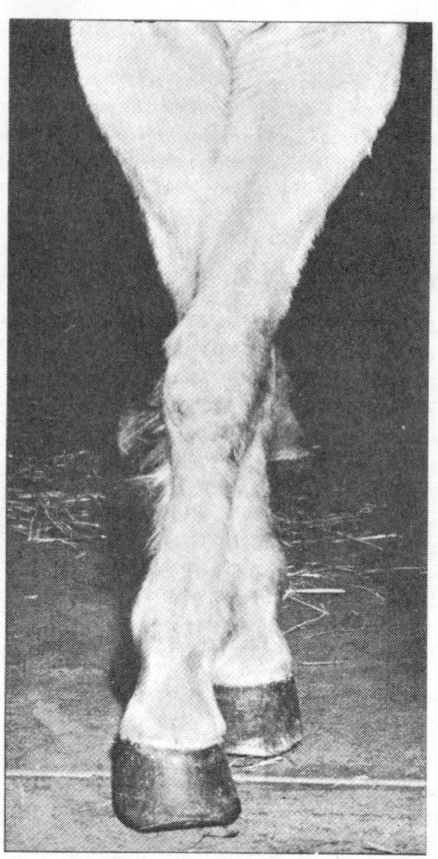

FIG. 247. Occasionally the legs would be crossed and held in this position for several minutes.

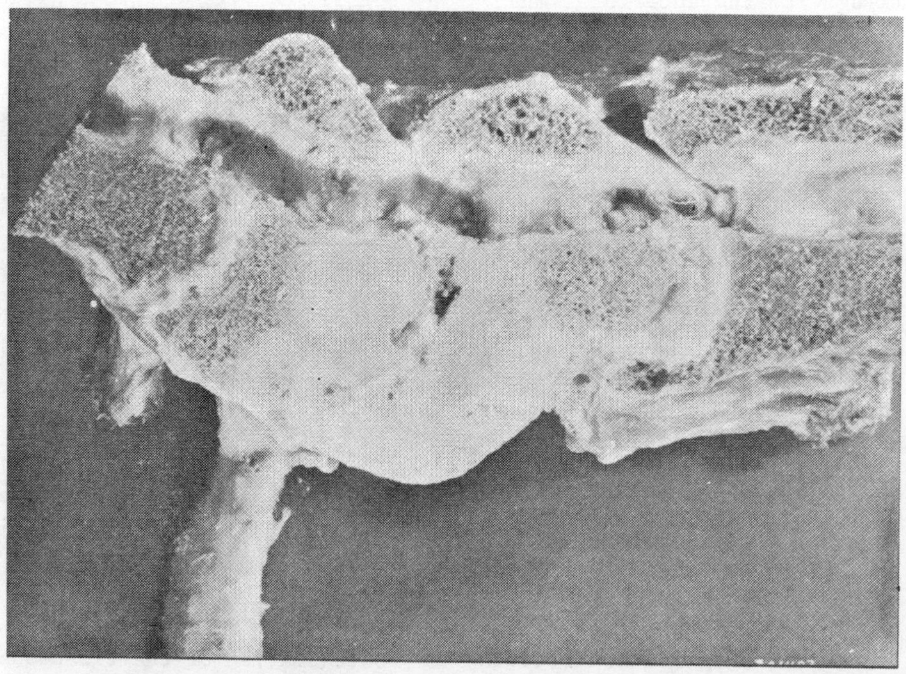

FIG. 248. Spondylarthritis of articulation between last cervical and first thoracic vertebrae, note first rib.

usually occurs without any treatment in four to six weeks. However, the use of blisters during this period may hasten recovery.

When it is apparent the atrophy is permanent irritants should be injected along the course of the affected muscles. One that does not cause abscess formation or sloughing is composed of equal parts of turpentine and chloroform. One cubic centimeter is injected at a point and the points are made two inches apart. A preparation that can be used on nervous highly sensitive individuals is a two per cent solution of silver nitrate.

The owner should be told that pronounced swelling of the area will occur and the animal will be reluctant to use the leg for several days. If the area does not completely fill in, it may be necessary to inject it again or at least some areas.

Inflammation of the Bursa Intertubercularis

The bursa intertubercularis is a very extensive bursa found between the biceps brachii muscle and the bicipital groove of the humerus. The biceps brachii is practically all tendon except at the bicipital groove where it becomes almost cartilaginous. The movement of the biceps brachii over the groove is made easier by the presence of this bursa. This bursa and sometimes the tendon is frequently affected with an acute or chronic inflammation and frequently diagnosed as shoulder lameness.

ETIOLOGY. Probably the most frequent cause of inflammation of the bursa is a severe traumatism at the point of the shoulder. Strain of the biceps brachii may also affect the bursa. An infection may localize in the bursa.

SIGNS. The outstanding sign is shown when the animal is in motion. He is unable to advance the leg but carries it while making a short jump forward on the sound limb. He cannot or will not make any attempt to lift the foot off the ground. However, when backing he may use the limb in almost a normal manner. When standing the foot is back of its normal position and usually resting on the toe. Pronounced signs of pain are pronounced when the leg is suddenly carried backward and upward.

In mild cases signs may be similar to navicular disease and when the condition

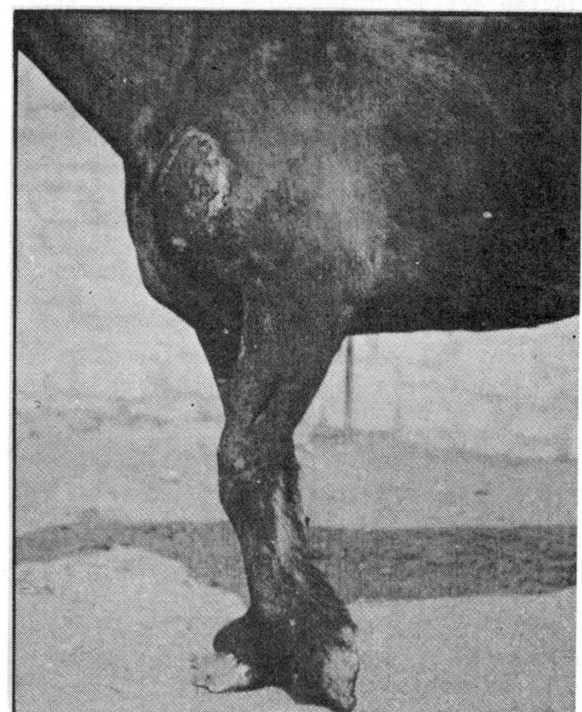

FIG. 249. Typical attitude of the limb in acute bursitis intertubercularis.

is bilateral it will need to be differentiated from laminitis.

TREATMENT. During the acute stage the use of cold water over the area for six to eight hours daily for two weeks is beneficial. Then for a week daily massage of the tissues with application of a liniment is helpful. Counter-irritation is then indicated and it is best obtained by injecting deep into the tissues over and around the point of the shoulder a subcutaneous irritant. The following may be used: Iodine crystals 20 grains, potassium iodide 40 grains and distilled water one ounce.

Inject two cubic centimeters deeply at a point about two inches apart over the front and sides of the shoulder. To hasten recovery it may be advisable to repeat this treatment in a month.

Paralysis of the Radial Nerve Musculo-spiral Nerve

The radial nerve is usually the largest branch of the brachial plexus and most of the fibres are derived from the first thoracic root of the plexus. One branch of the radial nerve supplies the tensor fasciae antibrachii before it reaches the musculo-spiral groove of the humerus. It then passes obliquely downward and outward and reaches the flexion surface of the elbow joint detaching muscular branches to the three heads of the triceps and the anconeus. Below the elbow, branches are supplied to the extensor carpi and the common and lateral extensors of the digit The radial nerve innervates the extensors of the elbow, carpal and digital joints and the lateral flexor of the carpus.

ETIOLOGY. There are many theories as to the cause of radial paralysis but some of those given are not very logical. One of the theories most frequently advanced is that radial paralysis is caused by fracture of the first rib. In a number of cases the two conditions may be present together but the same signs may exist without injury of the rib. Probably the most frequent cause of radial paralysis is overstretching of the nerve or the injury may involve only one of its branches. This has been observed to occur when the patient was restrained by means of a casting harness or in some cases when the patient was confined on the operating table. The trouble may originate in the muscle tissue and the changes in the nerve are only secondary.

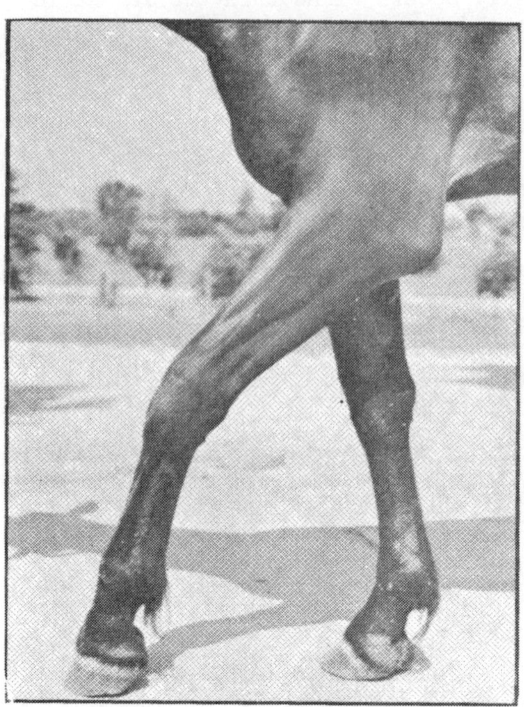

FIG. 251. Position of the limb when there is paralysis of the nerve to the triceps brachii muscle, note relaxation of the muscle and dropping of elbow.

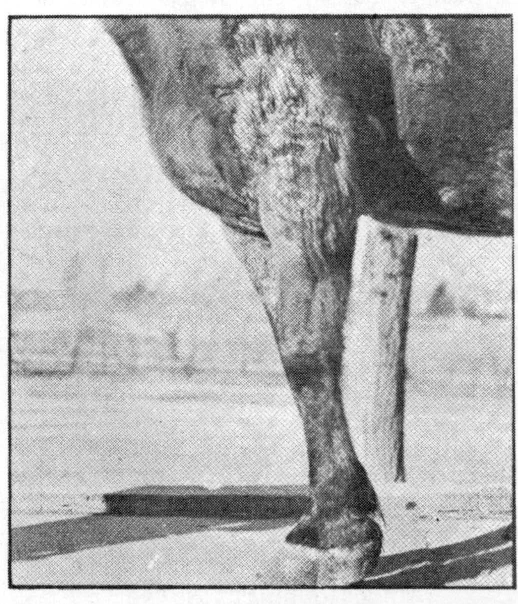

FIG. 250. Horse has difficulty in extending digit due to paralysis of nerve to the extensors.

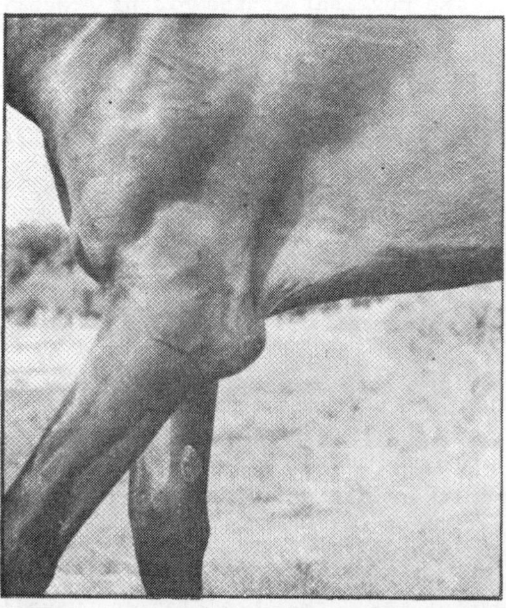

FIG. 252. Pronounced atrophy of the triceps brachii muscle had occurred two months after paralysis of the nerve.

SIGNS. The signs will vary with the extent and degree of paralysis. When the branch of the radial nerve supplying the extensors of the digit is affected the signs are characteristic. If the animal moves slowly and on a smooth surface nothing in particular may be noticed. In case an obstacle is encountered the foot is not sufficiently extended so it strikes against the obstacle, the leg may collapse and the horse fall. If there is complete paralysis of this branch of the radial nerve in the horse the stumbling may occur frequently. This lameness is characterized by stumbling, particularly on an uneven surface and later by a sliding motion of the foot when the limb is extended.

If there is complete paralysis of the branch of the radial nerve to the triceps brachii muscle the signs are characteristic. The foot is advanced forward to a normal position but due to loss of function of the triceps brachii muscle the horse is unable to extend the elbow joint and straighten the leg to a normal position for supporting weight. Note the relaxation of the muscle.

In complete paralysis of the radial nerve the animal stands with the shoulder and elbow joints extended and the knee and phalanges flexed. The toe of the foot is the only portion which rests on the ground. The triceps brachii muscle being relaxed allows full extension of the elbow joint. To an untrained observer the affected limb may appear longer than the sound one. When an attempt is made to move the horse he first advances both hind legs with the object of relieving his weight from the fore limbs. The patient attempts to advance the lame leg but is unable to carry it forward beyond half of the ordinary stride where it comes to rest, the toe on the ground with the knee and fetlock flexed. When the foot is brought forward by the hand until the sole rests on the ground and if pressure is brought to bear upon the fore arm just above the knee the animal will complete his stride and continue to advance just as long as the limb is extended for him and supported.

PROGNOSIS. In most of the cases it is favorable. However, uncertainty of movement may remain for sometime after the disappearance of the lameness. In some cases recovery occurs in ten days to six weeks or it may require a number of months for complete recovery to occur.

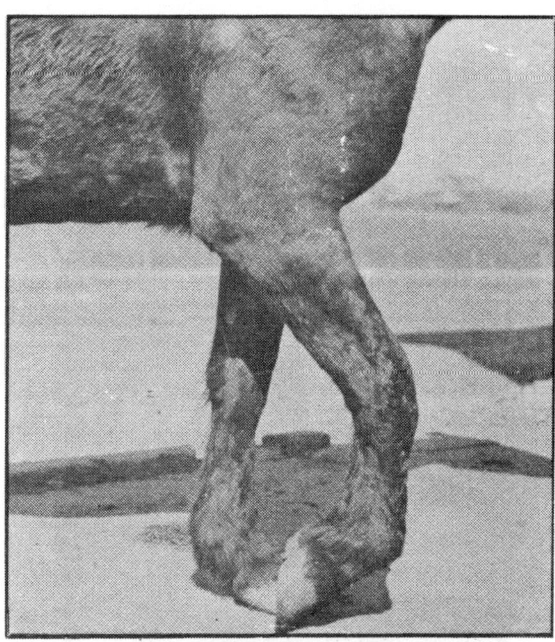

FIG. 253. Characteristic attitude of the limb in paralysis of the radial nerve.

TREATMENT. In most of the cases no particular treatment is necessary. Provision should be made for the affected animals to exercise daily on a smooth surface and it will be observed this is accompanied by gradual improvement. Some method should be devised to provide for normal movement of the limb during exercise.

Olecranon Bursitis, Capped Elbow, Hygroma, Shoe Boil

This condition is characterized by an inflammation of the subcutaneous bursa at the point of the elbow, and usually accompanied by a parabursitis and thickening of the tissues.

ETIOLOGY. Usually due to repeated traumatism of the bursa and subcutaneous tissues from long heel calkins or a hard surface. Infection may gain entrance during the course of an infectious disease.

SIGNS. It is most frequently seen as a chronic condition producing a thickening of the walls of the bursa and the surrounding tissue and varying a great deal in size. It is usually painless and does not cause lameness.

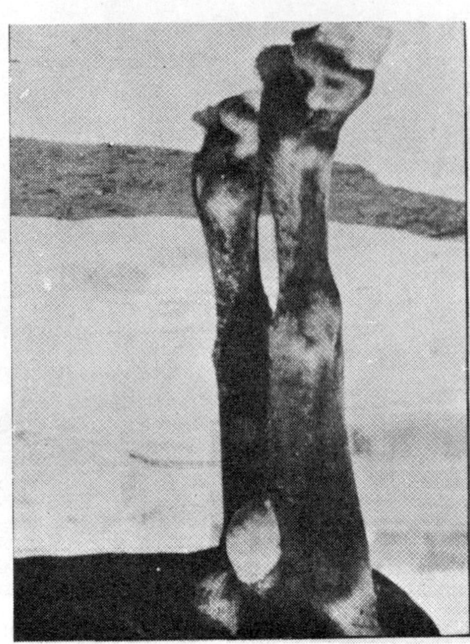

FIG. 254. A typical case of olecranon bursitis or shoe boil.

However, in some cases there is a hot, diffuse painful swelling on the point of the elbow with an extensive area of edema around it. This type of swelling usually indicates the presence of infection. Lameness is pronounced in a case of this type. In the suppurative condition rupture of the tissues may occur and one or more fistulous tracts develop.

PROGNOSIS. The condition is not usually serious but is in a location difficult to treat.

TREATMENT. First remove cause of irritation by removal of shoe and use of various type of pads to provide protection to the area. Plenty of bedding should be provided, a thick pad can be fastened under the sternum at night or a roll adjusted around the coronet may prevent further bruising.

In the acute painful cases, cold applications and astringent packs as white lotion. When a chronic enlargement is present the most successful form of treatment is surgical removal. An elliptical incision may be made over the enlargement and the excess tissue dissected out. The edges of the skin are sutured together and then the usual wound treatment is used. Some operators recommend removing the entire mass and treating as an open wound. The most important after care consists in preventing any irritation to the area until healing is complete.

Paralysis of a Pectoral Nerve

This condition occurs only occasionally in the equine and most often affects young colts. It may be either unilateral or bilateral with the affected limb or limbs assuming a pronounced bowed appearance.

According to the history given by the owner the colt that is pictured with this condition was strong and apparently normal at birth. For six weeks the colt's front legs were straight and well developed. At this time it was noticed the left fore leg was bowing slightly at the knee but the colt was not lame. There was a gradual but pronounced change in the shape of the limb for the next three months. At five months of age the colt began to favor the

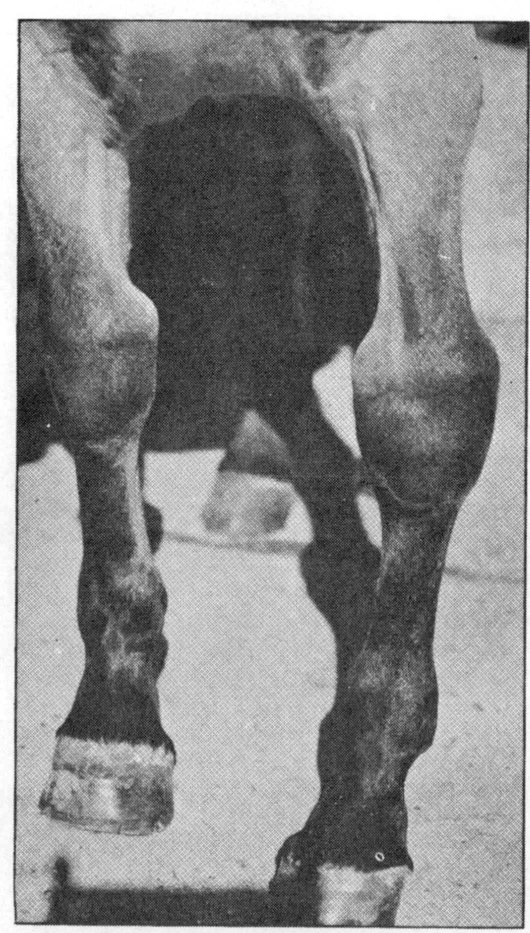

FIG. 255. Bowing of the limb that occurred after paralysis of a pectoral nerve.

limb and when running would show marked lameness sometimes carrying the limb.

Clinical examination revealed a well muscled strong colt with a pronounced outward bowing of the left front limb at the knee and an inward rotation of the digit. The elbow was abducted and the superficial pectoral muscles especially the posterior one atrophied. The colt walked with a slight limp and when forced to trot was very lame.

Post-mortem findings confirmed the clinical diagnosis of paralysis of a pectoral nerve. The left posterior superficial pectoral muscle was smaller than that of the opposite side and lighter in color. The change in the shape of the limb is one of compensation. The action of the superficial pectoral muscle is adduction of the limb and loss of action of this muscle permits its abduction.

Amputation of Anterior Limb

Amputation of a portion of the forelimb is indicated occasionally in the bovine. If the distal portion of the limb is affected with some incurable condition or severe injury amputation will hasten recovery. Also some animals that would have to be destroyed can be fattened for market or retained for breeding purposes.

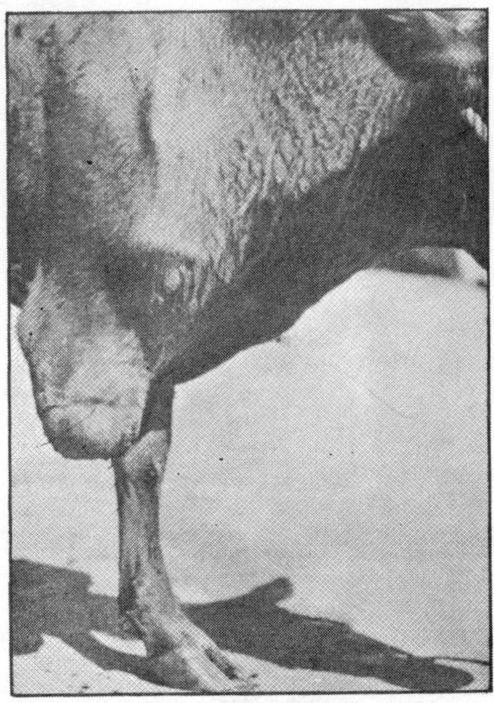

FIG. 256. After amputation of a portion of the limb.

OPERATION. The limb should be amputated high enough so the end of the stump will not be continually reinjured by striking on the ground. The operation is performed at the junction of the upper and middle third of the radius. A liberal area around the limb is shaved and prepared for an aseptic operation.

The skin and subcutaneous tissue is anesthetized by injecting a one per cent solution of a local anesthetic. The muscle and periosteum are anesthetized by infiltration with a two per cent solution of a local anesthetic. A tourniquet is fastened around the limb above the operative area.

Two elliptical incisions are made through the skin, one on the medial side and one on the lateral side of the limb. The incisions are made low enough so when the bone is removed at the junction of its upper and middle thirds the muscle and skin will cover over the end of the bone. The incisions through the muscles are similar to the skin incisions but shorter. The object of this procedure is to reduce the quantity of muscle tissue and to provide space for the post-operative swelling. There is usually some post-operative swelling and if provision is not made for it suture necrosis is apt to occur. Hemorrhage is controlled by ligation of the larger vessels. The soft tissue is dissected away from the bone up above the point where the bone is to be removed. The bone is removed with a bone saw at the junction of the upper and middle third of the radius. Suture the ends of the muscles together with No. 4 chromic catgut so the muscle tissue covers over the end of the bones. Unite the two flaps of skin with mattress sutures leaving an opening at the bottom for drainage. The sutures and edges of the skin are covered over with flexible collodion.

After treatment consists in keeping the drainage opening free of exudate and the removal of any necrotic tissue.

Rupture of the Common Digital Extensor in Foals

The above condition is not of common occurence but W. L. and W. G. Stevenson of Canada report having a few cases in their practice every year. These cases occur during the foaling season but do not occur in any particular community or farm. Probably many cases of rupture of the common digital extensor foals has been erroneously diagnosed and improperly treated.

The condition is usually observed when the colt attempts to stand after birth. It may go over on its knees and seems to be unable to extend the knee joint. The affected colt may be able to stand but goes over on its knees when it attempts to move. In a few cases the colt may not show any signs until the second or third day after birth.

The diagnostic sign is the animals inability to extend either the fetlock or knee joint.

DIAGNOSIS. This condition may be confused with contraction of the deep digital flexor tendon or paralysis of the branch of the radial nerve to the triceps brachii muscle. In both of these conditions the signs might be similar. However the diagnosis would be established by feeling the enlarged free end of the ruptured extensor under the skin. This free end is usually found over the carpus where there is some swelling. Rupture of the tendon occurs at the upper limit of the carpus and the end drops down into the carpal sheath.

TREATMENT. The treatment which is surgical is best performed when the colt is five to ten days old. At this age the colt will not die from shock and tissue will not have formed adhesions. The operative area is on the anterior surface of the carpus where the ruptured end of the tendon can be felt. After the usual preparation of the skin the tissue in the area is infiltrated with a one per cent solution of a local anesthetic. The incision through the skin is made over the end of the tendon. This incision is continued through the tissue until the loose end of the tendon is exposed. The end of the tendon is grasped with forceps and pulled up until all of the discolored portion is exposed. This portion which is usually two or three inches long is removed. The incision in the skin may or may not be sutured and receives the usual care. Improvement is usually rather gradual but in thirty days the colt has regained almost normal use of the limb. For horses used at slow gait the results are very satisfactory but they probably would not be in horses used for running and jumping.

Epiphysitis

Epiphysitis of the epiphyseal cartilage at the distal end of the radius is frequently seen in young colts. One or both front limbs may be affected. The inflammation of the epiphyseal cartilage stimulates the development of more than the normal amount of cartilage on the lateral or medial side. Due to the increased thickness of the cartilage on one side the distal end of the limb is displaced laterally or medially. The extent of the displacement will depend upon how much excess cartilage is formed.

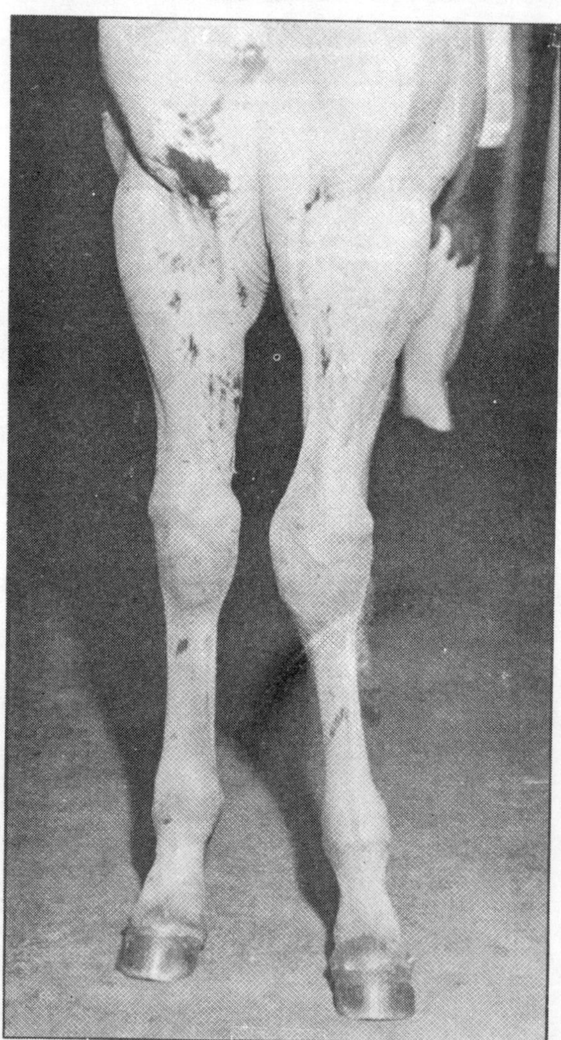

FIG. 257. Epiphysitis at distal end of radius and on medial side.

FIG. 257.

TREATMENT. A very successful method of treatment is to keep the colt confined in a box stall until the leg is normal.

Blemished Knee

The operation on a blemished knee is to remove a large scar or blemish to improve the appearance of the limb.

OPERATION. To obtain the best results from the operation the animal must be securely confined preferable on an operating table but the casting harness may be used for confining on the ground.

Anesthesia may consist of general anesthesia or enough to quiet the patient, supplemented with local anesthesia of the tissues in the operative area. In the largest percentage of cases probably a general anesthetic should be used.

PROCEDURE. Proper precautions should be taken to perform an aseptic operation as the desired results are only obtained when healing occurs by first intention. The operative area is shaved, and the operative area prepared for an aseptic operation.

Elliptical incisions are made extensive enough to include the scar and with their long axis parallel with the limb. The skin enclosed within the incisions are carefully dissected from the underlying tissue. Care should be taken not to injure any of the underlying tissue. One longitudinal incision should be made through the skin on each side of the elliptical incisions. These incisions should be as long as the elliptical incisions and about one inch on either side. The object of these incisions is to take the tension off the uniting sutures. The edges of the elliptical incisions are brought into close and complete apposition with closely placed interrupted sutures. A splint should be applied on the posterior surface of the limb from the fetlock to the elbow to prevent any bending of the knee. It may be necessary to keep the animal in slings to limit movement of the limb. Examine the operative area frequently to make sure there is no infection developing in the wound. The sutures may be removed in two weeks and the limb should be immobilized for three weeks.

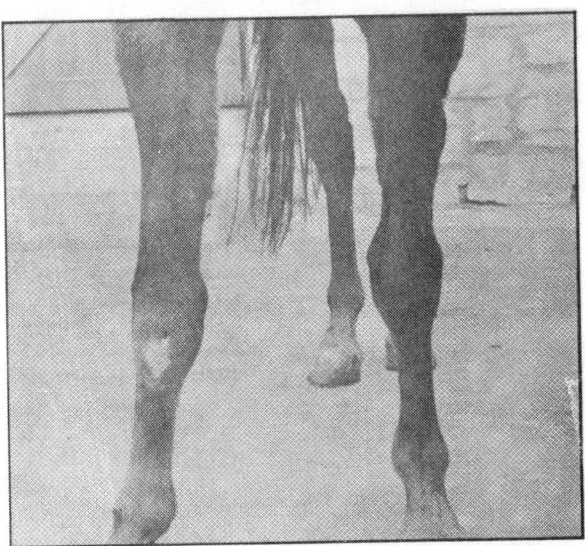

FIG. 258. Blemish on anterior surface of carpus.

Flexion of the Carpus, Acquired

Flexion of the carpus may occur in mature animals when there is severe strain of the tissues. Also when horses are required to pull heavy loads over a long period. The condition is referred to as bent knees,

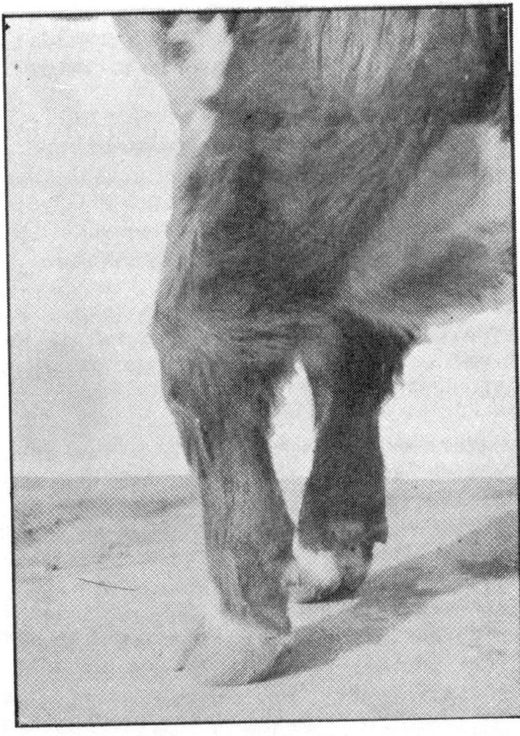

FIG. 259a. Flexion of the knee due to contraction of the flexor carpi ulnaris and ulnaris lateralis muscles.

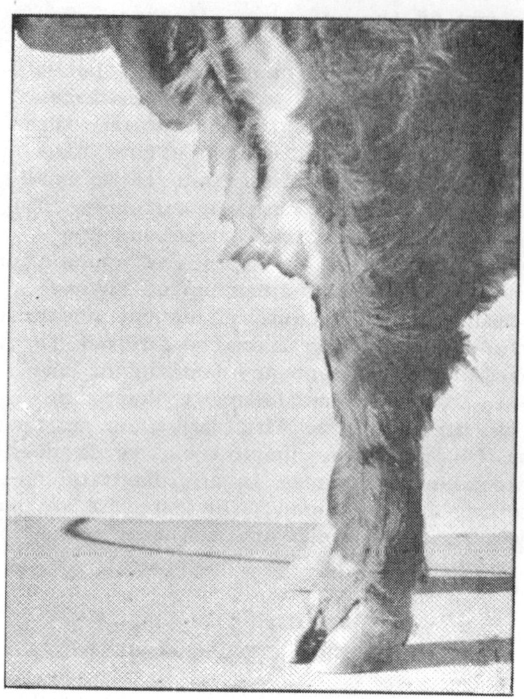

FIG. 259b. Tenotomy of the tendons of the flexor carpi ulnaris and ulnaris lateralis muscles corrected the flexion of the knee.

knee sprung or buck knees. In mature animals it is due to the contraction of the ulnaris lateralis and flexor carpi ulnaris muscles and the tendons insert on the accessory carpal bone.

TREATMENT. Supercarpal tenotomy of the tendons of the ulnaris lateralis and flexor carpi ulnaris tendons is indicated to relieve acquired flexion of the carpus. The operation is performed on the posterior surface of the carpus and dorsal to the accessory carpal bone where each tendon can be palpated. Usually the operation can be performed with the patient in the standing position.

The operative area is prepared for an aseptic operation and the tissues anesthetized by infiltration with a local anesthetic. By palpation the depression between the two tendons on the posterior surface of the limb is located about one inch dorsal to the accessory carpal bone. A knife with a narrow blade is introduced through the skin and first one tendon and then the other tendon is divided. The cutting of the tissue should stop as soon as the tendons are divided to prevent injury to the ulnar artery. The wound should be bandaged and kept covered until the small wound has healed. There is usually a rapid recovery from the operation.

Flexion of the Carpus, Congenital

Congenital flexion of the carpus may be seen in the young of most of the domesticated animals. The front legs are flexed at the carpus and cannot be extended. This flexion is due to two ligaments on the posterior surface of the carpus, one at the lateral and one at the medial edge. When these two ligaments are divided the carpal joint can be extended. The operative areas are prepared for aseptic operations and then infiltrated with a local anesthetic. A narrow bladed knife is introduced through the skin and the ligaments divided. The wounds are kept bandaged until healed. The patient may never have normal use of the limbs.

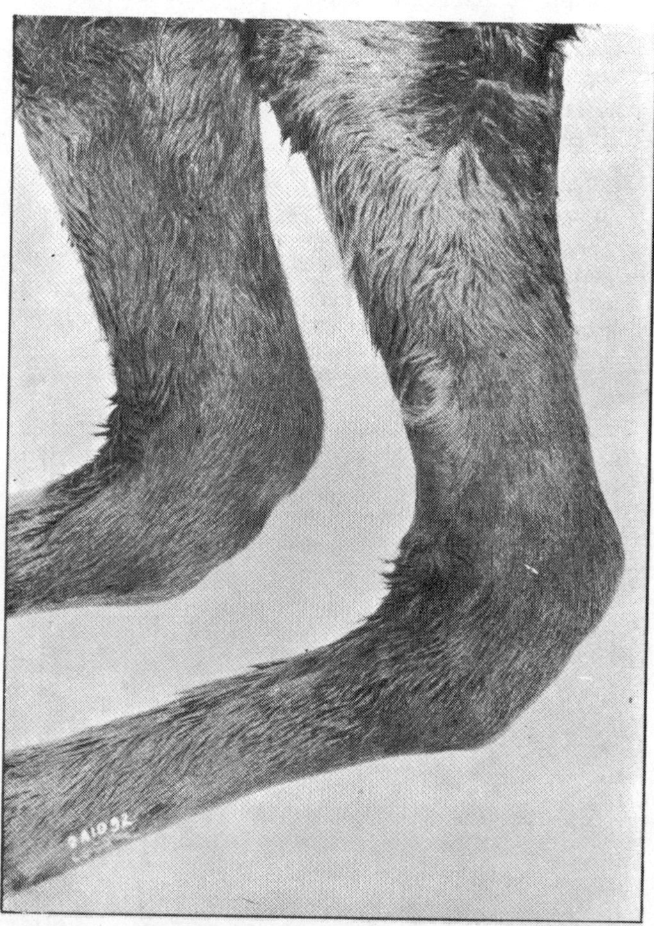

FIG. 260. Congenital flexion of the carpus in day old colt.

Arthritis of Carpal Joint

The carpal joint is frequently the seat of lameness and one or both carpal joints may be affected. When this condition occurs in the race horse the owner may say this horse has, "popped a knee". Arthritis or inflammation of the tissues of the carpal joint occurs most frequently in those horses used at fast gaits.

SIGNS. In the average case there is no observable enlargement of any of the tissues of the joint. Also no lameness is shown until the patient is used at a fast gait, when lameness develops in the affected limb or limbs. When the carpal joint is examined the outstanding symptom is the distention of the joint capsule, due to an increased quantity of synovial fluid. With rest the lameness and the excess synovial fluid disappears only to reappear with vigorous exercise. Examination may in some cases reveal an enlargement of some of the bones of the carpal joint or inflammatory tissue over the anterior surface of the joint.

PROGNOSIS. The prognosis will be favorable except in those cases where some of the carpal bones show some enlargement.

TREATMENT. A very successful form of treatment is the use of the actual cautery on the anterior surface of the carpal joint. Anesthesia of the operative area may be obtained by infiltrating the skin and subcutaneous tissue with a two per cent solution of a local anesthetic. The patient will not object to this infiltration of the tissue if small needles are used. A 25 gauge needle is used to anesthetize a small area in the skin, then a 21 gauge needle one inch long is inserted through this anesthetized area to complete the infiltration of the tissues over the anterior surface of the carpal joint. The actual cautery with a sharp point is used to place a series of points that just penetrate the skin.

A series of vertical imaginary lines about one inch apart may be drawn on the anterior surface of the carpal joint. The points are then placed about one inch apart on these lines. After the points have been placed a blister composed of one part red iodide of mercury and four parts petrolatum is massaged over the area for ten minutes. A thick layer of cotton that is extensive enough to extend above and below the carpal joint is placed around the leg and bandaged securely in position. The cotton is left on for ten days and then removed. The best results will be obtained if the patient is then rested for two or three months.

Hygroma of the Bovine Carpus

Hygroma of the carpal joint occurs most frequently in those animals that are confined on concrete floors or other hard surfaces. The repeated bruising of the tissues on the anterior surface of the carpal joint produces enlargements that will vary a great deal in size and also consistency or contents. In some cases the subcutaneous bursa is primarily involved, in others it is the subcutaneous tissue or the sheath of an extensor tendon and occasionally all three structures are affected. When a hygroma occurs in the bovine on pasture it is usually produced by a sudden severe bruise.

The hygroma may show an acute inflammation of the affected tissues which is very painful on palpation. When the hygroma is of slow development there may be a marked thickening of the affected tissues and there may or not be a large quantity of fluid present. An abscess may be present due to infection of the contents of the hygroma.

TREATMENT. For any treatment of hygroma to be successful the animal must be confined on a surface that will not bruise the tissues. This is most easily accomplished by confining on a dirt floor that is heavily bedded with straw.

For the cases of acute bursitis Ferguson recommends the following procedure as very successful in its treatment. The treatment for the first six hours consists in keeping cracked ice in contact with the tissues on the anterior surface of the carpal joint. Then for six hours hot applications are used. Then a good blister is used on the skin until it shows evidence of irritation.

The treatment for the chronic case will be determined by the changes that have occurred in the tissues. The operative area over the front and sides of the hygroma are shaved and prepared for an aseptic operation. The patient should be confined in lateral recumbency. A general anesthetic may be used or the skin infiltrated along the proposed lines of incision with a local anesthetic. For the hygroma of average size that contains fibrous tissue incisions may be made at the top and bottom

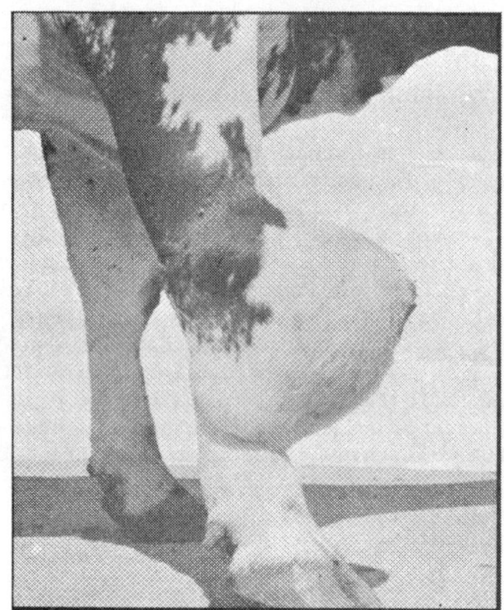

FIG. 261. Hygroma of the carpus.

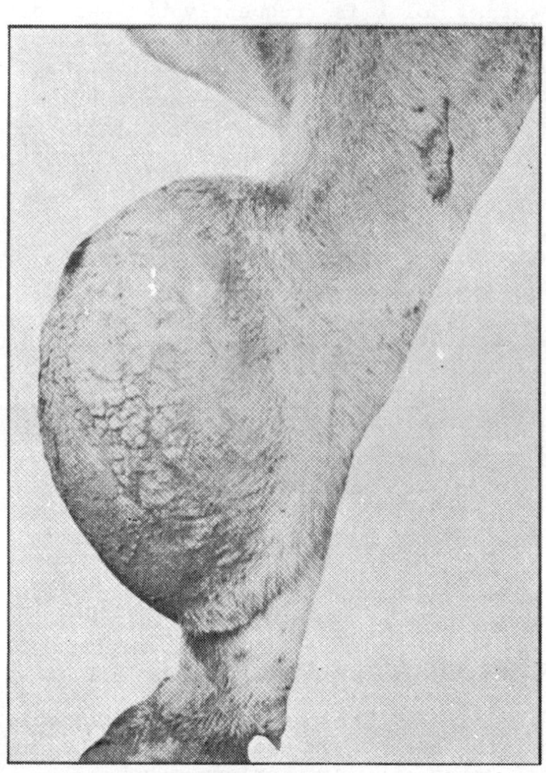

FIG. 263. Unusually large hygroma that was filled with fluid.

FIG. 262. Thirty days after the operation on the hygroma of the carpus.

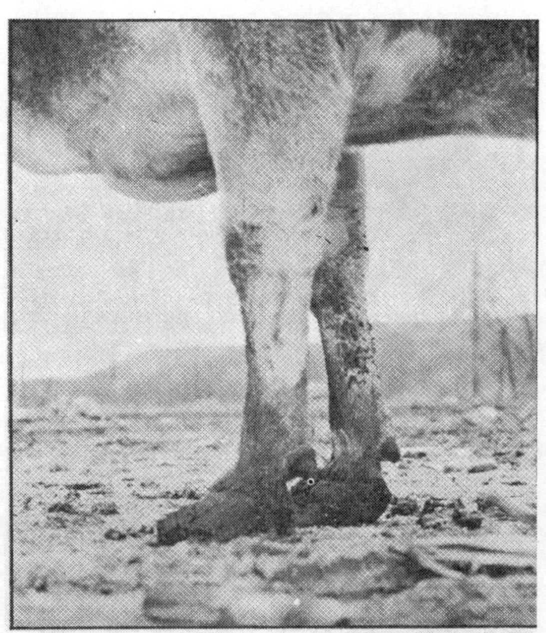

FIG. 264. The limb is now approximately normal size.

of the enlargement. In some cases it may be more desirable to make the incisions on the lateral and medial sides of the enlargement. By making the incisions in this manner no wound is made through the skin on the anterior surface of the carpal joint.

After the incisions are made through the skin the fluid contents are removed and the inflammatory tissue is dissected away from the skin. The tissue most adherent to the joint capsule is not removed because of the danger of opening the joint capsule. A thin layer of gauze that is impregnated with some form of iodine is placed in the cavity. The entire region is then firmly bandaged. The wound is examined in three days and retreated as often as it seems to be indicated. In most cases more rapid healing will be obtained if movement of the tissues is limited by a metal splint on the posterior surface of the limb.

A different technique was used in Figs. 261 and 263 where the unusually large swellings were due to an abnormal quantity of fluid. The skin on the anterior surface of the swelling was markedly thickened. The area was prepared for an aseptic operation by the usual technique. An incision through the skin released the large quantity of fluid in the hygroma. After the fluid was evacuated there was an excessive quantity

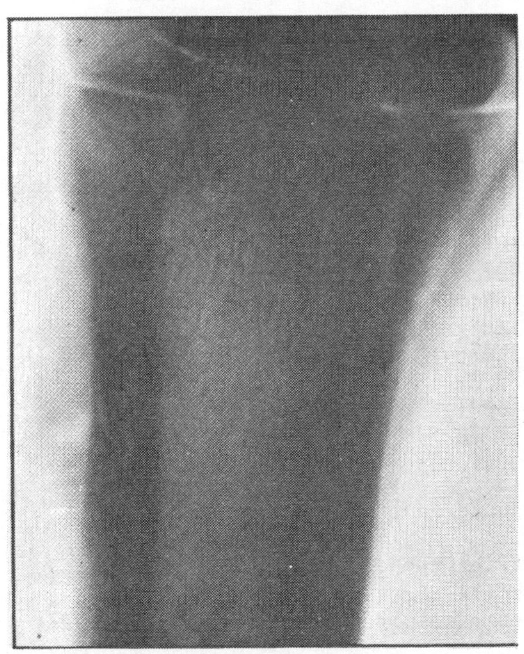

FIG. 265. A splint on the medial side of the right front limb.

of skin on the anterior surface of the knee joint. By bringing this excess skin over to the medial side of the limb, normal skin covered the anterior surface of the carpal joint. A local anesthetic of one per cent procaine hydrochloride was injected into the skin where it was planned to insert the sutures. A series of mattress sutures composed of a double strand of umbilical tape were inserted through the two layers of skin close along the lateral side of the limb. The large quantity of redundant skin was removed by an incision about one inch lateral to the line of sutures. An antiseptic pack was placed over the operative area and bandaged in position. A metal splint that extended from the foot to the upper third of the radius was placed in position on the posterior surface of the limb. This prevented movement of the knee joint which permitted rapid healing of the wound. The wound was retreated as often as it seemed to be advisable.

Splints

The term splint refers to those exostoses that occur along the large and small metacarpal or metatarsal bones and may involve only one or both of the bones. On the front limb they are usually found on the medial side and the lateral side on the hind limb and in some cases both sides are involved. Usually occur in horses under five years of age or before ossification occurs between the large and small metacarpal or metatarsals.

LOCATION. They are usually found below the head of the small metacarpal or metatarsal bone and more commonly in the middle third of this area. Usually there is one well defined enlargement or there may be a number of smaller enlargements occurring the entire length of the smaller bones. If the exostosis occurs on the splint bone close to the knee joint it is sometimes referred to as a knee splint. In some cases the exostosis occurs on the posterior surface of the metacarpal or metatarsal bone and becomes so extensive as to interfere with the suspensory ligament or movements of the flexor tendons.

ETIOLOGY. Splints occur frequently in young horses used for fast work on hard surfaces. Faulty conformation or improper shoeing may produce excessive strain on the medial side of the limb. Traumatisms to the area may produce a periostitis and exostosis.

PROGNOSIS. Depends on the location and extent of the splint. When they occur in the usual location the prognosis is favorable. However, when a splint occurs close to the knee joint or interferes with the suspensory ligament or movement of the flexor tendons the prognosis becomes unfavorable or guarded.

SIGNS. A typical splint lameness is a warm lameness, that is, it becomes more marked with exercise. It is also more noticeable at the trot over hard ground or going down hill. The horse may not show any lameness at the walk. Palpation of the affected area in the early stages may disclose a soft edematous swelling which is very sensitive. As the acute inflammation subsides the enlargement becomes more firm and finally ossification occurs. In some horses well developed splints are found and there is no history of the horse ever being lame.

DIAGNOSIS. Do not usually occur in horses over five years of age. In examining the limb for the presence of a splint careful palpation should be made along the lateral and medial sides of each splint bone for presence of any sensitive area. Examine carefully in front of the tendons to see if an exostosis is present that will interfere with the tendons.

TREATMENT. When acute inflammatory symptoms are present cold and astringent applications should be used until the acute symptoms subside. In about two weeks a biniodide mercury blister may be applied to the area and the horse should be permitted to exercise. If the lameness continues firing with a few deep points should be made into the area. In rare cases it may be necessary to remove the exostosis when it is interfering with the movements of the tendons.

Affections of the Synovial Sheaths and Bursae

The movements of the tendons over the limbs are simplified by the presence of bursae and tendon sheaths. Theca is a sheath like structure. Thecocentesis is the aspiration of synovia from a synovial sheath or bursa. Tendosynovitis or tendovaginitis is inflammation of tendons and tendon sheaths while bursitis is inflammation of a bursa. The sheaths of the flexor tendons are more extensive than the extensor tendons, so injuries and infection of the flexor sheaths are the most serious.

Acute Synovitis or Serous Synovitis

Normally synovial fluid is secreted by the synovial membrane and absorbed by the lymphatics. When the smooth glistening synovial membrane is injured or infected it becomes inflamed as do other tissues throwing out an excessive amount of synovial fluid for protection. The membrane becomes thickened and rough and is therefore swollen and painful. This is known as synovitis and demands rest of the part.

ETIOLOGY. In acute synovitis distension of the affected sheath appears very suddenly. Traumatic injury of the extensor sheaths may occur from bruising against the manger, wall, or hard floor. Small foreign objects as thorns may penetrate into the sheath producing a synovitis. In the largest percentage of cases synovitis occurs from overwork or it may result from strain of the tendon.

SIGNS. In the acute stage there is a pronounced distension of the affected sheath, heat, and sensitiveness upon palpation. If the inflammation is very acute lameness may be shown when the extensor tendon sheaths are affected. Synovitis of the flexor sheath is a rather serious condition and produces a marked type of lameness.

PROGNOSIS. In most cases the prognosis is favorable if appropriate treatment is applied during the early stages. However, in some old animals and in improperly treated cases they may linger for months with lameness and thickening of the affected tissues.

TREATMENT. In distensions of the extensor tendon sheaths there may be an absence of lameness. In some horses where appearance is not important, the condition may be only a blemish. When the flexor tendon sheaths are affected the lameness may be pronounced and rest is always indicated. During the acute inflammatory stage some type of antiphlogistic treatment is used for several hours daily. Then a thick layer of cotton that is thoroughly moistened with white lotion or a saturated solution of magnesium sulphate is bandaged over the part.

If after the acute symptoms subside there is still some swelling and lameness, a blister composed of one part red iodide of mercury and four parts of vaseline may be applied on the skin and thoroughly rubbed for fifteen minutes. A thick layer of cotton is applied over the area and bandaged firmly in position and is to be left on for ten days. Blistering of the skin may be prevented by applying vaseline to the skin at the top and bottom of the bandaged area to exclude the air.

Chronic Synovitis

The chronic condition may follow the acute without any decrease in size of the dis tended sheath. Also the chronic inflammation may appear without any apparent cause. In old chronic cases the contents of the sheath may have become fibrinous and the enlargement is firm to the touch.

TREATMENT. A sterile needle or trocar should be introduced into the sheath under strict aseptic precautions and the synovia aspirated. Various preparations may be injected into the sheath and at the present time one of the corticosteroides may be used. If the tissues are thickened and the fluid has become organized the repeated application of a blister may give good results.

Acute Suppurative Synovitis

Infection may gain entrance into the sheath through a wound or it may occur during the course of an infectious disease as influenza or strangles.

SYMPTOMS. There is an intense acute inflammation of the sheath that is very painful. The horse will in many cases refuse to bear any weight on the limb. There is a pronounced increase in the rate of the pulse, temperature and respirations. If there is a marked decrease in the appetite there is a loss of condition. The discharge from the wound consists of synovia and a purulent exudate.

PROGNOSIS. Prognosis is always guarded as any infection of a flexor tendon sheath is a serious condition. During the course of the infection the tendons may become infected, the tissue is weakened, and may rupture when there is any strain of the tissue.

When infection occurs in a tendon sheath there is the possibility of two serious conditions developing if the infection is not properly treated. The infection may spread throughout the sheath and lead to an extensive sepsis. Also the infection may invade and destroy the tendon tissue or cause an early breakdown when the tendons are used. To prevent development of any of the conditions named above early surgical drainage of the sheath is indicated. If the pressure of the excess fluid in the sheath is maintained within the sheath it will disturb the delicate blood supply of the tendon tissue. When this disturbance in blood supply is maintained for too long a period of time it may result in an early breakdown of the tendon tissue. After drainage of the infection from the sheath it is indicated to use one of the antibiotics in the sheath. This method of treatment seems to shorten the prolonged period of suppuration which usually followed surgical drainage.

Tendinitis

Inflammation of the flexor tendons occurs rather frequently in the horse and the tendons in the front legs are the ones usually affected.

ANATOMY. The muscular portion of the deep digital flexor also known as the flexor perforans has its origin on the humerus, radius, and ulna, and becomes tendinous about three or four inches above the carpus. Passing through the carpal canal it is included in the carpal synovial sheath with the superficial flexor tendon. In the middle of the metacarpus it is joined by the subcarpal check ligament which is a continuation of the posterior ligament of the carpus. The tendon then passes through the ring at the fetlock formed by the superficial flexor tendon. Also at the fetlock it is wider as it passes over the flexor surface of the distal sesamoids to be inserted on the semilunar crest of the third phalanx.

The superficial flexor tendon or flexor perforatus has its origin on the humerus. A strong fibrous band called the superior check ligament joins the tendon near the carpus. The tendon passes through the carpal canal enclosed in the carpal sheath with the deep digital flexor. As it approaches the fetlock, the tendon widens and at the fetlock it forms a ring for the passage of the deep flexor tendon. The tendon divides into two branches near the distal end of the first phalanx which diverge to reach their points of insertion on the proximal extremity of the second phalanx and distal extremity of the first phalanx.

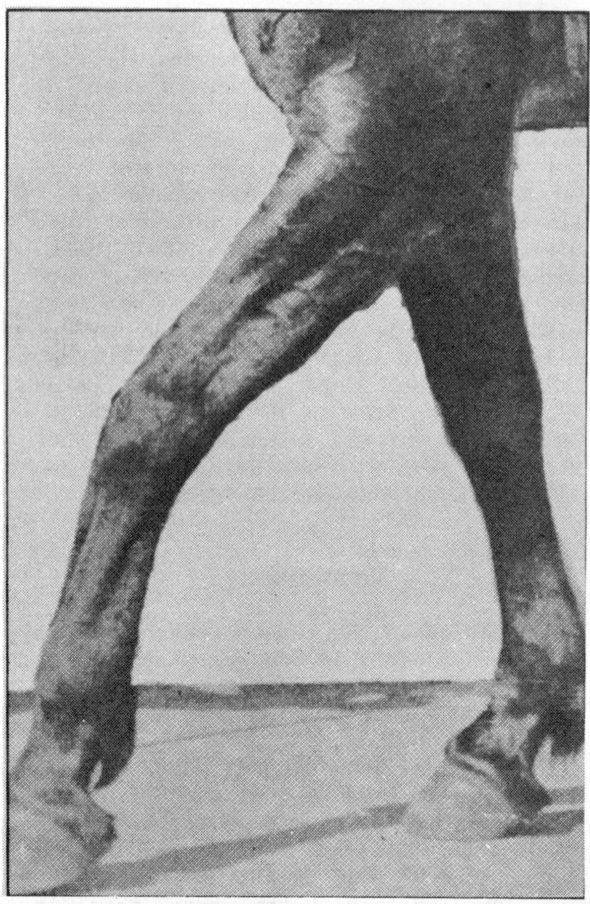

FIG. 266. Attitude of the limb in a case of inflammation of the suspensory ligament.

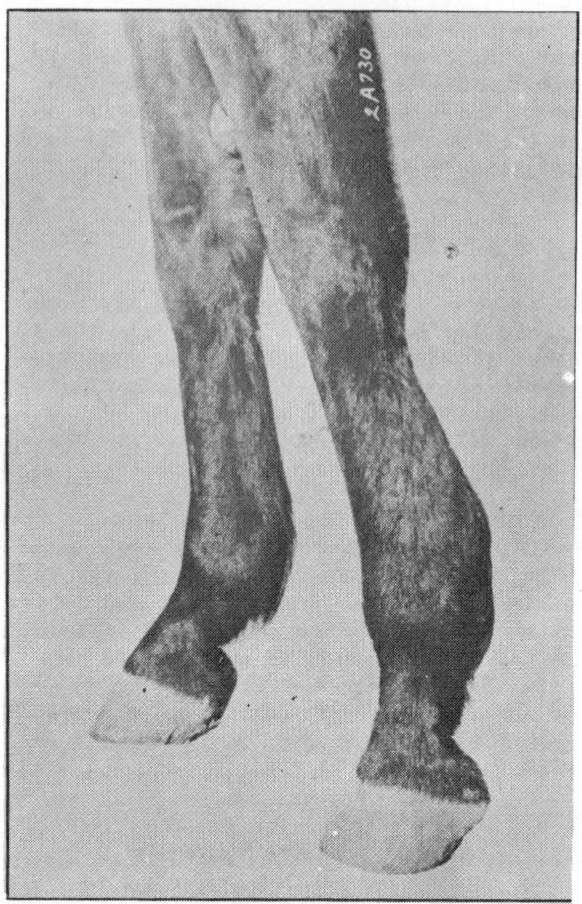

FIG. 267. A so-called "bowed tendon" increase in size may be due to synovitis of tendon sheath.

The suspensory ligament is a wide thick band that attaches to the distal row of carpal bones and the proximal surface of the large metacarpal bone. It divides into two branches at the lower fourth of the metacarpus, each branch passing to the abaxial surface of its sesamoid to which it is intimately attached. The branches continue downward to the dorsal surface of the first phalanx where they join the extensor tendon.

Strain of the Flexor Tendons and Suspensory Ligament

Strain of the flexor tendons or tendinitis varies a great deal in severity and amount of injury to the tissue. The injury may be limited to some of the peripheral fibres or a variable portion of the deeper fibres may be affected. Strain of the tendons may occur at most any point from the carpus to their insertion. The strain of the suspensory ligament usually occurs at its bifurcation or one of its branches. Probably strain of the subcarpal or check ligament occurs more frequently in draft horses than in light horses. In light horses strain is more frequent in the suspensory and deep digital flexor tendon.

ETIOLOGY. Poor conformation or leaving the toes too long and heels low, favors strain of the structures in the flexor apparatus. Tendons even though large may be of poor quality and are easily strained. In young horses forced training before the tendons are well developed may be the direct cause of strain. Hard, fast work, such as racing, hunting, and heavy work, fatigue the muscles, thus placing all of the support on the tendons, is a frequent cause of severe strain. In some cases synovitis precedes the tendinitis or the synovitis and tendinitis may be associated together.

SIGNS. When there is injury of the tissues of the flexor apparatus the symptoms of an inflammation as, heat, pain and swelling will be evident to a variable degree. If the inflammatory reaction in the tissues is severe the affected area is very sensitive and it may extend from the carpus to the fetlock. With proper treatment the inflammation may subside but there usually is some thickening of the affected tissue. The patient may not be rested a sufficient period of time for the tissues to make a complete recovery from the original injury. When used again the tissues are reinjured with more extensive injury to the damaged tissue. A change may be observed, as viewed from the side, in the straight line from the carpus to the fetlock with the development of the so-called "bowed tendon". This condition may occur from the carpus to the fetlock and when the bowed tendon occurs close to the fetlock joint it is considered to be the most serious. For many years it was thought that a bowed tendon occurred when the tendons were injured and there was an increase in the size of the tendons at the point of injury. Now it has been observed that the tendon sheaths may also be affected and the change in the appearance of the tissues is due to a thickening of the tendon sheath and the tendons. Also in many of the cases there is an increase in the synovial fluid in the sheath. The fluid may become organized adding to the increase in size of the affected area. In some cases of tendinitis palpation of the superficial flexor tendon will reveal it is thickened and is the only tissue that is affected.

PROGNOSIS. Will depend upon the tissues that are affected and the severity of the injury and its location, but it is usually guarded.

TREATMENT. Rest is a very important part of the treatment and this should last until all of the inflammation has disappeared from the tissue, usually from six months to a year. If the tissues are subjected to strain too quickly they are easily reinjured and the damage is more severe than it was the first time.

For the first forty-eight hours antiphlogistic treatment should be used to reduce the inflammation. This is followed by moist warmth including saturated solutions of magnesium sulphate supplemented by proper bandaging. A long roll of cotton gauze about one inch in diameter may be placed along each side of the tendon and these should be fixed by bandaging rather firmly in position. These are used not only to give support but also to maintain pressure on the affected structures and this pressure stimulates absorption of the exudate. If the tissues are edematous massage is beneficial to hasten its absorption. This massage should be in the direction of the venous flow and for one-half hour periods one or two times a day.

The injection of one of the corticosteroids into the tendon sheath should be beneficial in reducing the inflammation of the synovial membrane. When only the superficial flexor tendon is affected point firing may be used with excellent results.

Contraction of the Flexor Tendons

Contraction of the flexor tendons is of frequent occurrence in both young and mature animals and the contraction may be either congenital or acquired. Congenital contraction of the flexor tendons is seen most frequently in colts and occasionally a calf is presented with contracted tendons.

Congenital Contraction of the Flexor Tendons

In congenital contraction of the flexor tendons one or both tendons may be affected in one or more limbs. The cause of congenital contraction of the flexor tendons has never been explained.

The degree of contraction may vary a great deal in different cases. When the deep digital flexor tendons are contracted and in the largest percentage of the cases this is the tendon that is affected. The affected individual is able to stand on its toes but when they attempt to move, go over into the fetlock joints. In some cases the heel is raised and it is impossible to touch the heel to the ground. When both flexor tendons are affected there is complete flexion of the fetlock joints. If the contraction is bilateral only the anterior surface of the fetlock joints can be placed on the ground. When the contraction of the flexor tendons is not corrected the soft tissues are bruised and lacerated and infection may gain entrance into the joint.

PROGNOSIS. The prognosis is favorable if the contraction is corrected before injury and infection has occurred in the tissues. When infection has gained entrance into the joint cavity the prognosis is unfavorable.

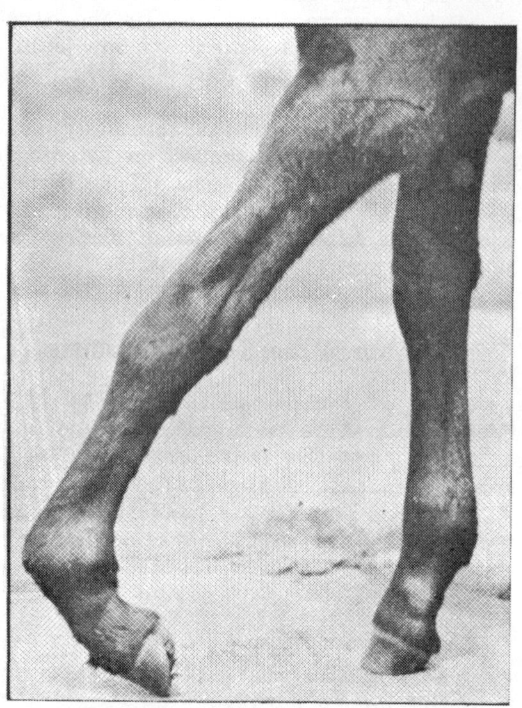

FIG. 268. Congenital unilateral contraction of the flexor tendons.

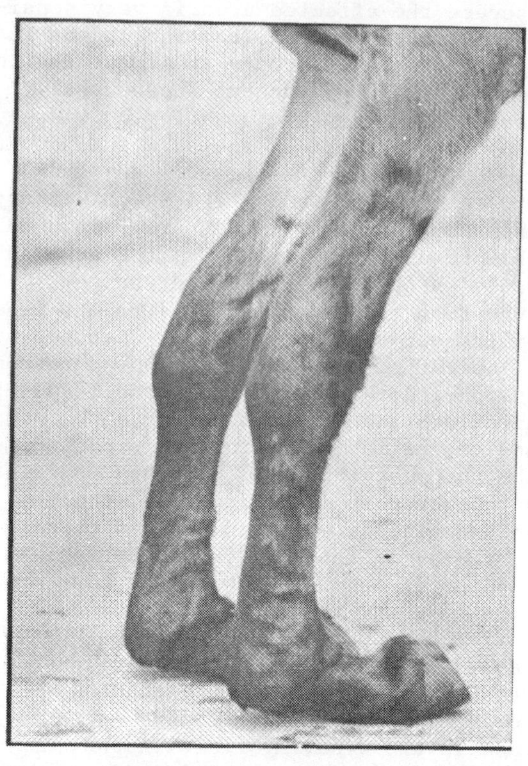

FIG. 269. Congenital bilateral contraction of the flexor tendons.

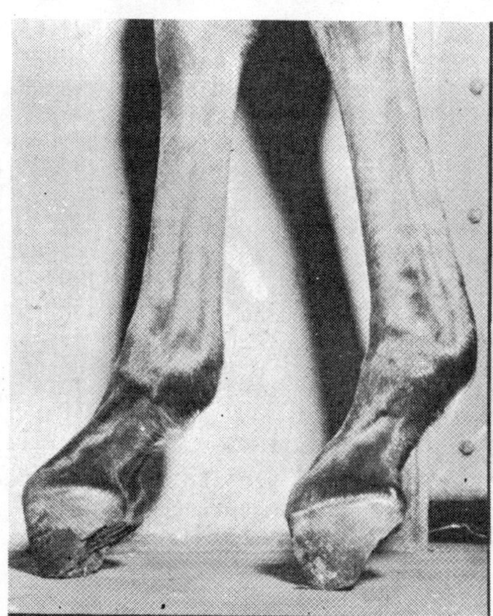

FIG. 270. Congenital contraction of deep digital flexor tendons in colt four months of age, heels are raised, affected since birth.

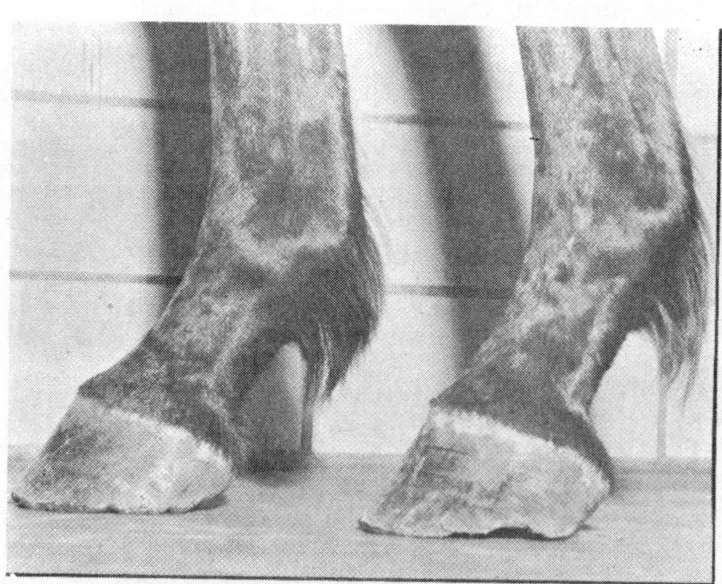

FIG. 271. Appearance of the limbs in Fig. 269, two years after the tenotomy of the deep digital flexor tendons.

FIG. 272. Acquired contraction of the deep digital flexor tendon, heel cannot be placed on the ground.

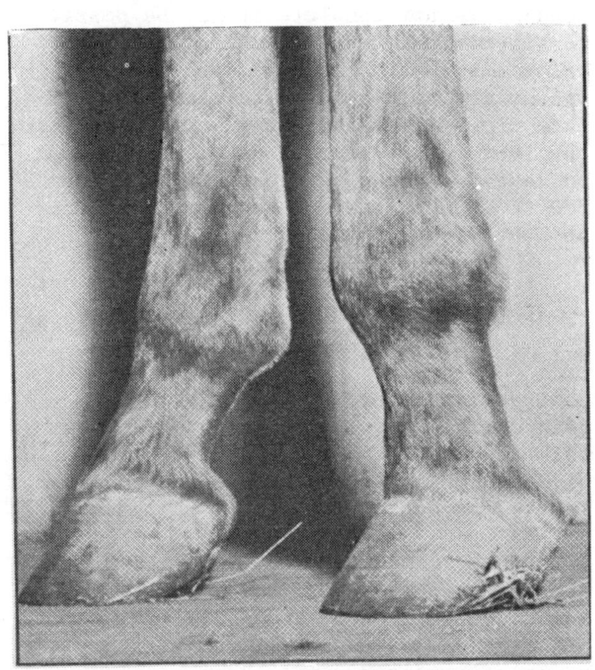

FIG. 273. Contraction of deep digital flexor tendon, fetlock joint is flexed when weight is placed on limb.

FIG. 274. The symptoms in this case were typical of contraction of superficial flexor tendons but tenotomy of both superficial and flexor tendons was necessary.

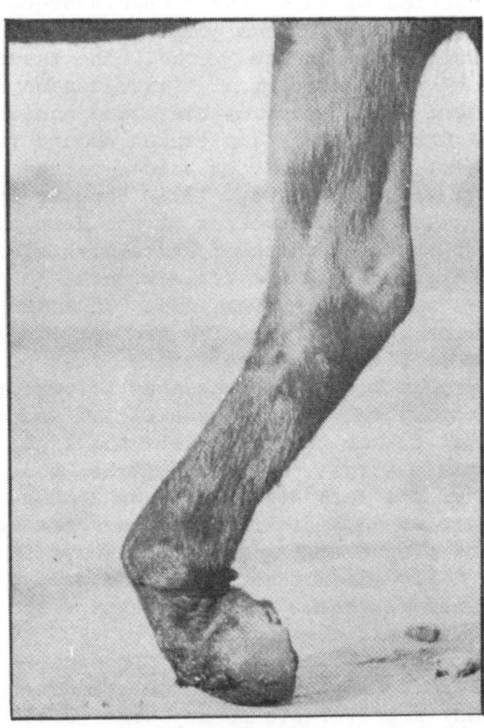

FIG. 275. Acquired contraction of the deep digital flexor tendon, only the front of the wall can be placed on the ground.

TREATMENT. When the contraction of the tendons is not complete it may be possible to stretch the tendons sufficiently to bring the foot to a normal position. A splint may be placed on the anterior surface of the limb and bandages used to hold the foot in the normal position. However in cases as shown in Figs. 268, 269 and 270 it is necessary to perform a tenotomy on the affected tendons.

Contraction of the Flexor Tendons In Older Animals

Contraction of either the superficial or deep digital flexor tendon may occur or both tendons may be affected. The deep digital flexor tendon is the one contracted in the largest percentage of the cases.

ETIOLOGY. In some cases contraction of the tendons may occur for no apparent reason. Contraction of some tendons have occurred following synovitis of either the carpal or great digital sheaths. Injury to the tendon tissue may result in contraction of the injured tendon or tendons.

With the insertion of the superficial flexor tendon on the first and second phalanges, contraction of this tendon should produce flexion of the fetlock joint with the foot remaining flat on the ground. The insertion of the deep digital flexor tendon on the semi-lunar crest of the third phalanx the contraction of this tendon should raise the heel so it cannot be placed on the ground as shown in Fig. 272. However in many cases of contraction of the deep digital flexor tendon the foot remains flat on the ground and the fetlock joint is flexed as shown in Figs. 273. In some cases as shown in Fig. 274 the fetlock joint is flexed and the foot is flat on the ground but it is necessary to perform a tenotomy on both the superficial and deep digital flexor tendons before the limb assumes a normal position. Marked contraction of the deep digital flexor tendon may produce so much flexion that only the wall can be placed on the ground as shown in Fig. 275. After tenotomy of the deep digital flexor tendon the foot returns to a normal position as in Fig. 276.

OPERATION. When possible the standing position is preferable to any other position of the patient when performing a tenotomy as the fibres of the tendon are tense and cut very easily. The tissues in the operative area may be anesthetized by blocking

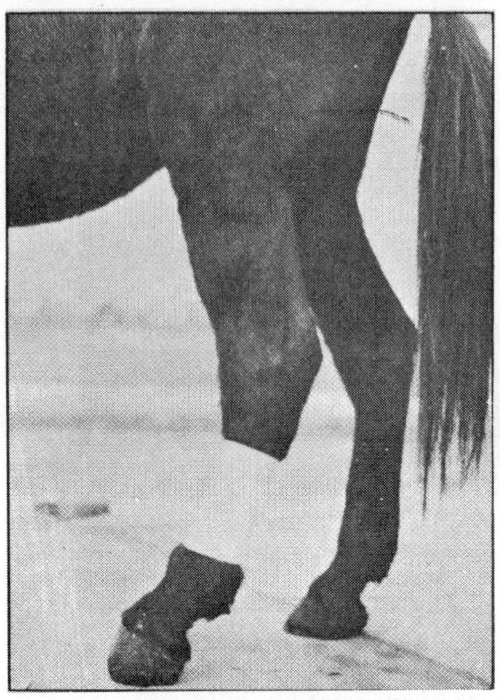

FIG. 276. After tenotomy of the deep digital flexor tendon the foot has returned to a normal position.

FIG. 277. Acquired contraction of the superficial flexor tendon.

either the volar or plantar nerves above the area. Prepare the operative area for an aseptic operation. A scalpel with a narrow blade as the No. 10 B-P is introduced between the superficial and deep digital flexor tendons. The cutting edge is turned toward the deep digital flexor tendon and it is divided. As the fibres are cut a definite sound is produced so the operator can tell when all the fibres of the tendon have been divided. The wound is bandaged and changed as indicated for ten days. The patient should be kept quiet in a box stall for one month. It should be at least three months before patient is used for hard or fast work.

In the young animal and those difficult to control the best results may be obtained in performing a tenotomy with the patient in lateral recombency. The patient should be placed in lateral recumbency with the affected limb down. Anesthesia of the tissues in the operative area may be obtained by blocking the volar or plantar nerves above the area. The struggling may be controlled with the drug that is indicated for the individual being confined. The operative area in the middle of the metacarpal or metatarsal region on the medial side is prepared for an aseptic operation. To tense the tendon tissue in the young animal one hand may be placed against the anterior surface of the carpus and with the other hand pull the foot forward. For the larger animal the carpus should be fastened so that it is stationary then a rope is fastened around the pastern and carried forward over the plantar surface of the foot. A twitch with a long handle may be used in the same way to tense the tendon tissue. The scalpel with the narrow blade is used to divide the deep digital flexor tendon and also the superficial flexor tendon is divided, when that is necessary for a normal limb. In most cases it is necessary to put a splint on the limb so it will be held in a normal position for a few days. Exercise should be limited until the wound has healed and the limb is being used in a normal manner.

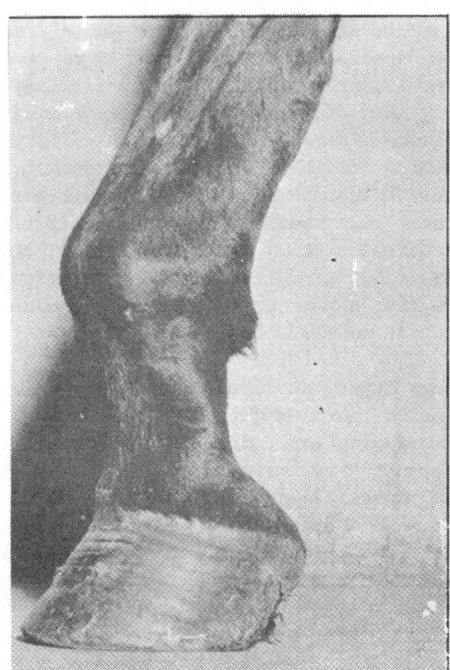

FIG. 278. Marked flexion of fetlock joint due to contraction of deep digital flexor tendon.

When it is necessary to divide both flexor tendons some support must be provided for the fetlock joint, except in the young animal. One method of providing support for the fetlock joint is to extend the heels of the shoe posteriorly. A vertical bar is extended up from the extension at each heel with a ring at the top of the bar. The sling to support the fetlock joint and that is fastened to the rings should be strong but composed of material that will not irritate the skin that rests on the sling. It is necessary to support the fetlock for several months as tendon tissue heals very slow.

Traumatic Division of the Flexor Tendons

The traumatic division of the flexor tendons may occur in any of the domesticated animals but is seen most frequently in the equine and bovine. When the equine strikes, kicks or backs into a sharp object the tendons may be divided, this injury may also occur in the bovine. The sharp object may not only divide the flexor tendons but also the suspensory ligament. If the deep flexor tendon is divided below the fetlock joint the toe turns upward and there is dorsal flexion of the phalanges, only the heel touches the ground. When the flexor tendons are divided above the fetlock joint there is a loss of some of the support of the fetlock joint and it sinks below its normal position. If the suspensory ligament is also divided the fetlock joint descends to the ground as it has lost all of its supporting tissue. When the flexor tendons and suspensory ligament are divided the

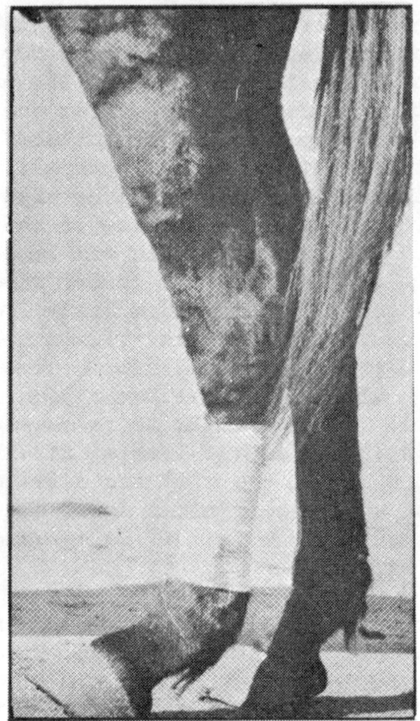

FIG. 279. Traumatic division of both flexor tendons dorsal to fetlock joint, toe is turned up and fetlock joint below normal position.

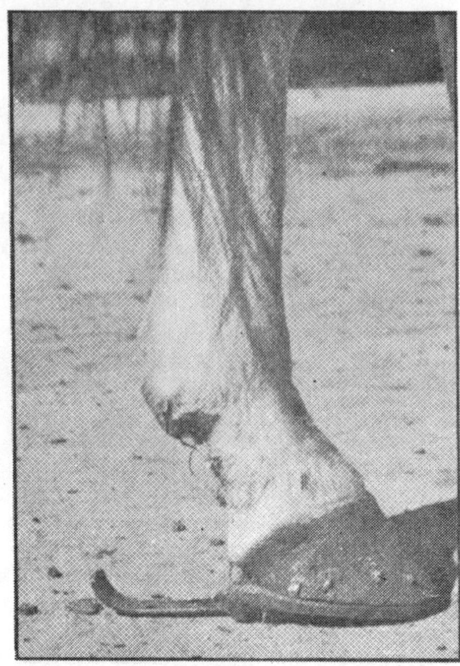

FIG. 280. Type of shoe used when deep flexor tendon is divided below fetlock joint.

arteries and veins have usually been divided and there is no blood supply to the tissues ventral to the wound. If this has occurred, in five to seven days the tissues will feel cold, which indicates gangrene of the tissue has developed.

PROGNOSIS. The prognosis should be guarded.

TREATMENT. When the wound occurs below the fetlock joint the great digital sheath is opened and infection may have been introduced into the sheath. If the deep digital flexor tendon is divided it will be indicated by the turning up of the toe and dorsal flexion of the phalanges. To hold the foot in its normal position and keep the ends of the tendon in close apposition to facilitate good healing, a special shoe is used. The shoe is prepared by using a piece of iron one and one-quarter inches wide, one-quarter of an inch thick and long enough to extend beyond the heels about three inches is welded on a bar shoe. The end of the bar is welded at the toe, a piece is cut out of the bar in the center so the iron will be level with the bar and the two pieces are welded together. To keep the end of the iron from catching in the ground the end should be turned up. If this type of shoe is put on a front foot the end should be turned up about three inches so the hind foot will slide off the iron. If the end of the iron is not turned up, the shoe comes off when stepped on by the hind foot. The shoe should be worn by the horse for four to six months. The wound should receive special attention and kept covered with antiseptic pack until it is closed. If the great digital sheath becomes distended above the fetlock joint it is an indication of infection in the sheath. The sheath should be opened at the most prominent point and the interior of the sheath treated with antiseptics and antibiotics. If the infection in the sheath is not treated there is danger of serious damage to the tendon tissue.

When the injury occurs above the fetlock joint both the superficial and deep digital flexor tendons are usually divided. This will permit the fetlock joint to drop below its normal position and the toe to turn up. The ends of the tendons should be held in close apposition so excess tissue does not fill in between the ends and the tendons will be longer than their normal length. To provide the support necessary to hold the fetlock joint in its normal position the shoe previously described may be used. The wound should receive the

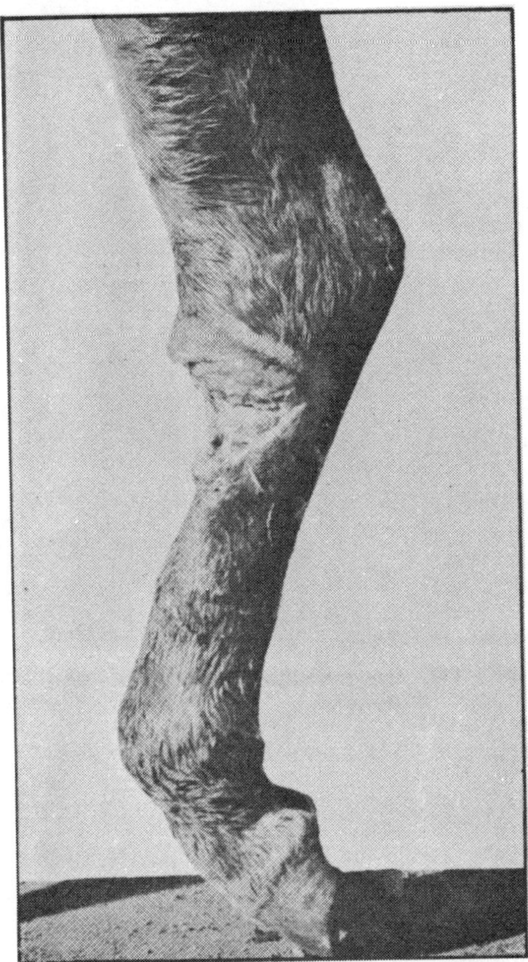

FIG. 281. A frequent location of the injury when the long extensor tendon is divided.

treatment indicated for each case. The shoe should support the fetlock joint until the tendons are able to provide the necessary support, which might be several months.

Sore Shins

This is a term frequently used for the periostitis and resulting swelling occurring on the anterior surface of the large metacarpal or metatarsal and sometimes the first phalanx. It usually occurs in two year old race horses in training.

ETIOLOGY. The condition usually appears after a work out so concussion is probably an important factor. Injuries to the periosteum from a traumatism may produce it.

SIGNS. The condition is readily recognized as the area affected is painful to palpation. The tissues feel tense due to the edema that is present. Lameness increases in severity with exercise and the stride is shortened. At rest the horse rests the affected leg and when both legs are affected the weight is shifted from one to the other.

PROGNOSIS. Is favorable when the condition is recognized as soon as symptoms appear and proper treatment used.

TREATMENT. Rest is the first essential if complete recovery is to occur. During the acute stage daily irrigation with cold water is used for an hour, two or three times a day. An antiphlogistine pack should then be applied.

When the acute symptoms subside in a few days, massage is beneficial, using a mild linement. In a few days a light blister may be applied to the area. Point firing may be used in those cases that are slow in responding to treatment.

Wind Galls

These are slight distensions of either the tendon sheath or joint capsule. They occur just above the fetlock joint on the lateral and medial side and in the form of two soft swellings about the size of hazel nuts. Swellings due to distension of the joint capsule appear between the suspensory ligament and the posterior surface of either the large metacarpal or metatarsal bones and are called articular wind galls. When the swellings appear between the deep flexor tendon and the suspensory ligament they are called tendinous wind galls.

In most cases wind galls are of little practical importance and treatment is not attempted. When attempts are made to reduce these swellings it is usually unsuccessful as they invariably return. In some cases wind galls may be due to a weakness of the part affected and are an indication of a serious unsoundness.

Sesamoiditis

In inflammation of the proximal sesamoid bones either the anterior or posterior surface of one or both bones may be affected. This inflammation may be either acute or chronic. Periostitis and ostitis may occur with ulceration and roughening of the articular surfaces. The ligaments of the sesamoid bones may also be affected.

ETIOLOGY. Any unusual strain placed upon the limb may produce sesamoiditis. The condition occurs most frequently in hunters, jumpers, and running horses, but is occasionally observed in draft horses.

SIGNS. In the acute stage pain is evident on local manipulation. There is some swelling and increase in temperature of the area. Pain is most marked when weight is placed on the limb and the animal is often unwilling to place any weight on the limb. If the inflammation becomes chronic marked proliferation of tissue may occur with exostoses and limitation in movement of the joint.

TREATMENT. The acute inflammation may be treated with cold packs or alternating hot and cold applications may be used. Also packs of white lotion seem to be beneficial in the acute stage. The sub-acute and chronic stage may be treated by point or line firing followed by blistering but the lameness may recur with use. In horses used at slow gaits a neurectomy may prolong their period of usefulness. The proper nerve or nerves to operate on to relieve the lameness should be determined by nerve blocking.

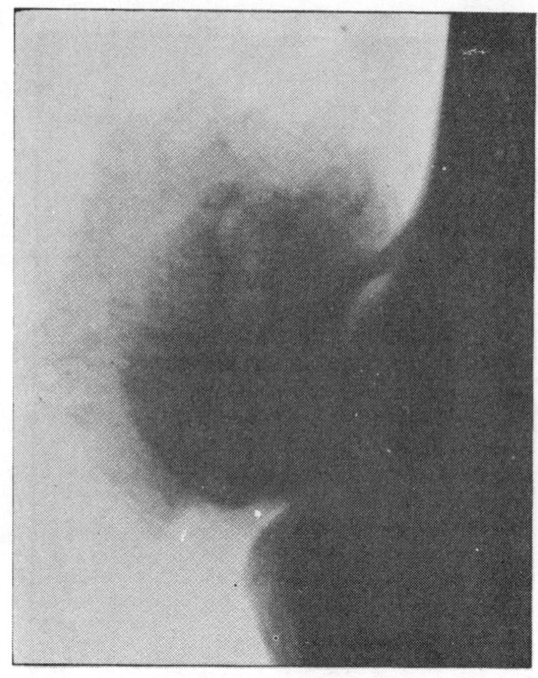

FIG. 282. Osteoperiostitis of the proximal medial sesamoid.

Osteo-periostitis of the Sesamoids

Inflammation of bone develops the same as inflammation in any of the other tissue. When there is inflammation of the periosteum it is called periostitis and of the bone, ostitis. When both tissues are affected it is osteo-periostitis.

ETIOLOGY. Inflammation of the proximal sesamoid bones may be caused by any irritation in any portion of the sesamoidean apparatus. Because of their location concussion is probably an important factor in producing irritation of the sesamoids. Irritation of the periosteum may develop at the points of insertion of some of the ligaments.

SIGNS. When the irritation first develops there may be all the symptoms of an acute inflammation as heat, swelling, and infiltration of the tissues in the area affected. Lameness is pronounced with little weight placed on the limb. The condition may

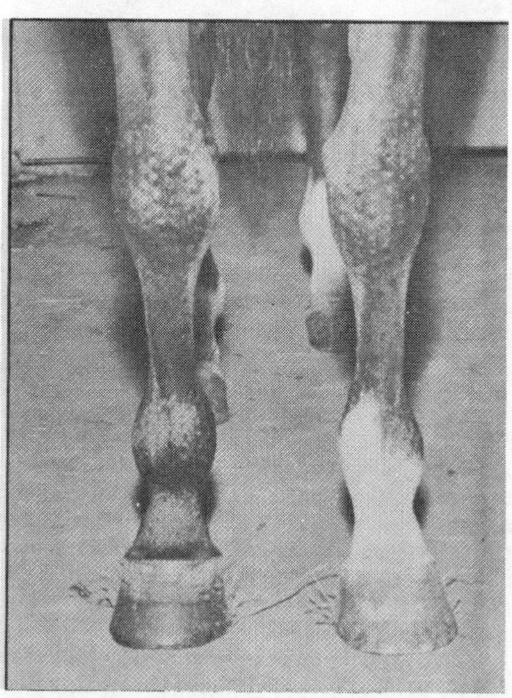

FIG. 283. Increase in size of the joint is observed in the equine and bovine.

develop as a subacute or chronic inflammation with only a slight lameness present. However, if the enlargement becomes so large that it interferes with movement of some of the parts lameness may be pronounced.

TREATMENT. The acute signs are treated by rest and the usual antiphlogistic measures. In the chronic stage it may respond to repeated applications of blisters or firing. However, when the enlargement becomes extensive median neurectomy seems to be the only treatment that gives relief from the lameness. In some cases it may be necessary to also perform an ulnar neurectomy. A median neurectomy was performed in the case of Figure 282 and ten years later the horse was still free from any lameness. In those cases where the involvement of the affected sesamoid bone is not too extensive a medial or lateral volar neurectomy may relieve the lameness.

Arthritis of the Fetlock Joint

Arthritis of one or both fetlock joints is occasionally observed in the bovine. The affected joint becomes larger than normal and the animal shows a variable amount of lameness.

Treatment for arthritis consists in point firing the joint with the same technique that is used in firing the equine. The points are placed on the lateral, medial and anterior sides. It is important that the point penetrates the skin and down to the periosteum. The blister, composed of one part of red iodide of mercury and four parts of vaseline, is rubbed over the area that has been fired for five minutes. A thick layer of cotton is bandaged over the fetlock joint, and left on for ten days. No further treatment is used after the removal of the cotton. If it is an uncomplicated case of arthritis the animal recovers from the lameness in a short time.

When the swelling of the joint appears rather suddenly and a certain area is sensitive a radiograph of the joint should be taken. The radiograph may reveal an unsuspected fracture with only a small piece of bone separated away from the distal end of the metacarpus. If the fracture involves only a small portion of the bone, immobilizing of the limb with a splint is unnecessary and good healing will occur with rest.

Ringbone

The above term has been rather loosely used to designate any exostosis on the phalanges as a ringbone. However, there is a great deal of difference in the importance of an exostosis that occurs on the shaft of the bone as compared with those occurring around the articulations. The usual location for the typical ringbone, or the one occurring most frequently, is in the region of the pastern joint. These are frequently referred to as high ringbones. A low ringbone occurs between the second and third phalanges. This usually produces the condition discussed under pyramidal disease. Another classification is to refer to ringbones as articular and periarticular. Probably most of the ringbones originate as a periostitis and ostitis on the shaft of the bone and with the production of bone tissue it may extend to and interfere with the movement of the joint.

ETIOLOGY. One of the most popular theories now is concerned with the necessary quantity and proportion of minerals in the ration. The statement is made that if the feed is rich in the proper minerals, especially calcium and phosphorus, bone affections such as ringbone rarely occur. Heredity in some cases may be a factor.

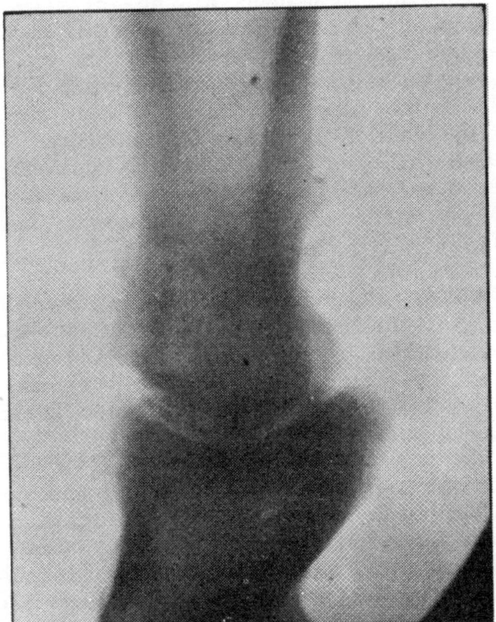

FIG. 284. Lateral view of the pastern showing exostoses present on the first and second phalanges.

Through inheritance of defective bone tissue or poor conformation the offspring may develop ringbone at a rather early age. Injuries to the periosteum from wire cuts are sometimes a cause of ringbone in the region of the pastern joint.

SIGNS. The presence of the exostosis may be visible at a distance or it may require careful palpation to determine its presence. The growth of bone is usually felt around the edge of the articulation. The lameness manifested is that of foot lameness, the most pronounced signs are shown when the foot receives its greatest concussion. The horse may not be lame at the walk but may be severely lame at the trot. Also it may be more noticeable when the horse is turned in a circle. The condition sometimes referred to as a "false ringbone" is a localized periostitis and later ostitis that occurs on the shaft of the bone. This may occur as the result of a bruise or irritation at the attachment of some of the ligaments to the periosteum. During the acute inflammation the horse is temporarily lame until the exostosis develops. When the inflammation subsides and the lameness disappears this condition does not interfere with the animal's usefulness.

FIG. 285. Lateral view of pastern joint showing exostoses so extensive as to produce a mechanical lameness.

In the early stages of the development of a ringbone when there is acute inflammation of the periosteum the lameness may be pronounced. If the cause of the inflammation soon subsides, lameness disappears with the development of only small exostoses on the affected tissue. If the condition is allowed to go untreated or the exciting cause is not removed a mass of bone may develop that interferes with complete movement of the joint. In this type of case there is a true mechanical lameness that may be devoid of pain or sensitiveness.

PROGNOSIS. Prognosis will depend upon the extent of the bony enlargement. If there is mechanical interference with the articulation the prognosis is unfavorable and with any well established ringbone the prognosis is guarded.

TREATMENT. In the acute stage antiphlogistic treatment with cold water irrigation or ice packs, with complete rest. Bone meal should be added to ration to increase the calcium and phosphorus, one ounce daily is sufficient. The foot must be trimmed so that it is level, to take undue strain from any of the ligaments and joint. If the lameness continues deep point firing should be used over the area placing the

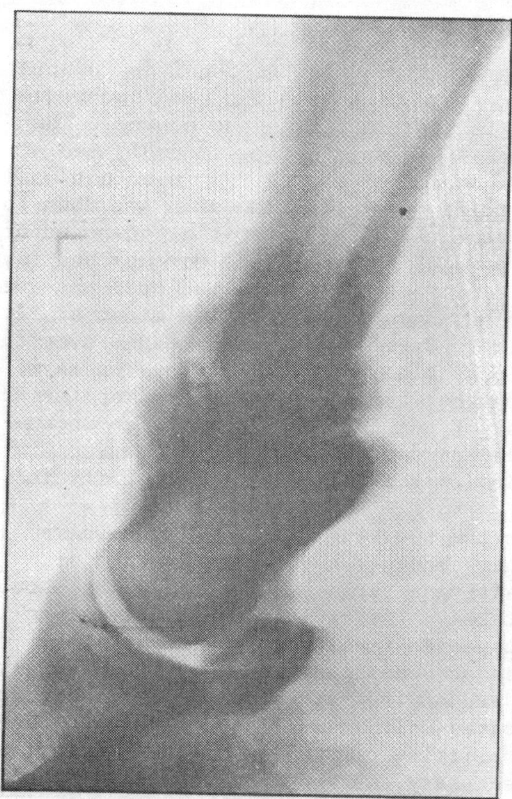

FIG. 286. Ringbone, extensive exostoses has produced ankylosis of pastern joint.

points about one inch apart. A one to four red iodide of mercury blister is rubbed into the area for fifteen minutes and a thick layer of cotton bandaged over it. The bandage should be left on for two weeks. Also shoe with a roller motion shoe. If it seems advisable the blister may be repeated. During this period the horse should have complete rest.

When this treatment fails to give relief either median or double volar neurectomy should be performed, but first determine by nerve blocking if it is a painful or mechanical lameness. Also by the nerve blocking the operator will be able to determine which nerve or nerves should be operated on to relieve the lameness. A neurectomy should not be performed above the fetlock joint on a horse that carries a rider.

Pyramidal Disease

In pyramidal disease there is a periostitis and ostitis with the formation of an exostosis on the extensor process. The term pyramidal disease originated when the extensor process was known as the pyramidal process. The exostosis varies a great deal in size and extent. As the exostosis develops the wall is gradually pushed outward the horse's foot is changed from a more or less U shape to a more pointed or V shape. The change in shape of the foot is more pronounced at the top of the wall. As the change in the shape of the foot becomes more pronounced there is usually an increase in the severity of the lameness. However there is an occasional case of pyramidal disease with a well developed exostosis that has never been lame.

More pronounced changes occur in the shape of the foot and the soft tissues dorsal to the top of the wall when there is a fracture of the extensor process. There is an extensive exostosis in the area of the extensor process and also an exostosis on the second phalanx. The change in the shape of the foot is suggestive of a, "Buttress" so that it is called a "Buttress Foot". The lameness in these cases is severe, when the horse is turned out in the evening he is alright, the next morning he will not touch the foot on the ground. For three to six months there is little improvement in the lameness until there is ankylosis of the coffin joint. As soon as there is ankylosis of the coffin joint the patient is able to work at a walk.

TREATMENT. Various methods of treatment have been tried to relieve the lameness due to pyramidal disease without improving the lameness. A volar neurectomy may relieve the lameness but there is usually a breakdown of the affected tissues.

Dermatitis Eczematosa (Cracked Heels, Scratches)

Scratches is an acute inflammation of the skin on the posterior surface of the pastern. Occurs rather frequently in light horses and occasionally in horses of the heavy breeds.

SIGNS. In acute cases the skin is hot, painful, and thickened. The skin usually cracks, small blisters may form and a rather thick exudate sticks the hairs together. It is very painful and the horse will frequently point the foot of the affected limb.

TREATMENT. Cleanse the area thoroughly with green soap and water and brush. Dry thoroughly and apply white lotion pack twice daily when inflammation is severe. Then the following may be applied: tincture of iodine, chloride of iron and gly erine equal parts. Apply twice daily with brush. Zinc oxide ointment may be rubbed in thoroughly twice a day. When the cracks are moist and discharging five per cent of tannic and salicylic acid in alcohol is very good.

Dermatitis Verrucosa (Grease Heel)

This is a chronic, usually progressive inflammation of the skin on the posterior surface of the pastern and fetlock region and may extend up to the hock or knee. The condition may develop from a case of scratches or from injury of the skin. However, the direct cause of grease heel is unknown.

SIGNS. In the acute stage the skin may be hot, swollen, and painful, and there is formed on the skin a fatty, ill-smelling, grey material. There is a marked thickening of the skin, most of the hair falls out and those that remain stand erect. After the condition becomes well established wart or grape-like growths develop on the skin called "grapes".

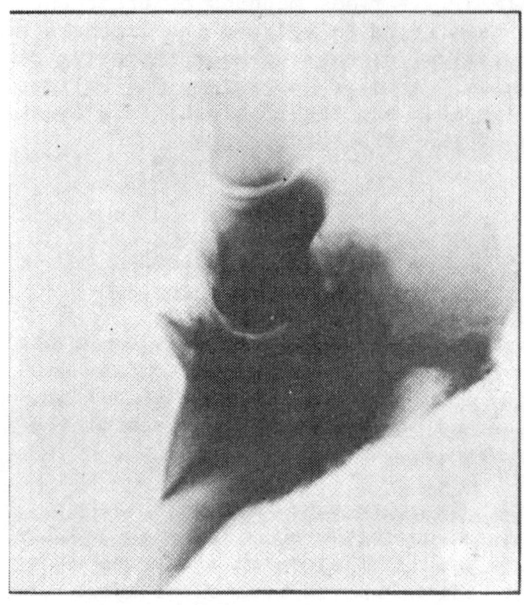

FIG. 287. Exostoses on extensor process of third phalanx.

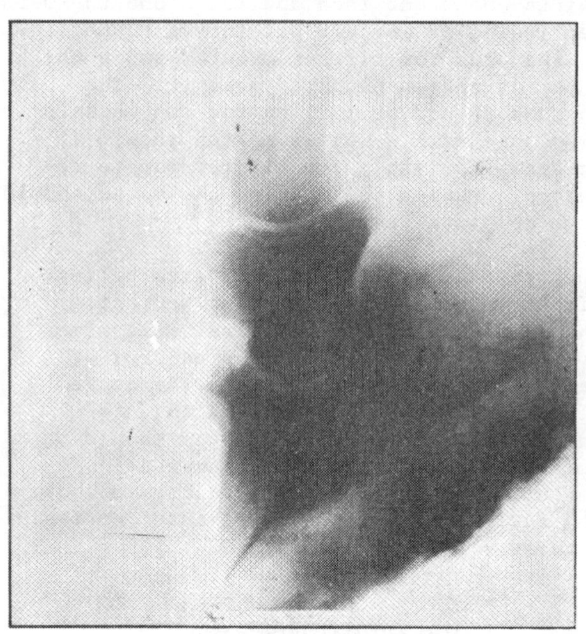

FIG. 289. Extensive exostoses of the second and third phalanges producing "Buttress" foot.

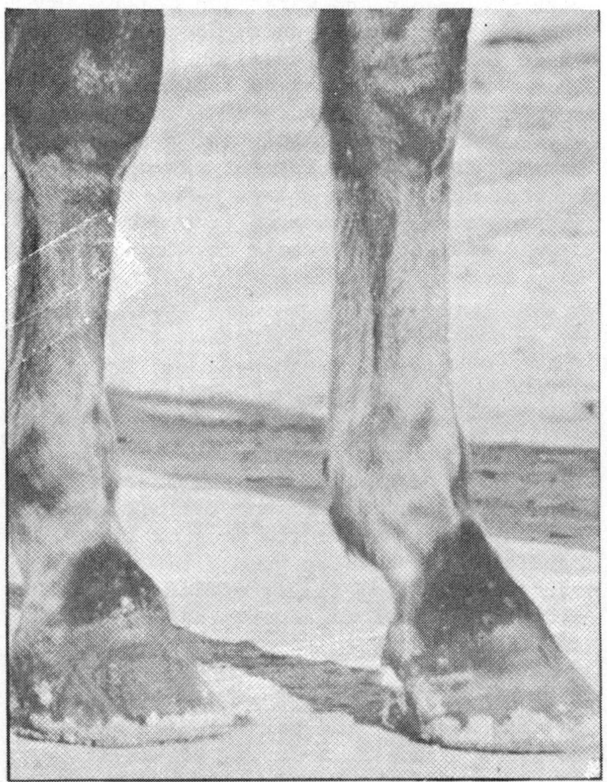

FIG. 288. Horse affected in both front feet, showing characteristic change in shape of feet.

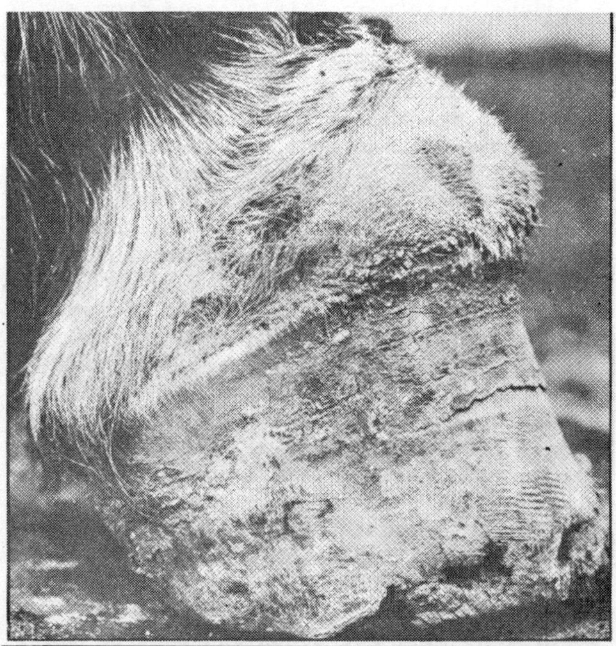

FIG. 290. A typical case of so-called "buttress" foot.

PROGNOSIS. The condition is very resistant to treatment and in most cases the prognosis is guarded.

TREATMENT. The most important part of the treatment is to thoroughly cleanse the skin and keep it clean by using antiseptic solutions, as two to three per cent solution of creolin, then dry the skin thoroughly and saturate it twice a day with five to ten per cent lotion of zinc sulphate and alum. The use of crude oil is recommended. The grapes should be removed with the actual cautery.

Thrush

In this condition there is an affection of the frog that is characterized by a moist dark discharge from the sulci. It occurs most frequently in the hind feet.

ETIOLOGY. Standing in wet and filthy surroundings has been given as a common cause but it occurs frequently under ideal conditions. Lack of proper frog pressure with atrophy of the frog seems to favor the development of this condition.

SIGNS. There is a fetid discharge from the sulci of the frog and usually a loosening of the horny frog from the sensitive tissue. Lameness may be pronounced with inflammation of the tissues at the heel.

TREATMENT. Remove all the affected tissue and all loose pieces of horny frog. Put in clean surroundings. Lower wall so there will be good frog pressure. Apply to the area a solution of ten per cent formalin, calomel, or equal parts of iodine and phenol.

Acute Laminitis

An aseptic spontaneous inflammation of the sensitive laminae. It may affect one foot, both front feet, both hind feet, or all four feet.

Synonyms used are derived from some of the exciting causes; colt founder, following difficult case of dystokia, retained placenta or metritis; water founder, after drinking a large quantity of cold water; car founder, after railroad journey; food founder, after case of impaction or overfeeding on grains, or superpurgation; road founder after long journey over a hard surface at fast gaits.

SIGNS. Will depend upon the severity and acuteness of the condition. It starts as an acute hyperemia of the sensitive laminae and is more marked in the anterior part of the foot. The sensitive laminae become thickened and infiltrated and exudation follows if the case is not properly treated. At first in a mild case the signs may not be very definite. But when the acute symptoms occur there is a rapid pulse, horse sweats in patches, with congestion of the conjunctiva. The affected feet are hot, sensitive to percussion, with an increased pulsation of the digital arteries. Temperature will vary from 103 to 106 degrees F. with an increase in the pulse rate.

When only the front feet are affected they are advanced as far forward as possible and the hind feet are placed well under the body to support as much of the weight as possible. If they move forward practically the same position of the feet will be kept. They also move forward in a crouching position. The heels are placed on the ground first, and the feet lifted quickly when the weight comes forward on the toe. If turned in a circle he will pivot on the hind feet, placing as little weight on the front feet as possible.

When the hind feet are affected the front feet are placed backward under the body to support as much of the weight as possible, and the hind feet are thrust forward to bear as much of the weight as possible on the heels. If all four feet are affected they stand in almost a normal manner, but when forced to move the effort almost produces spasms.

PROGNOSIS. Will depend upon the severity of the case, but in most cases it is favorable. Usually more serious in heavy horses than light horses. Also more unfavorable when all four feet are affected.

TREATMENT. Administer 125 to 150 cubic centimeters of whole blood or normal horse serum subcutaneously or intramuscularly. A rapid acting purgative should be given as it seems to be very beneficial. If the horse is shod the shoes should be removed.

Local treatment consists in the application of cold water to the feet. If a cold stream is available it is fine; may be necessary to dig holes for them to stand in and kept filled with cold water. When the condition is especially severe it may be advisable to add ice to the water and in some cases ice cream salt may also be added. During the first few days the feet should be kept in contact with cold water most of the time. The patient should be forced to lie down some of the time; it may be necessary to cast with ropes.

If there is absorption of toxic products from the digestive tract, four ounce doses of alum may be given two or three times a day.

When the laminitis is due to infection in the uterus this should be treated. First irrigate the uterus with a non-irritating antiseptic to remove all the infection from the uterus. Inject into the uterus a pint of mineral oil to which has been added ½ oz. of bismuth subnitrate and 1 oz. of iodoform. Also give pitruitrin or some other drug to stimulate the involution of the uterus. A laxative and diuretic should be used to stimulate elimination of waste products.

Chronic Laminitis

This may follow acute laminitis or develop as chronic laminitis. The changes that occur in the form of the affected feet are very characteristic in chronic laminitis. The wall usually becomes elongated and narrow. Just below the coronary band the wall may become almost vertical, while toward the toe it assumes the horizontal. Characteristic rings are formed on the wall parallel with the coronary band, wide behind and closer together in front. So called "dropped sole" may occur due to a contraction of the deep flexor tendon and a rotation of the third phalanx on its transverse axis. The anterior border of the third phalanx pushing down on the sole causes it to become flattened. A characteristic gait develops with the horse walking on his heels or may walk as if his feet hurt.

DIAGNOSIS. Is made on the changes in shape of the feet and the characteristic gait.

PROGNOSIS. Should be guarded, but this will depend upon the extent of the changes in the tissues in the feet.

TREATMENT. Some very unfavorable cases have responded to the following operation that was first described by a French veterinarian. The affected feet should be trimmed to as near the normal shape as possible. Then two grooves, one-fourth of an inch wide, are made in the wall at the toe and extending from the top of the wall to the bearing surface of the wall. These grooves are one and one-half inches apart or three-fourths of an inch on either side of the median line and down

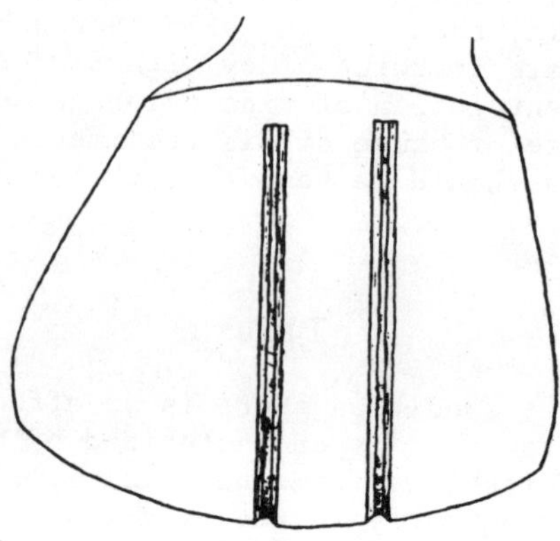

FIG. 291. Grooves on each side of the median line extend from the top to the bearing surface.

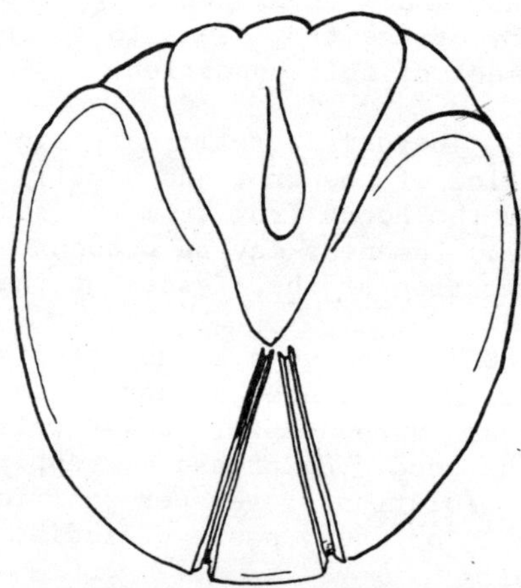

FIG. 292. Grooves extend from the wall on to the sole to the point of the frog.

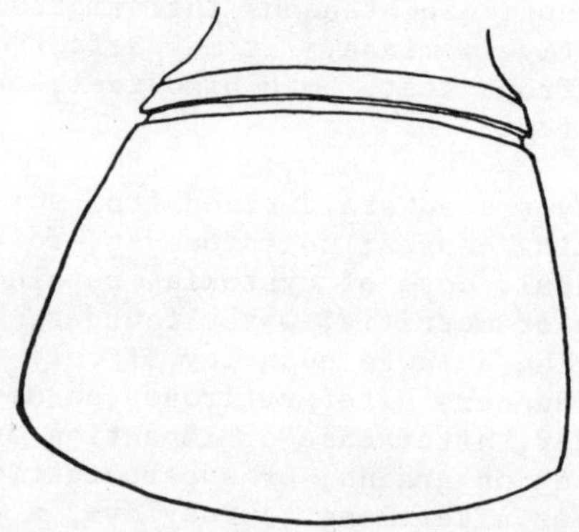

FIG. 293. Groove in the wall extends from one heel to the other one.

to but not deep enough to injure the sensitive laminae. These grooves are then continued on the sole to terminate at the point of the frog. It is also recommended that a shoe with heel calkins three-fourths of an inch long be put on the feet to relax the deep digital flexor tendon. The grooves should be maintained until complete recovery has occurred.

In some cases of chronic laminitis the wall will be vertical for approximately one inch below the top of the wall. In this type of case it is necessary to perform a different type of operation. In this operation a groove one-fourth of an inch wide is made one inch below the top of the wall. The groove extends around the wall from one heel to the other. Improvement of the lameness following this operation is not as rapid as from the preceding operation.

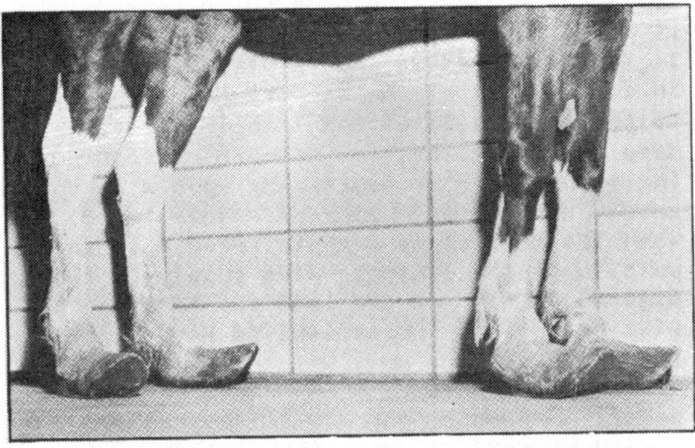

FIG. 294. In some cases of chronic laminitis there is a stimulation to rapid growth of wall as shown above, feet must be trimmed frequently.

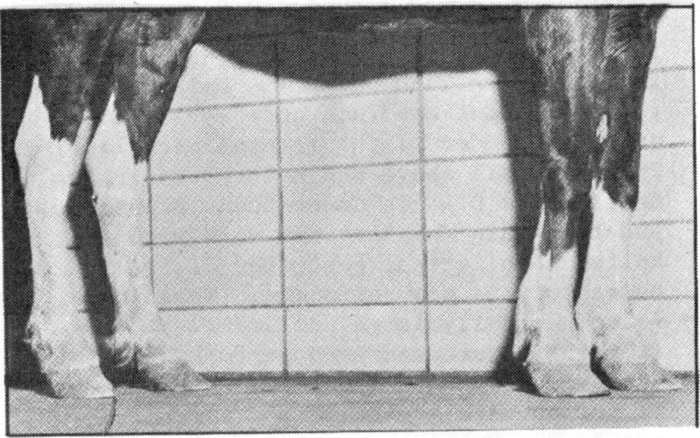

FIG. 295. After the feet were trimmed to normal shape.

Sidebone

A side bone is formed when there is ossification of the lateral cartilage and one or both cartilages may be affected. The side bone varies a great deal in size in different cases, from those that are just starting to develop, to those that are enormous in size and extent.

ETIOLOGY. The true cause of sidebone is not definitely known but there are a number of theories advanced as to the probable reasons for their development. There is a tendency for sidebones to develop in heavy horses where they are worked on hard surfaces at rapid gaits. However unusually large sidebones occur in heavy horses where they have only been worked on soft dirt on the farm. They may occur frequently in horses that are shod with high heel calkins and worked on a hard surface. Injury of the cartilage will stimulate ossification of the cartilage. There is, also, a tendency for sidebones to develop in certain breeds of horses, while it has been said that sidebones do not occur in the Thoroughbred.

SIGNS. The normal lateral cartilage is very flexible but as ossification occurs this gradually disappears until it feels as solid as bone. Generally ossification starts at the lower anterior end of the cartilage where it is attached to the third phalanx. As ossification of the cartilage develops there is an increase in its size and some sidebones become enormous. A sidebone may be lateral or medial but in most cases both cartilages are affected. One or both front feet may be involved and in rare cases they may be found in the hind feet. Ossification of the cartilage is non-inflammatory and the symptoms of pain are due to compression of the sensitive tissues of the foot.

DIAGNOSIS. When the lateral cartilage has lost its flexibility it is easy to diagnose a sidebone. If the ossification of the lateral cartilage involves only a portion of the cartilage a radiograph is of particular value in those cases where the ossification occurs only in the anterior portion of the cartilage.

PROGNOSIS. In draft horses worked on the farm sidebones seem to cause little trouble until the horses are used on a hard road. However when the sidebones become enormous there is usually a continuous lameness regardless of where they are worked. Sidebones are very serious when they occur in horses doing fast work.

TREATMENT. If the sidebones are not causing lameness they are not usually treated. When sidebones are small it is not always possible to say they are not responsible for some of the lameness.

For the average case of lameness due to well developed sidebones the following method of treatment has been very successful. A groove is made in the wall three-fourths of an inch below the hairline from the heel about one inch anterior to the anterior border of the lateral cartilage. Thin the wall above and below this groove until it is pliable under thumb pressure, and then thin the bars and sole with the knife. A bilateral posterior digital neurectomy is now performed. When there is an unusually large unilateral sidebone it might be necessary to perform a unilateral volar neurectomy. Also a bar shoe is put on with a leather and tar and oakum pack. The wall at the toe should be rounded so the foot breaks over more easily. The horse should receive moderate exercise every day.

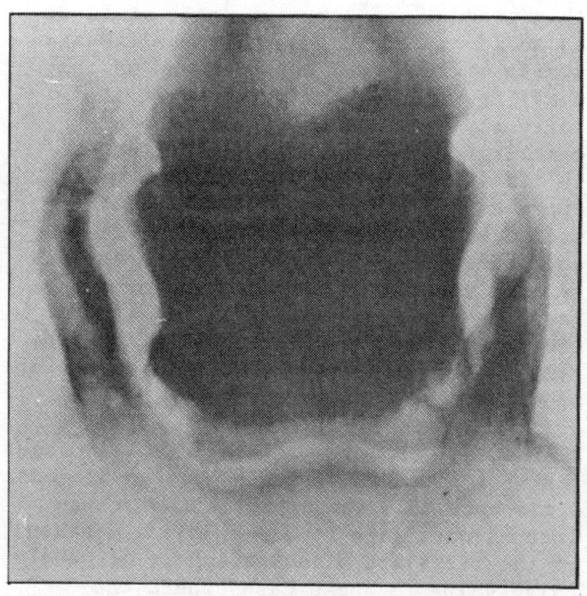

FIG. 296. Large well developed side bones.

Neurectomies Upon Anterior Limb

A neurectomy is the removal of a section of a nerve to destroy the ability of the nerve to transmit the sensation beyond the operative area. Neurectomy of a sensory nerve is performed to prolong the usefulness of an animal. The operation should only be performed for the relief of pain in a chronic condition that is incurable. Before performing a neurectomy the nerve should be blocked to be sure the neurectomy will be successful in relieving the lameness. Also by blocking the various nerves the operator can by a process of elimination determine upon which nerve it is necessary to perform the neurectomy. It is not advisable and is very dangerous to destroy all of the sensory nerve supply to the lower part of the limb in horses used at fast gaits, for example, performing a double volar neurectomy upon a race horse, hunter, polo pony or saddle horse. When the neurectomy has destroyed a large portion of the sensory nerve supply to the digital portion of the limb the results will be best if the patient is used only for light work.

Before performing any neurectomy the owner should be told of some of the disadvantages of the operation. The horse may step on a nail without feeling it and develop an incurable infection without showing any signs of lameness. Also some of the structures may break down as rupture of the flexor tendons, ligaments of the joints or separation of the horny wall and sole from the underlying corium any time after the operation, if a double volar neurectomy has been performed.

DIGITAL NEURECTOMY. A bilateral posterior digital neurectomy is usually indicated for the relief of lameness due to chronic navicular disease. The nerves operated upon are the posterior branches of the volar nerves. Anesthesia for the operation may be obtained by blocking the volar nerves above the fetlock joint. If the animal is not too nervous and the operator is experienced the operation may be performed with the patient in the standing position.

The operative area is located by palpating for the triangular area just below the fetlock joint on the posterior surface of the first phalanx. The base of the triangle is formed by the head of the first phalanx, one side of the triangle anteriorly by the shaft of the first phalanx and the other side of the triangle by the edge of the deep digital flexor tendon.

The nerve is in rather close contact to the edge of the deep digital flexor tendon with the digital artery and vein more anterior and deeper in the tissue. Prepare the area in the usual manner for an aseptic operation. The incision through the skin is started at the base of the triangle and extends along the edge of the deep digital flexor tendon. The incision about one inch long is made through the skin, subcutaneous tissue and fascia. One structure frequently encountered just beneath the skin is the ligament of the ergot. It crosses the field obliquely from above downward and either laterally or medially. This ligament is a wide flat band of tissue, glistening, yellowish white in color and its general direction is toward the ergot. When the ligament is grasped with forceps and traction is exerted the ergot is freely movable. A section of the ligament of the ergot should be removed to permit free access to the nerve. The loose areolar tissue is broken down with forceps until the rounded outline of the nerve is exposed lying along the edge of the deep digital flexor tendon. After the nerve has been isolated for a short distance it is picked up with a pair of forceps or neurectomy hook. The nerve should be separated from the surrounding tissue the entire length of the skin incision. A small amount of tension is exerted upon the nerve before dividing it at the superior commissure of the incision. When the nerve is divided under tension the proximal end retracts under the skin and is not caught in the healing process. The nerve is again divided at the distal commissure of the wound so about one inch of the nerve is removed. The other digital nerve is operated on using the same technique. The edges of the skin incision should be approximated with closely placed interrupted sutures. Apply an antiseptic pack over the wounds and bandage in position.

VOLAR NEURECTOMY. Neurectomy of one or both volar nerves is indicated for the relief of pain due usually to ringbone or sidebones or some chronic conditions producing an incurable lameness. If the above condition will not respond to any form of treatment a neurectomy offers the means of prolonging the usefulness of the patient. The volar nerves divide into anterior and posterior branches just above the fetlock joint so the operation is performed about two inches above the fetlock joint. The operative area for the two volar nerves is along the lateral and medial edge of the deep digital flexor tendon. Prepare the operative area for an aseptic operation by the usual procedure. Anesthesia for the operation is obtained by infiltrating the skin and subcutaneous tissue and the nerve in the operative area. The procedure for performing a volar neurectomy is very similar to that described for the digital neurectomy. The nerve should be found in close contact to the edge of the deep digital flexor tendon with the vein just anterior to the nerve and the artery ventral to the vein. When a double volar neurectomy has been performed all of the sensory nerve supply to the distal portion of the limb has been destroyed. After a double volar neurectomy has been performed the plantar surface of the foot should be examined frequently to see if there is a nail or other foreign object in it. Also after this operation there is more danger of some of the structures degenerating after the operation.

MEDIAN NEURECTOMY. This neurectomy is to be preferred to a double volar neurectomy as there is still some sensation supplied to the limb by the ulnar nerve. If the lameness of a chronic ringbone is relieved by blocking the median nerve, a neurectomy offers a method of prolonging the usefulness of the animal.

In most cases the patient will have to be confined in lateral recumbency on the affected side so the medial surface of the limb is exposed. The operative area is determined by measuring a hands breadth from the ventral surface of the thoracic wall. At the point where the end of the extended thumb touches in the groove just posterior to the radius is the approximate location of the operative area. The area is prepared in the usual manner for an aseptic operation. Anesthesia of the operative area may be obtained by infiltrating the skin and underlying tissue and also the median nerve with a two per cent solution of a local anesthetic.

OPERATION. The skin incision approximately two inches long is made just posterior to and parallel with the radius. It may be necessary to make the incision a little higher or lower than planned to avoid injury to the cephalic vein which crosses the operative area obliquely just beneath the skin. The skin incision is continued through the superficial and deep fascia and parallel with the posterior border of the radius. The slight hemorrhage which occurs may be controlled by the use of sponges. When the edge of the skin and fascia are retracted posteriorly the flexor carpi radialis muscle is exposed and this muscle overlaps the nerve slightly. It is important for the operator to remember that the nerve lies in close contact with and posterior to the large, thin walled, posterior radial vein and is superficial and usually posterior to the radial artery. By the use of the forceps the loose areolar tissue may be broken between the muscle and radius until the posterior radial vein is easily seen. This vein has a very thin wall so the operator should proceed very carefully with the dissection to expose the nerve which is in contact with and posterior to the large posterior radial vein, and enclosed in the same sheath. The nerve is more superficial and usually posterior to the radial artery. When the operator recognizes the nerve it should be carefully separated from the thin walled vein by inserting an instrument between the two structures. As the nerve is separated from the vein it is gradually lifted up until the nerve is divided at the upper commissure of the incision and again at the lower commissure. If the vein is injured during the operation it will be necessary to pack the wound to control the hemorrhage and retain the pack with sutures. If the vein has not been injured the edges of the skin are approximated with interrupted sutures leaving a small opening at the lower commissure for drainage. As a general rule it is not possible to obtain healing by first intention and there may be some suppuration before healing occurs, so the wound heals slowly.

ULNAR NEURECTOMY. Only rarely is an ulnar neurectomy indicated and then for some condition between the knee and fetlock that is not relieved by a median neurectomy. The operative area is approximately four inches above the accessory carpal bone on the posterior surface of the forearm. The ulnar nerve is located in the depression or groove which can be palpated between the ulnaris lateralis and flexor carpi ulnaris muscles. In this area the nerve is covered only by the tough antibrachial fascia and the skin. Prepare the operative area in the usual manner for an aseptic operation. Anesthesia for the operation may be obtained by infiltrating the skin and underlying tissue and the nerve. The operation may be performed in the standing position or with the animal in recumbency depending upon the preference of the operator.

OPERATION. The incision about one inch long is made exactly in the center of the groove and through the skin and thick fascia. Retract the edges of the incised tissues and sponge any blood from the wound. If the incision was made in its proper position the nerve about two millimeters in diameter will be observed lying in close contact to the vein. In some cases the blue walled vein will be most easily recognized first and the operator will know he will find the nerve in close contact to the vein. If he does not see either structure forceps should be used to break the tissue on the under surface of the fascia on each side of the incision. The most common mistake that is made is to search too deeply in the tissue for the nerve. After the nerve is exposed it may be picked up with forceps or neurectomy hook and freed from the surrounding tissue the length of the incision. The nerve is divided at the two commissures of the wound removing a section of nerve about one inch long. The edges of the incision through the skin and fascia are approximated with interrupted sutures and the wound closed with flexible collodion. Healing of the wound should occur by first intention.

Quittor

A quittor is necrosis of the lateral cartilage and characterized by one or more fistulous openings discharging through or above the coronary band. The necrotic portion of the lateral cartilage is recognized by its pea-green color.

ETIOLOGY. Probably direct injury of the lateral cartilage is the most common cause, as severe wire cuts invading the cartilage, injury from calkins, and puncture wounds.

Infection extending from a suppurating corn or infection resulting from a nail wound in the foot and involving the lateral cartilage. Necrosis of the lateral cartilage is apt to become very extensive because of its very poor blood supply and inability to withstand infection.

SIGNS. There is an inflammatory swelling over the affected cartilage. The swelling may be small or it may be very extensive, extending over the entire cartilage. Also it may be very prominent, bulging above and usually overlapping the coronary band. The area is usually very sensitive to palpation. The sinus usually has one or more openings through or above the coronary band discharging purulent material. When the discharging opening is between the coronary band and the top of the wall it is due to suppurative laminitis, or so-called "gravel". Lameness is usually well marked, but in some cases it is absent and in others only slight, depending upon the extent and location of the lesion. Usually if the lesion is located in the anterior part the lameness is more severe than when the posterior portion only is involved.

The infection may involve other tissues, producing serious complications as infections of the coffin joint, the sensitive laminae, aponeurosis of the deep digital tendon or even necrosis of the third phalanx.

PROGNOSIS. If the discharge is profuse it is indicative of extensive involvement of cartilage and may prove very resistant to treatment.

DIAGNOSIS. Diagnosis is usually based on the swelling over the cartilage and the presence of one or more openings discharging purulent material.

TREATMENT. An attempt may be made to destroy the infection and flush out the necrotic tissue by using a caustic preparation. This preparation should be injected into the cavity with some pressure.

The following are some of the preparations used; however, any caustic may produce the desired results if it reaches the diseased tissue. (1) Hydrochloric acid (c. p.) 1 part; hydrargyri Bichloridum, 3 parts; denatured alcohol, 20 parts. (2) Hydrargyri Bichloridum, 2 ounces; Hydrochloric acid, 1½ ounces; water q. s. 1 pint. (3) Hydrargyri Bichloridum, 17 parts; wood alcohol, 140 parts; Hydrochloric acid, 2-4 parts; lead acetate, 34 parts.

Hughes used the following treatment with very good results. The tracts or sinus are first irrigated with a formalin solution using one ounce in a quart of water. A syringe with a long nozzle is used to introduce a solution of bichloride of mercury, two ounces; hydrochloric acid, one and one-half ounces; and water enough to make a pint to the bottom of the sinus.

Another method is that recommended by Lomas. He stresses the importance of using gum elastic tubes to introduce to the bottom of the tracts or sinus. The preparation used is made by dissolving one dram of bichloride of mercury in sixteen ounces of boiling water. When the receptacle is taken away from the heat, one and one-half drams of glacial acetic acid is added. Best results are obtained if the weight is off the foot when the injection is made. The injections may have to be repeated every two days.

Some good results have been reported from introducing bichloride of mercury into the sinus. Another method is to cauterize the sinus with the actual cautery, which should come in contact with all the diseased tissue.

If it is desirable to remove the affected portion of the cartilage, the following simple operation devised by Perrier, a French veterinarian, may be performed.

The operative area over and around the affected portion of the cartilage should be shaved and a good skin antiseptic applied. Anesthesia of the tissue may be obtained by blocking the volar or plantar nerve above the fetlock joint. A tourniquet should be applied just below the fetlock joint to control the hemorrhage.

An elliptical incision should be made in the skin and enclosing the openings in the skin and any diseased skin. Also the opening should be large enough to expose the cartilage to permit examination and complete removal of all affected cartilage. The necrotic cartilage is recognized by its pea-green color. All the necrotic cartilage, together with any other diseased tissue, should be removed with knife and currette. If it is necessary to remove all the cartilage, the foot should be extended to tense the joint capsule, drawing it away from the cartilage. This reduces the danger of invading the joint capsule.

When all of the diseased tissue is removed it will be necessary to bandage it tightly to control the hemorrhage that will occur when the tourniquet is released. The gauze that is used to tamponade the cavity should be impregnated with Bipp or the camphor-phenol antiseptic.

The bandages should be removed in twenty-four to forty-eight hours, and the cavity wiped clean with dry cotton. A fresh antiseptic is reapplied to the area. The wound is treated as often as it seem necessary, always wiping out the discharge with dry cotton, and antiseptic powders may be used, such as salicylic acid, boric acid, calomel, and others. With this type of treatment the largest percentage of cases make a very satisfactory recovery.

Navicular Disease

The tissues affected in navicular disease may be a bursitis affecting the navicular bursa, inflammation of the aponeurosis of the deep digital flexor tendon or an ostitis, chrondritis or caries of the navicular bone. The periostitis and ostitis affecting the navicular bone may produce exostoses along its edges and especially at the ends of the bone.

The disease practically always occurs in the front feet but in rare cases may be found in the hind feet. It occurs most frequently in the light horses, hunters, jumpers and saddle horses but only occasionally in heavy horses.

ETIOLOGY. The actual cause is unknown but it does occur most frequently in light horses doing fast work on hard surfaces and is apparently due to the concussion. Also the excessive strain placed on the tissues in this area in hunting and jumping seems to be a factor. Usually occurs in horses seven years of age or older. Navicular disease usually develops rather slowly and is well established before the horse is presented for examination.

SIGNS. When only one foot is affected the characteristic pointing of the foot is noticed at rest. The foot is advanced slightly ahead of the normal position with the heel raised. If both feet are affected, first one foot is rested then the other foot, apparently this is to relieve the pressure of the tendon over the navicular bone. When first noticed the patient may seem a little tender, then if rested for a few days is apparently all right. As the condition progresses the lameness becomes more pronounced, the stride is shortened and the horse may stumble occasionally. Due to the shortened stride there is a tendency to regard the shoulders as the seat of the lameness. Generally the lameness is most marked when first starting to exercise and then diminishes or may disappear as the horse warms up. If the condition is well developed the lameness may be continuous.

The typical navicular foot is usually narrow, contracted and upright at the heels with pronounced atrophy of the frog. In cases where there is restricted use of the limb pronounced atrophy of the shoulder muscles may occur.

DIAGNOSIS. A number of procedures may be used to aid in the diagnosis of navicular disease. When a radiograph is taken certain changes may be apparent but it will be difficult to evaluate their importance. The blocking of the posterior digital nerve seems to be the most significant and valuable procedure that can be used to localize the seat of the lameness. It will, also, help in determining if treatment will be of any value.

When a case of lameness is presented it is examined thoroughly for any condition that might cause lameness. If we are unable to find any changes in the tissues we resort to the blocking of the posterior digital nerves. If the patient goes sound it is an indication that the seat of the lameness is in the posterior part of the foot, and in the tissues supplied by those nerves.

A bilateral posterior digital neurectomy is recommended when the horse goes sound after the nerves are blocked. Neurectomy of the posterior digital nerves has been an operation that has prolonged the usefulness of many horses. The operation has been performed on Jumpers, Hunters, Thoroughbreds, Quarter Horses that were used for cutting, roping and general all around cattle use, gaited horses, parade horses, walking horses and only occasionally is there one that would not stand hard usage.

The following case is a rather typical history of a horse with navicular disease. The horse was lame in the right front during the summer, then during the winter became lame in both front feet, and the lameness gradually increased in severity. A bilateral posterior digital neurectomy was performed. The owner was roping calves with him two weeks after the operation was performed and the horse has not shown any lameness since the operation.

It is recommended to rest the horse for ten days after the operation so the wounds can heal. In some cases, however, they have not been rested this long and made the usual good recovery. Occasionally a case is presented with the history of being lame in the front limbs for several years. Blocking of the posterior digital nerves relieves the lameness and a neurectomy is performed. It may take these cases several months before they recover from the lameness.

Sand Crack

A sand crack is in the wall of the hoof, starting at the coronary band and may extend only a short distance or all the way down the wall. These cracks appear more frequently on the quarters of the front feet and at the toe of the hind feet.

ETIOLOGY. May be due to excessive growth of horn, injury to coronary band results in weakened horn growing out which on pressure splits easily. The weakening of the wall from excessive drying or thinning may contribute to splitting of the wall.

SIGNS. The presence of the split in the wall is the outstanding sign. The sensitive laminae may become pinched between the edges of the crack causing a severe lameness. If infection has gained entrance to the sensitive laminae there may be a discharge of pus and a blood exudate.

DIAGNOSIS. Is made on the presence of the crack which is usually easily found.

PROGNOSIS. Will depend upon whether it is a simple or complicated crack, simple crack is usually favorable.

TREATMENT. For a complete toe crack, start one-half inch on each side of the crack and bevel the wall down to the sensitive laminae.

This creates a V shaped groove in the wall extending from the coronary band to the bearing surface of the wall. Also a portion of the bearing surface of the wall should be removed so it will not come in contact with the shoe.

For sand cracks at the quarter several procedures are recommended. One of the most efficient methods of immobilizing this portion of the wall is to arrange two grooves about the crack in the form of a V. The grooves should be made as deep as possible without injuring the sensitive laminae. The operator should also be careful not to make the grooves high enough to injure the coronary band as this may stimulate the formation of new cracks. The bearing surface of the wall just below the crack should be removed so as not to come in contact with the shoe. Then a good bar shoe is put on.

Another method is to thin the wall at the quarter with a rasp until the wall gives under light pressure. Remove bearing surface of the wall below crack and shoe with good bar shoe.

Keratoma, Keraphyllocele

This is a horn tumor which is found on the inner surface of the wall of the hoof. The growth may vary in size from a diameter of one-fourth to three-fourths of an inch. It may extend only a short distance up the wall or all the way. The shape may vary from a semicylindrical form to those that are pyramidal, conical or irregular in form. The tissues may be solid or there may be a tract extending part or all the way through it.

ETIOLOGY. Keratoma usually occurs from a chronic irritation of the coronary band or sensitive laminae. It may develop at the coronary band following a severe injury to this tissue thus causing an excessive quantity of new tissue to be formed. A nail that is driven too close to the sensitive laminae or a sand crack may result in the formation of a keratoma. In some cases the keratoma may appear to develop without any irritation of the sensitive laminae.

SIGNS. Lameness may or may not be present depending upon the location and size of the tumor. In other cases the signs are those of a foot lameness. If the keratoma is due to chronic irritation of the sensitive laminae there may be a discharge either watery or purulent in character. A keratoma can only be definitely diagnosed by finding the tumor when the plantar surface of the foot is examined.

PROGNOSIS. This should be guarded as the patient may not recover from the lameness

TREATMENT. If the tumor is not causing lameness it is best to leave it alone. When the horse is shod a portion of the wall below the tumor should be removed so that portion of the wall will not bear on the shoe. Blocking of the nerves may be tried to see if a neurectomy will relieve the lameness.

Operative treatment consists in removing that portion of the wall to which the tumor is attached. A groove is made through the wall on each side of the affected area. These grooves extend from the top of the wall to the plantar surface. This portion of the wall is then removed. The area thus exposed is then kept covered with antiseptic packs until it is protected by a new horn. In some cases there is a recurrence of the tumor.

Corns

A corn is produced when there is injury to the sensitive laminae of the sole, bar or quarters in the angle formed by the wall and bar. In most cases the injury affects the sensitive tissue of the sole.

ETIOLOGY. Corns occur most frequently on the inner angle of the front feet and are rarely found on the hind feet. This is probably due to the greater weight born by the front feet thus greater concussion occurs on the sensitive structures during movement. If too much horn is removed at the buttresses it weakens the foot where it should be strong. This may result in contraction of the quarters or heels and bruising of the sensitive laminae at the quarters. Improper trimming of the feet, lack of frog pressure, excessive concussion and bruising of the coronet from treads and over reaching are frequent causes of corns. If the heels are too low the sensitive tissue in the posterior part of the foot is more susceptible to bruising. If toe and heel calks are used they prevent the elastic structures, as the plantar cushion, from functioning normally so there is more concussion of the sensitive tissue. Defective conformation as long, weak fetlocks and abnormally narrow feet favor the development of corns. If the foot is abnormally narrow, corns usually occur on the bar while in a wide foot the corn is more likely to occur on the sole. Corns occur only rarely on unshod feet.

PROGNOSIS. As a general rule corns respond favorably to the proper treatment. However if the tissue has become infected serious complications may develop that are difficult or impossible to correct.

SIGNS. The location of the lesion and the changes in the horn are very characteristic. Lameness may or may not be present depending upon the changes in the tissue. Corns are usually classified into dry, moist and suppurating. A dry corn occurs when there is capillary hemorrhage at the inner surface of the horn from bruising of the sensitive tissue. The red spots produced may appear as fine points but are generally large red stains. With age the corn varies in color and depth. Usually the more superficial the corn the older it is. Moist corn is produced when the injury has been severe and the affected tissue becomes infiltrated with serum or it may accumulate beneath the horn. A suppurating corn occurs when infection gains entrance to the affected tissue through a break in the horn. Also it may occur if the horn is pared excessively. The corn becomes complicated when there is necosis of the sensitive laminae, lateral cartilage, plantar aponeurosis or the digital cushion.

The local signs will depend upon the extent of the lesion. If there is acute inflammation present there will be a varying degree of lameness. Pain is shown when compression is applied to the affected area. Increased heat may be felt on palpation. Removal of some of the horn in the affected area will reveal the presence of the stained horn which may vary from a yellowish appearance to deep red. In moist corn the horn is either infiltrated with serum or it has accumulated beneath it.

In suppurating corn pus escapes when an opening is made in the sole. The removal of the pus and treatment of the infection gives marked relief.

TREATMENT. In some cases the removal of the offending shoe may be all that is necessary to give relief. Also removing some of the tissue over the corn may relieve some pressure but it should not extend deep enough to invade the sensitive tissue. Shoes should not be put on until the tissues are normal. When the foot is dry and hard the foot should be soaked in water daily until the tissues are again moist and elastic. When shoeing a foot with a dry corn the foot should be examined for any contraction of the heels, ossification of the lateral cartilages or any evidence of navicular disease. If normal the foot is balanced and all pressure of the wall is removed from the shoe from just in front of the corn back to and including the buttress. A bar shoe is then put on, the foot is packed with tar and oakum and covered with a leather pad. If the heels are contracted the wall at the quarters should be weakened by removing two-thirds of the thickness of the wall from the top of the wall to the bearing surface. The bar shoe with tar, oakum and a leather pad is used. If a stronger shoe is required, a bar shoe with a bar that does not come in contact with the horny frog may be used. For a moist corn the same procedure is used for shoeing the foot.

When pus is present an opening should be made that will provide complete drainage. The foot should then be put in an antiseptic bath for one to two hour periods daily until there is no discharge. Any exuberant tissue that develops is removed with a scalpel or caustic. If any complications develop they are treated according to general principles. When the foot is ready to receive a shoe the entire wall over the affected area should be removed. The foot is then shod with a bar shoe, pack with tar and oakum and a leather pad. The shoe should be prepared so the bar will press where the horny frog is the heaviest. This procedure is employed so the digital cushion will support the weight that would have been carried by the portion of the wall that was removed. The horse is exercised daily and in two or three weeks is ready for regular work.

Contracted Heels

This condition is often called contracted hoof but the contraction usually occurs in the region of the quarters and heels. It occurs more commonly in the front feet than the hind feet.

ETIOLOGY. Some of the factors mentioned as contributing to the development of contraction heels are: (1) Removal of periople which permits drying and contraction of the wall. (2) Cutting the bars so the support of the quarters are weakened. (3) Shoeing with calkins or leaving the wall long removing the frog from contact with the ground. It is thought one frequent cause of this condition is an ossification of the lateral cartilages. This results in a thickening of the lateral cartilages a pododermatitis and a loosening of the bars and quarters with drying and contraction of hoof.

SIGNS. The deformity of the affected foot is noticeable when viewed from in front. The plantar surface of the foot shows the most marked change with the contraction of the quarter and heel. The bars are not as divergent posteriorly as normal but may be almost parallel. The frog is atrophied with the lateral sulci slit like.

TREATMENT. When lameness is present with the quarters definitely contracted the following operation recommended by Asmus is indicated.

Make a groove three-fourths of an inch below hairline from the heel about one inch anterior to the anterior border of the lateral cartilage. Then thin the wall above and below this groove until it is pliable. Thin the bars and sole with the knife. A bar shoe is put on with a leather and a tar and oakum pack. The wall at the toe should be rounded off so the foot breaks over more easily. Exercise the horse moderately every day. It may be necessary to repeat the operation in six months if the expansion is not complete.

Canker

Canker is an affection of the feet characterized as a chronic hypertrophic moist eczematous dermatitis. This condition originates in the frog and spreads to the sole and sometimes involves the wall. The hind feet are most commonly affected but sometimes all four feet are involved.

ETIOLOGY. It occurs more frequently in horses kept standing in manure and urine so the feet are moist continously. But also occurs in horses kept in apparently ideal surroundings. Lack of proper frog pressure seems to be an important predisposing factor.

SIGNS. Canker may develop insidiously and a large amount of damage to the tissue occur before its presence is recognized. When the disease is well established there is a softening and raising of the horn of the frog and appears to be soaked with moisture. Later the horn of the sole is affected and presents the characteristic loosened, ragged and moist appearance. When the pressure of the normal horn is removed the characteristic vegetations, or finger-like growths make their appearance. The whitish exudate has a very offensive odor. Even in apparently well advanced cases there may be little or no lameness.

DIAGNOSIS. Is based on the loosening or the horn, the profuse discharge with putrid odor, the characteristic growths, and the moistened horn.

PROGNOSIS. In most cases the prognosis should be guarded as it requires very intensive treatment to obtain a cure and then it may reoccur. If all four feet are affected or the tissue destruction extensive the prognosis is unfavorable.

TREATMENT. Consists in removal of all loose horn, excess tissue and the finger-like growths making sure all affected tissue is removed. Apply to the affected parts an antiseptic astringent preparation with pressure. Frequent changing of the antiseptic dressing is important. Antiseptics used have been calomel, tartar emetic or the following preparation, flour, four ounces; lead nitrate, two ounces. Mix in a mortar, add two drams of formalin and enough mineral oil to make a soft paste. Apply liberally and bandage renewing every third day. Excellent pressure can be obtained over the area by the use of shoes and fastening a piece of boiler plate to the shoes with screws. When the tissue begins to show definite improvement mild antiseptic powders should be used.

Wounds of the Plantar Surface of the Foot

Injury of the plantar surface of the foot is usually caused by a nail but it may be produced by any sharp piece of iron or rock.

SIGNS. Lameness is usually the first sign of injury of the plantar surface of the foot. The lameness may be severe or mild depending upon the degree of injury to the sensitive tissue. If the injury is in the region of the toe the animal steps more on the heel and vice versa. When the injury first occurs the animal may not be very lame but with the development of infection and inflammation of the sensitive tissue lameness may be severe.

DIAGNOSIS. Is easy when the causative agent is still present. The puncture wound may be found when the foot is thoroughly cleansed. In using the hoof testers some of the inflammatory exudate or purulent discharge may be forced out thru the wound in the sole or frog disclosing the point of injury.

PROGNOSIS. In most cases the prognosis is favorable. If the plantar surface of the foot is divided into three parts anterior, middle and posterior a puncture wound in the middle region is apt to be the most serious. Most of the important structures of the foot are above the middle region. If it occurs in the anterior region the third phalanx may be fractured. Injuries occurring in the posterior region are usually not so serious. However the type and virulence of the bacteria may produce a serious infection in any part of the foot. The severity of the lameness the attitude and temperature of the patient may be important guides as to the seriousness of the injury.

TREATMENT. In all foot injuries of the horse administer a prophylactic dose of tetanus antitoxin. If the examination reveals the presence of pus open the sole just enough to provide adequate drainage. Irrigate the cavity with any efficient antiseptic. Foot injuries make a quicker recovery if the foot can be kept in a hot antiseptic foot bath for about two hours a day. One of the best methods of providing protection for any injury to the plantar surface of the foot is to put on a shoe. Then a piece of boiler plate large enough to cover the plantar surface of the foot is fastened on the bottom of the shoe.

Penetrating Wounds

A penetrating wound is produced when a foreign body penetrates a bursa, joint cavity or tendon sheath. If a sharp object like a nail penetrates the middle region of the foot there is danger of injury to the navicular bursa, navicular bone, tendon or coffin bone. If the patient has a high temperature, does not eat, is depressed and severely lame with sometimes a discharge of synovial fluid from the wound resection of the deep digital flexor tendon is indicated. This operation is performed to enable the operator to make an accurate diagnosis and prognosis and institute the proper treatment.

Operative Treatment of Traumatic Inflammation of the Navicular Bursa With Preservation of the Deep Flexor Tendon

The foot should be thoroughly cleansed and the sole frog and bars trimmed down until they are pliable. Then an antiseptic pack is applied to the foot for twenty-four hours.

The patient is secured in lateral recumbency. Complete anesthesia of the foot is obtained by blocking the two volar nerves. A tourniquet is applied above the fetlock joint.

A transverse incision is made thru the frog so as to remove the anterior two-thirds.

This incision extends thru the horny and sensitive portion and the digital cushion to the deep digital flexor tendon. Two incisions extending forward along each side of the frog are made to its apex and the loosened portion of the frog is now dissected free from the deep digital flexor tendon. The exposed tendon may be normal in color, there may be areas of necrosis or it may be covered with reddish granulation tissue. The location of the navicular bone can be determined by flexing and extending the digit.

A small rectangular opening is made thru the tendon directly over the navicular bone. This permits examination of the navicular bone. This permits examination of the navicular bursa and the navicular bone and the operator may also determine if the nail has entered the articulation. If there is a fracture of the navicular bone it should be removed. Also any other treatment that is indicated as removal of all necrotic tissue and establishment of drainage. The aftercare consists in the use of antiseptic packs, irrigation of the area with proper antiseptics and removal of all diseased tissue.

Forssell of Stockholm recommends a different technique to reach the navicular bursa. He believes the chief objectives in operating are to remove all necrotic tissue in the tendon and remove all of the cartilage from the flexor surface of the navicular bone. Also in the operative procedure there should be a minimum of injury to the flexor tendon.

The bars, frog and adjacent portions of the sole should be thinned. A semi-circular groove is cut in the sole extending around the point of the frog to the angles between the wall and the bars at each side. This portion of the sole is now carefully elevated from the underlying tissue. A probe may be passed into the puncture wound to determine the extent of the injury to the underlying tissue especially the tendon.

A mid-line incision is made in the corium from the point of the frog to the bulbs of the heels. The extent of the navicular bone may be determined by flexing the digit. A longitudinal incision is made through the tendon in the mid-line from its insertion to the posterior border of the navicular bone. The tendon should be examined thoroughly and all necrotic tissue removed. The flexor surface of the navicular bone is examined by flexing and extending the digit. A currette is used to remove all the cartilage from the navicular bone. The cartilage is removed to stimulate the formation of granulation tissue. The bursal cavity is irrigated with hydrogen peroxide and then tincture of iodine is applied liberally. A strip of gauze is inserted through the incision in the tendon. The operative area and foot is then bandaged in the usual manner. The wound should be rebandaged as it seems necessary. The patients usually make a rather slow recovery and lameness is severe for several weeks. In about three months they are able to do light work and then the improvement is rapid.

Atrophy of the Third Phalanx

Atrophy of the third phalanx may occur when the foot is injured in a young animal. A four year old horse was presented with a front foot smaller than the other three feet. When the horse was four months of age a wire had penetrated the bottom of the foot producing a severe injury. The horse was lame when it was presented for examination. When the posterior digital nerves were blocked the horse went sound. A posterior digital neurectomy was performed to relieve the lameness.

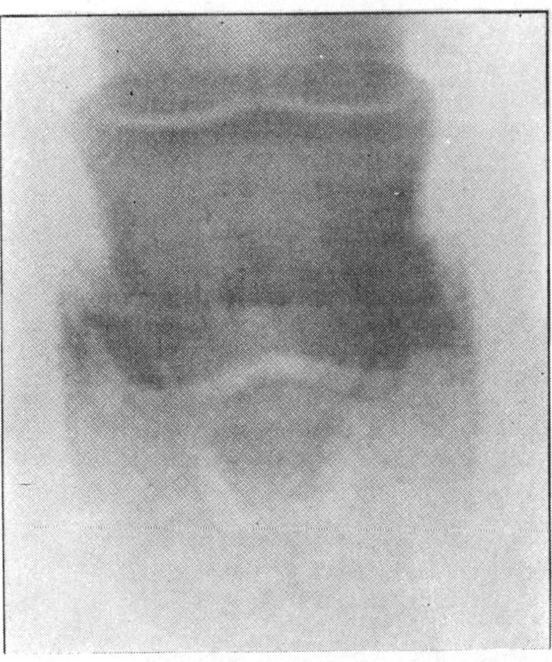

FIG. 297. Atrophy of the third phalanx that developed after injury to the foot when a young colt.

Infectious Pododermatitis Foot Rot, Foul Claw, Foul in the Foot

In the bovine infectious pododermatitis or foot rot is the most frequent cause of lameness. When dairy cows are affected there is a marked loss in milk production and in fattening cattle it may be the cause of a pronounced loss in condition.

ETIOLOGY. The most generally accepted cause of this condition is the organism Actinomyces necrophorus, a saprophyte that becomes pathogenic upon entrance into living tissue. Whenever the disease is prevalent in the feet of cattle it is also frequently found affecting the tissues of the lips, cheek, tongue, larynx, and liver. In some localities it is more prevalent during the summer season when the cattle are on soil that is extensively infected. This is most likely to occur when the animals have access to mud holes that are almost dry and containing filthy mud. This situation provides ideal conditions for the organism as it is anaerobic and wet airless soil favors its development. It is also of frequent occurrence during the winter and early spring months when cattle are confined in muddy lots. Infection in the tissues may be preceded by a traumatic injury from stones, sharp pieces of iron, nails or stub of brush or weed. If mud accumulates between the claws it may dry into a hard mass that abrades or lacerates the skin in the interdigital space and the infection gains entrance into the deeper tissue.

SIGNS. Some of the first noticeable signs will be frequent raising of the foot or feet, lameness, a decrease in appetite and the affected animals may spend most of their time lying down. Examination of the interdigital skin in the early case may disclose only a reddened, swollen, sensitive area. It may begin at the posterior part of the interdigital space, bulbs of the heels, fleshy sole or the inflammation may be most noticeable around the coronary band. In other cases the pastern may be upright or knuckled with the coronet red or bluish in color, hot, swollen and extremely sensitive. As the deeper tissue is affected a suppurating wound may develop, an abscess or sinus with the formation of necrotic tissue. The necrosis of tissue is recognized by its yellowish grey color and surrounded by an inflammatory, suppurating zone with the development of a line of demarcation or separation between the healthy and necrotic tissue. The infection may be confined to the skin and subcutaneous tissue or it may involve the interdigital ligaments or tendons. The coffin or pastern joints may become infected with the development of a septic arthritis. The symptoms then increase in severity with a marked rise in temperature, severe lameness and a fetid, purulent synovial discharge.

PROGNOSIS. When the lesion involves only the skin and subcutaneous tissue it responds rather readily to treatment. However, when the tendons and ligaments are involved recovery is slow. When the joints become infected satisfactory recovery is only obtained with removal of the affected joint.

TREATMENT. When the lesion involves only the skin, local applications of antiseptics may be all the treatment necessary. However, the antiseptic used should not be irritating to healthy tissue or have an escharotic action. Some antiseptics used with good results have been calomel, 10 per cent ointment of tartar emetic and lanolin, powdered copper sulphate, saturated solutions of copper sulphate or potassium permanganate have all given good results and there are many others. A piece of cotton or gauze just wide enough to fit in the interdigital space is used to hold any of the above preparations in contact with the affected tissue. The bandage which is used to hold the pack in position should not be so large the claws are forced apart.

In some cases the infection in the tissue produces a cellulitis which may involve both claws and extend above the fetlock joint. When this occurs there is extensive swelling of the tissue and a severe type of lameness. The use of antiphlogistic treatment, hot packs, poultices or soaking the area in hot antiseptic solutions may abort the infection or localize it in the tissue.

If the infection localizes in the tissue necrosis of this tissue occurs which is recognized by its yellowish grey color. A line of demarcation or separation develops between the healthy and necrotic tissue. This necrotic "core" of tissue should be removed and the area treated with the usual antiseptics. If the inflammation is very extensive in the surrounding tissue antiphlogistic treatment should also be used in reducing the inflammation in the tissues.

When the infection occurs in the feed lots it may be necessary to remove the animals from the lots to control the infection. In other outbreaks the infection may be controlled by having the animals walk through troughs containing antiseptics. These troughs may be set in the doorways or gates and contain either solutions or dry antiseptics. Some practitioners prefer copper sulphate in a one to three per cent solution, lime and sulphur dip one in fifteen, slaked lime or five pounds of copper sulphate mixed with one hundred pounds of lime may be used. For cattle out in pasture "Schmidt" recommends scattering two to four hundred pounds of this mixture around the salt licks. It is also advisable to either fill in or fence all mud holes in the pasture.

In 1946, Forman reported that one single intravenous injection of sodium sulfapyridine was a specific in the treatment of foot rot in cattle. He recommends using 60 grams of sodium sulfapyridine dissolved in 500 cubic centimeters of distilled water as specific and non-toxic in animals varying in weight from 500 to 1000 pounds. For larger animals more beneficial results may be obtained if the dose of the drug is increased, particularly in those cases where there is extensive involvement of the soft tissue. When cases of foot rot are treated by this method the infection does not require any local treatment of the affected tissues. It has been observed that following treatment there may be a reduction in milk flow for a few days. Good results cannot be expected in those cases where the infection has gained entrance to either the coffin or pastern joints. For in these cases the articular cartilage may be eroded or destroyed producing a permanent lameness even though the infection is destroyed by the treatment.

Chambers recommends the administration of 1,500,000 units of penicillin intramuscularly in the treatment of foot rot. Also he reports that a number of cases in which there was extensive involvement of tissue have recovered by giving two ounce doses of sodium sulfapyridine and 1,500,000 units of penicillin every other day for three treatments.

AMPUTATION OF CLAW. Whenever the infection gains entrance into either the coffin or pastern joints it produces a suppurative arthritis that does not respond to external treatment. If the affected articulation is not removed surgically the lameness and inflammation of the tissues persists for weeks and months and shows little tendency to heal. Also the affected animals lose condition and in milk cows there is a marked decrease in milk production. When the articulation is removed there is a quick and marked improvement in the condition of the animal.

ANATOMY OF THE FOOT. The cow's foot is very similar to that of the horse except the bones, tendons, ligaments and joints are doubled from the fetlock joint downward. The distal end of the large metacarpus or metatarsus is bifurcated to articulate with the two sets of phalangeal bones. The two metacarpal or metatarsal phalangeal joints communicate so that amputation of the digit should not be made higher than the middle of the first phalanx. There is no frog as in the horse, but its place is taken by the bulb or ball of the foot. If the coffin joint is infected an exarticulation through this joint may be performed.

ANESTHESIA. The operation may be performed under the influence of a local anesthetic. Depending upon the disposition of the animal it may be confined in the stanchion or cast in lateral recumbency. For the hind limb the plantar nerves should be blocked about three inches below the tarso-metatarsal or carpo-metacarpal articulation. To block both nerves, five cubic centimeters of a 2 per cent solution of a local anesthetic should be injected on the lateral and medial edge of the deep digital flexor tendon. Also the tissue on the dorsal surface of the limb just above the fetlock joint should be infiltrated with the local anesthetic. A tourniquet is then fastened tightly above the fetlock joint to control the hemorrhage. The claw may be removed with a surgical saw or obstetrical wire using the fetotome to guide the wire. The incision through the claw should be approximately one-fourth of an inch below the coronary band. As the extensor process of the os pedis is left attached to the articulation it should be removed. The wound should be covered with an antiseptic pack and bandaged tightly in position. After care of the wound will depend upon the infection present and how the wound is healing.

AMPUTATION OF CLAW THROUGH THE MIDDLE OF THE FIRST PHALANX. If the infection has invaded the tissue above the coffin joint or the pastern joint, amputation through the middle of the first phalanx should be performed.

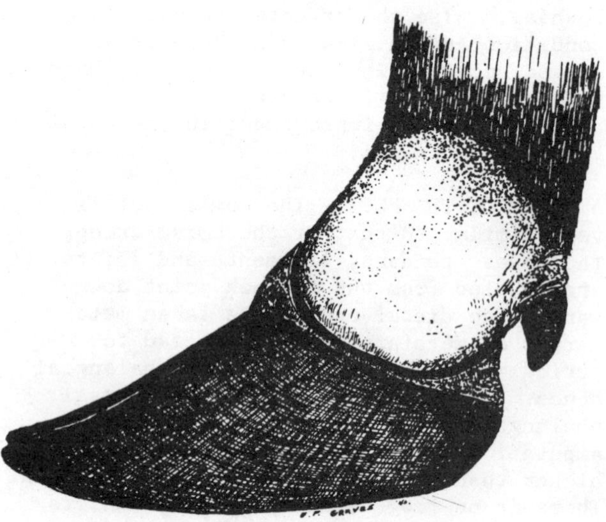

FIG. 298. The incision through the skin on the lateral side of the first phalanx.

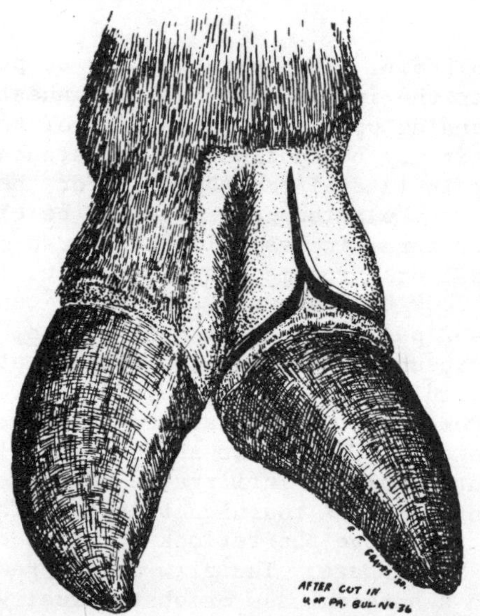

FIG. 299. The uniting of the two incisions.

The animal should be confined in lateral recumbency with the affected claw uppermost. Prepare the operative area by shaving the skin from the coronary band to the fetlock joint. The skin in the interdigital space and claw should be cleansed thoroughly. Cleanse the skin with a fat solvent as carbon tetrachloride and then apply an efficient skin antiseptic. Anesthesia of the operative area may be obtained by blocking the volar or plantar nerves about three inches below the tarso-metatarsal or carpo-metacarpal articulation. Also infiltrate the soft tissue below the fetlock joint and between the digits with a one per cent solution of a local anesthetic. A tourniquet should be applied tightly above the fetlock joint.

The incision through the skin and subcutaneous tissue may be started just below the dew claw and in the center of the first phalanx and apply sufficient pressure so all the soft tissue will be cut down to the bone. Continue the incision downward until as it approaches the coronary band it curves slightly forward and is continued above the coronary band. As the incision approaches the anterior surface of the first phalanx it curves upward and is continued over the center of the first phalanx to a joint just below the fetlock joint. The next incision is begun where the first incision starts to curve to the lateral side and is continued on the medial side of the digit in the same manner, saving all the skin possible, until it meets the first incision on the anterior surface of the first phalanx. Dissect the soft tissue free from the first phalanx on the lateral and medial sides of the bone above the point where you expect to remove the bone. Reflect the lateral flap of skin and with a bone saw cut through the middle of the first phalanx in a slanting direction downward and outward. Remove the digit and loosen the tourniquet to see if any blood vessels are going to bleed enough to require ligation. It is important to control the hemorrhage as decomposing blood in a wound delays healing. The edges of the two flaps of skin are now sutured together with interrupted sutures leaving an opening one and one-half inches wide at the bottom for drainage. An efficient non-irritating antiseptic should be used in the wound. To keep the antiseptic in contact with the tissues and control the hemorrhage gauze is packed tightly in the cavity. A pack that has been sprinkled liberally with an antiseptic powder is applied over the area and bandaged tightly in position. As the last bandage is wrapped in position water glass is applied to a dressing that is impervious to urine, water, and manure. In most cases the bandage should be removed in three or four days so the case can be retreated. The after treatment will then depend upon the freedom from infection in the wound and the progress made in the healing of the wound.

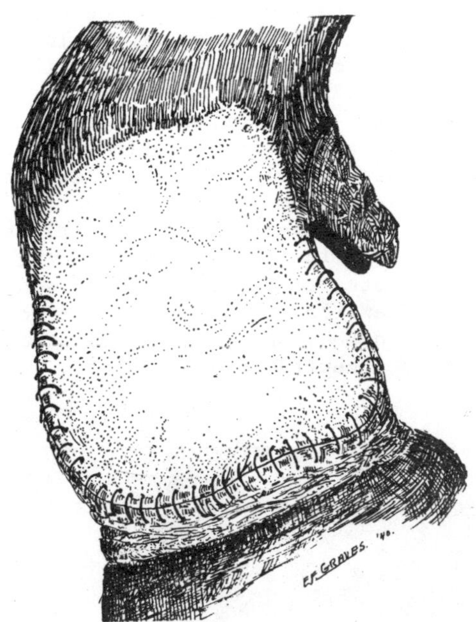

FIG. 300. The operative area after the skin is sutured.

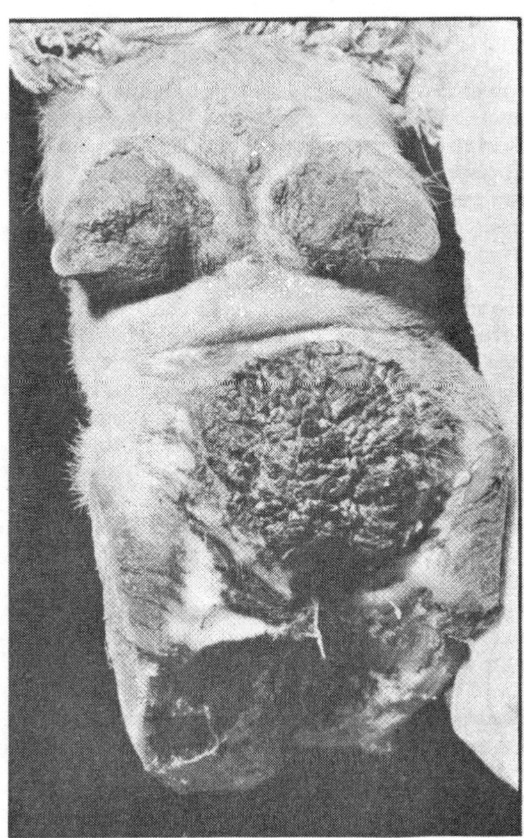

FIG. 302. A papilloma that is approximately two inches in diameter.

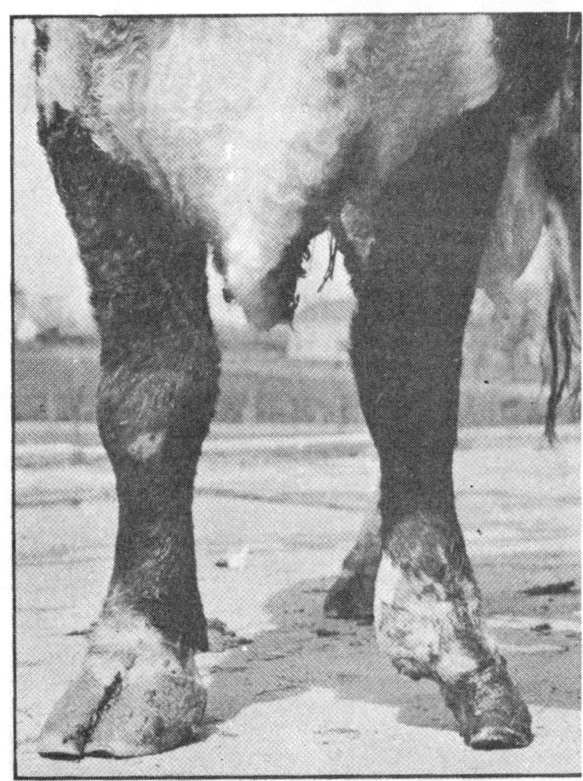

FIG. 301. After the wound has healed and the foot is being used in a normal manner.

FIG. 303. Chronic wound with unhealthy tissue must be removed surgically.

Papilloma

A papilloma may arise from cutaneous, mucous and serous surfaces, outgrowths of tissue composed of living cells and subjacent connective tissue occur in many portions of the body and in a variety of forms to which the general term papilloma is applied. The form of the papilloma is chiefly determined by the local conditions surrounding the tumor. Irritation leading to overgrowth of surface epithelium may occur where the skin is subjected to more or less continuous trauma. This irritation occurs on the posterior surface of the pastern region of the hind feet of cattle so that a papilloma frequently develops in the skin. These papillomas vary in size from those one inch in diameter to one that may extend onto the bulbs of the heels. The papillomas that occur in this area usually cause lameness and they are observed when the foot is examined for the seat of lameness.

Treatment consists in surgical removal of the papilloma. To prevent a reoccurrence of the tumor the operator must be sure that all of the neoplastic tissue is removed. The incision extends through the entire thickness of the skin and out in the normal healthy skin. After the neoplastic tissue is removed the wound is bandaged so it is protected from dirt, manure and other foreign matter. This is the most important part of the aftercare of the wound.

Chronic Wound

In Fig. 303 is shown a chronic wound that had been treated for a long time with various antiseptics. This tissue presents the appearance of a papilloma but the tissue is softer and more spongy when palpated. It was necessary to remove this tissue surgically and keep the area bandaged until the wound was healed.

Interdigital Vegetative Dermatitis

In interdigital vegetative dermatitis there is a proliferation of the skin and subcutaneous tissue in the interdigital space. This condition is sometimes referred to as a corn. As a general rule they are found most frequently in the hind feet but may occur in the front feet or all four feet. They are found most frequently in bulls and may cause a severe and persistent form of lameness that interferes with their usefulness for breeding purposes.

ETIOLOGY. The reason for the development of an excessive amount of tissue in the interdigital space is usually ascribed to a chronic inflammation. However an examination of the tissue that is removed does not reveal changes in the skin suggestive of a chronic inflammation. In between the skin will be found fat and connective tissue that is apparently normal. It has been observed that development of the tissue progresses to a certain point and then stops. When the above factors are considered it would seem the excess growth of tissue is an inherited characteristic.

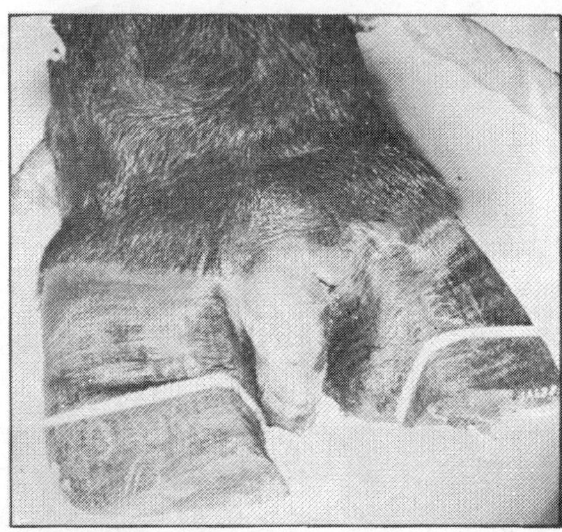

FIG. 304. Right front foot with smaller growth of tissue than the left front foot.

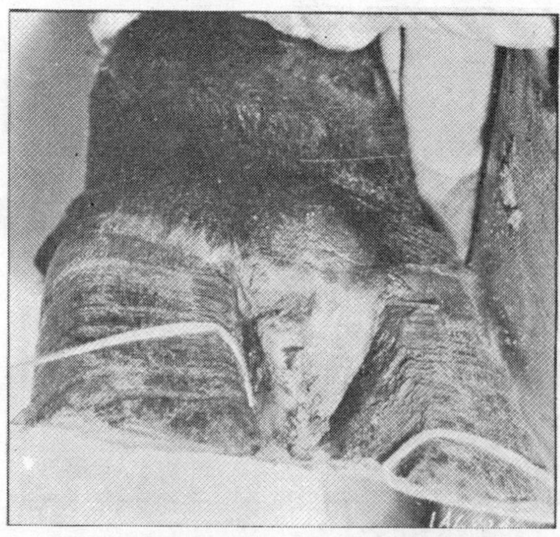

FIG. 305. Left foot excess tissue fills interdigital space.

SIGNS. The outstanding sign is a persistent type of lameness. Examination of the interdigital space reveals the growth of tissue which varies a great deal in size and extent in different individuals. Also there may be a wide variation in the size of the tissue in different feet on the same individual. In some cases the excess tissue may completely fill the interdigital space and extend down to the ground. In other individuals it will be small and thin and extend a variable distance. When the growth of tissue becomes pronounced in size it is subjected to pressure from the claws and the claws may be pushed apart. This lameness then becomes more persistent and severe until the excess tissue is removed from the interdigital space.

TREATMENT. The most successful method of treatment is surgical removal of the excess tissue between the claws. The patient should be confined so the foot can be held securely for the operation. Prepare the skin in the usual manner for an aseptic operation. Anesthesia for the operation may be obtained by infiltration of the tissue with a solution of a local anesthetic. All of the affected tissue is removed by incising through the skin on each side close to the claws. The area between the claws is covered with a layer of cotton which has been impregnated with a mild antiseptic and then bandaged in position. As a general rule it is not necessary to rebandage the foot very often, probably once a week for two or three times. However, the area should be protected from dirt and manure until there is complete healing.

Dislocation of Coffin Joint in Bovine

Dislocation of the coffin joint or the distal interphalangeal articulation of one claw of the bovine is rather rare. One case in which this dislocation did occur produced a very severe lameness. The lateral claw was affected and the toe was turned laterally. There was little external evidence of the dislocation. Due to the firm unyielding tissue surrounding the coffin joint there was no evident swelling of the tissue.

TREATMENT. Amputation of a portion of the claw.

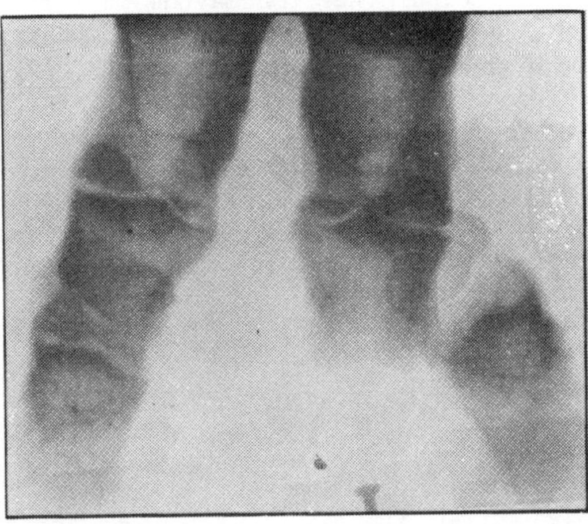

FIG. 306. Dislocation of the coffin joint or the distal interphalangeal articulation in the bovine.

Foreign Body in Interdigital Tissue

The examination of the plantar surface of the claws and interdigital space is indicated in cases of lameness in the bovine. Various objects as stones and pieces of wood have been found wedged between the claws in the interdigital space. In one case a large nail had penetrated the tissues to a depth of three inches in the interdigital space between the bulbs of the heels. Occasionally a nail is found that has penetrated through the sole and introduced infection into the coffin joint.

Treatment will be determined by the injury that has occurred to the tissue. If the foreign body has not invaded any important structure it is removed and the area bandaged with an antiseptic pack. In many cases it would be advisable to give a prophylactic dose of tetanus antitoxin. When the foreign body has penetrated the coffin joint the quickest recovery will be obtained by removal of the claw.

Fractures of the Phalanges

Fracture of one of the phalanges is sometimes observed in the bovine. The fracture usually causes a very severe lameness. Many of the fractures of the phalanges are comminuted or it is one in which it is impossible to obtain satisfactory healing. The quickest and best results may be obtained by removal of the affected claw. If it is a simple fracture the foot and distal part of the limb may be mobilized with a splint. There is the possibility that a good callus will be formed.

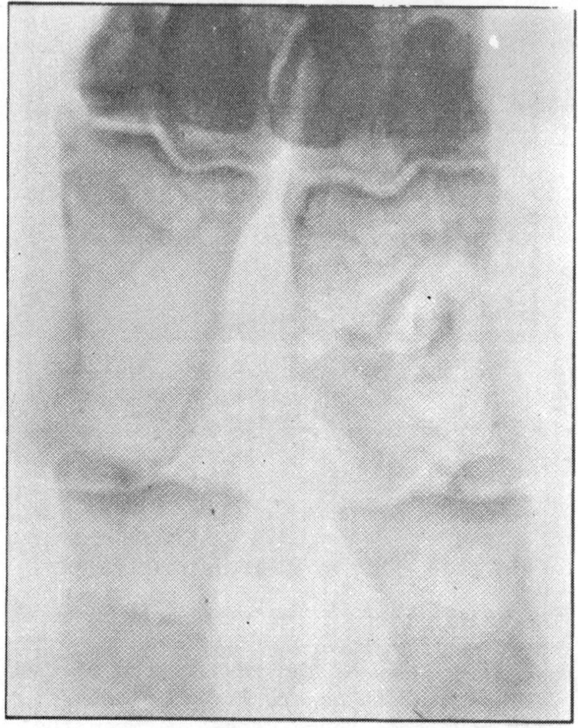

FIG. 307. Comminuted fracture of the first phalanx in a bull.

Elongated Hooves

Feet that need to be trimmed can be responsible for as much lameness as any other condition that may affect the bovine In some cases one foot may be affected, two feet or all four feet may need to be trimmed. Examination will reveal the feet that need to be trimmed. Examination of the affected feet may reveal that the wall at the quarters is too long, and that it has turned in under so the animal is walking on the wall. The toes may be elongated and because the sole is not in contact with the ground there is an excessive amount of tissue on the sole.

In trimming the foot or feet an attempt is made to remove the excess tissue so the foot is of normal shape. If the wall at the quarter curves in under an attempt should be made to remove the curved portion, so the wall is straight and the weight will be borne by the edge of the wall. All of the excess tissue should be removed from the sole until it gives under pressure with the thumbs. The sole is normally slightly concave and the final trimming should produce this shape of the sole.

The removal of the excess tissue may reveal an opening in the sole that has permitted dirt and manure to gain access to the sensitive tissues. The irritation of the sensitive pododerm will produce a very painful condition.

Treatment consists in flushing out all of the foreign material in the space between the sole and pododerm. If the irritation of the tissue has stimulated the formation of unhealthy granulation tissue this may be removed with an escharotic, such as powdered copper sulphate. The opening in the sole must be kept covered until it has filled in with healthy tissue.

REFERENCES

Chambers, E. E., Penicillin in the Treatment of Foot Rot in Cattle, The North American Veterinarian, Vol. 32, (July, 1951), No. 7, pp. 470-480.

Forman, Charles R., Single Injection Treatment for Foot Rot in Cattle, J.A.V.M.A., 109, (833), pp. 126-128.

Forsell, Gerhard, The Operative Treatment of Traumatic Inflammation of the Navicular Bursae With Preservation of the Deep Flexor Tendon, The North American Veterinarian, Vol. 11, February, 1930.

Frank, E. R. and McLeod, W. M., Paralysis of a Pectoral Nerve, The North American Veterinarian, 17, (1936), No. 2.

Gibbons, W. J., Amputation of the Claw in the Cow, The Cornell Veterinarian, XXIX, (1939), No. 3, pp. 294-296.

Law, J., Textbook of Veterinary Medicine, Vol. IV, 3rd Ed., Ithaca, N.Y., 1912.

Lomas, Harry, Quittor, The Veterinary Journal, (November, 1940), pp. 419.

Schmidt, A. H., Diseases of Feeder Cattle, The North American Veterinarian, Vol. XXIII, (1942), pp. 20-25.

Stevenson, W. L. and W. G., Rupture of the Common Digital Extensor in Foals, Canadian Journal Comp. Med., 6, pp. 197.

Chapter VIIII
AFFECTIONS OF THE THORACIC AND ABDOMINAL CAVITIES

Affections of the Back

Sore backs are of common occurrence in riding horses but most of the injuries can be prevented.

ETIOLOGY. Some of the most frequent causes of sore backs are poorly fitting saddles, failure to use a blanket that is clean or one that is not properly folded. When the rider lounges in the saddle it may result in injuries to the back. If the horse loses condition the saddle becomes ill-fitting and if proper adjustments are not made the tissues are injured.

Abrasions of the skin may occur when the epidermis is softened by sweat and is rubbed off exposing the sensitive tissue. This area is sensitive and the serous discharge which occurs dries and forms a scab.

Gall is characterized by the appearance of circular edematous shaped swellings in the saddle bed. This condition is produced when laceration of the subcutaneous tissue occurs. These areas are very sensitive and show the characteristic pitting on pressure.

Hematoma, rupture of blood vessels producing a hematoma may occur when excessive pressure is produced at one point. This may occur when the weight is improperly distributed or there is unevenness of the padding or saddle blanket. At first the swelling is soft and fluctuating but when the blood coagulates the contents are firm and crepitate on pressure.

Sit fast, when extreme continuous pressure is produced on the tissues the blood supply may be diminished or destroyed. An area of dry gangrene develops in the skin and sometimes extending into the deeper tissue forming a sitfast. The affected tissue is cone shaped in form with the base of the cone on the surface. With the formation of the dead tissue separation of the dead and healthy tissue usually occurs.

TREATMENT. Abrasions of the skin may be treated with white lotion, antiseptic powders or the pyoktannin blue preparation.

Galls, cold applications may be used at first, then hot applications with gentle massage of the area. This should be followed by the application of cold packs or ice packs which are held in position with a surcingle or bandage. The small hematomas may respond to the same treatment or it may be necessary to open them and remove the blood. In some of the large hematomas if the blood is not removed it may become infected and an abscess develops. After the blood is removed apply tincture of iodine to the lining of the cavity.

SITFAST. The separation of the dead and healthy tissue may be stimulated by the application of hot packs. As a general rule the sitfasts occurring in the saddle bed have a small diameter at their base and extend only through the skin. The sitfast may be dissected out of the tissues and the area treated as an open wound by the application of mild antiseptic powders. The most efficient method is to prepare the area in the usual manner for performing an aseptic operation. Anesthesia for the operation may be obtained by infiltrating the tissues with a local anesthetic. Two elliptical incisions are made so as to remove all of the sitfast. The edges of the skin are sutured together with closely placed interrupted sutures using fine suture material. The area is then covered with flexible collodion.

Injuries or bruises of the spine should be treated with cold packs or irrigation with cold water but the area should not be massaged.

Thoracentesis

This procedure consists in inserting a hollow needle or trocar into the pleural cavity. It is performed with the object of removing an excessive quantity of fluid from the pleural cavity or for diagnostic purposes.

In the horse it may be performed on the left side at the 8th intercostal space just above the vein and close to the anterior border of the rib. On the right side, it is performed at the 7th intercostal space. The area should be shaved and an efficient skin antiseptic applied. Push the skin upwards so the puncture thru the skin and muscle will not communicate directly. Slowly push the instrument thru the tissues until the resistance ceases and hold it still with the fingers. When the fluid stops flowing freely one end of a piece of rubber tubing should be attached to the instrument and the other end should be inserted below the surface of a liquid. This is to prevent the aspiration of air into the pleural cavity. After the instrument is removed the opening in the skin should be covered with flexible collodion.

Resection of the Fifth Rib

The resection of the fifth rib is performed to provide access to the pericardial sac. In traumatic pericarditis the pericardial sac is usually distended with a variable quantity of a purulent exudate, in some cases one or more liters, that should be removed. The mortality is high in traumatic pericarditis due to the unfavorable pathological changes that have usually occurred in some of the vital tissues. There is an occasional case that will recover without the operation. The operation may be performed for the owner who requests the operation in an effort to save the patient.

OPERATION. The location of the fifth rib may be determined by counting nine ribs forward from the last rib. Operation to provide access to the thoracic cavity requires the removal of a four or five inch portion of the distal end of the fifth rib. The operative area five inches wide and extending upward from the distal end of the rib for eight inches is prepared for the operation. Anesthesia for the operation is obtained by infiltration of the skin and subcutaneous over the section of rib to be removed. Also the tissue on the anterior and posterior edges of the portion of rib

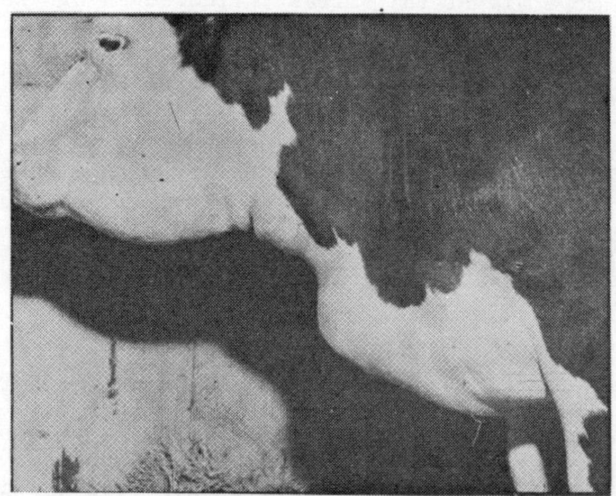

FIG. 308. Advanced case of traumatic pericarditis, note extensive edema of brisket, neck and tissues ventral to mandibular space, patient died two hours after picture was taken.

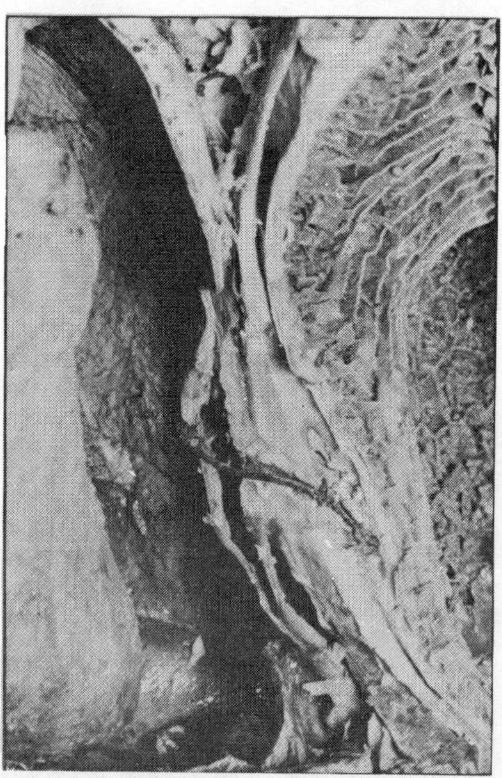

FIG. 309. A case of traumatic pericarditis showing the wire in position in the reticulum, diaphragm and pericardial sac. Courtesy Dr. W. M. McLeod.

to be removed are infiltrated and the medial surface.

An incision is made in the skin over the rib from a point about one inch below the costo-chondral articulation upward for a distance of six inches. Then carefully dissect the soft tissues from the surface of the rib and the anterior and posterior edge. Injury to the blood vessels which are in close contact with the posterior edge of the rib may be avoided by careful dissection along the edge of the rib. The pleura is closely attached to the medial side of the rib and may be separated from the rib by careful blunt dissection with the fingers.

After the portion of rib to be removed is separated from the surrounding tissue, a piece of obstetrical wire saw is passed between the pleura and rib. The rib is then cut through at the upper end of the skin incision. This piece of rib is grasped and bent outward until it is disarticulated at the costo-chondral articulation. The pleura is now exposed and may be freely incised as the pleura and pericardium are usually adhered together. If no adhesions are present, a small opening is made in the pleura and the opening gradually enlarged so air will slowly enter the pleural cavity and not embarrass the functioning of the lung. The pericardial sac should be freely opened and complete drainage established. Insert the hand into the pericardial sac and search for the foreign body and remove it if possible.

The after care is the same as for any infected cavity, irrigation with antiseptic solutions and removal of all purulent exudates.

The Abdominal Wall

The ventral and much of the lateral abdominal walls are formed by muscles and fascia. The muscles are named from the direction of their fibers. Hence, we recognize external and internal oblique, transverse, and rectus (straight) abdominal muscles. Two structures concerned with the insertion of the abdominal muscles are the lina alba and prepubic tendon.

The lina alba is formed when the embryonic tissues fold inward to enclose the body cavity. It is a distinct median line extending from the sternum to the prepubic tendon. Slightly behind its middle is the umbilicus. When the lina alba was formed, the fusion of the right and left sides was interrupted by the presence of the umbilical vessels, urachus and yolk stalk. When the cord breaks at birth the umbilicus has served its purpose and normally is closed by fibrous tissue. Occasionally its closure is more or less incomplete thus providing an avenue for umbilical hernia.

The prepubic tendon is the medium of insertion for the abdominal muscles with the exception of the transversus. It is a short, strong, rather broad structure attaching to the anterior border of the pubis and separates the medial angles of the inguinal canals. Since the abdominal muscles, particularly the rectus are important in maintaining the arch of the back, this tendon is of prime importance. Occasionally it ruptures. This rupture not only modifies the contour of the top line but interferes with the support of the abdominal viscera and the operation of the abdominal press.

The fascia is both superficial and deep. The superficial fascia is areolar in structure and more abundant than on other parts of the body. The portion of the cutaneous muscle of this region is in this fascia as well as fats in amounts varying with the condition of the animal. Superficial fascia is very abundant above and anterior to the stifle. The deep fascia is known as the abdominal tunic. It is elastic and therefore of a yellowish color, muscle in structure to accommodate changes in size of the abdomen and is said to be capable of supporting the weight of the viscera without the aid of the abdominal muscles. Since its chief function is support, it is confined to the ventral and adjacent part of the lateral wall. It does not extend into the upper part of the flank. It is attached to the ribs with the origin of the external oblique, crosses the belly of this muscle and fuses to its aponeuroses and joins its fellow at the linae alba. The ligamentum suspensorium of the mammary glands and much of the septum scroti are derived from the tunic. In addition to support, the abdominal tunic has a passive, but very definite function in normal expiration.

The external oblique is the most extensive of the abdominal muscles. Its fibers are directed downward and backward and are rather short, about 8 to 10 inches. The extensive aponeurosis attaches to the prepubic tendon and linae alba. The portion attaching to the prepubic tendon lies against the medial side of the flank and forms the posterior wall of the inguinal canal. This part is the inguinal or Poupart's ligament. The external inquinal ring is a slit in the aponeurosis extending outward, parallel and close to the thigh. The medial angle is at the border of the prepubic tendon, is very definite and is subcutaneous.

The internal oblique arises from the tuber coxae and is directed downward and forward to the last rib and linae alba. It forms the second muscular layer in the flank where its fibers are at a right angle to those of the external oblique. A portion extends medially and downward to the prepubic tendon and abdominal floor forming the anterior wall of the inguinal canal and the anterior margin of the internal ring. The inguinal canal is between the posterior parts of the oblique muscles. The extensive aponeurosis fuses with that of the external oblique to form the aponeurotic layer of the abdominal floor.

The transversus is a thin muscle forming the third muscular layer of the flank. In this region its fibers are vertical. In the abdominal floor the fleshy part is succeeded by an aponeurosis which crosses the rectus to reach the linae alba. The rectus abdominis extends from the sternum to the prepubic tendon and is, therefore, entirely on the abdominal floor. It is the strongest of the abdominal muscles and is of prime importance in maintaining the arch of the back as well as supporting the viscera. It is firmly attached to the combined aponeurosises of the oblique muscles by seven to nine transverse inscriptiones tindinae.

In incisions through the abdominal floor lateral to the linae alba one encounters in succession the skin and superficial fascia, a connective tissue layer formed by the abdominal tunic and combined aponeurosises of the oblique muscles, the rectus abdominus and the aponeurosis of the transversus. The amount of fat between the transverse muscle and peritoneum depends upon the condition of the animal.

The Peritoneal Cavity

The peritoneum consists of the visceral peritoneum which covers the intestines, liver and other abdominal organs. That portion of the peritoneum which is continued onto the inside of the abdominal wall is called the parietal peritoneum. While the peritoneal cavity if only a potential space it may become distended with a variable quantity of fluid (ascites).

PHYSIOLOGY OF THE PERITONEUM. The peritoneum is a smooth membrane covered with endothelium and lubricated with a small amount of fluid that facilitates the movement of the intestine. In the deeper layers of the peritoneum is a very rich network of blood vessels and lymphatic spaces. The peritoneum will absorb very readily hypotonic and isotonic fluids as well as microscopic foreign bodies. Most of the absorption occurs by means of the capillaries of the portal system and also the lymphatics. It has never been definitely determined which system is the most important in the protection mechanism.

The peritoneum is very resistant to infection so when bacteria come in contact with it they are rapidly destroyed. Probably the most important factor in the destruction of infection is phagocytosis by polymorphonuclear leucocytes. It is well known that the peritoneum is more resistant to infection than other tissues. This is demonstrated by the development of a severe infection in the tissues as a result of contamination during an operation but infection does not develop in the peritoneal cavity. However if peritonitis does develop it is a very serious infection and may result in a high mortality. When this occurs it is usually the result of a very virulent organism or a continued contamination. In human surgery it has been observed that there is less tendency for peritonitis to develop when there have been a number of operations on the intestine. The peritoneum seems to be able to develop an immunity to infection. If an infection does develop in the peritoneum only the increase in intestinal movement seems to interfere with the normal protective mechanism of the peritoneum against infection.

The omentum is a very important part of the protective mechanism of the abdominal cavity. It seems to have the ability to locate and localize an infection thus preventing a diffuse peritonitis. The omentum is frequently referred to as the "policeman" of the abdominal cavity because of its ability to envelop and localize an area of infection.

Etiologic Factors in Peritonitis

When inflammation of the peritoneum occurs it may be due to trauma, infection or chemicals but that due to infection is the most serious. If peritonitis due to infection becomes generalized it is very serious and the mortality is rather high. When the infection is localized and becomes isolated by the formation of adhesions there is little general reaction and a low mortality. However if the infection is highly virulent death may occur from absorption of toxins. While the peritoneum is very resistant to infection it does not resist continuous infection as may occur when the intestine is perforated. In these cases the peritonitis becomes generalized and is usually fatal. When toxemia develops along with peritonitis it is usually thought that various strains of gas bacilli are responsible for the infection.

Peritonitis may result from a number of different etiologic factors some of which are listed below.

1. Peritonitis may develop as a complication following a laparotomy and due to contamination of the peritoneum.

   Some of the factors responsible for the development of peritonitis may be leakage from the digestive tract or the uterus depending upon the tissue operated on, or source of infection.

2. Puerperal infection, the infection may pass through the uterine wall resulting in a generalized fatal peritonitis.

3. Peritonitis due to trauma frequently occurs from a foreign body puncturing through the wall of the reticulum. When the wall of the reticulum is perforated it permits bacteria and food material to contaminate the peritoneum. This contamination may produce either a localized or generalized peritonitis.

4. Rupture of the bladder may occur when the urethra is occluded with a urethral calculus. The peritonitis that occurs may be due to chemical irritation and also secondary infection.

Laparotomy

This operation may be performed for examining the peritoneal or abdominal cavity for diagnostic purposes. It is also used in ovariectomies, reduction of torsion of the uterus or intestines, intussusception of the intestine, and traumatic gastritis. Also for Cesarean section, rumenotomies, removal of neoplasms and rarely for extirpation of a kidney.

The operation may be performed in either the right or left flank and preferably in the standing position. It is usually possible to operate by infiltrating the operative area with a local anesthetic but in addition some individuals may require a sedative. The amount of sedatives used will depend upon the size and disposition of the patient and it may be administered either intravenously or into the stomach.

In most cases the operative area is between the last rib and the external angle of the ilium. This area should be thoroughly prepared for an aseptic operation. The skin and underlying tissues may be infiltrated with a local anesthetic.

The incision in the skin may be started just below the transverse processes of the lumbar vertebrae and its length will depend upon the purpose of the operation. It may vary from six inches long for exploratory purposes to one fifteen or eighteen inches long for Cesarean section. The same scalpel that is used for the skin incision should not be used to divide the deeper tissues as it is usually contaminated by bacteria in the skin. Division of the external and internal oblique muscles may be made in the direction of their fibers but in most cases it is best to incise the muscles and peritoneum in the same direction as the skin incision.

After the operation is performed the laparotomy wound may be closed in the following manner. The peritoneum may be sutured separately with a continuous suture of catgut or linen. The muscles may be sutured with No. 2 or 3, 20 day chronic catgut using a continuous suture. All sutures must be closely placed so the edges of the muscles are in close apposition thus preventing the formation of air pockets. The sutures should be so placed that they grasp more of the fascia than muscle tissue. Fascia will withstand suture tension while muscle tissue has a tendency to develop suture necrosis. The skin incision may be closed with mattress or interrupted sutures of silk, linen, umbilical tape, or other suture material. The skin incision and sutures should be covered with flexible collodion. All the skin sutures may be removed in ten days to two weeks.

Rumenotomy

This operation is performed in suspected cases of traumatic gastritis, impaction of the rumen and ingestion of the fetal membranes with the development of toxic symptoms.

TECHNIQUE OF OPERATION. It is preferred to have the patient in the standing position but it may be performed in the recumbent position. The laparotomy incision should be six to seven inches long and performed as described for the laparotomy operation.

When the rumen is exposed an umbilical tape suture about one foot long is inserted through the wall of the rumen at the upper end of the incision and the ends tied. Another suture of the same type is inserted through the rumen about two inches anterior to the first one. Two similar sutures are placed in the rumen at the ventral commissure of the skin incision. Traction on these sutures will bring the wall of the rumen out through the laparotomy incision. A vertical incision is made through the wall of the rumen halfway between the anterior and posterior sutures and approximately six inches long.

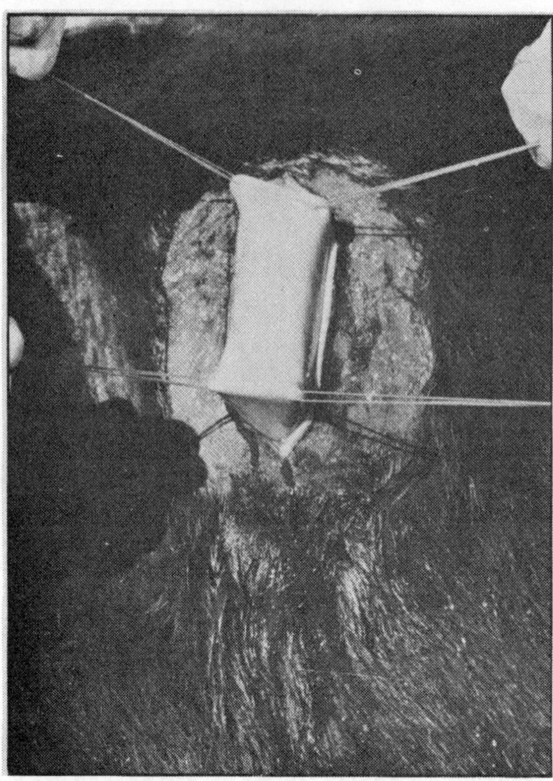

FIG. 310. The stay sutures are holding the wall of the rumen so it can be opened with a vertical incision.

A metal embroidery hoop six inches in diameter fastened in the middle of a yard square of a rubber sheet or other impervious material, is passed through the opening in the rumen. The hoop is turned in a vertical direction into the rumen and then turned so the rumen contents may be removed through the lumen of the hoop. The sheet protects the edges of the incision from contamination by the rumen contents as they are removed.

However, when the contents of the rumen are characterized by a mixing of the gas throughout the food content of the rumen, a different procedure is employed. In these cases when the laparotomy incision is completed the wall of the rumen is sutured to the edges of the skin before it is opened. If this method is not used, prevention of contamination of the edges of the incision is practically impossible.

A careful examination should be made of the interior of the reticulum for the detection and removal of any foreign bodies present. If the operation was performed because of the ingestion of fetal membranes these should be removed. The rubber sheet is now removed. The edges of the incision in the rumen and abdominal wall are thoroughly cleansed of any blood or food material. The incision in the rumen is closed with two rows of continuous Lembert sutures, using No. 2, 20 day chronic catgut, the second row burying the first row. As the second row of sutures are placed the stay sutures in the rumen are removed and that portion of the rumen wall is included in the sutures. The rumen is now released. The laparotomy incision is sutured as described in the laparotomy operation.

FIG. 311. The rubber sheet is in position protecting the edges of the incision.

Traumatic Gastritis

Traumatic Reticulitis

The ingestion of metallic foreign objects occurs frequently in the bovine and most of them eventually reach the reticulum. These objects vary in size and sharpness and consist usually of baling wire various lengths, nails, bolts, nuts and pieces of tin are most frequently removed from the reticulum. Occasionally a bovine is operated that has chewed tin cans into small pieces and in one case two pounds were removed from the reticulum. When the foreign body has a sharp end it can easily penetrate the wall of the reticulum. The end may be caught in the honey-combed arrangement of the mucous membrane and due to the muscular activity of the organ it penetrates into and sometimes through the wall of the reticulum. As soon as the object penetrates the wall there is an immediate disturbance in the functioning of the digestive tract. There may be almost complete loss of motility of the rumen. When this occurs and the rumen is full of food the examiner may diagnose impaction of the rumen and fail to examine further for the presence of a foreign body. Also if the rumen contains food that forms gas readily it quickly becomes distended with gas. Again due to loss of motility of the rumen and reticulum eructation does not occur and there is an accumulation of gas. The examiner may make a diagnosis of tympany of the rumen and does not complete the examination to determine if a foreign body is penetrating the tissues.

The signs will vary in different individuals, and for this reason a thorough examination of the patient should be made to eliminate the presence of a foreign body. If the foreign body is not removed there are usually repeated attacks of complete or partial loss of appetite, reduced milk flow and a marked loss in condition. There may be a pronounced stiffness of gait with a reluctance to move, and they may grunt or groan when walking. Some patients will be restless, first lying down and stretching out, then getting up as if seeking relief from pain. There is frequently an increase in the rapidity of the respirations and the pulse rate may vary from normal to 125 per minute. If the jugular veins are distended and tense it is an indication the blood is having difficulty returning to the heart. When this sign is present the foreign body has penetrated the pericardial sac. Rumen motility may or may not be present.

DIAGNOSIS. The correct diagnosis of an early case of traumatic gastritis is frequently very difficult as the signs will vary with different cases. In traumatic gastritis the mortality is very high when compared with other diseases of the bovine and this may be due to the failure to make a correct diagnosis when the condition is still favorable for a successful operation. Those conditions that produce similar signs should be eliminated before making a diagnosis of traumatic gastritis. Some conditions that may produce similar signs are metritis, pylonephritis, enteritis, acetonemia, lymphocytoma, and traumatic pericarditis.

The patient may show pain when pressure is exerted upward in the area of the xiphoid cartilage. A metal detector may be used in the examination of the patient to determine if metal is present in the reticulum. However the metal detector does not indicate if the foreign body is penetrating the tissues. If the foreign body is a non-magnetic metal the metal detector would not indicate its presence.

When signs are suggestive of traumatic gastritis a complete blood count is a valuable aid in the diagnosis. If the patient has been treated with antibiotics or sulfonamides the differential leucocyte count will not be accurate. The following blood counts are typical of those found in cases of traumatic gastritis and in which foreign bodies were penetrating the wall of of the reticulum.

R.B.C.	W.B.C.	Juvenile	Stab	Segments	Atypical Lymphocyte	Large Lym.	Small Lymphocyte
5, 500, 000	22, 250	23	18	25	11	6	13
6, 000, 000	10, 550	7	35	18		11	29
3, 330, 000	17, 300	5	50	25	4	6	10

There will be cases in which the blood count is almost normal but the signs are so typical of traumatic gastritis, it is indicated to perform an operation.

In ten cases of experimental bovine traumatic gastritis Kingrey found there is an increase in the total leucocyte count with the onset of signs. The percentage of non-segmented neutrophils increased in general in direct proportion to the total white cell count and to the percentage of segmented neutrophils. He considered from these findings the change in the blood count is consistent and should be considered significant in those cases suspected of being affected with traumatic gastritis.

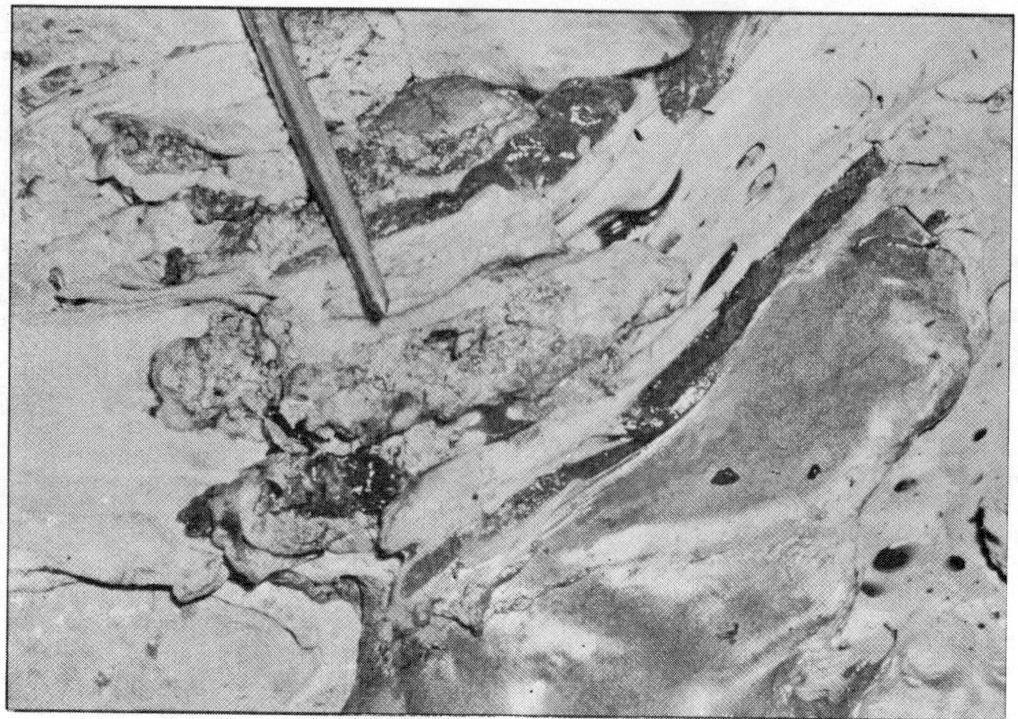

FIG. 312. Thrombus in the posterior vena cava.

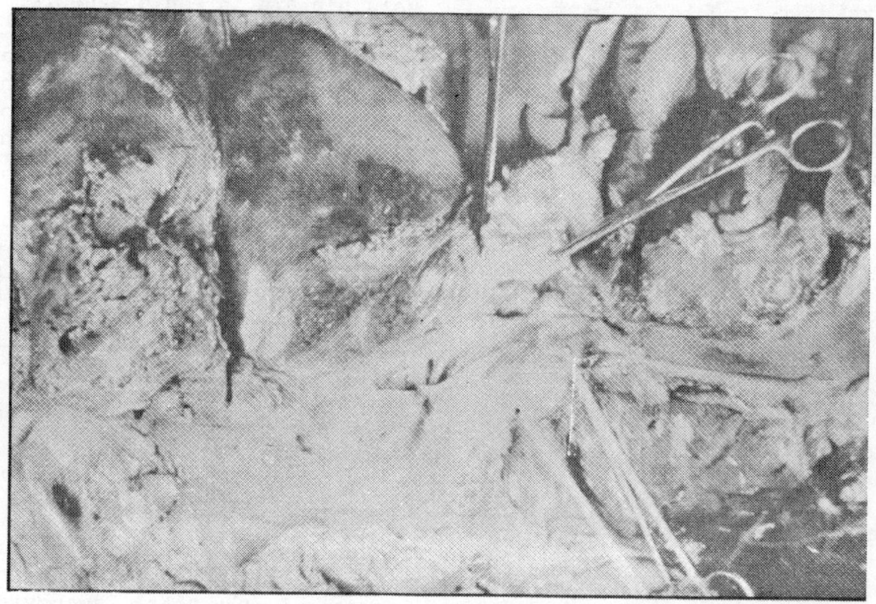

FIG. 313. Stricture of the posterior vena cava.

Dougherty in experimentally induced cases of traumatic gastritis found there was a distinct neutrophilic leukocytosis with band cells predominating. The shift to the left began as soon as four hours after the penetration and usually lasted two to three days and then the blood count gradually returned to normal. He also states that the total and differential white counts can be made very easily and are extremely valuable in making the correct diagnosis.

In a report on five hundred cases Carroll and Robinson found the differential leukocyte count to be of definite value in making a diagnosis of traumatic gastritis. When the differential blood count shows a definite shift to the left it is of definite value. The value of the blood count was determined as rumenotomies were performed on all of the cases. Occasionally a patient will have a good appetite but is gradually losing weight and a foreign body is present in the wall of the reticulum. Some cases become chronic and there is a history of repeated attacks of indigestion with signs suggestive of traumatic gastritis. The operator should give a guarded prognosis in these cases if the owner wants an operation. However many of these cases make a good recovery as the foreign body may be encapsulated in the wall of the reticulum. When the foreign body is loose in the reticulum it may cause trouble by repeatedly penetrating into its wall. The foreign body may pass through several folds of the mucous membrane but has not invaded the wall of the reticulum but these cases will show the typical signs. Due to the difficulty of making an accurate diagnosis in many of the cases an operation may be indicated to definitely eliminate the presence or absence of a foreign body.

The use of magnets in an attempt to prevent a foreign body from penetrating the wall of the reticulum seems to have value. One method in use is to introduce a magnet, a two and one-half by one inch cylinder, into the reticulum by way of the mouth. When some of the magnets were removed six months later a number of pieces of metal were adherent to the magnet. There were no pieces of metal free of the magnet in the reticulum. Another method of using a magnet has been to introduce a magnetic retriever into the reticulum through the mouth. It is recommended that all bulky food should be withheld for twelve to eighteen hours before passing the magnet. The magnet attached to a non-magnetic chain is passed through a stomach tube. When the magnet reaches the reticulum it is left there for approximately one minute. Before removing the magnet it is moved around by twisting the stomach tube. The magnet is pulled to the end of the stomach tube. Then the stomach tube, chain and magnet are brought to the outside. This apparatus was successful in removing seventy per cent of the foreign bodies in the reticulum. After the foreign body has penetrated the tissues it is questionable if the magnet is of any value in removing it or stopping its further progress.

TREATMENT. A rumenotomy is the treatment of choice when the examination indicates there is a foreign body. When so many incurable and fatal conditions develop as a result of foreign bodies in the tissues they should be removed. Of the many conditions that may develop the foreign body may penetrate the wall of the reticulum with adhesions developing between it and the diaphragm producing a localized peritonitis. In some cases the peritonitis becomes generalized with very extensive adhesions developing between all of the organs in the abdominal cavity.

The foreign body may penetrate the liver permitting infection to gain entrance into the tissues with the formation of one or more abscesses. When the abscess is in contact with the posterior vena cava it may cause an erosion of its wall and penetrates through the wall into the lumen. The inflammatory reaction that occurs in the tissues stimulates the formation of a thrombus. The thrombus which is composed of fibrin may become so extensive that it occludes the lumen of the posterior vena cava. When the blood is unable to pass through the posterior vena cava it is responsible for congestion of the blood in the liver. In some cases the abscess does not cause an erosion of the wall of the posterior vena cava but stimulates the formation of fibrous tissue. The formation of fibrous tissue may become so extensive that stricture of the posterior vena cava is produced with closure of the lumen.

When the foreign body is directed anteriorly and penetrates the wall of the reticulum an abscess may develop between the reticulum and diaphragm. The abscess may be small or contain a large quantity of purulent material. If the foreign body penetrates through the diaphragm an abscess may develop in the thoracic cavity. These abscesses seem to contain very toxic material and the absorption of the toxins is responsible for a severe reaction in the animal. When the foreign body penetrates the diaphragm it provides a way for infection to gain entrance into its tissues. An abscess may develop in the diaphragm so that a weakness or opening is developed in the tissues. The opening in the diaphragm may be large enough to permit all or a portion of the reticulum to pass into the thoracic cavity. Due to the inflammatory reaction in the tissues extensive adhesions develop between the reticulum and surrounding tissues including the lungs.

When a foreign body is a piece of wire it may pass through the side of the reticulum and the wall of the thoracic cavity. When this occurs a swelling is observed in the subcutaneous tissue immediately posterior to the point of the elbow. Examination of the subcutaneous tissue through a skin incision will reveal a wire. If a rumenotomy is performed an adhesion about two inches in diameter is found between the reticulum and thoracic wall where the wire passed through the tissues. Owners will occasionally report finding the end of a wire that has penetrated through the skin. When it is removed it will be a piece of baling wire four or five inches long. In removing retained fetal membranes Erichsson found a wire that had passed through the wall of the uterus.

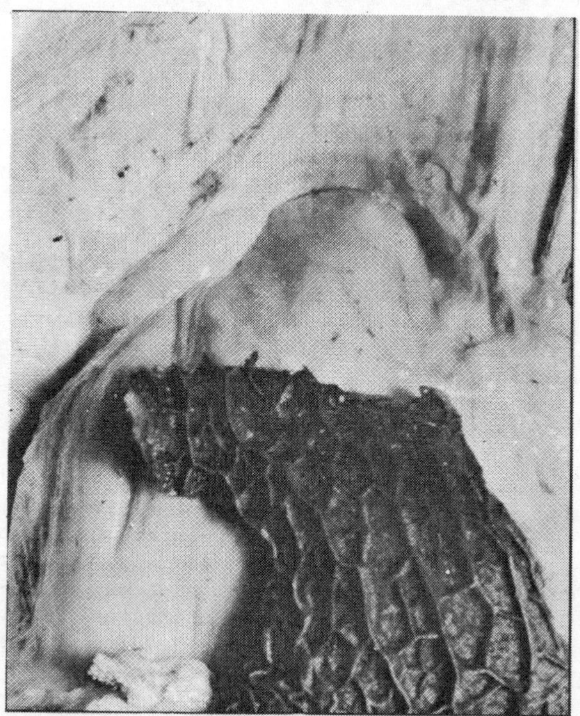

FIG. 314. Approximately one-half of the reticulum has passed into the thoracic cavity.

In the examination of the reticulum for a foreign body it is important to remember the arrangement of the mucous membrane. The mucous membrane is raised into folds which forms cells and are responsible for the honey-comb appearance of the reticulum. Each of these cells or spaces must be examined for the nail or wire as only the end may still be in the reticulum. If the foreign body is penetrating through the ventral surface of the reticulum it may be covered over with sand or other material of that nature. This sand must be removed or the operator may fail to find the foreign body. In one case a shingle nail had penetrated the ventral surface of the reticulum to the head and this was covered with sand. During the examination of the reticulum a magnet may be carried in with the hand. This magnet will attract pieces of metal that would be difficult or time consuming to pick up with the fingers.

Examination of the reticulum may not reveal a foreign body but an abscess may be palpated in the wall. In these cases a needle with a large lumen is introduced into the cavity of the abscess. A syringe is fastened to the needle and the pus is removed by suction. The size of the abscess will determine the amount of penicillin to inject into the cavity.

Treatment after the operation may not be necessary if the foreign body did penetrate through the wall of the reticulum. However if there is a marked increase in temperature, it is indicated to use sulfonamides or antibiotics to combat the infection.

Intestinal Obstruction

Intestinal obstruction is an important and serious surgical condition. When there is an interruption to the passage of intestinal contents death may occur very quickly due to the secondary changes resulting from the obstruction.

Acute intestinal obstruction is more important from a surgical standpoint than chronic intestinal obstruction. There are many kinds of obstructing agents but the following are some of those seen most frequently. Mechanical obstruction of the lumen may occur from stricture of oesophagus, adhesions, enteroliths, neoplasms and fibrous bands. Also extrinsic agents as neoplasms and abscesses may occur in any portion of the intestinal tract. When there is interference with the blood supply the lesion may be due to strangulated hernias, intussusception, torsion, mesenteric thrombosis or a loop of intestine may pass through a slit in the mesentery.

When an intestinal obstruction occurs it is characterized by occlusion of the lumen and the blood supply. One of the first effects of acute intestinal obstruction, regardless of the cause, is occlusion of the lumen. The occlusion may only be partial at first but gradually becomes complete due to the local changes that occur in the tissues. These changes are due to the vigorous attempts on the part of the bowel to force the contents through the constricted lumen. The tissues of the bowel wall become edematous so the thickened tissues gradually close the lumen.

If the distention of the intestine is not relieved but continues to increase and finally becomes great enough to occlude the blood flow. As the blood flow decreases loss of viability and necrosis of the entire wall of the intestine may occur. Thus a simple mechanical obstruction of the lumen may if neglected cause the same damage to tissue that occurs in strangulation.

In lesions such as torsion, intussusception and strangulated hernia closure of the blood vessels occurs very rapidly. Also in these cases closure of the intestinal lumen occurs several hours before the blood vessels are affected. Within a few hours after complete strangulation occurs, injury to the tissue develops very rapidly. In a short time gangrene occurs and the lumen contains many virulent bacteria. The combination of gangrenous tissue and bacterial infection produces toxic material that is rapidly absorbed. Absorption from a volvus of the intestine is very rapid but in the case of a strangulated hernia the sac is so tight the mass is walled off and there is little or no absorption.

Incarceration and strangulation of the intestine occurs frequently in hernias or occasionally by fibrous bands. The above conditions are seen most frequently in swine and occurs in both umbilical and scrotal hernias. When incarceration occurs the affected animal will stop eating and the hernia is irreducible. As the contents of the hernia become strangulated the skin of the sac becomes very tense and even cold to the touch. If a stallion shows symptoms of abdominal pain after service he should be examined for an inguinal hernia. A rectal examination will reveal if any intestines are in the internal inguinal ring. If the hernia is not reduced, in a few hours strangulation may occur.

When an incarceration of the intestine is suspected in the abdominal cavity of a bovine it is indicated to perform an exploratory laparotomy. Intussusception occurs when one portion of the intestine telescopes into the portion behind. This condition occurs most frequently in the bovine but has been observed in practically all species of animals.

Signs are those observed in abdominal pain, uneasiness, kicking at the abdomen with the hind feet and shifting the weight from one hind foot to the other. The patient is depressed, with loss of appetite and peristalsis is absent. A rectal examination may reveal a sausage shaped swelling, which is very firm, in the right side of the abdominal cavity. The rectum is usually empty of feces but contains a thick sticky mucus that may be blood stained.

Treatment consists in performing an intestinal anastomosis removing the affected portion of the intestine.

Volvulus or torsion of the intestine occurs as an acute obstruction. It may involve either the large or small intestine but the small intestine is affected in the largest percentage of cases. In torsion of the large colon there is a rotation on its longitudinal axis. With volvulus of the small intestine the torsion may affect the mesentery or one portion may be twisted around another portion of the intestine.

SIGNS. Volvulus of the intestine is characterized by almost continuous pain that may become violent at times. When the pain is severe the animal may walk continuously in a circle. In these cases there is marked depression, an anxious expression, sweating and at times maniacal movements. A dog sitting position may be observed in some cases.

In many cases it is possible to make a positive diagnosis on rectal examination for occasionally the twisted mass of small intestines may be palpated. As a general rule volvulus or torsion of the intestine is incurable.

Cesarean Section

Cesarean Section is the removal of the young from the mother through incisions in the abdominal and uterine walls. The successful performance of this operation may result in the saving of either the mother, the young, or both. Many pregnant cows have been destroyed that could have been saved by a Cesarean section. This is one of the most serious operations performed on animals and if the patient is to live, good judgement must be used in selecting the cases to be operated on. If the cases are selected with care a high percentage of the animals operated on will recover. When the mortality is high this very necessary and usually successful operation may come to be regarded with disfavor by the clients.

INDICATIONS. It is particularly indicated in the young female where the pelvic inlet is too small to admit the fetus. Also in those cases where there is a deformity of the maternal pelvis that will not permit the passage of the fetus. In many cases of fetal monsters it is much easier to perform a Cesarean section rather than an embryotomy operation. Whenever a case is presented with induration of the cervix a Cesarean section is indicated. From the results obtained in operating on cases of emphysematous fetuses, we believe a Cesarean section is the best procedure to relieve this condition. Many practitioners, Ferguson, Witt, Glenney, Curtis, Simpson, Isham, and others, have reported the excellent results and satisfaction they have obtained from Cesarean section in the bovine.

CONTRA-INDICATIONS. The operation is contra-indicated in thin, weak females but it may result in saving the fetus. When extensive and crude efforts have been made to deliver the fetus this operation should not be performed. For in many of these cases there are severe and extensive lacerations of the genital tract and virulent infections have been introduced into the tissues.

Technique of Operation

The type of anesthesia used will vary with the preference of the operator. Some operators prefer to give a basal anesthetic of either chloral hydrate or nembutal and then infiltrate the tissue along the proposed line of incision with a solution of a local anesthetic. Regional nerve blocking may be used and this procedure is also known as paravertebral lumbar anesthesia. This method consists in injecting ten cubic centimeters of a two percent solution of a local anesthetic over each of the last thoracic and first two lumbar nerves. Epidural anesthesia may be used; the amount and strength of the local anesthetic solution will vary with the size of the patient. For small heifers forty cubic centimeters of a two per cent solution of procaine hydrochloride is sufficient, while for older and larger cows it may be necessary to use fifty cubic centimeters of a two and one-half per cent solution of procaine hydrochloride.

Operative Area

The location of the operative area will vary with the preference of the operator and the individual case. Probably in the largest percentage of cases the operation is performed in the flank regions. The incision, usually twelve to eighteen inches long, is made through the skin, muscles, and peritoneum. Gotze, of Germany, performs the operation through an incision on the ventral surface of the abdominal cavity three inches lateral to the left subcutaneous abdominal vein. We prefer to make the incision on the right side of the median line and half way between it and the subcutaneous abdominal vein.

On the right side of the median line an area ten inches wide is shaved from the udder forward as far as the umbilicus. The skin is prepared for an aseptic operation.

A skin incision approximately twelve inche long is made half way between the median line and the subcutaneous abdominal vein. It usually extends from the udder as far forward as the umbilicus. The posterior portion of the body is now rotated so it is in dorsal recumbency. Sterile rubber gloves are put on, and the operative area is covered with a sterile shroud. The incision through the aponeurosis of the oblique abdominal muscles and peritoneum corresponds to the skin incision. It can be made with a scalpel or scissors, preferably with scissors. When the peritoneal cavity is opened the omentum is usually found covering the uterus. By grasping its posterior edge the omentum can be pulled forward and this exposes the uterus. One hand is introduced into the peritoneal cavity to locate the end of the pregnant horn and bring it through the incision. The horn should completely fill the opening to prevent the prolapse of any intestine. The posterior portion of the cow is now returned to lateral recumbency.

The incision through the wall of the uterus should be made so that none of the cotyledons will be injured. Their location

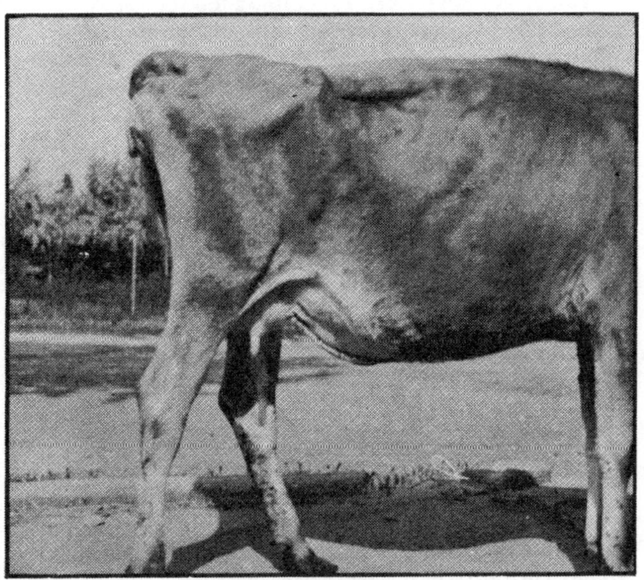

FIG. 315. The location of the wound when the incision is made on the right side of the median line.

can usually be determined by palpation of the uterine wall.

To prevent laceration of the uterine wall the incision should be large enough to permit passage of the fetus. After the fetus is removed the placenta should also be removed if it is not too tightly attached. If the placenta is removed at this time the uterine involution occurs very rapidly. The exposed portion of the uterus should be moistened and cleansed with sterile physiological saline solution.

The incision in the uterus is closed with two rows of continuous Lembert sutures. We prefer to use No. 1, 20 day chromic catgut with atraumatic needle for suturing of the uterus. The exposed portion of the uterus is again moistened with sterile physiological solution before it is returned to the abdominal cavity. The incision through the aponeurosis and peritoneum is closed with one continuous suture using one strand of umbilical tape to bring the edges of the incision in close apposition.

The after care of the patient is an important part of the operative procedure. Immediately after the operation 500 cubic centimeters of a 25 per cent solution of dextrose is given intravenously. It is also important to assist the patient to assume the normal position of sternal recumbency.

If the uterine muscles are atonic and they seem to need stimulation ten cubic centimeters of pituitary extract within twenty-four hours is used. This is usually administered into the epidural space. By experimental work Benesch found that for five days following parturition if pituitary extract is given epidurally it produces a stronger, longer, and more continuous action. If the placenta is not expelled in forty-eight to seventy-two hours attempts should be made to remove it. If there is any infection in the uterus various antiseptics may be placed in the uterus. This treatment may be repeated every twenty-four or forty-eight hours or whenever it seems to be indicated. The skin sutures should be removed in ten to fourteen days.

Cesarean Section in the Sow

This operation is frequently indicated in the sow but too often the owner has permitted her to labor too long. As a result the pigs are dead and the sow is suffering from toxemia. In many cases attempts have been made to remove the fetuses without regard to asepsis and frequently the genital tract is also lacerated.

The operation is indicated most frequently in gilts that are small and fat. In some cases there may be some abnormal condition present in the genital tract that prevents normal delivery. A higher percentage of recoveries will occur when the operation is performed within a few hours after the onset of labor. It is usually not advisable to operate if the sow has been laboring more than twenty-four hours. However, there may be a small percentage of recoveries when the operation is performed seventy-two hours after the onset of labor.

The patient should be confined on the operating table in lateral recumbency preferably with the right side upper most. If it is necessary to operate at the farm the sow can be roped in a standing position to a gate. The gate with the sow attached is turned sideways and placed on supports that will provide a convenient height for the operator.

OPERATION. Prepare the region in the right flank by shaving and preparing the skin for an aseptic operation.

The type of anesthesia used will depend upon the condition of the patient and the preference of the operator. In gilts epidural anesthesia is easily administered and provides complete anesthesia of the abdominal cavity. For a 225 pound gilt, 20 cubic centimeters of a two per cent solution of procaine hydrochloride is usually sufficient. If this type of anesthesia is used the patient's body should be kept level so the anesthetic solution will not gravitate too far forward and affect some of the vital centers.

If the sow is suffering from toxemia only a local anesthetic should be used. Anesthesia of the operative area is obtained by infiltrating the skin, muscle tissue and peritoneum, along the proposed line of incision with one and one-half per cent solution of a local anesthetic. A general anesthetic like ether that produces its effect quickly and the patient also recovers quickly from its effects may be used. Also ten cubic centimeters of nembutal may be given intravenously together with local infiltration of the tissues with a local anesthetic.

A vertical incision is made in the skin starting just below the transverse processes of the lumbar vertebrae and halfway between the last rib and external angle of the ilium. The incision should be liberal extending downward a distance of six to eight inches. A sterile rubber sheet is placed over the operative area with an opening in it corresponding to the skin incision. The muscles and peritoneum may be divided with an incision corresponding to the skin incision or the muscles may be divided in the direction of their fibers. In some cases it is well to remove the fat overlying the peritoneum. The peritoneum can then be opened with a vertical incision.

A sterile square of muslin is now placed over the rubber sheet and an opening made corresponding to the skin incision. Introduce one hand into the peritoneal cavity and locate the end of the horn and bring it to the outside. Each fetus is grasped separately and assisted through the incision until all the horn that contains fetuses is on the outside. An incision large enough to permit the easy removal of the fetus is made on the dorsal surface of the horn. The incision may be made over the posterior fetus or it may start at the bifurcation of the horn. In some unusual cases it may be necessary to make an incision over each fetus. The fetuses are carefully forced along the uterus back to the incision. The fetuses should be kept rather close together as they are moved along, so the uterus cannot contract too rapidly at one portion and prevent the backward movement of the remaining fetuses. If the fetal membranes are easily detached they are removed, otherwise they are left in the uterus to pass out later. The horn is now sponged lightly with a mild antiseptic solution and all of the horn is returned to the abdominal cavity except the portion containing the incision to be sutured. The other horn is brought to the outside and the fetuses removed in the same manner as described for the preceding horn. The portions of the uterus that are retained on the outside should be kept moist with warm physiological saline solution. Each incision in the uterus is closed with a double row of continuous Lembert sutures. If there is evidence of infection in the uterus it is advisable to inject a pint of liquid Bipp into each horn before closing the incisions. The remainder of the uterus is returned to the abdominal cavity and the laparotomy wound sutured. The incision in the peritoneum and transverse muscle can be closed with one continuous suture of catgut. Also the muscle incisions can be closed in the same manner. The edges of the skin incision are approximated with interrupted sutures of tape. Flexible collodion is applied over the skin sutures to keep the area from becoming contaminated. If infection was present in the uterus, or if the uterine muscles are atonic, one to three centimeters of pituitrin should be injected intramuscularly to stimulate a more rapid involution of the uterus and the elimination of any purulent exudate.

Hysterectomy

When an operator plans to do a Cesarean section, but examination of the uterus shows that it will not be successful, removal of the uterus may save the life of the animal. If the examination reveals the fetuses are dead, decomposed, and infection of the uterus has occurred, a Cesarean section is contra-indicated. However, removal of the uterus is not without danger due to the volume of tissue that is removed with its engorged blood vessels and also the already weakened condition of the patient.

If amputation of the uterus is indicated the uterine and ovarian arteries are ligated and the broad ligament may be divided by tearing with the fingers. The body of the uterus may be divided posterior to the bifurcation and the stump inverted into the vagina. The incision through the abdominal wall is closed in the usual manner

Hernias

A hernia is formed by the passage of some of the abdominal organs through a natural or artificial opening in the abdominal wall to form a swelling covered by skin and usually peritoneum.

The essential constituents of a hernia are: (1) The ring, (2) The sac which is composed of skin, subcutaneous tissue and peritoneum, (3) The contents which may consist of a loop of intestine called enterocele, omentum called epiplocele, stomach, gastrocele, uterus, metrocele.

The opening or ring may be formed by the umbilical opening, the inguinal ring or inguinal canal or it may be due to a rupture of the abdominal wall resulting in a ventral hernia. There may be a protrusion from the abdomen not covered by peritoneum or skin which is known as evisceration.

According to their location hernias may be classified as (1) umbilical hernia (omphalocele), (2) inguinal hernia (bubonocele), (3) scrotal hernia (oscheocele), (4) ventral hernia, (5) perineal hernia, (6) diaphrammatic hernia.

Reducible hernia is one in which the contents can be easily returned to the abdominal cavity.

Irreducible hernia is one in which the contents cannot be easily replaced in the abdominal cavity. This may be due to adhesions between the contents and the peritoreal portion of the sac. Also incarceration of the contents may occur when they become too voluminous to pass through the ring. The incarcerated hernia may become strangulated when sufficient pressure is exerted by the ring to reduce circulation to the contents. If this condition persists for a sufficient period of time there is gangrene of the affected tissue.

ETIOLOGY. Hernias especially umbilical and inguinal may be congenital or may appear shortly after birth. Imperfect closure of the umbilical opening may occur as a result of infection of the umbilical cord. Abscesses frequently weaken the tissues of the abdominal wall so that hernias develop. Traumatisms to the abdominal wall are the most frequent cause of ventral hernias.

PROGNOSIS. In most cases it is favorable and many umbilical and inguinal or scrotal hernias that are present at birth or shortly afterward disappear before the animal is one year of age. If the hernial ring is unusually large or the edges of the ring very thin the prognosis is guarded or unfavorable. Differentiation must be made between other swellings or enlargements that occur on the abdominal wall. To determine definitely the nature of the contents it may be necessary to make an exploratory puncture as the swelling may be an abscess, hematoma, neoplasm or hernia.

Umbilical Hernia

This type of hernia occurs most frequently in colts and pigs and sometimes in other species. The umbilical hernia may be present at birth or appear in a few days or weeks. In colts it is best to wait until they are about one year old before treatment. It has been observed that congenital umbilical hernia in calves frequently disappear in a few months after birth. However if the hernia has a tendency to become progressively larger or incarceration occurs it is advisable to operate as soon as possible.

When the hernia is definitely reducible, the edges of the ring firm and the ring is not more than three inches in diameter the

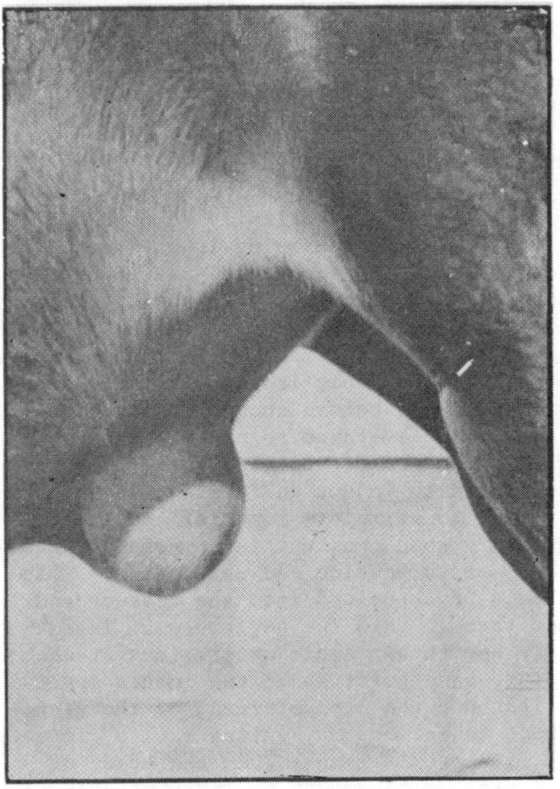

FIG. 316. A reducible umbilical hernia in a yearling colt.

hernial clamp may be used. It is easy to apply on colts and the results are uniformly successful.

OPERATION. The use of an anesthetic is not necessary as there is practically no pain inflicted during the application of the clamp. However, in particularly vigorous individuals it is advisable to give a sedative dose of chloral hydrate. This dose will usually vary from one-half to one and one-half ounces administered either intravenously or into the stomach and is sufficient to control the struggling. Also other methods of sedation may be used. The colt is then cast in the dorsal position as for the castration operation. The area around the base of the sac where the clamp is to be applied should be shaved and a skin antiseptic applied to the area.

Palpate the sac carefully to make sure the contents can be completely reduced and the peritoneal portion of the sac remains with the skin. The metal clamp is opened just enough so it will slip over the fundus of the sac. A pair of forceps are fastened to the end of the sac to assist in exerting traction on the sac. The clamp is now pushed toward the hernial ring and at the same time exerting traction on the forceps to pull the sac through the clamp. The progress of the clamp is facilitated by sliding it backward and forward as it is pushed toward the ring. When as much of the sac as possible is pulled through the clamp and the clamp is pressed firmly against the ring the screws are tightened. By putting the clamp on the sac in this manner there is practically no possibility of any contents remaining in the sac. The screws should be tightened just enough so the clamp is held firmly in position. If the clamp is properly adjusted the sac with the clamp should come away in ten to twelve days. If the clamp is too tight the sac will come off before enough inflammatory tissue has developed to close the ring. When the edges of the ring feel thin it is advisable to inject an irritant into the tissues to stimulate more inflammation. One very good irritant is composed of equal parts of turpentine and chloroform. This should be deposited into the tissues and not through into the peritoneum. Inject only one to two cubic centimeters at each point, each point about two inches apart all around the circumference of the ring. These injections may extend back a distance of five or six inches from the edges of the ring. The amount of irritant used will vary from fifteen to thirty cubic centimeters. The patient is now released and after it is on its feet straps or tapes fastened to the clamp are adjusted around the body to support the weight of the clamp. It is advisable to administer a prophylactic dose of tetanus antitoxin. If the patient is a mule it is advisable to adjust a jockey stick so they are unable to reach the area with their teeth. The patient should now be tied up until the clamp comes off.

Some operators prefer to ligate the sac after the clamp is adjusted and then remove the clamp. One method is to thread two straight needles on a double strand of umbilical tape which has been sterilized and one method that can be used is to dip it into tincture of iodine. Start suturing along the edge of the clamp furthest from the body. The needles are inserted through the same opening from opposite sides of the sac and each stitch is about one-half inch long. Each stitch as it is finished is pulled very tight and this procedure is repeated until the base of the sac is sutured. The clamp can now be removed the sac allowed to slough off from the tension of the sutures. This method of operating must be performed aseptically as it would be easy to infect the peritoneum.

Another method of inserting the sutures recommended by Fowler is as follows: Only one straight four inch needle is required and it should be threaded with about two and one-half feet of heavy suture material as No. 16 silk suture. The suture is started after the clamp is placed in position as described above. Starting at the posterior end of the clamp the needle is passed through the sac and about two-thirds of the suture material should be drawn through after the needle. The free end of the suture material is tied to the other portion. The needle is again passed through the sac about one-fourth inch below and one-fourth inch behind the first needle hole. The needle is brought forward about three-fourths of an inch and again tied tightly. Again the needle is passed through the sac one-fourth inch below and one-fourth behind the preceding needle hole. After which the needle is passed through the sac three-fourths of an inch further forward and another knot tied. This type of suturing is continued across the base of the sac. The clamp can now be removed and the sac together with the suture should drop off in about ten days.

Radical Operation

This type of operation is used on colts when the operator is not sure the contents are reducible. Also when the ring is too large or the edges of the ring seem too thin for a clamp or sutures to be successful. In practically all cases of incarcerated or strangulated hernia it is necessary to do this operation. In other species as the calf and pig it apparently is the most successful method to use.

Preparation of the patient if it is a colt should consist of first keeping all food away for thirty-six hours, in the other species this is not so important unless the hernia is unusually large. The patient should be cast on its back in dorsal recumbency with all the legs flexed.

General anesthesia may be used or some sedative administered to control all struggling. Then a one per cent solution of a local anesthetic is injected into the skin and deeper tissues to complete the anesthesia.

The operative area is carefully prepared by shaving and cleansing the skin thoroughly and the area prepared for an aseptic operation. A sterile shroud is placed over the operative field.

TECHNIQUE OF OPERATION. Either a linear or elliptical incision should be made over the fundus of the sac depending upon whether there is abraded areas or excess skin to be removed. The incision should extend down to the peritoneum and then the skin portion of the sac is separated from the peritoneal portion by blunt dissection. This dissection extends to the ring and over the fascia surrounding the ring for a distance of approximately one and one-half inches. If the peritoneal portion of the sac is extensive enough a purse string suture of silk is inserted through the neck of the sac close to the ring. After the peritoneum is inverted into the abdominal cavity the purse string suture is tightened and tied. The object of this procedure is to obtain adhesions between the peritoneal surfaces and develop a pad of tissue over the ring and this should assist in preventing a recurrence of the hernia.

If the edges of the ring are firm and fairly thick sutures are inserted so as to produce an overlapping of the tissue. This procedure should bring from one to one and one-half inches of tissue in close contact. When adhesions have developed between the two surfaces they are usually strong enough to prevent a recurrence of the hernia. To produce an overlapping of the tissue the sutures may be inserted as illustrated. To produce an overlapping of the tissue it may be necessary to use strong suture material as a double strand of umbilical tape. After the tissue is overlapped it is anchored with interrupted sutures of silk steel wire or some other nonabsorbable su-

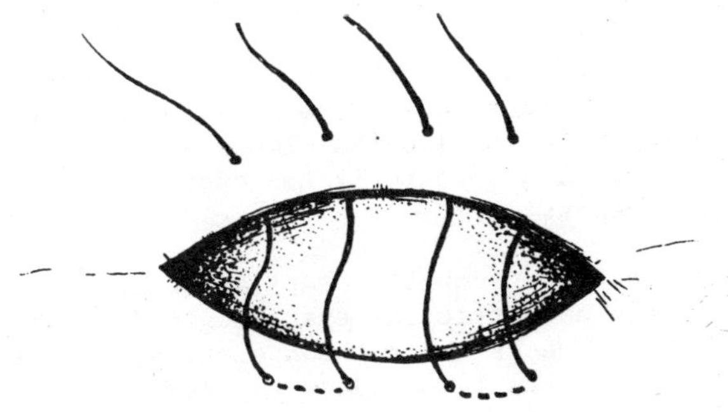

ture material. The skin is closed with interrupted or mattress sutures.

For those hernias that in the past have been unfavorable to operate or the method of operation was unsuccessful we now have another technique available. It consists in using some type of wire mesh and one of the best is a stainless steel wire mesh. In using the mesh the usual procedure of separating the peritoneal portion of the sac from the skin is used. This dissection is continued until the skin is separated from the underlying tissue a distance of one or two inches from the edge of the ring. After the peritoneal portion of the sac is everted into the abdominal cavity the edge of the ring are brought into close apposition with a continuous suture using one strand of steel wire. A piece of steel wire mesh large enough to cover the area previously prepared is now placed in position. A series of interrupted sutures using steel wire are inserted in the tissue and through the edge of the mesh. The granulation tissue infiltrates into the spaces of the mesh providing strong support to the area. The skin is closed in the usual manner.

The operation for umbilical hernia as just described may be used in any of the species of animals. In the pig there are some other conditions that will have to be considered. Quite frequently in pigs an abscess occurs on the peritoneal portion of the sac and it can usually be removed without rupturing if the operator is careful. Also in male pigs the sheath may cover the ring. A U-shaped incision may be made around the end of the sheath and then the sheath is reflected backward. Another method is to make two elliptical incisions lateral to the sheath so as to include the excess part of the skin portion of the sac. By blunt dissection the peritoneal portion of the sac is separated from the prepuce and the dissection is continued until the sac is completely isolated from the surrounding tissue.

In most cases of umbilical hernia where the radical operation has been performed the after care is almost as important as the operative procedure if the operation is to be successful.

The patient should be kept as quiet as possible restricting the amount of exercise for two weeks after the operation. It is very important to reduce by one-half the amount of feed consumed and this is especially true of the bulky portion of the feed. In a large animal if the ring was large a bandage around the body is beneficial in giving support to the area.

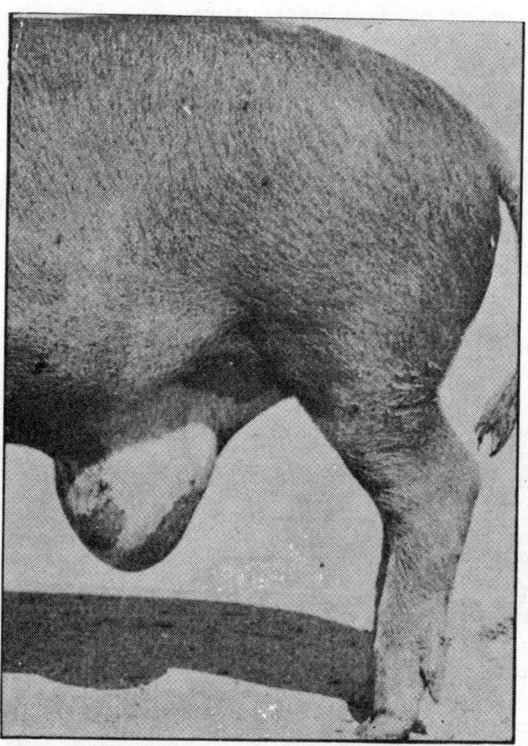

FIG. 317. A reducible umbilical hernia in a pig.

Inguinal and Scrotal Hernia

The passage of some of the abdominal organs, intestine, omentum or both through the internal inguinal ring forms an inguinal hernia. If the organs should pass into the scrotum a scrotal hernia is formed.

These hernias are of common occurrence in pigs and colts but occur only occasionally in cattle. In most cases occurring in colts and pigs the condition is congenital or appears within a few days after birth. Warwick found that scrotal hernia in swine is heritable; the percentage of hernias increasing from 4.19 per cent to 45.0 per cent in the fifth generation. Thus by careful selection of the breeding stock the occurrence of scrotal hernia can be reduced.

When colts a few days old affected with scrotal hernia are presented for operation the owner is advised to wait a few months. This is true unless the hernia is unusually large, exhibits a tendency to increase in size or shows a tendency to become incarcerated. Practically all scrotal hernias in colts disappear within a few months after birth.

In mature animals it occurs more frequently in the stallion. During service by the stallion a loop of intestine may slip through the internal ring into the inguinal canal. A few cases of inguinal hernia have occurred in geldings several years after they were castrated.

SIGNS. When it occurs in stallions during service, within a short time they show signs of abdominal pain. A rectal examination should be made and a careful search made in each internal ring to see if a loop of intestine is present in the canal. At this time the loop of intestine can usually be removed with but little traction. In other cases where the internal ring is greatly enlarged the intestine may pass down into the scrotum and not cause the stallion any inconvenience.

DIAGNOSIS. Is usually easy but when there is any doubt, it can be determined by rectal examination if a loop of intestine has entered the inguinal canal.

PROGNOSIS. In most cases it is favorable but when the intestine has become strangulated it is guarded or unfavorable.

OPERATION. The type of anesthesia used will depend upon the vigor of the patient and the preference of the operator. The patient should be cast as for the ordinary castration and held in dorsal recumbency. Thorough preparation of the operative field is then cast as for the ordinary castration and held in dorsal recumbency. Thorough preparation of the operative field is then made for an aseptic operation. An incision parallel to the median raphe is made through the scrotum and it should be liberal enough to permit the necessary operative procedures. The tunics should be separated from the scrotum by blunt dissection and this separation should be continued until the cord is exposed well down into the inguinal canal. The contents of the sac are most easily and efficiently reduced by having an assistant insert a hand into the rectum. Then by gentle traction the contents usually small intestine can be returned to the abdominal cavity. However, if the contents are incarcerated it may be necessary to introduce a probe pointed bistoury to the lateral commissure of the internal ring. The ring should then be enlarged enough to permit the reduction of the contents.

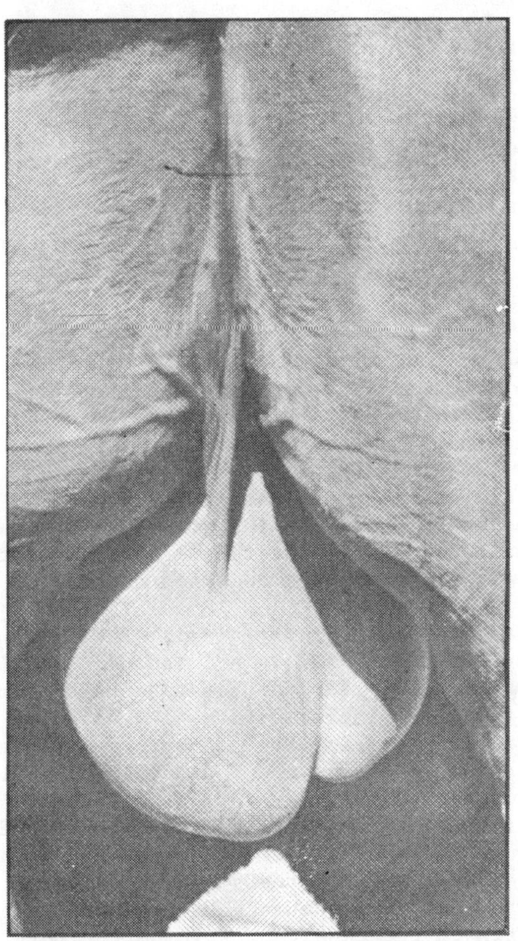

FIG. 318. Acquired scortal hernia in a five year old stallion.

With the testicle held in its normal position a sterile ligature of braided silk or some other strong material is placed by fixation through the tunics and cord. This ligature is placed as far down on the cord as possible. The ligature is passed around the cord several times tying it each time with the last knot tied very securely. The cord is then divided beyond the ligature and the end of the cord examined for any bleeding vessels. The stump of the cord is then pushed as far down into the inguinal canal as possible. Tamponade the inguinal canal and scrotum with sterile gauze and close the skin incision with mattress sutures. The sutures and gauze should be removed in 48 hours and the horse exercised daily.

Scrotal Hernia in the Bull

Scrotal hernia occurs when some of the abdominal contents, usually small intestine, pass through the internal inguinal ring into the scrotum. This type of hernia is observed most frequently in the mature animal but cases have been presented in the bull calves less than one year of age. As a general rule the hernia is unilateral but after one side has been operated on a hernia may occur on the other side at a later date. It is rather unusual for a scrotal hernia to become incarcerated as the ring seems to dilate enough for the passage of the contents However, it does occur and is manifested by uneasiness, occasional symptoms of abdominal pain and variable appetite. Before making a definite diagnosis of scrotal hernia, the surgeon must determine whether it is fat or intestine in the scrotum. In most cases it is almost impossible to differentiate between fat and intestine by palpation of the scrotum. When there is an excessive deposition of fat in the scrotum it is called lipomatosis. Occasionally we will find both fat and intestine are responsible for the increase in size of the scrotum. A rectal examination is one method of making a definite diagnosis. Palpation of the two internal inguinal rings will reveal that intestines are passing through the ring on the affected side. In most cases it will be possible to determine that the edges of the ring are further apart on the affected side than the normal ring. If there is an excessive amount of fat in the abdominal cavity it may be impossible to make a def-

FIG. 319. Lipomatosis or excessive deposition of fat in the scrotum.

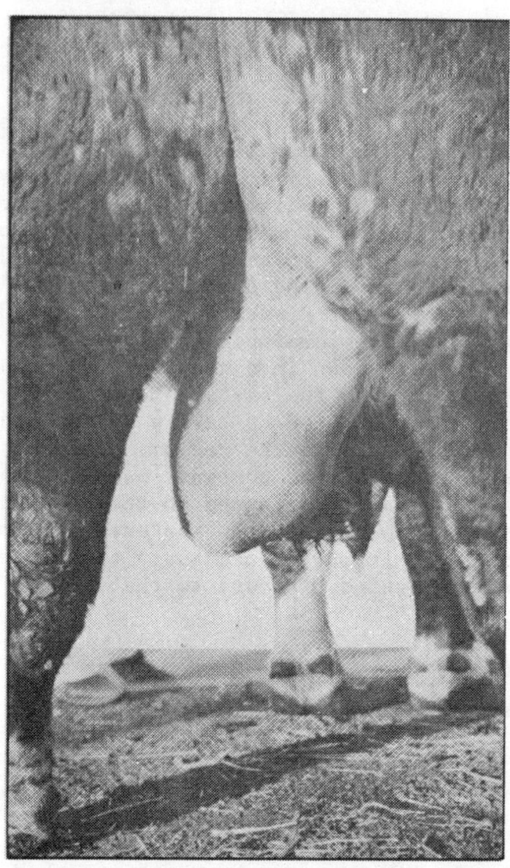

FIG. 320. Acquired scrotal hernia in a six year old bull.

inite diagnosis of scrotal hernia by rectal examination. When a positive diagnosis is necessary a laparotomy may be performed and it can be definitely determined if the swelling in the scrotum is due to any of the contents from the abdominal cavity.

In two cases of scrotal hernia in the bull the bladder had passed through the internal inguinal ring into the scrotum. By a rectal examination the operator may be able to palpate the ureters passing downward through the internal inguinal ring. Also if the bladder has filled with urine, pressure on the swelling in the scrotum will cause urine to be expelled from the penis. In operating on these cases it is very important to operate within a few days after they occur or wait at least one month. If they are not operated within a few days extensive adhesions develop between the bladder and surrounding tissue. When the operation is performed within a short time after the adhesions are formed, excessive hemorrhage may occur, when the adhesions are broken as the tissues are separated. If the operation is not performed for one month, the acute inflammation will have subsided and when the tissues are separated excessive hemorrhage does not occur.

If the contents of the hernia are intestine and the hernia is not reduced, within a short time after the hernia occurs, some of the following conditions may develop. There is a possibility the hernia will remain the same size and not cause the bull any trouble. The hernia may continue to increase in size until the scrotum touches the ground. Then due to the weight of the intestine and pain the bull refuses to serve. Usually the longer the intestines remain in the canal and scrotum the more extensive the adhesions. When the adhesions are first formed they are fragile and easily broken. In a short time the adhesions may become fibrous and the reducing of the hernia is a more difficult procedure. Some hernias become incarcerated and the patient is in constant pain until the hernia is reduced. Occasionally the hernia will become strangulated and a condition develops that cannot be corrected. As a general rule scrotal hernias should be reduced as soon as they are diagnosed as they are most easily corrected at this time.

A definite diagnosis is necessary if the proper treatment is to be used. In the young bull either intestine or fat in the scrotum may be responsible for the bulls failure to complete service. He may mount the cow and then before making the thrust stop and dismount. The weight of the fat or intestine seems to cause enough pain or discomfort that the bull will not serve. A mature bull may have a large quantity of fat or intestine in the scrotum and still serve in a normal manner. When there is an abnormal quantity of fat in the scrotum the concentrate portion of the ration should be reduced. This may result in a gradual reduction in the amount of fat in the scrotum.

The treatment of scrotal hernia will be determined by the individual case and the preference of the operator. The operation may be performed by making an incision through the scrotum over the testicle. By blunt dissection, the testicle enclosed in the tunics, is separated from the skin of the scrotum. This dissection is continued until the cord is separated from the surrounding tissue to the external inguinal ring. A ligature by fixation is placed in the cord as close to the external inguinal ring as is possible. The cord is then divided about two inches ventral to the ligature removing the testicle and tunics. The stump of the cord is pushed up close to the internal inguinal ring and maintained in this position by packing the area with sterile gauze. The gauze is maintained in position by placing a series of mattress sutures through the skin. In forty-eight hours the sutures and gauze are removed and the area is treated as an open wound. This method of operating is indicated when the hernia is unusually large and has been present for a long time. In these cases extensive adhesions are present and will have to be divided before the contents can be returned to the abdominal cavity.

The second method that can be used to correct a scrotal hernia in the bull is to perform a laparotomy, reduce the hernia and suture the internal inguinal ring. This method of operating has a number of advantages, one is the conservation of the testicle and the retention of the shape of the scrotum. The second reason is that a hernia may develop through the other inguinal ring at some later date so there is a better chance of prolonging the breeding usefulness of the bull.

If the operator is right handed the right paralumbar fossa is prepared for an aseptic operation. Anesthesia for the operation is obtained by infiltration of the tissue with a two per cent solution of a local anesthetic.

OPERATION. The incision seven inches long in the skin is started just below the transverse processes of the lumbar vertebrae and halfway between the last rib and the tuber coxae. The external oblique muscle is divided in the direction of its fibers which is downward and backward. Similarly the internal oblique muscle is divided in the direction of its fibers which is downward and forward. The fibers of the transversalis are separated parallel to their course. The hand and arm covered with a sterile glove and sleeve is inserted through the incision and peritoneum to the inguinal rings. Palpation will disclose the contents from the abdominal cavity passing through the inguinal ring on the affected side of the scrotum which is usually the left side. The contents are usually too voluminous and heavy to lift out at one time. With an assistant lifting up on the scrotum the operator can gradually return the contents of the hernia to the abdominal cavity. Occasionally we find there are some adhesions preventing a complete reduction of the hernia. These adhesions are usually easily broken with the fingers. The ring is sutured by using a No. 30 full curved needle threaded with a strand of umbilical tape and the two ends tied together. A loop about twelve inches long is produced when the two ends of the tape are tied together. The loop is slipped over the hand and the needle is grasped between the thumb and finger. Starting at the lateral commissure of the internal inguinal ring the needle is inserted through the anterior edge of the ring which is composed of rather tough fibrous tissue. The needle is then inserted through the peritoneum. As the suture material is pulled through the tissue the loop over the hand is slipped over the fingers. At the same time the needle is pulled through the loop until the two tissues are together and the first suture is complete. A continuous suture is used to complete the closure of the internal ring. After the last suture is inserted the needle is inserted in the tissue so the suture material is locked and cannot slip. A Bard Parker blade is carried in to cut the suture material and the needle is removed. The incision in the peritoneum and transverse abdominal muscle is closed with a continuous suture using No. 2 chromic catgut. The fibers of the internal and external oblique muscles are approximated with continuous sutures using No. 2 chromic catgut. The skin incision is closed with interrupted sutures using umbilical tape and then covered with flexible collodion. For approximately two weeks after the operation there will be some inflammatory swelling of the scrotum but it gradually subsides. The skin sutures are removed in ten days to two weeks.

Inguinal Hernia

Inguinal hernia does not occur very frequently in the heifer. A heifer two days of age was presented with a large inguinal hernia. The operative area was prepared for an aseptic operation. Anesthesia was obtained by giving the calf ten cubic centimeters of nembutal intravenously. Also the skin and abdominal wall were infiltrated with a two per cent solution of procaine hydrochloride. The incision in the skin was made over the most ventral portion of the hernial sac. By blunt dissection the peritoneal portion of the sac was separated from the skin. The peritoneum was everted through the inguinal ring into the peritoneal cavity. A continuous suture of No. 25 stainless steel wire was used to close the inguinal ring. The skin incision was closed with mattress sutures.

Scrotal Hernia in the Porcine

Scrotal hernia occurs frequently in pigs, inguinal hernia is less frequently observed in the female. It is unusual for spontaneous reduction of scrotal hernias to occur in pigs. Quite frequently the hernia appears to be corrected but examination of the inguinal rings will reveal the ring is still enlarged on the affected side. If the ordinary castration procedure is employed evisceration of the intestine frequently occurs when the animal is released.

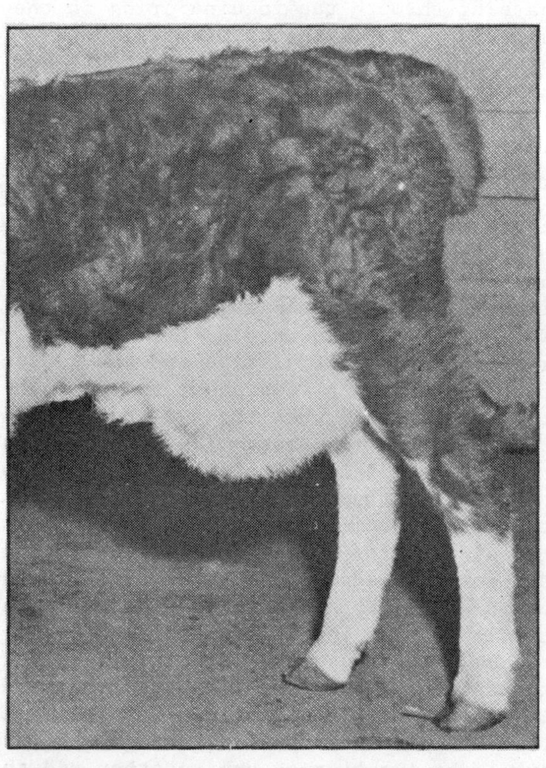

FIG. 321. Inguinal hernia in a two day old heifer calf.

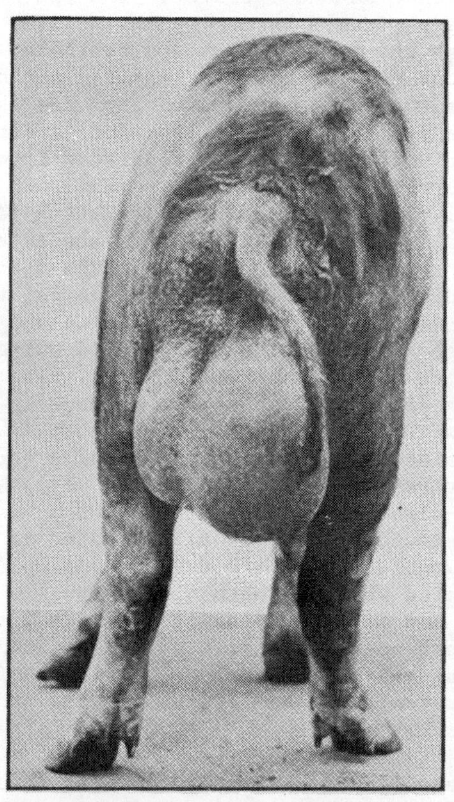

FIG. 322. Scrotal hernia in a boar.

OPERATION. The animal is placed on its back in dorsal recumbency and the area over the inguinal ring prepared for an aseptic operation.

This operation may be performed painlessly by injecting the skin along the proposed line of incision with a one per cent solution of a local anesthetic. Also deposit some of the anesthetic in the tissue forming the inguinal ring.

An incision about three inches long is made through the skin and subcutaneous tissue starting at the anterior commissure of the ring and extending backward along the course of the cord. The fingers are used to break through the thick white fascia surrounding the tunica. When the tunics are exposed the intestines contained within them can be easily seen. If young pigs are being operated on the tunics must be handled carefully as they are easily torn. The fingers are inserted around the tunics and steady traction exerted on the tunics and cord and at the same time the testicle is pushed out of the scrotum with the other hand. As the testicle is pushed out of the scrotum with the one hand it is grasped with the fingers of the other hand and the tunics pulled loose from their attachment to the scrotum. The fingers may be used to force the contents into the abdominal cavity. A ligature is placed through the cord by fixation as close to the ring as possible and the cord is divided beyond the ligature. The two edges of the ring are brought together with a continuous suture of catgut or silk. The skin incision may be closed with a continuous or mattress suture.

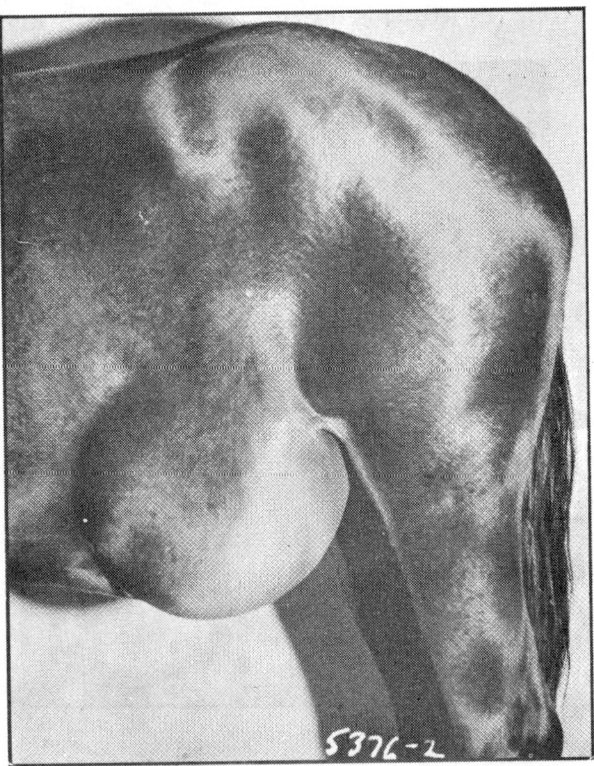

FIG. 323. Ventral hernia, occurred during eighth month of pregnancy similar hernia on other side of median line.

Ventral Hernia

Ventral hernia occurs when some of the contents of the abdominal cavity pass through an unnatural opening in the abdominal wall. In some of the ventral hernias the peritoneum is intact while in some of the hernias the peritoneum has ruptured and the contents are in contact with the skin. The opening through the abdominal wall, usually is the result of an external injury as a kick, blow, horn thrusts, becoming cast on an upright post or stake, falling on blunt objects and rupture of prepubian tendon. In the equine ventral hernias occur frequently along the posterior border of the last rib. The size of the opening will vary from a small opening to one that is eighteen inches in diameter.

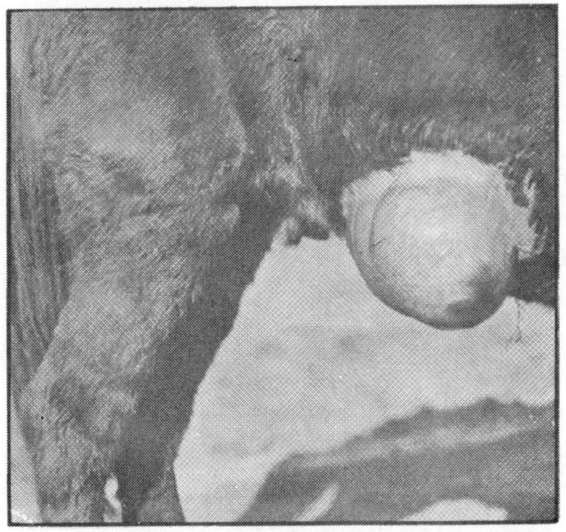

FIG. 324. Ventral hernia in the abdominal wall of a mule with a ring approximately ten inches in diameter.

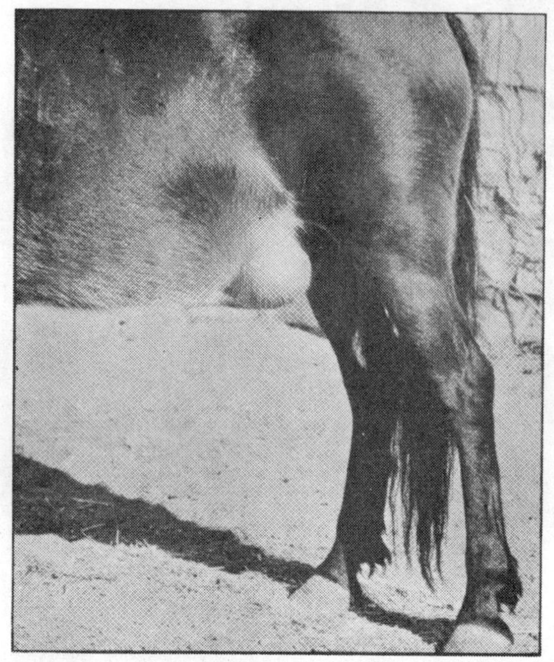

FIG. 325.

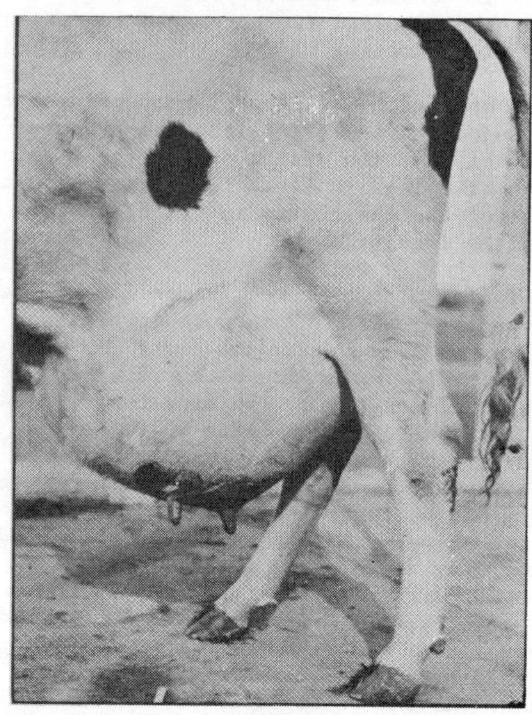

FIG. 327.

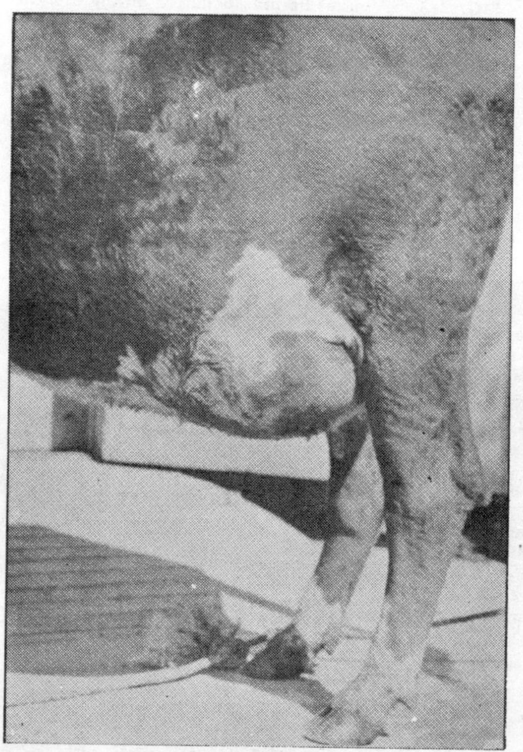

FIG. 326.

Figs. 325, 326 and 327 are ventral hernias due to rupture of the prepubian tendon and are inoperable.

PROGNOSIS. The prognosis will depend upon many factors, size and location of the opening, thickness and firmness of the tissues forming the edge of the opening.

OPERATION. In the case of a large opening food should be withheld for thirty-six hours before the operation. The operative area should be prepared for an aseptic operation. Depending upon the location of the opening and the facilities the patient may be confined on a table or the ground. In most cases a general anesthetic should be used so there is complete relaxation of the tissues. If the opening is unusually large a trachea tube might be indicated for a few days to prevent any undue strain on the operative area.

The operation will be described for the ventral hernia with a large opening. A linear incision is made through the skin over the center of the sac. By blunt dissection and use of the scalpel when necessary the peritoneum, if intact, is separated from the skin. The dissection and separation is continued for a distance of two inches past the edge of the ring. The ring is closed by overlapping the edges of the ring. For suture material heavy unbleached muslin is cut into strips one and one-half inches wide. The sutures are inserted in the edges of the ring so as to produce an overlapping of the edges. The

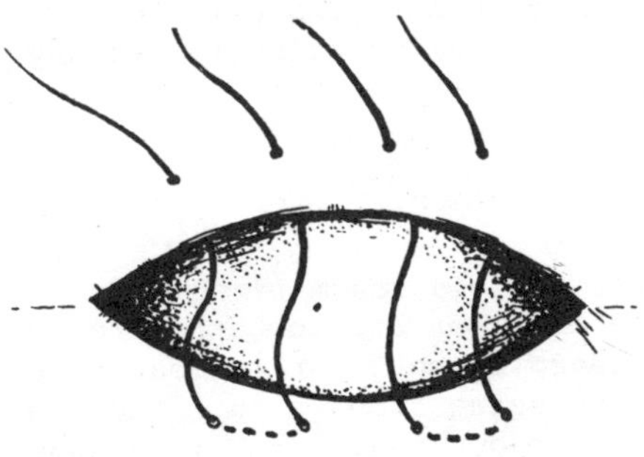

method of inserting the sutures is shown in the drawing above. It will be necessary to insert a variable number of sutures depending upon the size of the ring. After the necessary number of sutures are inserted they are gradually tightened and tied. A number of interrupted sutures of stainless steel wire are in the edge of the overlapping tissue to bring the tissue into closer apposition. The excess skin of the sac was removed and the skin incision closed with a series of mattress sutures. For two weeks the patient should be kept in a box stall. The bulky portion

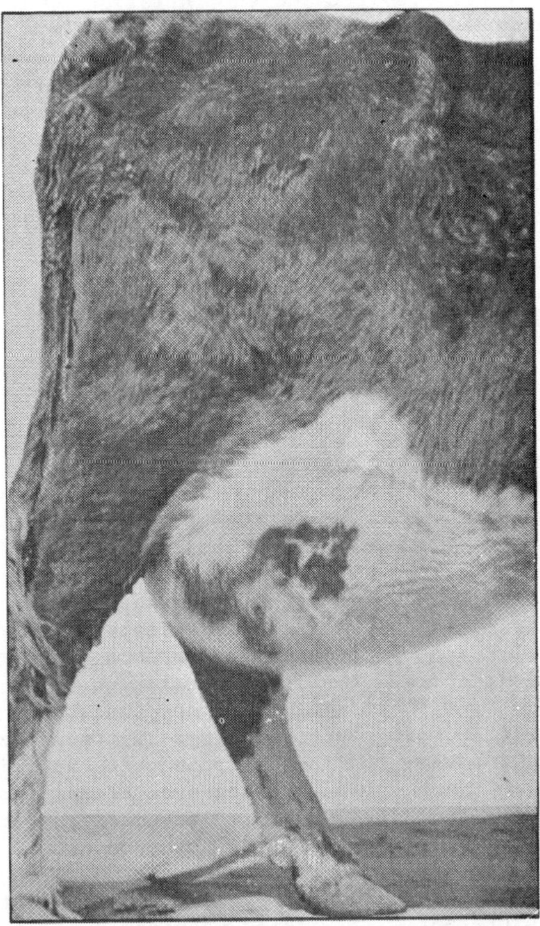

FIG. 328. A ventral hernia that occurred ten days before parturition.

of the ration should be reduced and the grain increased. Remove the skin sutures in two weeks.

The opening in the abdominal wall in Fig. 328 was a vertical slit like opening about six inches long through the abdominal wall. This opening was located about half-way on on the side of the abdominal wall. Most of the small intestines had passed through this opening into the subcutaneous tissue and gravitated ventrally to form a sac medial and ventral to the fold of the flank.

The skin over the opening was prepared for the operation. Anesthesia of the tissues was obtained by infiltration with a local anesthetic. A vertical incision through the skin was made over the opening. With the patient in lateral recumbency attempts to return the intestines to the abdominal cavity were unsuccessful. After ropes were fastened around the hocks, the posterior part was elevated and the intestines were returned to the abdominal cavity. The opening in the abdominal wall was closed with continuous sutures using No. 4 chromic catgut. The skin incision was closed with mattress sutures using umbilical tape. When extensive injuries of the abdominal wall occur a few days before they are due to calve, the patient should receive help at the time of parturition to relieve strain on the operative area.

Affections of the Teats and Mammary Gland

Successful surgery of the teat requires a thorough knowledge of its anatomy and aseptic technique must be used if the best results are to be obtained. The location of the udder exposes it and the teats to many adverse conditions such as moisture, filth, cold, infection, and various types of trauma. In many cases serious injury occurs to the teats and udder from the feet of other cows, or a cow may step on her own teats. Striking the udder and teats against solid objects frequently traumatizes the tissues. Of the sharp objects barb wire is a common cause of extensive lacerations of the teats and udder. A traumatic injury of the udder or teats may not produce a visable break in the tissue, but may lower its resistence to pathogenic bacteria that are present. If milking machines are not operating efficiently they may be responsible for the development of mastitis and traumatic damage of the tissue.

The teat is a membranous tube that provides a passageway for the milk from the sinus of the gland to the outside. There is a wide variation in both the length and diameter of the teats, depending upon their shape. The length may vary from one to seven inches and the diameter from two to three inches at its base while the distal end may be small. The wall of the teat is of a uniform thickness and is composed of mucous membrane, connective tissue, muscle and skin. There are a large number of folds of the mucous membrane that vary a great deal in size from the microscopic to those that are rather prominent. The folds may extend in a longitudinal direction and also transversely to the long axis of the teat. Many of the longitudinal folds begin in the streak canal and extend up into the milk sinus. The mucous membrane of the teat canal reacts very quickly to any form of irritation with the development of inflammatory tissue that may become extensive enough to occlude the lumen. Operations that involve this tissue may be unsuccessful because of the formation of scar tissue.

The papillary duct or teat canal extends from the teat sinus to the teat orifice, and is about one centimeter in length. Many of the longitudinal folds of the teat canal also extend into the papillary duct. Under the mucous membrane there is a heavy mass of connective tissue. The sphincter of the papillary duct is separated by smooth muscle bundles from the deeper part of the layers of connective tissue. The skin covering the teat extends up into the papillary duct and terminates very abruptly at the dorsal end of the duct.

When teat surgery is performed there is a certain amount of danger to infection so it should be performed only when necessary. The operation may be performed with faultless technique but bacteria already present in the tissues may cause an infection due to the decreased resistence of the tissue.

If teat tubes have been used prior to the presentation of the animal for treatment surgery should not be performed for seventy-two hours. When teat tubes are used they may have caused some injury to the tissues and may have introduced some infection into the tissues. Anesthesia for the operation may be obtained by infiltration of the tissue with a local anesthetic or by topical application. In some cases, where the animal is difficult to restrain for the operation, it may be necessary to use a general anesthetic.

Trauma

When the teat is traumatized it may occur from lacerations due to barb wire or some other sharp object, but in most cases it is due to being stepped on. The cow may step on her own teat or it is stepped on by another cow. The conclusion of many authorities is that the largest percentage of trauma are self inflicted. A common cause of injury may also occur when the teat is traumatized when the cow is getting up, between the point of the hock and floor.

For those lacerations of the teat that do not extend completely through the wall the best treatment will be determined by the damaged tissue. If the patient is presented promptly after the injury occurs the tissue may be sutured. If the edges of the wound are dry they should be debrided to create fresh surfaces. The suture material that is used should be non-irritating and most of the suture materials made from synthetic material are satisfactory. For the small wounds, collodion or aeroderm may be used to cover and protect the wound. It may be desirable to use tape around the teat to provide some support to the sutures. When the wound is several days old, if the tissue is edematous, stiff, and thickened due to the inflammatory reaction, the best results may be obtained when it is treated as an open wound.

If the end of the teat is injured without involving the papillary duct, the small irregular portions of tissue may be trimmed off. When the papillary duct has been injured a plastic teat tube with the removable cap is used until the injured tissue has healed.

When the laceration extends through the wall of the teat, of a cow in production, milk will come through the opening. If the case is presented when the wound is only a few hours old the edges may be sutured together. Any small, almost loose pieces of tissue on the edges of the wound are even and smooth. The hemorrhage can be controlled with a tourniquet around the base of the teat. To bring and hold the surfaces of the wound in close apposition stainless steel wire, size 30 or 32 may be used. The sutures are started about one-fourth of an inch from the edge of the wound down to but not through the mucous membrane. The needle penetrates the tissue on the other side of the wound in the same manner. Sutures are placed about one-fourth inch apart so the edges of the wound are brought into close apposition. The edges of the skin are approximated with closely placed interrupted sutures.

MAMMARY HEMATOMA. Hematomas of the udder usually occur on the rear quarters due to a contusion and rupture of a subcutaneous blood vessel. In most cases the glandular tissue is not involved. Injury of the large subcutaneous abdominal vein anterior to the udder may result in the development of an unusually large hematoma.

TREATMENT. The smaller hematomas of the udder should be opened, the blood clot removed and the cavity packed tightly with gauze to prevent further hemorrhage. If the cavity suppurates afterward the pus should be prevented from collecting on the end of the teat and infecting the quarter.

The large hematomas that occur anterior to the udder should not be opened for several days or until there is definite evidence the blood has clotted. If they are opened too soon a hemorrhage may occur that is difficult to stop. In some cases the blood is gradually reabsorbed. In other cases it may be advisable to let the hematoma go until infection has developed an abscess. The abscess may be opened and the pus drained out without danger of hemorrhage.

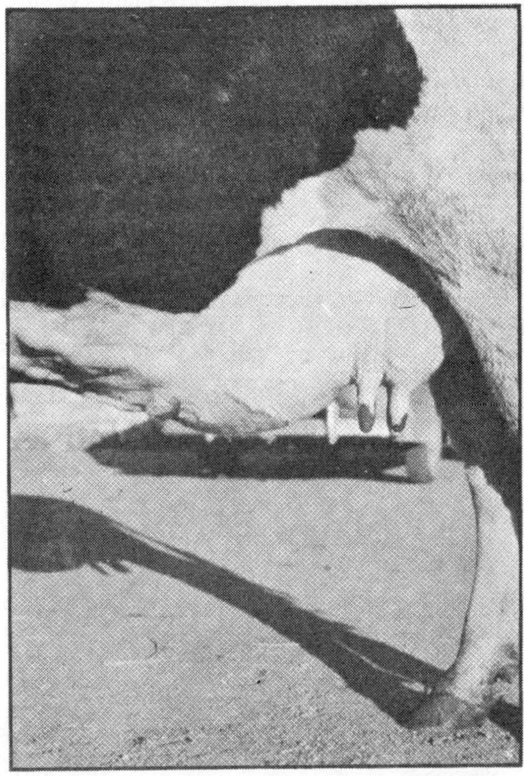

FIG. 329. A large hematoma anterior to the udder.

Necrosis of Skin

This condition is characterized by necrosis of the skin in a circular area about two inches in diameter. The area is located at the anterior border of the udder on the median line between the halves of the udder. A slight purulent discharge is always present and a very fetid odor.

TREATMENT. The following preparation may be applied liberally to the area daily, pyoktannin blue one ounce, alcohol 70 per cent one gallon or equal parts of tincture of iodine and formalin. In some cases it may be necessary to surgically remove the necrotic tissue.

Sore or Chapped Teats

This condition occurs most frequently during the winter and spring months. Sore teats may occur as the result of irritation from sucking of the calf, wet milking, wet bedding and damp conditions in the stable.

The skin may first become rough and later wrinkles are formed which become hard and deep. The wrinkles may develop into deep fissures which break open and the area is swollen and very sensitive to manipulation. When the area is very sensitive the cow may be difficult to milk or for the calf to nurse. If the end of the teat becomes affected the infection may gain entrance to the quarter and cause mastitis.

TREATMENT. The affected teats should be dried after each milking and a softening antiseptic preparation applied. Some of the preparations are: 20 per cent of tannic acid in glycerine is very good for the superficial cracks; one ounce of phenol in one pint of glycerine; one part tincture of iodine and four parts glycerine. A very excellent preparation consists of one pound of liquefied phenol, two pounds of gum camphor and three pounds of mineral oil.

Accessory Teats

Accessory teats frequently interfere with the milking process and are objectionable on show animals. It is best to remove these teats when the animal is young or in the case of an older cow when she is dry.

Anesthesia of the operative area may be obtained by infiltrating the tissue at the base of the teat with a one per cent solution of a local anesthetic. The teat may be removed at its base with a scalpel making two elliptical incisions. Also the emasculatome may be used to pinch the tissue at the base of the teat and its removal completed with a sharp instrument. Two or three interrupted sutures of catgut are inserted to hold the cut edges together. The area is then covered with flexible collodion.

Imperforate Teats

The absence of an opening in the end of the teat may be congenital or acquired. In most cases the opening is covered by a thin skin.

TREATMENT. The end of the teat should be cleansed thoroughly with an efficient skin antiseptic. Grasp the teat so it will be distended with milk and insert a large sterile needle through the skin at the point where the opening should be. After each milking a large size antiseptic teat dilator is inserted with proper antiseptic precautions into the opening. This procedure is continued until a permanent opening is established.

Teat or Milk Fistulae

A teat fistula may be congenital or acquired through injury to the teat. The opening of the congenital fistulae are usually located close to the base of the teat. As a general rule these fistulae have a secreting tissue of their own. Injuries to the teat that involve the teat canal frequently occur early in the lactation period and there is a more less constant escape of milk. This discharge interferes with complete healing of the wound and a fistula is produced.

TREATMENT. If the wound is treated a short time after it is produced complete healing of the wound may occur by first intention. The edges of a small wound may be held in close apposition with strips of adhesive tape around the teat. In extensive wounds the best results may be obtained by the insertion of interrupted sutures to hold the cut edges closely together. Strict antiseptic precautions must be used in treating wounds of the teat to prevent infection gaining entrance to the quarter.

Most teat fistulae should be operated on if possible when the cow is dry. Various methods of treatment have been advocated to obtain healing of fistulae. Tischhauser recommends the following treatment as being very successful for milk fistula. The cow should be dry when she is treated. To prevent irritation of the skin around the opening in the teat, petrolatum may be applied to the skin. The small ends of two toothpicks are covered with a few strands of long fibre cotton. A toothpick is dipped into the butter of antimony, the surplus wiped off, and then inserted into the tract of the fistula and rotated. The second toothpick is used in the same manner. No further treatment is necessary and all cases have responded to this treatment. Cauterization of the fistula may be performed with a wire heated to a cherry red color or with a stick of potassium hydroxide or silver nitrate. The teat should be prepared for an aseptic operation by first cleansing it with alcohol.

The operative method of treatment is to dissect out the cicatricial tissue lining the fistula. Anesthesia of the area is obtained by infiltrating the tissue around the operative area with a one per cent solution of a local anesthetic. An elliptical incision large enough to include the fistula is made through the skin and underlying tissue to the lumen of the teat. To suture the incision No. 0 catgut fastened to a full curved atraumatic needle is used. The first suture which is continuous includes only the tissue between the mucous membrane and skin. It is important the tissues are brought into close apposition at both commissures of the wound. If the operator fails to do this it may result in the development of another fistula. A continuous suture is used to close the skin incision. The area is then covered with flexible collodion. If the fistula is congenital the same operation is performed except the incision does not extend into the teat canal. When the opening is permanently closed the secreting tissue ceases to function. Another method of treatment recommended by Sweet, of New York, is as follows. The fistula is milked dry and then a good skin antiseptic is applied to the skin around the opening. To destroy the secreting tissue, five cubic centimeters of three parts of a ten per cent solution of silver nitrate and two parts of glycerin are used. A fine needle is inserted through the opening, then a syringe is used to inject the solution with considerable force. This treatment may cause some swelling of the tissue in a few hours and the next day a brownish purulent discharge can be milked out. The discharge should be removed daily for about two weeks when a permanent cure is obtained. When the opening of the fistula is too close to the end of the teat to be operated on the end of the teat can be removed. The portion of the teat to be removed should also include the fistula. There will be a new sphincter formed to retain the milk. After the operation the end of the teat should be immersed in a warm 1-1000 solution of bichloride of mercury or saturated solution of magnesium sulphate several times a day for fifteen to thirty minutes at a time until healing of the cut surface occurs.

Contracted Sphincter, Hard Milker

This condition is of frequent occurrence in dairy cows and one or more or all four teats may be affected. Because of the extra effort and time required to milk cows so affected the owner appreciates the correction of this condition.

TREATMENT. The most successful method of overcoming a contracted sphincter is to divide it one or more times. For this operation a Case's teat bistoury may be used. The teat should be cleansed thoroughly with alcohol and then an efficient skin antiseptic used around and over the end of the teat.

A few streams of milk should be forced from the teat before introducing the bistoury to remove any infection in the teat. The sterile closed bistoury is introduced through the end of the teat until the cutting edge is in contact with the sphincter. The cutting edge of the knife is exposed enough so the sphincter can be rocked over it and divided. The sphincter should be divided in one or more places until it permits the milk to pass through freely and this can be determined by milking a few streams of milk. By using this method of operating, the skin at the end of the teat is not injured so there is little possibility of infection gaining entrance to the quarter. The first few streams of milk at the beginning of each milking should be vigorously expelled for this procedure tends to break any adhesions that may have developed.

Growths in the Teat Canal

These growths may vary in size from a pea to those extending the length of the canal. When the pea size growth are located close to the end of the teat and are pedunculated they may act like a valve and prevent milk from passing out. The large growths may almost fill the teat canal.

TREATMENT. The pea size growths are easily and most efficiently removed with Trump's teat rollers. When the growths are extensive in the teat canal it is best not to attempt surgical interference. The growth will finally produce a complete obstruction and the quarter will become distended with its own secretion. This secretion is soon suspended the contents are absorbed and the quarter becomes functionally inactive.

Membranous Obstruction

Spider Teats

These membranes are usually located close to the base of the teat and prevent or partially prevent the milk from passing into the teat canal from the sinus. These membranes may be thick or thin, partial or complete. They may be present in one or two or all four teats may be affected. The usual history of the case is the cow was milking alright when she was turned dry. Then when she freshened the milker was unable to obtain any milk from the affected teat or teats. The presence of the membrane is easily determined by rolling the teat between the thumb and fingers.

TREATMENT. If the membrane is thick it is best not to operate but allow the quarter to become functionally inactive. However, if the membrane feels thin an operation is usually successful. The teat is thoroughly cleansed with a 1-1000 solution of bichloride of mercury in alcohol. A sterile Case's teat bistoury is introduced through the end of the teat until the point has passed through the membrane at one side. If the membrane is thin the cutting edge of the knife is exposed and the membrane cut to its center. It is then cut to the center from the opposite side. This procedure is repeated until the membrane is cut into quarters permitting the cut portions of the membrane to fall to the sides of the teat canal. However, if the center of the membrane is markedly thickened the rather thin attachments at the edge are cut. This permits the membrane to fall to one side of the teat canal. After treatment consists in leaving some milk in the teat at each milking to prevent the cut edges of the membrane from healing together. Probably the most important after treatment procedure is to place one hand on either side of the milk cistern and force milk down into the teat. This procedure tends to break any adhesions that have developed in the operative area.

Lacteal Calculi

The terms lacteal calculi or milkstone are applied to those concretions that are found in the udder. The stones may result from the accumulation of lime salts from the milk. They are freely movable in the teat canal, vary a great deal in size and are very hard with an uneven surface.

TREATMENT. When small they may be removed by manipulation during the milking process. It may be necessary to crush the larger calculi with a pair of forceps introduced through the end of the teat. In some cases it may be desirable to enlarge the opening at the end of the teat by dividing the sphincter one or more times.

Amputation of the Teat

This operation is indicated in purulent mastitis to provide complete drainage from the milk cistern. In some cases it is impossible to obtain complete drainage through the teat due to partial closure of the teat canal and thick character of the pus.

OPERATION. The teat and operative area should be cleansed with alcohol. Anesthesia of the operative area may be obtained by infiltrating the skin and underlying tissue at the base of the teat with a one per cent solution of a local anesthetic.

The incision is made through the tissues at the base of the teat with the blade of the scalpel inserted into the milk cistern. By removing the teat in this manner it assures complete drainage from the milk cistern. The rather profuse hemorrhage that occurs is effectively controlled by suturing the skin and mucous membrane together with a continuous suture.

Extirpation of the Udder

This operation may be indicated in some cases of gangrene of a portion or all of the udder. Also in cases of neoplasms, actinomycosis or some incurable infection of the udder and the owner wishes to save the cow for breeding purposes. In some cases of gangrene of the udder there is less reaction and more cows will be saved if the udder is not extirpated. Instead numerous liberal incisions are made into the affected tissue to provide drainage for the toxic fluids. There is a gradual separation of the gangrenous from the healthy tissue.

ANATOMY. The operator should know the important structures of the udder. The udder of the cow is divided into two equal halves but incompletely divided into quarters. Each half is suspended by a ligament from the abdominal tunic attached along the median line. The lateral surface of the gland is covered by the lateral ligament. Its large blood supply is derived principally from the external pudic artery which passes through the inguinal canal accompanied by its vein and nerves. The blood is drained from the udder anteriorly by the large subcutaneous abdominal vein and passing backward is the perineal vein and the external pudic vein through the inguinal canal.

OPERATION. Anesthesia of the operative area may be obtained by injecting 40 cubic centimeters of a three per cent solution of procaine hydrochloride into the epidural space.

If only one-half of the udder is to be removed cast the cow with the affected side uppermost. Prepare the skin for an aseptic operation. Start the skin incision on the median line at the upper posterior border of the udder and extend it downward and across the lateral side of the udder forward to the median line in front of the udder. The skin flap is loosened from the lateral fascia by blunt dissection until the inguinal region is exposed. Incise the lateral fascia and palpate for the inguinal vessels which are easily recognized by the pulsation of the artery. The artery, vein and nerve are gathered into one group and a strong silk fixation ligature is fastened tightly around these vessels. A similar fixation ligature is applied about two inches below the first ligature. The vessels are then divided about halfway between the two ligatures. The lateral fascia is cut along the base of the udder and the areolar tissue between the udder and abdominal tunic separated with the fingers. Isolate the perineal vein and the subcutaneous abdominal vein, ligate and divide between the ligatures. The suspensory ligament belonging to this half of the udder is divided close to its attachment to the abdominal wall. The other half of the udder may be removed in the same manner. The cut edges of the skin are sutured together and the cavity packed with gauze that has been impregnated with an antiseptic powder. The area usually heals as an open wound.

Actinomycotic Mastitis

The above condition is observed quite frequently in the sow and one or more mammary glands may be affected.

Infection of the mammary gland may occur through abrasions of the skin and its contact with infection. It has also been suggested that infection may gain entrance through injuries caused by the teeth of suckling pigs. The lesions are the same as occur in the soft tissue in any other part of the body. This consists of a thick fibrous capsule inclosing a thick tenacious, granular creamy white pus. The actinomycotic enlargement may be lobulated or it may have a regular outline. If the surface becomes eroded there may be several openings discharging the characteristic thick pus

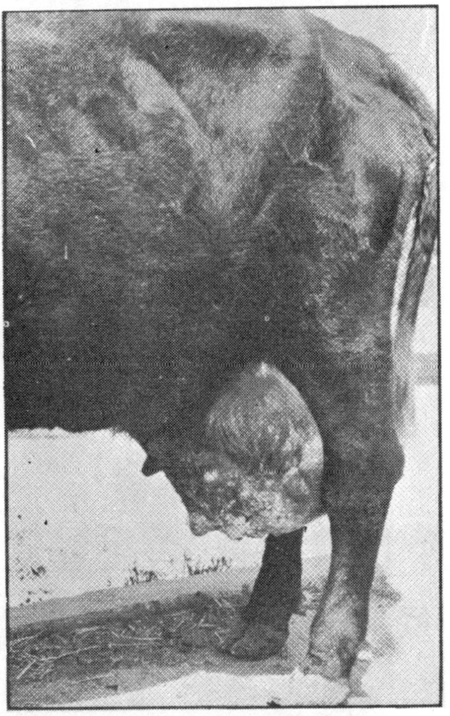

FIG. 330. Actinomycosis of the udder of a cow, when removed it weighed approximately 100 pounds.

to the exterior. When the condition is allowed to go untreated the affected mammary gland or glands may become enormous as shown in the picture.

TREATMENT. If treatment is started while the enlargement is small the internal administration of iodine is very successful. However, when the involvement of tissue becomes pronounced the administration of iodine does not seem to alter the course of the infection.

Surgical extirpation of the affected tissue is indicated when internal medication is contraindicated or unsuccessful. A general anesthetic may be used or a one per cent solution of a local anesthetic may be used to infiltrate along the proposed lines of incision. After the incision is made through the skin most of the dissection may be continued by blunt dissection with the fingers. The most important point to consider during the dissection is the control of hemorrhage.

In an operation on the mammary gland the area is very vascular and if the operator is not careful excessive hemorrhage may result in shock and death of the patient. Forceps are used on all bleeding vessels and the larger ones are ligated. If the

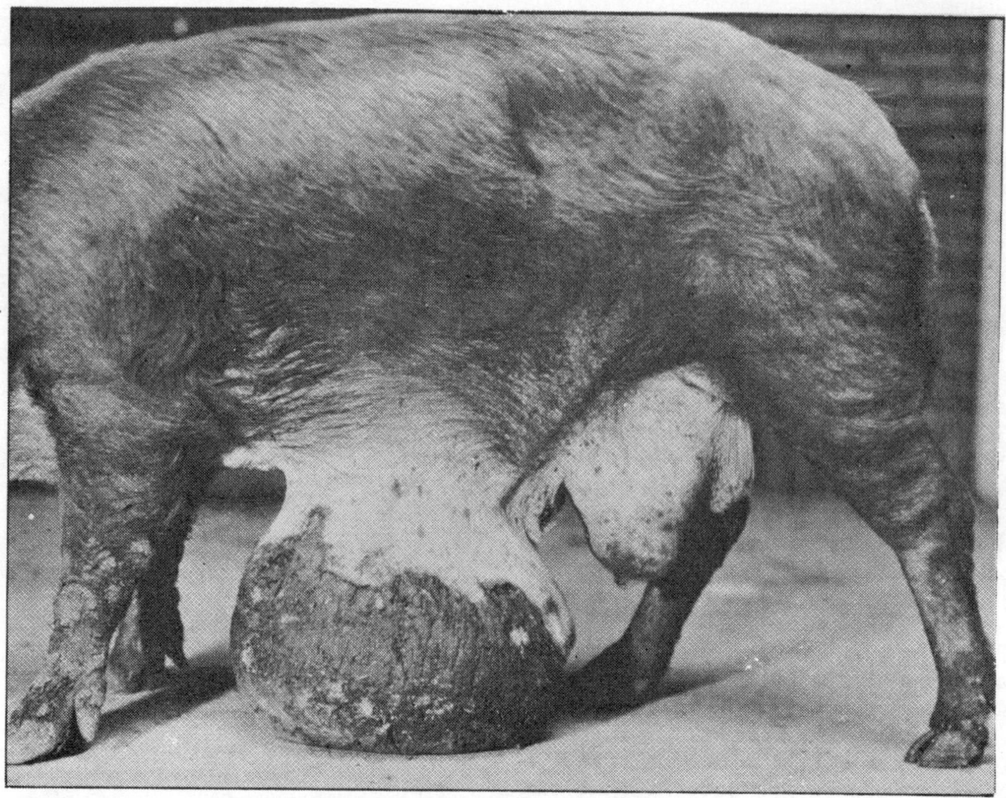

FIG. 331. Actinomycotic mastitis, several glands are affected.

patient bleeds excessively it is advisable to keep up the blood pressure by the administration of dextrose or saline solution administered intravenously. The edges of the skin incision are united with interrupted silk sutures. The wound then receives the usual after care.

Congenital Union of Teats

Occasionally in heifers two teats will be found congenitally united together This may occur due to a fusion of their walls or by a web of skin and subcutaneous tissue. Before treatment a careful examination should be made to determine if the condition is due to a fusion of the walls and then an operation is contra-indicated. When the union is due to skin and connective tissue it may be divided.

OPERATION. The tissue to be operated on may be infiltrated with a one per cent solution of a local anesthetic. Incise the skin between the teats but divide the subcutaneous tissue by blunt dissection. The edges of the skin wound of each teat may be united by closely placed interrupted sutures of fine catgut. Apply flexible collodion over the sutures and healing by first intention should occur in seven to eight days.

Orchitis

Orchitis is inflammation of the testicle and occurs in all species of domestic animals. The inflammation may occur as the result of traumatism. In those cases where the traumatism is severe large hematomas may form in the testicle. Infection is probably the most frequent cause of orchitis and in the bovine Bacillus abortus and Actinomyces Bovis have been isolated from cases of orchitis.

SYMPTOMS. The symptoms of acute orchitis are easily recognized as the affected testicle or testicles are swollen and painful with extreme sensitiveness to the touch. The affected tissue is warm or hot and if the scrotal skin is white there is redness. If the inflammation is severe there is general depression with a decrease in appetite. In a few days adhesions develop between the tunics and the testicle and may also develop between the tunics and scrotum.

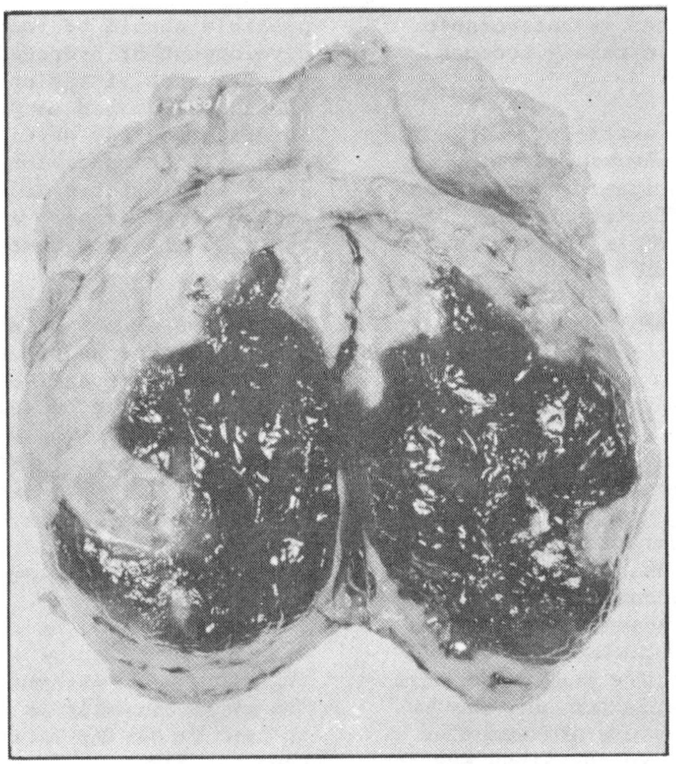

FIG. 332. Hematoma in a bovine testicle.

FIG. 333. Unilateral orchitis in a bull.

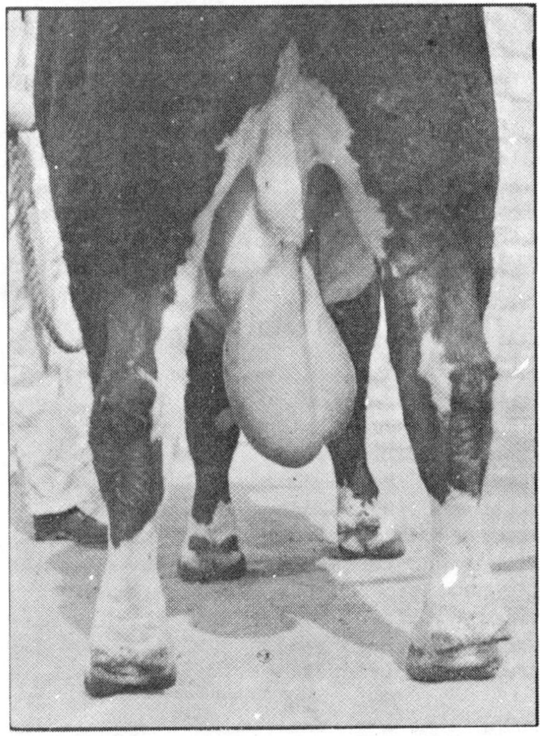

FIG. 334. Cystic orchitis in a bull, complicated with scrotal hernia and adhesions of intestine to testicle.

PROGNOSIS. In most cases is unfavorable as the affected testicle rarely becomes normal again.

TREATMENT. The use of antiphlogistic measures and rest are always indicated in the early stages. A suspensory should be used to support the affected tissue. If the affected testicle fails to show any response to treatment in a week or ten days it is surgically removed. The removal of the affected testicle may prevent affection of the other testicle. Also the animal's general condition shows a rapid improvement. In removing the testicle, if possible, the cord should be divided where it is healthy, removing all affected tissue. Anesthesia for the operation may be obtained by infiltrating the scrotum along the proposed line of incision with a local anesthetic. Also anesthetize the cord by injecting a local anesthetic into the tissue at or above the proposed site of division of the cord. The incision in the scrotum extends its entire length and high enough so all of the affected cord may be removed. Due to the severe inflammation in the testicle extensive adhesions develop between the testicle and tunics and between the tunics and scrotum. The adhesions between the tunics and scrotum are broken down by blunt dissection until there is complete separation of the tunics from the scrotum. If possible the separation of the tissue is continued until the healthy portion of the cord can be reached. A ligature is placed around the cord to control the hemorrhage and the cord is divided below the ligature. The testicle enclosed within the tunics is now removed and the area is treated as an open wound.

Castration

Removal of the testicles from the equine, bovine, ovine and suis is universally practiced. The principal reason in the equine is they are more easily handled in the presence of the female or other males. In the species used for food purposes the castrated animals fatten more easily and quicker and the flesh is of a more desirable quality. Also it permits careful selection of the male animals that are to be retained for breeding purposes and the inferior individuals castrated.

EQUINE. As a general rule the equine is castrated at approximately one year of age. In the equine it is important that complete drainage be established from the operative area. As much of the tunics as possible should be removed to prevent the development of hydrocele or "water seed". Also as much of the cord as is possible should be removed to prevent it becoming infected and the development of a scirrhous cord. If the operator is careful to include sufficient tissue in the emasculator so the blood vessels are tightly closed there is little danger of excessive hemorrhage.

Castration of colts is contra-indicated during the course of any infectious disease as distemper or influenza. The castration operation should be delayed if the colt is in poor condition because of parasites or inferior quality of feed. If there is any history of the colt ever being affected with a scrotal hernia a careful examination should be made of the inguinal canals at the time of castration.

The operation may be performed in the standing position or in recumbency depending upon the preference of the operator. The operation will be described with the patient in the recumbent position and with the legs flexed. To control the patient during the casting and confinement in dorsal recumbency one of the general anesthetics is given in sufficient amount to control the struggling. Anesthesia of the tissues is obtained by infiltration of the scrotum along the proposed lines of incision and infiltration of the cords at or above the proposed point of removal.

For the straight castration the operative area is prepared for the operation. It is almost needless to say the instruments should be sterile and the hands of the operator as clean as possible. Grasp the skin at the anterior end of the sheath with one hand and tense the skin of the scrotum upward and forward. Then with a sharp knife and starting at the anterior end of the scrotum two parallel incisions are made through the scrotum one-half inch on either side of the median line and approximately five inches long. The testicle and cord below the intended point of removal are freed from the loose areolar tissue surrounding them by breaking it loose with the fingers. Special attention is directed to the large scrotal veins that are frequently in close contact to the cord or tunics. The veins are carefully pushed away from the tunics so they will not be crushed or severed by the emasculator. If any of these veins are cut by the emasculator they are usually the source of any excessive hemorrhage that occurs following the castration operation.

After the testicle and cord have been freed from the surrounding tissue the cord is grasped in one hand just below the testicle. An incision long enough for the testicle to pass through is made in the tunics over the testicle. The hand grasping the cord forces the testicle out through the incision in the tunics. The emasculator is placed around the tunics and closed just enough so it can be pushed down the cord. The emasculator is introduced well down on the cord and the tunics and cord divided. By forcing the testicle out through the incision in the tunics, when the cord is divided the end of the cord retracts and the tunics are left longer than the cord. By this method the end of the cord is not likely to become infected with the formation of a scirrhous cord.

The interior of the scrotum is examined to see if the fascia was incised to the same extent as the skin. If the fascia tends to form any pockets it is incised so complete drainage is established from the scrotum. The section of skin between the two parallel incisions is now removed so the scrotal incisions will not heal together too quickly.

All castrated colts should be turned out in a pasture and observed to see if they take sufficient exercise. In some cases it may be necessary to force them to take the necessary daily exercise required to prevent excessive swelling of the sheath.

BOVINE. The shape and position of the scrotum in the bovine are different from the equine but the principles of castration remain the same.

The operation may be performed in the standing position or in lateral recumbency. The incisions in the scrotum may be made over the front, the side or the back of the scrotum and directly over each testicle. Start the incisions at the approximate heighth of the rudimentary teats and continue through the bottom of the scrotum. The testicle enclosed within the tunics is brought out through the incision. The emasculator is put on over the tunics and cord and all the structures divided as high in the scrotum as possible. If there is very much fat in the scrotum much of it should be removed as it interferes with drainage and healing of the scrotal wound. The bottom of the scrotum may be cut off but it results in an unsightly shaped cod which is objectionable to many owners.

The emasculatome is used a great deal on the bovine and ovine and it has several advantages. No open wound is produced so there is no danger of infection or infection by larvae.

In using the emasculatome the cord should be pushed firmly against the side of the scrotum. The emasculatome is adjusted so the entire cord will be crushed but only include as much of the scrotum as is necessary. The action of the emasculatome should not extend across the median septum of the scrotum or the lower part of the scrotum will slough off.

Vasectomy in the Bovine

The vasectomy operation consists of removing from each of the vas deferens a section approximately one inch long. The operation has increased in importance due to the increase in popularity of artificial insemination. The use of a vasectomized bull to identify cows that do not show pronounced symptoms of oestrus is very important. When these cows are not identified valuable time is lost in getting them pregnant. The bull that is to be operated on should be a young bull that has never been used for breeding purposes. Also the bull should be examined for any infection of the genital tract before the operation is performed.

The operation may be performed on the anterior or posterior surface of the scrotum. Also it is possible to perform the operation with the bull in the standing position if he is of a quiet disposition. The operation will be most easily performed, however, with the patient confined in lateral recumbency. The operative area from two to three inches above the base of the testicle is prepared for an aseptic operation. The incision is made about two inches long through the skin and subcutaneous tissue to the cord. Both cords may be operated through one incision or an incision may be made over each cord. A pair of curved forceps is introduced beneath the cord and it is elevated through the incision. The vas deferens enclosed in a special fold of the tunica vaginalis propria can be palpated between the thumb and finger and recognized as a small hard tube. The serous membrane is incised so the vas deferens is freely exposed. It is optional as to the advisability of ligating the vas deferens before a section is removed. After removing the

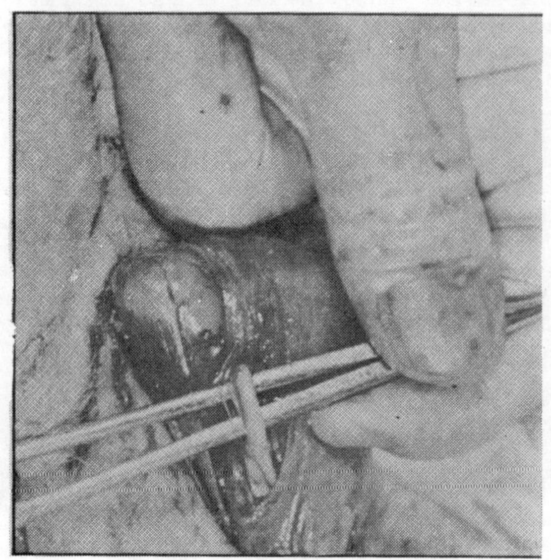

FIG. 335. Vas deferens is a firm cord like structure.

ection of the vas deferens the cord is released and allowed to return to its normal position. The other cord may be operated on with the same technique. The operation is completed by closing the incision or incisions in the skin with two or three interrupted sutures. The vasectomy may be performed at the ventral extremity of the testicle.

OVINE. The same technique that is used in castrating the bovine is used on the ovine. Most lambs are castrated about two weeks of age and the small emasculatome is very convenient to use.

PORCINE. Most pigs are castrated at a rather early age when they are from one to several weeks of age. They seem to mature quicker than pigs castrated when they are older. If the pigs are to be fitted for show purposes castration is delayed until they weigh about 100 to 150 pounds.

In castrating swine one incision in the scrotum is sufficient. This method has been used on boars weighing up to 800 pounds with excellent results. Start the incision in the median line about the middle of the scrotum and extend it an equal distance below the bottom of the scrotum. The fingers are inserted around the tunics and by traction the attachments of the tunic to the scrotum are broken. The testicle enclosed within the tunics is brought out through the incision and the cord and tunics are divided at the anterior end of the incision. It is usually necessary to make an incision through the median septum of the scrotum to reach the other testicle and it is removed in the same manner.

Castration of Large Boars Using Chloroform Anesthesia

The use of chloroform to produce genera anesthesia in the castration of large boars is not only humane but is also important as a means of restraint. A chloro form bag may be made similar to the feed bag for horses except it has a short canvas extension with a draw string around it. The bag should be drawn over the boars snout up to the eyes. Some operators prefer to wrap several layers of sacking around the snout. A piece of gauze may be folded several times and moistened with one-half ounce of chloroform and then introduced into the bag which is left open to insure plenty of air will be mixed with the chloroform. When the boar relaxes a little the concentration of the chloroform should be increased by partially closing the bag. Also additional amounts of chloroform may be given adding it slowly and carefully and noting the character of the respirations. For the average boar it will require one ounce of chloroform, some will take less others will require one and one-half ounces. Complete anesthesia takes place very rapidly with the boar, as they roll over on their side. A rope may be used to fasten the posterior limbs forward from the operative area. The liberal incisions that are made over each testicle should extend to the bottom of the scrotum When the operation is completed the boar should be returned to a normal sternal position to recover from the effects of the chloroform.

Castration of Large Boars Using Nembutal

Nembutal may be given intravenously in th ear vein of large boars as an important aid in their restraint or enough may be used for complete anesthesia. When nembutal is injected intravenously its effect is noticed very quickly as the boar may go down before the operator has time to give the desired dosage. The boar usually goes down very easily and rolls over onto its side. The patient is then easily restrained in the recumbent position for the operation. For large boars fifteen to thirty cubic centimeters of nembutal may be used with the patient recovering in two or three hours. The advantages of nembutal is its ease of administration and safety. There may be marked variation in the dosage of nembutal for each case and only enough should be given to obtain the desired results.

Castration of the Equine Cryptorchid (Ridgling, Original, Rig)

The term cryptorchid refers to a hidden testicle. The testicle may be found in the abdominal cavity or in the inguinal canal. If located in the abdominal cavity it is called an abdominal cryptochid, and when one is present it is unilateral and if both are retained the term bilateral is used. When it is retained in the inguinal canal the term inguinal cryptorchid, (high flanker) is used and may be unilateral or bilateral.

When the term monorchid is used it may mean the testicle is retained or has not developed and the term anorchid is used when both are retained or undeveloped.

The successful operator must know and understand the anatomy of the parts he will invade in his search for the hidden testicle. Also it is important to know the position of the testicle in the embryo and the course of its descent into the scrotum.

DIAGNOSIS. If no attempt has ever been made to castrate the patient the diagnosis of retention of one or both testicles is easy and the side on which they are retained is readily determined. Examination of the external ring may disclose the testicle just above or in the ring. In some cases the mass of inflammatory tissue which may develop on the cut end of the cord may lead to an incorrect diagnosis as to the location of the testicle. A rectal examination is usually of little value in these cases as the cryptic testicle is usually difficult to palpate. Failure to definately feel the testicle may lead to an erroneous conclusion as to its presence or absence.

The information as given by the owner or attendant may not be of much assistance to the operator. If the horse has been purchased recently the owner may not know if either testicle has been removed. The owner may know that one testicle was removed but does not know which one. Other owners have been present when the horse was castrated and are sure they know which testicle was removed but this information may later prove to be erroneous. Occasionally the owner is able to give the operator very reliable information. But the operator should not form a definite opinion until the horse is down and he has examined the scrotum for scars and the inguinal canal for the end of the cord.

ANATOMY. In operating on cryptorchids in any species the operator must know the anatomy of the structures he will invade. Also he should know about the development of the testicle in the embryo and the route of its descent into the scrotum. The term inguinal canal refers to a passage through the posterior part of the abdominal wall. Its anterior wall is formed by the fleshy posterior part of the internal oblique muscle and the posterior wall by the strong tendinous inguinal ligament. The average length of the canal is about four inches. The internal inguinal ring is formed by the thin margin of the internal oblique muscle in front and behind by the inguinal ligament. The external inguinal ring is formed by a slit in the aponeurosis of the external oblique muscle.

In the embryo the testicle develops in the sublumbar region above the parietal peritoneum. The spermatic artery, a branch of the posterior aorta, joins the testicle and suspends it anteriorly. The epididymi develops posterior to the testicle and is attached to it by tissue which becomes the ligament of the epididymis. This tissue varies in length and in the cryptic tissue may be rather long so the testicle is not close to the epididymis. The ductus deferens, a continuation of the epididymis, passes back to the pelvic cavity where it enters the edge of the genital fold and terminates at the urethra.

Another embryonic structure, the gubernaculum testes, extends from the tail of the epididymis to be attached in the vicinity of the internal ring. There is a continuation of the gubernaculum testes to the bottom of the scrotum and it shortens as the testicle descends and eventually becomes the ligament of the scrotum. With the development of the fetus the testicle usually gravitates toward the internal ring and the structures accompanying it are enclosed in a fold or peritoneum. Some cryptic testicles when found have not moved from their original position. If the testicle does not descend into the canal three structures may be used to locate it, the gubernaculum testes, which is usually attached close to the internal ring, the vas deferens, which is easily picked up where it passes through the edge of the genital fold and the vascular fold anteriorly which is not easy to locate.

The testicle is preceded into the canal by an evagination of the parietal peritoneum, the processus vaginalis. In the center of the processus is an area about an inch in diameter where the peritoneum feels thinner called the vaginal ring. When the hand is introduced into the inguinal canal to the wrist the operator should be able to feel the vaginal ring with the tips of his fingers.

Operation

PREPARATION. Every precaution should be taken to perform an aseptic operation. The instruments that are sterilized should include both an emasculator and ecraseur as in some cases the cord is so short the testicle cannot be removed with an emasculator. Other instruments consist of a knife, scissors, forceps, suture needles, suture material, and a roll of sterile gauze.

Some form of anesthesia should be used to control the pain and struggling. If excessive struggling occurs during the operative procedure it may result in severe trauma to the tissues and a delay in healing of the wound. The anesthesia that is used will depend upon the preference of the operator but it should control the struggling and the pain of the operation.

The patient is then cast in dorsal recumbency and the hind legs so tied they are fully abducted. Wrap the hind feet in clean cloths to assist in keeping the operative area clean. The skin in the scrotal and inguinal region is thoroughly prepared for an aseptic operation. Also the operators hands should be thoroughly cleansed by scrubbing with brush, soap, and water and the liberal application of an efficient skin antiseptic.

If there is some doubt as to which testicle is retained the scrotum should be examined thoroughly for the presence of scars. When only one scar is present it is a fairly reliable indication the testicle has been removed from that side. When two scars are present it may mean one testicle has been removed, or both, and in some cases neither one has been removed. We have castrators that make one incision and attempt to remove both testicles through the one incision. If the available evidence fails to disclose which testicle is retained the left side is operated on first.

The incision may be made the same as for a normal castration or over the external ring. Any hemorrhage that occurs should be completely controlled. In most cases an incision about four inches long is made over the external ring. The fingers are used to break the loose areolar tissue over and in the ring until its edges are clearly exposed. A careful examination is made to see if the gubernaculum or epididymis are in the ring. When either of these structures are found they will lead directly to the testicle. Failing to find any structure the operator should cleanse the hand thoroughly that is to be inserted into the canal. The best procedure is to put a sterile rubber glove on the hand that is to enter the canal and probably the abdominal cavity. If the cut end of the cord is found it is definite evidence the testicle has been removed from that side.

With the tips of the fingers together the hand is inserted into the canal using the tips of the fingers to break any adhesions that may be present. As the hand is advanced down the canal the fingers are constantly feeling for the gubernaculum, epididymis or even the testicle itself. Failing to find any recognizable structure the hand is inserted into the canal up to the wrist. Careful palpation is then made for the internal ring which is most easily identified by finding the vaginal ring. This ring is about one inch in diameter and composed of one layer of peritoneum which feels very thin. If the tips of the fingers are pressed against the internal ring the testicle may appear in the hand. If no structure is palpated the vaginal ring is punctured with the index finger or in some cases it is advisable to use a long pair forceps as the peritoneum may be rather tough. The index finger is then inserted into the abdominal cavity and with it flexed, a search is made for the gubernaculum where it is usually attached close to the posterior edge of the internal ring. If it is not found insert another finger through the ring and attempt to pick up the epididymis. In a large percentage of cases this is the structure that is usually located. It may be necessary to insert the hand into the peritoneal cavity to search for the testicle. When this fails the other hand should be inserted into the peritoneal cavity to find the genital fold

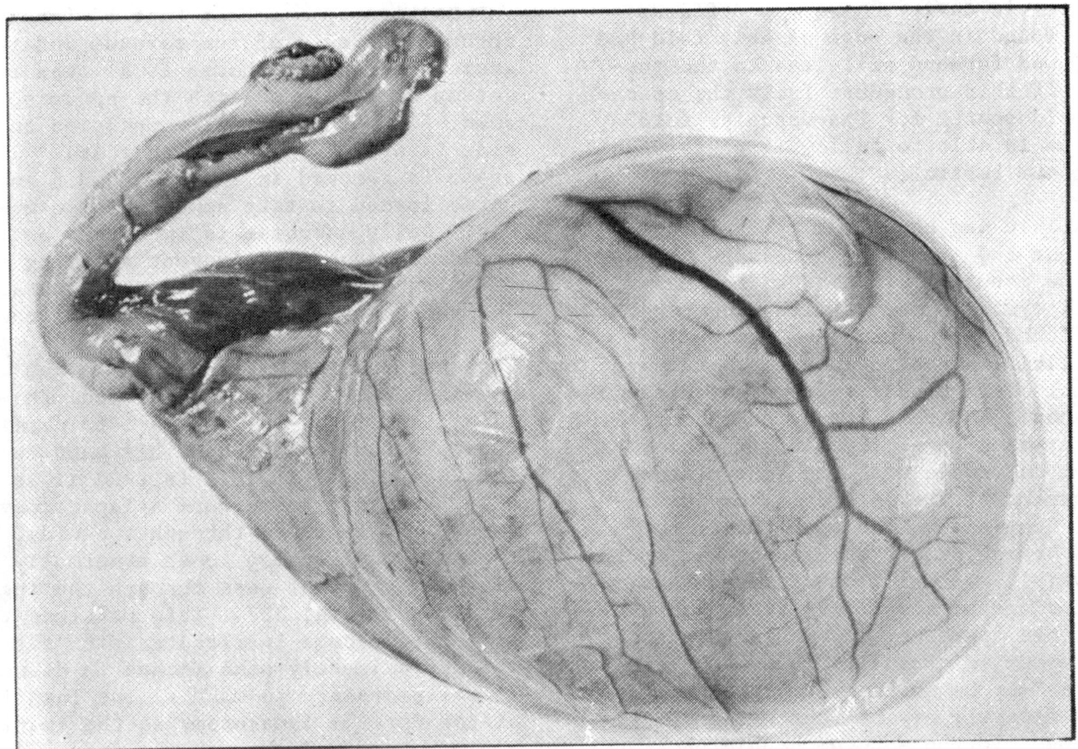

FIG. 336. A cystic testicle removed from the abdominal cavity of a two year old colt.

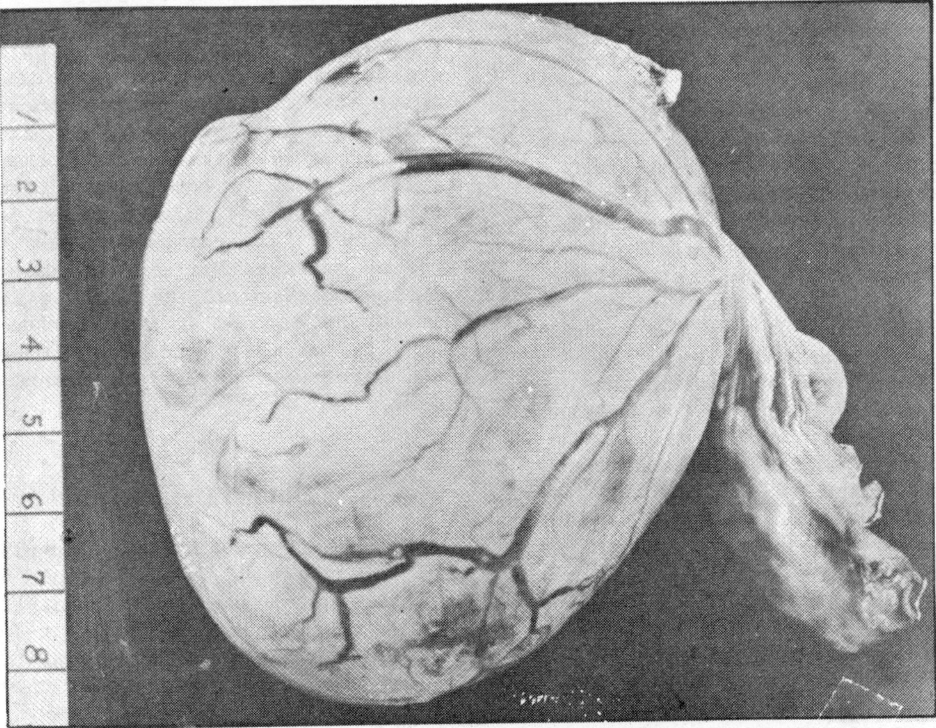

FIG. 337. This was a retained testicle in the abdominal cavity of a two year old, that became infiltrated with fat and weighed nine and one-half pounds.

in the pelvic cavity. The vas deferens will be found in the edge of this fold and if followed forward will lead to the testicle. If this procedure fails the operator should search for the vascular fold and if he is able to follow it, this should lead to the testicle.

The testicle may be unusually large due to a tumor and it may be necessary to enlarge the internal ring. When the testicle is cystic a needle with rubber tubing attached may be used, to remove the excess fluid. Cryptic testicles that are abdominal or inguinal vary a great deal in size, shape, and consistency so the operator should examine carefully the structures he is going to remove with the emasculator. The ligament of the epididymis may be unusually long and if the operator is not careful he may remove only a portion of the epididymis. Another type of case, that may be confusing the first time it is encountered by the operator, is one in which the vas deferens is unusually long, and this condition may be unilateral or bilateral. The vas deferens may be long enough to extend down into the scrotum double back up the inguinal canal to be attached to the testicle in the abdominal cavity. After making the incision through the scrotum the operator will find the curved portion of the vas deferens covered by the tunics and may wrongly conclude the testicle has been removed or he may remove this curved portion for a small testicle. However there will be an absence of inflammatory tissue which would be present if it is the end of the cord. If the operator will cut through the tunics he will find the two portions of the vas deferens and by exerting traction first on one portion, then the other, the operator will be able to determine to which portion the testicle is attached. This is usually revealed by the portion to which the testicle is attached will give, as traction is exerted. The testicle may be removed by passing the hand along the vas deferens to the internal ring and enlarging the opening in the vaginal ring with the fingers until the testicle will pass through. The testicle is then removed in the usual manner. If the other testicle is also cryptic it should be removed at this time.

If only one or two fingers are introduced through the internal ring the canal is not packed with gauze. However when the hand has been introduced through the internal ring the canal should be packed with gauze to prevent any intestine from passing through the ring. The gauze is maintained in position by a suture that is inserted through the skin of the scrotum and the gauze. Before the horse is allowed to get up he is placed with the operated side down. If both sides were operated on, one side is usually packed with gauze. The gauze is removed in 24 to 36 hours and the horse forced to take some exercise every day. Daily exercise is important as this tends to reduce and prevent swelling of the tissues and force out any suppuration or wound secretion in the inguinal canal.

When the testicle is retained in the abdominal cavity of a Shetland pony the inguinal canal may be too small to permit the operator to introduce his hand to the internal ring. If this is true it is usually necessary to perform a laparotomy and remove the testicle through the side. The testicle may develop to an abnormally large size so it cannot pass through the inguinal canal as in Fig. 337. This retained testicle had become infiltrated with fat and was approximately nine inches in diameter. It was necessary to make a nine inch incision for the laparotomy so the testicle could be removed through the side.

Teratomas

Teratomas in most cases start their development in embryonic life and are composed of more than one of the three primary germ layers, the ectoderm, mesoderm and entoderm. Most of the teratomas occur in either the ovary or testicle. The different tissues are all mixed together in a mass that usually consists of cartilage, connective tissue, bone and epithelial structures. The growth of the various tissues may vary but in most cases it is of slow development, but with a true teratoma there must be active growth. Occasionally one of the tissues becomes malignant with rapid growth and metastasis may occur.

Bovine Cryptorchid

It is rather rare to find a cryptic testicle in the bull. The testicle is usually ectopic, not in the scrotum but situated in the subcutaneous tissue. It may be located beneath the skin alongside the penis, the ventral surface of the abdomen or out in the fold of the flank. When the testicle is located in the subcutaneous tissue an incision is made through the skin and the testicle removed at that point.

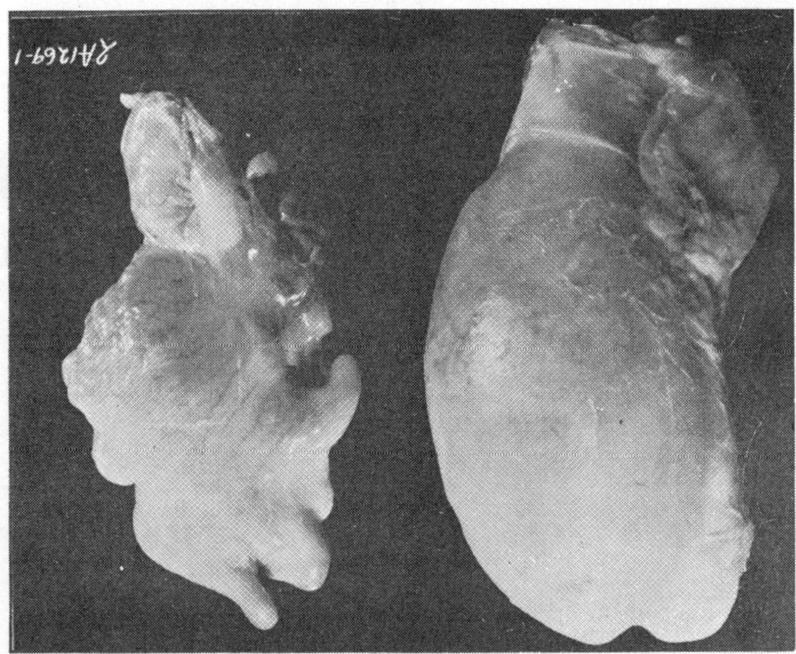

FIG. 338. Left testicle retained in abdominal cavity of two year old, edge of retained testicle very irregular.

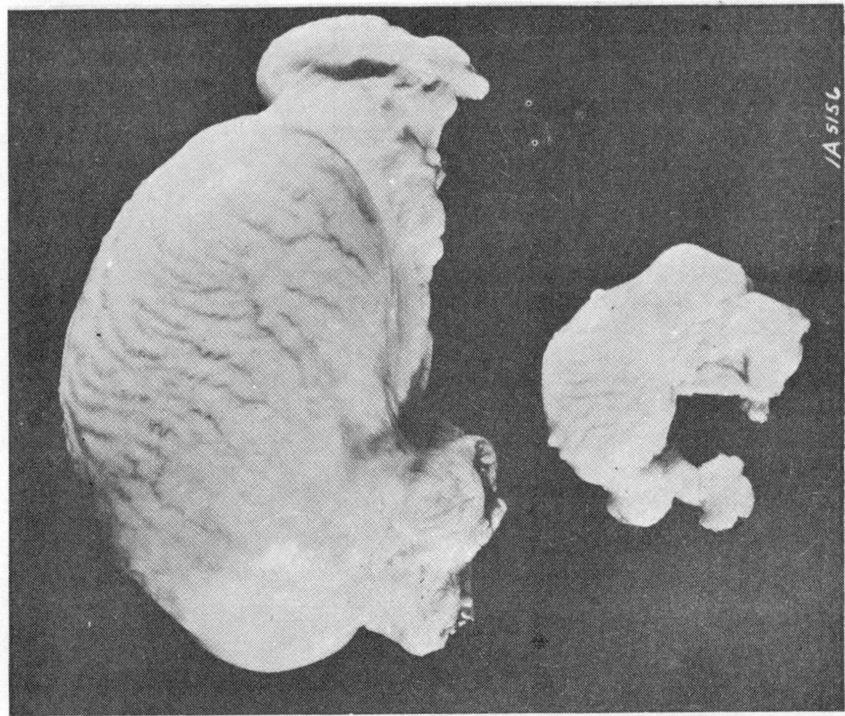

FIG. 339. The difference in size between a normal testicle in the scrotum and one retained in the inguinal canal in a two year old.

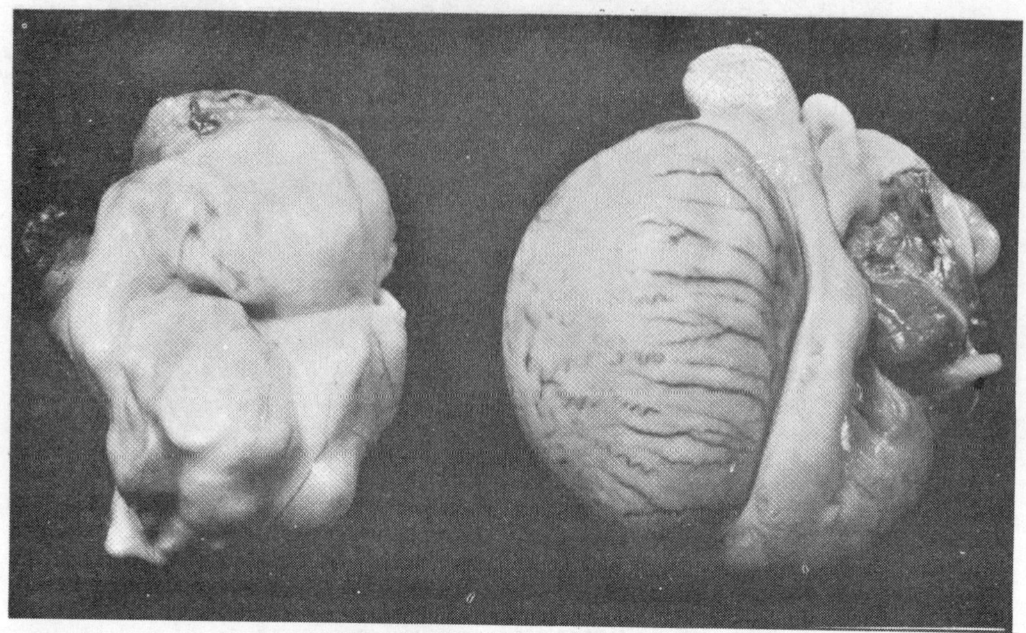

FIG. 340. Teratoma of left testicle retained in abdominal cavity of two year old. Courtesy of Dr. J. C. Catlin.

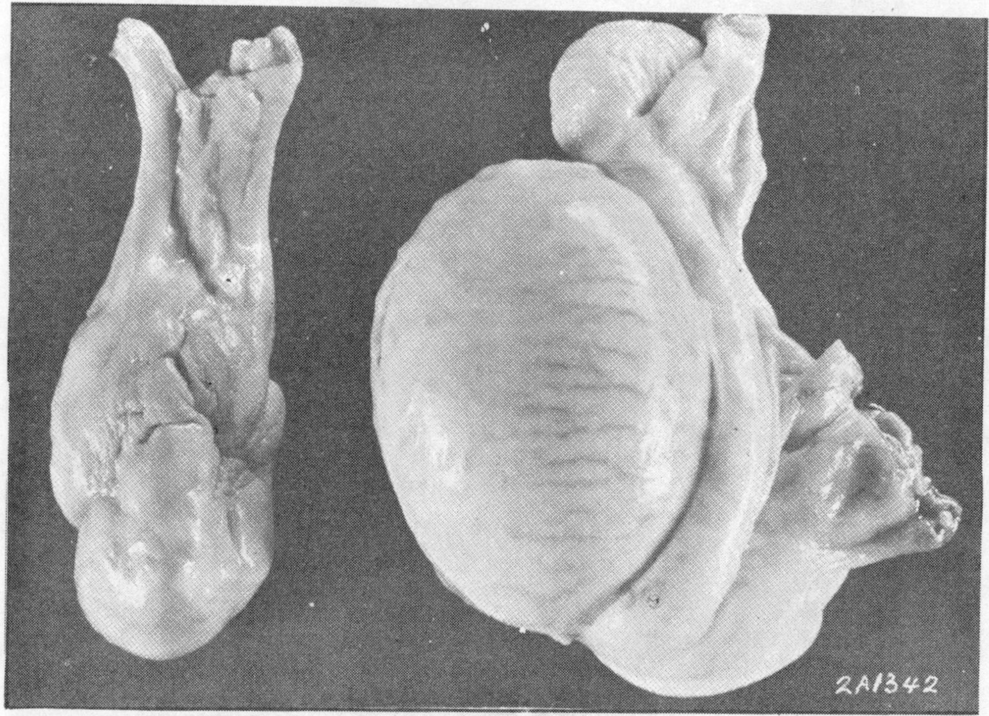

FIG. 341. Testicular dermoid in a testicle retained in the abdominal cavity on the left side in a three year old.

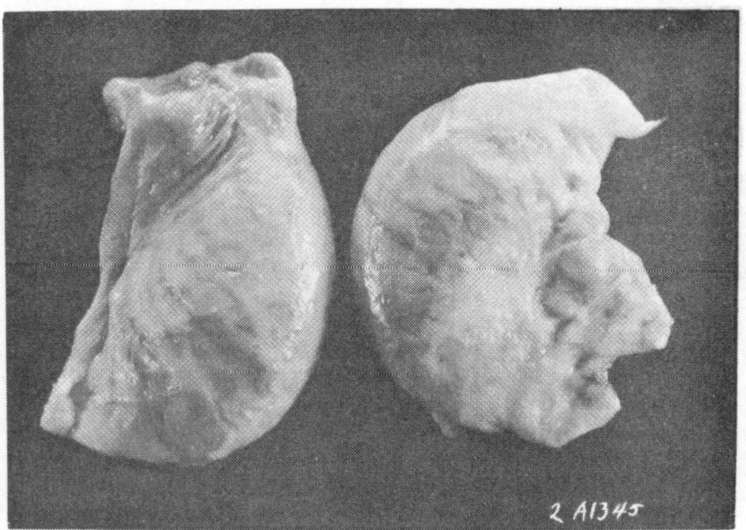

FIG. 342. Both testicles retained in abdominal cavity of two year old.

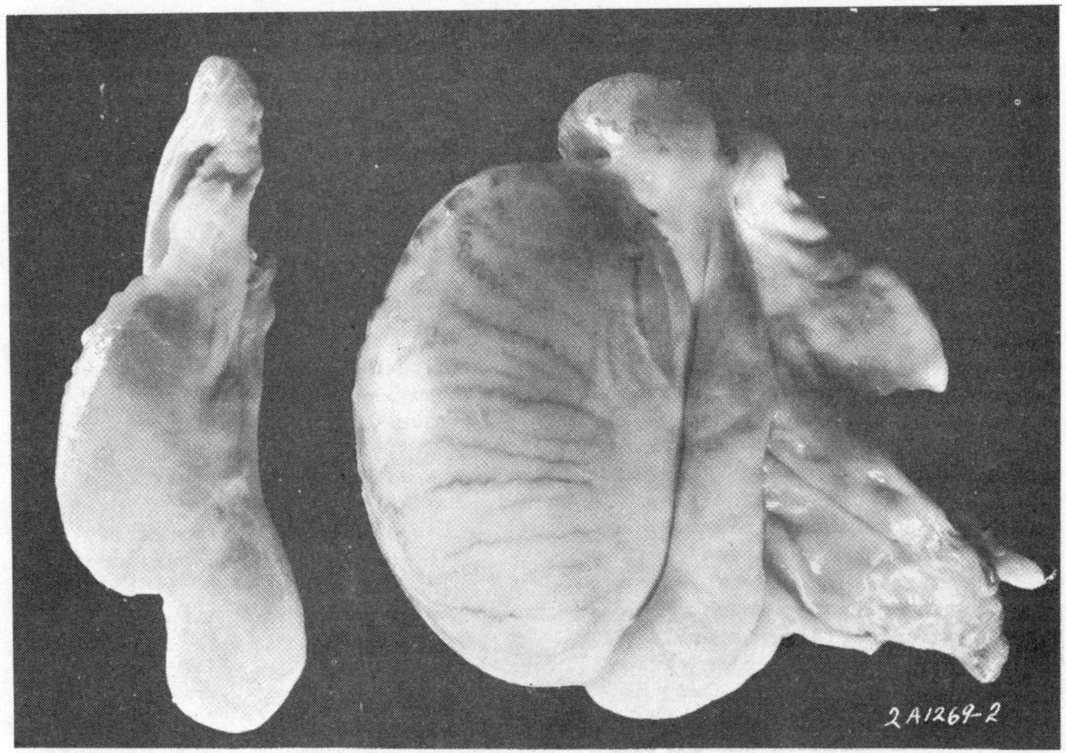

FIG. 343. Left testicle retained in abdominal cavity of two year old.

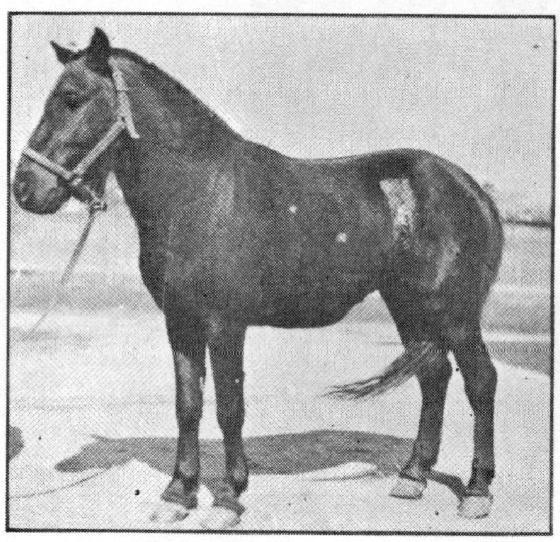

FIG. 344. In this case it was necessary to perform a laparotomy to remove the testicle.

If the testicle is in the abdominal cavity a laparotomy is performed in the right or left flank. The same guides that are used to find the cryptic testicle in the equine are used in the bovine. The testicle is also removed in the same manner.

Porcine Cryptorchid

Crypic testicles occur frequently in swine and in many cases both testicles are retained. The operation may be performed through the side or in the inguinal region. Some form of anesthesia should be used, either general using chloroform or nembutal, infiltration of the tissues with a local anesthetic or epidural anesthesia may be used.

Usually we operate by making an incision over the internal ring through the skin and subcutaneous tissues down to the ring. The ring is carefully examined for any vessels passing through it that might lead to the testicle. The index finger is inserted through the peritoneum and a search made for the gubernaculum, epididymis or the testicle itself. If none of these structures are found a search is made for the genital fold in the pelvic cavity. The vas deferens will be found in the edge of the genital fold and if followed forward is a definite guide to the testicle. The

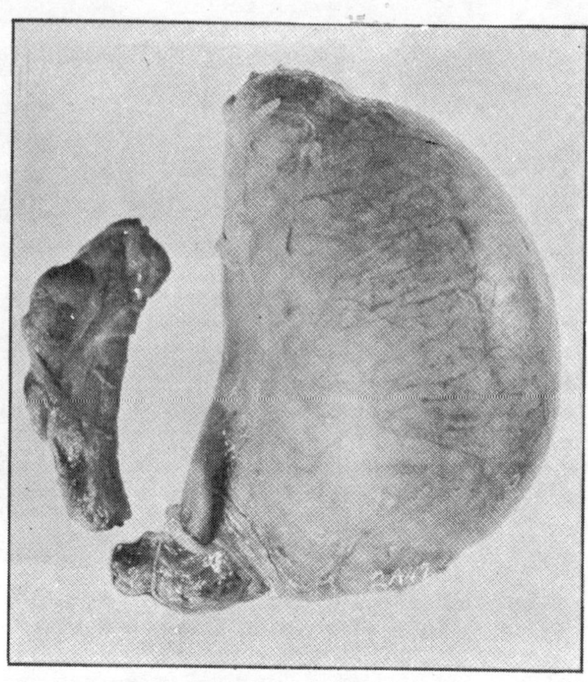

FIG. 345. Testicles removed from boar both in the scrotum.

testicle when found is brought out to the incision, the cord ligated and the testicle removed. The internal ring is closed with a continuous catgut suture. The incision is closed with a mattress suture.

Complications that may occur following castration:

1. Hemorrhage may be severe enough to endanger the life of the animal. Excessive hemorrhage is usually due to injury to some of the large scrotal veins. An attempt should be made to find the bleeding vessel and ligate it. If this is unsuccessful it may be necessary to pack the inguinal region tightly with sterile gauze. This is retained in position for twenty-four hours by closing the scrotal incision with mattress sutures.

2. Prolapse of the omentum may occur when the patient assumes a standing position. The patient should be cast and a little more of the omentum pulled out. A catgut ligature is placed around the omentum and the omentum distal to the ligature is removed. The omentum is placed well down into the inguinal canal and the cut ends of the tunics are picked up and sutured together or the cord may be ligated.

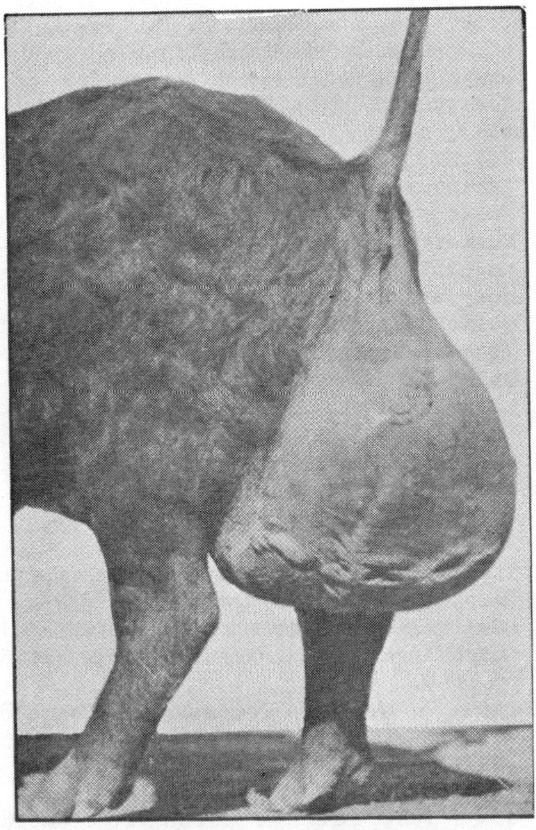

FIG. 346. Unusually large scirrhous cord in a pig.

If prolapse of the intestine occurs it should be protected from injury with antiseptic packs until the animal can be cast. The prolapsed portion is then carefully cleansed with a non-irritating antiseptic solution or a physiological saline solution. The intestines are most easily returned to the abdominal cavity by inserting a hand into the rectum and exerting steady traction on the intestine. The cut ends of the tunics are picked up and sutured together. In some cases it may be advisable to pack the inguinal canal with sterile gauze and retain it in position for twenty-four hours.

Scirrhous Cord

The most frequent complication following castration in pigs is scirrhous cord, only occasionally do we have a case presented in horses and cattle. When present its appearance is characterized by a firm adherent practically painless enlargement in the scrotal and inguinal region. There is usually a slow but gradual increase in its size with the development of usually one or more openings discharging to the exterior. It should be treated as soon as observed for there is a gradual increase in the development of inflammatory tissue and adhesions with the surrounding tissue.

Since the introduction of the antibiotics and the use of penicillin in the treatment of scirrhous cords it has not been necessary to surgically remove the infected and inflammatory mass of tissue. The penicillin is injected intramuscularly and either the procaine penicillin or penicillin in oil may be used. The amount to use will be determined by the amount of infected tissue. However the dosage will vary from one to two million units and even more may be indicated in an unusual case. In some cases it may be necessary to repeat the dosage in a week to ten days if there is still some inflammatory tissue. The results from the use of penicillin in the treatment of scirrhous cords have been excellent.

Hydrocele - Water Seed

In this condition a variable quantity of fluid is found between the layers of the tunica vaginalis due to chronic inflammation of these tissues. The symptoms may resemble a scrotal hernia except that most of the swelling is confined to the lower part of the scrotum.

Treatment consists in making an incision through the skin over the swelling. Blunt dissection is used to separate the tunics from the surrounding tissue and as much of the tunics are removed as is possible.

REFERENCES

Arthur, G. H., The Diagnostic Value of the Blood Leucocyte Picture in Traumatic Reticulitis And Pericaditis of Bovines, The Veterinary Record, (August 1946), pp. 365-366.

Baker, D. D., Obstetrics in Swine, Veterinary Medicine, Vol. XXXII, 1937, No. 3.

Bemis, H. E., Castration of the Normal Male Animal, North American Veterinarian, Vol. II, (1930), No. 3, pp. 17-19.

Bemis, H. E., Scrotal and Inguinal Hernia, North American Veterinarian, Vol. II, (1930), No. 6.

Bemis, H. E., Cryptorchid Castration, North American Veterinarian, Vol. II (1930), No. 4, pp. 25-27.

Bemis, H. E., Umbilical Hernia, North American Veterinarian, Vol. II, (May, 1930), pp. 17.

Carroll, R. E., Magnets in the Control of Traumatic Gastritis, J.A.V.M.A., (1955), pp. 311-312.

Carroll, R. E. and Robinson, R. E., The Differential Leukocyte Counts in the Diagnosis and Prognosis of Bovine Traumatic Gastritis, J.A.V.M.A., 132, (1958), pp. 248-249.

Cooper, H. K., A Proposed Procedure for Controlling Traumatic Gastritis, J.A.V.M.A., 127, (Dec. 1955), pp. 477-481.

Curtis, H., Caesarean Section in the Cow, North American Veterinarian, Vol. XX, (March, 1939), pp. 21.

Dougherty, R. W., Induced Cases of Traumatic Gastritis in Dairy Cattle, J.A.V.M.A., 94, (1939), pp. 357-362.

Ferguson, T. H. and S. E., Caesarean Section in Cattle, The North American Veterinarian, Vol. 15, (1934), No.9, pp. 25.

Fowler, G. R., Umbilical Hernia in a Horse, Jen-Sal Journal, (September-October, 1937).

Frank, E. R. and Roberts, S. J., Caesarean Section in the Bovine, North American Veterinarian, Vol. XI, (Sept., 1940), pp. 1946.

Frank, E. R., Some Hernias in the Equine and Bovine, J.A.V.M.A., Vol. XCI, (1937), N.S., Vol. 44, No. 6, pp. 639-646.

Fuller, J. R., Surgical Treatment of Hernia in Horses, North American Veterinarian, Vol. 16, (1935), No. 3., pp. 32-34.

Glenney, W. C., Caesarean Section in Large Animals, North American Veterinarian, Vol. XX, (Dec., 1939), pp. 43

Isham, R. R., Caesarotomy in a Cow, North American Veterinarian, Vol. X, (August, 1929), pp. 39.

Kettel, E. W. and Snook, M. D., Prevention of So-Called "Hardware Disease" in Cattle Using a Magnetic Metal Retriever, J.A.V.M.A., 131, (1957), pp. 285-286.

Kimball, Alice, B. S., Twiehaus, M. J., D.V.M., M.S., Frank, E. R., D.V.M., M.S., Actinomyces Bovis Isolated From Six Cases of Orchitis, American Journ. Vet. Research, Vol. XV, No. 57, (Oct., 1954), pp. 551-553.

Kingery, B. W., Experimental Bovine Traumatic Gastritis, J.A.V.M.A., Vol. 127, (December, 1955), pp. 477-481.

McCahon, J. V. and Bond, W. P., Use of a Magnet to Locate and Remove Foreign Bodies From the Reticulum, Proc. 90th, Am. Mtg. J.A.V.M.A., (1954), pp. 70-72.

Ouderkirk, R. E., Successful Caesarotomy in a Cow, North American Veterinarian, Vol. IX, (Sept., 1928), pp. 29.

Schipper, I. A., Witz, Richard and Eveleth, D. R., Magnetic Apparatus for the Removal of Metal From the Bovine Reticulum, North American Veterinarian, 36, (1955), pp. 640.

Simpson, W. M., Caesarotomy Saves Cow and Calf, North American Veterinarian, Vol. VIII, (July, 1927), pp. 23.

Tischhauser, L. A., Milk Fistula of the Cow's Teat, North American Veterinarian, Vol. XXII, 3, (1941), pp. 166.

Turner, J. P., Castration of Large Boars Using Chloroform Anesthesia, Veterinary Medicine, XXXIII, 4, (April, 1938), pp. 156.

Witt, B., Veterinary Obstetrics, Veterinary Medicine, (Jan. 1937), pp. 24.

Chapter IX
AFFECTIONS OF THE TAIL, ANUS, RECTUM, VAGINA AND PENIS

Subcutaneous Caudal Myotomy

Tail Setting

The object of performing a myotomy on the depressor muscles of the tail is to assist the horse in elevating the tail higher than normal when in motion. Some horses will carry the tail the desired height and will not require or be benefited by the operation. In saddle horses there are usually two types of tails presented for operation, the limber tail and the stiff tail. It may be impossible to obtain a high elevation of the limber tail because of lack of stiffness, the tail will not be carried or stand very high without curving to the right or left. The stiff tail usually develops a high elevation which is very desirable when it has the proper curve. As a general rule the horse should become accustomed to wearing the tail set before the operation is performed. However horses that have unusually strong depressor muscles may object to the use of the tail set. In some cases the tail will be held stiff and straight while others may become crooked. The use of the tail set should be discontinued for those cases, that are held stiff and straight, for two or three months and then the tail setting operation may be performed. The principal object in using the tail set is to hold the tail at the desired angle with the body. Also with the tail resting in the crupper which is nine to eleven inches long the end of the tail hangs over the end of the crupper which after a period of time produces a curve which adds to its beauty when held at the proper height.

OPERATION. The operation is performed with the patient in the standing position by the application of a twitch to the upper lip and the use of breeding hobbles to prevent kicking. A side line may be used in some cases or the horse can be backed up to a low partition which will prevent the operator from being kicked.

Anesthesia for the operation is obtained by infiltration of the tissues with a two per cent solution of a local anesthetic. With the tail elevated over the back and held firmly in position the ventral surface of the tail close to the body is prepared for an aseptic operation. A 24 gauge needle is used to produce an insensitive area in the skin about one-half inch to the right of the median line. This insensitive area is made as close to the body as possible for this is where the muscle should be divided to obtain the best results. A 22 gauge needle one and one-half inches long is now used to infiltrate the muscle to be operated on and usually fifteen cubic centimeters of the local anesthetic is used. The same procedure is used to anesthetize the tissue to the left of the median line. It is very important that the tissue is completely infiltrated so that the patient does not feel any pain during the operation. The tail is now released and sufficient time is allowed to give the anesthetic time to exert its full effect.

The tail should again be elevated over the back and held firmly in position on the median line and the operative area again prepared for the operation. It does not make any difference which muscle is operated on first as this can be determined by the preference of the operator. If the muscle to the right of the median line is to be operated on first, the nicking knife is introduced through the skin one-half to three quarters of an inch to the right of the median line. The medial edge of the sacro-coccygeus ventralis muscle which may be palpated is used as a guide as the point to insert the knife. The point of the knife with its side against the muscle should be directed upward, forward and slightly laterally to avoid injury to the vertebrae. Introduce the knife until its cutting edge is beneath the skin then turn the cutting edge until it is against the muscle. The muscle tissue is divided to the skin and the knife introduced deeper and the cutting continued until the muscle is divided which is indicated by a separation of the ends. The operator should determine by palpation that all of the tissue has been cut to the skin but the skin should not be injured. The same procedure

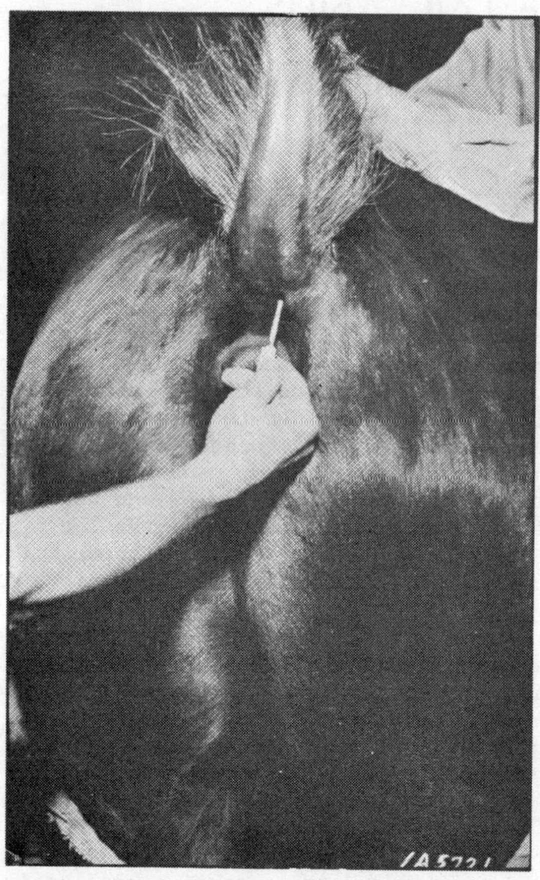

FIG. 347. Nicking knife in position to cut right sacro-coccygeus ventralis muscle.

Crooked Tail

A horse is frequently presented with the request that an operation be performed to correct a crooked tail. The tail may become crooked because of an improperly performed tail setting operation, elevating a stiff tail too high with the tail set, improper use of the tail set or it may be a congenital condition. The tail may also be injured producing a marked crook of the tail as shown in Fig. 348.

OPERATION. The operation to correct a crook of the tail consists in cutting the sacro-coccygeus dorsalis muscle one or more times depending upon the extent of the crook. The horse is confined the same as for the tail setting operation. To determine the exact location of the crook the horse should be walked after a little ginger has been introduced into the rectum to stimulate the elevation of the tail. When the exact point of the crook has been determined the tissue may be infiltrated with a few cubic centimeters of the two per cent solution of the local anesthetic. When the area is anesthetized the nicking knife is introduced through the skin and the dorsalis muscle is divided transversely. If the crook is used to cut the corresponding muscle of the opposite side. To ensure complete division of all the fibers of the muscles the thumb tips are forcibly inserted into the area to force the cut ends apart. If the operator is careful not to cut any more tissue than is necessary, he can prevent a great deal of the hemorrhage that occurs when blood vessels are unnecessarily injured. When excessive hemorrhage occurs it may be controlled by the use of the tail set and elevating the tail higher than normal. The after care consists in the daily application of an antiseptic to the small skin wounds until they are healed. Also the tail should be carefully elevated over the back each day with the object of keeping the ends of the muscles from healing together. The space between the ends of the muscles should fill in with connective tissue. If the best results are to be obtained from the operation the tail set should be worn daily for three months after the operation.

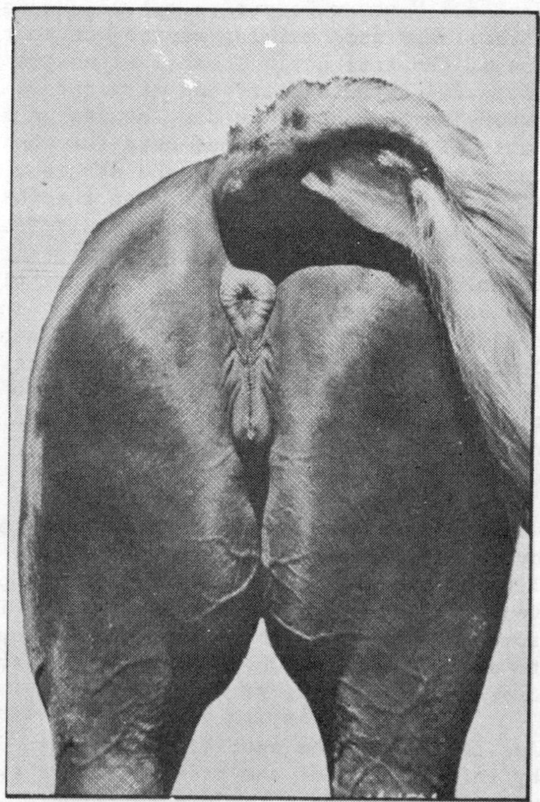

FIG. 348. A crooked tail.

is only slight it may only require a partial division of the muscle. When the crook makes a pronounced curve as in Fig. 348 the muscle is divided three times about two inches apart. After the operation the horse should again be exercised and the tail should be carried straight or slightly in the opposite direction if the operation was properly performed. In some cases it may be necessary to divide the muscle one inch closer to the body from the original incision. The slight hemorrhage that usually occurs from the operation may be controlled by the use of a pressure pack applied over the area for a few hours. The tail should be tied around to the side opposite to which it curved before the operation. Each day the horse is exercised and when it bends in the opposite direction the tail set may be used. Whenever the tail shows a tendency to curve again it may be tied around to the side. The success of the operation is determined by constant care and good judgement before it will be carried perfectly straight.

Amputation of the Tail

A portion of the tail is frequently amputated to supposedly improve the appearance of the animal. The operation may also be indicated in the case of injury or neoplasm of the tail.

OPERATION. This operation is performed with horse in the standing position and using breeding hobbles or a side line for restraint. The point at which the tail is docked will depend upon the breed and the horses conformation. As a general rule in draft breeds the tail is removed slightly below the floor of the pelvis while ponies are docked a little shorter.

Anesthesia may be obtained by infiltrating the tissue in the operative area with a two per cent solution of a local anesthetic. Also epidural anesthesia may be used by injecting fifteen cubic centimeters of a one per cent solution of a local anesthetic into the epidural space. A tourniquet is adjusted tightly at the base of the tail. The operator should determine by manipulation the point to disarticulate the vertebrae. The hair at this point is turned upwards and fastened. The hair in the operative area is removed by clipping closely or shaving. An efficient skin antiseptic is applied to the area.

In performing the operation a dorsal and ventral flap are made of the skin and soft tissues. The dorsal flap is made slightly longer than the ventral flap. The knife is introduced into the tissues at the proposed point of disarticulation of the vertebrae. A semi-circular incision is made down and across the tail to the opposite side.

The ventral incision is made in the same manner except that it is shorter. Bend the tail sharply at the proposed point of disarticulation of the vertebrae and insert the knife into the articulation. The amputation is completed by cutting all the remaining soft tissues. Interrupted sutures are used to bring the edges of the flaps together. A tourniquet is placed around the tail just above the operative area and removed in about two hours. The tourniquet at the base of the tail is removed.

Proctitis Inflammation of Anus

Rectitis Inflammation of Rectum

The presence of congenital malformations of the anus and rectum are of frequent occurrence in domestic animals. The two structures develop from two distinct areas in the embryo and unite to form one passage. When either structure fails to develop in a normal manner certain malformations occur, (1) Rectum is fully developed but the anus is absent. (2) There is absence of both rectum and anus. (3) Only a thin membrane may separate anus and rectum. (4) There may be a slight constriction between the anus and rectum.

When there is complete obstruction the animal strains more or less continuously and there is a gradual increase in size of the abdominal cavity. If passage for the meconium is not established within a short time the animal will die.

Atresia Ani

When only the anus is absent a circular piece of skin about one-half inch in diameter is removed at the usual location of the anus. The mucous membrane is then sutured to the cut edges of the skin.

Atresia Ani et Recti

It is usually necessary to remove a circular piece of skin as for the preceding operation to determine if the rectum is absent. In many cases where the rectum is absent a bulging outward of the skin occurs, due to the abdominal pressure. If the end of the intestine cannot be located in the pelvic cavity it is usually advisable to destroy the animal. However, if it is present, the end may be sutured to the edges of the skin incision. In most cases the end of the intestine is in the abdominal cavity and humane destruction of the animal is advisable in these cases.

If there is only a thin membrane or a portion of the membrane separating the anus and rectum it is rather easily ruptured with a blunt instrument.

Paralysis of the Rectum

Paralysis of the rectum occurs most frequently in the equine but has been observed in the bovine. More cases have been observed in mares than males. When paralysis of the rectum occurs other structures are usually affected as the bladder, tail, and sometimes the posterior limbs.

ETIOLOGY. Paralysis of the rectum may be produced by affections of the spinal cord, neoplasms of the lumbar and sacral region, toxins of infectious diseases and in some cases no apparent cause can be found. In a few cases paralysis of the rectum has occurred spontaneously and progressively with involvement of the rectum, bladder, tail and even the posterior quarters may be affected. The paralysis of the different structures may be complete or incomplete.

SIGNS. The first sign observed may be the passage of large quantities of feces at infrequent intervals. After the wall of the rectum becomes stretched from the accumulation of feces it is unable to expel the feces. In some cases the tail is limp and becomes soiled also the anus may be relaxed. When the bladder is affected the urine may be passed involuntarily. With the bladder distended with urine some is expelled at the time of service and becomes part of the semen. The urine has a harmful effect on the spermatazoa lowering the value of the bull for breeding.

PROGNOSIS. Will depend upon the cause but the largest percentage of the cases are incurable. If there is only a partial paralysis of the rectum the condition is not so serious as the accumulated feces can be manually removed. When the paralysis has been caused from injury as a fracture between the sacrum and first coccygeal vertebrae complete recovery has occurred in a month.

TREATMENT. The treatment consists in relieving the signs, as manual removal of the feces several times daily. If the bladder is paralyzed a catheter should be passed twice a day to remove the urine. However, the paralysis is usually progressive and shows no response to treatment. Various nerve tonics may be administered but their use produces little if any benefit.

A two year old pure bred stallion was presented in the clinic with the following history: One day the horse was noticed lying down more than usual. Examination the next day revealed the rectum was filled with feces and there was a continual dribbling of urine. He was also quite restless and wanted to roll. The feces were removed manually and an enema of soapy water was administered. It was necessary to manually remove the feces every day and in three days it was necessary to remove the urine with a catheter two times a day. This procedure was kept up for two weeks when he was presented at the hospital.

The above procedure was continued in the hospital with daily manual removal of the feces and the urine was removed with a catheter two times a day. He was also given various drugs that are recommended as tonics and nerve stimulants. After the above treatment was used for a month he failed to show any improvement. The horse was euthanized but a careful post mortem failed to reveal any lesion or nerve degeneration that would produce paralysis of the rectum and bladder.

Prolapse of the Rectum

Rectal prolapse occurs in all of the species of domestic animals but is observed most frequently in the bovine, porcine and ovine with only an occasional case in the equine. The condition is observed more commonly in the young than the adult animal. There may be some congenital defect in the firmness of the fibrous attachments between the various layers of the rectum as a possible cause of rectal prolapse. If the prolapsed tissue is not reduced, in a short time the spasm of the sphincter may interfere with the blood supply to the

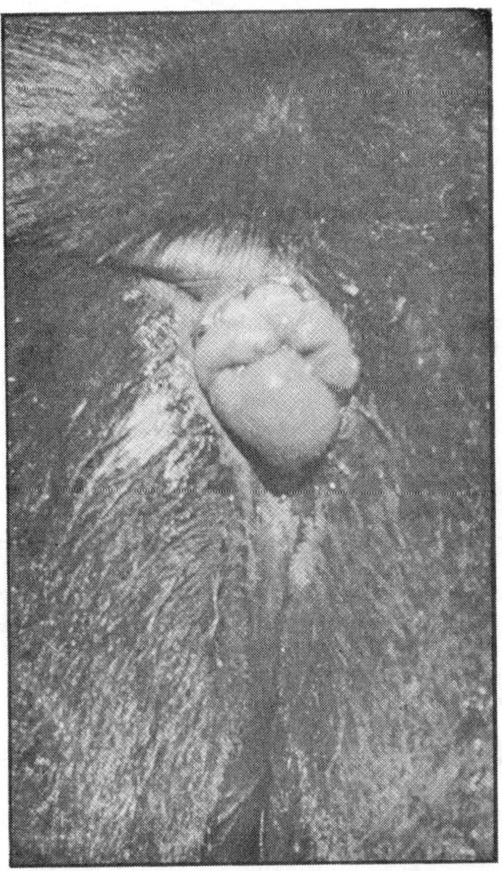

FIG. 349a. Prolapse of the mucous membrane of the entire circumference of the rectum.

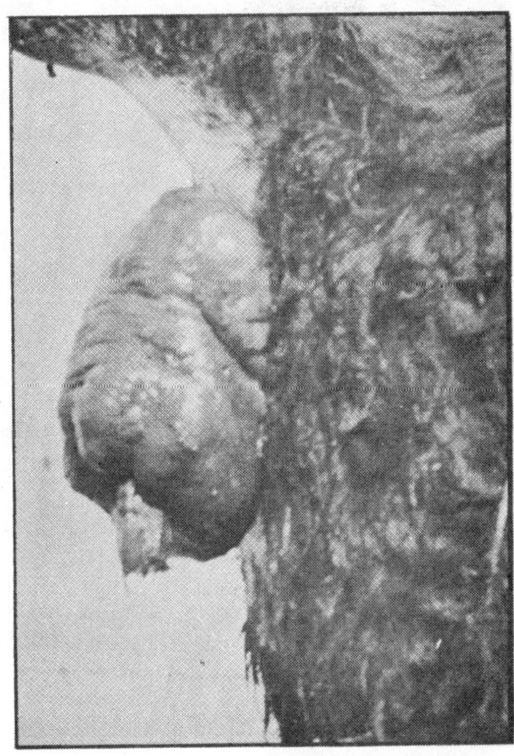

FIG. 349b. Complete prolapse of the rectal wall.

prolapsed tissue. The tissue then becomes edematous and cyanotic and in many cases gangrene may occur. When prolapse of the rectum occurs in the normal adult animal it is usually due to some condition that stimulates excessive straining or an increased intra-abdominal pressure probably plays an important role.

Two types of prolapse of the rectum are seen, the mucosal and a complete prolapse of the rectal wall. The mucosal prolapse is seen frequently and in most cases occurs without any apparent cause. In this type of prolapse the protrusion of the mucosa is unaccompanied by the musculature of the rectum. The prolapse may involve all or only a portion of the entire circumference of the bowel. If the prolapse is of recent occurrence and the mucous membrane is normal it is returned to its normal position. A purse string suture is placed in the skin around the anus but not involving the sphincter. The suture is tightened so the tissue cannot prolapse but is loose enough to permit the passage of feces. It is advisable to remove the purse string suture in three or four days.

When the prolapsed mucous membrane is not reduced the contraction of the sphincter may interfere with the blood supply. This results in edema and cyanosis of the prolapsed tissue. If this condition is allowed to persist the fluid becomes organized and the tissue becomes firm and interferes with defecation. The prolapsed mucous membrane must be removed surgically. With a curved pair of scissors the mucous membrane is cut close to the rectal wall at both ends of the prolapsed tissue. Any blood vessels that bleed freely are ligated. Usually these cases do not require any after care.

In Fig. 350 a very extensive prolapse developed from a prolapse of the mucous membrane on the floor of the rectum. The prolapse of the mucous membrane started approximately six inches anterior to the sphincter. The prolapse gradually became

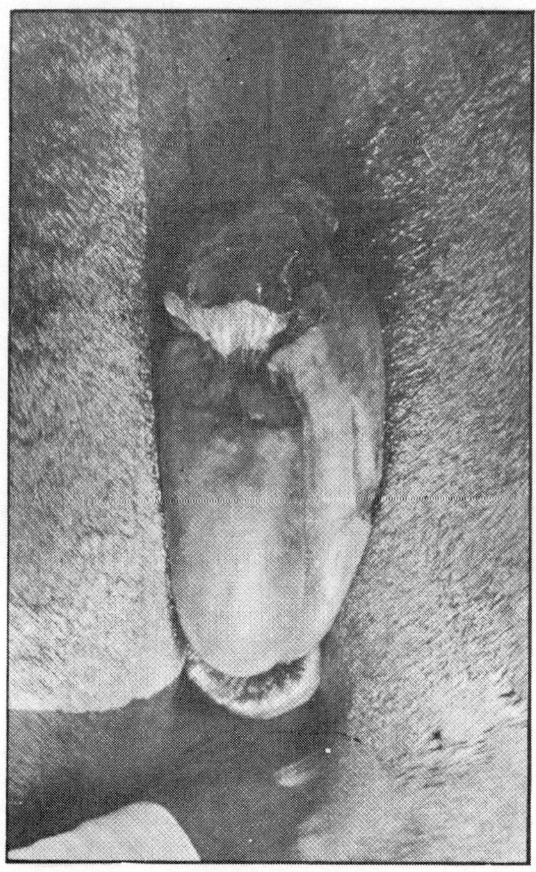

FIG. 350. Only a portion of the mucous membrane has prolapsed but has become extensive due to the edema.

more extensive over a period of six months. When small the tissue would prolapse during defecation but would return to its normal position when the rectum was empty. As it became more edematous and larger it was necessary to replace it manually whenever it prolapsed. The tissue finally became so extensive that it was necessary to remove it surgically. A series of mattress sutures were placed through the mucous membrane close to the rectal wall. The tissue was divided one-half inch posterior to the sutures.

Complete prolapse of the rectum involves all of the structures of the bowel including the muscularis so that it may become very extensive. This protruding mass is covered with mucosa except at the point of exit from the anus where the skin runs on to it and joins the mucosa at the mucocutaneous line.

Treatment will be determined by the amount of tissue that is prolapsed and whether it is edematous and lacerated. If the tissue has only been prolapsed for a short time, is uninjured and not more than six inches of the rectal wall is affected the tissue is returned to its normal position. A purse string suture is inserted around the anus and tied just tight enough to prevent a reoccurrence of the prolapse. The suture may be removed in three or four days. When the tissue has been prolapsed for some time and the mucous membrane is edematous the treatment will be determined by the extent of the prolapse. If the prolapse does not involve more than six to eight inches of the rectal wall and the mucous membrane is edematous a submucous resection may be performed. In performing this operation Johnson recommends the following technique. The area is prepared in the usual manner, cotton is packed in the rectum to prevent the passage of feces. Epidural anesthesia should provide complete anesthesia for the operation. Slight traction is exerted on the prolapsed portion of the rectum and two eight inch fourteen gauge needles are used to hold the tissues. The needles are placed through the tissues in opposite directions and close to the body. The object of the operation is to remove the affected mucous membrane and not injure the underlying tissue. A longitudinal incision is made through the mucous membrane from the anorectal line to the apex of the prolapse. Then circular incisions are made through the mucous membrane at each end of the longitudinal incision. Using blunt dissection the mucous membrane is separated from the healthy underlying tissue. It is important to control any appreciable hemorrhage as it develops. When the mucous membrane has been separated for some distance catgut sutures are placed in position. The sutures as they are inserted bring the cut edges of the mucous membrane in apposition. As the dissection is continued more sutures are put in, some interrupted and other continuous. This procedure is continued until the mucous membrane is removed and the sutures have united the edges of the circular incisions. The two needles and cotton are removed and the prolapsed tissue is returned to its normal position. In most cases it is advisable to insert a purse string suture to prevent a recurrence of the prolapse.

Amputation of the rectum seems to give the best results when more than eight inches of the rectum is prolapsed. Also if the tissue has been prolapsed for some time and all of the tissues are adhered together as a result of the severe inflammation.

When there are extensive adhesions in the tissue of the rectum and the mucous membrane is not edematous it will be necessary to perform an amputation. Stricture of the rectum may occur if it is returned to its normal position after being prolapsed for some time and there is extensive irritation of the mucosa. Due to the inflammatory reaction in the tissues fibrous tissue is laid down, encircling the rectum leading to a stenosis or stricture. It is usually possible in these cases to produce a prolapse of the affected tissue and perform an amputation. Prolapse of the rectum occasionally occurs in bulls at the time of service but is easily returned to its normal position. However if this tendency to prolapse persists over a period ot time it gradually becomes more difficult to replace the prolapsed rectum. Surgical removal of the tissue that prolapses is the surest method of correcting the condition.

Amputation of the rectum may be performed by inserting a series of interrupted mattress sutures around the circumference of the bowel. In placing the sutures one or two fingers should be in the lumen of the bowel or in large animals the entire hand may be introduced to assist in placing the sutures. Depending upon the size of the animal, one or two strands of braided silk or umbilical tape threaded on a full curved needle is used for suturing. As the sutures are inserted in the tissues the rectum is pulled posteriorly as much as possible so there is tension on the tissues. When the prolapsed portion of the bowel is removed after the sutures are in position the remainder of the bowel will retract pulling the sutures anterior to the sphincter. Also the fingers in the lumen are used to direct the point of the needle outward when it enters the lumen. A sufficient number of sutures are inserted to hold the tissues in apposition but if too many sutures are inserted it may result in the formation of a stricture. Depending upon the circumference of the bowel usually five to seven mattress sutures are inserted in the tissues. The prolapsed portion of the rectum is removed with an incision through the tissues about one inch posterior to the sutures. All large bleeding vessels should be ligated. If the patient shows a tendency to strain excessively after the operation this should be controlled with epidural anesthesia for a few days after the operation.

In swine the tissue that is prolapsed may involve only the mucous membrane and this may be removed surgically. If there is a complete prolapse of the rectal wall quite frequently there is edema of the mucous membrane. The edematous mucous membrane may be separated from the normal underlying tissue by blunt dissection with the ends of the fingers. The loosened mucous membrane is then divided with scissors at each end where it becomes normal. After the remainder of the rectum is returned to its normal position a purse string suture is inserted for three to four days. When the tissue has been prolapsed for some time and has been injured or frozen the usual amputation is performed.

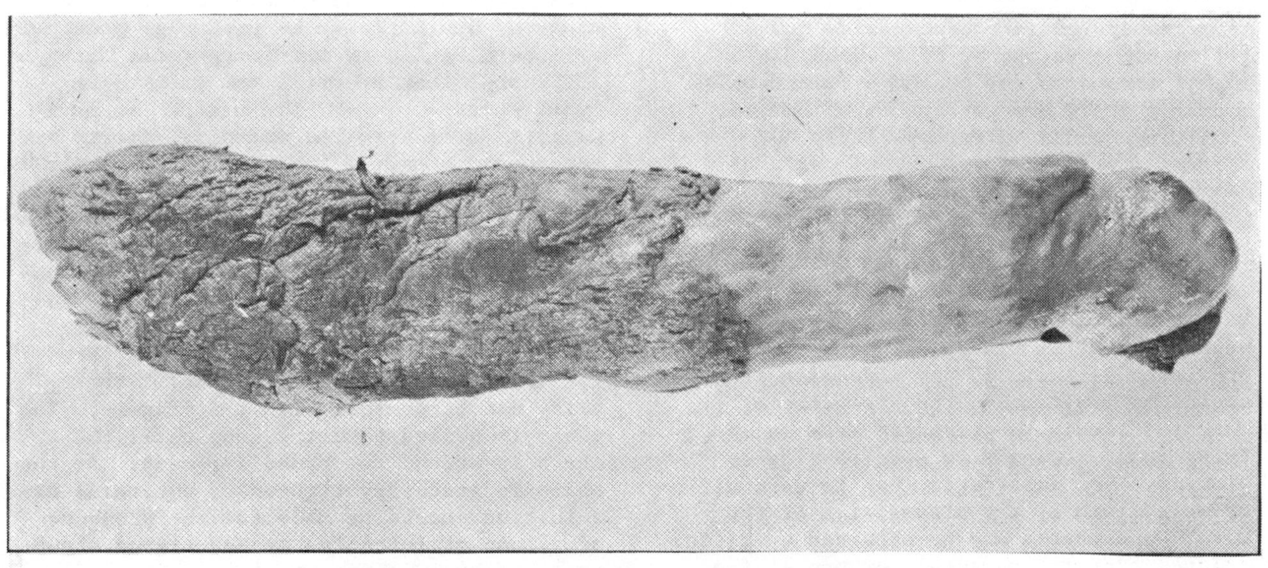

FIG. 351. Anomaly that was removed from the rectum of a cow.

Teratology

Teratology is the subdivision of embryology that deals with abnormal development and its end products. The anomalies occur during the formation of various tissues of the body, so most of the anomalies date from the early weeks of development. The anomaly shown in Fig. 351 occurred in the rectum of a mature cow. The large end was protruding through the anal sphincter and the other end was attached to the wall of the intestine approximately fifteen inches anterior to the sphincter. The attachment of the anomaly to the intestine was divided with a mare spaying ecraseur.

Oophorectomy or Spaying

Oophorectomy may be performed in the mare so she will be more tractable when she is around strange horses. In some cases there may be an irritation of the ovaries that will cause her to show signs of nymphomania. When removed the ovaries may be enlarged due to a variable number of cysts, they may be smaller than normal or normal in size. The ovaries may not show any changes in the tissues when examined macroscopically or microscopically. Some of the mares may have a prolonged oestrous cycle in others the oestrous cycle will be shorter than normal. Some mares may be in oestrum all the time. The removal of the ovaries may not produce any change in the disposition of the mare. A mare may have the history of normal oestral periods but does not become pregnant. Examination of the ovaries reveals that one ovary is much larger than normal due to a large number of cysts or the increase in size may be due to the development of fibrous tissue. If the mare does not become pregnant this enlarged ovary should be removed but if pregnancy occurs it is apparently not causing any trouble. When one ovary is removed and the other ovary is normal, the mare will become pregnant, in many cases, in a short time.

OPERATION. The operation will be described with the mare in a standing position. The vaginal route should not be used for the operation if there is any infection in the uterus or vagina. In the restraint of the mare she should be prevented from backing, lying down, moving from side to side or kicking. The anesthetic that is used will be determined by the disposition of the mare. Anesthesia may be obtained by giving chloral hydrate, nembutal, or one of the tranquilizers. If it is desirable to control straining, which is very objectionable during the operation, epidural anesthesia may be used. For the average case ten cubic centimeters of a two per cent solution or twelve cubic centimeters of a one per cent solution of a local anesthetic is very effective.

The external genitals should be thoroughly cleansed and the tail wrapped. A warm, mild antiseptic solution may be used to stimulate the ballooning of the vaginal walls and then all of the solution should be removed. However in many cases this procedure is not used as the vagina may dilate with the introduction of the hand into the vagina. All instruments used during the operation should be sterile. Also the hands and arms of the operator should be prepared for an aseptic operation. Sterile rubber gloves are used for all operative procedures.

With the vagina ballooned, a sharp scalpel with the sharp edge held in close contact with the index finger, is carried into the vagina and the point is placed one or two inches above the cervix. The cutting edge is directed upward with the point of the knife directed downward and forward. The vaginal wall and peritoneum are punctured with a thrust forward of the scalpel. As the scalpel is removed it is drawn upward so as to enlarge the opening. It is very important that the peritoneum is punctured with the first thrust of the scalpel. The incision should be large enough to admit one or two fingers. The scalpel should be directed so as to avoid injury to the posterior aorta and the rectum dorsally and the uterus. The incision is gradually enlarged by inserting one or two fingers and then additional fingers until the opening is large enough to admit the hand. The hand is introduced into the abdominal cavity and each ovary examined for size and position.

The mare spaying ecraseur with the chain extended back along the dorsal surface of its shaft is passed along the operators arm until the chain can be grasped with the fingers. The chain is opened with thumb and fingers and the fingers are slipped thru the loop formed by the chain until the ovary can be grasped with the fingers. The ovary is pulled thru the loop until the chain is around the broad ligament. As the chain is gradually tightened, a careful examination should be made for the presence of a loop of intestine or any tissue other than the broad ligament. When the chain is tight the cutting of the tissues should be completed as quickly as possible. The ovary is carried out thru the incision and dropped on the floor of the vagina. The ecraseur is held in the vagina and the chain is reset. The other ovary is removed using the same technique.

The patient is tied in a stall so that it cannot lie down and is kept quiet for six or seven days. During this period of time it is fed lightly and with food of a laxative nature. Complications that may occur are prolapse of the intestine or rectum, hemorrhage, peritonitis or abscess in the vagina. The presence of an abscess is indicated by straining, increase in temperature and vaginal palpation will reveal a hard, painful swelling in the region of the operative area. When present the abscess is drained into the vagina.

Hypertrophy of Ovary with Hematoma

The genital tract of a mare was examined and the right ovary was enlarged, cylindrical in shape, smooth and larger than normal. When the ovary was examined three months later it had doubled in size and was more elongated. In two weeks there was a definite bilateral distension of the abdominal cavity. A needle introduced through the abdominal wall revealed blood was responsible for the distension of the abdominal cavity. The blood was gradually absorbed and the abdominal cavity assumed its normal size. The mare was euthanized and a necropsy was performed. Examination revealed the large amount of blood that had been present in the abdominal cavity came from the right ovary.

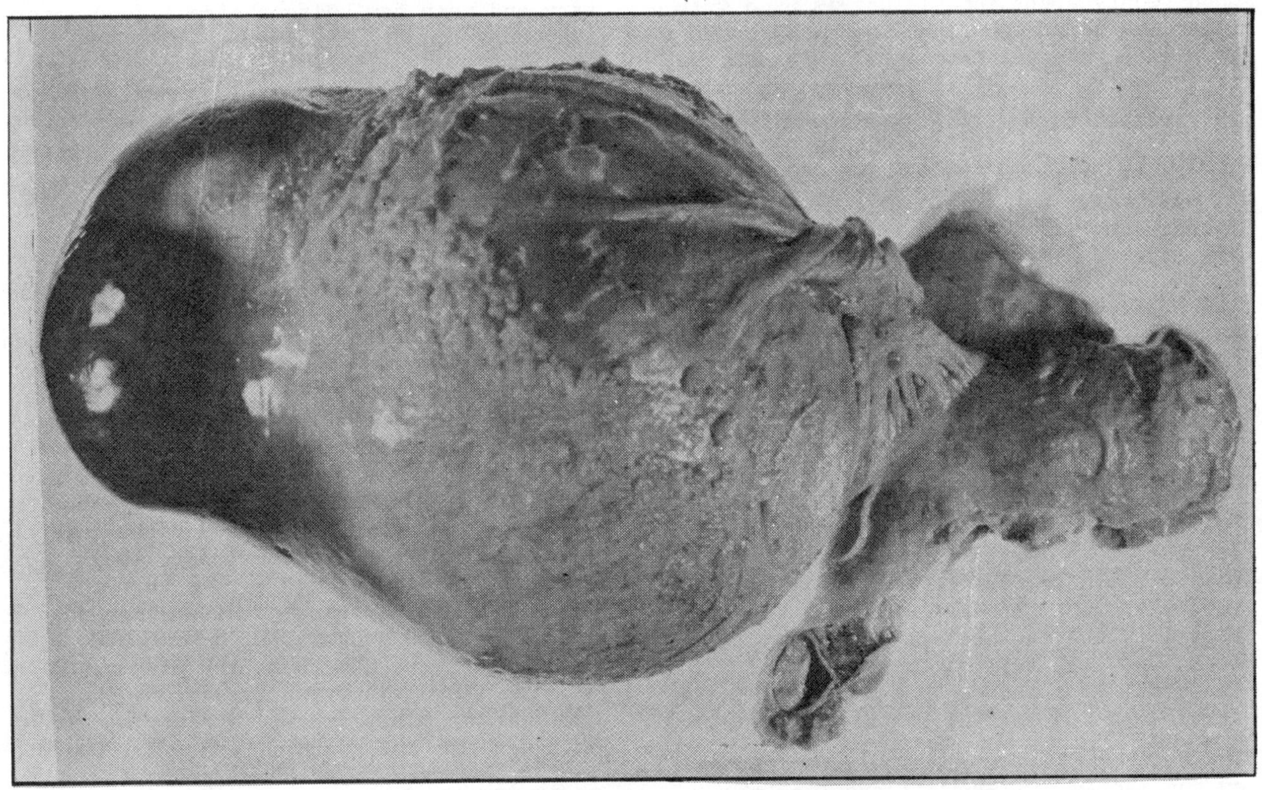

FIG. 352. Hypertrophy of right ovary with hematoma, note minute size of left ovary.

Spaying Heifers

This operation may be performed on heifers at any age but it is usually performed when they are six to eighteen months of age.

The advantages of spaying heifers is they can be ranged with steers or a bull, fatten more easily and quicker. Also they are not coming in heat every twenty-one days. If they are not marketed until they weigh eight or nine hundred pounds they bring more than unspayed heifers in some years.

An efficient operator can spay on the average one hundred and twenty-five to one hundred and fifty heifers a day. The number will also depend upon the equipment and the efficiency of the crew that are restraining the heifers.

RESTRAINT. The following method of restraint is efficient and practical for heifers up to about eight months of age. It consists of two upright poles set about fifteen inches apart and about twelve feet high. A cross piece is fastened at the top for the attachment of a block and tackle to raise the heifers. To restrain the hind feet and raise the heifer a bar of wood twenty-eight inches long is used with two holes about two inches apart bored near each end. A one inch rope is threaded thru the holes so a loop can be placed around the heifers hind legs just above the fetlock joints. Two such pieces of equipment should be prepared and set far enough apart so one heifer can be released and confined without interfering with the operation on the other one.

The heifers are prepared for the operation by withholding feed for twenty-four hours, but permitting them to have some water. The advantages of this method of operating is a much smaller wound is made and it is in a perfect position for drainage of any wound secretion.

OPERATION. The heifers are roped and brought to the poles where the loops are placed above the fetlock joints of the posterior limbs. The posterior part of the body is elevated until only the shoulders, head, and neck rest on the ground. Further restraint is obtained by a man holding the front legs and sitting on the head and neck.

The hair on the operative area, which is on the median line just in front of the udder is removed with clipper or scissors. The area is then painted with a skin antiseptic. An incision is made thru the skin starting about two inches in front of the udder and is made large enough to admit two fingers or about two inches long. The incision is continued thru the tissues to the peritoneum. Care should be taken in cutting thru the peritoneum not to injure the rumen and this may be prevented by using a groove director or picking up a fold of peritoneum before it is incised. The location of the incision in the abdominal wall may vary a little in some individuals. Two fingers are inserted thru the incision into the abdominal cavity and either one horn or the ovary is grasped and brought thru the incision. A pair of forceps are clamped just back of the ovary to hold it, while the horns are followed around to the other ovary and it is brought to the outside and the two ovaries are removed with emasculator or spaying shears. Two or three interrupted umbilical tape sutures are used to close the incision and both sutures are inserted thru the skin and the tissues down to the peritoneum, but the needle does not penetrate the peritoneum.

The heifer is now released by loosening the block and tackle rope and the heifer will kick loose. No further treatment is necessary and very few heifers miss a feed after the operation.

Cattle chutes are now available that are very efficient in controlling heifers for the spaying operation in the standing position. If two chutes are available the heifers may be operated on very rapidly. While one heifer is being operated another heifer can be confined in the second chute and prepared for the operation. The heifers may be confined on the ground with the front feet forward and the hind feet stretched backward.

The area for performing the operation is in the left flank at the site described for a rumenotomy. The hair is clipped from the area and a vertical or U shaped incision made thru the skin and the muscles divided in the direction of their fibres. After the hand breaks thru the peritoneum it passes along the rumen to the pelvis. One ovary is located and grasped between the thumb and finger. A spaying shear is passed back along the arm and the ovary removed by cutting close to the thumb and finger. The first ovary may be retained in the hand and the second ovary grasped and removed. The skin incision is closed with two or three interrupted sutures.

Spaying Older Cows

This operation is performed quite frequently in old cows after they have passed their usefulness as breeders. It has been observed they fatten more quickly and the meat is of better quality. Older dairy cows may be spayed so they will fatten more quickly and produce a more desirable beef carcass. Also in dairy cows the period of lactation can be increased up to two years and in some cases four or five years. However, the cows must be operated within four to six weeks after parturition if the lactation period is prolonged. Where the operation is performed for this purpose cows eight or nine years old are operated to prolong their period of usefulness. In cows that have had several calves the best method is to operate thru the vaginal route. The same technique that was described for spaying mares thru the vagina may be used in the cow.

Affections of the Vulva, Vagina, and Rectum

Injury of these tissues usually occurs during the act of parturition. The injuries are usually of three kinds: (1) A tear of the tissues at the superior commissure of the vulva extending to the anal sphincter. (2) Opening or communication established between the rectum and vagina permitting feces to pass into the vagina. (3) The injury may extend through the recto-vaginal wall and the anal sphincter down to and including the superior commissure of the vulva producing a common opening. These cases are commonly referred to as fluter, flutering or gil-flirters.

Wind Sucking Through the Vulva

The sucking of air into the vagina through the vulva is an important factor in introducing infection into the vagina and uterus. This usually results in the mare being sterile until the condition is corrected or it may cause permanent sterility.

ETIOLOGY. Some of the factors responsible for the development of this condition may be injuries to the vulva and rectum, abortion, dystokia and conformation of the vulva. A vulva that is near or over perpendicular and the partial horizontal seem to favor the development of the habit. In other cases the rectum appears to set too far forward.

SIGNS. The most apparent sign is the sucking or gurgling sound produced by the air passing through the vulva. In some cases the sound may not be noticeable and the shape and appearance of the vulva may be the only indication of the condition.

TREATMENT. The operation to prevent wind sucking consists in closing the lips of the vulva from the superior commissure to at least one-half inch below the floor of the pelvis. The vulva is cleansed thoroughly and prepared for an aseptic operation. Anesthesia of the operative area is obtained by infiltrating the tissue along the edge of the lips of the vulva and the superior commissure of the vulva with a one per cent solution of a local anesthetic. A strip of tissue one-half inch wide is scarified along each edge of the vulva. The lips of the vulva should be scarified so they can be closed completely from its superior commissure to one-half inch below the floor of the pelvis. The two scarified surfaces are brought into close contact by metal suture clips or interrupted sutures placed about one-quarter of an inch apart. After care consists in applying a mild antiseptic ointment to the area daily.

The Vagina

The vagina is a tubular passage that extends through the pelvic cavity from the uterus to the vulva. It varies in length from six to eight inches in the mare to eight to ten inches in the cow. In the mare the recto-genital pouch of peritoneum usually extends posteriorly between the vagina and rectum for approximately two inches and in the cow it extends backward about five inches dorsally and two inches ventrally. The vagina is slightly longer and larger in diameter in the cow than in the mare. The vaginal wall is composed of muscular and mucous coats and in the muscular coat there is a thin layer of longitudinal fibers and thicker circular muscular layer. That portion of the vagina that is retroperitoneal is surrounded by loose connective tissue and some fat.

RUPTURE OF THE VAGINAL WALL. Occasionally rupture of the vagina wall occurs in heifers at the time of parturition. This occurs when there has been an abnormal quantity of fat deposited between the vaginal wall and pelvis. Due to the extreme pressure produced during parturition the fat is forced out through a rupture in the wall of the vagina. The fat may be observed by the attendant protruding between the lips of the vulva before or after parturition. If the hand is inserted into the vagina it can be easily determined where the fat has passed through a rupture in the vaginal wall. By removing all of the fat that can be pulled through the opening there is then little tendency for more fat to be deposited in the area. The opening in the vaginal wall may be allowed to heal without suturing if it is too far anterior to permit the introduction of sutures.

Prolapse of the Vagina

Vaginal prolapse occurs in all species of animals but is observed most frequently in the pregnant cow and ewe. In some cases the prolapse occurs before parturition, then it may occur after parturition and again it may occur both before and after parturition. The prolapsed portion of the vagina may involve one or both of the side walls but the floor of the vagina is the portion that is prolapsed most frequently.

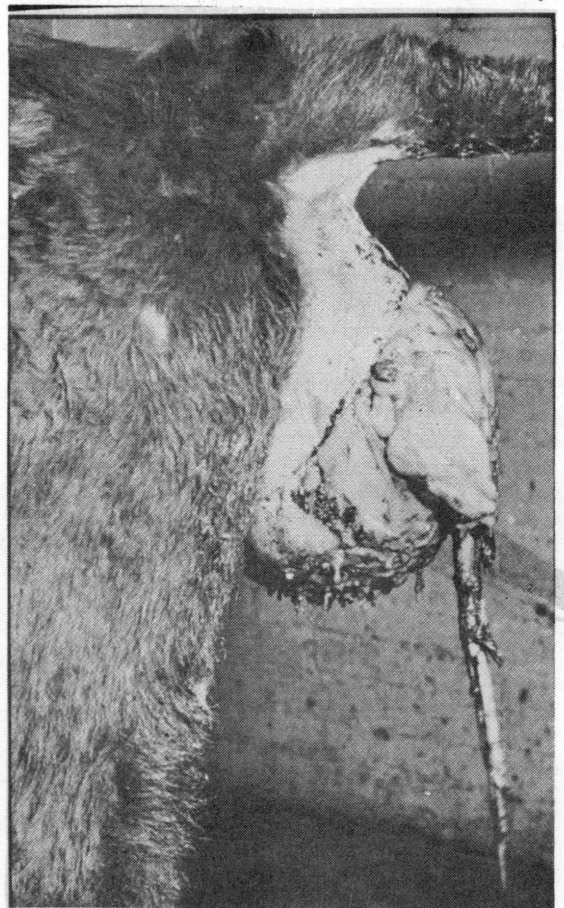

FIG. 353. Prolapse of the floor of the vagina, and contained within is the bladder filled with urine.

When prolapse of the floor of the vagina occurs it may also contain the bladder filled with urine and is referred to as a vaginal cystocele.

ETIOLOGY. When prolapse of the vagina occurs before parturition it may be due to the voluminous contents in the abdominal cavity. The prolapse of the vaginal wall may only be observed when the cow is lying down and disappears when she is standing. If the tissue continues to prolapse it becomes irritated from exposure to the air and possibly contact with objects which are irritating. The injured tissue stimulates straining so that more of the vaginal tissue is prolapsed and remains exposed to outside influences. The exposure to air, rubbing of the prolapsed tissue on hard objects and irritation from manure produces a marked inflammatory reaction in the exposed tissue. If the straining becomes severe enough a prolapse of the rectum may also occur.

Prolapse of the Vagina and Cervix

When a complete prolapse of the vagina occurs the cervix is also included in the prolapsed tissue. If the prolapse is not corrected the tissue undergoes those changes produced by outside influences.

TREATMENT. The prolapsed tissue should be returned to its normal position as soon as possible. Anesthesia to control straining is obtained by using epidural anesthesia. The anesthetic that is used will be determined by the extent of the prolapse and the amount of irritation of the tissue. Some of the anesthetics that have an oil for a base will control straining for twelve to twenty-four hours. When a local anesthetic is dissolved in water it is only effective for two or three hours in controlling straining. If straining can be controlled, for several days the patient will usually make an uneventful recovery.

Before returning the tissue to its normal position, it should be thoroughly cleansed with a non-irritating antiseptic. To prevent the prolapse from reoccurring some method should be used to retain the tissues in the vagina. One method that may be used is to place interrupted sutures composed of two strands of umbilical tape for each suture. The two top sutures are placed in the thick skin about two inches from and on either side of the lips of the vulva. Place the two top sutures slightly above

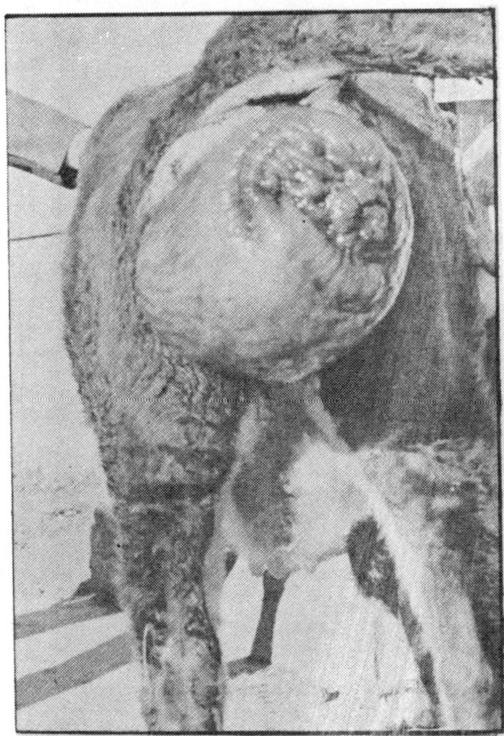

FIG. 354. Prolapse of both the vagina and cervix.

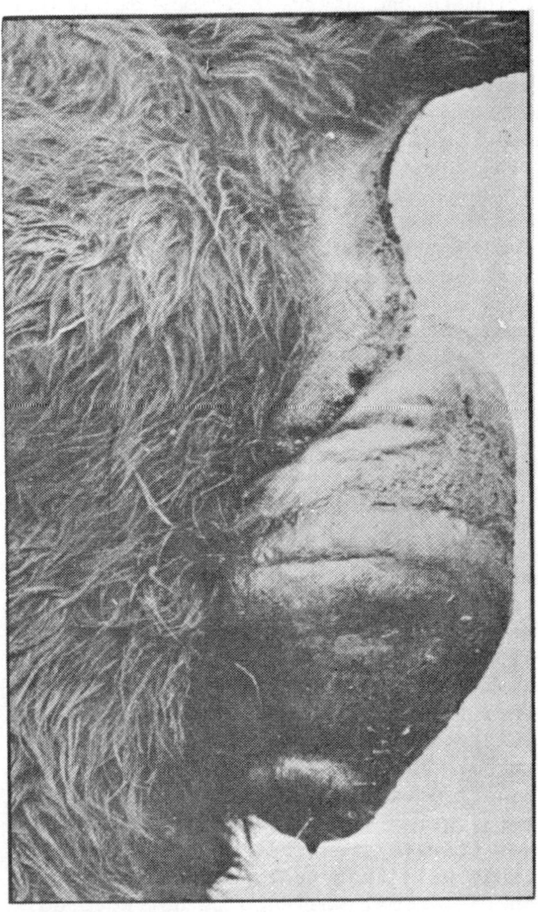

FIG. 355. Complete prolapse of the vagina and cervix.

the superior commissure of the lips of the vulva. In tying the sutures rather large loops are formed so tapes may be passed through the loops. The two lower sutures are placed so they extend just below the inferior commissure of the vulva. Two more sutures are placed halfway between the upper and lower sutures. A strand of bandage material four inches wide is passed through the loops in both a horizontal and diagonal direction. In tying the tapes the lips of the vulva are pulled tightly together. By using this method of suturing, the lips of the vulva are not injured or lacerated. Also the tapes can be removed and reinserted without difficulty.

Chronic Prolapse of the Vagina

When a persistent prolapse of the vagina extends over a period of time the tissues should be examined carefully in an effort to determine the cause. There are a number of reasons why a cow will continue to prolapse the vagina before or after parturition. In a recent parturition infection and inflammation of the uterus or vagina is a frequent cause of persistent straining. The vagina should be examined for lacerations and contusions of the tissues of the vagina as they may be the cause of the persistent straining. If the mucous membrane of the vaginal wall becomes edematous it may be the reason for a chronic prolapse of the vagina. When a portion of the vaginal wall prolapses over a period of time a chronic inflammation of this tissue occurs. Examination of the tissue will reveal that it is much thicker than normal tissue and composed of inflammatory or fibrous tissue. In many of the cases of chronic prolapse there will be an excessive quantity of fat between the vaginal wall and pelvis.

PROGNOSIS. Is always guarded in chronic prolapse of the vagina as the vagina may continue to prolapse after the operation. However, this recurring prolapse after an operation, occurs in only a small percentage of the cases.

TREATMENT. The treatment or surgical operation that is performed will be determined by the cause of the prolapse. If the prolapse is due to irritation from infection in the uterus this may be treated in the usual manner. When that portion of the mucous membrane that covers the prolapsing portion of the vaginal wall becomes edematous it should be removed. Incisions should be made through the mucous membrane at the junction of the edematous and normal mucous membrane. The edematous mucous membrane separates rather readily from the underlying tissue by blunt dissection. After the membrane is removed the edges of the mucous membrane are united with closely placed interrupted sutures of catgut. Part of the treatment should consist in injecting oil into the uterus as this will coat over and soothe the irritated tissue.

If the prolapsing portion of the vaginal wall is thickened and composed of inflammatory and fibrous tissue it should be removed. Two elliptical incisions are made through the normal vaginal wall so as to remove all of that portion of the vaginal wall that is abnormal. The space between the vaginal wall and pelvis should be examined for the presence of an excessive quantity of fat and if present should be removed. The edges of the vaginal wall are united with closely placed interrupted sutures using chromic catgut. In some cases it will seem that the portion of the vaginal wall that prolapses is thicker than the normal wall and is not covered with mucous membrane. We remove this portion of the vaginal wall also any fat that may be present. The edges of the vaginal wall are sutured together with catgut.

There will be an inflammatory reaction in the tissues after the operation on the vagina and this will stimulate straining. After operations on the vagina all straining should be controlled by the use of epidural anesthesia for approximately six to ten days.

Prolapse of the Vagina and Rectum

Prolapse of one structure usually occurs, then due to the excessive straining, the other prolapses.

In the treatment of this condition, best results have been obtained by amputation of the prolapsed portion of the rectum. The vagina is replaced and held in position by means of the sutures that have been described.

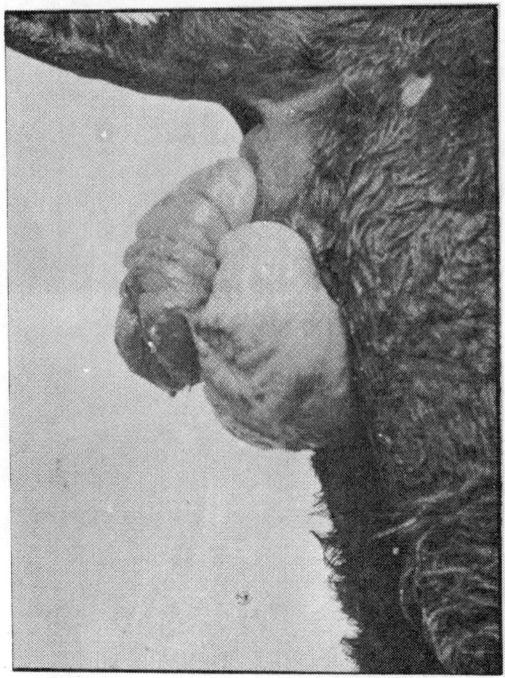

FIG. 356. Prolapse of the rectum and vagina.

When attempts have been made to return both structures to their normal positions excessive straining has resulted and the after results have been unsatisfactory.

Recto-Vaginal Fistula

A recto-vaginal fistula is produced when the foot of the fetus is forced up through the roof of the vagina and the floor of the rectum. Thus a communication is established between the rectum and vagina for the passage of feces into the vagina.

OPERATION. If the principles recommended by Forssell for operating on this condition are closely adhered to, good results are obtained. The four principles are (1) there must be the least tension possible on the sutures, (2) there must be good contact of the fresh wound surfaces, (3) use suture material strong enough to hold the tissues in good apposition, and (4) reduce the amount of feces in the rectum. It is usually advisable to reduce the bulky portion of the feed for one week to ten days before the operation. This is accomplished by feeding only a small amount of hay or pellets and increasing the amount of grain fed. The addition of some mineral oil to the daily feed helps to soften the feces.

The operation is most convenient to perform in the standing position. Anesthesia may be obtained by injecting 10 to 15 cubic centimeters of a one per cent solution of procaine hydrochloride into the epidural space, and it may be necessary to inject more during the operative procedure. In the case of a very nervous horse it may be necessary to give enough chloral hydrate, nembutal or tranquilizer to quiet the patient.

Just before the operation the contents of the rectum are removed manually with the hand. The lumen of the rectum is then carefully cleansed with pledgets of cotton that have been moistened with a nonirritating antiseptic.

To provide a separate rectal wound and vaginal wound the rectal wall and vaginal wall must be separated by an incision that separates the two structures. This incision is continued until it extends beyond the anterior edge of the fistulous opening about two inches. In making the incision care is taken to leave the rectal wall at least one-half inch thick if possible. If complete closure of the rectal wound is obtained the tissue must be strong enough to hold the sutures and develop good adhesions. A uniform thickness of the rectal wall may be obtained by keeping one hand in the rectum and checking the thickness of the tissue as the incision is made. On each side the tissues are separated for a distance of at least one inch. The incision separating the two structures is made with a scalpel manipulated with the hand in the vagina.

The rectal wall and vaginal wall should be included in the same suture as this procedure seems to supply more support to the sutured tissues. The suture is started in the vaginal wall with a Lembert type suture so the edge will be turned into the lumen of the vagina. The suture is continued into the rectal wall so the edge will be turned into the lumen of the rectum. Also the fresh surfaces of each structure will be brought into close apposition when the sutures are tightened and tied. The sutures are placed about one-half inch apart. The suture material that is used will depend upon the preference of the operator. In inserting the sutures in the rectal wall care should be taken that the needle does not penetrate the mucous membrane of the rectal wall. The ends of the sutures should be left long enough so they can be located in ten to fourteen days and the sutures removed. A narrow bladed knife is inserted dorsally and the anal sphincter is divided. The division of the anal sphincter permits feces to pass more easily relieving some strain on the operative area. The diet that was recommended pre-operatively is continued post-operatively until the sutures are removed.

Laceration of the Vulva and Anus

This injury occurs at the time of parturition and the laceration of the tissue extends from the superior commissure of the vulva up through the anal sphincter creating a common opening. The injury to the rectal wall varies from a slight laceration to one several inches long. The chief difficulty in the repair of this injury is the healing together of the ends of the anal sphincter. Any attempt to repair the laceration immediately after the injury is usually unsuccessful. This is due to the intense inflammatory reaction and extensive edema that occurs in the

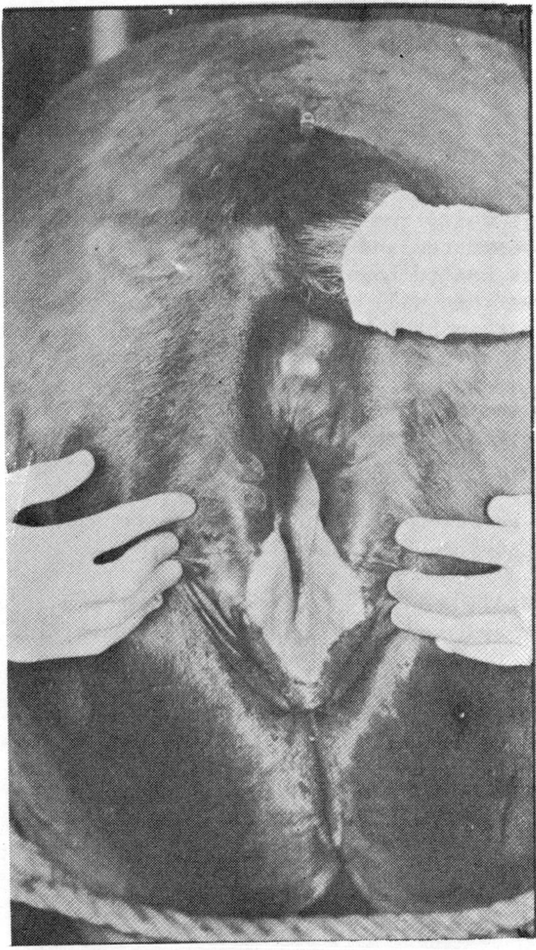

FIG. 357. Laceration of the vulva and anus.

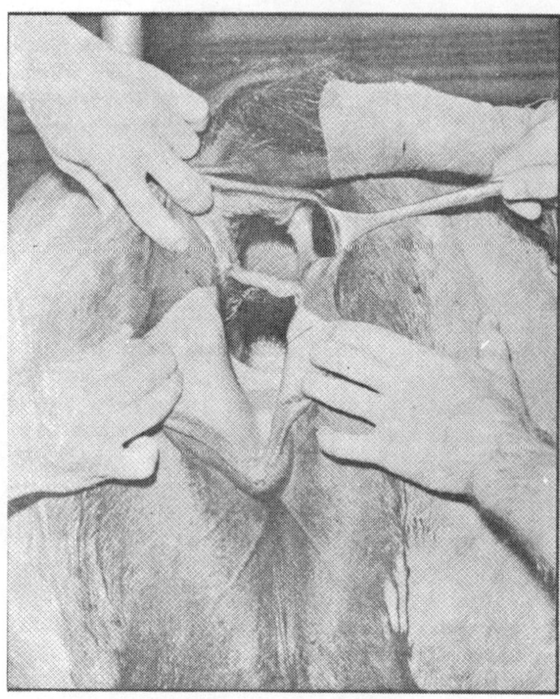

FIG. 358. Shelf that is formed with the healing together of the rectal and vaginal walls.

lacerated tissues so they are not able to initiate the physiologic processes of repair at this time. The operator should wait until the inflammation and edema has disappeared and the edges of the tissues have healed together. Examination of the area then will reveal the mucous membrane and skin have healed together and the ends of the sphincter have healed over with inflammatory tissue. It will also be observed there is a shelf formed by the healing together of the edges of the rectal and vaginal walls at the anterior edge of the opening. The preliminary preparation of the patient is the same as for the recto-vaginal fistula.

OPERATION. All of the feces that can be removed manually are removed at this time. The tissues are carefully cleansed with cotton moistened with a mild antiseptic. Anesthesia of the operative area is obtained by injecting 12 to 15 cubic centimeters of a one per cent solution of procaine hydrochloride into the epidural space. One of the most important steps in the operation is the careful dissection of the tissue. The operator may start at the original location of the superior commissure of the vulva at the junction of the skin and mucous membrane. About one-half inch of fresh surface is exposed during the dissection. The incision is continued upward to the end of the anal sphincter which is exposed by removing the inflammatory tissue which has formed over it during the healing process. It is necessary to separate the rectal and vaginal walls by careful dissection leaving the rectal wall the thickest of the two structures. The separation of the rectal and vaginal walls is continued one to two inches anterior to the edge of the shelf. The dissection described for the one side is continued around to the other lip of the vulva. If the dissection of the tissue has been carefully performed the rectal and vaginal walls are again separate structures, the ends of the anal sphincter are exposed and the structures may be united with interrupted sutures using chromic catgut. A full curved needle is used to insert the sutures in the rectal wall and vaginal wall they should be started just anterior to the edge of the laceration in the rectal wall. A Lembert type of suture is inserted in the vaginal and rectal wall so that about one-half inch of fresh surface is brought into close contact and the edges turned up into the lumen of the rectum and the edges of the vaginal wall into the lumen of the vagina. If the tissue of the rectal wall is carefully approximated, when the sphincter is reached the ends will automatically come together. A number of interrupted sutures are inserted through the ends of the sphincter so this tissue is brought into close contact. Several interrupted sutures are inserted deep into the tissues immediately posterior to the sphincter to supply additional support for the sphincter sutures. The success of the operation is usually determined by the healing that occurs at the sphincter. The edges of the lips of the vulva are brought into close contact by closely placed mattress sutures. If healing is going to occur the tissues should be firmly united in ten days and the sutures may be removed at this time.

Prolapse of the Bladder

Whenever a rupture occurs in the floor of the vagina there may be a prolapse of the bladder through the opening. This injury to the vagina usually occurs during the act of parturition and is most frequently observed in the sow. Although it has been observed in the cow and mare.

In most cases the symptoms are characteristic as the round red fundus of the bladder will be observed protruding between the lips of the vulva. The size of the bladder will depend upon the amount of urine it contains. The urine can pass into the bladder but cannot pass out due to the closure of the urethra. Examination of the floor of the vagina will reveal the rupture with the tissues of the bladder passing through the opening.

Treatment consists in returning the bladder to its normal position. Before this can be accomplished it may be necessary to remove the urine through a needle passed into the bladder. A syringe can be attached to the needle and the urine removed very quickly. With proper aseptic precautions the bladder should be returned to its normal position. When possible the opening in the vagina should be closed with sutures. However in those cases in the sow where this has not been possible uneventful healing has occurred.

Eversion of the Bladder

The above condition occurs more frequently in the mare due to the larger and more easily dilatable urethra. Eversion of the bladder may occur before, during or after parturition due to the high intra-pelvic pressure produced at this time.

The signs usually presented in this condition makes the diagnosis rather easy. A pear-shaped swelling covered with mucous membrane is observed between the lips of the vulva. Palpation of this structure will reveal that its tissues pass through the urethral opening. Also present on either side near its neck will be found the two openings of the ureters. It will be observed there is an almost continual escape of urine either drop by drop or in small forceful jets from these openings.

PROGNOSIS. In a recent case is favorable but if allowed to go without treatment it becomes unfavorable.

TREATMENT. If eversion of the bladder occurs before or during the act of parturition the bladder should be returned to its normal position before the passage of the fetus. One practitioner reported he was able to prevent the re-eversion of the bladder during parturition by placing a collapsible rubber ball in it. This was removed after parturition and the bladder remained in position.

Before replacing the everted bladder, all exposed tissue should be thoroughly cleansed with a mild antiseptic solution. If there are any tears or perforations of the bladder these should be carefully sutured. However, if any of the tissue is irreparably damaged it should be removed but the operator must be sure the functioning of the ureters is not interfered with.

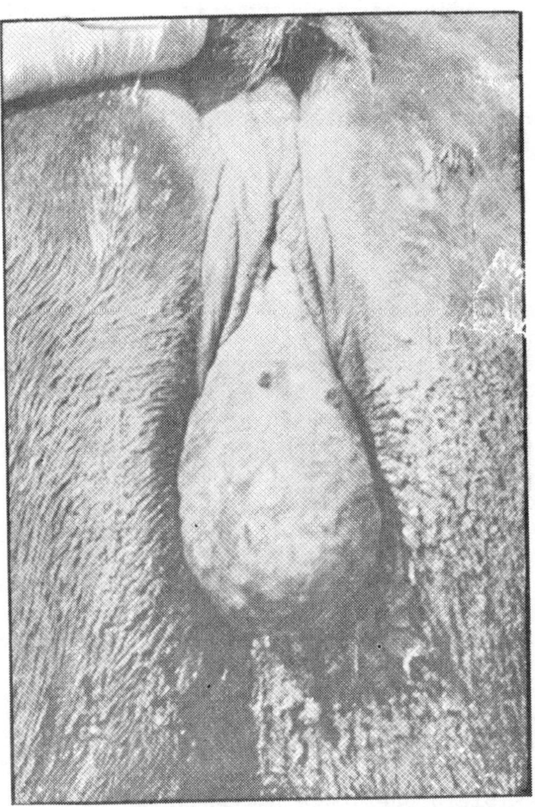

FIG. 359. Eversion of the bladder, note the two small uretral openings close to the neck of the bladder

In treating and returning the bladder to its normal position the straining on the part of the patient may be prevented by injecting an anesthetic into the epidural space. Usually fifteen cubic centimeters of a one per cent solution of procaine hydrochloride is sufficient.

Before returning the bladder to its normal position, it may be necessary to reduce the engorgement of the blood in its tissues. This is accomplished by exerting steady pressure over the entire mass with both hands. When the tissues return to normal size and consistency the bladder is gradually returned through the urethral opening to its normal position.

Chronic eversion of the bladder is of rather rare occurrence but in Fig. 359

the bladder has been everted for approximately four months. The mare was presented for treatment with the following history. The mare was attempting to foal one day early in June and after some difficulty a dead foal was delivered. In a few minutes an enlargement about the size of a coconut was noticed protruding between the lips of the vulva. This enlargement was the bladder and a cresol compound was applied to its surface daily during the summer months. When the mare was presented at the clinic early in October the wall of the bladder was markedly thickened and the mucous membrane bled freely when manipulated. The act of urination which occurred frequently was accomplished with severe straining. The urine was forced from the ureters in drops or in fine streams that sometimes spurted six feet.

Treatment at first consisted in massage of the bladder in an attempt to reduce the thickness of the walls and make it more pliable. However, after ten days treatment very little improvement was observed and it was decided to amputate the fundus portion of the bladder.

Flexible probes were passed into the ureters to determine their exact location. A series of mattress sutures of umbilical tape were placed across the bladder posterior to the ureters. The fundus portion of the bladder posterior to the sutures was then removed. The mare was able to urinate without any apparent difficulty. Also the stump of the bladder was retained in the vagina most of the time.

Affections of the Penis

Infantile Male Genital Organs

Bulls are occasionally examined when they reach breeding age and it is found the genital organs are not fully developed. The bull may be able to protrude its penis only four or five inches. It will be found the testicles are smaller in size than normal but of almost normal consistency. Treatment is of no value and the affected animals should be castrated and fattened for food purposes.

Congenital Adhesions of the Penis

A young bull is occasionally found with adhesions between the penis and prepuce. It is observed that when the bull attempts to serve there is a downward curvature of the end of the penis. On examination it will be found there is an adhesion between the penis and prepuce. This fold of tissue is rather easily cut and the difficulty is corrected.

A bull fourteen months of age was presented for examination with a very unusual history. For eight months the owner had noticed that when urinating the bull would have a slight prolapse of the rectum. When he began to use him for breeding purposes the prolapse of the rectum would be more extensive. It was also observed that after service the penis would be curled up at the end of the sheath. Examination of the penis revealed an adhesion, one and one-half inches long, between the ventral surface of the glans penis and the prepuce. When this tissue was incised it permitted the penis to protrude in a normal manner.

Erection Hemorrhages

It is sometimes observed that in young bulls at the time they are ready to serve hemorrhage occurs from the glans penis. The hemorrhage may consist of a few drops or may come out in a fine stream. Examination may reveal small elevations on the glans penis that are openings of fistulous tracts from the corpus cavernosum tissue. On erection blood is forced through these small openings. When blood mixes with the semen at the service it materially reduces the fertility. Surgical interference in these cases is of little value. Some of the cases make a complete recovery when they are withheld from breeding for several weeks.

Affections of the Sheath and Penis

Posthitis or acrobystitis is inflammation of the prepuce. Balanitis is inflammation of the glans penis.

The glans penis of the horse is the enlarged free end of the penis. Just above the urethra in the glans penis is a sinus. This diverticulum is sometimes filled with smegma that may become almost as hard as stone. When the urethra becomes occluded or partially occluded the horse will show the same signs as when a calculus is present. Whenever a horse shows difficulty in urination the diverticulum should be examined for the presence of smegma and when present it should be removed.

In the Pig

The umbilical pouch or preputial diverticulum in the upper wall of the sheath of the pig may become distended with urine or its own secretion.

SIGNS. Swelling and inflammatory signs are observed in the affected region. The swelling resembles that produced by an umbilical hernia.

TREATMENT. Treatment consists in forcing the accumulated fluid out by pressure. Sometimes, however, due to inflammation a stricture of the opening in the sheath has developed and it is necessary to enlarge the opening. This is accomplished by removing a triangular portion of skin from the ventral surface of the sheath. The base of the triangle is anterior and includes the opening in the sheath. The incisions to remove the triangular portion of skin should not extend into the prepuce. When the skin is removed an incision is made on the median line through the prepuce. The prepuce is sutured to the corresponding edges of the skin on each side of the triangle.

Phimosis

The above term is used when the animal is unable to protrude the penis from the sheath. This may be due to a stricture of the preputial orifice or the development of inflammatory tissue in the sheath as the result of infection or traumation. In some cases a neoplasm of the penis may be the cause of the phimosis.

TREATMENT. When due to infection of the prepuce and the development of inflammatory tissue and sheath may be irrigated daily with a non-irritating antiseptic solution. If a stricture has developed at the end of the sheath the operation previously described is performed. A neoplasm may be the cause of the phimosis and amputation of that portion of the penis is indicated or it may be possible to remove the neoplasm.

Phimosis, recurring

The above diagnosis seems justified when the phimosis only occurs when the following circumstance develops. If erection of the penis occurs before the end of the penis enters the preputial orifice the penis is directed upward and forward. This seems to occur as the result of unusually vigorous contractions of the muscles on the ventral surface of the sheath. Due to the vigorous attempts to protrude the penis the tissues are forced anteriorly creating the impression a pocket is present dorsal to the preputial orifice but a pocket is not present. If the penis is protruded through the preputial orifice before there is complete erection the bull is able to breed in a normal manner.

Operation to relieve the phimosis consists in removing a triangular area of skin from the ventral surface of the sheath. Prepare the operative area and the tissues may be anesthetized by local infiltration. The base of the triangle about one inch long is made at the junction of the skin and prepuce on the ventral surface of the sheath. The sides of the triangle three inches long extend posteriorly and are made so the point of the triangle is on the median line. The incisions extend through the skin but do not invade the prepuce. After the triangular area of skin is removed the prepuce is incised on the median line from the base to the point of the triangle. The edges of the prepuce are sutured to the corresponding sides of the triangle with closely placed interrupted sutures. These cases recover without any after care. After the tissues are healed the bull is able to breed in a normal manner.

Paraphimosis

Paraphimosis occurs when the animal is unable to retract the penis into the sheath.

ETIOLOGY. The paraphimosis may develop after castration when infection stimulates excessive swelling of the sheath and inguinal region and prevents retraction of the penis into the sheath. When paralysis of the retractor penis muscle occurs there is inability to retract the penis into the sheath. A large neoplasm on the penis may cause paraphimosis.

TREATMENT. The treatment for paraphimosis will depend upon the cause of the condition. When due to a paralysis of the retractor penis muscle it is usually necessary to amputate a portion of the penis. If the neoplasm is not too extensive it may be removed or it may be necessary to remove a portion of the penis.

Prolapse of the Prepuce

Prolapse of the prepuce occurs frequently in the bovine and is seen occasionally in the ovine. The prepuce may be lacerated at the time of service and infection gains entrance into the deeper tissues. Some bulls have a tendency to prolapse a portion of the prepuce at frequent intervals. The prolapsed portion of the prepuce is injured from contact with bushes, rocks, the ground and other hard objects. The damaged tissue becomes edematous, infection may occur with extensive inflammatory reaction in the tissue. If the tissue does not receive the proper treatment fibrous tissue is formed with the development of a stricture and the bull is unable to protrude the penis. Due to the thickened prepuce the bull may or may not be able to retract the prepuce into the sheath. The bull should be kept by himself so he will not be stimulated to protrude the penis. Each time he attempts to force the penis through the stricture the tissue is reinjured and there is a stimulation to the formation of more inflammatory tissue. As a general rule it is a good procedure to partially close the end of the sheath with a suture, after the prepuce is returned to its normal position. If the injured portion of the prepuce can be protected from the drying effects of air and further injury from foreign objects there is a chance for recovery.

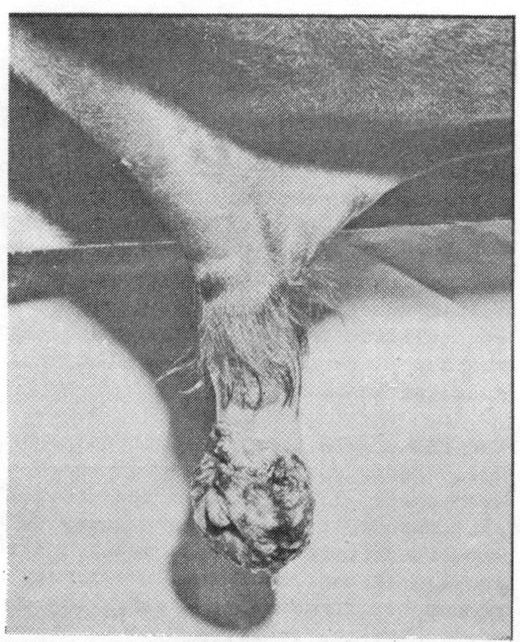

FIG. 360. Extensive laceration of prepuce.

OPERATION. The treatment will be determined by the location of the injury in the prepuce and how extensively the tissues have been damaged. When the prepuce is injured there is a marked inflammatory reaction to the injury to the tissue with the development of an excessive amount of inflammatory tissue. If the injury to the prepuce occurred to the posterior portion antibiotics may be used to control the infection. Also the bull should be separated from other individuals so he will not be stimulated to protrude the penis.

If the injury to the tissues is limited to the most anterior portion of the prepuce and it does not respond to treatment the damaged tissue may be removed. In some individuals the prepuce is short in length and only a small portion may be removed. The operator should determine how much of the prepuce will have to be removed. If the end of the penis will be held close to the end of the sheath after the operation the bull will not be useful for natural service.

The bull may be operated in the standing position or confined in lateral recumbency depending on the facilities that are available for restraint. Prepare the tissues for the operation. Anesthesia for the operation may be obtained by infiltration of the tissues with a local anesthetic. The sutures are inserted through the skin and prepuce at the end of the sheath using either mattress or interrupted sutures. As the sutures are inserted it facilitates the suturing to incise the tissues a short distance anterior to the sutures. To prevent the development of a stricture it is necessary to enlarge the opening at the end of the sheath by removing a triangular area of the skin. The base of the triangle is anterior about one inch long and at the edge of the skin. The sides of the triangle are two to three inches long and terminate on the median line. The incisions to remove the triangular area of skin extend to but do not injure the prepuce. Incise the prepuce on the median line from the base to the top of the triangle. The edges of the prepuce are sutured to their respective sides of the triangle with closely placed interrupted sutures. There will be some swelling of the tissues but this gradually subsides and a permanent opening is formed.

Neoplasms on the Penis of the Bovine

Neoplasms occur rather frequently on the penis of the bovine and usually in animal

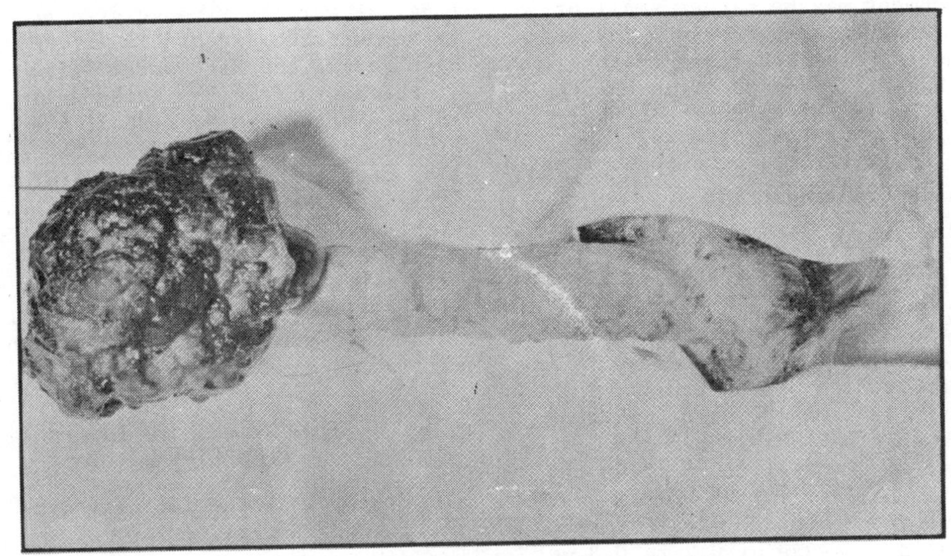

FIG. 361. Fibrosarcoma involving the glans penis of a bull one year of age.

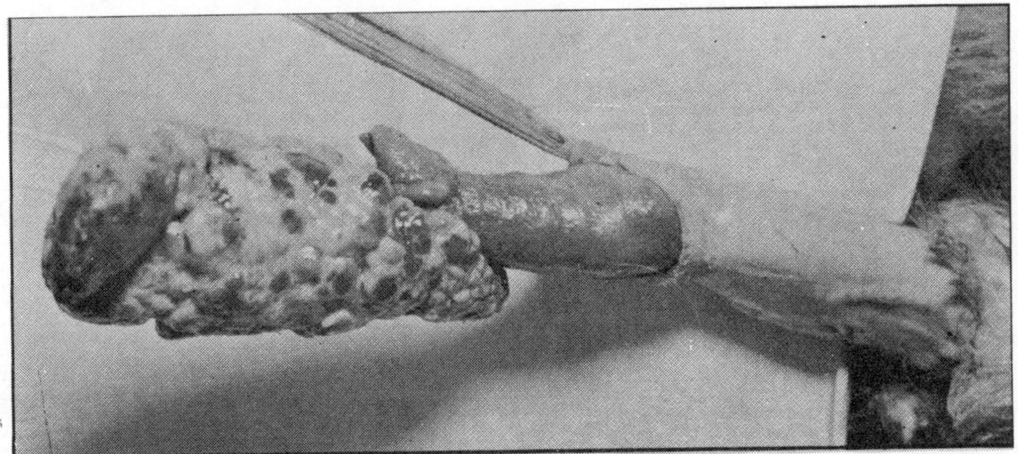

FIG. 362. Fibropapilloma with a small area of attachment to the penis.

from one to two years of age. If a number of young bulls are together the neoplasms may occur on a rather high percentage of the group. The neoplasms vary a great deal in number on each penis from one to five. Also they vary a great deal in size from the rather minute to one that was four inches long and three inches wide. The base of attachment may be rather small or it may be extensive. The neoplasm may cause a phimosis or paraphimosis in some cases hemorrhage is observed or an enlargement may be seen in the sheath. In the largest percentage of the cases the neoplasms are fibropapillomas but fibromas and carcinomas have been reported.

TREATMENT. If there is any difficulty protruding the penis from the sheath so it can be held for the operation a number of methods may be used for the procedure. Usually the ejaculator is very effective in producing a protrusion of the penis. The pudendal nerve block may be used with good results. But in some individuals the pudendal nerve block may fail to relax the penis so a tranquilizer may be used. Chlorpromazine hydrochloride may be given intravenously in a dosage of 0.2 to 0.3 mg for each pound of body weight. For a two thousand pound bull the dosage would be 250 mgs injected into the jugular vein. Relaxation of the penis should occur within five minutes after the drug is given intravenously.

In most cases when all of the neoplastic tissue is removed there is no tendency for the neoplastic tissue to recur. However if it does recur there may be a rapid and more extensive growth of tissue. For those neoplasms with a small base of attachment, two elliptical incisions may be made so as to remove all of the neoplastic tissue. The edges of the incisions are united with fine catgut using interrupted sutures. If the neoplasm has a broad base of attachment it may be possible to remove all of the neoplastic tissue and treat the area as an open wound. For those cases in which the neoplastic tissue involves the end of the penis the following technique may be used to remove the end of the penis.

A piece of gauze bandage fastened around the penis may be used to hold it in position for the opertion. The exposed portion of the penis should be cleaned thoroughly with a mild antiseptic solution. Anesthesia of the operative area may be obtained by infiltrating the penile tissue with a one percent solution of a local anesthetic. A tourniquet should be placed around the penis to control the hemorrhage during the operation. To determine the exact location of the urethra a metal probe is inserted in the urethra beyond the operative area. A triangular area of tissue is removed from over the urethra so that it is exposed. The base of the triangle is anterior with the sides and base approximately one inch long. After the triangular area of tissue is removed the urethra is incised from the base to the tip of the triangle. One edge of the urethra is now sutured to the tissue of the corresponding side of the triangle with closely placed interrupted sutures of fine silk or catgut. To control the hemorrhage a ligature by fixation is inserted about one-half inch anterior to the base of the triangle. The penis is then divided with a transverse incision one inch anterior to the ligature. Most of the bulls operated on by this procedure continue to be of service as sires.

Blocking of the Internal Pudendal Nerve

The blocking of the pudendal nerve relaxes the retractor penis muscle so the penis may be easily examined. The penis is anesthetized so it may be manipulated or various operations may be performed painlessly. The technique that is the most consistently successful in producing the desired results is to introduce the needle in the ischiorectal fossa. One hand should be in the rectum to direct the point of the needle until it is contact with the nerve.

The area for inserting the needle is in the deepest part of the ischiorectal fossa. This fossa is in an area which is bounded ventrally by the ischial tuberosity, laterally by the sacrotuberous ligament, and on the medial side by the rectum and base of the tail. In the beef animal that is very fat it may be easier to palpate the edge of the sacrotuberous ligament, and insert the needle so it will pass on the medial side of this ligament.

Preparè the site for the insertion of the needle in the skin so the sterile needle will not push any skin infection into the deeper tissues. A small area in the skin is anesthetized for the introduction of the cannula. For the large bulls that are thick fleshed and fat the needle will need to be fifteen gauge and six inches long. If the needle is not stiff it will be difficult to direct the point of the needle through the tissue. The average animal may only require an eighteen gauge needle five inches long.

To block the right internal pudendal nerve the left hand is inserted into the rectum. The location of the nerve is most easily found by palpating for that portion of the lesser sciatic foramen that is anterior to the coccygeus muscle. Palpation of this area gives the impression of a weak spot in the sacrosciatic ligament rather than a definite opening. The pulsation of the internal pudendal artery as it passes through the foramen will help to identify the foramen. With the identification of the foramen the hand is moved a few inches forward, and then brought backward with the fingers pressing against the sacrosciatic ligament. The nerve about the size of a light cord should be felt dorsal to the artery.

As the needle is inserted through the tissue some of the anesthetic solution is injected so the tissue will be anesthetized ahead of the needle. When the end of the needle can be palpated with the left hand it is directed into close contact with the internal pudendal nerve. Usually twenty-five cubic centimeters of a two per cent solution is injected around the nerve and somewhat dorsal to the lesser sciatic foramen. Before injecting all of the anesthetic solution, the point of the needle is directed a little higher so the middle hemorrhoidal nerve will, also, be blocked. Habel concluded from his dissection of the nerves in this area that it would be necessary to block another nerve to obtain complete anesthesia of the perineum, penis, or vulva. After injecting the anesthetic solution over the internal pudendal nerve and the middle hemorrhoidal nerve the point of the needle should be directed more ventrally and just inside the lesser sciatic foramen. The ventral branch of the pudendal nerve may be blocked by injecting some of the anesthetic solution in this area.

Some operators may prefer to keep the left hand in the rectum to block the nerve on the left side, while for some, the procedure is facilitated by keeping the right hand in the rectum.

For blocking the pudendal nerve in either the stallion or bovine Getty recommends inserting the needle one inch ventral to the anus and one inch lateral to the median line. The needle will need to be inserted a distance of approximately two to two and one-half inches. Anesthesia of the nerves will occur if ten cubic centimeters of two per cent solution is deposited over each nerve.

Hematoma of the Bovine Penis

The diagnosis of hematoma of the bovine penis may be incorrect in many cases. The hematomas occur dorsal to the penis and there is a great variation in their blood content. The average quantity of blood removed may vary from one pint to a gallon of clotted blood. In most cases the blood comes from the corpus cavernosum through a rupture in the tunica albuginea that occurs during the act of service. There is an intense inflammatory reaction in the tissues following the formation of the hematoma. There is extensive swelling of the sheath and a variable portion of the prepuce is prolapsed from the sheath. In some cases the end of the penis may protrude from the sheath. The injury usually occurs at the time of service as the swelling may be observed within a short time after the bull dismounts. It has been necessary to operate on bull calves nine months of age for hematoma. Practically all of the hematomas occur anterior to the scrotum but one occurred posterior to the scrotum.

PROGNOSIS. In the average case where there is one to two pints of clotted blood in the hematoma the operation should result in a good recovery. The prognosis is more guarded or unfavorable with the increase in the amount of blood in the hematoma. When there is as much as one gallon of clotted blood in the hematoma the inflammatory reaction in the tissues is so extensive the prognosis becomes very unfavorable. If the blood is not removed an abscess may develop with one or more openings through the skin discharging purulent material to the outside. The blood may not become infected but is gradually absorbed but a thick fibrous capsule is formed around the cavity with extensive adhesions to the surrounding tissues.

OPERATION. After the inflammation of the tissues has subsided and the prepuce has returned to its normal position the extent of the swelling can be readily determined by palpation. The ideal time to operate on the average case is about ten days after the appearance of the hematoma when the acute inflammatory reaction in the tissues has subsided. In some cases where the injury has been rather severe it may be desirable to wait two weeks before operating. The tissues seem to return to normal very rapidly when all of the inflammation in the tissues from the injury has subsided before the operation. The operation should be performed on the side of the swelling where

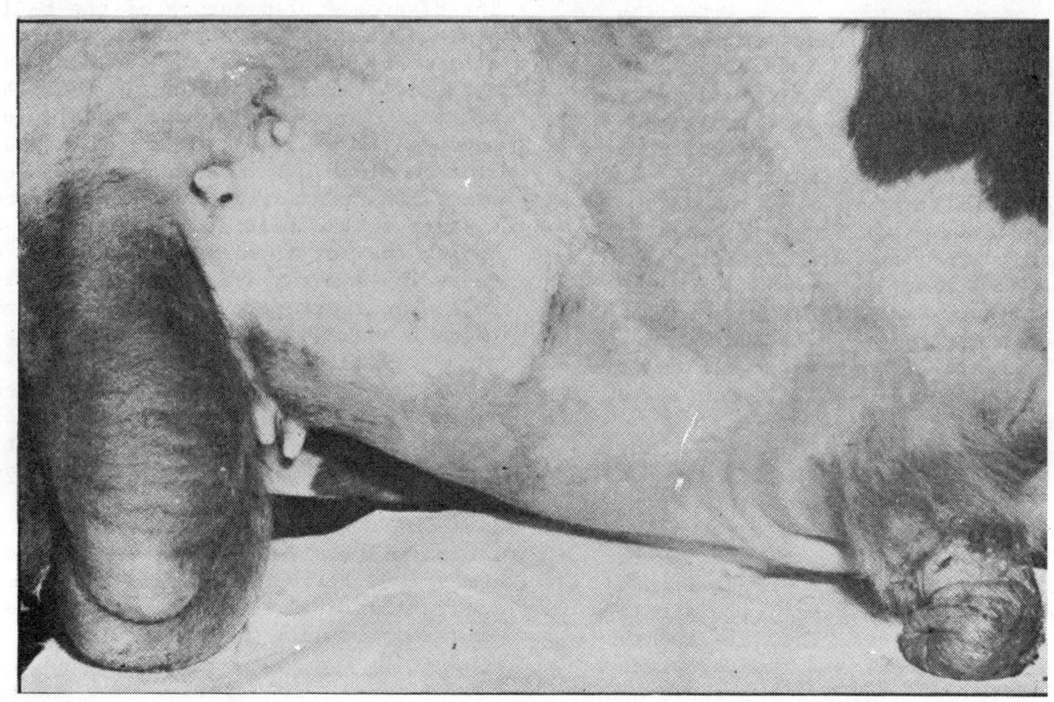

FIG. 363. Hematoma anterior to scrotum extensive inflammation of the sheath and prolapse of prepuce.

it is the most prominent as most of the blood is in this portion of the cavity. The operation is most easily performed with the patient in lateral recumbency although it can be performed with the patient standing. Prepare the operative area for an aseptic operation. If the operation is to be successful it is essential to keep all infection from the cavity.

The tissues may be infiltrated with a local anesthetic along the proposed line of incision. A vertical incision about three inches long is sufficient for the average case. An opening large enough to permit the introduction of a finger into the cavity is made at the most prominent point of the swelling. The opening is now enlarged by using the finger to guide the cutting of the tissue. The opening should be large enough so two fingers can be easily introduced into the cavity. As the blood clot is broken into small pieces with the fingers the pieces are removed. Also pressure is applied on the outside of the cavity to force some of the blood through the opening. The cavity is not smooth and round on the inside but there are many small cavities that extend from the main cavity that contain blood. It is very important to remove all of the clotted blood. The incision should be closed with closely placed sutures and coated over with collodion. As a general rule the bull should not be used for natural service for two to three months after the operation.

Affections of the Prepuce and Penis

Stricture of the Preputial Ring in the Equine

Stricture of the preputial ring in the equine seems to be a congenital condition as the signs are observed from birth. The stricture of the preputial ring is responsible for the retention of some of the urine so there is more or less constant dribbling of urine from the end of the sheath. These cases may not be presented for examination and treatment until the patient is several years of age. Examination of the preputial ring will reveal the ventral portion of the ring is thicker and more prominent than the normal ring. In operating on this stricture the desired results have been obtained by incising through the preputial ring. The incision is started on the median line at the preputial orifice incising the sheath and prepuce through the preputial ring. The edges of the prepuce

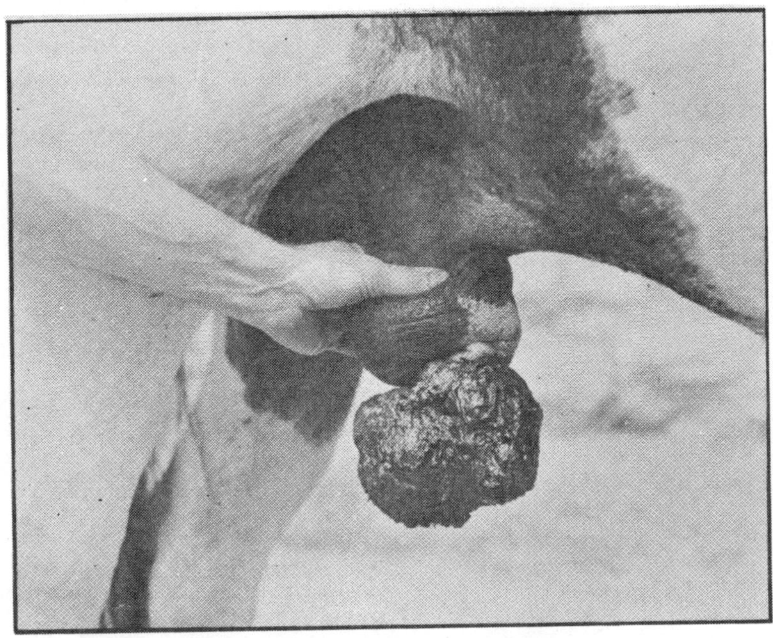

FIG. 364. A carcinoma on the prepuce.

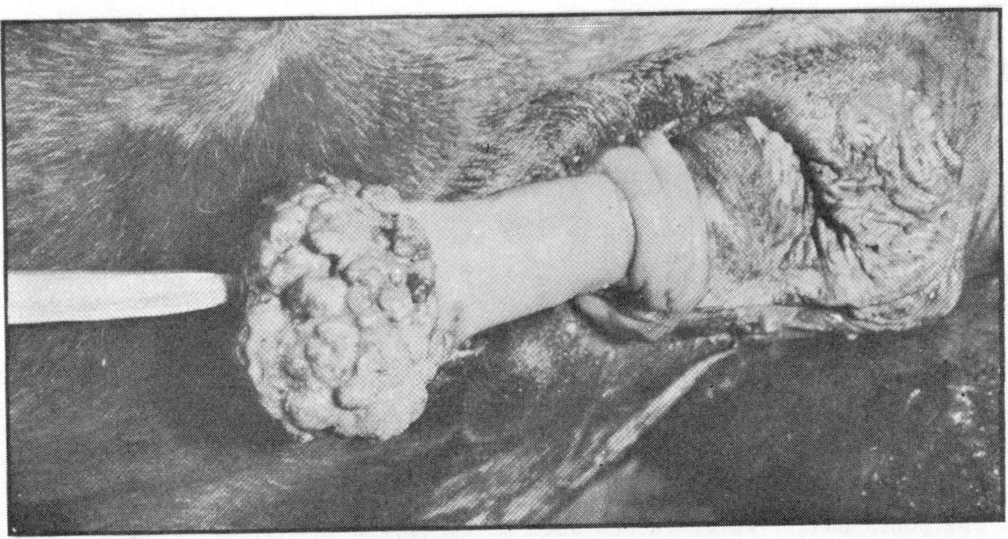

FIG. 365. A carcinoma involving the glans penis of the horse.

and skin on each side of the incision are sutured together with mattress sutures. The blood supply to the tissues is rather profuse and mattress sutures seem to control the hemorrhage better than other type of suture. Very little after care is required in these cases except to use a fly repellent during the fly season.

Carcinoma on the Prepuce

Neoplasms occur rather frequently on the prepuce and in the largest percentage of the cases they are carcinoma. The neoplasms vary in size from those that are small to rather large masses of tissue as shown in Fig. 364. There is a tendency for neoplastic tissue to recur after removal from the prepuce. The operation may be performed in the standing position after anesthetizing the prepuce by infiltration with a local anesthetic. In removing the neoplastic tissue two elliptical incisions are made so that all of the neoplastic tissue is removed. The edges of the incisions are united by closely placed sutures.

Operations on the Equine Penis

Operations are indicated on the equine penis for paralysis of the penis, neoplasms on the penis, paraphimosis following castration and calculus in the urethra. The operation that is performed will depend upon the preference of the operator and the indication for the operation. If the penis is paralyzed and it is desirable to save the end of the penis the reefing operation may be performed. With this operation the prepuce is not injured so a stricture of the urethra does not occur following the operation.

Reefing Operation on Equine Penis

If the paralysis of the penis occurs in a stallion he should be castrated at least one month before the operation. The patient may be confined in lateral recumbency and given a general anesthetic. With the penis fully extended a circular incision is made through the skin about five inches from the end. The position of the next circular incision is approximately two-thirds of the distance from the end of the sheath to the end of the penis. In other words, if the penis hangs twelve inches out of the sheath, the width of the cuff to be removed will be about eight inches. The hemorrhage will be negligible, because the large veins in the loose subcutis need not be injured. Join the circular incisions by one longitudinal incision and dissect away the cuff, avoiding the large veins lying upon the tunica albuginea. The edges of the circular incisions are united by four mattress tape sutures equally spaced around the penis. Place three interrupted silk sutures between each two tape sutures. When healing has occurred in two or three weeks the end of the penis should be held one to two inches anterior to the end of the sheath. The sutures may be removed in two weeks.

Vinsot's Operation

When it is necessary to amputate the end of the penis in the equine Vinsot's operation may be performed. One objection to the operation is the tendency to develop a stricture.

The operation is performed with the patient in lateral recumbency and under general anesthesia. The penis is drawn out of the sheath as far as possible and a catheter inserted into the urethra. A tape may be fastened around the penis to hold it in position for the operation. The tissues are cleansed as thoroughly as possible. A triangular opening with the base one inch long and the sides one and one-half inches long and with the base of the triangle directed posteriorly, is made directly over the urethra. This triangular area of tissue is removed exposing the urethra. The urethra is incised on the median line from the base to the apex of the triangle. The edges of the urethra are now sutured to the corresponding sides of the triangle with closely placed sutures. A fixation suture and drawn tight enough to control the hemorrhage is placed around the penis one inch anterior to the base of the triangle. The end of the penis is amputated with a transverse incision one-half inch anterior to the suture. No after care is necessary.

Dissection of the Urethra

The dissection of the urethra is another operation that may be performed when it is necessary to amputate the end of the penis. In those cases where the penis is involved in neoplastic tissue, is gangrenous or extensively injured this operation could not be performed. A stricture is not supposed to occur following this operation but sometimes one does develop.

OPERATION. The patient is confined in lateral recumbency under the influence of a general anesthetic. The penis is drawn out of the sheath and the tissues prepared for the operation. A piece of rubber tubing is used as a tourniquet and adjusted around the penis posterior to the proposed point of amputation. A catheter,(metal is preferred) is inserted into the urethra. The first incision is made through the skin over the urethra from the proposed point of amputation to the end of the penis. At the end of the penis the incision is continued through the corpus cavernosum urethra tissue to the urethra. The blunt pointed end of the blade of a pair of scissors is inserted between the urethra and the corpus cavernosum urethra and this tissue is incised to the proposed point of amputation. The urethra is exposed and with a little care it is separated from the surrounding tissue. To control hemorrhage from the penis a ligature is fastened in position one inch posterior to the proposed point of amputation. The urethra is not included in this ligature. A transverse incision is used to divide the penis about one inch anterior to the ligature. The tourniquet is loosened and any definite bleeding points are ligated. The stump of the penis retracts into the sheath with the urethra hanging out of the sheath. In the healing the urethra retracts a little, shrivels up and later breaks off. However in the healing of the penis, the urethra develops a good opening with very little tendency to develop a stricture.

Urethrotomy, Ischial

Urethrotomy at the ischial arch is indicated when it is necessary to remove all of the penis and prepuce in the sheath. There is probably less tendency to the formation of a stricture of the urethra with this operation than with those operations previously described on the urethra. If a stricture should develop it is located where it can be easily corrected. In Fig. 366 there is extensive involvement of the penis and prepuce with carcinoma and it was necessary to perform a urethrotomy at the ischial arch. The urethrotomy is most easily performed with the patient in a standing position as there is no displacement of the tissues. Anesthesia of the operative area may be obtained with either epidural anesthesia or infiltration of the

FIG. 366. Extensive involvement of penis and prepuce with carcinoma

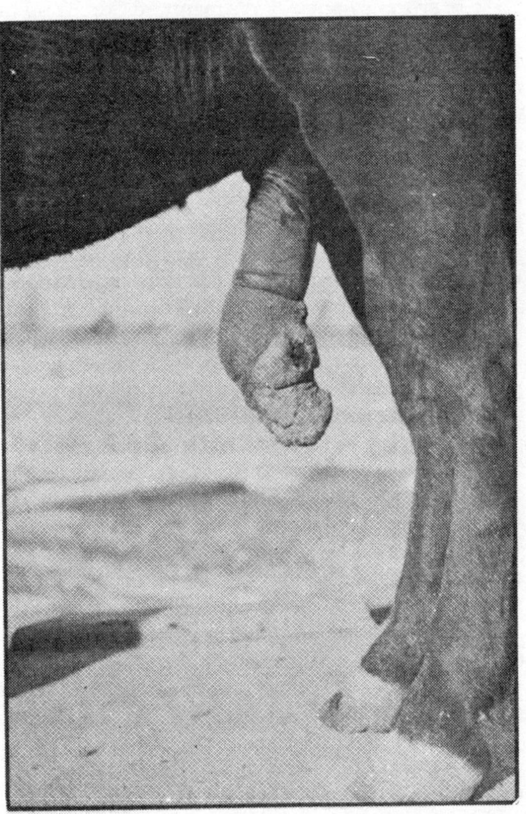

FIG. 367. Paraphimosis that developed after infection of a castration wound.

tissues with a local anesthetic. Prepare the tissues ventral to the anus for an aseptic operation.

The incision through the skin is started on the median line about one inch dorsal to the floor of the pelvis. The incision is continued ventral to the floor of the pelvis until it is about two and one-half inches long. If it has been possible to pass a catheter, but in many of these cases it may not be desirable, the urethra is more easily recognized when it contains a catheter. The dissection and separation of the deeper tissues is continued on the median line. If the operator does not stay close to the median line in the dissection profuse hemorrhage may occur which will interfere with the operation. The urethra will be found in close contact with the bony tissue of the ischial arch. When the urethra is identified it is separated from the surrounding tissue very carefully as in some cases it is thin and tears easily. The separation of the urethra is continued until the operator feels the urethra can be divided and the end brought to the edges of the skin incision. After the urethra is divided by a transverse incision the end is brought out to the edges of the skin. The urethra is sutured to the edges of the skin with closely placed interrupted sutures and so the end of the urethra is on the same level as the floor of the pelvis. Antiseptic wound dressings may be used daily for a week.

After the urethrotomy the horse with the carcinoma of the penis and prepuce received a general anesthetic and was confined in dorsal recumbency. The operative area over the sheath was prepared for the operation. A four inch skin incision was made on the median line posterior to the reflection of the prepuce onto the penis. The penis was separated from the surrounding tissue and ligated. The penis was divided with a transverse incision one inch anterior to the ligature. The penis and prepuce was separated from the surrounding tissue by blunt dissection and removed through the preputial orifice. It was necessary to pack the wound with gauze to control the hemorrhage and this was removed in forty-eight hours. The patient was returned one year later for an examination of a firm swelling in the sheath. This swelling was about six inches in diameter, firm and circumscribed. It was removed and proved to be a carcinoma. Healing was uneventful and the area has remained free of neoplastic tissue.

The described operation may be used for cases such as shown in Fig. 367. The penis is composed of inflammatory and fibrous tissue and cannot be returned to the sheath.

Hermaphroditism

The presence of the genital organs of both sexes in one individual is observed in all species of domestic animals and is called hermaphroditism. This intersexuality manifested by the presence of both internal and external genitalia in one individual is probably due to some heritable disturbance of the factor that determines sex differention.

Pseudohermaphrodites

Individuals called pseudohermaphrodites may occur in which the gonads of one sex may be combined with the external genitalia and the internal parts of the genitourinary system may resemble those of the opposite sex. One method of classifying these cases is to refer to a patient with developed testes as a male pseudohermaphrodite and one with the ovaries developed, as a female pseudohermaphrodite.

In the horse there is a tendency toward the development of testicles which may be retained close to their point of development or may descend into an imperfect scrotum. The mammary glands may develop moderately and resemble in appearance those of the mare. The erectile tissue may be located halfway between the clitores of the mare and the usual location of the penis of the horse. In one case presented for castration the erectile tissue protruded at the anterior edge of the pubis and the sheath was absent. There was no observable scrotum but the testicles were located in the external inguinal rings.

In the illustration the erectile tissue is shown protruding backward approximately twelve inches below the ischial arch. The penis which was seven inches long was suspended in a fold of skin which extended downward from the ischial arch. There was no definite scrotum but the testicles could be palpated close to the external inguinal rings.

The owner did not like the appearance of the animal with the erectile tissue protruding backward and wanted it removed.

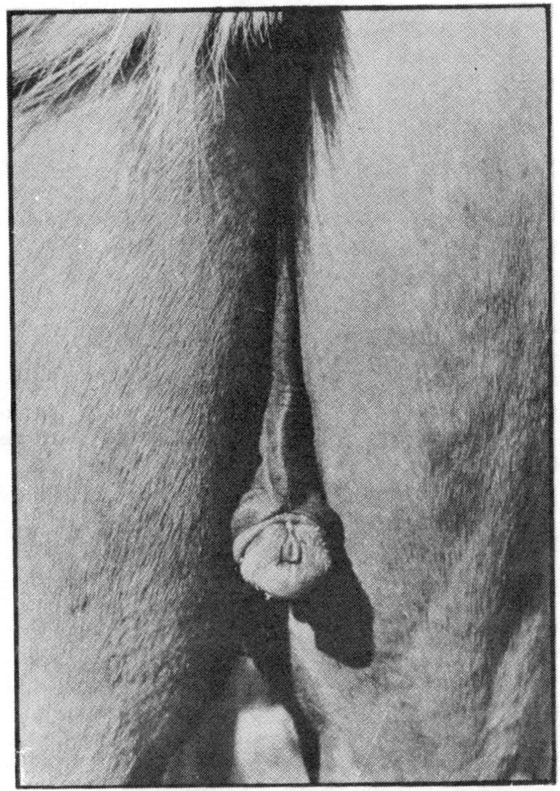

FIG. 368. Male pseudohermaphrodite.

The horse was castrated about one week before performing the plastic operation.

Anesthesia for the operative area was obtained by injecting fifteen cubic centimeters of a one per cent solution of procaine hydrochloride into the epidural space. The operation was performed with the animal confined in lateral recumbency. A median incision starting about five inches below the ischial arch was made through the skin to the opening of the urethra. The urethra was then dissected loose from the surrounding tissue to the beginning of the skin incision. The erectile tissue was also dissected free from its surrounding tissue to a point where it was attached about five inches below the ischial arch. A fixation ligature was inserted in the tissue at this point and the tissue was divided one-half inch posterior to the ligature. With the removal of the penis there was an excessive amount of skin left on each side of the incision. The skin was approximated to the contour of the body by a series of mattress sutures and the excess skin removed beyond the sutures. It seemed best to establish the permanent opening of the urethra at the beginning of the skin incision. The excess portion of the urethra beyond this point was removed. Then the end of the urethra was sutured to the edges of the skin by closely placed interrupted sutures of No. 1 chormic catgut. Healing was uneventful and the operation produced a marked improvement in the appearance of the animal.

Urinary Calculi

Urinary calculi occur frequently in the male bovine and ovine but only occasionally in the equine.

ETIOLOGY. A number of theories have been advanced as to the cause of urinary calculi, The consumption of hard water has been suggested as a factor in the formation of calculi but they probably occur as frequently in animals receiving soft water. Many investigators feel that a deficiency of water is a more important factor than the kind of water. A deficiency of vitamin A or the feeding of excessive amounts of calcium and phosphorus may be important factors in the formation of calculi. Composition of the urinary calculi occurring in the male bovine and ovine has been found to be calcium, magnesium and aluminum salts of phosphoric acid. The urinary calculi of the equine seem to be composed mostly of calcium carbonate.

Urinary calculi occur so frequently in the male bovine and ovine during the winter months that any unusual signs manifested by the affected individual may be due to urinary calculi. To determine the presence or absence of a calculus a thorough examination of the bladder and urethra should be made. Some of the first signs that may be noticed in the bovine are uneasiness or restlessness also attempts to urinate with only a few drops of urine passing or none at all. If careful palpation is made over the urethra at the ischial arch at this time the pulsating urethra filled with urine may be felt. However severe straining may cause a wave like motion to pass along the tissues that suggests a pulsating urethra. What feels like a pulsating urethra should not be considered diagnostic until it is correlated with more definite findings. Examination of the preputial hairs may disclose slight or extensive collections of precipitated salts attached to the hairs and in many cases the deposits resemble calculi in shape. But these accumulations on the hairs should not be regarded as definite evidence of calculi as the accumulations may be seen when there are calculi present and also when calculi are not in the urinary tract. The patient may kick at the abdomen, lie down and immediately get up, also may make short side or wiggling movements with the base of the tail and at the same time back for several steps. If the acute painful signs subside unnoticed the patient seems to spend most of the time in recumbency and there may be a complete loss of appetite.

The signs in some cases presented for examination are not always suggestive of a urethral calculus. A two year old bull was presented for the treatment of a slight prolapse of the prepuce. A rectal examination revealed a distended bladder and a lead wire passed up the urethra disclosed a calculus about eighteen inches from the end of the penis. It is always advisable to make a rectal examination and if the bladder is distended with urine it can be palpated anterior to the edge of the pubis. The wall of the bladder will be tense and the dorsal surface of the bladder is about level with the floor of the pelvis.

In some cases the first signs are not observed and the first indication of a urethral calculus may be due to a rupture of the urethra. If these cases are not treated urine gravitates into the subcutaneous tissues and with the inflammation that occurs a swelling four to six inches thick may develop on the ventral surface of the body. The Stockmen refer to these cases as "water belly". In other cases the bladder ruptures and the urine collects in the peritoneal cavity. If the rupture occurred a short time before the examination there is usually a tenseness of the abdominal wall with an appearance of being full. A rectal examination usually reveals a collapsed bladder and sometimes the opening in the bladder can be palpated. If these cases are not treated, in a few days, there is a pronounced bilateral distention of the abdominal cavity. In some cases as much as twenty or more gallons of fluid have been removed from the peritoneal cavity.

TREATMENT. If the affected animal is in excellent condition for food purposes and the calculus has recently lodged in the urethra, in most cases it is advisable to recommend immediate slaughter. In some fat individuals unfavorable changes have occurred in the urinary tract and they do not respond to treatment. When a valuable breeding animal is affected and the calculus has recently lodged in the urethra an

FIG. 369. When the urethra ruptures the urine gravitates into the subcutaneous tissues of the ventral surface of the abdominal wall.

FIG. 370. Bilateral distension of the abdominal cavity occurring after rupture of the bladder.

attempt should be made to find the exact location of the calculus. To relax the penis for the examination either a tranquilizer or epidural anesthesia may be used. The penis may be straightened out and a No. 20 lead wire passed up the urethra. When the end of the wire comes in contact with the calculus a distinct grating sound is heard. The calculus is in some cases composed of soft material so the grating sound is not produced but the wire will not go any further. As small an incision as possible is made through the urethra over the calculus and it is removed. If the calculus has not produced too much irritation of the tissues the urethra may heal without developing a definite stricture. The incision in the urethra is allowed to heal as an open wound.

In other cases where the calculus has been present for some time or the urethra has ruptured another procedure is used. In the largest percentage of cases the calculus has stopped at the beginning of the S shaped flexure or is more anterior.

The skin just posterior to the base of the scrotum or cod should be prepared for an aseptic operation. Epidural anesthesia may be used or the skin and subcutaneous tissue may be infiltrated with a one per cent solution of a local anesthetic. An incision approximately three inches long is made in the median line just above the base of the scrotum. The fingers are inserted through the skin incision and the rather loose tissue broken down until the penis can be grasped. By straightening out the S shaped flexure the penis can be brought out to the skin incision. The urethra should be palpated to see if the calculus can be located.

If the urethra has ruptured or there is extensive inflammation of the tissues around the calculus the following operation is performed. In this case the blade of the scalpel is inserted flatwise between the dorsal artery of the penis and the two structures separated for a distance of three inches. The penis and urethra are then divided so the end will be just long enough to protrude out through the skin incision and sutured to the edges of the skin. If the urethra is open to the bladder some urine is expelled through the end of the urethra. However, if the bladder has been distended with urine for some time it may not be able to expell the urine readily. To hasten the recovery of the animal a needle is inserted through the ventral wall of the abdomen just anterior to the pubis and into the bladder. If a syringe is attached to the needle the bladder is quickly evacuated. If the urine is permitted to remain in the subcutaneous tissues gangrene of the skin, occurs in a short time and extensive sloughing of the affected tissue will occur. The gangrene may be prevented by making incisions through the skin on each side of the median line, inserting a hand through the incisions and breaking the loose subcutaneous tissues releasing the urine.

Repair of Urinary Bladder in the Bovine

When the bladder in the bovine ruptures a larger percentage of these cases will live if the opening is closed with sutures. The opening in the wall of the bladder will vary in size and amount of damage that has occurred to the tissue. Urine may pass through the wall of the bladder in an area where all of the tissues have not ruptured. In other cases there will be a small opening through the wall of the bladder. Then again there may be extensive gangrene of the walls of the bladder with a large opening. These perforations may occur on the dorsal, lateral or ventral surface of the fundus portion of the bladder. A urethrotomy should be performed.

The operation on the bladder is most easily performed with the posterior part of the patient raised so the operative area is a convenient height for the operator. After ropes are fastened to the posterior limbs above the fetlocks the posterior part may be elevated by means of a block and tackle. The posterior part of the body is elevated until only the shoulders, head and neck rest on the ground. The operative area is immediately in front of the brim of the pelvis and lateral to the penis.

Anesthesia of the operative area may be obtained by infiltration of the tissues with a two per cent solution of a local anesthetic. The incision through the skin and abdominal wall is made long enough so the hand and arm can be introduced into the abdominal cavity. With the hand grasping the end of a stomach tube it is carried through the incision until it is below the level of the fluid. Practically all of the fluid may be removed by siphoning if the fingers are kept over the end of the tube. The fingers are used to prevent tissue from being drawn into the end and closing the lumen of the tube. After the fluid is all removed two to three liters of sterile physiological saline is introduced into the abdominal cavity. This fluid is flushed over the tissues to remove all of the urine and is then siphoned out of the abdominal cavity.

The fundus of the bladder is brought out through the incision so the opening through the wall of the bladder may be repaired. If the edges of the opening are necrotic this tissue should be removed. The opening in the bladder is closed with two rows of continuous sutures bringing the serosal surfaces in close contact, and using No. 1 chromic catgut. The incision in the abdominal wall is closed with the usual technique.

Urethral Calculi in the Ovine

The signs of urethral calculi in the ovine are practically the same as those described for the bovine. The treatment is also the same except that occasionally in the ovine the calculus is found in the process urethra. This is easily determined, if excessive edema of the sheath has not occurred. When the sheath is normal the patient may be placed on its buttocks and the end of the penis pushed forward out of the sheath. If a calculus is present in the process urethra it is easily seen through the thin membrane. The process urethra may be divided posterior to the calculus. Removal of this process urethra does not seen to interfere with the ability of the ram to breed. In some cases in the ovine a portion or all of the urethra may be tightly packed with fine sand like calculi. These cases are very difficult to treat successfully due to extensive involvement of urinary tract.

The incidence of urinary calculi can be reduced by the addition of two to three percent of salt to the ration.

Vesical Calculi in the Equine

The bladder is the most common location for calculi in the equine. Usually there is one large calculus, round or egg shaped and rough or smooth.

SIGNS. The presence of the calculus in the bladder may cause the patient to walk with a stilted gait, kick at the abdomen, stretch out and intermittent straining. Some of the signs most frequently observed may be an almost continual dribbling of urine from the penis or vulva. There may be some blood or clots of blood in the urine especially after exercise. The straining to pass urine may be accentuated after breeding and only a small amount is expelled. If the calculus has been present for some time there may be a gradual loss of condition and even emaciation.

DIAGNOSIS. If a rectal examination is made when the bladder is empty the calculus will be felt in the bladder or lodged in the neck of the bladder. When the bladder is distended with urine a careful examination should be made of the urethra and bladder for calculi.

TREATMENT. A urethrotomy is indicated for the removal of calculi from the bladder of a male animal. If possible the operation should be performed with the animal in the standing position. Anesthesia may be obtained by injecting fifteen to twenty-five cubic centimeters of a one per cent solution of a local anesthetic into the epidural space. Cleanse the skin thoroughly in the operative area which is just below the anus.

A catheter is passed into the bladder to assist in finding the urethra. The incision in the skin is started just below the anal sphincter on the median line and extends downward to just below the ischial arch. The incision is continued through the tissues until the urethra is exposed which is easily recognized by the presence of the catheter. A longitudinal incision is made in the urethra long enough to admit a pair of small animal obstetrical forceps. The forceps are passed through the incision forward into the bladder. The grasping of the calculus with the forceps is facilitated with one hand in the rectum to guide the forceps. When the forceps have a firm hold on the calculus they are rotated and moved back and forth until the calculus is raised out of the mucous membrane in which it is usually embedded. If the calculus is deeply embedded it may be necessary to use one half of the forcep to work the mucous membrane away from the calculus. It is sometimes necessary to pry the calculus out of its deep implantation in the mucous membrane before it can be removed. As the calculus is brought out through the incision it may be necessary to free the calculus from the mucous membrane with a blunt instrument. To control the hemorrhage which is sometimes very profuse it may be necessary to pack the bladder with gauze. The gauze may be removed in twenty-four hours and the bladder irrigated with a mild antiseptic solution. The opening in the urethra should not be sutured but allowed to heal as an open wound.

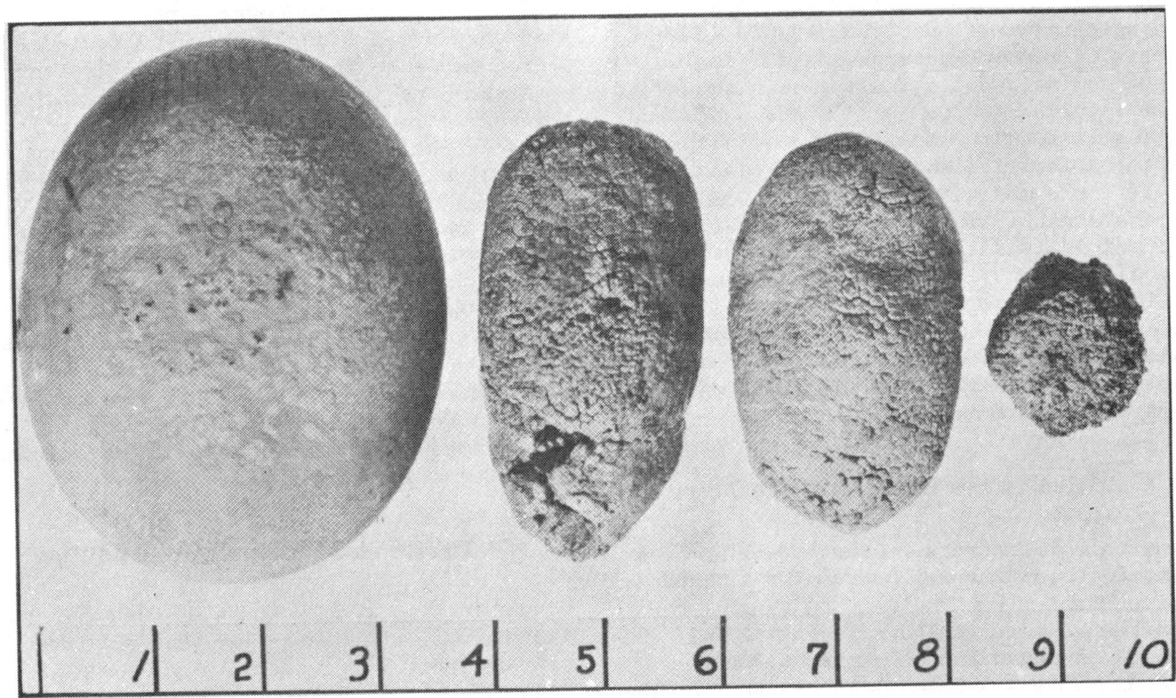

FIG. 371. Vesical calculi of Equine origin, the largest one weighs one pound and nine ounces.

FIG. 372. Vesical calculus of equine origin that weighed fifteen pounds was ten inches long and twenty three inches in circumference.

If the calculus is too large to pass through the urethra, and cannot be reduced in size, it may be removed through an incision in the abdominal wall. The incision should be made anterior to the edge of the pubis and in the mare on the median line. In the male the incision should be far enough lateral to the median line to prevent injury to the sheath. The bladder is usually contracted so it will require some tension to bring it to the incision in the abdominal wall. After the calculus is removed through an incision in the wall of the bladder the incision is closed with two rows of sutures. The incision through the abdominal wall is closed with the usual technique.

Calculus in the Bladder of the Mare

When a calculus occurs in the bladder of the mare it can usually be removed through the urethra. A picture of a calculus removed from a mare is shown in Fig. 373 weighed one pound and four ounces and a diameter of approximately four ounces. The mare was operated in the standing position after fifteen cubic centimeters of a one percent solution of procaine hydrochloride was injected into the epidural space. The urethra was gradually dilated by introducing

FIG. 373. Calculus removed from bladder of mare, approximately four inches in diameter, weight one pound four ounces. Courtesy Dr. J. C. Catlin.

first one, two and three fingers into the urethra until finally the hand could be introduced into the bladder. The introduction of the hand into the bladder will not be possible in all mares. A pair of canine obstetrical forceps were used to grasp the calculus. Attempts to remove the calculus through the sphincter were unsuccessful until the sphincter was incised dorsally. The calculus then passed through the sphincter to the outside very easily. In some cases it may be necessary to incise the sphincter dorsally and also laterally and there are no contra-indications to this procedure. The bladder should be irrigated with a non-irritating antiseptic solution to remove any material that might stimulate the formation of another calculus.

Urethral Calculus in the Equine

Occasionally a calculus will lodge in the urethra of the equine male and it is surprising how large a calculus will pass into the urethra. The usual signs of a urethral calculus occur, as uneasiness, straining to pass urine and only a few drops is expelled or none at all. If the calculus is large it may be palpated to determine its location or a metal catheter passed up the urethra. When the metal catheter strikes the calculus a grating sound is heard. The calculus may be loosened from its position in the urethra by the catheter and expelled.

TREATMENT. Depending upon the location of the calculus it may be possible to operate on the equine in the standing position. The anesthesia used will depend upon the animal and the location of the calculus. The tissues in the operative area may be infiltrated with a local anesthetic. The incision is made on the median line into the urethra and the calculus removed. The incision heals as an open wound.

Rupture of the Bladder in the Foal

Rupture of the bladder may occur in the foal as it is passing through the birth canal. When rupture of the bladder does occur it is probably tightly distended as the foal starts through the birth canal and enough pressure is produced to rupture the bladder. Crowhurst of England, personal communication, stated that he had treated five cases in practice. The signs observed in the equine are the same as in the bovine uneasiness and frequent straining. If the condition is allowed to progress there is a gradual distention of the abdominal cavity.

The treatment is surgical and the foal should be confined in dorsal recumbency. Nembutal is ideal to use as a general anesthetic in the foal and the average case will require fifteen cubic centimeters when given intravenously. The operative area is on the median line anterior to the edge of the pubis. Prepare the area for an aseptic operation. The incision in the female may be made on the median line while in the male it will need to be lateral to the median line to avoid injury to the penis. After the abdominal cavity is opened all of the excess fluid should be removed. It is desirable to introduce two or three liters of sterile physiological saline solution into the abdominal cavity and then it should be removed. The bladder is then brought to the incision so the opening may be repaired, with a double row of sutures. The incision in the abdominal wall is closed in the usual manner.

REFERENCES

Bemis, H. E., A New Operation for Recto-vaginal Fistula, North American Veterinarian, Vol. XI, (1930), No. 2, pp. 37-40.

Caslick, E. A., The Vulva Vulva-vaginal Orifice and its Relation to Genital Health of the Thoroughbred Mare, The Cornell Veterinarian, (April, 1937), pp. 178.

Farquharson, James, Surgical Treatment of Third Degree Perineal Lacerations, North American Veterinarian, 24, (1943), pp. 220-225.

Frank, E. R., Urethral Calculi, North American Veterinarian, Vol. XI, (1930), No. 5, pp. 25-27.

Getty, R., Sowa, J. A., Lundvall, Richard, L., Local Anesthesia and Applied Anatomy as Related to Nerve Blocks in Horses, J.A.V.M.A., 128, (1956), pp. 583-587.

Habel, Robert E., A Source of Error in the Bovine Pudendal Nerve Block, J.A.V.M.A., 128, (1956), pp. 16-17.

Johnson, Harry W., Submucous Resection, Surgical Correction Prolapse of the Rectum, J.A.V.M.A., 102, (1943), pp. 113-115.

Kingrey, B. W., Repair of Urinary Bladders in Steers, Veterinary Medicine, (April, 1956), pp. 157-158.

Larson, L. L., The Internal Pudendal (Pudic) Nerve Block for Anesthesia of the Penis and Relaxation of the Retractor Penis Muscle, J.A.V.M.A., 123, (1953), pp. 18-27.

Magens, H. J., Cystic Calculi of Sheep and Goats, North American Veterinarian, Vol. XV, (1934), No. 9, pp. 28-29.

Newsom, I. E., Urinary Calculi with Special Reference to Cattle and Sheep, J.A.V.M.A., Vol. XCII, (1938), N. S. 45, pp. 495-502.

Wegner, E. E., The Urethral Sound and the Catheter for the Bull, North American Veterinarian, Vol. XIII, (1932), No. 3, pp. 25-26.

Chapter X
AFFECTIONS OF THE POSTERIOR LIMB, CARE OF THE FEET, LAMENESS, UNSOUNDNESS AND COLORS

Thrombosis of the Posterior Aorta or Iliacs

The presence of a thrombus in the posterior aorta or the iliacs of the equine is not a rare condition. A thrombus may occur in the brachial artery producing the same signs in the anterior limb.

ETIOLOGY. The exact cause of thrombi has never been definitely determined. In some cases strongyles seem to be the primary cause, while in other cases it seems to occur as the result of strangles, influenza, or some other systemic infection.

SIGNS. The onset of the signs will vary with the size of the thrombus and the occlusion of the blood vessel. If the thrombus is small, the lameness may not appear until after the horse has been exercised vigorously. While at rest the blood supply to the muscles is maintained by the collateral circulation. When the lameness appears and the animal is forced to continue exercising, there is severe pain and sweating is profuse, except on the affected limb.

THE OUTSTANDING CHARACTERISTIC OF THIS CONDITION IS. The intermittent lameness which appears with exercise disappears with rest. If the thrombosis is bilateral or in the aorta the animal may have difficulty supporting the hind parts for any period of time.

DIAGNOSIS MAY SOMETIMES BE CONFIRMED BY. Making a rectal examination which may reveal the position of the thrombus or the difference in size of pulsation of the arteries to the limbs.

TREATMENT. As a general rule treatment is of no value. However the horse may be exercised regularly with the hope of stimulating the formation of more collateral circulation or that the thrombus may be absorbed.

Epiphyseal Separation

A number of cases of separation through the epiphyseal cartilage at the head of the femur have occurred in young horses. These cases usually occur in colts less than three and one-half years of age as ossification of this cartilage has usually occurred at this age, although in one case in a mule separation through the epiphyseal cartilage occurred at five years of age.

SIGNS. The signs are usually characteristic of this condition. The lameness appears very suddenly and never gets any worse, nor does it show any improvement. The neck of the femur is displaced upward, and the great trochanter is more prominent.

TREATMENT. There is no practical method of treatment available at the present time.

Trochanteric Bursitis or Trochanteric Lameness

This is an inflammation of the bursa beneath the tendon of the middle gluetus where it passes over the great trochanter.

ETIOLOGY. The condition may be caused by a bruising of the bursa from a blow or fall, or a strain of the tendon. It may follow or occur during an attack of influenza or strangles.

SIGNS. In a case of acute bursitis there is swelling and pain on pressure over the great trochanter. It may be necessary to exert pressure from both sides as the horse may normally move away from pressure on one side. At rest the limb may be flexed, although in some cases the limb will appear normal until the horse is exercised. When exercised the forward stride is shortened with the hind parts carried over to the sound side, sometimes referred to as traveling "dog fashion".

This is due to the sound leg being carried further forward and weight is placed on the inside of the affected limb.

In the chronic cases atrophy of the gluteal muscles may occur between the internal and external angles of the ilium.

COURSE. With the proper treatment recovery occurs in four to six weeks. However, if the injury to the bursa or tendon is severe, the condition may become chronic.

TREATMENT. During the acute inflammation, absolute rest is indicated and either hot or cold applications may be used. In the later stages Lugol's solution may be injected into the tissues around and over the bursa and tendon. Two cubic centimeters are deposited at a point and the points are placed two inches apart.

Coxitis

Inflammation of the coxo-femoral articulation occurs occasionally in cattle, but is of rather rare occurrence in the horse.

ETIOLOGY. Inflammation of the joint has occurred in horses following a fall on a hard surface. It has also been observed when a horse has been forced to violent effort in pulling a load and has slipped.

SYMPTOMS. At rest the attitude of the limb is usually diagnostic. The affected limb is held extended with the toe turned out. At the walk the limb is carried forward in almost a normal manner. The symptoms of pain occur when the limb is vertical as the weight is borne by the limb. In most cases the signs remain about the same, they never get any worse nor do they show any improvement. The signs are practically the same in the bovine.

PROGNOSIS. In most cases in equine and bovine the prognosis is unfavorable as the affected individuals show little, if any improvement.

TREATMENT. As in most cases of lameness rest is always indicated.

An irritant composed of 20 grains of iodine and 40 grains of potassium iodide in one ounce of water is injected into the tissues. A two inch needle is used to inject it into the tissues around the joint. Two cubic centimeters are injected at a point, and the points are placed about two inches apart. The treatment may be repeated in three or four weeks, but it rarely results in complete recovery.

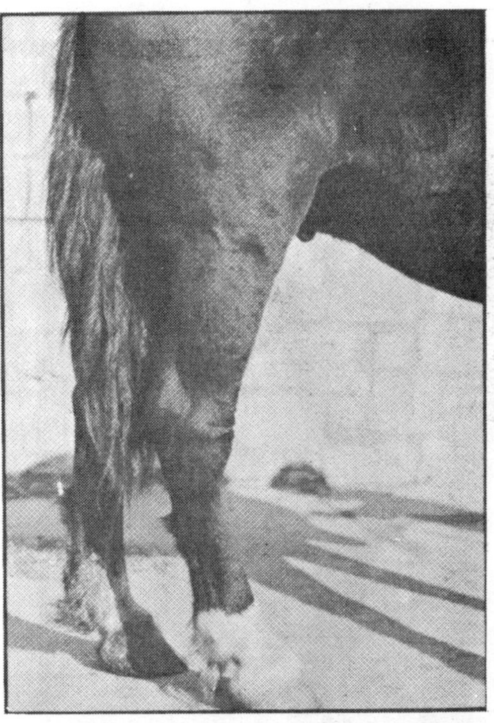

FIG. 374. Typical attitude of the limb in coxitis.

Dislocation of the Coxo-femoral Articulation

Dislocation of the coxo-femoral articulation is of rather frequent occurrence in the bovine but is considered rather rare in the equine. The frequency of its occurrence in the bovine is due to the difference in anatomy of the hip joint. In the bovine the acetabulum is comparatively shallow, its superior border is deeply notched, and the articular head of the femur has a smaller radius of curvature. The ligament is entirely intra-articular and sometimes absent while the accessory ligament is always absent.

A ten year old Jack was presented for examination, lame in the left hind leg. The Jack had been confined in a box stall and the pronounced lameness had appeared without apparent cause. Examination of the limb revealed the proximal extremity of the femur was freely movable. Also the affected limb was apparently shorter than the normal limb. A post-mortem examination revealed a complete dislocation of the head of the femur with rupture of the joint capsule.

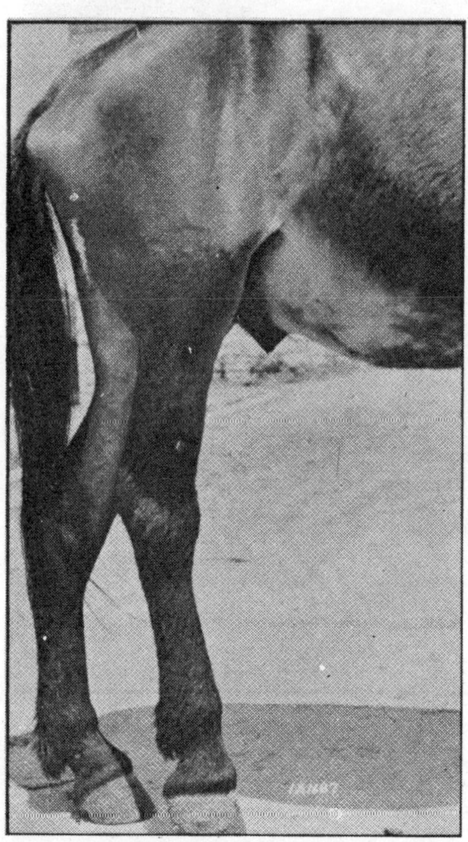

FIG. 375. Dislocation of the hip joint in a twelve year old mule.

SIGNS. When the dislocation occurs the head of the femur is displaced upward and forward. The characteristic signs are limited abduction, easy adduction, a pronounced shortening of the limb with unusual prominence of the great trochanter. Note shortening of limb and prominence of the great trochanter.

For approximately a week after the dislocation occurred there was a great deal of swelling of the soft tissue along the femur and around the hip joint.

TREATMENT. The dislocation may be reduced by pulling the leg downward and forward. At the same time the operator should manipulate the head of the femur through the notch into the acetabulum. However, there is usually a recurrence of the dislocation and in large animals it is usually impossible to prevent.

Paralysis of the Sciatic Nerve

Paralysis of the nerve occurs occasionally in the equine and bovine, and may be unilateral or bilateral. Bilateral paralysis is usually of spinal origin and may be due to an abscess or neoplasm pressing on the nerve. In some cases lymphoid tissue replaces the nerve tissue. The paralysis may develop following a fall.

SIGNS. The affected limb hangs loosely due to loss of function of the muscles of the quarter with the exception of the quadriceps femoris muscles. When forced to move the quadriceps femoris muscles jerks the limb upward and forward, and due to inability to extend the phalanges the front of the foot rests on the ground. However, when the foot is placed in its proper position the limb is able to support weight.

PROGNOSIS. Recovery will depend upon the cause of the paralysis.

TREATMENT. Support in slings and exercise of the affected limb is the most important form of treatment. When the animal is made to exercise with each step the foot should be brought up to and placed in a normal position.

Spastic Paresis of Hind Limbs

The disease spastic paresis of the hind limbs also called "contraction of the Achilles Tendon" is very descriptive as that structure seems to be drawn as tight as possible. With the limbs stretched tight and joints extended the tuberosity of the tuber calcis is pulled close to the distal extremity of the tibia.

SIGNS. There may be some disturbance in the normal movements of one or both posterior limbs early in life but this may not be noticed if the signs are slight. Probably in most cases the signs do not appear until the animal is two to six months of age, and at this age the signs are very apparent. There does not seem to be any disturbance in the general condition as long as the animals receive a good diet. In the young animals milk in the diet seems to be very important. As the animal becomes older the general condition may not be as good as that of normal animals of the same age. There is no indication of paralysis of either the bladder or rectum.

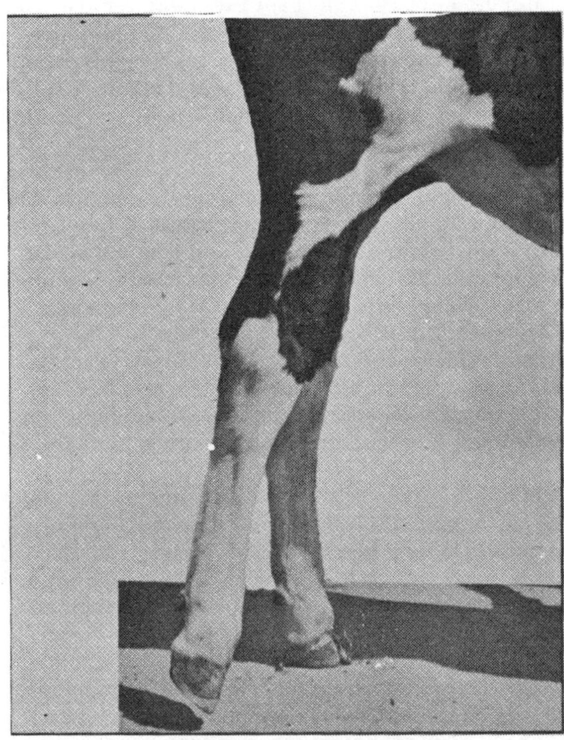

FIG. 376. Spastic paresis.

The characteristic signs that are shown in one or both posterior limbs will vary in degree with different individuals. When the condition is well developed only one limb is affected with marked extension of the hock joint and the marked contraction of the tendon of achilles. The limb seems to be shortened and may only touch the ground with the point of the toe. If the limb is observed closely it will be noticed the stiff joint is elevated higher than normal, and the hock joint seems to be small, due probably to the marked extension of the joint. When the limb is palpated there is no indication of inflammation of any of the structures of the limb. The outstanding finding will be the marked spasm of the quadriceps and gastronemius muscles, and the tenseness of the tendon of achilles. It will be noticed the limb is adducted due to the contraction of the adductor muscles. There may be some difficulty in the animal getting up depending upon the severity of the spasms of the muscles. The most pronounced contractions of the muscles occur when the animal is getting up and when it finally stands on its feet. When the spasms subside the joints of the limbs may be flexed without difficulty, provided this is performed gently. If the limb is manipulated vigorously, however, it will be impossible to flex the joints due to the violent spastic reaction of the muscles. In the less severe cases the gait of the animal is not affected but in a well developed case there is definite interference with the gait. The affected leg swings backward and forward like a pendulum with the toe barely touching or in some cases not even reaching the ground. It might be necessary to differentiate between spastic paresis, gonitis or upward fixation of patella, but if the signs are evaluated carefully it should not be too difficult to diagnose the condition.

TREATMENT. The signs in about fifty per cent of the cases may be relieved or alleviated by an operation of the tendon of achilles. The operative area is approximately two inches anterior to the tuber caleis on the lateral and dorsal surfaces of the tendon of achilles, and is prepared for an aseptic operation. Anesthesia for the operation is obtained by infiltrating the skin and underlying tissue with a local anesthetic. A narrow bladed scalpel is introduced through the skin so the blade passes ventral to the tendon of gastroenemius. The sharp edge is turned toward the tendon and the incision is made through the tendon of gastroenemius until it is divided. Introduce the scalpel blade in the center of the superficial flexor tendon and transversely divide one half of the tendon. One interrupted suture is used to close each of the two openings in the skin.

Femoral Paralysis (Crural)

Paralysis of the femoral nerve affects the quadriceps femoris muscle.

ETIOLOGY. Probably most cases occur as the result of myoglobinuria or azoturia. Some cases appear suddenly without any apparent cause, and the signs disappear in a few days with rest. Injury to the nerve may occur from overstretching during excessive exertion, from kicking or slipping.

SIGNS. The most marked signs occur during movement of the limb as weight cannot be supported by the affected limb. As soon as weight is placed upon the limb all of the joints are flexed. At rest the limb is held with the stifle and the joints of the limb flexed, and the affected quarter appears lower than the other quarter.

Marked atrophy of the quadriceps muscles may occur if the paralysis persists for some time and when used fibers may stand out as thick cords. Atrophy of muscles arise from disuse, overwork, trauma, from prolonged pressure, from interference with circulation or from central or peripheral lesions of motor nerves.

The muscles become smaller and flaccid. Their functional power decreases slowly or rapidly and atrophy may progress to the complete loss of contractile substance. The anatomic alterations vary and depend on etiology. In atrophy due to non-use and fibers though smaller in size are normal in structure and appearance. This type of atrophy is seen frequently in lameness of horses when the affected limb is not used in a normal manner. When the cause of the lameness is corrected and the limb is used in a normal manner, the muscles resume their normal size and function.

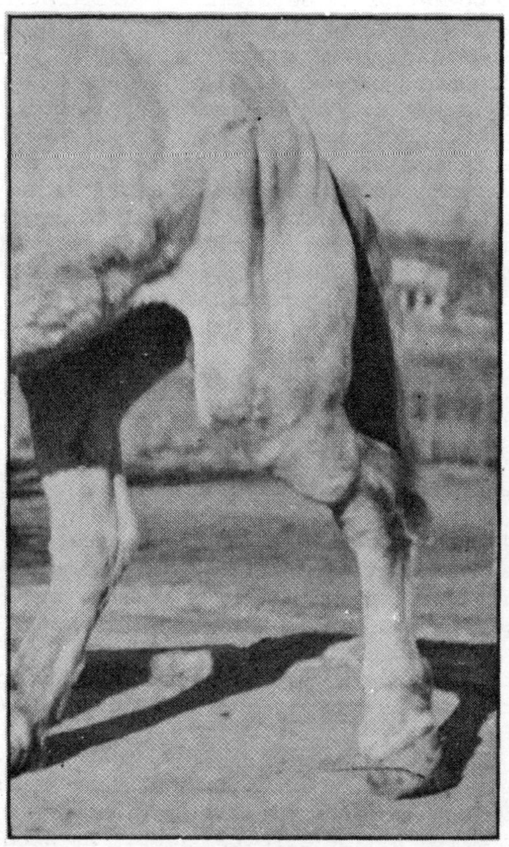

FIG. 377. Femoral paralysis with marked atrophy of quadriceps femoris muscle, note inability to support weight.

In atrophy resulting from interference with the nerve supply the fibrils degenerate into granules of fat which later on are absorbed and the whole muscle is transformed into fibrous connective tissue which finally produce the deformed and permanent attitude of the parts.

There are two other conditions in which the signs would be the same as femoral paralysis. In lateral luxation of the patella and rupture of the quadriceps femoris muscle the signs would be similar. However in lateral luxation of the patella the examination would disclose the patella on the lateral side of the stifle joint. By palpation the examination would reveal the rupture of the quadriceps femoris muscle.

PROGNOSIS. The injury to the nerve is usually of short duration but the paralysis may persist for weeks and months. In a severe case of azoturia the paralysis of the nerve may be permanent and the muscle never regains its function.

TREATMENT. Exercise is the most important part of the treatment and sufficient time for the injured nerve to recover its function.

Obturator Paralysis

The obturator nerve is most frequently injured during the act of parturition. It may be injured by the fetus where the nerve passes over the prominence of the lumbosacral articulation and at the edge of the obturator foramen.

SIGNS. These are very characteristic as the adductor muscles of the limbs are affected. If the condition is unilateral the animal is able to walk but the affected limb is carried in abduction. If both nerves are affected the limbs are completely abducted and the affected individual drops upon its pubis. However if the limbs are maintained in a normal position the weight is supported without difficulty.

TREATMENT. The treatment consists in maintaining the animal in slings and fastening the legs so they are held in a normal position. Where possible exercise hastens recovery, which may occur in a few days, weeks or months.

Paralysis of Deep Peroneal Nerve (External Popliteal Nerve)

This nerve supplies the long and lateral extensors of the digit and the tibialis anterior.

ETIOLOGY. Injury of this nerve may result from falls, slipping, running away, or may follow some infectious disease. In some cases it appears without any apparent cause.

SIGNS. Paralysis produces a partial or complete loss of function of the tibialis anterior and the extensor muscles. In the standing position the limb is able to bear a normal amount of weight, if the foot is in its normal position. However, if there is complete paralysis the hock is extended, the fetlock is flexed with the front of the foot resting on the ground. In walking the limb at first appears to hestitate, then is extended rigidly backwards with the hock extended and the fetlock flexed. The limb is then brought forward by the extensors of the stifle, until the front of the foot and sometimes the fetlock rest on the ground. At a faster gait the horse may carry the limb with the fetlock and front of the foot dragging on the ground.

PROGNOSIS. As in most cases of paralysis should be guarded.

TREATMENT. Exercise is the best form of treatment and with each step use some method to bring the limb forward and the foot up to a normal position.

Paralysis of the Posterior Tibial Nerve (Internal Popliteal Nerve)

The muscles on the posterior surface of the tibia are supplied by this nerve.

SYMPTOMS. With paralysis of this nerve the hock cannot be extended nor the foot flexed. However, when flexion of the hock occurs there is automatic flexion of the phalangeal joints. When advancing the limb all of the joints are flexed and the foot is held higher than normal and is set on the ground with an uncertain movement. After the foot is in position the leg is able to bear weight as the hock is fixed by the Achilles tendon.

PROGNOSIS. Guarded.

TREATMENT. Exercise during which, an attempt should be made to produce normal movement of the limb.

Affections of the Stifle Joint

The stifle joint is a large and complicated joint and is composed of two separate articulations, the femoro-patellar and the femoro-tibial. The joint capsule is very extensive and it usually communicates with the medial sac of the femoro-tibial joint cavity by a slit like opening. There is usually a smaller communication with the lateral sac of the femoro-tibial joint capsule.

Hydroarthrosis of the Stifle Joint

Animals affected with this condition are frequently presented within a few weeks after birth while others may be five or six months old. It usually indicates a weakness of the affected joint, and one or both joints may be affected.

The joint capsules are excessively distended causing the colt to extend the hind legs.

FIG. 378. Hydroarthrosis of the stifle joints in a six months old colt.

In some cases the lameness is not severe until there is excessive distension of the joint capsule. When colts only a few weeks old are affected in one or both legs the legs seem to be weak.

PROGNOSIS. Guarded as it is usually an indication of a weakness of the joint.

TREATMENT. Aspiration of the excessive quantity of joint fluid and blistering has not proved to be of much value. In a few cases recovery may occur without any treatment but usually there is little or no improvement.

Acute Gonitis

Acute aseptic inflammation of the stifle joint or ligaments may occur as the result of a strain or traumatism. The joint capsule may be distended due to a marked increase in joint fluid. Palpation of the joint will in many cases reveal the tissue along the edge of the tibia is sensitive on the medial side of the joint. The stifle joint is kept flexed with the toe just touching the ground and the patient refuses to bear any weight on the limb.

TREATMENT. Absolute rest is the most important part of the treatment. The use o cold water daily on the joint may help to reduce the inflammation. The value of various preparations injected into the joint cavity is questionable.

Chronic Gonitis

In chronic inflammation of the stifle joint, ulceration of the articular surface of both the femur and tibia may occur. In many cases there is inflammation of the synovial membrane and the inner surface presents a granular appearance. Palpatior of the stifle joint will in many cases reveal exostoses at the proximal end of the tibia on the medial side. Also there may be a marked enlargement of the proximal end of the tibia. When a loud clicking

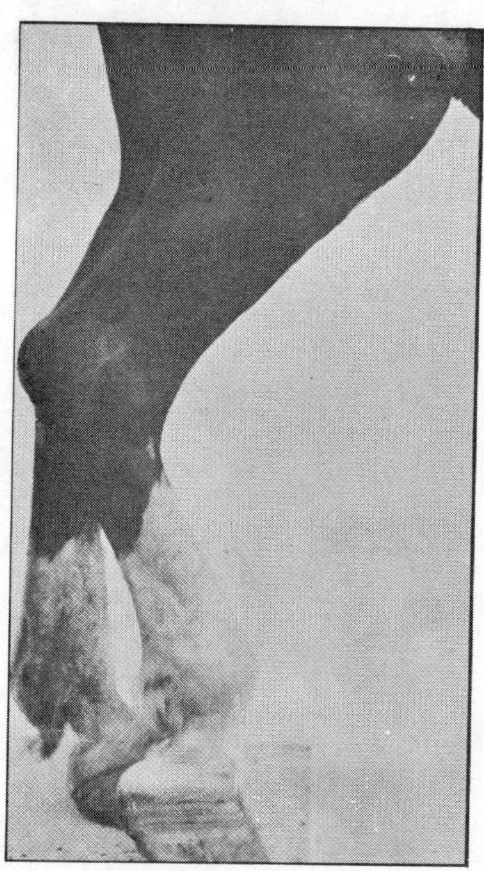

FIG. 379. Typical attitude of the limb in a severe case of gonitis.

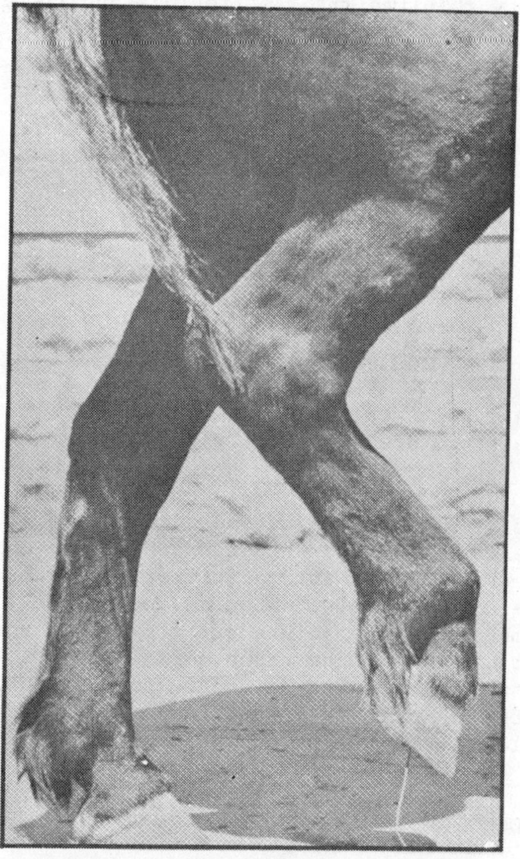

FIG. 380. Typical attitude of the limb in gonitis.

sound is heard as the patient walks there is a lack of joint fluid and it is a dry joint. The stifle joint is kept flexed and there is a reluctance to put any weight on the limb and pressure on the joint surfaces.

TREATMENT. Rest is the most important part of the treatment. Direct treatment of the joint cavity rarely produces any beneficial results.

Gonitis in the Bovine

Inflammation of the stifle joint is one of the most serious lamenesses that occurs in the bovine. This is particularly true of the bull as with a painful condition in the stifle joint they usually refuse to breed. It is one of the most common causes of bulls becoming useless for natural service. Chronic gonitis also occurs in the cow and is a frequent cause of a chronic lameness.

Examination of the bovine for lameness should always include the foot as it is frequently the seat of lameness. If the foot seems to be normal the stifle joint should then be examined very carefully.

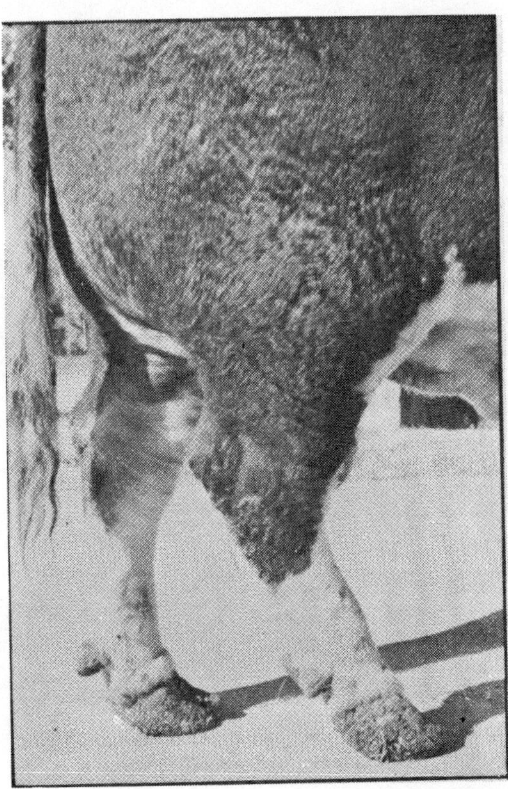

FIG. 381. Typical attitude of the limb in gonitis in the bull.

The examination may reveal there is an absence of joint fluid and a clicking sound will be heard as the animal walks. In some cases there may be an increase in joint fluid which will be determined by palpation of the joint capsule. The joint capsule may be tightly distended with joint fluid or the distention may involve only the anterior portion of the joint capsule. One of the most constant changes observed in chronic gonitis is bone hypertrophy. The cause of the hypertrophic type of chronic arthritis is unknown. Probably one of the most important contributing factors is local joint trauma. The trauma need not be excessive but may comprise the strains and stresses on inferior joint structures. Also a sudden severe strain may occur in one of the stifle joints during the breeding act. In the young bull epiphyseal bone changes may occur in which the underlying bone becomes thickened and denser than normal. Occasionally the periosteum near the articular margin proliferates and forms osteophytes.

Examination of the joint for evidence of bone changes is performed most efficiently by digital examination from the rear of the animal. The surgeon will find the most pronounced bone changes have occurred at the proximal extremity of the tibia on the medial side. By using both hands the width of the affected and normal joints may be compared and in some cases it is very pronounced.

TREATMENT. The most benefit seems to be obtained from rest of the animal. The patient should be confined in a small enclosure and exercise limited until the lameness disappears.

It is advisable to use hand breeding when the patient becomes serviceable again. If the activity of the patient is controlled he may be useful for a number of years. However excessive use may reinjure the joint and the second time it may not respond to rest so the lameness becomes incurable. During the period of rest one of the corticosteroids may be injected into the joint cavity.

Fracture Through Epiphyseal Cartilage at Proximal End of Tibia

Fracture through the epiphyseal cartilage at proximal end of tibia occurs most frequently in the bovine when they are two to three years of age. After three years of age there is ossification of the epiphyseal cartilage and fractures of the tibia occur on the shaft of the bone. Fractures through the epiphyseal cartilage usually occurs from a traumatism on the lateral side of the tibia at the proximal extremity. The lateral side of the tibia is covered with heavy muscle tissue while on the medial side the bone is subcutaneous. When the fracture occurs the proximal end of the tibia is displaced medially. If the patient is lying down there is a marked crease in the soft tissue on the lateral side of the hock joint. A casual examination of the limb gives the examiner the impression this is the location of the fracture. However palpation of the tibia will reveal the proximal end of the tibia has been displaced medially and the flat roughened surface of the end of the tibia may be felt.

PROGNOSIS. The prognosis is guarded as there is little tendency toward the formation of a callus. Even when the fracture has been immobilized and the surfaces held in close apposition the surfaces have remained smooth and no indication of callus formation. A very small percentage of the cases have developed fibrous tissue around the fracture so the limb was usable.

Seroma

A seroma is characterized by the presence of a thin fluid that is tinged with blood so that it is a reddish-brown color. In some cases they may represent a degenerative state of a hematoma as there is frequently a hematoma in the cavity. There is frequently some lymphatic drainage from the traumatized tissue into the cavity. The seromas occur most frequently as a cavity in the subcutaneous tissue and is filled with a variable quantity of fluid. Seromas usually occur on those areas of the body that are more easily traumatized as the brisket or pectoral region.

Treatment consists in making a liberal incision through the skin at the most ventral portion of the swelling. The contents of the cavity should be evacuated and the interior of the cavity should be examined for fibrin, and when present it is removed. The cavity may be packed with gauze moistened with tincture of iodine, removing the gauze in twenty-four hours. In a large seroma healing occurs rather slowly as the skin may have been separated from the underlying tissue over a large area.

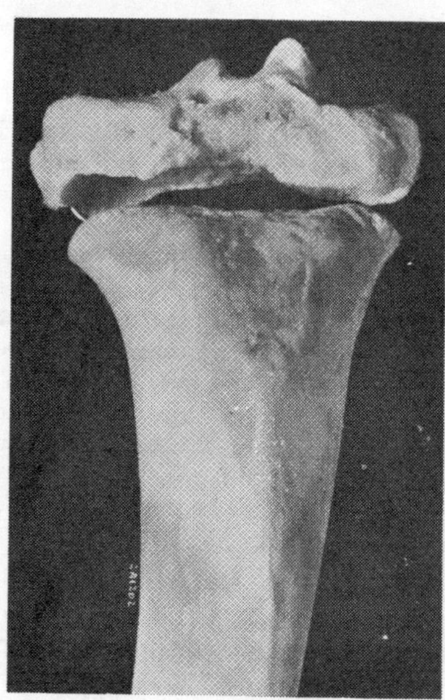

FIG. 382. Fracture that occurred through epiphyseal cartilage at proximal end of tibia.

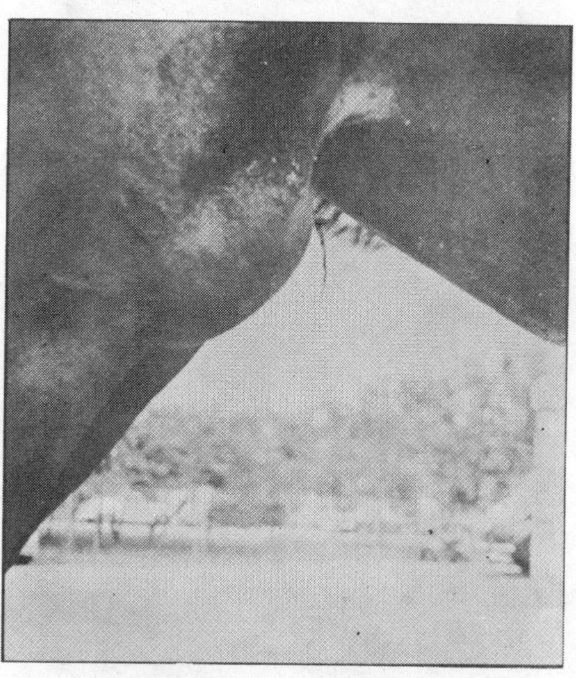

FIG. 383. Seroma may occur in any location. This one is medial to the stifle joint.

Luxation of the Patella

In the horse the patella may become fixed above the medial lip of the trochlea or there may be a lateral luxation of the patella. Upward fixation of the patella may be either partial or complete. Upward fixation of the patella occurs when the stifle joint is fully extended. It occurs more often in stabled horses especially on those that have been lying down, and get up and stretch extending first one, then the other posterior limb backwards.

SIGNS. The signs of momentary, recurrent or complete upward fixation of the patella are characteristic and easily recognized.

In momentary luxation at the trot, the foot appears to hesitate for a moment as it leaves the ground. Or the patella may be fixed temporarily and the leg will be carried, extended backwards for a few steps. After a variable period of time the signs disappear and the gait becomes normal.

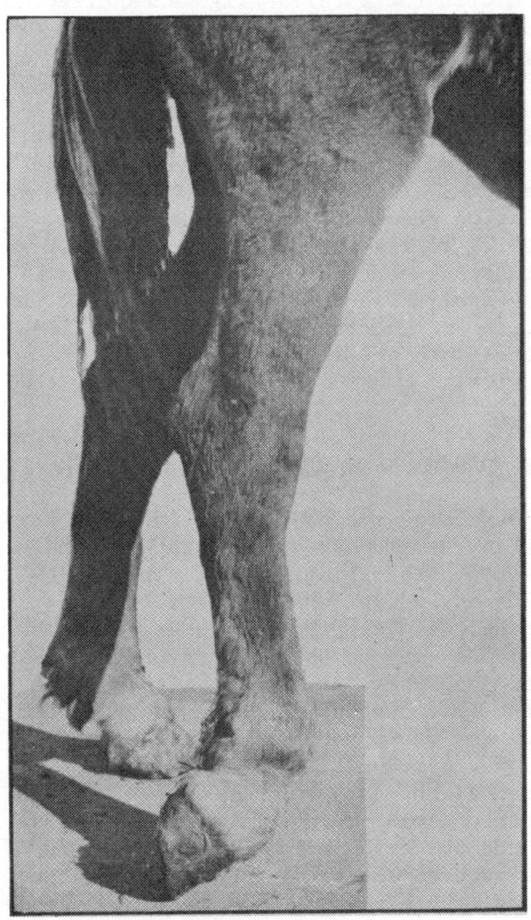

FIG. 384. Characteristic attitude of the limb with stifle and hock joints extended.

In upward fixation of the patella the signs are very characteristic. The stifle and hock joints are fully extended and cannot be flexed with the fetlock and the front of the foot resting on the ground.

When the horse walks the leg is carried in this position with the front of the foot dragging on the ground. Palpation of the trochlea reveals the absence of the patella and the tenseness of the patellar ligaments. Prognosis is favorable in most cases of luxation and upward fixation of the patella. Congenital luxation of the patella is unfavorable.

TREATMENT. In some cases the signs disappear almost as quickly as they appeared. When the horse is forced to back quickly it may be sufficient to dislodge the patella. The usual treatment is to fasten a rope below the fetlock and pull the leg forward. At the same time the operator may place one hand on either side of the patella and attempt to displace it. In a few rare cases it may be necessary to give the patient a general anesthetic to thoroughly relax the tissues. It might be necessary to cut the medial patellar ligament as described for recurrent luxation of the patella with locking. When the patella slips into position flexion of the stifle and hock joints occurs.

Operation for Recurrent Upward Fixation of the Patella with Locking

This operation is performed when there is repeated upward fixation of the patella with locking. The three patellar ligaments which arise from the patella, and are attached to the tuberosity of the tibia are easily identified by palpation. The medial patellar ligament is cut as close to its attachment to the tibia as possible.

Operation

If the patient can be controlled the operation is easily performed with the patient in the standing position. The operative area is located by palpating for the middle straight patellar ligament and then for the V shaped depression between it and the medial patellar ligament. This depression is just above the attachments of the ligaments to the tuberosity of the tibia. The medial ligament is about one-half inch wide but the posterior edge blends in with the fascia which makes it difficult to palpate its width. The tail setting knife can be used to divide the medial patellar ligament. Prepare the skin over the V shaped depression in the usual manner for an aseptic operation. The skin and underlying tissue is infiltrated with a two per cent solution of a local anesthetic. Also the tissue on each side of the ligament is infiltrated with the anesthetic solution. Palpate for the anterior edge of the medial patellar ligament and introduce the knife directly through the skin and fascia at this point. The knife is held with its flat surface against the ligament. After the point of the knife passes the edge of the ligament it is directed posteriorly along the deeper surface of the ligament. When all of the cutting edge of the knife has been introduced through the skin the sharp edge is turned against the ligament. The ligament is then divided through out its entire width and the knife withdrawn. As the opening in the skin is less than 1/4 inch long it is not necessary to insert any sutures. The small opening in the skin may be covered with flexible collodion. In most cases the horse should be rested for a week or ten days after the operation. In some cases we find it is necessary to cut some of the fascia posterior to the ligament before the patella will remain in its normal position.

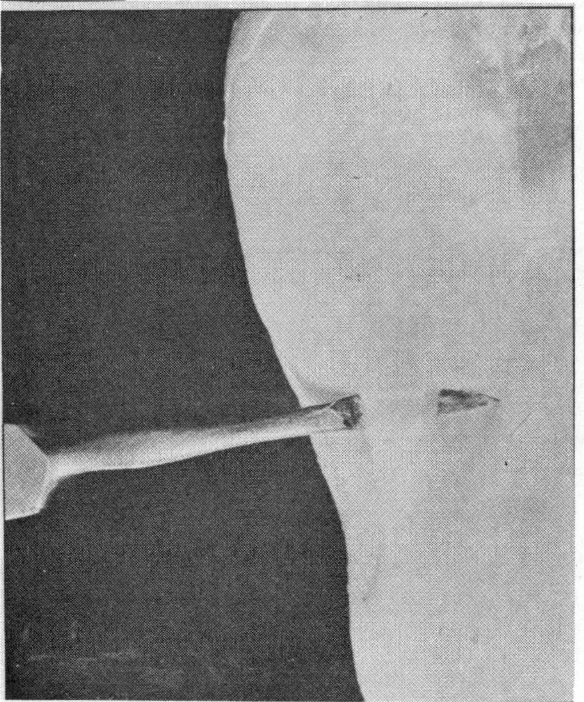

FIG. 385. Knife inserted to show width of medial patellar ligament preparatory to dividing the ligament.

Lateral Luxation of the Patella

This is a rather rare condition in large animals, but it does occur in horses and cattle. A case of congenital bilateral luxation of the patellas in a three months old calf was presented at the clinic.

SIGNS. Clinically the signs of lateral luxation of the patella resemble those of femoral paralysis. When the animal attempts to put weight on the limb it is unable to bear any weight and there is flexion of all the joints. At rest the limb is held with all the joints flexed and only occasionally touching the toe to the ground. Palpation of the stifle joint reveals the patella in an abnormal position with the patellar ligaments directed obliquely upwards and outwards. Also examination of the trochlea reveals the absence of the patella.

TREATMENT. A rope attached to the limb below the fetlock may be used to extend the limb. At the same time digital manipulation should be used to return the patella to its normal position. If it shows a tendency to recur, twenty cubic centimeters of a two and one-half per cent solution of tincture of iodine may be injected into the tissues lateral to the patella.

Fracture or Defect of the Fibula

In examining the posterior limbs for the seat of a lameness a radiograph may be taken of the tibial region. The radiograph may reveal what appears to be a fracture of the fibula. These so-called fractures may be open spaces or non-ossified epiphyseal cartilage. It has been noted that osseous union of the head and body and various portions of the shaft may never occur. Many of the signs of lameness that are attributed to fracture of the fibula are observed in affections of the posterior limbs. In Yugoslavia two hundred and fifty horses healthy and sound were examined using both roentgenologic and anatomic examinations and it was found that osseous union of various portions of the fibula never take place.

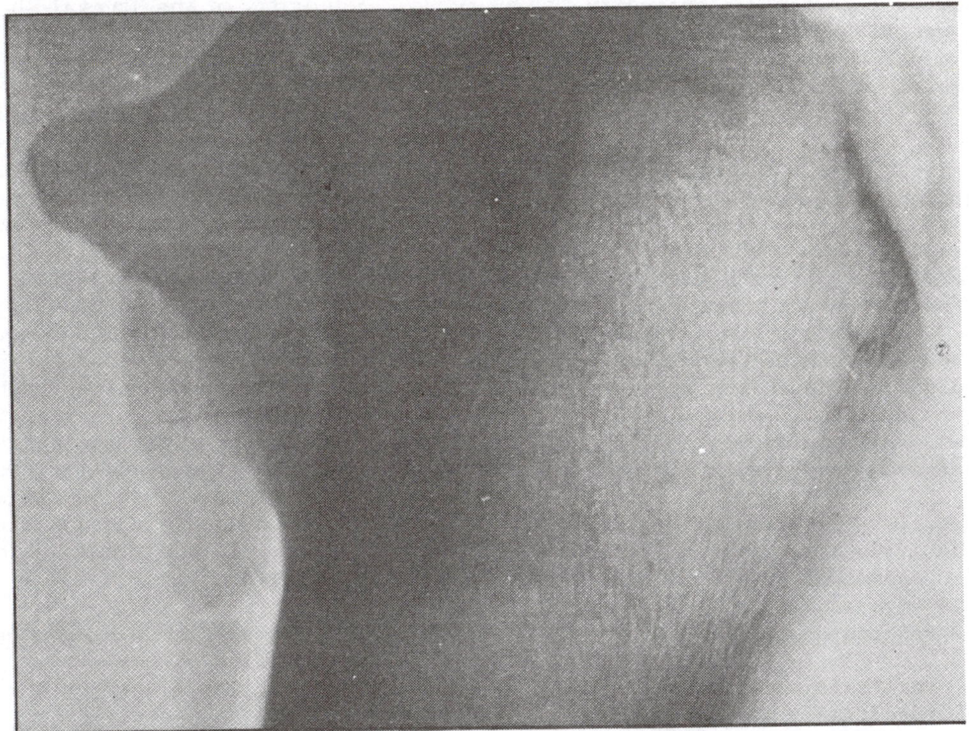

FIG. 386. A case of so-called fracture of the fibula.

FIG. 387. Appearance of the limb after amputation below the stifle joint.

It is concluded that the discontinuity which has been diagnosed as a fracture represents a normal phenomenon which occurs in approximately fifty per cent of healthy horses.

Amputation of a Posterior Limb.

This operation is indicated when the lower part of the limb is affected with some condition that would not respond to local treatment. In some cases this operation might not be an economical procedure but certain individuals could be fattened for meat purposes that would otherwise have to be destroyed. Also valuable breeding animals can be saved for breeding purposes.

In performing the operation on the hind limb the operative area is at the junction of the upper and middle third of the tibia. The stump is high enough so it will not be injured by striking on the ground.

OPERATION. Anesthesia of the limb may be obtained by injecting forty cubic centimeters of a two per cent solution of procaine-hydrochloride into the epidural space. The patient may be confined in lateral recumbency on the operating table or the ground. Prepare the operative area by shaving and the application of a good antiseptic. An old stomach tube makes a good elastic tourniquet to apply on the limb above the operative area.

Two elliptical incisions are made through the skin one on the medial and one on the lateral side of the limb. The incisions are made so the bone can be divided at the junction of its upper and middle thirds and the skin and muscle can be sutured over the end of the bone. The skin incisions are continued thru the muscle tissue to the bone. The muscle tissue is dissected away from the bone above the point where the bone is to be divided. A bone saw is used to divide the bone. The ends of the muscles are sutured together with No. 4 chromic catgut so they will form a pad of muscle over the end of the bone. Unite the edges of the skin with two continuous sutures of umbilical tape, each starting at the upper ends of the incisions and terminating so there is an opening for drainage at the lowest point. The skin sutures are covered with flexible collodion. After treatment consists in keeping the opening free of exudate so there is complete drainage. In ten days to two weeks the skin sutures may be removed.

Synovitis of the Tarsal Sheath

The tarsal sheath or the synovial sheath of the deep digital flexor tendon in its course over the medial surface of the hock. It is a very extensive sheath as it extends from approximately three inches above the medial malleolus of the tibia to about three inches down on the metacarpus.

Inflammation of the tarsal sheath may occur as the result of a traumatism or a strain of the tendon called tenosynovitis. When inflammation of the sheath occurs there is an outpouring of an excessive amount of synovial fluid. Palpation will reveal tenderness along the course of the sheath and when the tendon is used there is evidence of pain. If the excess fluid remains in the sheath fibrous tissue may replace the fluid and fibrin which results in a limitation of motion.

SIGNS. The sheath is distended and sensitive to palpation. Lameness is pronounced with little weight placed on the affected limb.

TREATMENT. Same as described for other cases of acute synovitis.

Purulent Synovitis of Tarsal Sheath

When infection occurs in the tarsal sheath it is a serious condition. As a result of the infection necrosis of the tendon may occur producing an incurable condition. The signs are those of a very painful condition, painful lameness, intense pain and a partial or complete loss of appetite. Palpation of the sheath reveals that it is tightly distended, hot and very sensitive to the touch. Usually the patient does not bear any weight on the leg but stands with the leg flexed.

TREATMENT. The introduction of antibiotics has simplified the treatment of purulent synovitis if the treatment can be started early in the infection. The infected fluid may be removed with a needle and syringe and an antibiotic injected into the sheath. This treatment is repeated every day or two until recovery has occurred. If treatment is delayed until the infection is well established in the sheath it may be necessary to establish drainage from the sheath. A full therapeutic dosage of an antibiotic should be given systemically. This opening should be made at the lowest point of the distention of the sheath.

After all of the purulent material has been removed from the sheath it may be re-injected with an antibiotic.

Chronic Synovitis of the Tarsal Sheath (Thoroughpin)

Chronic inflammation of the tarsal sheath may develop from an acute synovitis or it may be of slow development. There is considerable variation in the distention of the sheath and also in the degree of lameness in Fig. 388.

A thoroughpin is characterized by a swelling of the tarsal sheath in front of the tendon of Achilles and about on a level with the tuber calcis. A thoroughpin may vary a great deal in size and there may be a gradual increase in the distention of the sheath. Lameness is usually absent but in some cases it is present all the time and very resistant to treatment.

PROGNOSIS. Is guarded when there is lameness associated with the chronic synovitis. In most cases it is difficult to permanently reduce the sheath to its normal size.

TREATMENT. Probably the most successful form of treatment is to aseptically aspirate the contents and inject an antiseptic into the sheath. The antiseptic may consist of three parts glycerine and one part Lugol's solution. Also the following blister may be applied to the area daily four ounces of tincture of iodine, one ounce of turpentine and ten drops of croton oil.

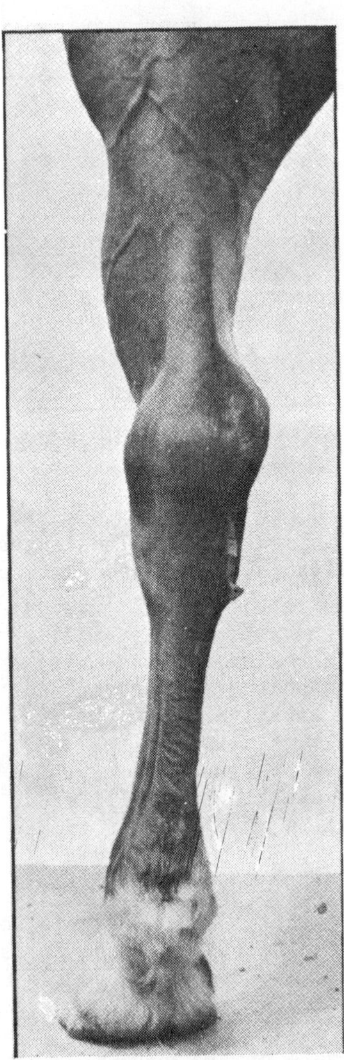

FIG. 388. Pronounced distension of the tarsal sheath.

Rupture of the Peroneus Tertius

The peroneus tertius is entirely tendinous and unites the stifle and hock joints. Its action is to mechanically flex the hock when the stifle joint is flexed.

ETIOLOGY. Rupture of the peroneus tertius usually occurs from over extension of the hock joint. It may occur when the leg becomes caught and the horse struggles violently to free the limb. If the limb is drawn too far backward and then if violent efforts are made to free the limb it may result in rupture of the peroneus tertius.

SIGNS. When rupture of the peroneus tertius occurs the signs are very typical. As the animal moves it is easy to diagnose the condition from a distance. Due to the loss of function of the peroneus tertius the hock joint is not flexed when flexion of the stifle joint occurs. The portion of the limb below the hock joint is carried and hangs inert. This marked change in the normal action of the limb may lead a careless observer to make a diagnosis of a fracture. If the lower part of the limb is pulled backward the hock will be excessively extended and it will be observed the Achillis tendon is relaxed.

PROGNOSIS. In the average case this is favorable as the ends of the tendon do not retract very far. Occasionally a case may not recover due to the location of the rupture. The average case will make a complete recovery in two to three months.

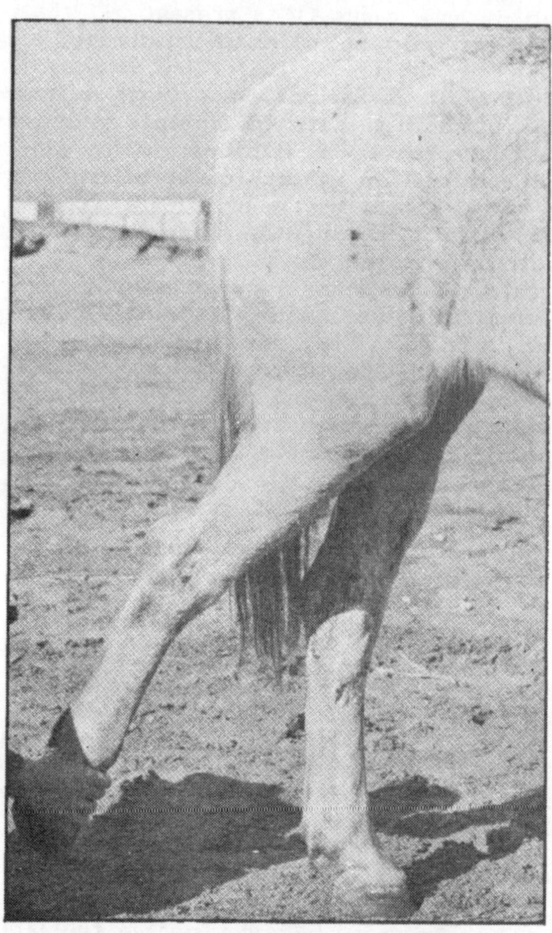

FIG. 389. Rupture of the peroneus tertius, note over extension of the hock joint.

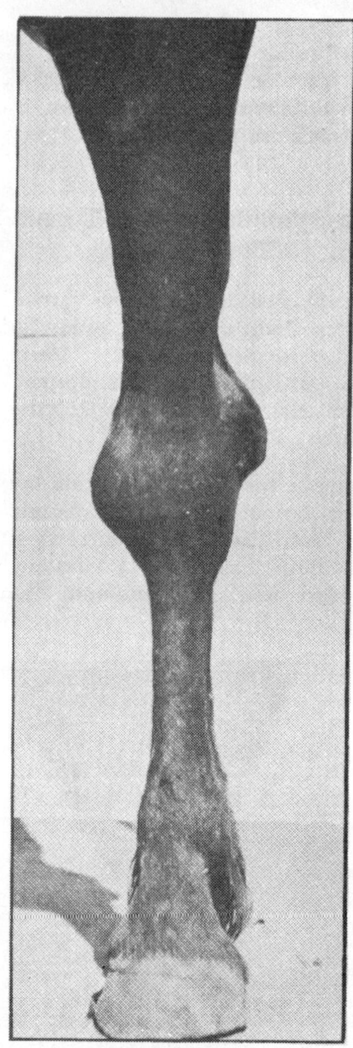

FIG. 390. Bog spavin, with unusually large swelling.

If the horse is put to work too quick the recovery may not be complete.

TREATMENT. Rest is the most important part of the treatment and the animal should be kept as quiet as possible. If the animal is exercised too much the tendon may heal but will be longer than normal with impairment of action.

Bog Spavin

A chronic distention of the joint capsule of the tibial articulation as the result of a chronic synovitis. The term "blood spavin" is sometimes used by the laymen when there is a bog spavin and a very prominent saphenous vein.

When a bog spavin is present it is easily recognized by the three characteristic fluctuating swellings. The largest of the three swellings is situated antero-internally at the level of the inner lip of the trochlea, the two smaller swellings located one on either side of the posterior surface of the hock joint at the junction of the tibial tarsal and fibular tarsal bones. These swellings vary in size in different cases. When pressure is exerted on any one of the swellings it will cause an increase in size of the other two swellings.

ETIOLOGY. Probably in most cases bog spavin develops because of a weakness of the hock joints. If the leg is too straight the function of the excessive joint fluid may decrease the concussion of the articular surfaces. In some cases it seems to develop following an unusually severe strain of the joints. When there is a painful condition in one posterior limb so that it is not used in getting up and down the normal limb may develop a bog spavin as a result of the excessive strain that is put on the normal limb.

PROGNOSIS. The prognosis should be guarded when there is lameness and a distention of the joint capsule. In many of the cases the horse is not lame so that it does not interfere with his usefulness.

TREATMENT. When a horse has bog spavin and is lame we have used a blister on the three swellings with some success. The blister consists of Tincture of Iodine four ounces, Turpentine one ounce and Croton Oil, ten drops, applied daily to the three areas for ten days. In ten days the skin may become irritated so treatment should be discontinued for a week or ten days. The treatment may be repeated with the possibility the lameness will disappear. However, there is usually little or no decrease in the quantity of fluid in the joint cavity. The actual cautery may be used in some cases and with considerable success in producing a permanent reduction in the excessive quantity of synovial fluid, in the joint cavity. A number of points are inserted through the skin over each of the three swellings. A blister is then used on each one of the three areas. This treatment has frequently produced a permanent reduction in the amount of fluid in the joint cavity.

The use of one of the corticosteroids injected into the joint cavity has proved to be very beneficial in a number of cases. Prepare the skin over the anterior medial swelling so a needle may be introduced through the skin without introducing any infection into the joint cavity. The skin and deeper tissues may be anesthetized by local infiltration. When the needle has been introduced into the joint cavity the excess joint fluid may be removed by suction with a syringe. The corticosteroid is then injected into the joint cavity. It may be necessary to repeat this treatment two or more times at weekly intervals.

Bone Spavin
Arthritis, Chronica Deformans Tarsi

SYNONYMS. 1. Visible spavin where there is a definite exostosis present. 2. Occult or blind spavin a case which shows typical spavin lameness but no visible exostosis. 3. High spavin, in which the exostosis is located close to the true hock joint. 4. Jack spavin, is the term used when the exostosis is unusually large. The usual location of a bone spavin is on the medial side of the hock joint and involving the proximal end of the large metatarsal bone and distal row of tarsal bones.

A true spavin probably starts as an ostitis. In the majority of cases a rarefying ostitis affects the deeper portions of the bone and then extends toward the periphery or may extend toward the articular surfaces of the bone or both. The rarefying ostitis produces cavities in the bone which fill in with granulation tissue osteosclerosis may then occur and also ankylosis and exostosis. If the ostitis extends only peripherally ankylosis

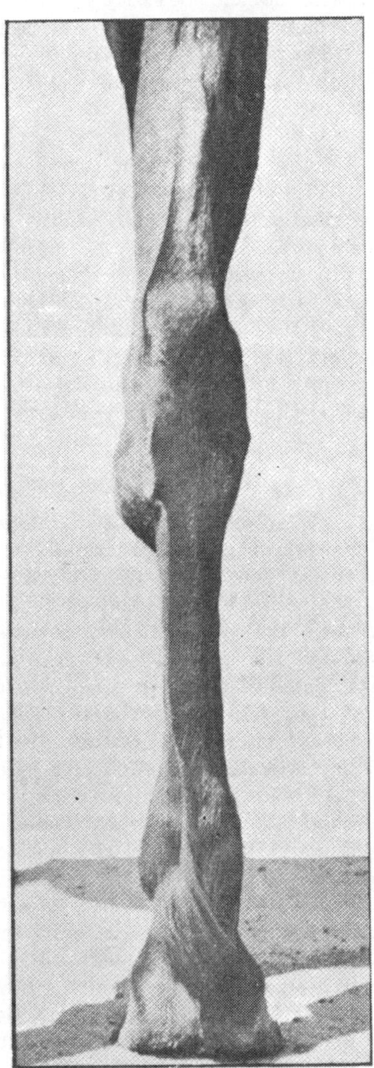

FIG. 391. Bone spavin with unusually large exostosis, horse was never lame.

may occur without any involvement of the articular surfaces. In other cases ulceration of the articular cartilage occurs and ankylosis develops without the formation of any visible exostosis. These cases are the so called occult or blind spavins.

ETIOLOGY. A number of theories have been advanced as to the cause of spavin. One of the theories is poor conformation of the hock but there are probably just as many spavins present on apparently perfectly formed hocks as those of poor conformation. Hereditary predisposition is listed as a factor but no definite statement as to what is inherited. Upright conformation of the hind limb may be a factor in the production of more concussion on the bones of the hock. Deficiency of phosphorus in the ration may be the most important factor in stimulating the formation of many of the bony conditions that occur.

SIGNS. In the examination of one or both posterior limbs for the seat of the lameness the region of the hock joints should be examined very carefully. When there is lameness in a posterior limb the hock joint is the seat of the lameness in the largest percentage of the cases. When the seat of the lameness is in the region of the hock joint, a bone spavin is the cause of the lameness in the largest percentage of the cases.

The typical bone spavin lameness is a cold lameness. When the horse first starts to move after resting, the lameness may be evident for a few steps or a variable distance. The lameness disappears as long as he continues to move and the tissues are warm. However if he is rested a sufficient time until the tissues are cold then when he starts to move again there is lameness. In some cases there is lameness evident most of the time and these cases never warm out of the lameness. Other cases will be alright when they are moving straight ahead but if they are turned on the affected limb they show lameness. One case refused to go straight forward but would try to deviate to one side or the other. Examination revealed a bone spavin in each hock. After each spavin was operated on the horse would go straight in a normal manner. Other cases may not show any lameness until an unusual strain occurs on the limb.

The only indication of a bone spavin may be imperfect flexion of the hock joint with a tendency to drag the toe. Failure to completely flex the hock is due to the pain produced when the hock joint is completely flexed. It may be noticed that with imperfect flexion of the hock joint there is exaggerated hip action. With the tendency to drag the toe more weight is put on the toe so the wall at the toe or the toe of the shoe is worn excessively. The patient when at rest may flex the hock in a spasmodic manner. It may be noticed the shoe is worn more on the lateral side due to more pressure on that side.

Examination of the hock for bone spavin may consist in first viewing the hock from different angles. A direct view of the hocks may be obtained by standing in front of the patient and compare the two hocks by looking between the front legs. Stand to one side of each front limb and look obliquely at the inner aspects of the hocks. If there is any pronounced enlargement it is easily detected. Any exostosis present or inflammatory changes in the tissues can usually be determined by passing the fingers over the usual location of a spavin. If the other hock is normal, examination of this hock will help in detecting changes that have occurred in the affected hock.

The spavin test consists in grasping the leg above the fetlock joint and completely flexing the hock joint for a short time. When the leg is released the patient should trot for a short distance. If a spavin, causing lameness is present there should be a pronounced lameness for a few steps. However this test is not always diagnostic, as other conditions especially in older horses may cause increased lameness after forced flexion of the limb. In an obscure case it might be desirable to block the plantar nerves, the posterior tibial and deep peroneal nerves to determine if the seat of the lameness is in the region of the hock joint.

PROGNOSIS. The prognosis should be favorable in the largest percentage of the cases. If the exostosis is very extensive and extends high dorsally and far forward the prognosis is guarded. Some cases with large exostoses have never been lame.

TREATMENT. The spavin should not be treated until the patient can be confined for one month. During this period of confinement the patient should not receive any exercise. A number of treatments have been recommended for the treatment of bone spavin. Those treatments mentioned the

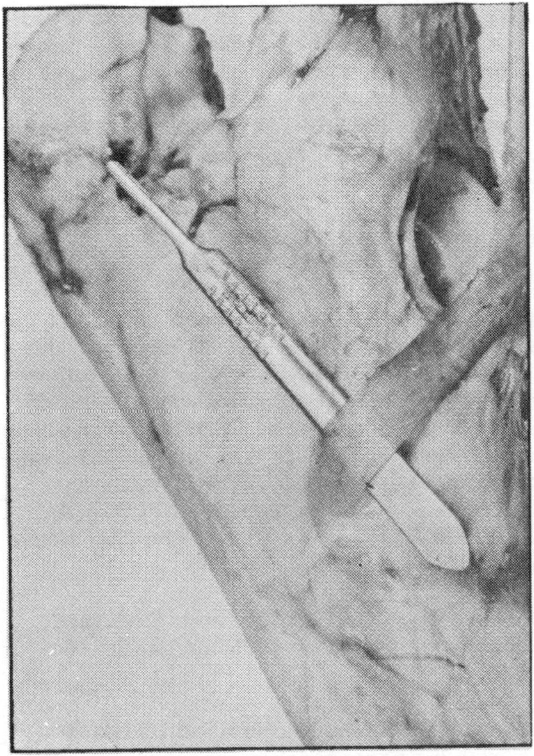

FIG. 392. A scalpel handle has been inserted under the cunean tendon just before its insertion on first tarsal bone.

most frequently, blistering, point firing and tenotomy of the cunean tendon. The tenotomy of the cunean tendon is the most logical treatment and has given consistently good results. Some operators may prefer to perform a tenotomy of the cunean tendon and point firing of the area. The tendon may be located by palpation of a notch on the anterio - medial surface of the hock joint. After passing through the notch the tendon crosses the medial surface of the hock joint in a direction down and backward to insert on the first and second tarsal bones. The tendon is about one-half inch wide and can usually be palpated beneath the skin.

The operation may be performed with the patient in lateral recumbency or in the standing position. It is the unusual patient that can not be operated in the standing position. Anesthesia of the operative area is obtained by infiltration of the tissue with a local anesthetic. A scalpel with a sharp point and narrow blade with sharp cutting edge three-fourths of an inch long is preferred for the operation. The knife is introduced through the skin ventral to the cunean tendon with the cutting edge directed anterior or posterior. With the knife blade in the subcutaneous tissue it is pushed dorsally until the cutting edge is over the cunean tendon. The knife blade is turned until the cutting edge is in contact with the tendon. The cunean tendon is divided two times, one cut is made toward the medial malleolus of the tibia and the second cut toward the point of the hock. As the tough fibres of the cunean tendon are cut a grating sound is heard so it is easy to determine when the tendon is divided. The small opening in the skin is not sutured.

When the exostosis is so extensive that it extends above the edge of the tendon on each side, the tendon will be in a depression in the bone. To cut the tendon it will be necessary to introduce the knife through the skin over the tendon and do the cutting of the tendon with the point of the knife.

If improvement in the lameness does not occur with treatment, a neurectomy of the posterior tibial and deep peroneal nerves may be performed as a last resort. However, the results from this operation are not usually satisfactory.

Capped Hock

Capped hock is a general term that is used for a swelling that occurs on the tuber calcis. The involvement of tissues on the tuber calcis rarely causes lameness but is a very prominent blemish.

The tissues that may be affected in capped hock are the skin and subcutaneous tissues. Probably a ditension of the bursa ventral to the skin is seen most frequently in capped hock. That portion of the superficial digital flexor tendon that covers the tuber calcis and a bursa ventral to this tendon are rarely affected.

ETIOLOGY. Capped hock is produced when there is traumatic injury to the tissues on the tuber calcis. Those individuals that are chronic kickers bruise the tissues severely when they strike the tuber calcis against some hard object, a great many times. The most severe injury to the tissues has occurred when animals were too closely confined and struggled violently to get loose.

SIGNS. The presence of the swelling on the tuber calcis is easily seen. The size of the swelling will depend upon the tissues that are injured and the reaction of this tissue to the traumatism.

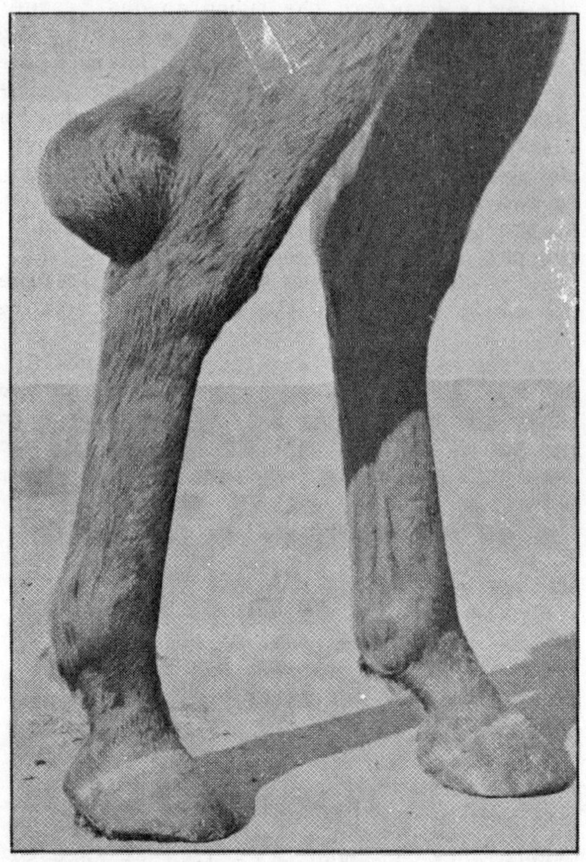

FIG. 393. A capped hock.

TREATMENT. By careful palpation of the swelling the operator may be able to identify the tissues that are responsible for the swelling. If the affected tissues can be identified the operator will be able to use the treatment that will give the best results. When the skin and subcutaneous tissues are thickened vigorous daily massage of the area is usually beneficial. The massage may be applied by the palm of the hand after iodex ointment has been applied to the skin. When the bursa is distended the excess fluid should be removed and a corticosteroid injected into the cavity, this treatment may need to be repeated. An operation should only be performed as a last resort as a wound may be created with a chronic discharge that will not heal.

Curb

Curb is an inflammation and thickening of the plantar ligament. This produces an enlargement on the posterior surface of the limb with the most prominent part posterior to the tarsal metatarsal articulation.

ETIOLOGY. Curb may occur in normal shaped hocks as well as poorly formed hocks. However the sickle-shaped or tied in hocks are supposed to be the most susceptible to the development of a curb. A strain of the ligament may occur when the horse is jumping or from heavy pulling.

To recognize a curb the limb must be viewed from the side. When present the most prominent part of the enlargement is posterior to the tarsal metatarsal articulation. There is a gradual decrease in size of the enlargement above and below the most prominent part. If the curb developed rapidly there is usually an acute local inflammation of the tissues and a varying degree of lameness. At rest the foot is held with the heel off the ground to ease the strain on the inflamed ligament. In motion the horse has a tendency to go on the toe.

DIAGNOSIS. By viewing the limb from the side the presence of a curb is easily determined.

PROGNOSIS. In hocks of poor conformation a curb may be resistant to treatment. In hocks of good conformation the curb usually responds to treatment. Curb is always a blemish and technically is an unsoundness.

TREATMENT. The acute inflammation is treated with cold water either by irrigation or cold packs. As the inflammation subsides vigorous massage will produce a marked reduction in the size of the enlargement. When the inflammation of the ligament has become chronic a blister or point firing seem to give the best results.

Stringhalt

Stringhalt is an involuntary flexing of the hock of one or both hind limbs during progression. It is of frequent occurrence in the hind limbs but rarely affects a fore limb.

ETIOLOGY. Temporary or symptomatic stringhalt often appears as the result of some irritation in the lower part of the limb. In the great majority of cases of stringhalt nothing can be detected to account for the condition and many theories have been put forward as to its etiology, such as articular lesions of the hock or stifle, muscular tendinous and aponeurotic lesions, nervous lesions.

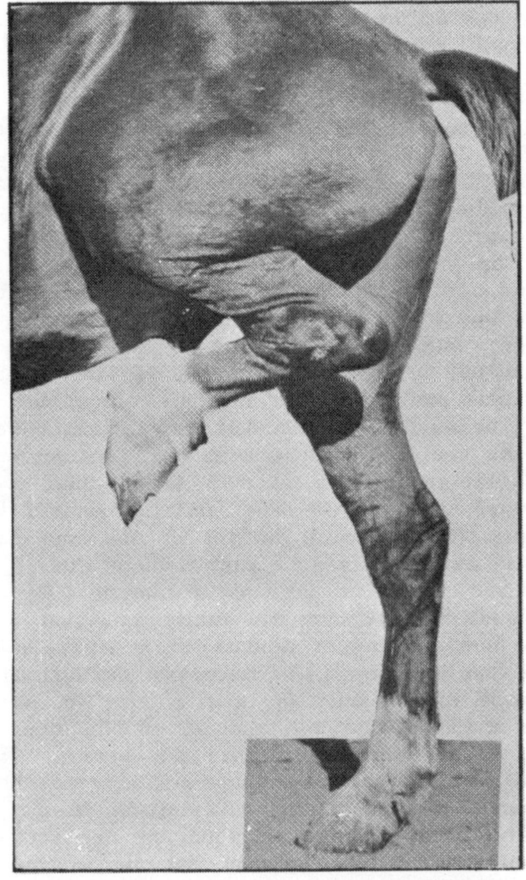

FIG. 394. Typical action in a case of stringhalt.

SIGNS. When stringhalt is present it is easily recognized as it may be so marked that the hind foot almost touches the abdomen. It is best seen when the horse is walked after resting or when turned in short circles. In some cases the foot after being spasmodically lifted is brought to the ground with great force whereas in others it strikes the ground in a normal manner.

DIAGNOSIS. The only difficulty about diagnosis is that the stringhalt might be absent at the time of the examination.

PROGNOSIS. As a rule stringhalt does not interfere with the horse's usefulness but occasionally the affected individual tires easily. Most cases of stringhalt recover a short time after the operation.

TREATMENT. This is surgical and consists in the removal of the tendon of the lateral digital extensor. The patient should be confined on the table or ground in lateral recumbency with the affected leg uppermost. The operation may be performed with the patient in the standing position if it has a good disposition. An area over the tendon just before it joins the long digital extensor is shaved and another area just above and posterior to the lateral malleolus of the tibia. The areas should be prepared for an aseptic operation.

Anesthesia of the operative areas can be obtained by infiltration of the tissues with a two per cent solution of a local anesthetic.

An incision one quarter of an inch long is made in the skin and through the subcutaneous tissues directly over the tendon just before it joins the long digital extensor tendon. A tenotome is passed through the incision and introduced flatwise under the tendon and the cutting edge turned upwards. The tendon cuts easily and the ends usually retract and are easily palpated showing that the tendon has been completely divided. The lower end of the second incision is on a level with the upper part of the lateral malleolus of the tibia and is made directly over the tendon. The incision extends upwards a distance of one and one-half inches through the subcutaneous tissues down to the tendon. A curved blunt pointed instrument is introduced under the tendon to lift it up through the incision.

Some traction is usually required to break the adhesions which many times develops around the tendon in its course over the tarsal bones. The entire tendon about seven inches in length is pulled through the upper incision and then divided removing a small portion of the muscle tissue with the tendon. The two skin incisions are closed with interrupted sutures and covered with flexible collodion. In most cases it takes several weeks before complete recovery occurs.

Neurectomies of the Posterior Limbs

POSTERIOR DIGITAL NEURECTOMY. There is seldom any indication for performing a posterior digital neurectomy in the posterior limb. However the technique of performing a digital neurectomy of the posterior limb is the same as that described for the anterior limb.

PLANTAR NEURECTOMY. Those conditions for which a volar neurectomy is indicated in the anterior limb are seldom present in the posterior limb. The field of operation, relation of structures and technique of the operation is the same as the volar neurectomy.

TIBIAL NEURECTOMY. A tibial neurectomy may prolong the usefulness of an animal affected with a chronic incurable lameness in the hock or the distal portion of the limb. In distribution of nerve supply it corresponds very closely to the median nerve as it furnishes the chief sensory nerve supply to the lower part of the limb. The operative area is about four inches above the point of the hock on the medial side of the limb. The tibial nerve is a rather large nerve located on the posterior border of the deep flexor muscle accompanied by the artery and vein. With the fingers on one side of the tendon Achilles and the thumb on the other side, the nerve will be felt to roll between the thumb and fingers by palpating deep into the tissue posterior to the deep flexor muscle. The patient is confined in lateral recumbency with the affected limb down. Prepare the operative area in the usual manner for an aseptic operation. The incision about two inches long is made over the nerve and extends through the skin and subcutaneous tissues to the heavy fascia. At this point the preferred technique is to puncture the heavy fascia and insert a probe pointed bistoury through this opening. The fascia is then opened with an incision corresponding to the skin incision. Retract the edges of the skin and fascia to expose the posterior edge of the deep flexor muscle. The nerve will be found in close contact with this muscle. If there is any difficulty encountered in finding the nerve the tissues can be palpated to determine its exact location. A neurectomy hook can be inserted around the nerve and passed the length of the incision to separate the nerve from the surrounding structures. The nerve is elevated up to the incision and divided at the superior commissure of the wound. It is again divided at the inferior commissure of the wound removing about two inches of the nerve. The edges of the skin and fascia are sutured together by a series of interrupted sutures and the wound covered with flexible collodion. If infection occurs in the wound, remove the sutures and treat as an open wound.

DEEP PERONEAL NEURECTOMY (ANTERION TIBIAL). Neurectomy of the deep peroneal nerve is indicated when neurectomy of the tibial nerve has failed to destroy all sensation of the affected part. The deep peroneal nerve is located on the lateral side of the tibial region between the long and lateral digital extensor muscles. It is a small nerve about two millimeters in diameter and lying in contact with the thin edge of the tibialis anterior muscle.

OPERATION. The animal is confined in lateral recumbency on the sound limb. The operative area is on the lateral surface of the limb just distal to the most prominent portion of the two muscles. Prepare the operative area for an aseptic operation. Anesthesia for the operation may be obtained by infiltrating the tissues with a local anesthetic or a general anesthetic may be used. Palpate for the division between the long and lateral digital extensor muscles and make a skin incision about two inches long. This skin incision should be along the posterior border of the long digital extensor muscle and through the tibial fascia to the muscle sheath. By palpation determine the exact location of the heavy muscular septum which separates the two muscles. The incision through the muscle sheath must be anterior to the septum dividing the two muscles or the operator will be unable to find the nerve. The small amount of hemorrhage present may be removed with sponges. A blunt pointed forceps may be used to separate the loose connective tissue between the two muscles. Then with a forcep in each hand insert the ends rather deeply into the wound and press downward and laterally upon the two muscles. The pressure produced forces the tibialis anterior muscle up into the wound and the nerve will be seen lying on the thin edge of this dark red muscle. Grasp the nerve with forceps and lift it up to the edge of the wound. A section about one inch long is removed by dividing it in the usual manner. The edges of the skin and fascia are approximated with interrupted sutures and the wound covered with flexible collodion. Healing of the wound should occur by first intention.

Spondylitis in the Bovine

This is one form of polyarthritis in which the lesions are located in the articulations of the vertebrae. There is very little to be found in the literature on the subject. It has been suggested that Bacillus abortus might be the causative organism. However, all the cases examined have been negative to the abortion test. Probably this condition has often been diagnosed as rheumatism or lumbago.

The symptoms are very characteristic and constant in all the cases observed. The muscles of the back and hind leg become rigid and remain in this position for a few seconds and the leg is then jerked forward. This continues for the first few steps that the cow takes and then the gait becomes almost normal. The signs are most pronounced when the cow first gets up after she has been lying down for a few hours. The signs are also more pronounced when she gets up on a cold morning or if she is confined in a stanchion. The signs have been noticed for about a year and have remained rather constant in Fig. 395.

One Holstein cow was affected very severely in one hind leg and would show the characteristic signs for several minutes after getting up, especially if she was confined in a stanchion. Some cows will exhibit the signs when they are made to back or are pushed from one side to the other of the stanchion.

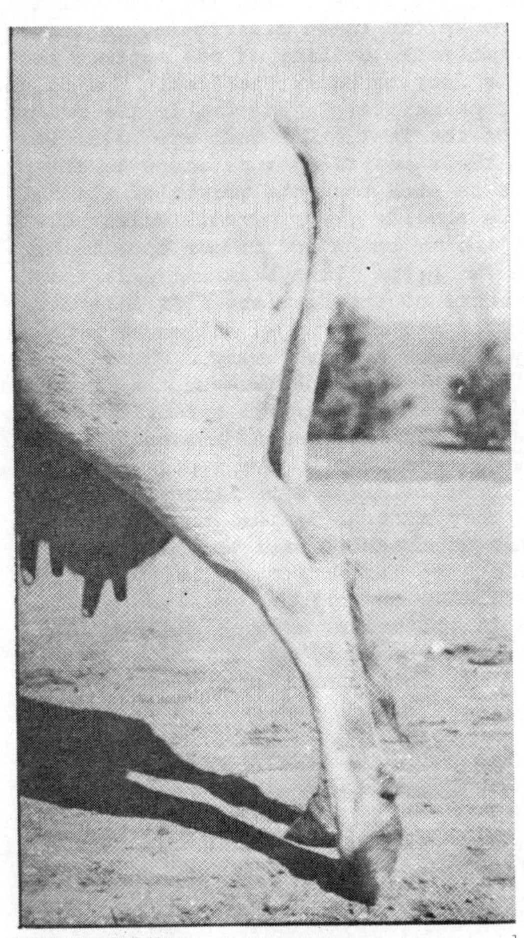

FIG. 395. Characteristic position of hind leg in spondylitis.

A valuable Holstein bull was able to be purchased in one of the northern states because it was said the extreme cold weather made his rheumatism worse. Both hind legs showed the characteristic signs to a marked degree. First one leg would be extended rigidly backwards then the other leg and he would continue to do this for several minutes without taking a forward step. However, he was able to serve a cow without any noticeable difficulty.

During the course of a year the signs seemed to increase in severity and would last longer. Also toward the end of the year it was apparently more difficult for him to get up. At the end of the year he was completely paralyzed in the posterior limbs.

Post mortem examination revealed a proliferative periostitis and ostitis involving the affected articulation, which was between the last thoracic and first lumbar vertebrae. The exostosis involving the articulation was extremely large producing pressure on the spinal cord.

The prognosis in these cases is always guarded. Due to the location of the affected area it is impossible to determine the extent of the pathological changes that have taken place. However, if the signs are of unusual severity an unfavorable prognosis might be indicated.

Treatment has not been attempted in any of the cases. With the exception of the bull and the cow now under observation, the affected animals have made gradual but slow recoveries.

Shivering

This condition is defined as a nervous or neuro-muscular disease characterized by involuntary muscular movements of the limbs and tail. In most cases both hind limbs and the tail are affected, but in some cases it is the forelimbs that are involved. In a few instances the eyelids flicker, the ears are tremulous, and the commissure of the lips are drawn backward.

ETIOLOGY. The exact cause of shivering is unknown although some cases have developed after an attack of strangles, influenza, or some other systemic disease. It is found affecting horses of all ages but occurs most often in the heavier breeds.

SIGNS. In slight cases, the signs may be difficult to detect, although in most cases the signs are very characteristic. Even in well developed cases affecting the posterior limbs, signs may not be shown when the horse is standing still or moving forward. The most characteristic signs occur when an attempt is made to back the affected individual. A hind foot is jerked from the ground and held in mid-air and abducted with the leg semi-flexed and quivering or shaking violently. The tail is elevated and exhibits rapid, quivering movements. After the quivering ceases, which is in a few moments, the foot and tail return slowly to a normal position. The signs return when further attempts are made to force him to back. In other cases the signs may be shown when he is turned, forced to step over, or a foot is lifted up

When an anterior limb is affected it is elevated and abducted with the knee flexed and the muscles above the elbow quivering until the foot is brought to the ground.

PROGNOSIS. The prognosis is unfavorable in pronounced cases as there is a tendency for the signs to slowly increase in severity, decreasing the usefulness of the animal. It is impossible to back many of the cases affected in the posterior limbs.

TREATMENT. Treatment is usually valueless.

Care of the Horses Feet

Since the serviceability of the horse may depend upon the condition of the feet, the Veterinarian should be qualified to supervise their care. An intimate knowledge of the anatomy of the feet as well as the functions of the various parts must be known if successful shoeing is to be accomplished. Satisfactory shoeing is accomplished only by adherence to the fundamental principles of horseshoeing which are based upon the anatomy and the physiological requirements of the feet.

The fundamental principle is to protect the hoof by shoeing and at the same time interfere as little as possible with the physiological functions of the different structures of the foot. Shoes though fitted and applied by the best methods known are still detrimental to the proper functioning of the foot. Any nail driven into the wall destroys some tissue and weakens the weight bearing part of the foot. The shoe, also, raises the foot from the ground and prevents the proper functioning of the frog and elastic structures. The resistance against injury depends a great deal upon the elasticity of the tissues.

The strength of the horn structure of the feet depends a great deal upon a normal amount of moisture in the tissues. The moisture will be supplied from the blood circulating through the feet or where they are in contact with a moist surface where they are standing. When the horse is removed from his natural surroundings and used on hard dry surfaces, the blood may be unable to supply enough moisture to keep the horn structures of the foot in a normal condition. When this occurs additional moisture must be provided, as described in the care of the feet between showing periods.

By close application of the principles of horseshoeing many of the faults in the gait of the horse may be corrected or improved. It is necessary for the weight of the animal to be distributed in accordance with the ability of the various parts of the foot to carry the load. One of the first principles in shoeing is the balancing of the feet. The feet are balanced when their position in relation to the limbs is such that the weight of the animal is equally distributed. Unless the feet are balanced one cannot hope to balance the gait. In a balanced gait the movements of the feet and legs extending backward and forward in alignment with the body without lateral swing. There is also sufficient clearance between the front and hind feet in action with sufficient elevation to clear the ground properly in the forward extension of the feet. If the feet are to be extended in alignment with the body they must be in that position at the moment of breaking over and leaving the ground. By the proper use of shoes it is possible to control the position of the foot at the moment of breaking over and leaving the ground; and the rapidity with which the foot breaks over.

Physiology of the Foot

When weight is placed on the leg, the third phalanx descends slightly and causes the sole to descend and flatten. The plantar cushion and horny frog are compressed between ground below and the structures above. This compression causes these tissues to spread carrying outward the lateral cartilages and bars, and the wall at the quarters. This is called expansion. When weight is removed from the leg, the plantar cushion becomes thicker and narrower. The lateral cartilages and quarters move inward to where they were before they extended. This is called contraction. The elastic lateral cartilage is the flexible extension of the wing of the third phalanx and it and the bars seem to have been designed for the expansion and contraction that occurs at the quarters.

The plantar cushion has the important function of breaking the jar when the foot strikes the ground, and also assists in the circulation of the blood through the feet. If the horse is made to exercise vigorously after resting, severe injury may occur to some of the structures of the foot as the circulation and structures of the foot should have time to become adapted to the change from rest to rapid movement.

The wall of the healthy foot is by weight about one-fourth water, the sole more than one-third, and the frog almost one-half of the total amount. The frog is capable of absorbing moisture from the ground. The periople which covers the wall prevents the evaporation of water, and should never be removed. As there is no similar covering for the sole and frog the layers of horn on their exposed surfaces dry out and die. The dead layers are hard and brittle and gradually fall or flake off. In preparing the hoof for shoeing the dead layers of horn on the sole should not be removed as they help to preserve the moisture in the underlying healthy tissue.

Normal Shoeing

The term "normal shoeing" means the shoeing used on a horse having sound feet, good leg conformation and correct gaits. Normal shoeing should not be used on horses with abnormal feet. If there is faulty conformation of the limbs the animal should have a special type of shoe.

A careful preliminary examination of the gaits, the conformation of the limbs, and the condition of the feet should be made in order to determine the correct method of shoeing to be used for the particular animal to be shod. Examine the horse to determine whether there is any abnormality in his gait. This is best done by having the horse shown under normal working conditions. Next, the following examinations should be made to assist in performing the shoeing in the most intelligent manner. Have the horse stand on a level surface and view the feet and legs from a position in front of the animal. Are the bones of the pastern and foot in a direct line with the upper bones of the leg, or is the toe directed inward (toe in); or is the toe directed outward (toe out); and are the limbs too close together (narrow chest)? In the examination of the feet note if they are the same size in width of quarters and length of toe. Is the length of the wall from the hair line to the lower border equal on both sides of the foot, and are the feet circular, or narrow with pointed toes? In observing the animal from the side note if the length of toe and height of heels follow the conformation of the pastern. Are the heels the same in height; and does the angle of the wall at the front part of the hoof coincide with the slope of the pattern?

The old shoes should be examined to determine balance of the foot and its position at the moment of breaking over and leaving the ground. Also note the general condition of the feet to see what type of shoe is best suited for this particular horse, and to ascertain if there is any malformation of the feet or evidence of irregularities in the gait. If these conditions are found the type of shoe and fitting should be such as to correct the irregularity.

The horseshoer, having the foot in a secure and comfortable position, removes the shoe. using care to avoid breaking away the wall, With a knife pare away the dead horn over the white-line to ascertain the amount of surplus horn that may be removed in preparation of the foot for the shoe. Consider the size of the feet compared with the size and weight of the animal, and the nature of work to be performed. Some classes of work such as marching over hard surfaced roads, polo, hunting and jumping, require a greater amount of hoof than is required for ordinary work. If this precaution is not taken, the feet, especially the sensitive sole, are more easily bruised and a variable degree of lameness may be shown. To retain the elasticity of the live horn of the sole and frog and to protect the sensitive sole and frog against bruising, a covering of dead horn is essential. To cut away the bars or open the heels weakens the foot and usually results in contraction of the quarters and heels. Where a great accumulation of dead horn is present on the sole, it is advisable to remove a portion of it, being careful to leave a sufficient amount to protect the structures. Too great an accumulation of dead horn on the sole is detrimental to the proper functioning of the inner structures of the hoof. This condition results in contraction of the feet and is found only in a foot that has a very arched sole. There is a great difference in the thickness of the horny sole between cup shaped and flat feet. The horny sole of the flat foot is naturally thinner than that of the cup shaped foot. Great care should be exercised in its preparation as the dead horn readily flakes off as it dries out. The wall of the foot is trimmed to a more oblique angle than in the cup shaped foot. In order to use the machine made shoe on a foot of this type, in which the creasing does not conform to this type of foot, it is necessary to remove a part of the outer edge of the wall at the lower border so the nails may be driven in the outer edge of the white-line when securing the shoe to the hoof. Cutting away the outer layer of horn on the lower border of the wall weakens that horn structure so that it is more susceptible to drying out and becoming brittle. When the flat foot is prepared for shoeing, and the outer lower border of the wall is not removed and a machine made shoe is fitted to the outline of the foot, the nail holes are over the bearing surface of the wall lateral to the white-line. If the nails are driven into the wall outside of the white-line the wall will break away to the height where the nails penetrate the wall. In making shoes for flat feet use bar steel so the nail holes in the shoe will conform to the white-line. This will insure firm nailing and a good strong wall. If it is necessary to use a machine made on flat feet a portion of the wall should be removed so it will produce the least damage to the wall.

When the horseshoer is preparing the feet for shoeing the nippers and hoof knife should be used when there is much horn to be removed, otherwise the rasp only is used. The balance of the foot from toe to heel is most easily maintained when the surplus horn is removed first from the toe and quarters. If too much horn is removed from the heels it will leave the foot in a broken back condition which retards the breaking over of the foot. When this occurs there is an increased susceptibility to stumbling, forging, strained tendons and a weakening of the hoof. The strength of the hoof will depend a great deal on the condition and amount of horn at the buttresses. The foot should be examined frequently during its preparation making sure that it is balanced.

The foot will be most accurately balanced if the foot is examined on a level surface to observe the position of the foot in relation to the limb. The usual practice of sighting over the plantar surface of the foot in a raised position to see if the foot is balanced is not as accurate as observing the foot when it is on the ground. Abnormalities occur frequently in the feet and in some cases the coronet close to the bulb of the heel may be in an abnormal position. This may occur when there is a contraction on one side of the foot and when this condition occurs in a flat foot there is an uneven distribution of weight and the coronet is forced upward causing a permanent malformation of the foot to develop if it is not corrected. In most cases it is practically impossible to determine with any degree of accuracy the balance of a malformed foot if the examination is not made with the foot on a flat surface.

The plantar surface of the foot should be examined to determine the regularity of the foot bearing surface for the shoe. A foot may have good balance but there will be irregularities of the bearing surface so there is incomplete contact between the wall and shoe. Occasionally a horse is presented with one foot smaller than the other feet. This atrophy of the foot may be due to injury when the animal was young and the foot did not develop to a normal size. When the feet are being prepared for shoeing the larger foot should be prepared first, and the preparation of the smaller foot should be governed by that of the larger foot. The length of toe and height of heel should be the same for the smaller foot as for the other feet. This practice will tend to prevent irregularities of gait.

In shoeing hunters and jumpers a foot adjuster should be used as these horses require greater accuracy than can be determined with the eye. If there is a fraction of an inch difference in the height of the heels or the length of the toes on corresponding feet the difference in the rapidity of the breaking over of the feet may be responsible for an irregularity in gait. The knife should only be used on the frog to remove ragged pieces that would permit dirt and manure to become lodged in the tissues and be responsible for thrush.

The size, weight and type of shoe should be governed by the condition of the feet and the conformation of the horse. When the shoe is properly prepared for the foot it should provide the greatest possible protection. It should also aid the foot to break over and leave the ground with the correct position and rapidity to ensure proper elevation and stride during flight. The weight of the shoe on the foot has a tendency to increase elevation during flight. To provide lateral support to the foot at the moment of breaking over the shoe should have some roundness at the toe. If the shoe is pointed at the toe it may cause the horse to interfere, stumble or forge. When the toe is in the act of breaking over it is carrying much of the body weight and if at this moment the weight is thrown on the side of the foot the balance of the body is upset so there is a defect in the flight of the feet and legs. The size of the shoe at the quarters will be determined by the condition of the feet, whether they are contracted or normal, and the type of work the horse is doing. For horses with normal feet and doing ordinary work the shoe should be an eighth of an inch wider than the wall at the heels to allow for expansion of the wall at the heels and growth of horn between shoeing periods. If there is contraction of the heels it is desirable to allow more fullness for expansion. The front feet of the horse support a large percentage of the weight of the body so that a shoe that has a wide web and is not too thick should be used. For the hind feet a web that is not so wide and a lighter shoe may be used.

When the horny sole has been prepared for the shoe it should be thinner at its outer border than in any other portion. The shoe should have a web that is sufficiently wide to cover the horny sole at its junction with the wall, so the sensitive sole will not be bruised. If the shoe covers only the edge of the wall and white-line it will not protect the sensitive sole against injury on a hard surface. Also the shoe should have sufficient width at the heels to cover the buttresses to supply support to the hoof where it receives the most concussion.

It is very important to have the nail holes properly spaced as the stability of the shoe and strength of the wall will be determined by this important part of the shoeing. The number of nails used should be held to the minimum number that will hold the shoes securely, and the nails should not penetrate the wall any higher than is necessary to hold the shoe. The spacing of nails will be determined by the size of the foot, and the position of the first nail hole is approximately one inch posterior to a line parallel to the toe. For the quarter nail a hole is made at the rear bend of the quarters, and the third hole is placed an equal distance between the toe and quarter holes on both branches of the shoe. In the machine made shoe the holes are not made so the nail will enter the white-line. The nails enter the edge of the wall and may cause the wall to crack as high as the nails penetrate the wall. Also the nail holes are too close together so with several shoeings the wall is not strong enough to hold the shoe securely. The ideal shoe for the riding horse may be made from a bar of mild steel of suitable width and thickness, and with three nail holes in each branch so placed to conform to the width of the bearing surface of the wall at the toe and quarters. The nail holes in the shoe should be of the same shape and size of the shank of the nails, and made at an angle corresponding to the shape of the wall, so the nail will enter the wall to ensure strong nailing. If the nail heads are seated properly they should project a slight distance beyond the surface of the shoe.

Care of the Feet Between Shoeing Periods

If the feet receive the proper care between shoeing periods it will prevent many disorders of the feet from developing. When horses are stabled they are deprived of the moisture which they would obtain under natural conditions. Moisture in the horn structures is essential to maintain the elasticity which is necessary to reduce the concussion on the feet and at the same time maintain solidity of the hoof. The front feet are affected more by stabling than the hind feet. The hind feet absorb much moisture from standing in the droppings. As a general rule the tissues of the hind feet are soft, pliable, and in a normal condition, while the front feet do not receive a sufficient supply of moisture from exterior sources. The horn fibers of the hoof are nourished by the flow of blood throughout the foot and consist of a large percentage of moisture, by weight. In some localities there will be seasons when the rainfall is deficient, causing the turf over which the horse is worked to become hard and dry. Under these conditions the moisture supplied by the blood is not sufficient to keep the hooves supplied with a normal amount of moisture, and the front hooves rapidly deteriorate. This condition causes the hoof to become narrower, the horny frog to atrophy, the quarters and heels to contract, and the horn structure in general to become inelastic. This last condition increases the concussion on the feet due to the loss of the elastic cushion afforded by the horny frog and other structures such as the digital cushion and lateral cartilages. This can cause many of the disorders of the feet to develop. When the horse is groomed the feet should be carefully cleaned to remove any filth that may have accumulated around the horny frog and over the horny sole. The foot should be examined for evidence of injury as nails penetrating the horny frog or sole, or a stone may be lodged between the branch of the shoe and the frog. When the horny frog is healthy it is somewhat the consistency of rubber. Examine the shoe for evidence of wear and position on the foot, noting also, the security of nailing and smoothness of the clinches. The need for moisture of the remaining horny structures can be determined by the condition of the horny frog. When the horny frog becomes hard and dry the other horn structures will need moisture. There are two practical methods of keeping the horn structures in a normal elastic condition. One method would be to supply the horn with moisture from exterior sources, another way would be to avoid the evaporation of moisture supplied by nature.

Moisture may be supplied to the horn structure, of those horses that require it, by cleaning and packing the front feet with moist white rock or clay filling the space between the branches of the shoe over the horny sole and frog. The horn structures being porous will absorb the moisture contained in the white rock and clay when packed over the sole and frog.

Oil of tar applied to the horny sole, frog wall fills the pores in the horn structures thus eliminating evaporation of the moisture supplied from the blood circulating throughout the foot. Oil of tar should be applied with a short, stiff bristle brush and in freezing temperatures this method of treatment is preferable for maintaining elasticity of the hoof.

The frequency of packing the feet with white rock or clay, or dressing the hoofs with oil of tar, should be governed by the requirements of the horn structures. Since climatic conditions affect the elasticity of the hoof, it is advisable to have a clay stand adjacent to the stable for the purpose of softening the hoofs and reducing fever in the feet. The clay stand may be constructed in the corral and the animals led through just prior to tying them in their stalls. The feet will fill with the moist clay, which will remain in the feet unless removed until all moisture has been absorbed by the horn structures of the hoof. It is advisable to locate the clay stand near the water trough in order that it may be sprinkled each day.

Gaits

The gaits to be considered are the walk, trot and gallop. Horses are classified as the riding horse, the harness horse, and the draft horse. At the walk the horse lifts one foot at a time in diagonal sequence. The left front foot is followed by the right hind foot and placed down in the same order. The trot is a diagonal movement in which the left front foot and the right hind foot leave the ground and again strike the ground at the same time. The gallop is a gait in which the horse springs into the air from one front foot and has all four feet off the ground at once. The diagonal hind foot is the first to strike the ground, and then the other hind foot, next the front foot opposite the one from which the spring was made, and last the foot used for the spring.

In a well balanced gait the movement of the feet and legs is made without any lost motion or interference. The feet and legs extend backward and forward in alignment with the body without lateral swing and there is sufficient elevation to clear the ground properly in the forward extension of the feet. When horses are shod for the purpose of altering the gaits it will be fount that no two cases may be treated alike because of the difference in conformation and condition of the feet.

Some of the faults in the gait of the horse are stumbling, interfering, forging, over reaching and scalping. These irregularities in the gait may be due to permanent causes such as undeveloped muscle, poor general condition and unbalanced feet. Other causes may be shoes that are not of the proper weight, or shoes that are not applied correctly to the feet. When certain principles are followed they may produce beneficial results in gaiting horses. The desired results will not necessarily be obtained in the riding horse by shoeing alone, since a great deal may depend upon the use of the rein and the adjustment of the saddle together with the adjustment of the weight of the rider. Those horses with faulty conformation of the limbs are the most apt to have some irregularity in their gait. If the faulty conformation affects the flight of the feet and legs it may be impossible to completely correct the fault in the flight of the feet. The irregularity in the flight of the feet may be corrected enough, however, so the feet do not traumatize any soft tissue. The type of shoe that is used should supply protection, be comfortable to the foot, and it should correct if possible the fault in the gait.

The success of the corrective shoeing will depend upon the correct diagnosis as to the cause, and then upon the proper balancing of the feet. There may be a number of horses affected with the same irregularity of gait but each horse may require some specific change in the shoeing.

When the horse is in motion the flight of the foot is governed by the rapidity with which it breaks over and leaves the ground. If the breaking over of the foot is retarded it stimulates a long stride with little elevation. When the foot breaks over rapidly there is a greater flexing of the knee and hock, an increased elevation in the flight of the foot, and a decrease in length of the stride. The correct shoes can control the rapidity with which the foot breaks over and starts its flight as well as its position to alignment of the body. If the foot is to be carried forward in alignment with the body it must be in that position at the beginning of its flight. The pendulum swing of the front and hind legs must coordinate if balance of the gait is to be obtained.

Forging

Forging is a fault in the horse's gait that is characterized by the toe of the hind foot overtaking and striking the bottom of the front foot or branches of the shoe on the same side. This occurs at the moment the front foot is breaking over and starting its flight, but it is too slow in leaving the ground to miss the hind foot. When forging occurs in a pacer the inner quarter or the under surface of the inner branch of the front shoe is struck with the toe of the diagonal hind foot and is called, "cross firing". The sound produced by forging is very unpleasant to hear and could be dangerous to the horse. It would be easy for severe injury to occur to the heels of the forefeet, and the coronet of the hind feet.

Some of the factors that are considered to be responsible for forging are improper shoeing, faulty conformation, leg weariness, poor adjustment of the saddle and improper riding. Forging may occur more frequently in those horses that have a short body and relatively long legs, or the front legs may be short and the hind legs are long.

When the feet are not properly prepared or improperly shod the front feet may break over too slowly and decrease the

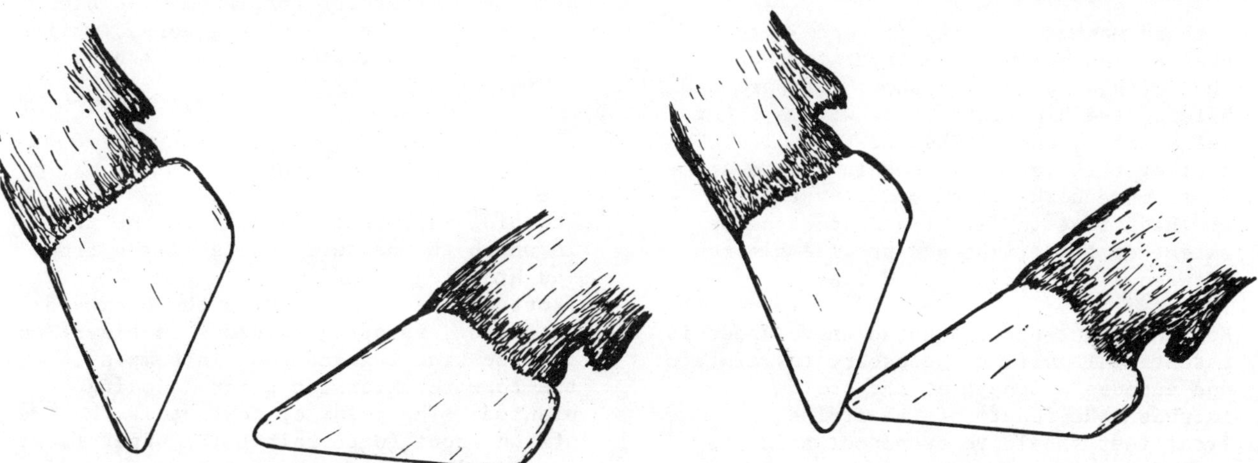

FIG. 396. Co-ordination of front and hind feet in flight.

FIG. 397. Forging.

height of their action. Forging may occur in young horses with good conformation and with proper balance of the feet, but it occurs due to the underdevelopment of the muscles.

To correct the average case of forging a rolled or rocker-toe shoe is used on the front feet, and normal shoes on the hind feet. This method of shoeing should cause the front feet to break over more quickly with a greater elevation of the feet.

For those cases that do not respond to the simpler method of treatment other types of corrective shoeing may be used. Prepare the front feet so they are balanced and shoe with rocker-toe shoe, using a light weight machine shoe. The hind feet should be prepared by leaving the toes longer than normal, and shoe with light weight shoes. The shoes should extend to the point of the toe, and the heels should extend one-half or three-fourths of an inch beyond the buttresses and turned out slightly. By shoeing in this manner the front feet should break over more quickly and delay the breaking over of the hind feet.

Another method is to prepare the front feet and shoe with a plate shoe equal in weight to the light pattern. The hind feet should be prepared and balanced, and then shod with heavy-weight shoes with trailers, having the weight and trailer on the outside branch of the shoe. By this method of shoeing the flight of the hind feet are extended forward with an outward swing. The hind feet are carried forward on a line outside of the path of the front feet as they leave the ground.

A third method that may be used is to prepare and balance the front feet and shoe with a rocker-toe shoe. Prepare and balance the hind feet, shoe with a light weight shoe, heel calks and toe. The object of this method of shoeing is to stimulate more hock action and elevation of the hind feet in flight and shorten the extent of the flight and provide clearance between the front and hind feet.

For the light harness horse where speed is essential it will be necessary to maintain and encourage length of the stride. To increase the length of the stride the front feet should be prepared, balanced and shod with a toe-weight shoe. The hind feet are prepared and balanced and shod with a side-weight shoe with trailer, the weight and trailer on the outside branch of the shoe. By this method of shoeing the front feet are extended forward with little elevation. The hind feet and legs are extended with an outward swing and planted outside of the line of the front foot where it leaves the ground.

Over-Reaching

Over-reaching is that fault in the gait in which the toe of the hind foot overtakes and strikes the quarter and heels of the front foot as the foot is breaking over preparatory to starting its flight. This fault in gait may occur in both the riding and harness horse at the trot.

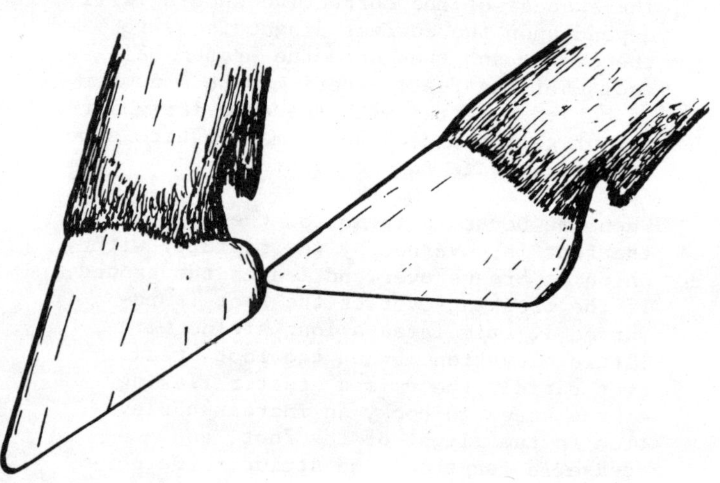

FIG. 398. Over-reaching.

In correcting over-reaching methods 1, 2 and 3 submitted for forging may be used with success for the riding horse, while method 4 is indicated for the harness horse.

Scalping

Scalping is a fault in gait at the trot in which the pendulum swing of the front and hind legs conflict at a time when the front foot and leg, during the backward extension, is being raised into elevation and the hind leg and foot is completing the forward extension prior to being planted. The point of contact is the toe of the front foot against the upper front foot against the upper front surface of the wall, coronet or lower end of the pastern. The irregularity is common with the light harness horse at speed.

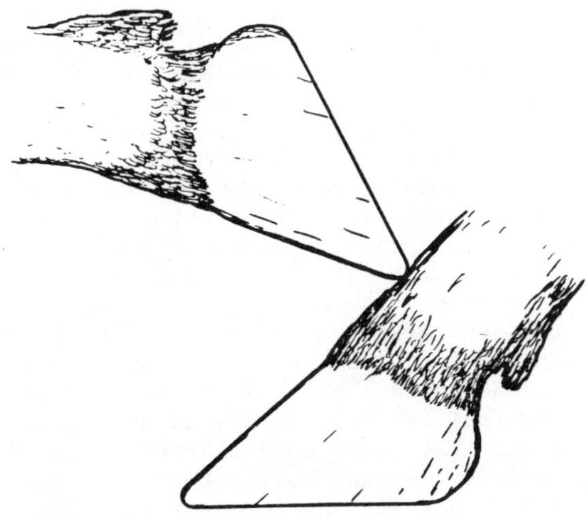

FIG. 399. Scalping.

The shoeing should be directed toward co-ordinating the flight of the feet and legs and as a precautionary measure scalping boots should be worn on the hind feet.

Interfering

Interfering occurs when the foot in motion strikes some portion of the opposite supporting leg. The front limb may be injured from the coronary band to the knee and the medial side of the fetlock joint of the posterior limb. Interfering occurs more frequently in the posterior limbs and may cause lameness.

Some of the temporary causes of interfering may be too wide hoofs, faulty preparation of the feet, improper shoeing, trimming the inner wall too low, using shoes that are too heavy, and nail heads protruding too far below the surface of the shoe. The permanent causes may be toeing out, narrow chest, front legs too close together and narrow behind with hind legs too close together. If interfering is to be corrected the clearance between the legs must be increased by removing any projection on the inside of the foot or shoe and causing the foot to break over at the center of the toe.

When interfering is due to a faulty position of the limbs an examination should be made to determine exactly the part of the foot that is causing the trouble. The shoe should be made straight along the area that is striking. If the interfering is producing serious injuries a shoe should be used that has no nail holes in the inner branch. When the toe is pointed there is no lateral support when the foot breaks over disturbing the balance of the horse. This condition is responsible for many of the faults in gait. The preparation of the affected foot is apparent. When the feet toe out in front and the front feet break over at the inner side of the toe, the foot is carried forward with an inward swing. In preparing the feet and outlining of the shoe the object is to produce lateral balance when the horse is at rest. The shoe is fitted full on one diagonal and close on the other. When the extension is made at the inner portion of the toe it prevents the toe from breaking over at that point but allows it to break over at the center of the toe. By having the foot start its flight in alignment with the body the tendency toward an inward swing is reduced.

When there is toeing-out behind prepare the hind feet in the same way as described for the front feet with the exception of the outside heel which should be three quarters of an inch longer than normal and turned out.

Stumbling

This is a fault in gait in which the front feet and legs lack sufficient elevation to properly clear the ground. When the stumbling is due to faulty preparation of the feet, shoes that are too heavy or improperly fitted, the cause may be corrected. If the stumbling is due to faulty conformation a shoe suitable for the work to be performed should be used. The foot can be made to break over more quickly by using a rocket-toe shoe to increase the elevation of the stride.

Paddling

Paddling is an irregularity in gait characterized by the front feet and legs being carried with an outward swing. The feet break over the outside portion of the toe when leaving the ground and the outside half of the foot is carried with highest elevation. Beneficial results may be obtained in the young undeveloped horse but very little improvement is obtained in the mature horse with developed muscles and confirmed gait. When a horse has a toe-in standing of the feet there will be a natural lateral swing of the feet. If the elevation of the feet is increased the lateral swing will be increased.

The lateral swing in the young horse with good conformation may be helped by using a light weight square toed shoe. When the toe-in standing is due to faulty conformation the feet should be balanced. A greater amount than the normal hoof is prepared so the greatest length of wall is at the outside portion of the wall and approaching the bend of the quarter with the lowest point at the heel. The horse is shod with the lateral extension-toe shoes and with the shoe fitted full on the outside branch from the toe to the first or second nail hole and close from that point back to the heel. The inside branch of the shoe fitted close at the toe and full from the bend of the quarter back to the heel. With the extension of the shoe at the outside portion of the toe it induces a straight forward breaking over of the feet, there is a lessening of the elevation of the stride and a decreasing of the lateral swing of the foot.

Polo Shoeing

The polo horse requires considerable speed, stamina and, most of all, sound feet and strong leg tendons. The shoeing practice on the polo horse is done with the object of attaining the greatest assistance to the horse in speed, starting, turning, and stopping.

In general practice, little consideration is given to the horn structures of the hoof. Shoes best suited for attaining speed are not sufficient weight and strength to properly protect the feet, resulting (at the end of the playing season) in a broken down condition of the horn structures of the hoof.

During the training season, it is advisable to use a slightly heavier shoe than is required for fast work. The heavier shoe gives better protection to the horn structures. While in training, use the "full swedge shoe" heavy pattern, front and hind. The front shoes should be fitted plain (no caulks); the hind shoes fitted with heel caulks one-half inch in height, the outside heel caulk turned at right angle to web of shoe, muled out slightly, and the rear part of the caulk hot rasped smooth and rounded. The inside heel caulk should be diamond shape or triangular. A toe clip should be placed at the point or sides of the toe to assist in holding the shoe in position. The type of caulk on the hind shoes give firm footing and permits the horse to turn short and quick on the haunches with the minimum strain on the ligaments and tendons of the lower part of the leg. The branches of the front shoe should terminate with the buttresses with very little fullness of the shoe beyond the outline of the wall from the bend of the quarter to the buttress. The heel of the shoe so finished that the ground surface of the shoe is shorter than the foot surface thus avoiding casting the shoe. The "full swedge shoe" is manufactured for use in shoeing trotters, pacers, riding horses, and polo horses. This type of shoe has but three nail holes in each branch, whereas the general type of machine shoe has four nail holes in each branch. The nail holes in the "full swedge shoe" are placed a greater distance apart thus reducing the number of perforations in the wall, thereby insuring a stronger job of nailing with less damage to the wall. The hoofs on the polo horse should not be trimmed as low as practiced on horses doing ordinary work. A greater amount of horn on the hoof will increase its strength and better resist the effects caused by traveling at rapid gaits and frequent reshoeing.

During the playing season, it is advisable to use a shoe lighter in weight than that used when training. The "full wedge shoe" medium pattern, is suitable for this period of the work. The condition of the field and rules of the game govern the use of toe grabs on the shoe. For the front shoes, the toe grabs give the horse the advantage of a firm footing for a quick getaway and avoids slipping. For the hind shoes toe grabs in addition to heel calks further aid in preventing slipping when starting or stopping suddenly.

The shoes for the front feet should be concaved on the ground surface, thereby insuring a firmer footing. The hind shoes should be fitted with heel calks and toe clips.

When the playing season is over, the feet of polo horses should be examined with care for evidence of malformation of the hoofs and general disorders of the feet. Examine the condition of the horny frog, is it of normal size and healthy. Do the quarters and heels show evidence of contraction. Examine the horny sole at the angle of the wall and bar for evidence of corns. In general, if the feet are not in normal condition, there should be no delay in correcting the irregularities.

For horses with sound feet at the close of the playing season, it is advisable to remove the shoes, round the outer lower border of the wall, and allow the horse to go without shoes for a period of two or three months. In case of abnormal conditions, such as contraction of the quarters and heels, or corns, the animal should be treated to remove or overcome the irregularity before being allowed to run free from shoeing. Normally, shoeing in connection with the remedial treatment gives quicker and better results than when the horse goes unshod.

Shoeing the Horse for Hunting

The shoeing for this type of horse and class of work will differ from the shoeing of horses used for ordinary riding purposes. The nature of the work is such that consideration must be given to secure footing, casting of shoes and excessive concussion on the foot structures. The horse should carry more foot than is the case in ordinary riding, the shoes should be fitted with heel calks about one-half inch in height.

Since there is a great danger of cast shoes in this class of work, the outline of the shoe at the quarters and heels should be less full and a trifle shorter than ordinary shoeing.

Shoeing the Horse for Jumping and Show Ring Purposes

In jumping and other show ring work, more hoof is required than for ordinary work and minute detail in balancing the feet is essential to effect good performance. It is believed that a shoe of suitable weight, and width of web made from bar steel (hand forged) with but three nail holes in each branch is best suited for this class of work.

The shoes should be fitted as described for hunting. A shoe with three nail holes on each side covering the space occupied by the four nail holes in the machine made shoe will insure a stronger job of nailing with less damage to the wall.

It is advisable during the training period to shoe the front feet with a plate shoe and replace the plate with a calk shoe when horses make exhibition performances. The effects of concussion on the foot structures is not as severe on the plate shoe as with heel calks. The hind shoes should be fitted with heel calks at all times. If the front feet become the least bit tender, the horse will not take kindly to the jumps. Constant use of heel calks on the front feet is very likely to develop soreness.

When changing the plate shoe for the calk shoe the change should be made at least three or four days before the horse is shown for exhibition in order that the animal may adjust his movements with the change made in shoeing. If heel calks are to be used on the front feet for long periods, the outer surface on the upper web of the shoe from the bend of the quarter to the point of the heel should be beveled to aid in expansion of the foot. Constant use of heel calks on the front feet tend to encourage contraction of the quarters and heels and produce soreness.

Lameness

This is manifested in the act of progression, by one or more of the limbs, of pain, disease, weakness, deformity or impediment. Among our equine patients lameness is of frequent occurrence and the difficulty of locating the exact seat of the trouble in many cases makes it a subject of prime importance.

In examining an animal for a lameness the tendency in many cases is to make a diagnosis before a thorough and systematic examination has been made. To arrive at an accurate diagnosis the examiner should have a systematic method of examination which is invariably followed.

Anamnesis

If a complete and accurate history of the case can be obtained it may be very helpful in arriving at a diagnosis. However, the examiner must be careful as the history may be misleading either because of deceit or lack of accurate observation. A history of intermittent lameness is suggestive of a certain lameness. When lameness is most pronounced when the animal is first moved and disappears with exercise it is known as a cold lameness. A bone spavin is a typical case of cold lameness. When a case of lameness increases in severity with exercise, as splint lameness, it is known as a warm lameness.

EXAMINATION. Before resorting to palpation of any part the animal should be observed at rest from a distance of at least twenty feet. The attitude of the limb may be significant of the seat of the lameness. It may be assumed the animal holds the limb in a certain position to allow relaxation of an inflamed tendon, ligament or part. Also the positions of abduction, adduction, or undue flexion or extension of the limb may be of considerable significance.

As a general rule when the seat of the lameness is in the lower part of the limb the foot is held ahead of the normal position. If the seat of the lameness is in the region of the knee the foot is held in about the normal position. Whenever the seat of the lameness is located in the upper part of the limb the foot is held back of the normal position. In the hind limb if the seat of the lameness is in the region of the hip joint the affected limb is held extended with the toe turned out. Quite frequently when the seat of the lameness is in the region of the stifle joint all of the joints of the limb are held flexed with the toe resting on the ground.

MOVING THE ANIMAL. In some cases of lameness it may be necessary and desirable to move the animal at the walk and trot. However, the animal should be moved only enough to exhibit the degree of lameness as it is not necessary to move the patient to cause unnecessary pain. If the affected limb is not readily apparent it may be desirable to move the animal at both the walk and trot.

The animal should be led at a normal walk toward the examiner. The flight of the feet should be noted, whether they are carried in or deviate from a straight line. Also the contractions and relaxations of the muscles should be noted.

The animal is led directly away from the examiner so the movements of the posterior limbs may be observed. It should be observed if the feet move forward in a straight line and if they are carried to the same height. Also the contractions and relaxations of the muscles are noted.

The animal should be led past the examiner so it may be observed whether the feet are placed squarely on the ground. If the seat of the lameness is in the posterior portion of the foot most of the weight is placed on the toe. When the seat of the lameness is in the anterior portion of the foot most of the weight is placed on the heel. The foot is also picked up quickly when the weight comes over on the toe.

It may be necessary to determine in which leg the animal is affected and if it is a front limb the animal should be trotted toward the examiner. The animal should be allowed free use of his head and the rein should be grasped about two feet from his head. The movements of the head are important in determining which limb is affected. When the weight comes down on the lame limb the head is raised and when the weight comes down on the sound limb the head drops.

If the lameness is located in a hind limb the animal should be trotted away from the examiner to determine which limb is affected. In hind leg lameness at the trot the croup is raised when the weight is borne by the affected limb. The croup is lowered when the weight is supported by the sound limb.

It may be desirable to have the horse turned in a small circle. The lameness is always increased when he is forced to pivot on the affected limb.

After the animal has been moved at the walk and trot and the seat of the lameness is not obvious, a careful manual examination should be made.

The limbs should be palpated carefully and thoroughly from the withers or croup to the foot. Each individual structure should be examined thoroughly, noting any evidence of pain, enlargement, or increase in temperature. The tendons, ligaments, joints, and common seats of lameness should receive special attention. When apparently areas of pain or enlargements are found the opposite limb should also be examined to see if it may be the same in both limbs.

In practically all cases of lameness the foot should receive a thorough examination. The foot should be picked up and its condition observed, especially the wearing surface and the wall. If it is shod notice whether any part of the shoe is worn excessively. The frog should be examined to see if it is of normal size or atrophied. To complete the examination of the foot the hoof testers should be used on every portion of the foot to see if there are any sensitive areas.

If the seat of the lameness is still not obvious nerve blocking should be resorted to. The blocking of different nerves is discussed under nerve blocking or neurectomy. After blocking the nerves to a part the animal should not be exercised excessively as rupture or fracture of the affected tissue may occur.

The x-ray may be used to take radiographs of the various areas and it may disclose obscure lesions, especially in the foot.

In lameness of the hind limb, a rectal examination may disclose the cause of the lameness. This is especially true in young animals.

In some cases of obscure lameness in the horse a deficiency of phosphorus in the ration has been the causative factor. Young horses are more subject to this deficiency than older horses and those horses doing heavy work or speed horses are more susceptible than horses doing less strenuous work. A persistent lameness or a shifting lameness without any visible cause is in many cases due to osteomalacia. There is usually no significant change in the total calcium in the blood but there is a marked decrease in the inorganic phosphorus of the blood. In a rather extensive study of the blood sera of horses Errington found the following amounts of inorganic phosphorus in the blood. For horses four years of age and over the mean was 3.55 mg. per 100 cc.; for colts 2 to 3 years of age the mean was 5.13 mg. per 100 cc.; for colts 23 to 43 weeks of age the mean was 4.95 mg. per 100 cc. of blood. If analyses of the blood reveals there is a marked decrease in the inorganic phosphorus of the blood the addition of phosphorus is indicated to the ration. Either ground bone meal or dicalcium phosphate may be added daily to the ration in one-half ounce doses. In the average case it is usually about two weeks before the horse shows definite improvement.

REFERENCES

Churchill, Frank, G., Horseshoeing, The Cavalry School, Fort Riley, Kansas.

Delahanty, D. D., Defects-Not Fracture of the Fibula in the Horse, J.A.V.M.A., 133, (1958), pp. 258-259.

Errington, B. J., Inorganic Phosphorus and Calcium Content of the Blood, The Cornell Veterinarian, XXVII, (1937), pp. 1.

Gotze, R., Spastic Paresis of the Hind Extremities in Calves and Young Bovines, Abstract in Modern Veterinary Practice, 39, (1958), pp. 41.

Hunting, William, The Art of Horse-Shoeing, Printed by William R. Jenkins.

Lundvall, R. L., Fracture of the Fibula in the Horse, J.A.V.M.A., 129, (1956), pp. 16-18.

Lungwitz, A., A Textbook of Horse Shoeing, Translated by John W. Adams, from Tenth German Edition, J. B. Lippincott Company, (1910).

Schmidt, H., Calcium and Phosphorous Deficiencies in Horses and Cattle, Clinical Picture, Treatment and Prevention, J.A.V.M.A., XCVI, 757, (April, 1940), pp. 441-456.

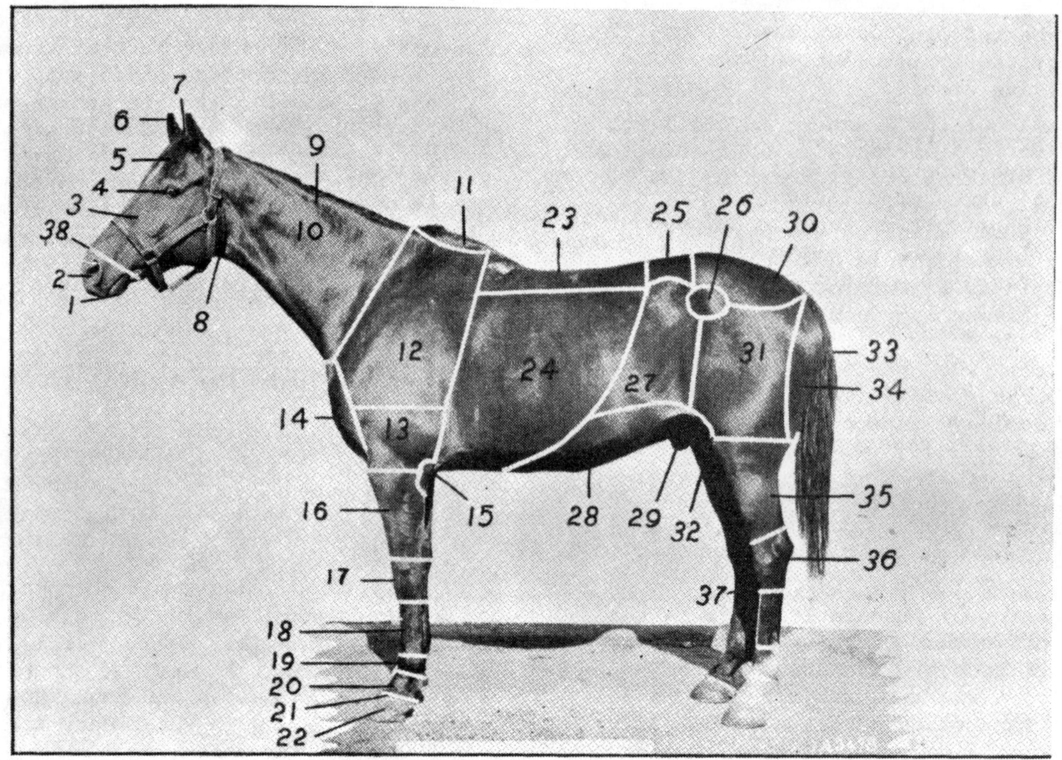

FIG. 400.

Regions of the Horse

1. Lips - upper and lower.
2. Nostril.
3. Face. From the muzzle to a line connecting the inner corners of the eyes. Bounded on the sides by lines from the outer corners of the eyes to the corresponding nostril.
4. Eye. Includes eyelids.
5. Forehead. From the upper border of the face to the poll. Bounded on the sides by a line from the outer corner of the eye to the base of the ear.
6. Ears.
7. Poll. The prominence between the ears.
8. Throat.
9. Crest. Upper border of neck bearing the mane.
10. Neck.
11. Withers.
12. Shoulder.
13. Arm.
14. Breast. A single region bounded by the neck, the region of the arm and below by a horizontal line at the level of the elbow joint.
15. Elbow. Corresponds to the ulna.
16. **Forearm.**
17. Knee. Corresponds to the knee joint.
18. Cannon.
19. Fetlock or fetlock joint.
20. Pastern.
21. Coronet. Corresponds to coronary band.
22. Hoof.
23. Back.
24. Costal region. Region of ribs. Back border and lower border follow the line of the ends of the ribs.
25. Loin.
26. Point of hip.
27. Flank.
28. Abdomen or belly.
29. Sheath.
30. Croup.
31. Thigh.
32. Stifle. Corresponds to stifle joint.
33. Tail.
34. Buttocks.
35. Leg. Lower part of this region also known as gaskin.
36. Hock.
37. Chestnut. (Also on foreleg above knee.)
38. Muzzle. Includes lips, nostrils, and nose, or space between the nostrils.

Regions Not Numbered on Figure 400

<u>Intermaxillary space</u>: The depression between the branches of the mandible or jaw.
<u>Jaw</u>: The branches of the jaw or mandible and including the sides of the head below the face and temple.
<u>Temple</u>: The area just back of the eye.
<u>Interaxillary region</u>: The space back of the breast and between the fore legs.
<u>Axilla</u>: The space between the fore leg and body.
<u>Groin</u>: The region between the inner surface of the hind leg and belly.
<u>The Dock</u>: The fleshy portion of the tail.
<u>Ergot</u>: The small growth of horn appearing in the tuft of long hair on the back of the fetlock.

Reprinted from, Horsemanship and Horsemastership, Academic Division The Cavalry School, Fort Riley, Kansas.

Colors and Markings

When used for the purpose of identification colors and markings should be noted exactly as they are and recorded.

<u>Bay</u>: Bay horses vary from a light, golden, or yellowish which might almost be called a dun to a very dark rich shade which merges into brown and between these extremes there is the bright blood bay with a coat like polished mahogany. The bay has a black mane and tail and usually has black on the limbs.

<u>Brown</u>: Brown is a mixture of black and chocolate pigment in the body coat. The hair on the muzzle will show whether it is bay or brown.

<u>Bay-Brown</u>: The predominating color is brown with muzzle bay, the limbs, mane, and tail are black.

<u>Black</u>: When the coat is composed of uniform black hairs.

<u>Chestnuts</u>: This is a whole color which may vary from the chestnut which is a medium golden color, the light chestnut which includes sorrel to the dark chestnut which includes liver chestnut and mahogany chestnut.

<u>Ysabella</u>: A color group having flax or silver manes and tails:

1. <u>Red ysabella</u> - red sorrel-like; flax mane and tail.
2. <u>Palomino</u> - a golden yellow; silver mane and tail.
3. <u>Pseudo-albino</u> - very light cream to white; silver mane and tail; often have 'glass' or blue eyes.

Ysabella, commonly considered identical with Palomino, is here suggested as a name for the group of immediately related colors.

<u>Greys</u>: This color is applied to the coat when it contains an equal number of white and black hairs. The color will vary from a light grey in which the white hairs predominate to dark grey in which the dark hairs predominate. The iron grey is a bluish shade of grey and includes blue and greyish blue coats. A flea bitten grey has a dark grey coat intermixed with small patches of whitish hairs.

<u>Roan</u>: Roan is applied to a color where there is intermingling of the red, white and black hairs. Blue roan the body color is black or black brown with a mixture of white hair which gives it a blue tinge. Strawberry roan the body color is chestnut with a mixture of white hairs.

<u>Dun</u>: This color may vary from a mouse color which is an ashy grey shade to a golden dun. Mule markings down the back and across the shoulder and zebra stripes across the arms and thighs are generally well marked on animals of this color.

<u>Buckskin</u>: Is a term applied to a coat of uniform yellowish colored hairs.

<u>Appaloosa</u> or <u>Morocco</u> <u>Spotted</u> <u>Horse</u>: These horses have in common a white rump interspersed with dark spots. These spots may cover the horse and may vary in color and shade. The horse may be of any color from white on down through the varying shades of brown. The only thing that the horse must have as far as color is concerned is a spotted white rump.

<u>Piebald</u>: The body coat consists of well defined large irregular patches of black and white.

<u>Skewbald</u>: The body consists of well defined large irregular patches of white and any other color except black.

Markings on the Head

<u>Star</u>: A white mark on the forehead. May be described as large, small, irregular, or faint when necessary.

Race or Stripe: A narrow white stripe usually down the center of the face and may be short, broad, or faint.

Snip: A white mark between the nostrils or may extend to one nostril when its position should be specified.

Blaze: A broad white mark down the face usually involving the whole width of the nasal bones. It may be distinct from the star and snip or it may include both.

White Face: The face is white from the forehead to muzzle.

Markings on the Limbs

White Pastern: The white extends from the coronet to just below the fetlock joint.

White fetlock or quarterstocking: The white extends from the coronet to an inch or two above the fetlock joint.

Threequarterstocking or sock: The white extends to halfway between the fetlock and knee or hock.

Full stocking or stocking: The white extends to or includes the knee or hock.

Cowlicks are characterized by the hair showing an inverse circular growth. When present they should be recorded as they are permanent characteristics.

Ray or list are terms used for a dark stripe sometimes seen along the backs of horses and mules.

Cross, dark line over the withers from side to side.

Examination of Horses as to Soundness

The general rule as to soundness is that at the time of sale if the horse has any condition that interferes with his natural usefulness or which may in time interfere with his natural usefulness that horse is unsound. Animals purchased for breeding purposes are examined to see if they are free from any heredity unsoundness or any defect that may interfere with their use for breeding purposes. If horses are sold as serviceably or practically sound they are examined to see if they are capable of performing the work for which they are purchased. Horses advertised or described as a "good worker" "quiet to ride or drive" are examined to see if they conform to this description. There are very few horses over five years that are absolutely sound. Usually they have one or more unsoundnesses that do not interfere with their usefulness but do lower their market value. Even though a horse is sound he may have certain vices or undesirable characteristics that makes him undesirable to purchase.

The examination of the horse should be made in an orderly manner so no unsoundness or defect will be overlooked. This is especially important in the examination of the legs and feet. After the examination has been completed the horse should be walked and trotted and then examined as to wind.

It is well to examine carefully the usual locations where neurectomies are performed. If the operations have been performed scars or nodules will be present. There will also be a noticeable loss of sensation to the part or parts supplied by the nerve or nerves operated on.

All skin affections should be carefully examined to see if they will respond to treatment. Some skin conditions are benign or easily treated while others may not respond to treatment. Skin affections frequently encountered are ringworn, galls, mange, cracked heels, grease and others. Chronic cases of grease may be practically resistant to treatment.

The region of the head is examined for any bulging of the bones of the face, for facial paralysis, cysts, openings discharging along the ventral border of the mandible are indicative of alveolar periostitis or there may be a unilateral nasal discharge. The examination of the teeth may reveal some serious dental defect that may be an unsoundness. Any cough should be regarded with suspicion as it may be chronic and should be regarded as an unsoundness. The jugular vein on each side of the neck should be distended to see if they are both patent. If only one is functionless it is a blemish but if both are affected it is an unsoundness. The pulse should be taken and any irregularity noted for it may be advisable to auscultate the heart. If any defect of the heart or lungs is found it is usually an unsoundness. The abdominal wall should be examined for the presence of various types of hernias. Any scirrhous cord is likely to get larger and have to be removed.

Neoplasms around the anal or perineal region should be examined carefully for they may be malignant especially in grey animals.

Horses submitted for examination seldom show serious defects in the upper part of the front limb. However any scar in the region of the withers should be examined carefully. If there is any evidence of a capped elbow it is not a serious defect but may prove to be a permanent one. The importance of a blemished knee is usually exaggerated but does lower the market value of the animal.

Below the knee the cannon region is examined for splints and affections of the tendons and tendon sheaths. Splints derive their importance from the lameness they produce and which is caused by their formation. Some large splints are so situated they interfere with a flexor tendon or the suspensory ligament, the prominence of the splint exerting pressure during movement on the tendon or tendon sheath. Old or fully formed splints in horses over six years of age are of little consequence except in those few cases in which the prominence of the splint is in contact with a tendon. However the existence of a splint should be mentioned in the certificate for it is a technical unsoundness.

Any strain of the flexor tendons should be regarded with suspicion as it may produce an intermittent type of lameness. If the affected tendon becomes swollen, edematous and painful with slight work the condition will usually become worse with steady work. Chronic thickening of the tendons at the fettock is particularly serious and very resistent to treatment. Most cases of flexor strain become gradually worse but the horse may be serviceable for a long time. However any degree of flexor strain is an unsoundness.

Windgalls when present should be examined carefully to determine what structure is affected. In many cases they are present and the horse has never been lame. It has been observed that tendinous windgall is more likely to develop a troublesome lameness than the articular windgall.

Ringbone disease is probably one of the most serious of the unsoundnesses. It may affect any of the phalanges but occurs most frequently on the first and second. In most cases the exostosis may become so extensive that it interferes with the movement of the joint producing a mechanical lameness. Very few horses with a true ringbone ever become sound in action.

Sidebones are usually found only on the front feet and may be either unilateral or bilateral. They are rarely found on the hind feet. The condition is more frequently observed in heavy horses than in the lighter breeds. When the sidebones are bilateral there is a hereditary predisposition toward sidebone, but their development is usually stimulated by constant work on hard surfaces. A unilateral sidebone usually develops as the result of an injury to the cartilage or from the extension of an infection from another area. Even though a sidebone is present and not causing lameness it is an unsoundness.

The feet should be a normal size and shape but even if they are not it may not interfere with the horses usefulness so it is not an unsoundness.

When a sand crack is present at either the quarter or toe it is an unsoundness. Whenever an open sand crack is accompanied by lameness it is always a serious condition as it may prove very stubborn about responding to treatment. A keratoma or horn tumor when present is an unsoundness. Thrush which often develops into a chronic condition when not treated is an unsoundness. Corns of any type are an unsoundness.

HIND LIMB. In some horses presented for examination there may be a fracture of the external angle of the ilium. After the inflammation subsides the lameness disappears and the condition does not affect the horses ability to work. Also a portion of bone may be fractured from the tuber ischii producing a marked deformity. While horses so affected are serviceably sound they cannot be described as sound.

In the hind limbs we find most of the unsoundness occurring in the region of the hock. Whenever a large curb is present in a saddle horse it should be regarded as an unsoundness. If a curb is present it should be mentioned in the certificate as it may give trouble later on.

When a bone spavin is present it is an unsoundness but if the animal is not lame it may never cause any trouble. Many horses have bone spavins and they have never been lame so their importance in many cases is over rated. In some cases a well developed exostosis may strengthen the hock so that it is stronger and will stand a good deal of hard work. However in cases where there is little or no exostosis present the lameness may be persistent and very resistent to treatment.

Bog spavin in its chronic form with distension of the joint capsule but without inflammation is frequently seen. These cases usually do not cause lameness unless the distension becomes excessive. When lameness is present it is very resistent to treatment. Another distension occurring in this area is that in the tarsal sheath producing a thoroughpin. This condition may also be very resistent to treatment. When the distension is small it usually does not cause trouble. Capped hock is frequently observed and in most cases is a blemish. However when it is produced from a distension of the bursa beneath the superficial tendon the lameness may be very resistent to treatment. The unsoundness occurring below the hock are the same as those discussed for the same region in the front limb.

Lameness is always an unsoundness and a horse should always be carefully examined for it. The horse should be examined at rest and the walk and trot. The horse should be moved on a smooth hard surface as he might fail to show lameness on a turf. The person leading the horse should have his hand about eighteen inches from the halter or bridle. This allows free movement of his head.

Stringhalt is always an unsoundness but it may not be serious enough to interfere with the horses usefulness. It may be intermittent or continuous and not pronounced. In some cases it may only be observed when the horse is forced to move sideways or turned in a small circle.

Shivering is a serious unsoundness that usually increases in severity finally rendering the horse almost useless. In some cases only slight symptoms will be observed when the horse is backed but the horse may become so severely affected it is unable to back. Horses used at fast gaits may tire easily or become unsafe for running or jumping.

EYES. The eyes should always be examined for any changes that may have occurred and will affect good vision. Horses are not often presented for an examination for soundness in which obvious changes have occurred. In some cases horses may be presented that have had recurring attacks of periodic ophthalmia producing permanent changes in some of the tissues. Shying may be a vice or due to inability to see clearly. Corneal opacities may be either temporary or permanent and their importance will depend upon size and location. As long as it is present a corneal opacity is an unsoundness. Cataract is always a serious defect but their importance is determined by their size and location. An extensive cataract may obstruct vision but a small one may not interfere with the horses usefulness. The importance of the cataract will depend upon its becoming more extensive but when present is an unsoundness.

AGE. The teeth and the various changes taking place that serve as a guide to the age of the horse have been discussed under dentition. Also some of the deformities of the teeth that are unsoundnesses are discussed.

WIND. Some of the principal unsoundnesses of wind are, roaring, broken wind, wheezing and chronic cough. In some cases other objectionable respiratory sounds may be made but unless due to some definite condition may be objectionable but not important.

Some horses may produce a grunt when forced to make a sudden movement or great effort. It has been noticed that some horses that are roarers will grunt when struck on the ribs and again when threatened with the stick. However all roarers do not grunt when subjected to the test. Some horses may make only a whistling sound while others make a definite roar. Roaring is usually indicative of a more serious condition as it usually increases in severity. In some cases individuals have progressed to where they could not perform any type of vigorous work.

THICK WIND. May occur rather frequently in old horses, that are too well fed but have not received enough exercise. However in some horses it may be a chronic condition that will gradually become worse. Some cases may be benefited by more care in feeding and regular exercise.

Broken wind is a condition that usually occurs in middle aged horses. These horses usually have a characteristic hollow cough. Other characteristic symptoms are a double movement of the flank on expiration and the so-called pumping of the anus. Horses so affected tire easily and cannot stand long continuous work.

TESTING THE HORSES WIND. The method or methods that are used for testing a horses wind will depend upon the facilities present. Saddle horses may be lunged or galloped while harness horses may be driven singly or with another horse. Horses used at faster gaits may be given a more strenuous work out.

All blemishes, scars and firing marks should receive a careful examination to determine their importance. Some blemishes may lower the market value of the animal. Areas that have been fired should be examined to determine the exact extent of the changes in the tissue. If the blemish does not interfere with the usefulness of the horse or is not likely to it should not be considered an unsoundness.

VICES. There are many vices some of which may seriously affect the animals health and constitute an unsoundness. Cribbing, wind sucking or both may be so chronic they affect the animals health. Licking may be a bad habit which may develop into an unsoundness. Weaving is another habit which may cause the horse to develop an unsteady gait. Some of the other vices or bad habits are being mean about shoeing, biting the rider, kicking, bad temper, running away and there are others that may be so serious they should be regarded as unsoundnesses.

OPINION. The veterinarian may give his opinion in writing in the form of a certificate. The certificate may state whether the horse is sound, serviceably sound, or any other term that describes the condition of the horse. It is also best to include in the certificate the sex, age and marks of identification.

Vices

There are many types of vices and habits some of which may develop into an unsoundness that interferes with the horses usefulness.

CRIBBING. In cribbing the horse grasps the edge of the manger or any projection between its incisor teeth and gradually wears it away. When this habit is continued long enough it produces the characteristic bevelling of the anterior edge of the incisor teeth. If a horse is a cribber he is usually also a wind sucker as the two conditions usually go together. However a horse may have one condition and not the other. Excessive wear of the edges of the incisor teeth may be caused by other conditions but its presence is suggestive the horse is a cribber. Poor condition of a horse with either one or both of these vices is cause for rejection.

WEAVING. This condition is manifested by a rhythmical shifting of the weight of the anterior portion of the body from one front leg to the other. A bear in the zoo will often show this habit of weaving. This habit or vice may in time lead to an unsteadiness in gait.

KICKING. The tendency for some horses to kick may be shown only at feeding time due to their impatience to be fed. Some horses never kick except when they are in the stable while other horses may kick with the intention of injuring other horses or the caretaker. This tendency to be a habitual kicker seems to occur more frequently in mares than geldings. A stable kicker may get all of his satisfaction from the noise that is produced. If the sides of the stall are padded it may discourage the kicking and also prevent injury to the horse.

TAIL RUBBING. This may start from some irritation in the tail or in the gelding a dirty sheath may be the cause. However after the practice is started they may continue to do it even if the cause has been corrected. In some cases the horse may have to be confined so he cannot rub his tail.

HALTER PULLING. Some horses develop the vice of pulling back on the halter. This may sometimes be corrected by placing a rope or chain across the stall back of them. Another method is to place a slip noose about the abdomen in the flank region. The end of the rope is passed forward between the front legs, through the halter ring and tied securely. After the horse tightens this noose about his body once he usually keeps the rope slack afterward. One other method is to tie a rope to a hobble around the pastern of one fore foot. The rope is then tied to the ring in the manger.

Many of the habits and vices of horses develop during periods of idleness. To prevent many of these conditions from developing it is important that the horse receive regular and sufficient exercise.

BOOK REFERENCES

The Anatomy of the Domestic Animals, Septimus Sisson, W. B. Saunders Co.

Animal Dentistry and Diseases of the Mouth, L. A. Merillat, (1919) Alexander Eger.

Diseases of the Horse's Foot, H. Carlton Reeks, (1906), Alexander Eger.

Dollar's Veterinary Surgery, General Operative and Regional, J. J. O'Connor, Alexander Eger.

Encyclopedia of Veterinary Surgery and Obstetrics, G. H. Wooldridge, Oxford Press

Lameness of the Horse, J. V. Lacroix, (1916), American Journal of Veterinary Medicine.

Regional Veterinary Surgery and Operative Technique, J. W. Dollar, (1920), Alexander Eger.

Veterinary Surgical Operations, Bemis, H.E., (1933), Worman Printery, Inc.

Veterinary Surgical Operations, L. A. Merillat, (1921), Alexander Eger.

INDEX